Decision at Midnight

Michael Hart
with Bill Dymond and Colin Robertson

DECISION AT MIDNIGHT: INSIDE THE CANADA-US FREE-TRADE NEGOTIATIONS

Foreword by Donald Macdonald
with cartoons by Alan King of the *Ottawa Citizen*

UBC PRESS / VANCOUVER

Printed in Canada on acid-free paper ∞

ISBN 0-7748-0514-5

ISSN 0847-0510

Canadian Cataloguing in Publication Data

Hart, Michael, 1944-
  Decision at midnight

  (Canada and international relations, ISSN 0847-0510; v. 9)
  Includes bibliographical references and index.
  ISBN 0-7748-0514-5

  1. Free trade – Canada. 2. Free trade – United States. 3. Canada –
Commercial treaties. 4. United States – Commercial treaties.
I. Dymond, Bill, 1943- II. Robertson, Colin, 1954- III. Title. IV. Series

HF1766.H352 1994   382'.971073   C94-910657-7

UBC Press gratefully acknowledges the ongoing support to its publishing
program from the Canada Council, the Province of British Columbia
Cultural Services Branch, and the Department of Communications of
the Government of Canada.

Cartoons copyright Alan King
Photos courtesy Canadian Press
Set in Galliard and Minion
Designer: George Vaitkunas
Copy-editor: Ann Webb
Proofreader: Stacy Belden
Indexer: Edward Hart

UBC Press
University of British Columbia
6344 Memorial Road
Vancouver, BC V6T 1Z2
(604) 822-3259
Fax: (604) 822-6083

To Mary Virginia, Pat, and Maureen, without whose support, forbearance, and understanding this project would never have been undertaken, let alone completed.

CONTENTS

CHARTS AND TABLES

FOREWORD

Donald Macdonald

The conclusion of a free trade agreement between Canada and the United States stands as one of the premier events in the twentieth-century history of Canada. The agreement represented the end-point of a course of deliberations between the two countries, and within the two, on eliminating barriers to trade stretching back into the last century to a time when Canada was not yet a nation. At various times the concept found warm support in one country or the other, and at others it was strongly opposed.

For Canada, the less powerful of the two countries, negotiations on free trade evoked both attraction and fear. Favourable access to the world's most affluent market was an attractive prospect, but underneath lay a nagging fear that more extensive commercial links might put Canadian political independence at risk. It was obvious from their very beginnings, that the negotiations would occasion a great national debate. Business, labour, churches, women's groups, native peoples, universities, and many other Canadians all made their views known, some in strident and even exaggerated tones. Whatever the stands taken, all agreed that the free-trade agreement would have a major and enduring impact on Canada and Canadian society.

Decision at Midnight was written by public servants who played a direct role in the negotiations and who were present during the great events which attended their launch, their conduct, and their conclusion. With full respect for the rules of cabinet secrecy and the confidentiality of official advice to ministers, the authors have crafted an exciting, yet thoughtful, account of the negotiations. The book reaches beyond a specialist audience and should appeal to a broad spectrum, specialist and non-specialist alike. It is refreshingly free of jargon and the turgid drafting so beloved in governments and large corporations.

The magnitude of the issues involved, particularly in Canada, lured thousands into the unfolding of events. In addition to the prime minister and president, their cabinets, premiers, MPs, senators and congressmen, and the hundreds of officials who backed them up, academics, businessmen, reporters, and a wide range of opponents and critics march across the pages of *Decision at Midnight*. Not only do the authors describe the main events of the negotiations themselves, but they also bring in the supporting roles of the International Trade Advisory Committee, the Sectoral Advisory Groups, the federal-provincial Continuing Committee on Trade Negotiations, the advocacy pro and con of the Canadian Alliance for Trade and Job

Opportunities, the Pro-Canada Network, and the daily commentary of the media. Never before had one issue dominated Canadian political life so completely and involved so many so intimately.

The book tells its story from the particular point of view of the authors as actors in a particular cause, and thus reveals only one slice of the whole. Others may wish to develop the story from other perspectives such as that of the American negotiators, of the political decision-makers, or of provincial or private-sector advisors. Given the importance of the agreement, it will undoubtedly provide grist for many books to come. Few, however, will match *Decision at Midnight* for its insights into why the negotiations took place and what happened. While this is a book by officials, this is not an 'official' book. Its examinations of issues and events is critical in the best sense of the word.

Although the main focus of the book is on the issues and events in the Canada-US negotiations, it indirectly casts light on the way modern governments reach major decisions and prepare for, organize, and conduct international negotiations. Students of public administration will find in these pages, therefore, an almost unique account of the pursuit of a major public policy issue from its conception to its conclusion.

Honourable Donald S. Macdonald, PC

PREFACE

Charles Ritchie remarks in one of his books on life in the Canadian diplomatic service that he kept a diary because he could not bear to let his life go by without some record. The origin of *Decision at Midnight* is largely the same. Due to experience, training, and good luck, we had the opportunity to contribute to the decision to launch the free-trade negotiations with the United States and to take part in them. To let them go by without recording what we saw, what we heard, and what we participated in would have been too hard to bear.

The successful conclusion of negotiations, marked by the formal signing of the agreement on 2 January 1988, signalled the culmination of a process that had started in 1846 when Britain repealed its Corn Laws and abandoned its colonies in North America to the vagaries of American competition in the British and home market. From the day realization of that consequence sank in, Canadians have sought an enduring, contractual relationship with the United States providing for the free and open exchange of goods. The scope and particular issues involved in the quest have changed over the years, but the basic dream has endured. The dream became reality in the 1980s not because it finally made economic sense – it always has – but because a combination of events and forces made an agreement sufficiently attractive to overcome traditional non-economic fears and concerns. While a spirited opposition, drawing on a wide range of arguments old and new, was mounted on the day the government announced its intention to negotiate an agreement, it proved insufficient to derail the project. The agreement went into effect on 1 January 1989.

The story of the successful negotiation of the agreement is an intensely political story. It took political courage to defy the conventional wisdom that bilateral trade negotiations with the United States were a potential death trap. It took political tenacity to stick with the negotiations in the face of American mismanagement and indifference, and relentless opposition at home. It took political vision and courage to rescue the initiative when it looked hopeless in the dark days of September 1987. Despite the success of the negotiations, the issue eventually had to be resolved in a federal election. Throughout the campaign, opponents portrayed the agreement in the most lurid colours and ensured that the election would settle once and for all whether or not Canadians wanted to proceed with it. On 21 November 1988, the Conservative government that had staked its future on free trade was returned with a solid national mandate to implement the agreement.

The key figures in this political drama were the prime minister and president, three trade ministers in Canada (James Kelleher, Pat Carney, and John Crosbie) and two in the United States (Bill Brock and Clayton Yeutter), Canadian Finance Minister Michael Wilson and US Treasury Secretary Jim Baker, Canadian Secretary of State for External Affairs Joe Clark and American Secretary of State George Shultz, the two leaders of the opposition parties, dozens of members of Congress, as well as provincial premiers and other federal and provincial cabinet ministers. But the story we tell in the pages that follow is not primarily the political story. While this story dominated the media for almost five years, its details remain to be told. We leave that challenge, however, for others, more qualified and less hemmed in by the proprieties of public service. Rather, we concentrate on the story of the negotiations themselves – the preparations for and conduct of the negotiations as well as the ideas and issues behind them.

The main protagonists in the story we tell are the normally anonymous public servants who negotiate on behalf of governments. Past trade negotiations have attracted virtually no public profile, but the intensity of these talks made the two chief negotiators, Simon Reisman and Peter Murphy, household names in Canada with a higher recognition factor than even some cabinet ministers. They occupy centre stage. They are assisted by a host of other officials in both national capitals. Simon Reisman is backed up by his deputy Gordon Ritchie and a team of more than a hundred assistant negotiators, issue specialists, policy analysts, and support staff. Outside of the Trade Negotiations Office, Derek Burney, successively assistant deputy minister (ADM) for US Affairs in the Department of External Affairs, associate undersecretary at External, and chief of staff in the Prime Minister's Office, plays a dominant role throughout the story. Bob Richardson and Gerry Shannon, successively deputy ministers of International Trade, and Don Campbell, Burney's successor as ADM for US Affairs, also play key roles. On the US side, Peter Murphy has assembled a team of experienced officials including Bill Merkin, his deputy, Ann Hughes and Jean Anderson from the Department of Commerce, Bob Cornell and Bill Barreda from the Treasury Department, Chris Hankin from the Department of Labour, Ralph Johnson from the State Department, and Bill Hart from the International Trade Commission. They too are assisted by a host of other specialists. From beginning to end, Ambassador Allan Gotlieb and the Canadian embassy in Washington push and cajole often indifferent American officials and legislators and bolster sometimes flagging Canadian spirits. In the closing stages of the negotiations, US Deputy Treasury Secretary Peter McPherson and Deputy

US Trade Representative (USTR) Alan Holmer prove indispensable. The two chief legal counsels, Konrad von Finckenstein and Chip Roh, with the help of a band of persistent and able lawyers, translate the negotiated agreement into a precise legal text, a task that proved almost as daunting as the negotiations themselves.

Decision at Midnight is the story of these people. All find their place in the narrative. It is thus mainly the story of the negotiations themselves and of the resulting agreement rather than of the political drama. Nevertheless, we do relate the two. The comprehensive nature of the negotiations which, unlike previous trade negotiations, were pursued in the glare of daily publicity, fed the fury of political controversy, while the intensity of the political debate in turn influenced the conduct and content of the negotiations.

We analyze the events and issues from the point of view of three middle-level participants who took part in the events from the beginning in the early 1980s to the conclusion of the negotiations in December 1988. It is the story as we experienced it and from that perspective touches on the political debate, on federal-provincial relations, on the media coverage of events, and on the academic debate, but primarily it focuses on the unfolding of the bureaucratic story. This is a dimension that is only infrequently exposed to public scrutiny but in this instance is critical to understanding both the agreement and the process that led to it.

We began the manuscript shortly after the formal negotiations commenced in the spring of 1986. All of the writing was done on our own time, at home in the evenings and on weekends. Many of our colleagues encouraged us; others wondered how an account of the negotiations could be written by public servants without breaching the rules of cabinet secrecy and the confidentiality of advice given by officials to the government. The rules have been respected fully; those looking for an inside peek at the cabinet room, for example, will be disappointed. Furthermore, the opinions and analysis in the book are our own. We take full responsibility for the selection of events and issues and for the analysis and opinions that hold them together.

The basic content of the book had been assembled by the end of 1987. During the winter of 1988, while teaching a course on the agreement at Carleton University, Michael Hart recast the manuscript, marrying narrative and analysis to create a single story.[1] The book was largely completed by the spring of 1988, at which time we sought permission to publish and entered into exploratory discussions with publishers. These exploratory discussions led to an offer from *Saturday Night* to publish an excerpt in its July 1988 edition. The excerpt was advertised but never appeared.

We did not receive permission to publish. Senior officials in the government were reluctant to see public servants become embroiled in the heated political debate that eventually led to an election dominated by arguments for and against free trade. We respected that decision. As career public servants, we accepted their judgment that we should not intrude into this political situation with a book that might be misconstrued for partisan purposes.

Six years have now passed and, while the FTA continues to be a politically charged issue, time has suggested that the publication of this account might help to dispel some of the more egregious tales now being told. The manuscript remains largely as it was when completed in the middle of 1988. In the intervening time we have done no more than add endnotes, clean up the text, and sharpen arguments. We decided not to take advantage of the opportunity to continue the story through the election. None of us participated in the drafting of the implementing legislation or in the agreement's implementation. The story, therefore, ends where our direct involvement ends: with the signature of the agreement on 2 January 1988 by the prime minister and president. In the conclusions we have taken the opportunity to respond to some of the more outrageous myths and allegations that have emerged, and provided some preliminary thoughts on the agreement's impact. More detail on these aspects, however, can be found in some of our subsequent writings.

While we have now received the permission to proceed with publication which, as public servants, we must have, we wish to dismiss any idea that this book represents an 'official' account. It is not a modern equivalent of Clair Wilcox's *A Charter for World Trade*, which was written in 1948 by the American deputy negotiator to the Havana Conference to convince a sceptical Congress and business establishment that American interests would be served by ratification of the Havana Charter for an International Trade Organization. Ours is an independent analysis and assessment of the negotiations. To the extent that others, including those in government, agree with our analysis, we are gratified. To the extent that they do not, we encourage them to respond and add to our efforts to demystify Canadian trade policy in general and the Canada-US trade negotiations in particular.

While the consequences can be far-reaching, trade policy is a specialty practised by a relatively small group of officials and fully understood outside of government by a small number of specialists. Until a few years ago, there was little literature outlining the nature of Canadian trade policy, Canada's place in the world trading system, and the conduct of Canadian trade negotiations. Nor was much available on specific negotiating issues. The free-trade issue not only brought trade negotiations into the public spotlight, but also stimulated the production of a torrent of academic and popular literature touching on trade policy. We hope that our own effort will contribute further to public understanding and knowledge of this important aspect of Canadian public policy.

We owe a special debt of thanks to friends and colleagues who reviewed the text for accuracy and advised us on events and issues with which they were more familiar. Gerry Shannon graciously agreed that one of us could spend a year as an academic visitor at the University of Western Ontario and at Carleton University, thus providing the time to think, teach, and write. Jean Anderson, Tom d'Aquino, Bob Bothwell, Derek Burney, Don Campbell, Percy Eastham, Jonathan Fried, Ingrid Hall, Bob Kymlycka, Alec Macpherson, Maureen Molot, John Noble, Frank Petrie, Frank Stone, Phil Stone, Chris Thomas, Brian Tomlin, John Whalley, and Gil Winham all read and commented on all or part of various versions of the text. All made valuable suggestions and offered their wisdom and advice. Any errors or omissions, as well as judgments, about the importance of the negotiations for Canada, the selection of events, and the role of the various players, however, are entirely our responsibility.

The book would not be what it is without the collaboration of three additional people. In order to illustrate the book, we turned to Alan King of the *Ottawa Citizen* and asked him if he would let us use the many fine cartoons he prepared during the negotiations. While it is a cartoonist's lot to dip his pen in acid, Alan does so with a difference; he is prepared to poke fun at all sides of an issue. If there can be such a person as a balanced cartoonist, Alan fits that bill. We are grateful for his agreement to let his good sense of humour enliven our narrative. We are also grateful to Greg Stevenson of Canadian Press for his determination and assistance in tracking down press photographs. Many were found but, in the end, only some were chosen. Finally, we want to thank Edward Hart for spending his summer on the painstaking task of building an index. It was not much fun, but it does make a difference.

We are also grateful to UBC Press for their willingness to take on a project that is somewhat different from the usual university press fare and for their enthusiasm in ensuring that the book tells the whole story, events, and policy as we experienced it. In preparing the manuscript for publication, we had the able assistance of Laura Macleod, Holly Keller-Brohman, and other members of the editorial staff. It was a learning experience for us all and the result is a better book.

Finally, a word about our wives and children. Our participation in the preparation for and conduct of the negotiations already put inordinate strains on normal family life. To have compounded these strains by simultaneously preparing a chronicle of events was an act of folly. Their continuing support and understanding made the strain and pressure bearable. This book is collectively dedicated to them and to their forbearance. While all three wives encouraged and forbore, Mary Virginia Hart also read and reread the manuscript to ensure a consistency and accuracy of style. We owe her an even greater debt of gratitude.

Michael Hart
Bill Dymond
Colin Robertson

Ottawa and Brasilia
5 September 1994

DECISION AT MIDNIGHT

THE FORK IN THE ROAD

Two roads diverged in a wood, and I –
I took the one less travelled by,
And that has made all the difference
– Robert Frost, *The Road Not Taken*

'Free trade' is one of the more opaque and lifeless phrases in the English language. In Canada, however, the two words seem to go to the root of nationhood, a trumpet call arousing fierce passions on both sides of the issue. When Sir John A. Macdonald uttered his immortal words, 'a British subject I was born, a British subject I will die,' he was not thinking of the Plains of Abraham or Queenston Heights, but of the tariff on ploughs from New York. For over a century, free trade had been a catchword for patriots, a rallying cry for radicals, and the object of hope and fear for thousands of ordinary Canadians. But few of them had any appreciation of what it really means. All this changed in the 1980s. Slowly, hesitantly, free trade began to creep into ordinary conversation. By the mid-1980s, the phrase had become the stuff of public controversy. Nowhere was this more true than in Toronto.

The Great Debate

The evening of 19 September 1985 was hot and muggy in Toronto. As elsewhere, ideas about free trade swirled in the air. Would the government, beset by the scandals of tuna inspection and election spending, proceed to a free-trade negotiation with the United States? Would it reopen an issue that had bedeviled the country since Confederation? Or would it take the safe course and continue to take refuge in multilateral trade negotiations under the auspices of the General Agreement on Tariffs and Trade (GATT) in Geneva? What would triumph, politics or economics? Would the government listen to the urgent call of business or heed the dire warnings of the nationalist establishment worried about Canada's future as an independent nation?

Two blocks in from the Yonge Street strip, in a lecture hall made available by Ryerson College, an audience assembled for what had been modestly billed the Great Free Trade Debate. Organized by the C.D. Howe Institute, the debate featured Dick Lipsey, its senior economist and ardent advocate of free trade, and David Crane, an equally spirited proponent of moderate economic nationalism and the voice of a *Toronto Star* column already hardened into implacable opposition. The debaters were formidable and articulate proponents of opposing views, and in the course of a three-hour discussion, the major lines of argument were vigorously asserted and opposed.[1]

The arguments had been rehearsed over the past several years in lecture halls and seminar rooms across the country. They had been debated in corporate boardrooms and government conference rooms, and had now reached the public stage and the front pages of the daily press. Even the electronic media had begun grasping at ways to inform listeners and viewers of the details of trade negotiations.

Lipsey took his principal arguments from his book, co-authored with Murray Smith, *Taking the Initiative, Canada's Trade Options in a Turbulent World*.[2] His presentation was a classic, lucidly argued defence of free trade. Crane was equal to the match, speaking from a flurry of handwritten notes on scraps of paper that occasionally flew in the air, as if caught by the poignancy of the argument. His views had been gathered together earlier in the year in a series of feature articles in the *Star*.[3]

Hugh Corbett, an experienced old trade hand from Australia and head of the distinguished Trade Policy Research Institute in London, was there to provide an international flavour and act as a neutral moderator. He found the atmosphere somewhat bewildering, but reminiscent of the debates in England a generation earlier on British entry into the European Common Market.

The debate would be the first of many to be held across the country in the months ahead. Free trade had become a matter of controversy. Populists and academics alike were prepared to do battle for the hearts and minds of Canadians. Of immediate concern were the politicians in Ottawa. Would they or would they not take the plunge and initiate negotiations?

For Lipsey and Crane that September night in Toronto, their common point of departure was that Canadians earn their bread by trade. They both accepted that the capacity of Canadians to generate wealth from the domestic economy alone is limited, and that the capacity to do so by international trade is limited only by how competitive Canadian products are on world markets. The crucial ingredient is secure and unimpeded access to export markets combined with access at world prices to goods and services Canadians cannot efficiently produce themselves. The difficult issue is the extent to which Canadians are prepared to integrate their economy further into world markets and accept the constraints that come with such integration.

In the mid-1980s, Canadians had come to a fork in the road: whether to stick with the tried and true or to break with the past and start anew. That was the issue Lipsey and Crane had come to Ryerson College to address. Lipsey had come to make the case that the old reality of a protected market and cumbersome multilateral negotiations was no longer viable. He was convinced that Canadians needed to turn to the opportunity and challenge of a bilateral agreement. Crane was prepared to argue that changing circumstances required even greater emphasis on multilateral negotiations and a more concerted approach to industrial policy.

Lipsey contended that the time had come to strike a new trading relationship with Canada's most important trading partner. Canada's place in a rapidly evolving world economy had changed. Postwar economic wealth had been built upon ready markets and the products of an abundant and low-cost resource base. But new competitors in developing countries, new technologies, substitute materials, and the increasingly higher costs of extraction had brought home the reality that Canada's resource base was no longer an assured source of wealth. More significantly, it had become clear that the resource base could no longer finance the maintenance of an inefficient manufacturing economy sheltered behind high tariff walls. Canadians had been able to enjoy a high standard of living despite being up to one-quarter less productive than Americans. But in the modern world, an economy based upon the century-old pattern of resource exports and small-scale manufacturing serving a small domestic market and sheltered from the winds of change was no longer feasible.

Lipsey argued that small economies dependent on trade with larger economies need free, stable, and secure access to at least one large market in order to reap the benefits of specialization and long production runs that are available to industries in Europe, the USA, and Japan because of large domestic markets. Such benefits could be made available to Canada through more open trade arrangements. In the 1960s some economists had opted for a North Atlantic free-trade area; in the 1970s a greater number had turned increasingly to a North American free-trade area. In both cases, their views ran counter to the lingering legacy of the National Policy of high tariffs that continued to dominate business and official views. In the 1980s, however, economists were finding the business community increasingly interested in more secure access to a large market and prepared to pay for this access by opening the Canadian market to US competitors. Official views had also become less hostile to negotiating the elimination of the remaining barriers to cross-border trade on a bilateral basis. Both business leaders and government officials had thus become more receptive to age-old economic arguments.

Economists had demonstrated long ago that open borders stimulate greater efficiency and lead to greater wealth and prosperity. Contrary to the general perception, trade barriers rarely increase employment or demand for goods. Tariffs and other forms of trade barriers tend to increase prices and reduce real income for consumers and, as a consequence, reduce demand for goods in all industries. They also raise the cost of inputs to manufacturers and thus make their products less competitive. Lipsey claimed that a Canada-US free-trade agreement would provide an opportunity to reduce barriers within a sensible and reciprocal framework of rules.

Crane was not comfortable with this neoclassical view of economics. While he did not dispute the general benefits of trade liberalization, he was apprehensive for other reasons. He was fearful that a free-trade agreement with the US would have dire consequences. He worried that strategic parts of the manufacturing sector would not be able to survive the onslaught of US competition as US branch plants would close down and the Canadian market would be served by an extra shift at the parent plant in the United States. As a consequence, free trade would bring an intolerable level of short-run unemployment.

Lipsey had the answers. He recognized that the small size of the manufacturing sector had worried Canadians throughout their history. They do not want to be hewers of wood and drawers of water. But Canadians had always been a little schizophrenic on the subject. Wages are high in the mining industry and production is located in the areas where employment is most difficult to generate. People who live in the north are very protective of the forestry industry; similarly, the people of Newfoundland are protective of fishing and its associated lifestyle. There are few realistic alternatives for these single-industry regions of the country. The resource industry also continues to generate national wealth and accounts for a substantial share of foreign exchange earnings. This, he argued, is as it should be. Canadians are exchanging that which is abundant in Canada for goods that are scarce or that can be produced more efficiently elsewhere. Canada's resource sector will always be relatively large whether or not there is free trade.

The risk of an investment pull-out, he insisted, was highly exaggerated; it made sense only for those who believe that Canada's comparative advantage lies in a small, protected domestic market. Yet fifty years of tariff cutting, first under the 1935 and 1938 bilateral agreements with the United States and then in seven GATT rounds, had always led to more, not less, investment. No responsible corporation simply walks away from a productive, profitable facility as a result of a change in protection at the border. The basic reality in the 1980s, he noted, is that Canadian investment is now going to the United States to get behind US protectionist barriers. Securing free access to the largest and most lucrative market in the world is the best inducement for investment, the surest means to exploit Canada's comparative advantage, and

HE WONDERS WHY THE GOODS DON'T MOVE

Arch Dale, *Winnipeg Free Press*, 14 April 1931

a guarantor of productive, long-term employment.

Indeed, he asserted, the threat of massive unemployment was also greatly overblown. As a result of the Kennedy and Tokyo Rounds of GATT negotiations, there had been substantial reductions in world and Canadian tariffs, although Canadian tariffs had remained relatively high. Most Canadian industries had adjusted without difficulty. The Canadian industries least able to cope under these more competitive conditions had been the same ones that were in difficulty long before the period of tariff reductions began. Their plight was by no means a uniquely Canadian problem. The same industries were and continue to be in distress in almost all industrialized nations. They are the ones characterized by low wages and labour intensive production.

The crux of David Crane's argument, however, was not economic but political. He, like many other economic nationalists, feared that Canada-US free trade would lead first to economic and eventually to political absorption by the United States. Crane insisted that the Canadian economy was already heavily dependent on the US economy and that the real challenge was to find a policy mix that would loosen these ties. He insisted that Canada had never made economic sense and that Canadians had always and would continue to be prepared to pay a price for being Canadians. A free-trade agreement, on the other hand, would lead to greater economic integration and eventually to political union as the natural and inevitable consequence of this integration.

Even if absorption could be fended off, he contended that a free-trade agreement with the United States would erode Canada's capacity to conduct an independent foreign policy. Canada's rationale for being a member of the economic summit would disappear. Canadian governments would inevitably be drawn into supporting US foreign policy adventures in Central America and elsewhere. Canada's role as an honest broker and voice of reason in world councils would be lost as it would increasingly be forced to parrot the American line in order to safeguard the trade agreement.

Lipsey did not agree. He believed that there was not a scrap of evidence indicating that closer trading ties lead inevitably to political union or even to a unified view of foreign policy. Efforts in Western Europe to follow economic union with political union had foundered repeatedly, particularly because of problems in developing a common view on international political issues. Where foreign policy is largely economic policy, as is the case at the OECD or GATT, there is already a close working relationship between Canadians and Americans because they often hold a shared view of the objectives of these organizations.

Crane further insisted that a Canada-US trade agreement would force Canada, the smaller partner, to align many of its domestic social and economic policies with those of the larger partner because the United States would regard many Canadian social programs, such as Medicare and unemployment insurance, as subsidies and Canada would be forced to get rid of them. Pressure to lower taxes that pay for these programs would come from corporations, faced with the need to reduce costs and become competitive in a free-trade environment.

Lipsey rejoined that Crane failed to appreciate that it is the high degree of integration of capital and financial markets between Canada and the United States that creates pressures to harmonize. The issue, therefore, is how a trade negotiation alters the pressure to harmonize. The change can be both positive and negative. The removal of the threat of unilaterally imposed countervailing duties is a plus; the need to limit government subvention practices may be a minus. It is the totality of changes required that must be measured, not each issue in isolation.

Crane was not satisfied. He was worried about how free trade would affect Canada's ability to protect and nurture its culture, ranging from the Grey Cup to the National Film Board. He was not comforted by assurances from free trade's advocates that the issue of whether or not specific Canadian or American cultural industries required special measures to assist them fell well outside the scope of trade negotiations. He was concerned that under free trade the future of *Maclean's* and CTV would be at risk. Lipsey insisted that this apocalyptic view was neither necessary nor real. It would be possible to exempt the cultural industries from any deal. Furthermore, Crane ignored the positive impact a trade negotiation would have on culture and sovereignty. Removing the threat of protectionist actions to individuals and firms, creating the conditions of security and predictability necessary for new investment and new jobs, and clarifying the rules of trade would enhance Canadian sovereignty, expand the scope for independent action, create additional wealth that could be devoted to cultural and other pursuits, and reinforce Canadian identity.

Lipsey also pointed out that Canada had had a comprehensive trade agreement with the United States for more than fifty years dating back to the 1935 reciprocal trade agreement. The current agreement, the GATT (a multilateral contract encompassing a series of bilateral agreements under which barriers to much cross-border trade have already been reduced or eliminated), imposes very substantial obligations upon both Canada and the United States in the conduct of bilateral trade relations, as befits an agreement managing the world's largest trading relationship. Other aspects of the relationship are governed by a host of other agreements and arrangements. Lipsey wondered how a free-trade agreement would append Canada to US foreign policy while the many hundreds of multilateral and bilateral agreements Canada enjoys with the United States in trade and other areas do not. Why any Canadian government would wish to give up some of Canada's advanced social programs for the sake of a new trade agreement was also a mystery. How a trade agreement would dispose Canadians to watch even more US television and movies and read more US books similarly defied explanation. The arguments were advanced that evening, however, with great relish and would continue to be the stock-in-trade of the debate to come.

Crane insisted that the alternative to bilateral free trade was continued efforts to strengthen and improve the multilateral trading system. He feared that Canada's multilateral heritage and duty would be betrayed by a radical and risky lunge into bilateralism. He assured the audience that his unease was prompted by neither anti-Americanism nor protectionism. Rather, he felt that Canada was plunging headlong down a path that it would later regret. He was apprehensive that the necessary homework on what Canadians would have to pay appeared not to have been done. He did not believe the government had a mandate to take Canada down this path. A massive communications effort was no substitute for healthy and informed debate. At a minimum, the government should be prepared to seek a mandate from the people to pursue this dangerous course.

Hugh Corbett sat with a bemused expression during this exchange of rhetoric. He did not know what the fuss was all about. He recalled that in 1960, the Treaty of Stockholm had been negotiated between the seven original members of the European Free Trade Association in two weeks after less than a year of preparation and little public debate. It proved a beneficial arrangement for its members. Australia and New Zealand similarly followed a bilateral course for more than twenty years to their mutual profit. He saw no reason why Canada and the United States, concurrent with a long-term effort to rebuild the GATT, should not move to negotiate a similar arrangement between them, an arrangement that would be better than anything that could be negotiated multilaterally. Indeed, it could stimulate interest in better multilateral rules on the part of the European Economic Community (EC) and Japan, starting with the proposed new round.[4] In his closing remarks, Corbett suggested that the GATT was in bad shape and that Canada and the United States were at the forefront of those trying to shore it up. Canada's commitment to the multilateral system was surely not in question.

As the members of the audience filed out of the auditorium, they felt drained. These were not easy issues. Over the months to come, they would hear them repeated again and again. The nuances and details might change, the rhetoric might become more shrill, and the anxiety more pronounced, but the basic thrust would be the same. Few changed their minds that night. By September 1985, most Canadians had developed a gut feeling about the issue. About half thought the government should proceed and give it a try; about a quarter were convinced that it was the wrong way to go. The remaining quarter was either indifferent or wavering between the two positions. Most of those at Ryerson that night fell in one of the first two camps, pleased with the effort of their champion, convinced that the other was a misguided fool. That would be the pattern in the months ahead. There would be little room for shades of grey.

For the government, however, the options had become steadily clearer and, at the end of September, it decided to proceed with negotiations. For the next two years, free trade dominated the agenda and consumed an ever growing amount of political and bureaucratic energy. By the end of September 1987, the game looked hopeless. Three years of preparations, discussion, consensus building, and negotiations appeared to have been for nought. The United States could not see its way clear to the audacious vision put forward by Canada, and Canada could not find a way to fall back to the cautious package on offer from the United States. Then, in a dramatic series of events culminating in a frantic weekend in Washington, the negative debris that had blocked progress was steadily cleared away. Even then, however, the key to success remained elusive. Not until minutes before the deadline imposed by the expiry of US negotiating authority did the two sides agree on the elements of the agreement. The decision made minutes before the stroke of midnight on 3 October 1987 ushered in a revolution in the Canadian economy. We now turn to the story of the making of that revolution.

PART ONE

SETTING THE STAGE

POLICY ORIGINS

Free trade, one of the greatest blessings which a
government can confer on a people, is in almost
every country unpopular.
– Thomas Babington (Lord Macauley), 1824

The debate at Ryerson that hot night in September indicated that free trade had become more than a matter of academic curiosity. It had become a hot topic. A decision by the government as to whether to proceed with negotiations was imminent. While the debate may have been as old as Confederation, its more recent origins could be traced to the fallout from a 1982-3 review of trade policy conducted by the Trudeau government. That review had taken place within the context of a growing body of support among business, governments, and academics prepared to reconsider the basic tenets of Canada's commercial relations with its trading partners, particularly with the United States.

In Canada, arguments favouring direct negotiations with the United States to dismantle remaining barriers had been set out in considerable detail by the Senate Standing Committee on Foreign Affairs in three separate reports issued in 1975, 1978, and 1982.[1] They were based on extensive public hearings and responded to an increasingly popular view among influential members of the Canadian business establishment.

The Senate report was also in harmony with the work of the Economic Council. In its 1975 report, *Looking Outward*,[2] the Council ranked its support for Canada-US free trade as the fifth among a number of possible strategies. Ahead of it were multilateral free trade; free trade among the United States, the EC, Japan, and Canada; free trade among the United States, the EC, and Canada; and free trade among the United States, Japan, and Canada. Its assessment was that a Canada-US free-trade agreement was probably the most attainable of all the options.

The Economic Council, in turn, had built upon the work of economists such as the Wonnacott brothers, John Young, Ted English, Harry Johnson, and others who had long contended that the small Canadian economy could not afford to isolate itself from the world economy by maintaining high barriers to imports.[3] This point of view had been summarized by John Young in his study for the 1957 Royal Commission on Canada's Economic Prospects chaired by Walter Gordon, as follows: 'The principal result of this analysis can be summarized in a sentence. In general and over the long run, increases in protection can be expected to lead to economic losses and decreases in protection to economic gains for the country as a whole. This follows not only from the direct effect the Canadian tariff has on the Canadian economy, but also from the effect Canadian commercial policy has on the treatment accorded this country's exports.'[4]

But since 1972, Mitchell Sharp's essay, *Canada-US Relations: Options for the Future*,[5] had reigned as the official view of the options for Canada-US relations. The essay was a response to the August 1971 'Nixon measures' whereby the United States broke from the postwar Bretton Woods arrangements which required fixed exchange rates. For Canada, the most severe component of the Nixon measures had been the imposition of a 10 per cent import surcharge on dutiable imports from all sources. The refusal of the Americans to exempt Canada from the surcharge and the potentially devastating effect that the surcharge, if maintained for any period, would have had on Canada, brought home to the government of the day the need to re-examine the comfortable assumptions underpinning the bilateral trading relationship. Sharp claimed that Canada had three options: one was to drift into progressively greater degrees of dependence on the United States; the second was to aggressively promote Canada-US economic integration and secure special treatment; and the third was to deliberately diversify Canada's trade and economic relations away from the United States by striking new partnerships with Europe and Japan.

The government had chosen to pursue the third option and the main vehicle for executing it became the 1976 framework agreements for economic cooperation with the European Economic Community and with Japan. For two years, Canada negotiated with its two principal overseas trading partners and achieved agreements that provided for consultation and cooperation, but yielded no useful trade or economic commitments. In effect, Canada succeeded in increasing political awareness of Canada's trade interests in Europe and in Japan and gained a commitment to periodically discuss those interests, but could not succeed in lowering a single tariff or other barrier to increased trade.

Fine words, high political commitment, and a substantial allocation of bureaucratic resources to add flesh to bones could not change harsh reality. The potential for governments of market economies to alter the flows of trade and investment in a fundamental way is limited; what potential does exist lies in the negotiation of contractual rights and obligations to lower barriers or otherwise reduce discrimination between the treatment of domestic and foreign goods, as has been done in the GATT and similar agreements. The third option contained neither scope for nor interest in going beyond the GATT; there was no desire on the part of either the EC or Japan to conclude preferential bilateral trading arrangements which might have induced such changes. Concurrent negotiations in the GATT (the Tokyo Round), however, brought only meagre gains in new Canadian access to the European and Japanese markets. In sum, neither Canadian nor European nor Japanese business was prepared to invest and expand trade that was not dictated by commercial advantage and real conditions of open and secure market access.

It was not surprising, therefore, that by the early 1980s, neither the EC nor Japanese arrangements had borne much edible fruit. While they remained useful expressions of an essentially political relationship, the inescapable conclusion was that framework agreements, unaccompanied by the exchange of new rights and obligations beyond those in the GATT, could not be effective instruments for gaining improved and more secure access to larger markets. They thus proved insufficient to stimulate the restructuring the Canadian economy needed to give it the more competitive edge required in the rapidly changing world. Sharp's analysis of Canada's growing and irreversible dependence upon the US market had been sound; his prescription for diversifying away from that market had ignored economic reality and had overestimated the willingness of other governments to make reciprocal concessions that could make a difference. The result was political rhetoric rather than new trade and investment patterns.

The patterns of Canadian trade, however, had changed in the 1960s and 1970s, as illustrated in Tables 1 and 2. The commodity composition of Canadian exports had become more diversified, even as their geographic makeup had become more concentrated. Canadian manufacturers, hitherto stout opponents of trade liberalization, had gradually realized that for this pattern to continue, they would need secure and free access to larger markets, especially the US market, to underwrite investment and to achieve economies of scale and specialization.

The pressures of the 1981-2 recession in Canada and apprehension about a nationalist lurch in Canadian energy and investment policies had further convinced the traditionally cautious and suspicious business community of the need for a change in direction in Canada's commercial relations with the United States. Early in 1983, for example, the Canadian Chamber of Commerce

Table 1

Commodity composition of Canadian exports, 1960-84 (%)

	1960	1970	1980	1983	1984
Food and agriculture	18.8	11.4	11.1	11.6	9.7
Crude materials	21.2	18.8	19.8	15.9	15.8
Fabricated materials	51.9	35.8	39.8	33.3	32.0
Manufactured end-products	7.8	33.8	29.4	38.9	42.1
Special transactions	0.3	0.2	0.3	0.3	0.4
Total	100.0	100.0	100.0	100.0	100.0

Source: Richard G. Lipsey and Murray G. Smith, *Taking the Initiative: Canada's Trade Options in a Turbulent World* (Toronto: C.D. Howe Institute 1985), 15.

adopted a resolution asking the Trudeau government to join with industry and the provinces to explore the 'benefits and adjustments required to facilitate a free-trade agreement with the U.S. to be effective by 1987.'[6]

A number of federal government policies adopted in the 1970s and directly attributable to the views of economic nationalists, had undermined Canadian business confidence in government economic policymaking and had added to the business community's determination to use trade policy as a vehicle to effect change in Canada's economic policy orientation. Many of these policies had first been suggested in the 1957 report of the Gordon Commission. They included: trade diversification (the third option), reviews of foreign investment proposals to determine whether they promised significant benefit to Canada (FIRA), Canadian control of the energy industry (NEP), and an industrial policy (DREE, then DRIE, and all the programs delivered by these two departments). These policies did not sit well with Canada's business community. Their unease had grown in the early 1980s. First, the National Energy Policy (NEP) had been badly received by Canada's trading partners, particularly the United States. US officials had zeroed in on the NEP, as well as the rumoured 'strengthening' of the Foreign Investment Review Act, as evidence of a Canadian government unconcerned about its international commitments and determined to develop the Canadian economy along lines fundamentally at odds with US policy developments. The Reagan administration's commitment to the free-enterprise system and deregulation had heightened US awareness of foreign practices that might undermine US business interests abroad. Second, the global recession had begun to take hold in Canada. Various government policies, such as a made-in-Canada oil price, had initially shielded Canada, but when the recession finally hit, it hit harder than in any other OECD country.

Table 2

Distribution of Canadian exports by trading areas, 1960-84 (%)

	1960	1970	1980	1983	1984
United States	55.8	64.4	63.2	72.9	75.6
United Kingdom	17.4	9.0	4.3	2.8	2.2
Other Western Europe	11.3	9.8	10.6	5.8	5.0
Japan	3.4	4.9	5.9	5.3	5.1
Other Asia	2.2	2.9	4.0	4.4	3.8
Other	9.9	9.0	12.0	8.8	8.3
Total	100.0	100.0	100.0	100.0	100.0

Source: Richard G. Lipsey and Murray G. Smith, *Taking the Initiative: Canada's Trade Options in a Turbulent World* (Toronto: C.D. Howe Institute 1985), 47.

Reviewing Trade Policy

The federal government's 1982-3 trade policy review provided the vehicle for analyzing these trends and matching them to Canadian needs and aspirations. Two studies resulted from the project: *A Review of Canadian Trade Policy* and *Canadian Trade Policy for the 1980s*.[7] Together they provided an overview and appreciation of the roles of trade and trade policy in the Canadian economy and a policy prescription for the future.

The review was initially begun in the Department of Industry, Trade and Commerce under the political direction of the minister for international trade. Ed Lumley had never been happy with the interventionist thrust of the early years of the Trudeau renaissance and in 1982 encouraged a review that would take a hard look at the benefits of greater reliance on market forces. His officials and their colleagues in Finance and External Affairs enthusiastically agreed. They relished the opportunity for a hard-nosed look at the place of trade policy in promoting domestic industrial and other economic objectives, at the interrelationship between trade policy and other economic policies, and at the role of trade policy in meeting Canadian foreign policy objectives.

Early in 1982, both Lumley and the review were moved from Industry, Trade, and Commerce (whose senior minister, Herb Gray, was the spiritual father of the nationalism that had underpinned the economic policies of the Trudeau government in 1980-1) to the Department of External Affairs. At External, Derek Burney, assistant undersecretary for trade and economic policy, took charge of the project team.[8] In a flurry of consultations in August and September of that year, first with a group of old trade hands, then with representatives of the business community and the provinces, Lumley and his team heard a very clear message: no more nationalist experiments and get the Canada-US relationship right. In a joint brief prepared subsequent to the consultations, for example, the provinces said: 'We must dramatically improve our economic relationship with the U.S. by all means. All the provinces see the repairing of our relationship with the U.S. as our No. 1 bilateral trade policy objective.'[9]

Soon after completing these initial consultations, Lumley was made minister of regional industrial expansion (DRIE) and his responsibility for trade was assigned to Gerald Regan. Lumley had brought a more market-oriented approach to the business of trade policy, and this was reflected in early drafts of the background papers. Reluctant to give up the trade policy review, he used the occasion of one of his first speeches as industry minister to tell the Atlantic Provinces Economic Council that arrangements similar to the autopact for textiles and chemicals and other sectors would help to resolve trade conflicts between the United States and Canada. While some officials may have viewed this unrehearsed departure from orthodoxy with some anxiety, the direction he wanted to take in re-orienting Canada's trade policy was clear.[10]

His successor, Gerald Regan, brought a Maritime perspective to the trade policy review. An experienced politician and former premier of Nova Scotia, he respected the traditions of the past and the advice of officials, but he had strong ideas of his own. One was that the golden age of Nova Scotia had been under the Reciprocity Treaty of 1854 which provided for free trade between the United States and the British colonies to the north. He reminded officials of this as the review made its tortuous way through the decision-making process.[11] As well, those he consulted constantly repeated the same two themes heard by Lumley: the US market is basic to Canada's economic well-being, and success in that market requires a stable Canada-US relationship; economic policies such as FIRA and the NEP are souring relations with the United States and interfering with good business judgment. Thus two different ministers heard the same message from the business community and indicated their interest in moving towards bilateral negotiations. Old traditions and orthodoxies, however, die slow deaths in official Ottawa.

While ministers waited, bureaucrats debated, largely within the confines of the Department of External Affairs. Two difficult policy issues needed to be addressed: the relationship between domestic economic policy and trade policy, and the approach to be taken towards the US relationship. They could not be avoided. The policy orientation towards these two matters would condition the approach to most other issues.

From the outset, Burney and his team had sought an approach based on domestic rather than international considerations, recognizing the fundamental link between trade and domestic economic policy. The consultations had demonstrated the strongly held view outside official Ottawa that a successful trade performance required a competitive domestic economy and that government trade policies should concentrate in the first instance on promoting competitiveness. While not quarrelling with this point of view, Bob Johnstone, Regan's deputy minister, was troubled with the concept of a trade minister going to his colleagues with recommendations that would go well beyond the traditional concerns of trade policy, such as market access, trade relations, export credits, import quotas, tariffs, and export promotion. If he followed the advice gleaned from the consultations, the final report would also need to include such matters as tax and monetary policy, investment policy, and industrial incentives. Ministers might be prepared to accept such a novel approach; bureaucrats would not. The Department of Finance, for example, would not tolerate non-Finance officials suggesting how the government might approach tax and monetary policy. Senior officials have a well-developed sense of propriety and sensitivity as to their individual and collective responsibilities. To succeed in convincing his minister to recommend a policy paper to his colleagues, Johnstone needed to be confident his counterparts in interested ministries would not undermine his advice by giving contrary views to their own ministers.

The second issue was equally sensitive. Concurrent with the trade policy review, another group was reviewing the Canada-US relationship more generally. That paper was for the signature of the secretary of state for external affairs and was being prepared under the direction of the deputy minister for foreign relations, de Montigny Marchand. It was not meant for publication and not based on broad consultations. Nevertheless, it would be important to ensure that two such basic papers were generally in agreement. In the fall of 1982, they were not. The US review was still very much cast in the mold of Mitchell Sharp's 1972 paper.[12]

The project team thus ran into the twin orthodoxies of trade policy limited to the instruments of protection and promotion and of foreign policy based on the principle of the third option. Both orthodoxies ran directly opposite to the message from the consultations, particularly from business executives whose profits were daily on the line and who had rejected policies that undermined their ability to export. They also contradicted the approach favoured first by Lumley and then by Regan, as well as the analysis in the background papers and the practice of the past ten years. A frontal attack, however, would not have been successful. No policy paper can proceed if it gains a lot of detractors. Bureaucrats thrive on consensus, but many have become experts at nitpicking. An experienced practitioner can nibble a policy document to death without seriously questioning its overall approach. 'I like your paper, but there are a few questions of detail that need to be tightened up,' is a familiar opening gambit.

It took six months to work the documents through the system. Cabinet considered the accumulated papers in various committee sessions over a period of months and endorsed the conclusions and recommendations. The whole process proved time-consuming and replete with frustrations but, in the end, successful. The government endorsed an important set of principles. Regan and his senior minister, Secretary of State for External Affairs Allan MacEachen, had proven enthusiastic supporters of the review and had jointly signed the preface to the documents to be published. These documents made available a range of information and analysis not readily found elsewhere. These led to a set of sober conclusions that reflected accurately the range and depth of genuine consultations and the underlying analysis. In effect, the documents provided a sophisticated if unexciting defence of the status quo. The release of the documents also marked a triumph of substance over process. By the mid-1980s, cabinet decision-making had evolved into a complicated process involving a myriad of committees and diffused responsibility. The process was geared more to the development of programs and the approval of expenditures than to policy discussion and the latter had become increasingly rare. The trade policy review turned out to be an exception.[13]

The results of the review were made public by Regan on Wednesday, 31 August 1983, at a sparsely attended press conference at the National Press Building across from Parliament Hill. Two days before the last summer weekend is not the most propitious time for government announcements, but the minister had promised to release the study before the end of August and was determined to live up to that commitment. The script called for the minister to hand down a Canadian trade policy for the 1980s reaffirming that Canada was strongly attached to the GATT multilateral system. It was and would remain the warp and woof of Canadian trade policy. A small space was reserved for bilateral negotiations with the United States on a sectoral or functional basis.

The minister, however, turned the emphasis around. There was little news value in a statement declaring that there would be little or no change in government policy. Instead, he proclaimed the death of the third option and the dawning of a new era in trade relations with the United States.[14] The driving force of the new policy would be bilateral agreements to eliminate trade barriers in selected sectors of the Canadian economy without raising the political nightmare of launching a full-scale free-trade negotiation. Any negotiations would be pursued within a multilateral framework. A sober and cautious reflection of months of bureaucratic study and carefully orchestrated consultations, the trade policy review thus inadvertently became a vehicle for a full-scale public debate on trade relations with the United States and the merits of a comprehensive Canada-United States trade agreement.

The press liked the theme. Finding little of interest in most of the analysis and background information, reporters zeroed in on the issue of sectoral free trade. The *Ottawa Citizen* headline trumpeted 'Canada to Pursue Free Trade with U.S.' and declared that 'the government's so-called "third option" is dead and the country now will pursue limited free trade with the U.S.' The Toronto *Globe and Mail* and *Star* were more cautious, both noting that the government had rejected complete free trade. Editorial opinion across the country supported the decision. On the East Coast, the Halifax *Chronicle-Herald* concluded that 'Canada cannot afford to abdicate any avenues, in any direction of the world, it cannot escape the fact that the American market is our biggest and our best, and it offers the brightest prospects for expansion.' The *Winnipeg Free Press* was more direct:

> It has taken more than a decade for the federal Liberal government to concede that the United States is and will remain the most important single export market on which most effort should be expended ... the unstated premise of the federal government's long-delayed discussion paper ... is that the Third Option is dead. It has been dead for most of the past ten years but the department of external affairs and the prime minister's office refused to issue a death certificate until now.[15]

While constituting only a small portion of the review, the sectoral free-trade initiative soon became the main focus of public discussion. Nevertheless, the choice made in the review to consider, however cautiously, sectoral arrangements with the United States was based on an assessment of the mood of the country and a pragmatic and deliberate decision that there was a need to consider a change in emphasis.

As indicated in Table 2 above, by 1985 three-quarters of Canada's exports went to the United States, and it was on the basis of a North American economy that the private sector increasingly made its investment plans. The proportion of manufactured end-products was even higher. Improved access could stimulate growth. Indeed, most business people naturally concluded that the US market was basic to their export success in third markets. They accepted that for many Canadian manufacturing companies, future diversification of Canadian trade patterns depended on a sound North American economic base. If these companies could not compete in the United States and find customers south of the border, they would not find them in Europe, Japan, or the Third World. Their views were summed up in an editorial in the *Montreal Gazette*: 'The real world is a harsh place. Among its cold facts are that the U.S. is there and that we need it, whether we like it or not. We do need to strike better deals. But they will have to be approached with extreme caution.'[16]

Business strongly held this view. All those consulted had stressed that while sound export and import policies were significant, more important for Canada's future economic development and trade performance were sound domestic policy instruments, i.e., sound fiscal, tax, and monetary policies supported by appropriate industrial policies. What trade policy should do is provide secure access to markets, particularly the United States market. Chamber of Commerce president Sam Hughes told the *Financial Post* that 'more and more of our members are looking at the U.S. market and saying that they want to ensure access.'[17]

Reaction to the review demonstrated that there was broad consensus in Canada about the objectives of Canadian trade policy. It was generally held that the government should use the instruments available to it to stimulate a stronger, more efficient, productive, competitive, and growing Canadian economy which would result in a greater integration of the Canadian economy into world markets and a more stable and open international trading environment. The arguments were about how to achieve these objectives.

Three Options Again
By the early 1980s, Canadian trade practice had begun to assume that bilateralism and multilateralism were mutually exclusive. One important contribution of the trade policy review was to point out that they were in fact complementary means of achieving the same end: negotiated improvements in access to markets and rules-based management of trade relations. The review pointed out that Canada and the United States had cooperated for almost fifty years in fostering first the establishment and then the preservation of a stable and strong multilateral trading order. Within that order, however, each had forged beneficial relations with various individual trading partners and particularly with each other. The rights and obligations contained in a range of multilateral and bilateral agreements were not mutually exclusive but rather complementary and mutually reinforcing means to the same end. The issue, therefore, was not about a choice between bilateralism and multilateralism, but about how best to increase and share wealth within Canada and with our trading partners. While many options were advanced during the debate, they can be reduced to three broad approaches, each reflecting its own philosophical underpinnings.

The first option revolved around an integrated industrial policy, i.e., nationalizing some industries, raising barriers to imports, and engaging in large-scale industrial subsidization in order to strengthen manufacturing and add to the coinage available for future trade negotiations. This was the

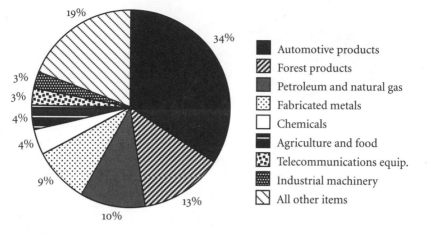

19%

34%

3%

3%

4%

4%

9%

13%

10%

- ■ Automotive products
- ▨ Forest products
- ■ Petroleum and natural gas
- ▦ Fabricated metals
- □ Chemicals
- ■ Agriculture and food
- ▨ Telecommunications equip.
- ▦ Industrial machinery
- ◩ All other items

Source: Statistics Canada

Chart 1: Distribution of major Canadian exports to the United States, 1984

answer of Canadian economic nationalists, left-wing academics, the NDP, and the union leaders. They did not share the liberal ideology of comparative advantage and free markets, preferring the mercantilist philosophy of government-determined comparative advantage and zero-sum calculations of the national interest. Such an interventionist policy had never been fully implemented in Canada, although some of the elements involved were pursued during the more nationalist periods of Grit rule. It had never garnered broad support in Canada, but it continued to be put forward with considerable vigour and conviction by the economic nationalists before and during the free-trade debate.

The flaw in this approach was that Canada would have to shelter itself from foreign competition by erecting major new barriers against imports, imposing foreign exchange controls and price controls, putting limits on private business, and setting up new crown corporations to undertake a number of domestic business activities. Such measures would be tantamount to declaring economic war on Canada's trading partners and would place at risk the nearly 30 per cent of GNP derived from international trade. This nationalist strategy thus presented a bleak alternative to further broad, comprehensive trade liberalization, whether achieved bilaterally or multilaterally.

The second option was the status quo. Canada would continue to rely largely on the multilateral system but, as opportunities presented themselves, it would enter into special arrangements – either sectorally or bilaterally. This had been the policy of successive post-war Canadian governments, a policy originally forged and implemented by politicians, such as Lester Pearson, Mitchell Sharp, and Bud Drury, who had learned their trade and

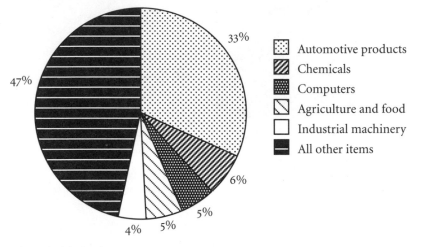

Source: Statistics Canada

Chart 2: Distribution of major Canadian imports from the United States, 1984

industrial policy as senior mandarins. It was a pragmatic approach, but increasingly reflected past realities. The multilateralists of the 1980s were by now struggling to come to grips with the new realities and found themselves stuck between a rock and a hard place: the policies of the left and a free-trade agreement with the United States.

The new third option was to grasp the nettle and pursue a free-trade agreement with the United States within the framework of rules provided by the GATT. Such an approach, while neither denying nor denigrating the continued pursuit of multilateral negotiations and improved trade relations with all potential trading partners, would recognize the higher priority of the Canada-US relationship. It would provide Canadian industry with a much stronger North American base from which to tackle world markets.

Much of the consequent debate tended to crowd out the middle position. The debate was couched in terms of either an industrial strategy or free trade with the United States. The idea that Canada could continue to pursue a rich mix of industrial policies as well as GATT negotiations simultaneously with a bilateral free-trade agreement seemed impossible for many Canadians to grasp or accept. More importantly, for many adherents to the first or second option, their real concern about the free-trade option appeared to have less to do with industrial or trade policy and more with concerns about Canadian identity and sovereignty. To compound the complexity of the debate, these critics seemed to have an unrealistic appreciation of more recent developments in the GATT and Canada's place in the world economy.

Throughout the discussion, the defendants of the status quo or second option were of the view that theirs was the position that had to be disproven. Proponents of Canada-US free trade were placed on the defensive and challenged to prove their case. But the options were decreasing for the supporters of the status quo. Their do-nothing approach would have led over time to a further reduction in Canada's competitiveness, output, employment, and real incomes. By the mid-1980s, apart from Australia, Canada was the only advanced industrial country in the world that did not have secure access to a large market of 100 million or more people. This lack of secure access to a large market threatened a deterioration of Canada's competitive trading position, and would result in higher costs for consumers and producers alike.[18]

Adherents of the status quo also seemed ready to ignore the subtle, gradual, and fundamental changes taking place in the capacity of the GATT rules to protect and advance Canadian trade interests with its principal trading partner. Whatever its strengths had been in providing a general framework of rules and a world forum for trade negotiations, GATT was proving insufficient to deal with the massive and complex Canada-US trade and economic relationship.

Changes in the International Policy Context

The foundation of the GATT rules which govern trade relations among industrialized countries is non-discrimination. The economic rationale for non-discrimination is security of market access as the basis for achieving economic growth through the application of comparative advantage and specialization. The legal expression of non-discrimination is most-favoured-nation (MFN) and national treatment, the two basic precepts of the General Agreement on Tariffs and Trade.[19]

The antithesis of non-discrimination is mercantilism. Mercantilists believe that exports are good and imports are bad and the purpose of international trade is to strengthen the state and weaken its rivals. International trade is thus a zero-sum game. If one party gains, then it follows that the other parties have lost. Thus the mercantilist regards a trade negotiation like a carpet sale: get as much as you can and give as little as you can. In modern trade policy, mercantilists practice their craft through sector by sector and product by product reciprocity and package it as industrial policy or managed trade.[20] For mercantilists, there is no inherent value in MFN or national treatment and hardly any place for rewarding competition, comparative advantage, and dynamic efficiencies. While much of the negotiation under GATT has always had a mercantilist or tit-for-tat flavour, it has been under-

pinned by a set of rules based on a shared acceptance of the value of competition and growth through trade and international specialization.[21]

Most-favoured-nation and national treatment are essential preconditions
to liberalization based on reciprocal trade negotiations. At the post-war conferences which established the GATT, agreement on most-favoured-nation
and national treatment enabled the first round of tariff cutting to succeed.
These principles provided assurance that the expanded trade opportunities
resulting from the reduction of trade barriers would not be denied through
measures of external or internal discrimination. Without such assurance, the
reduction of trade barriers would have been foolhardy and investment to
exploit comparative advantage and pursue specialization based on larger
markets no more than a gambler's throw.

In practical terms, as articulated in the GATT and practised by its contracting parties, most-favoured-nation treatment has had a chequered history. The unconditional obligation of most-favoured-nation treatment is
qualified by the entitlement under Article XXIV of the GATT for two or
more countries to enter into customs unions and free-trade areas to eliminate trade barriers between them and withhold such treatment from other
contracting parties of the GATT. The rationale for such a breach is that such
arrangements should be trade-creating and thus convey compensating benefits to non-participants. Nevertheless, it constitutes a denial of MFN. Over
the years, an increasing proportion of world trade had come under the cover
of such regional arrangements. Less easy to accept was the gradual move to
'managed' trade agreements such as the Multifibre Agreement, which is an
explicit and institutionalized denial of most-favoured-nation treatment on a
sectoral (textiles and clothing) basis.

By the mid-1980s, there had also developed an epidemic of voluntary
restraints and orderly marketing arrangements which denied all but in name
most-favoured-nation treatment. The spread of 'conditional' most-favoured-
nation treatment in the GATT codes negotiated in the Tokyo Round (1973-9)
had lent further help and comfort to the mercantilists by establishing
degrees of most-favoured-nation treatment. Qualified discrimination,
replacing unqualified non-discrimination, was proving extremely costly to
economic growth and destructive of international trade. To Canadians,
heavily dependent on trade with the United States, pressures in the US
Congress and elsewhere to impose reciprocity in access and treatment, product by product and country by country, seemed poised to erode non-discriminatory trade policies even further and make exclusive reliance on
GATT negotiations a foolhardy insistence on the virtues of the past.[22]

The principle of national treatment had become no less immune to assault. Here, the emergence of state intervention through subsidies, government procurement preferences, and the application of trade remedy laws had all but replaced tariffs and quotas as powerful and discriminatory instruments of protection. The GATT and its subsidiary agreements constituted valiant attempts to discipline the application of state intervention and trade remedy law, but all these instruments of intervention or protection introduced are inherently discriminatory. Subsidies and procurement preferences expressly favour domestic over imported products and seek to overcome lack of comparative advantage. Trade remedy laws – providing for the application of anti-dumping and countervailing duties and similar measures – are equally discriminatory. Imported products judged to benefit from injurious subsidies may be countervailed without regard to the existence of subsidies on the domestic product, subsidies that may have provoked the injurious subsidy in the country of export in the first place. The standards for countering price discrimination vary widely between domestic products, subject to the penalties of competition law, and imported products, subject to anti-dumping duties. There is no effective recourse for a domestic producer to obtain relief from lower cost competition from domestic products via a safeguard mechanism, yet such action against imported products is explicitly sanctioned in the GATT and widely practised in a discriminatory manner. Codes negotiated during the Tokyo Round of GATT negotiations had further entrenched the rights of members – particularly the United States – to practise such discriminatory policies.

In addition to the diminishing strength of multilateral disciplines, Canada was also finding that its ability to influence the final outcome of negotiations was declining. Since the first round of GATT negotiations in 1947, the GATT had by 1985 grown from twenty-three to ninety-six contracting parties with a further twenty-eight countries applying the rules of the GATT on a de facto basis. Consensus, accordingly, had become much more difficult to achieve. Most of the new entrants were developing countries which benefited from GATT rights until they became too competitive in traditional products such as textiles, clothing, and steel and were then subjected to import quotas or 'voluntary' export restraints. These countries accepted – perhaps with reason – few of GATT's obligations and consequently pursued mercantilist trade policies that sought to establish domestic manufacture of products that could be imported at lower cost from abroad. They were, moreover, wary of efforts led by the United States to extend GATT principles of non-discrimination into new areas such as services, intellectual property, and investment. The result had been the 'UNCTADization' of GATT, i.e., the breakdown of the contracting parties into regional groups with consensus on what to do resulting from arduous discussions of texts rather than policies.[23] While industrialized countries, of course, retained the capacity to negotiate within the framework of the GATT, the task of determining negotiating agendas and timetables had become enormously more difficult than in earlier years.[24]

A further adverse development had been the reduction in the number of developed countries determined to play an independent role. During the Kennedy Round of GATT negotiations (1964-7), Britain, Ireland, the Nordics, Austria, Switzerland, Spain, Portugal, Australia, and New Zealand, each as dependent as Canada upon the multilateral system, had all been full and independent participants. Together they formed a group of smaller countries with whom alliances could be forged in pursuit of common interests on particular issues and who could thus combine their bargaining power and leverage against the larger countries. By the time of the Tokyo Round (1973-9), most of the European members of this group had been gathered into the smothering embrace of the EC, either through accession as in the case of the UK, Denmark, and Ireland, or through free-trade agreements with the EC for industrial products, as in the case of Sweden, Norway, and other members of the European Free Trade Association. Such countries were no longer independent participants; furthermore, they saw their principal trade policy interest as the preservation of their preferred access to the enlarged European market. Multilateral trade liberalization no longer held the same attraction for them. By 1985, Western Europe was well on its way to becoming one large free-trade area governed by arrangements loosely blessed by GATT but essentially outside it. Even Australia and New Zealand had long since worked out a separate arrangement between themselves. Only Canada remained as a small, industrialized country heavily dependent on trade with one country but with a wholly independent trade policy. In these circumstances, with whom could Canada form alliances?

The results of the Tokyo Round were largely determined by the level of the lowest common denominator among the United States, Japan, and the European Community. Canada achieved only meagre gains in improved access to Japan and the EC while at the same time making substantial reductions in protection afforded Canadian producers in the bilateral tariff negotiations with the United States. The overall consequences of the Tokyo Round were perverse for Canada: the countries with which a special relationship had been sought earlier in the decade (the EC and Japan) paid little for their improved access to the North American market and the United States began to deploy, in a discriminatory manner, its trade remedy laws – as strengthened and given new legitimacy by codes negotiated during the Tokyo Round – as its principal instruments of protection.

As the 1980s dawned, Canadian trade dependence upon the US market started to grow prodigiously and a new multilateral round, forever the beacon of the old realities and the old trade policy, seemed far in the future. By the mid-1980s, not comfortable with the status quo and fearful of the consequences of the nationalist option, Canadians seemed ready to address the old and recurring option to further integrate the Canadian economy into the international economy and improve access to all markets, but especially the US market, by all available means, including a bilateral free-trade agreement. Changing realities had now made this an appealing option for more than just economists.

The Commission Addresses the Options
The focus for much of the debate in 1983-5 was the ongoing research and consultations of the Royal Commission on the Economic Union and Development Prospects for Canada,[25] chaired by Donald Macdonald. Throughout 1984, it was an open secret that the Commission was struggling with the issue of a Canada-US free-trade agreement and leaning towards a positive recommendation. Much of its work responded to the theme of letting markets work, in keeping with the more conservative tenor of society in the 1980s. Nationalists on the staff and at seminars lamented that the Commission had been captured by neoclassical economists. They complained that the Commission was responding to the views of the scions of Canadian business, such as Bell Canada chairman Jean de Grandpré and Bank of Montreal chairman William Mulholland who, in a joint appearance, told commissioners to favour policies that 'place greater reliance on market forces to determine the allocation of the bulk of Canada's resources in order to promote greater efficiency and productivity.'[26]

One of the staff economists at the Commission was John Whalley, an economics professor at the University of Western Ontario in London. His expertise lay in general equilibrium models. A recent research interest had been interprovincial barriers to trade. He was asked to take the lead in preparing research and background papers on trade policy. It did not take him long to decide that the only issue of any consequence was Canada-US free trade and he began to devote his considerable energy to organizing seminars and research projects that would examine the issue from every angle. He was amazed to learn from some of his more cautious colleagues, familiar with the ways of government, that he was dabbling in a hot and dangerous topic. Ottawa's traditionalism and orthodoxies even extended to research for royal commissions. Undeterred, he pressed on. By the time his assignment with the Commission came to an end, he had written, edited, or encouraged the production of seven volumes of research related to this theme.[27] More than any other person on the Commission staff, he ensured that the free-trade option gained a full hearing.

Within the political science cadre of researchers, Gil Winham, a professor from Dalhousie University in Halifax with an interest in trade policy and the conduct of negotiations, had come to the same conclusion. The issue to be addressed was free trade. A third research coordinator, Jack Quinn, a law professor at Osgoode Hall in Toronto, shared Whalley's and Winham's assessment that if the Commission wanted to make a statement about trade policy, it had to confront Canada-US free trade. Over the course of the summer of 1984, these three researchers began to put together the elements of a package for consideration by commissioners in the fall. By this time, it had become clear that Macdonald agreed with their assessment: the issue was free trade.

For Whalley, economic considerations were paramount. Economists have long sought to analyze and quantify the effects of trade liberalization. Their research has established that removing barriers multilaterally is better than removing them bilaterally, which in turn is better than removing them unilaterally, which finally is better than maintaining them. Canadian empirical research since the 1950s had been fascinated with the quantitative effect of bilateral free trade with the United States.[28] Various economists had suggested that bilateral free trade with the United States could increase Canadian GNP by as much as 10 per cent, although the margin had somewhat decreased over the years as part of the benefits of bilateral free trade were realized through multilateral negotiations. Whether achieved bilaterally or multilaterally, the increase in GNP would result in part because free trade would eliminate some distortion in relative prices. When consumers are given prices that more accurately reflect costs, they maximize their consumption in a way that minimizes the cost of the nation's resources and labour. This is the so-called classical economic argument for free trade. Empirical measurement indicated that gains from free trade of this sort would not be large. Marginal changes in protection, such as a gradual reduction in tariff protection over a period of years, would be unlikely to lead to dramatic changes in economic performance.[29]

While the price effects of free trade would be important, the economists further argued that the greatest part of the increase in GNP would come about through a rise in productivity achieved through economies of scale at the level of the producing firm. Canadian productivity had long lagged behind American levels because individual plants were not sufficiently specialized. Because of Canada's smaller market, production runs were necessarily shorter and the variety produced in each plant consequently greater. In the 1970s and early 1980s, Canadian manufacturers tended to be some 20 to 25 per cent less productive than their American counterparts. Multilateral tariff cutting, the autopact, and international rule making had already reduced that figure; thirty years earlier, economists had estimated the figure to be closer to 40 per cent.

These economic arguments, however, were not widely shared among Canadians. Few of them appreciated the extent to which success in the market is the best evidence of economic efficiency. Those firms that survive the market process are the ones that steadily contribute to achieving higher levels of national income. Additionally, well-meaning politicians, often because of the political influence of concentrated special interests, frustrate this process by introducing tariffs, taxes, and subsidies to support declining industries. Among various instruments available to governments to influence the economy, tariffs and other barriers at the border tend to be among the worst forms of market intervention. These measures provide short-term palliatives for the affected industry, but also result in rising prices and falling incomes for the economy as a whole. Declining industries that cannot meet the challenge of the market steadily contribute towards declining levels of national income. Tariffs, quotas, subsidies, and other support measures that keep them alive neither increase demand for goods nor raise employment in the long term. If, for example, as a result of tariffs or other trade barriers, Canadians must pay more for clothing or for shoes, they have that much less money with which to buy other goods; this, in turn, reduces demand for goods and services generally.

GETTING TO WORK ON FOREIGN MARKETS

Arch Dale, *Winnipeg Free Press*, 22 November 1930

From the point of view of economists, therefore, the removal of tariffs and other trade barriers would have a dramatic impact on Canadian industrial attitudes. With the entire North American market open to them, Canadian firms could lengthen their production runs and reduce costs by producing larger quantities and fewer varieties of goods. A free-trade arrangement with the United States could thus expand Canadian industries' potential market by a factor of ten or more.

The researchers recognized that if Canada and the United States were to enter into more open trade arrangements, some firms would undoubtedly experience difficulties in adjusting to the new situation. As is the case in the ongoing process of economic change, some enterprises and their work force would grow, while others would shrink. Evidence from past experience in Canada and a great number of other countries suggested that there would be a significant net gain in output and employment; the amount of adjustment would be manageable; and this adjustment would likely be within industries rather than between industries. The phased implementation of new trading arrangements would ensure that there would be adequate time to adjust to new export opportunities and new competition in the domestic market.

It would have been relatively easy to pick out sectors and companies which considered themselves threatened or which thought that the status quo would best serve their interests. Their representatives were quick to speak out and the Commission received a number of briefs to this effect. For economists, however, the reality is that change is constant and that the status quo is neither a viable nor a desirable option. There would always be weak firms and strong firms within every industry. Expanded trading opportunities would help both kinds of firms, whereas the absence of such opportunities would harm both kinds of firms. The purpose of trade negotiations with the United States was to expand opportunities in such a way as to benefit strong firms and encourage weaker firms to strengthen their competitive position.[30]

The Commission's staff economists concluded that the adjustment process would be very similar to that which had taken place when the European Economic Community had been formed. Products of a similar kind were both exported and imported in greater volume; individual firms became more specialized and expanded their exports; and imports increased, but total sales did not fall because a greater proportion of output was exported. The adjustment took place within firms and, accordingly, the amount of dislocation of labour and the amount of retooling was relatively small.

Commission researchers accepted that in a bilateral trade agreement with the United States, the problem of adjustment would be larger for Canada than for the United States. An agreement would directly affect a quarter or more of Canadian GNP, or half of the goods-producing sector of the economy. While the long-term benefits were clear, these could only be achieved if there were structural changes in the economy.

Would the same set of industries continue to locate in Canada after free trade, or more accurately, would the same industries locate in one of the Canadian or one of the American industrial regions because, with free trade, the nation of location would no longer be of such importance? Experience suggested that the regional location of any firm depended on a host of factors: the availability of specialized suppliers, the availability of specialized labour skills, infrastructure, costs, land rents, taxes, living costs. The list went on and on. The average wage would not be important. A correct assessment would be based on the wages paid for the skills required by a particular firm. Each firm would have a different set of requirements and would choose its most suitable location accordingly. The advantages which had brought Canadian industries to their existing regional locations would not disappear under free trade.

Industrial regions are often perceived to be far more unstable than they really are. The relative economic sizes of North American regions would change if the regions had different growth rates. None, however, actually needed to decline. In regions that grew the fastest, wages, rents, and other costs would rise and there would be corresponding relative declines in regions of slower growth.

Staff economists pointed out that in one respect free trade might make matters worse for Canada. Without bilateral free trade, there could be an incentive for foreign firms to establish branch plants in Canada to avoid payment of the Canadian tariff. With free trade, this incentive would be gone, at least for US-based firms. However, free trade would also remove a substantial disadvantage to location in Canada. With free trade, any firm located in one of the Canadian regions would no longer have to pay the American tariff or move to the United States to get behind the wall of tariff and other barriers for its exports to the United States.

The economists knew, of course, that the future competitiveness of Canadian industry and new employment opportunities would be affected by a host of considerations, of which trade policy would be only one. In the Canada-US context, it was clear that not all industries would be affected in the same way by new opportunities and competition. This was nothing new. Canadian industry had already been required to rationalize and reorganize as a result of previous trade negotiations and other exogenous factors. Even in the absence of a bilateral agreement with the United States, Canadian industry would continue to be challenged by technological innovation, international competition, and other factors.

These were the issues addressed by Whalley, Winham, Quinn, and their colleagues in their research and in seminars and colloquia over the course of the summer and fall of 1984. The direction of their thinking was clear; the arguments were about matters of detail. Gradually the shape of their recommendations began to fall into place.[31]

In November 1984, Donald Macdonald went public and declared that Canadians should be prepared to take a leap of faith that they had the necessary self-confidence to prosper in a more open trade relationship with the United States. While attending a conference[32] on Canada-US relations at Arden House in Harriman, New York, he gave *Globe and Mail* correspondent Bill Johnson a briefing to explain what he was telling the conference. He told him:

> Many Canadians are nervous about the prospect of putting in jeopardy that perhaps fragmentary structure of national sovereignty that was built in a country called Canada – a country that started off, after all, with a plain defiance of the north-south economic pressures ... If we do get down to a point where it's going to be a leap of faith, then I think at some point some Canadians are going to have to be bold and say, yes, we will do that ... It's another step in our evolution, and we've got enough confidence in ourselves to do it.[33]

While his choice of words may have proved unfortunate, he greatly advanced the credibility of those espousing free trade and brought the debate to the front page.

In many ways, Macdonald personified the changes in society. As a newly elected MP in the 1960s, he had prided himself on being labelled an economic nationalist. As a senior government minister in the 1970s, he had seen himself as a pragmatist in the mold of Lester Pearson, Mitchell Sharp, and Bud Drury. As chair of the Commission in the 1980s, he accepted the new realities and saw a need to return to the discipline of market-driven economics. It would be the theme of the Commission's report.

Late in November and again in February, commissioners met to discuss the trade policy aspects of their report. They listened to the conclusions of their researchers, they read synopses of hundreds of briefs and thousands of pages of testimony, they listened to the dissenting views of other researchers, they asked probing questions, they debated among themselves, and they concluded that they were prepared to recommend that Canada seek a free-trade agreement with the United States. They authorized Whalley and his collaborators to put together the necessary chapters to explain the rationale for their decision.[34]

For those who believed in the benefits of free trade, the Commission thus performed its most valuable service in further conditioning the country for a decision which many thought needed to be taken and which some even thought was overdue. The final report was not, however, unanimously accepted. Gérard Docquier, the lone voice of labour on the Commission, declared his opposition early in the debate and, with the help of CLC economists, penned an impassioned minority opinion.

Among the influential voices which joined the debate was that of Simon Reisman. Based on his considerable experience, first as a trade negotiator who had been part of the Canadian delegation to the 1947-8 Havana Conference which sought to establish an International Trade Organization, then as a senior mandarin to both Conservative and Liberal governments and, upon retirement, as a denizen of corporate boardrooms, he made a cogent case for free trade. Speaking on Canada-US relations at a conference in April 1984 sponsored by the prestigious Brookings Institution in Washington, he counselled:

> If the United States and Canada were able to work out a free-trade agreement it would be a good thing for both countries and a good example to the world. It would make both countries richer. It would also make us better neighbours, because it would remove many of the issues about which we have been squabbling for many years.
>
> A free-trade arrangement would not weaken Canadian sovereignty or Canadian resolve to remain independent. Indeed, by enriching Canada and by raising its confidence, the agreement would strengthen Canada's purpose and its ability to survive as a strong free nation.[35]

He also cautioned that for such an initiative to succeed it would require just the right chemical mixture of bad times in Canada and good times in the United States. In 1984, he questioned whether that mixture prevailed. A year later, speaking at a conference in Toronto sponsored by the *Financial Post*, he changed his tune; he concluded that it was time to proceed. In his view, there was sufficient business interest in Canada and political interest in the United States to make an agreement feasible. To his later regret he also suggested that should Canada add access to fresh water to the agenda, the job of negotiating a good agreement would be that much easier. In the fall of 1985, he privately advised Prime Minister Mulroney that the time to proceed was now.[36]

3

No Anchor, No Rudder, No Compass: The US Setting

Chaos umpire sits
And by decision more embroils the fray
By which he reigns; next him high arbiter
Chance governs all.
– Milton, *Paradise Lost*

C hanges in Canadians' perception of their place in the world and of the surety provided by the multilateral trading system in the early 1980s were matched by changes in US attitudes and policies towards its trading partners.[1] In the United States there was similar growing unease about continued reliance on multilateralism and about the easy assumptions of the immediate postwar era. American concerns and anxieties and their expression in renewed protectionism helped to convince Canadians of the need for a new approach to the management of Canada-US relations. Ironically, they also made Americans more receptive to a proposal from Canada. By the early 1980s, traditional US protectionism, which had been kept in check through two generations by a coalition of internationalists in successive administrations and congresses, broke through and again became the respectable, established view. Clothed in the rhetoric of 'fairness' and 'reciprocity,' the new protectionism was nothing more than old-fashioned mercantilism. These attitudes also found expression in a renewed interest in bilateral trade agreements.

The Development of Modern US Trade Policy
United States trade policy in the postwar years was built upon the success of the reciprocal trade agreements program introduced in 1934 by President Roosevelt's secretary of state, Cordell Hull, as an antidote to congressional protectionism. The latter had reached its zenith in the Smoot-Hawley tariff of 1930 that had contributed so much to deepening the global depression. Congress belatedly recognized that high tariffs did not lead to economic

Uncle Sam: "I can almost hear them singing 'The Star Spangled Banner' in Ottawa, Be gosh."

growth, and grudgingly granted the president authority to negotiate tariff reductions on a bilateral, reciprocal basis. As a harbinger of the changed times, Senator Reed Smoot of Utah and Representative Willis Hawley of Oregon, sponsors of the 1930 excesses of congressional protectionism, were defeated in the 1932 election, while Cordell Hull, one of its staunchest opponents as the ranking Democrat on the House Ways and Means Committee, had been elected senator from Tennessee and then appointed secretary of state by President Roosevelt. By the end of the Second World War, the administration had negotiated some twenty-nine agreements with twenty-five countries, including two agreements with Canada. Much progress had thus been made in reversing the protectionism of the 1930s.[2]

The reciprocal trade agreements program was renewed after the war, but the administration now added a new twist: it coupled the program with its new-found faith in multilateralism. Rather than negotiate new agreements on a bilateral, reciprocal basis, it now negotiated simultaneously with all interested countries through the new mechanism of the General Agreement on Tariffs and Trade (GATT) and extended the benefits of each agreement reached on a multilateral basis. Congress never accepted this revolutionary new policy. It expressed its disapproval by refusing to accept the 1948 Havana Charter for an International Trade Organization and in each subsequent renewal of the president's trade negotiating authority, reminded the administration that the GATT was nothing more than an executive agreement which the Congress had never approved.[3]

Successive administrations, however, remained committed to a multilateral trading system, seeing it as the best way of managing the United States' diverse trade relations with other countries. In the first decades after the Second World War, this policy was founded on the premise that eliminating barriers to the free exchange of goods among nations would benefit not only the United States, but others as well. Reducing tariffs, quotas, and similar trade restrictions made not only economic sense to US policymakers, but even greater political sense. Merchandise trade during this period occupied only some 5 per cent of US gross national product. United States competitiveness was assured: the US consistently ran a merchandise trade surplus and used this to finance investment, aid, and military assistance. Of greater significance to US policymakers, the industrialized world ravaged by war needed prosperity to maintain peace and establish a bulwark against the growing new threat of world communism.

Throughout this period, the role of the United States in the management and leadership of the international economy and international institutions cannot be overestimated. The negotiation of new international rules frequently involved the internationalization of US domestic legislation or ideology. This leadership also had its negative dimension: the accepted application of these rules was frequently determined by US practice. This phenomenon is well demonstrated by the chequered history of the application of rules to trade in textiles and clothing and the inability to extend liberalizing rules to trade in agriculture. The United States, for example, received a waiver from its GATT obligations in 1955 so that it could apply quotas on imports of agricultural products in order to maintain domestic price support programs. Similarly, in 1961 the US led the way in negotiating the Short-term Cotton Textile Arrangement, the first of many special trade-restrictive arrangements to follow. In both cases, US domestic politics determined that the application of liberal rules needed to be tempered in order to satisfy the protectionist needs of a powerful special interest group.

The pre-eminent role of the United States in the world and US perception of that role were captured rather wittily by Charles Ritchie. Reflecting on his term as Canada's ambassador to Washington in the 1960s, he wrote:

> Even when the sun of favour is shining, there are outer limits for a foreigner to exchanges of thought with the Washington higher management. For one thing, the President never listens – or at any rate never listens to foreigners. He talks them down inexhaustibly. The phrase 'consultations with allies' is apt to mean, in United States terms, briefing allies, lecturing allies, sometimes pressuring allies or sounding out allies to see if they are sound. The idea of learning anything from allies seems strange to official Washington thinking. The word comes from Washington and is home-made.[4]

During the 1950s and 1960s, US trade and economic policy and foreign policy were largely in harmony – a period of enlightened interest and unchallenged leadership. The US thus led a largely successful assault on the most blatant obstacles to trade among free-world nations. Those roadblocks were primarily tariffs and quantitative restrictions, the first targets of the original twenty-three signatories to the GATT. The success of GATT in the rounds that followed laid bare the more intractable barriers to trade. But GATT's success was accompanied by the continued cant of the mercantilists. Increasingly during the late 1960s and into the 1970s, new forms of protectionism crept into the shaping of trade policy throughout much of the world. The concept of reciprocity assumed a new meaning. Previously the cornerstone of a doctrine that rested on extending mutual trade concessions, reciprocity now came to be linked with pursuit of measures designed to counter, or retaliate against what were seen as unfair or restrictive trade practices by other nations. This brought new challenges to US trade policymakers.

Up until the Tokyo Round, the seventh in GATT's periodic negotiating conferences, US trade policy was largely subservient to foreign policy concerns. The US establishment of the Marshall Plan and its sponsorship of the Organization for European Economic Cooperation (the OEEC, forerunner of the OECD) were both dedicated to foreign policy objectives and provided impetus to efforts at intra-European cooperation and integration. The US backing of the 1958 Treaty of Rome establishing the European Economic Community (EC) explicitly recognized that although the EC would erect preferences and establish a discriminatory Common Agricultural Policy (CAP), US geopolitical interests were served by European unity and took precedence over narrow commercial interests. Early on, however, the US took exception to the discriminatory aspects of the EC's CAP and has continued to view it as the most distasteful consequence of European economic integration, most recently in a direct assault during the Uruguay Round of GATT negotiations.

Congress was never comfortable with this State Department view of the world and in 1962 established a new, cabinet-level official, the Special Trade Representative, to run US trade policy. This new official was placed in the executive office of the president but was to take direction from the Congress, in effect providing greater congressional oversight over the administration's exercise of its delegated authority. The shift was also evident in the attitude towards various EC enlargements starting with the entry of the UK, Ireland, and Denmark in 1973 and the renewal of the Lomé Convention in 1974 (the treaty that governed relations between the Community and the former colonies of its member states). These European developments were now judged on the basis of commercial interests rather than foreign policy attitudes. The State Department had been effectively replaced by a new and aggressive player. Similarly, US sponsorship of Japan's entry into GATT and into the family of nations in the 1950s was gradually supplanted by an aggressive resentment of Japan's commercial success and its chronic merchandise trade surplus with the United States.[5]

By the end of the Kennedy Round of GATT negotiations (1964-7), congressional tolerance of liberalism and multilateralism in administration trade policy had effectively come to an end. Congress rejected the anti-dumping code negotiated during the Kennedy Round and sought to shorten the negotiating leash it periodically gave the president. The Nixon administration, bedeviled by scandal, failed in its first two attempts to gain an acceptable new authority and, only belatedly, with its trading partners waiting in Geneva, received authority for the new Tokyo Round in the Trade Act of 1974. This new law established a new marriage of convenience between Congress and the administration: it gave the president extensive authority and established the 'fast-track' approval method for implementing the results of the negotiations, but it also rewrote much of US trade law and gave Congress additional oversight authority.

The Trade Act of 1974 began the change from a tariff-centred trade policy to the administered or contingent system of protection. It toughened the anti-dumping and countervailing duty statutes, rewrote the escape law provisions, and added new investigative authority. Thus the delicate balance that had been maintained between executive liberalism and legislative protectionism for nearly four decades began to tilt towards protectionism. The consensus favouring trade liberalization in the United States had been originally based on the secure knowledge that US industry had a broadly based comparative advantage. This had changed by the 1970s as differences in per capita wealth among OECD countries narrowed and the newly industrialized countries became more competitive. As a result, the consensus favouring continued trade liberalization eroded considerably. By the late 1970s, there developed a widely held view in the United States that excessive imports were a major cause of damage to US industries and that such imports should be curbed.[6]

By the 1980s, US trade policy was suffering from a gap between ideology and practice. US policymakers relied on a strong and traditional ideological orientation, but appeared confused about its day-to-day implementation. The Reagan administration's trade policy was characterized by a visible and vigorous pursuit of individual issues and by the extension of international discipline into new areas for the benefit of US traders. While some charitable analysts chose to characterize this trade policy as pragmatic, a more compelling assessment was that US policymakers were struggling to come to terms with the new realities of many more trading partners, diminished competitiveness in basic US industries, a burgeoning trade deficit fuelled by an overvalued dollar, and a growing budgetary deficit.

US Decision-Making: The Burden of Divided Power

The US political decision-making process virtually guarantees imprecision and frequent changes in direction. In Canada, while there are many actors and various levels of influence, in the final analysis federal policy emerges from one source: cabinet. A role for the provinces in the trade policy-making process emerged in the 1970s, but its final shape remains to be determined. In the United States, on the other hand, federal policy emerges from a highly brokered political market involving the administration, Congress, and various special interest groups. Successful policymaking requires coalitions, many of which are forged out of what appear to be unrelated interests.[7]

The much touted constitutional separation of powers in no way does justice to the very real dispersion of power within both the administration and Congress. The Congress had become notorious by the 1980s for the proliferation of internal and independent power centres, each represented or headed by one of the innumerable committee and subcommittee chairs. With the disappearance of the seniority system, the absence of any centralized direction or control over the institutions had resulted in near paralysis of the legislative system as individual interest group objectives got played off against each other. In many respects, the administration, even on the biggest issues, had become beset by the same kind of dynamics as different agencies and departments, or even factions within them, competed against each other in the promotion of their specific agenda. The political system had, in many ways, moved from the doctrine of separation of powers to that of the sub-separation of powers. One Canadian student of US policymaking wrote:

> Public disagreement between members of an American cabinet, both before and after the introduction of legislation, is commonplace. Cabinet officers freely advocate and promote particular policy objectives ... without regard for ... cabinet solidarity. There are many examples of a cabinet officer working hard, and sometimes successfully, to overturn policies advocated and even initiated by cabinet colleagues. The notion of cabinet secrecy is surely not a powerful one in a political culture which so values and cultivates leaks to the press as a standard part of the policy-making process.[8]

Within Congress, trade policy came to be viewed as an important ingredient in formulating domestic economic policy and in meeting the needs of individual interest groups. Congress became increasingly oriented towards a 'fair-trade' ideology. It preferred to strengthen legal processes in pursuit of US trade interests. Members of Congress tend to be preoccupied by current problems and by elections every two years. The increased desire of Congress to play a role not only in setting US trade goals but also in its precise implementation was demonstrated by the growing number of trade bills and resolutions being introduced in Congress. Throughout the postwar years, dozens of bills and resolutions per session were not uncommon. Few of these, however, reached the floor of either the Senate or the House; many served their purpose when read into the congressional record; others routinely died in committee. The 98th Congress (1983-4), however, witnessed the introduction of 882 bills and resolutions and a determined desire to pass them into law. The passage of the Trade and Tariff Act of 1984 marked the first time since the depression that Congress had foisted a major trade act on an unenthusiastic president.[9] Flushed with success, the 99th Congress returned to the fray with the reintroduction of many pet projects that had not been picked up in the 1984 Act. The days of clear administration leadership in trade policymaking were definitely over.

The Reagan Administration: Searching for the Right Mix

Speaking to the nation in his second state-of-the-union speech in January 1983, President Reagan made it clear that, in economic terms, the state of the union was more closely entwined with the state of the world than ever before: 'Every American has a role and a stake in international trade. One out of every five jobs in our country depends on trade. We export over 20 percent of our industrial production and 40 percent of our farmland produces for export.'[10] The theme was repeated throughout the speech and others that followed. Trade had become a major preoccupation of the Reagan administration. The reason, noted then United States Trade Representative and later Labor Secretary Bill Brock, was that the 1982 decline in trade had contributed greatly to unemployment in the US. The decline in trade, moreover, was also contributing to looming budget deficits.

Used to a low level of dependence on foreign markets, many Americans were unprepared for the impact which increasing dependence can have. The global recession of 1981-2 drove home to Americans its full implications. The effects of the recession were exacerbated by a new emphasis on mercantilism in the world, with governments adopting protectionist measures to increase exports and decrease imports. The US reaction was not a desire to become more competitive; rather, it was a conviction that foreigners were taking advantage of American generosity.

The approach of President Reagan and his emphasis on the virtues of free trade – 'as leader of the West and as a country that has become great and rich because of economic freedom, America must be an unrelenting advocate of free trade'[11] – reflected America's postwar approach. But times had changed. Only a decade earlier, trade issues did not receive much attention – but then trade still accounted for only a little over 5 per cent of US GNP during much of the 1970s. By the early 1980s, however, trade's percentage of US GNP had doubled. While the US economy remained far less dependent on foreign trade than other industrialized countries, a number of key domestic industries now relied heavily on export sales for survival and others had become particularly vulnerable to foreign competition, at home and abroad. As USTR Brock pointed out: 'In recent years, four out of five of the new US jobs in manufacturing have been created by international trade. One out of every three acres planted by American farmers is producing crops for export. Two trillion dollars of goods and services currently are being traded internationally and the potential for growth is unlimited.'[12]

In spite of action to correct the value of the dollar and the large decrease in the cost of oil imports as its price and volume declined, the US trade deficit worsened. For 1985, it was a record $148.5 billion – and the US International Trade Commission claimed that each billion dollar change in the trade balance affected at least 25,000 jobs. Many of the lost job opportunities were in manufacturing, where the deficit widened most rapidly. Between 1979 and 1982, employment fell by 39 per cent in the US auto industry, 47 per cent in steel, 19 per cent among shoe manufacturers, and 17 per cent in the apparel industry. (Not surprisingly, a number of these industries appeared before Congress to voice their concerns about a free-trade agreement with Canada). On the other hand, protectionist measures to save jobs proved costly. According to a study prepared by the Institute for International Economics, in the late 1970s US consumers paid an estimated $58,000 annually per job saved for protecting the domestic manufacturers of specialty steel, television sets, and footwear.[13]

Agricultural exports, long the mainstay of American export success, began to decline in the early 1980s, and by 1985 the surplus was only $11.4 billion, a decline of nearly $8 billion from 1984 and less than half of the $26.6 billion surplus recorded in 1981. The reasons were varied: the strength of the dollar; the 1980 grain embargo which brought US reliability into question and made traditional suppliers such as Canada and new suppliers such as Argentina look more attractive; the 1981 Farm Bill which made US agricultural exports less competitive on world markets at a time when world prices were declining; and increased self-sufficiency among importers, especially in the Third World. Subsidies, particularly in the European Community, also played a part.

If agriculture faced greater competition abroad for its sales, at home the US auto industry and steel producers faced increasing pressure as the domestic car market lost ground to foreign competition, especially from Japan. Even though iron and steel imports declined – partly as a result of agreements with EC producers and other restrictions on the import of foreign steel – domestic steel mills continued to operate at only 40 per cent capacity, and unemployment in the industry reached the 50 per cent mark.

Efforts were made by people like UAW president Douglas Fraser and Chrysler president Lee Iacocca to reverse the trend. Iacocca formed a group called the US Trade Policy Council with members from the steel, auto, and aviation industries dedicated to a 'level playing field.' Their efforts met with little success. The voices being raised in Washington in favour of protectionism were shrill and frequent and had the potential to become a chorus, but they could not agree on the harmony. The purveyors of protectionism failed to form a single protectionist coalition. Most of their ideas were industry-specific, with only a handful aimed at broader measures. For the most part, they remained a collection of soloists with only marginal successes in erecting, for example, new barriers on steel, textiles, and other products, or in attaching 'Buy America' provisions to some legislation.

The most highly touted market-access legislation was a proposal by Missouri senator Jack Danforth to open foreign telecommunications markets to US producers. If US sales did not increase then the bill required the president to limit access of foreign telecommunications to US markets. Another approach, imposing a 25 per cent import surcharge on goods from some countries with big trade surpluses with the United States was put forward by Representatives Dan Rostenkowski of Illinois and Dick Gephardt of Indiana and Senator Lloyd Bentsen of Texas. Eliminating unfair trade practices – subsidies and dumping – in an effort to create a level playing field was the objective of legislation introduced by senators like John Heinz of Pennsylvania. These legislators were also interested in limiting presidential discretion in trade disputes, fearing that trade considerations were too easily shunted aside to accommodate diplomatic concerns.

No More Mr. Nice Guy

To meet the surging protectionist tide, the administration went on the offensive on trade issues in 1985. It initiated investigations of unfair trade practices under section 301 of the 1974 Trade Act, at first timidly, but as the protection-

ist surge failed to dissipate, more and more stridently. Administration officials convinced themselves that the vigorous application of US trade law
would keep the protectionist forces at bay. They thus decided to fight the
congressional brand of protectionism with their own housebrand. For some,
Mr. Reagan's free-trade credentials had been suspect all along. Fred Bergsten
of the International Economics Institute, concluded that 'regardless of its
free-trade rhetoric, the Reagan administration has allowed more restrictive
measures in the past two years than any administration since the 1930s,' and
Harald Malmgren, a Washington-based trade consultant and former USTR
official, warned, 'the White House is worried about the election and is prepared to grant import trade restrictions to vulnerable industries.'[14]

The time for even more serious action was apparent when Congress
returned from its summer recess with increased fervour for its own protectionist brand of trade policy. The congressional leadership increasingly intimated that without administration leadership, some of the many bills being
considered would become law.

All along, the Achilles heel of the Reagan administration's foreign economic policy had been its failure to address the strong US dollar. On 22
September 1985 at the Plaza Hotel in New York, finance ministers of
Germany, France, Japan, and the UK finally persuaded the United States to
pursue a mix of policies that would bring down the overvalued dollar. The
mere announcement of these policies had an immediate impact on the
exchange markets. The next day, the president went on television and despite
strong personal misgivings, made a major statement on US trade policy
which emphasized a new 'get-tough' policy with unfair traders. The president's handlers had convinced him that in order to keep the protectionist
appetite in Congress in check, he would have to lash out at 'unfairness,' a
concept repugnant to his free-trade ideology. The president thus shifted the
administration's policy emphasis from free trade to fair trade and created a
special strike force to root out unfair trade practices under the leadership of
Commerce Deputy Secretary Bruce Smart.

To get the ball rolling, the administration initiated more unfair trade
actions: three against Brazil because of its restrictions on access by foreign
computer firms; two against South Korea because of its limitations on
opportunities for US insurance companies in its market and its failure to
protect US copyright, patent, and trademark rights; one against Japan's ciga-
rette and tobacco monopoly; and one against the EC under the GATT over
its wheat export subsidies. It also joined with industry to mount a 'Crafted
With Pride in the USA' sales promotion campaign that struck a responsive
nerve among consumers. Big-name personalities like Bob Hope donated

their time, and major retailers like Wal-Mart and J.C. Penney prominently featured US products.

The administration's 'get-tough' policy had a two-pronged, interrelated purpose: appease short-term pressures at home while moving on long-term interests abroad. Thus it sought simultaneously to respond to short-term, protectionist pressures and to take an active, forward-looking approach to the trade issues of the 1980s, using the elaboration of the multilateral trade policy agenda to demonstrate its continued, long-term commitment to a free-trade system. US officials identified a number of specific areas in which the administration wanted new or better international rules, including agriculture, trade in services, the trade aspects of investment (such as trade-related performance requirements), trade in counterfeit goods, the greater integration of developing countries into the GATT, and trade in high-technology goods. The president insisted that negotiating open markets would have long-term benefits and would result in adjustment to a stronger, more resilient world economy. This policy, however, failed to stem the tide: in Congress, because it did not sufficiently satisfy immediate demands from constituents at home to do something about unemployment, the trade deficit, unfairness, plant closures, and other symptoms of a troubled economy; abroad, because resistance to negotiating the administration's agenda was strong and concessions were given only grudgingly by the EC, Japan, and the major developing countries (LDCs), while resentment of individual trade actions grew.

A third plank in the administration's 1985 trade policy was renewed interest in bilateralism. Convinced that the EC was not committed to a new round of multilateral trade negotiations, that the Japanese were unlikely to make more concessions in the new round than they had in previous rounds, and that the major LDCs were essentially mischievous in their demands, the administration suggested that it was not necessarily committed to a new round. If the EC, Japan, and the major LDCs were not prepared to enter into a new round based on the US agenda, the United States would be prepared to satisfy its needs through bilateral negotiations. The bilateral trade agreement with Israel (negotiated in 1984 and brought into force in 1985) was touted as a harbinger of the new policy. If Canada was interested, the administration was prepared to negotiate with Canada. As early as 1983, USTR Brock told journalist Richard Gwyn:

> If not Canada, who? If we really and truly are willing to open ourselves to competition and to let the economic juices flow, to accept not only the rewards but the risks that come from doing that, I cannot imagine a more logical country in the world

than Canada. Isn't that a fabulous example to give to the rest of the world in terms of what can be achieved when people reduce trade barriers rather than raise them. We need some more examples. If Canada wants to do that, then it's worth a lot to us.[15]

Throughout this period, neither the administration nor Congress appeared to have clear plans as to what they wanted to do. The administration had an ideological attachment to the free play of market forces but in the face of political pressures, an increasing reluctance to pursue policies consistent with this ideology. Congress had a fair-trade ideology that in its practical application was protectionism, but it could not assemble broad enough coalitions for narrowly conceived single-issue causes. The result was stalemate and drift. Common to both, however, was the conviction that only the United States was playing by the rules and the time had come to even the odds. The theme of the United States as a patsy, while unfamiliar to its trading partners, had become deeply engrained in the US subconscious and thus contributed to the malaise and drift in US trade policy. The periods of creativity, purpose, and direction had been periods when at least the administration had been outward-looking and confident. The mid-1980s was not such a period.[16]

By the fall of 1985, the administration and Congress seemed finally to be on the same tack, but with divergent means and emphases and a mutual lack of trust. For America's trading partners, the message was ominous: now they faced both protectionist threats from the legislators and protectionist actions from the administration. The administration pleaded its tough actions were required to keep the protectionist horde under control, while Congress rationalized that its threatened new laws were required to restore fairness and a level playing field.

As an earnest indication of its continuing, get-tough policy, the administration released $280 million of mixed credits in October, combining loans with grants for export promotion, a reversal of its prior position. Similarly, a lingering dispute with the EC over European duties on US citrus products escalated into a major dispute when in November the administration retaliated by imposing a tariff on imports of pasta. In December, a major new farm bill offered higher direct subsidies than any previous policy, based on the dubious strategy that subsidizing farmers in the short-term would wean them from subsidies in the long run.

A complicating factor for the administration's management of its trade policy relations with the Congress was the move of Bill Brock from USTR to secretary of Labor in March 1985. Brock had been an able and experienced player on the Hill, as a member of Congress from Tennessee, as chair of the

Republican party, and as a cabinet officer. He had been under pressure for some time by White House chief of staff Donald Regan to take on the labour portfolio and had demurred, preferring the challenge of trade. There were suggestions that the president's closest advisors did not like Brock's independent power base and his excellent relations with Congress. They wanted him in a less visible assignment. His close ties with Republican Senate majority leader Bob Dole also disturbed the White House handlers. More positively, the problems generated by the forced resignation of former Labor Secretary Donovan over an alleged conflict of interest required a strong and clean successor. Brock fully fit that requirement.

It took the administration a month to find a replacement for Brock in Clayton Yeutter, a deputy USTR during the Nixon administration and most recently president of the Chicago Commodity Exchange. Trade policy veterans remembered him as a loud Nebraskan whose backslapping and corny sense of humour hid a shrewd politician. It took a further three months for Yeutter to gain Senate confirmation and begin to rebuild the trade representative's office in his own image. Yeutter started with the handicap of following a popular USTR, and had much less experience and rapport on the Hill than his predecessor. His job was not made any easier by the extended vacancy in the position. As criticism of the administration's trade policy mounted on the Hill, Yeutter appeared unable to deflect congressional frustration or harness it to the administration's own goals.[17]

The legislators, not to be outdone by the new zeal in the administration for protecting US trade interests, prepared competing omnibus trade bills involving reform of trade law, new multilateral trade negotiating authority, and monetary reform. On 22 May 1986, the House passed an omnibus trade bill (HR 4800) by a vote of 295 to 115. The legislation would make retaliation in unfair trade cases mandatory, require retaliation if other countries did not open up their telecommunications markets to US exports, auction off import quotas and use the money to help workers who lose their jobs due to imports, define denial of worker rights as an unfair trade practice, require action against countries with 'excessive trade surpluses,' and generally strengthen the USTR's hand on trade policy. In the Senate, a majority of the Senate Finance Committee, a coalition of Republicans and Democrats including John Chafee, John Danforth, John Heinz, and Daniel Patrick Moynihan, prepared their own omnibus trade bill (S-1860). But the senators, preoccupied with tax reform and other priorities, took no action before Congress rose for the mid-term election. As a parting shot, however, Congress passed legislation requiring a customs user fee and a differential tax on oil imports. In both cases, Canadian exporters were asked to make a large and discriminatory contribution to US domestic programs.

Throughout this period, both the administration and Congress had one eye cocked to the 1986 mid-term elections with the prize being control of the Senate. The slim Republican majority of 53 to 47 was vulnerable with more Republicans up for re-election than Democrats. Continued control of the Senate was considered vital by the president, although control had brought him small comfort from those Republican senators who nominally had his best interests at heart. On the trade front, Republican John Danforth, for example, had been an inveterate foe of the administration's policies. In the event, no amount of manoeuvring could retain Republican control. The 100th Congress would open with both Houses firmly under the leadership of the Democrats.

A trade bill was at the top of the new Congress's agenda early in 1987. Both the House and the Senate had bills ready and appeared eager to pass them into law. Additionally, the administration needed a bill because the president's authority to negotiate trade agreements would expire in January 1988 – long before the conclusion of the Uruguay Round of multilateral trade negotiations. The administration had built much of its trade policy on these talks and without negotiating authority in the hands of the Congress, serious negotiations could not begin.

The Canadian Dimension
For thirty-five years, the Canadian-US trade relationship had been comfortably lodged in the GATT and in two bilateral agreements on automobiles and defence products.[18] While individual disputes had been frequent – potatoes and fish in the east, lumber on the west coast, uranium and potash on the Prairies, and steel and border broadcasting in central Canada – they had been localized. Both sides had been careful to ensure that these disputes did not undermine the whole relationship. Except for episodic nationalist or protectionist lurches in both countries, the trade relationship had not called forth major expenditures of political energy to keep it running smoothly and profitably. Unlike the conflict between the Europeans and the Americans, the two countries had avoided chicken and pasta wars that risked calling into question the whole fabric of their relationship.

The Canada-US trade and economic relationship appeared to work fairly well without specialized bilateral institutions to support it. The ministerial committee that annually brought together large numbers of Canadian ministers and US secretaries was abandoned in the early 1970s as it was found to be too cumbersome and unproductive. Until the early 1980s, there were no annual trade meetings, no annual reviews of the state of the relationship, and no communiques by which diplomats earn their keep.

Canadians long assumed that proximity and neighbourliness assured them such a special relationship. But the indifferent reaction of John Connally, President Nixon's treasury secretary, to Canada's complaint that it had been included in the 1971 balance-of-payments measures, including a 10 per cent surcharge on all imports, had put paid to that notion. Nevertheless, there continued to be some evidence that Canadians were not regarded in the same light as the Europeans or Japanese. Indeed, in the periodic outbursts of protectionism in the early 1980s, Canadians had been spared the almost xenophobic US wrath against the unfairness of invidious foreigners. Canada had, however, suffered from the broad-brush nature of 'Buy America' provisions that were written into measures like the interstate highway construction bill and from the ever increasing trade remedy actions. As well, global trade actions on products such as steel had inevitably sideswiped Canadian trade interests.

By far America's largest trading partner and one of its fastest growing markets, Canada's relationship with the US remained, nonetheless, asymmetrical. While the US absorbed almost 80 per cent of Canadian exports in 1984 and supplied about 70 per cent of Canada's imports, Canadian trade accounted for only one-fifth of American imports and exports. Canadians thought they knew all about the United States – although many of their impressions were wrong or superficial – while most Americans had only the vaguest, and often wrong, impression of Canada. Acts of neighbourliness such as the 1980 Iran caper brought outpourings of warmth and affection, but made only small inroads into US awareness of Canada as anything more than the source of cold weather on the six o'clock news.

Traditionally, the United States had been indifferent to the negotiation of bilateral agreements with Canada. Negotiations in 1854, 1911, and 1947, and overtures at other times had almost invariably originated in Canada. The United States, with considerably less dependence than Canada upon international market forces, had been able to rely upon a dynamic and richly endowed domestic economy to secure and sustain its prosperity. Its pursuit of a multilateral trading order in the postwar years had been motivated more by political and security considerations than by economic policy. But by the early 1980s, the United States no longer enjoyed the same luxury of indifference to international economic developments. Its vulnerability to changing technologies, oil price fluctuation, low-cost competition from the newly industrializing countries, and currency movements, while less than that of Canada, was no less real. The power and interests of the Congress in trade legislation and in the multilateral and bilateral trade negotiations bore eloquent witness to the importance of a stable international trading environment for the US.

Diogenes, 18 June 1869

A PERTINENT QUESTION

MRS. BRITANNIA.—"IS IT POSSIBLE, MY DEAR, THAT YOU HAVE EVER GIVEN YOUR COUSIN JONATHAN ANY ENCOURAGEMENT."

MISS CANADA.—"ENCOURAGEMENT? CERTAINLY NOT, MAMA. I HAVE TOLD HIM WE CAN *NEVER* BE UNITED."

United States interest in a free-trade agreement with Canada thus needed to be assessed in the context of serious American national interest and American policy driven by a deteriorating trading climate, rising protectionism, disillusionment with America's trading partners, and strife between the two branches of government. That there was interest was clear. For many Canadians, free trade brought visions of either the threat of protectionism or the erosion of sovereignty; many Americans would be surprised to learn that trade with Canada was 'foreign' trade and far from free. Those who knew differently were a specialized and sophisticated audience.

This specialized audience could be divided into four groups: those with export interests; those with investment interests; those with interests in resources; and those worried about import competition. While by far the smallest group, the latter was most often heard from, especially during troubled times. Those in the first three groups rarely bothered to make their views known. When they did, their impact was general and anodyne. For example, in the 1979 Trade Agreements Act they called for agreements with countries in the 'northern half of the Western hemisphere,' and in 1980 then presidential candidate Reagan called for a North American accord. The benefits of good relations with Canada were taken for granted and the desirability of free trade was regarded as an obvious if not very pressing objective by those Americans who had a positive awareness of Canada. Such an attitude does not fare well in an era of rampant protectionism. It is the negative view that is usually publicized.

Whither US Trade Policy?
As Canadian interest in the negotiation of a free-trade agreement grew, US trade policy hovered on a knife edge.[19] Throughout the 1970s, US dependence on trade as a proportion of national wealth steadily increased, while US competitiveness and technological pre-eminence eroded as Japan and Europe rapidly caught up. In the trade acts of the 1970s and 1980s, Congress restored its constitutional prerogative to direct trade policy in the face of the administration's indifference or incapacity to deploy trade policy to serve national interests. Three features stood out:
- The management of trade policy had been separated from foreign policy.
- Because Congress could not direct day-to-day trade policy, it had progressively enlarged private rights through trade remedy law and thus subjected trade policy management to a litigious process heavily influenced by political pressures in defence of sectoral or regional interests.[20]
- Congress had increasingly rediscovered the ability – as it had in forging Smoot-Hawley and other horror shows of the past – to weld coalitions of diverse interests into support of legislative action at the expense of administrational discretion.[21]

These factors had a number of baneful consequences for US trade policy. One was that the administration had substituted posture for policy in multilateral and bilateral trade relations. On the one hand, the administration stood for trade liberalization and on the other, it vigorously enforced the instruments of retaliation and sectoral reciprocity bequeathed to it by the Congress. In multilateral and bilateral trade negotiations, for example, the administration designated new rules for trade in services as a priority, yet was unable to specify how such negotiations should proceed, what precise issues should be tackled, and what kinds of new obligations the United States would be willing to undertake. Similarly, the administration parroted congressional preoccupation with fairness and a level playing field, but reacted with indignation when other countries fought back. It castigated the Europeans, for example, for deploying subsidies to develop an aerospace industry to compete with a US industry built with defence appropriations, and Canadians for their use of countervailing duties to offset subsidies on US corn exports.[22]

Given this ambivalent situation, the prospect of a free-trade negotiation with Canada appeared a welcome alternative. Here was an issue to fire the imagination. Rather than bashing away at the entrenched protectionist policies of the Japanese and Europeans, here was an opportunity to open markets through mutually advantageous negotiations. But the professionals in Washington had learned in the 1970s that relations with Ottawa could be a delicate issue and that any free-trade overtures needed to come from Ottawa. Probes to gauge Washington's views by Canadian academic and other groups always met with polite interest and, sometimes, even enthusiasm, always with the careful caveat that any serious overtures would have to originate with the Canadian government. Until the mid-1980s, however, successive governments in Ottawa had carefully steered clear of the free-trade issue and thus taught US officials to do the same. The combination of rampant protectionism and a renewed interest in bilateralism changed that attitude in Ottawa and, as a consequence, interest in Washington as well. In 1983, the issue was no longer remote.

4

PREPARING THE WAY

The reward of a thing well done, is to have done it.
– Ralph Waldo Emerson

Two fundamental conditions must underpin any trade negotiation: the reduction and elimination of trade barriers should offer the potential to resolve economic problems that cannot be addressed by purely domestic measures, and the exchange of new rights and obligations should alter and improve the trading relationship between the countries involved. Between September of 1983 and September of 1985, the Canadian and US governments weighed the issues, consulted, and eventually concluded that these two conditions could be met. As the smaller partner, Canada had the larger stake and the more vigorous and far-reaching public debate. In the United States, the discussion was confined to senior levels of trade officials, the cabinet, and the White House. The decision to proceed was jointly reached after careful preparation and was grounded in a realistic and hard-nosed appreciation of the scope and prospects of negotiation.

The decision to proceed would take Canada down a well-travelled road. The landmarks were the same, although painted in modern colours. The story began in 1846-8 when the British abandoned the mercantilist system in favour of free trade, and Canadian grain, timber, and fisheries products lost guaranteed and preferred access to the British market. New markets were needed and those markets would be found in the rapidly expanding economy of the United States. Access to this market was assured through the 1854 Elgin-Marcy Reciprocity Treaty providing for duty-free trade for a wide range of natural products including grain, flour, breadstuffs, fish, meats, coal, and timber.[1]

This first reciprocity treaty was a casualty of the US civil war. Between 1866 and 1874, the new Canadian confederation made three separate attempts to negotiate a replacement and each time was rebuffed by either the US administration or the Senate. The failure to achieve free trade with the United

States enabled Canadian manufacturers to make a convincing case to Sir John A. Macdonald and the Conservative party that the domestic market should be reserved for them, and high tariffs became an integral part of the new National Policy introduced in 1879. Sir John underlined that higher Canadian tariffs could induce the Americans to take Canadian overtures for a reciprocity deal more seriously. But the National Policy suffered from a conflict among its principal objectives for it soon became evident that economic development hinged significantly on the ability to compete in export markets. High tariffs gradually stimulated the development of small-scale secondary manufacturing in Ontario, but they did not give Canadian exporters access to export markets for resources and manufactured products. The National Policy's tariffs raised consumer costs, reduced productivity, and discouraged the development of internationally competitive manufacturing based on Canada's comparative advantage in resources.[2]

1911: Helping Uncle

1912: Helping Father

The alternative, Canada-US reciprocity, involved controversial politics in both countries but almost became reality in 1911. An agreement negotiated with the Taft administration provided for free tariffs on primary agricultural and resource products and some manufactured goods, harmonized tariff levels on further processed products, and reduced duties on a larger list of manufactured goods. While the agreement was accepted by the US Senate, it was rejected by the Canadian electorate in the 1911 election. Canadian manufacturers feared the agreement was but the thin edge of the wedge of complete free trade. The combined effort of protectionist manufacturers ('no truck or trade with the Yankees') and nationalists committed to the British connection ('one empire, one flag, one fleet') overwhelmed the Laurier government and the agreement in a wave of nationalist, protectionist, and emotional sentiment. It would be another generation before any Canadian government felt confident enough to venture into reciprocity again.[3]

By the 1930s, the pattern of Canadian trade had altered considerably. Britain was no longer Canada's premier trading partner. The United States and Britain now each accounted for roughly the same quantity of Canadian exports, while the United States continued as the principal source of Canadian imports. Imperial preferences adopted at the Ottawa Conference of 1932, delivered little benefit. Thus by mid-decade, spurred by the bleak conditions of the depression, Canada once again sought to negotiate with its southern neighbour, accepting the open invitation of President Roosevelt's good neighbour policy. This time, the effort was crowned with success. In 1935 and again in 1938, Canada concluded limited tariff reduction agreements with the United States which incidentally also reduced preferences with the UK. Dana Wilgress, one of the architects of Canadian trade policy in the 1930s and 1940s, summarized the result as follows:

> The successful outcome of the triangular negotiations of 1938 served to stabilize trade relations with the two chief outlets for Canadian products. A goal had been achieved towards which Canadians had been striving ever since the days of Canada's immaturity as a nation. In reaching this goal Canada had won the respect and high regard of her trading partners. The basis was laid for that partnership, which would take the lead towards the promotion of world trade through multilateralism.[4]

It is a fascinating footnote of history that in 1947 Canada and the United States again engaged in negotiations for a free-trade agreement. The stimulus for these negotiations was the severe balance-of-payments problems encountered by Canada in the immediate postwar period. Canada's large trade surplus with the United Kingdom was more than offset by its deficit with the United States, but Canada could not use its sterling to pay for American goods nor could the British use US credits for purchases from Canada. To forestall Canadian restrictions on US imports that would inevitably become necessary to protect dwindling American dollar reserves, negotiations with the United States were conducted in secret for six months in 1947-8. To accommodate an eventual bilateral agreement, Canada and the United States collaborated in adding the concept of free-trade areas to the drafting of the Havana Charter, the document setting out the charter for the ill-fated International Trade Organization (and thus for Article XXIV of the GATT). With negotiations almost concluded, Prime Minister Mackenzie King took fright at the political consequences. He remembered the fate of Laurier in 1911 and was convinced that Canadian nationalists would once again confuse the reduction of customs duties and other trade barriers with the United States with patriotism. As secretly as the negotiations began, they were abandoned.[5]

Throughout the postwar years, the multilateral exchange of rights and obligations and GATT negotiations thus became the bedrock of Canadian trade policy. But in each of the seven GATT negotiations between 1947 and 1979, Canada-US negotiations were the most important. So long as Canada and the United States did not strike a special trading relationship, the achievement of Canadian trade objectives depended upon the surety which the GATT provided against abrupt protectionist lurches in US trade policy and on the capacity of the GATT to continue to serve as the forum for far-reaching and successful trade negotiations. As was indicated in the previous two chapters, however, GATT had increasingly failed to provide this surety and US policy had begun to drift away from the original principles of the GATT. The alternative of a contractual special relationship with the United States began to appear increasingly attractive to many Canadians.

Free Trade by a Thousand Cuts
The 1982-3 trade policy review laid the basis for a sectoral approach to bilateral trade liberalization. More indirectly, it stimulated public debate about the Canada-US relationship in general and the role of trade policy in particular. That debate, in turn, became the central focus of the hearings and research of the Macdonald Commission. By the time the Conservative party was elected with an overwhelming mandate in September 1984, free trade had reached the top of the public policy agenda.

The 1983 choice of sectoral trade agreements as the instrument for a new Canada-US commercial relationship articulated a long-standing impulse in Canada for more autopacts.[6] Close to twenty years after the negotiation of the original autopact, no one questioned the benefits that an arrangement confined to a discrete sector could bring to Canada in terms of increased production, investment, employment, and exports. The agreement had not been without its critics. Indeed, some of its strongest defenders in the 1980s were its staunchest critics twenty years earlier. All that, however, was history. In the mid-1980s, many argued that what was possible and beneficial for the automotive industry should be possible for other sectors in which growth and development were stunted by trade barriers on both sides of the border. But nostalgia alone, without the support of hard analysis, is a poor guide to policy, as was soon obvious.

The initial response from the United States government to the sectoral overture was positive. A few days following the announcement, United States Trade Representative Bill Brock stated, 'I believe that every opportunity to expand and/or liberalize international trade should be explored fully ... there may be considerable merit ... to potential sectoral trade pacts between the United States and Canada.'[7] The United States would go as far and as fast as Canada liked. US officials recognized that a US initiative would awaken long-standing fears of absorption among Canadians and that any precipitate US move was likely to provoke a quick and unseemly withdrawal by nervous politicians and terrified officials. Said Mike Smith, Brock's deputy, at a seminar sponsored by the Canadian Manufacturers Association to discuss the sectoral initiative: 'It is important to find easy sectors to negotiate quickly, to see how the water is, to catch the momentum, and to use it.' But the US government 'would take its lead from Canada, and was prepared to watch it, step by step, whether Canada chooses to walk or run.'[8] The pace was thus left for Canada to set.

An experienced Canadian trade hand, Tony Halliday, was appointed to implement the sectoral initiative. Four years earlier, returning to Ottawa from a four-year stint as head of the trade section at the Canadian Embassy in Washington, he had written a detailed assessment of Canada-US trade relations and the possibility of a free-trade agreement. It was this paper that had backed up the assessment in the trade policy review that a full-scale free-trade agreement with the United States did not make much sense at that time, but that sectoral or functional issues might well be pursued. He set to work to devise a work program, select candidate sectors, and meet with his US counterparts.

By December, he and his colleagues had determined that a decision to proceed had to be taken soon in order to maintain momentum. Arrangements were set in train for Brock and Minister for International Trade Gerry Regan to get together to consider a joint work program. They met in Washington on 17 February 1984 to begin formal consideration of the sectoral initiative and to agree on a bilateral dispute settlement process for safeguard actions affecting the two countries. Accompanied by a bevy of officials, neither expected to make much progress at the meeting and both declared themselves well-satisfied that they had been able to agree on a concrete work program. Regan told journalist Richard Gwyn that his 'purpose wasn't so much securing tariff reduction as such as in securing immunity for ourselves.' He was also quite candid about US motives: 'It's my best guess that, given the size of our market and its relative importance, they are motivated more by mood than by any considered strategy.'9 A number of sectors that had been suggested initially, including textiles and clothing, beef, forestry products, alcoholic beverages, furniture, and petrochemicals, were shelved for further study. Four sectors were chosen for immediate concentration in a work program to be concluded by May 1984. These were steel, urban transit industries, agricultural equipment, and informatics. Each in its own way demonstrated the strengths and weaknesses of the sectoral approach and of multilateral trade negotiations as means for achieving Canadian objectives.

Steel was an obvious candidate. Canadian exports were threatened by a safeguard action. To the industry, a sectoral trade agreement would head off quotas or higher tariffs and, since Canadian producers were more competitive than their US counterparts, increase exports at little risk to domestic production and employment. The blessings which this act of vision would bring to the United States were less apparent to the industry south of the border. It had other fish to fry: severely restricting import penetration into the US market, particularly from Japan, Korea, and the EC, was its priority. A sectoral trade agreement with Canada to eliminate barriers to trade was not only irrelevant to its central preoccupations, but smacked of dealing with the enemy. This line of reasoning proved persuasive with administration officials who declared that, notwithstanding their commitment to observe the pace established by Canada, they could not overcome the opposition of the domestic steel industry to a sectoral trade agreement.

The urban transit industry was no easier a nut to crack, but for different reasons. The United States has no domestic industry of significance competing with Canadian suppliers of light rail systems. Its market is largely served by imports. At the same time, the United States has a huge appetite for modern urban transportation systems of the type that Canada produces and exports efficiently. However, by virtue of the Surface Transportation Assistance Acts of 1978 and 1982, the federal funds that underwrite the enormous investment required carry onerous 'Buy America' requirements. Their removal was and remains a long-standing Canadian priority. The obstacle to this heaven-made match was balance. Since the Canadian market was saturated – all the major cities in Canada having up-to-date systems – and since the United States had no comparable industry, US officials felt the marriage contract needed further work; specifically, they suggested that Canada should open the procurement of provincial hydro-electric and telecommunications utilities to open bidding. In short, the marital bliss of the Canadian urban transit industry would be purchased at the expense of the suppliers to hydro-electric and telecommunications utilities who, in turn, would lose their preferred supplier status with the utilities but with no corresponding gains in access to the US market for their product. The result was stalemate.

The farm equipment sector presented different problems. In 1944, Canada and the United States had agreed to eliminate duties on an end-use basis for farm equipment. This policy had been implemented on a multilateral basis, but the nature of farming in North America had ensured that, as a practical matter, the benefits of duty elimination had gone largely to North American manufacturers. The object of a sectoral trade agreement would be to expand the list of farm equipment and parts trading free of duties which, because of the end-use definition, were excluded from the blessings of free trade. There was in principle no obstacle to doing such a deal although it was recognized that many months of painstaking, tedious tariff work lay ahead. Even with success, the farm equipment sector, although worthy in its own right, was clearly not the route to the new Jerusalem.

The informatics sector was the future. It was, however, vast and would take negotiators into uncharted territory. At issue were not only trade barriers on hardware and software, but the whole panoply of associated regulations. Officials dealing with the area were humbled by the inadequate statistical base and a policy framework outpaced by a technology racing along at breakneck speed. Here again, there was a fertile field for imagination but the benefits lay in the distant future, fraught with possibilities, but uncertain.

In June 1984, Regan and Brock met again to review the results of four months of work and to plan the next steps. Brock confirmed the obvious: sectoral trade agreements in steel and urban transit were not to be. Here, at least, the US pace was slower than the Canadian. Work was to proceed in farm equipment and inputs and informatics, and new sectors were to be considered, including forest products, furniture, petrochemicals, printing, non-ferrous metals and minerals, beef, alcoholic beverages, and cosmetics. To show good faith, Brock announced that the advice of the US International Trade Commission would be sought as an essential preparatory step on the US side to engaging in substantive negotiations. But the reality was that by the time of the June meeting the sectoral trade initiative was dead in the water.

There were important lessons learned from the year of the sectoral trade initiative. The first was that autopact-style arrangements were not for everybody. In fact, the particular corporate structure of the auto industry, as well as the market dominance in 1965 of North American-made autos and parts, were not replicated in any other sector. The immediate advantage of the sectoral approach – the opportunity to isolate particular sectors or sub-sectors for special treatment – depends on finding the right match. In 1983-4, there was no easy match of corporate, trade, and industrial policy interests in any major sector to underwrite a sectoral trade agreement.

The second lesson was that any sectoral arrangement presents severe problems of balance and symmetry. Oliver Smoot, executive vice president of the US Computer and Business Equipment Manufacturers Association, summed it up as follows: 'In general we're for zero tariffs and no non-tariff barriers, so this fits within that philosophy. But we think a lot of work has to be done on the part of the U.S. government to figure out what kinds of sectors they want to negotiate on. There has to be a balance between what's advantageous from the U.S. viewpoint and what's advantageous from the Canadian viewpoint or we're not going to have a deal.'[10] It also makes little political sense to buy benefits for one sector and pay for them at the expense of another that would stand to gain no benefit in terms of secure or expanded access in its export markets. The scope for cross-sectoral trade-offs possible in an economy-wide negotiation is virtually non-existent in a sectoral negotiation. As a result, sectoral agreements cannot command the broad coalition of support in the private and public sectors to ensure success. They draw out those with narrow (and sometimes honourable) interests to protect or advance. Whatever the economic sense of sectoral arrangements, they are short on vision and, without vision, trade agreements are next to impossible to conclude.

Third, to countries devoted by paternity and deeply felt attachments to the GATT, the most-favoured-nation obligation was a further formidable obstacle to sectoral arrangements unless these were to be extended to other countries. But extension to other countries would erode whatever support there existed in either Canada or the United States for sectoral arrangements – no outsiders need apply was a point which the Canadian steel and urban transit industries were quick to hammer home. Unless the two countries' other trading partners could be persuaded to take leave of their senses and grant a waiver to deny them the benefits of sectoral arrangements, only a free-trade area meeting the full requirements of GATT would provide the legal cover for sectoral arrangements. Brock argued that Canada and the United States could declare that the existing level of duty-free trade between them, about 70 per cent, constituted a de facto free-trade area in accordance with the provisions of the GATT and could thus justify any new sectoral arrangements. However, even for those who regard the MFN obligation of the GATT as the centrepiece of a boy-scouts' jamboree, such a transparent and self-serving sleight of hand held little attraction.

But from small acorns grow great oaks. To the surprise of some and chagrin of others, the initiative bore fruit, not in the form of brothers and sisters for the autopact, but rather in healthy debate. The sectoral trade initiative proved to be a prelude to the main event. Some rushed to welcome the free-trade option; others clamoured to keep the trade menace safely locked away; all contributed to a growing debate about the pros and cons of closer trading ties with the United States. Those who confused multilateralism with the objective rather than the means of Canadian trade policy, disdained the sectoral trade initiative as a bothersome and unimportant nuisance that would shortly be relegated to the dust-heap of history.

Among critics of the Grit sectoral initiative was Tory trade spokesman Michael Wilson. In March he told the *Globe and Mail*'s Patrick Martin that the talks were 'not moving fast enough ... we must move more quickly to get a deal because the protectionist influences in the United States are moving quickly.' He expected a Conservative government to pursue the matter with more vigour. 'There seems to be an inexorable pull toward it [a more liberal trading relationship]; Canada has been moving this way for 120 years; the only question has been how fast.' His view confirmed that of the vast majority of the members of his party. A year earlier, pollster Allan Gregg of Decima Research had found that 80 per cent of the delegates to the 1983 leadership convention favoured closer economic ties to the United States.[11]

The Penny Drops

With the election of a new federal government in Canada in September 1984 came the opportunity to take a fresh look at the issue. A week after the election, Derek Burney, now assistant deputy minister for the United States at External Affairs, convened a meeting in the small, cramped boardroom that adjoined his office. He had before him a long paper on the sectoral approach, its origins, results to date, and its future.

The new prime minister had not yet appointed his cabinet. Rumours about new ministers abounded. What the new ministers, once appointed, would think of the sectoral approach, the brainchild of the previous government, could only be surmised. One thing was certain: better relations with the United States or, to use the prime minister's term, refurbished relations, would be at the heart of the new government's foreign policy, and trade policy would have to play a central role.

The paper was a dog's breakfast. In some forty-five pages it reviewed the experience with the sectoral trade initiative, set out the options and the options within options, and explored the problems that separate sectoral trade deals would give Canada and the United States with their GATT obligations. It did not take long for the meeting to decide that a forty-five-page memorandum did not fit the bill. At a minimum, it needed to be tightened up and given a greater sense of purpose. There was no doubt, however, about proceeding with an options paper. With this reworked paper, Burney proceeded to place the issue before ministers. The choice before the government was reduced to three possibilities: to persist in a low-risk and, consequently, a low-gain exercise; to close down the initiative; or to launch a full-scale analytical and consultative exercise on the option of a free-trade agreement.

Concurrent with preparations to lay the trade options before the government, Burney was asked to arrange a quick visit for the new prime minister to Washington to meet with the president to confirm his commitment to better relations with the United States. On 26 September, the two conservative leaders met in the Oval Office and affirmed the warm mutual regard that had been evident during a June visit by Mulroney while still opposition leader. The *Globe and Mail*'s Bill Johnson used the occasion to write a background piece suggesting that 'the most portentous issue Prime Minister Brian Mulroney will deal with today when he meets President Ronald Reagan is that of free trade.' He went on to describe the sectoral initiative as drifting and the Americans as interested in going further. He quoted Bill Merkin, the USTR official responsible for Canadian affairs, as saying 'I've heard that at least some in the Conservative Government may be looking at that idea [a more far-reaching agreement], and others. It's an idea that we have heard before out of Canada, and I think we would be interested in looking at it, too, and I think it would be much more manageable.'[12]

Within official circles in Ottawa, the debate was initially confined to Minister for International Trade Jim Kelleher and Secretary of State for External Affairs Joe Clark and their officials in the Department of External Affairs, including Trade Deputy Sylvia Ostry. In October, the circle widened. While Burney and his staff had prepared the options paper as well as a paper outlining the rationale and means for 'refurbished' relations with the United States, Gerry Shannon, senior assistant deputy minister at Finance, and his staff had prepared drafts of a paper setting out the economic options for the government. Now Minister of Finance Michael Wilson announced his intention to make an economic statement to Parliament. Included with the statement would be an 'agenda' paper that would set out in broad terms how the government intended to manage economic policy over the life of its mandate. It too would promise 'refurbished' relations with the United States and an effort to explore with the private sector and the provinces all possible options 'to secure and enhance' Canada's market access to the United States.[13]

The economic statement propelled efforts already under way to bring a full review of the options before the government. With the agenda document had come promises of a series of discussion papers as vehicles for consultations and work proceeded apace on a trade options paper. Thus by early November, the Canada-US trade issue had already found a central place in the government's agenda. Nevertheless, the *Globe and Mail* continued to insist there needed to be more debate and that the government needed to find its place in the debate. On 1 November Jeffrey Simpson opined that

> the elements are gradually falling into place for a great national debate about our relations with the United States ... It will be a while, maybe a long while before the Government joins the debate. Ministers are still feeling their way into this politically tricky and economically complicated field. And ministers will find, when they finally enter the debate, that their own senior civil servants are divided, even at the upper reaches of the External Affairs Department.[14]

But ministers had already cautiously entered the debate. The week before, Joe Clark had suggested that 'closer economic relations with the United States, if played right, can enhance our voice and influence in international affairs ... Canada possesses a new maturity as a nation. The modern purpose of Canadian nationalism is to express ourselves, not protect ourselves.'[15] On 8 November the government's Throne Speech indicated the direction of its thinking and this was confirmed in Wilson's agenda paper. The government was prepared to move, but only cautiously and step by step, feeling out public opinion as it went along. An essential ingredient in this process was a trade discussion paper.

The drafting of an options paper at first went smoothly. Striving for a lay comprehension of some rather technical trade issues, the drafters tried for a succinct and untechnical approach. They sought to draw the options in bold colours: the status quo or a comprehensive free-trade agreement. But the colouring proved too intense for some and the supporting analysis too self-evident to admit of discussion for others. One deputy minister said that the paper reminded him of his mother's chicken broth – nourishing but nothing to chew on – and the drafters went back to work.

Several more versions were produced, this time relying upon an interdepartmental drafting committee. Not unexpectedly, the committee produced an indigestible mass of conflicting analysis, red herrings, and private agenda. On Christmas Eve, Burney took matters in hand. The indigestible mush produced to date did not serve the government's needs. He would rewrite the beginning and the end and other task force officials would concentrate on the middle. It had to have a coherent theme and a consistent message. The purpose of a discussion paper is to stimulate public discussion. Nothing to date had met this test, but it was not too late to do it right. He was ready to start, beginning Christmas day.

As the paper began to take on discernible shape, there were further problems. Traditionalists resisted any efforts that threatened Canada's established support for GATT and multilateral negotiations. Indeed, the imminence of a new round of GATT trade negotiations (finally launched at Punta del Este, Uruguay, in September 1986) should be given pride of place. More threateningly, the keepers of the multilateral flame maintained that Canada's multilateral heritage and duty would be betrayed by a radical and risky lunge into bilateralism.

There were also those who were suspicious of any trade liberalization. Officials in the Department of Regional Industrial Expansion argued against any move to open markets on a general basis. Their mission in life was to stimulate industry with government funds, even if the effect often led to protection for failing firms. A free-trade agreement would complicate their job by adding to the competitive pressures on those firms. Indeed, they were convinced that whole sectors of the Canadian economy would not survive under more open trading conditions. Hardened by years of dealing with companies in trouble, they had long ago convinced themselves that trade liberalization was an instrument of the devil and that the devil's cohorts worked in the Department of External Affairs. At most, they were prepared to concede the benefits of an enhanced sectoral approach.

The internal, bureaucratic debate was given further spice by others, echoing the views of the economic nationalists, who expressed caution about the political pitfalls in any full-fledged bilateral trade negotiation and sought refuge in some procedural means of addressing the call for Canada-US negotiations, such as by getting a bilateral headstart on impending multilateral negotiations. They argued that any free-trade agreement would inevitably lead to greater economic integration and eventually to political union as the natural consequence of this integration. As a second line of argument, they insisted that even if absorption could be fended off, a free-trade agreement with the United States would erode Canada's capacity to conduct an independent foreign policy.[16]

This romantic view of Canadian foreign policy did not impress Trade Minister Jim Kelleher, nor was he much taken by the bureaucratic infighting and concern with the multilateral trading system. He insisted on a strong dose of bilateralism and exposure of the real bilateral option. If this needed to be accompanied by a traditional litany on the virtues of multilateralism, so be it, but not at the expense of the real issue.

Kelleher was more impressed by the views expressed by Canada's business moguls who were worried about the protectionist threat in the United States, sceptical about early progress in launching a new round of GATT negotiations, and troubled by the absence of any formal dispute resolution mechanism that would take the politics out of the management of the Canada-US economic relationship. Early in 1985, Business Council on National Issues (BCNI) president Tom d'Aquino, on behalf of a business lobby representing Canada's largest 150 corporations, called for the negotiation of a framework agreement to provide just such a dispute settlement mechanism as well as a forum for future bilateral negotiations.

The time for hitting the street began to approach. Unless the document could be published by the end of January, the opportunity would be lost because the paper would not be delivered to the provinces in time for review prior to the Regina first ministers' conference in mid-February. Kelleher was also beginning to express concern that the possibility of opening negotiations with the United States would be lost if the government did not proceed soon. On 22 January a document was finally approved for release. It sought to cast the issue in terms of Canada's global trade interests and concluded by posing a number of questions as the focus of attention.

The document, *How to Secure and Enhance Canadian Access to Export Markets*, appeared on 29 January. Whatever the views of the bureaucrats, Kelleher had successfully insisted that the paper be responsive to his agenda. While there was a strong bow in the direction of the orthodox shibboleths of Canadian trade policy, the main message was clear. The paper was in three parts. Part I set the scene, describing Canadian trade in a rapidly evolving international trade environment. Part II rehearsed the background and prospects for a new round of multilateral trade negotiations. The main message was found in Part III which set out four options for Canada-US trade relations:

- preserve the status quo, i.e., continue as in the past managing trade relations through the GATT supplemented by bilateral arrangements – the glaringly obvious conclusion was tentatively advanced that this approach might not adequately serve immediate Canadian interests
- negotiate sectoral or functional arrangements on a limited basis – bearing in mind that these might not prove negotiable
- negotiate a comprehensive trade arrangement – the cat poking its head out of the bag
- negotiate a framework agreement for consultations and for possible negotiations – the reddest of red herrings.

The phrase 'free trade' had by this time been proscribed and did not appear in the final version. Nonetheless, the *Globe and Mail* in its headline declared that government 'Announces Free-Trade Policy' and characterized the paper as concluding that 'Canada may not have much choice but to work toward a comprehensive agreement, as the conservatives prefer to call free trade.'[17] Jeffrey Simpson was not impressed: 'The damp squibs that pass for policy papers now being released in Ottawa are disappointing only to those who do not know what the Mulroney Government is about ... Uncertain of where they want to take Canada, unwilling yet to make hard decisions, determined to massage rather than challenge voters, trapped by the intellectual unreality of their campaign, the Mulroney ministers are leading by following public opinion.'[18]

Whatever Simpson's views, by publishing the discussion paper, the government captured the debate and made it focus on the real issues. From now on the opposition was on the defensive and the case to be proven was that the government was wrong. The status quo had lost its place as the premier option.

The day before the paper was released, Mel Hurtig, the Edmonton publisher and publicist of nationalist causes, moved to organize a new lobby group to follow up the work of the Committee for an Independent Canada, disbanded as being no longer necessary three years earlier in the face of the nationalist lurch in Canadian policy in 1980. The Council of Canadians would become one of a number of groups that would dog the government throughout the negotiations and keep the debate interesting.

Quixotic, emotional, and exaggerated, the nationalist opposition provided an undertone of varying intensity throughout the preparatory period and into the negotiations. Rooted in fear of the unknown, its shrillness reflected a lamentable lack of seriousness in the day-to-day public debate. The historical echoes of their arguments were striking. In 1911, the opposition coalesced around the nationalists anchored in the imperial connection and the protectionists fearful of being swept away by US competition. In the 1980s, the new nationalists, shorn of their attachment to empire but devoted to a vibrant and independent Canada, made common cause with the new mercantilists who believed that Canada's comparative advantage lay in protecting the Canadian market from US industry and investment and devising a distinct Canadian industrial strategy to promote exports and keep out imports.

The house organ of the nationalist opposition was the *Toronto Star*; the chief acolyte its cherubic columnist, David Crane; the high priest Mel Hurtig, supported by a revived if diminished Council of Canadians; the intellectual apologists Jim Laxer, Mel Watkins, Abe Rotstein, and other veterans of the Committee for an Independent Canada who were also contributors to the nationalist journal, *Canadian Forum*.[19] Their views found an occasional echo in the ranks of the Liberal and New Democratic parties, but the real opposition on this issue was outside Parliament, among the mercantilist leaders of the Canadian Labour Congress and many of its affiliates, the

Bengough, *Grinchuckle*, 3 September 1869

UNCLE SAM KICKED OUT!

YOUNG CANADA.– "WE DON'T WANT YOU HERE."

JOHN BULL.–"THAT'S RIGHT, MY SON. NO MATTER WHAT COMES, AN EMPTY HOUSE IS BETTER THAN SUCH A TENANT AS THAT."

Canadian cultural industries, and the leaders of various single-issue groups which found that opposition to free trade gave them immediate headlines. Catholic bishops, professional feminists, hardened trade unionists, former ministers and mandarins, and cultural gurus, all felt threatened by the prospect of secure and enhanced access to a market most Canadians routinely take for granted.[20]

A year earlier, Hurtig had expressed concern with the sectoral initiative. Now it looked like the government was prepared to go even further, encouraged by a business community unconcerned by questions of sovereignty, culture, and independence. Someone had to warn Canadians. He had a mission.[21]

Setting Joint Goals

In March 1985, six weeks after the release of the trade discussion paper, the prime minister met with the president in Quebec City. Amid all the hoopla attendant on such major milestones in public diplomacy, the two leaders conducted some very serious business. At a meeting at the Chateau Frontenac on 17 March, attended by their closest foreign and economic policy advisors including Joe Clark, George Shultz, Michael Wilson, Donald Regan, Jim Kelleher, and Bill Brock, the two leaders put the finishing touches on a declaration on trade in goods and services. Both governments indicated that they wanted to examine seriously the broadest possible means for liberalizing trade between the two countries.[22] They set in train a process for joint preparation so that should negotiations eventually be joined, they could produce results quickly. This document, in effect, set the agenda for the negotiation of a free-trade agreement.

The Quebec meeting had been well prepared. In January, a hand-picked interdepartmental task force had been established to clear the ground on three key issues: acid rain, defence, and trade. Each involved careful analysis of what should and could be achieved, meetings with US counterparts, and the drafting of a declaration. The Canadian task force, formally headed by Dr. Fred Doucet from the prime minister's political staff, relied on Derek Burney for inspiration and guidance, while US officials took their direction from the president's national security advisor, Robert MacFarlane. Burney took personal charge of the trade declaration, insisting that it reflect the ongoing debate and provide a basis for setting common goals for the future and a framework for addressing these goals. At the same time, he wanted the two leaders to be in a position to resolve a number of bilateral trade irritants as an indication of the new and positive relationship the two leaders were determined to establish.

The two months of preparations demonstrated again what is a commonplace in Canada-US discussions. Canadian ministers and officials supply the vision and details; US politicians provide the enthusiasm; and US officials put on the brakes. The White House and USTR Brock were enthusiastic; officials lower in the hierarchy were cautious, short on vision, generally unprepared, and full of reasons why something could not be done (by the United States) or why something should be done (by Canada). This state of affairs is not a reflection on the ability of US officials but on the way things work in Washington. Things related to the United States are at the top of Canada's foreign policy and even domestic policy agenda; things Canadian are low on the US agenda. Thus there appeared, from the start, a gap between political rhetoric and the will and imagination to work out the practical details. The trade declaration, which originally was meant to be accompanied by a list of irritants which had been resolved and which demonstrated what two friends could do when they set their minds to it, had to stand on its own with much less impressive support from a press kit which outlined progress on a few of the lesser irritants.

That there was US interest in negotiating bilaterally with Canada was clear. In February, USTR Brock had told the US Chamber of Commerce:

The failure of the [world trading] system to move has put the U.S. in the position where we have to contemplate defending our own vital interests. One of the ways we can do that is to take one or more countries and set up a complete process by which we remove all trade barriers between us as an example of how good the world can be. The U.S. has to operate in its own self-interest and that means the priority has to be building up a global system ... I would not be in the least reluctant to have several examples for those countries which seem to have chosen a different path for the moment.

But Brock remained cautious about raising the spectre of the United States pushing Canada into a negotiation. The pace would continue to be set in Ottawa.[23]

Nevertheless, the declaration on trade in goods and services released by the two leaders on 18 March was an important step towards eventual trade negotiations. It set as the common goal of the two governments the establishment of an improved and more secure climate for bilateral trade. Kelleher and Brock were charged to report back in six months on 'a bilateral mechanism to chart all possible ways to reduce and eliminate existing barriers to trade.' Additionally, the declaration set in train a work program for resolving impediments to trade in eight specific areas. Thus, while consultations with business leaders and provincial officials continued, Brian Mulroney had already agreed to explore the potential for a comprehensive accord with the Americans.

One disquieting development immediately following Quebec City was the departure from the trade portfolio of Bill Brock, the very able and agreeable United States trade representative, who had been instrumental in nurturing

Irish eyes are smiling at Quebec City summit; amid all the hoopla, some serious business was transacted.
(17 March 1985)

support for a bilateral agreement within the administration. The goals of the Quebec trade declaration would be pursued by the new USTR, Clayton Yeutter, who was not fully in the saddle until mid-summer by which time valuable momentum had been lost.

Building Consensus
Throughout this preparatory period, the Canadian government showed a consistent determination to take the issue forward, but in a measured way, step by step. While it may have been intellectually convinced by the memoranda and advice flowing from the bureaucracy, it was not as yet politically committed. There was no question that the economic benefits were at the very least positive, but ministers were convinced that bureaucrats were not sufficiently wary of the political pitfalls. They would have been surprised to learn the degree to which this point of view was shared by the mandarins, many of whom were at best lukewarm. At cocktail parties all around Ottawa, those working on the initiative continued to be regarded as pariahs leading ministers down a reckless and uncharted trail. In the view of many (but not all) bureaucrats, the government would eventually come to its senses and leave the advocates of free trade high and dry.

Public Attitudes
The government, however, had a more constructive approach than carping at cocktail parties. It commissioned polls and it consulted with those who had a stake in the negotiations: business, labour, provincial politicians, and a host of other Canadians.

The election of 1911 had created the myth in Canada that governments that openly opted for the promise of the American market did so at their peril. Ironically, for more than two generations, a majority of Canadians, in every region but Ontario, had consistently backed the idea of freer trade with the United States, as Gallup polls dating back to 1953 illustrated (Table 3). Approval had been, moreover, remarkably consistent. In April of 1984, during the dying days of the Trudeau government, an Environics poll conducted for the *Globe and Mail* revealed that a huge majority – 78 per cent of Canadians – backed a trade deal with the United States with only 17 per cent against the idea. In a real sense, therefore, public support for free trade had always been at hand; what had been missing was a government willing to grasp the nettle and boldly take up the challenge.

With better political and economic relations with the United States being one of the planks in the Conservative campaign platform, it was natural for the Tories' pollster, Decima, to examine in some detail Canadian attitudes

Table 3

Results of Gallup polls on free trade, 1953-83 (%)

	Canada would be:		
	Better off	Worse off	Can't say
National			
1983	54	29	17
1968	56	27	17
1963	50	32	18
1953	54	28	18
By region, May 1983			
Atlantic	67	23	10
Quebec	60	19	21
Ontario	46	37	17
Prairies	53	29	19
British Columbia	58	29	13

Note: Percentages may not add exactly to 100, due to rounding.

towards closer economic relations with the United States. Their surveys revealed not only that the vast majority shared the prime minister's belief that closer trade and commercial links with the United States would benefit the Canadian economy, but also that, by a two to one margin, the potential benefits of such an arrangement were seen to outweigh the risks to Canada's independence. Nationalism had become less defensive. It was more concerned with Canada's place in the world than with Canadian culture or control of the economy.

The prime minister caught this spirit and expressed it best in a speech he made to the Economic Club of New York in December 1984 when, in announcing that Canada was once again open for business, he told the capacity audience that Canadians were now 'mature enough as a nation and confident enough in ourselves to recognize this reality and to take pride in an amicable relationship with a neighbour as powerful as the United States.' In early February 1985, a Gallup poll taken in December revealed that Canadians continued to favour a free-trade agreement. The figures, once again, revealed little change over the past three decades, but Trade Minister Kelleher told reporters that the government had an 'open mind' on the issue.

Press coverage of free trade continued to grow and remained very positive in most papers. That many Canadians approved of the prime minister's handling of the US relationship quickly became clear in the wake of the Shamrock Summit. Surveys showed a boost both in support for freer trade

Table 4

Results of Gallup polls on free trade, December 1984 (%)

	Canada would be:		
	Better off	Worse off	Can't say
National	54	29	17
By region			
Atlantic	44	31	25
Quebec	59	23	18
Ontario	52	32	16
Prairies	56	32	13
British Columbia	54	27	20

and in the public perception of Canada-US relations. However, as the Decima analysis taken at the time was quick to point out, Canadians were not overwhelmingly convinced that this issue was the most important on the agenda: acid rain and the environment received equal weighting with trade and economic issues. A majority believed that closer ties were in Canada's interest, but a majority also stated that establishing such ties should not be achieved at the expense of broadening Canadian relations with the rest of the world. In short, Canadians would support a trade initiative but in the context of a foreign policy that continued to be devoted to multilateralism and non-discrimination. The polls also revealed that support for the initiative was not based on a deep awareness of the issues involved and was, therefore, quite soft. A major campaign to promote awareness among Canadians, particularly among opinion-makers in business, labour, and especially, the media, was necessary to solidify support.

Opinion surveys taken in the days after the Quebec Summit revealed that the public supported the government's approach to the United States, but most of the reporting tended to dismiss it as a public relations exercise between two North American Irishmen. There was a nagging suggestion that the schmaltz of the summit did not sit well with Canadians. Canadian approval for Mulroney's handling of US relations became less positive after the Quebec meeting. Nonetheless, a clear link was drawn between the benefits of free trade and the peril of US protectionism. As the *Winnipeg Free Press* editorialized: 'Anybody who cares about employment in Canada must want to see our entry to the US market maintained and expanded. If we fail in that, increased joblessness will be the result.'[24]

The Ministerial Progress: Curb Service Trade Policy

In February 1985, Trade Minister Kelleher had been asked to approve a detailed program of cross-Canada consultations on his discussion paper. The program called for him to meet privately with national business associations, labour unions, and a whole range of individual industry associations whose views would be a critical component in any decision to launch a free-trade negotiation.

Kelleher rejected the plan. While the concept of a free-trade agreement represented bold, innovative thinking, confidential consultations, hid from public and press, were nothing but old-fashioned bureaucratic caution. The consultations would be public. Officials were horrified: the minister would only hear what he needed to hear in closed door meetings; publicly, he would get posturing; the groups proposed for consultations were a trade minister's natural constituency; they had a right to talk to him in private; it had always been done that way. Kelleher was adamant and, as it turned out, right.

From late March to mid-May, Kelleher, accompanied by his parliamentary secretary, Stewart McInnis, the Trade Deputy Bob Richardson, and various officials held meetings in fifteen cities from coast to coast. In each, Kelleher hosted a private breakfast or lunch, a grudging concession to cautious officials, gave a speech accompanied by a slide show, and invited all and sundry to meet him in a public forum.

The first consultation took place on a cold, rainy day in Halifax on 19 March. No one was sure what would happen; it could be a bust. The private meeting drew some twenty local business worthies; about 150 members of the public turned out for the public forum. Both privately and publicly, the interests were about equally divided between those wanting more and easier government export financing, those concerned with the pros and cons of a free-trade negotiation, and those seeking a remedy for a grievance. This pattern was repeated across the country, with attendance in the public forums varying between two or three dozen to several hundred. Meticulous notes were taken. When the minister reported to cabinet, it would not be hearsay, but what he had seen and heard. He was not averse, however, to tipping his hand a little. In Calgary, he told a luncheon audience:

> Now is the time to enter into some sort of agreement with the U.S., where they have mid-term elections in 1986 and 34 Senate seats are up for grabs. The feeling in the U.S. is that if we are not well along in negotiations before the mid-term elections, the window will close and there will be no other opportunity before 1988. We agree with this view and have every intention of beginning discussions during the late summer or early fall.[25]

The consultations in Montreal and Toronto were critical. The greatest impact and greatest adjustments in a free-trade agreement would be felt in the manufacturing industries of the central provinces. Kelleher travelled to Montreal on 1 April 1985. He had been warned by his officials to expect a protectionist front. Quebec had far more than its fair share of outdated, low-wage, highly protected industries, least able to survive a free-trade environment. His officials proved to be wrong. Quebec was ready, indeed eager, for free trade. The message, both privately and in public, was unambiguous; a kind of collective decision had been taken that the future lay in free trade with the United States, Quebec's largest market. The adjustment might be severe but it would have to be faced.

The Toronto consultation took its script from the Montreal meeting. The Ontario business community was ready to go. It had come out of the recession with its confidence in the old order of a small protected Canadian market shattered and shaken. Its leaders also pressed for a practical consultative mechanism that would give them real input in decision-making. The windows should be opened up. It would be essential that, unlike during previous multilateral trade negotiations, they know at least as much as their US counterparts.

The consultations were serious business, but they inevitably produced some bizarre moments. One exporter in the Charlottetown consultations complained bitterly about the expensive contortions necessary to evade government export control regulations. In Edmonton, a participant pressed his case for an export promotion grant on anyone he could buttonhole. He wanted $20 million – to open a trading house in Teheran. He could understand the need for detailed study before approval, but would be satisfied with an advance. An employee of the local Federal Regional Development Office appeared in the public forum in Toronto to press for a tariff reduction on imported European rock music; he could understand the need for protection against American recordings – they competed directly – but European rock was different. A Calgary oil executive, told by the minister that those who believed in a made-in-Canada exchange rate also believed in the tooth fairy, affirmed that in fact he did believe in the tooth fairy. In Kitchener, an autoparts representative announced that speaking for his company, he strongly supported free trade but the association, of which he was the president and spokesman, was opposed.

In Vancouver, Toronto, and Montreal, Kelleher held private meetings with labour leaders. Organized labour was wary, not quite believing that a Conservative government would adopt a free-trade policy, thumbing its nose at history. Its position had not yet hardened into implacable opposition, but neither free trade nor support of a Conservative government initiative was high on its agenda. Labour wanted an industrial policy to generate high-paying union jobs. Its leaders wanted more, not less, control over market forces. The CAW representative at the Toronto meeting captured the point well, arguing that the government should retard the adjustment process if jobs were threatened and not hurry it along by lowering trade barriers.

Thus, from the beginning, the only option seriously addressed by those consulted was whether or not to proceed with a comprehensive trade agreement with the United States. An overwhelming message came through: to get on with negotiations and get the best deal possible. In fact, there was a certain measure of impatience. The minister found that the ground, already ploughed by Donald Macdonald and his royal commission and a two-year national debate, was more than ready for planting.

The consultations demonstrated widespread dissatisfaction with the status quo: a high level of unemployment, especially among youths, limited optimism about the future, an inadequate investment performance, and few incentives for growth and new employment opportunities. The impatience was expressed despite the fact that Canada had a large merchandise trade surplus with the United States; many Canadian firms had become painfully aware of Canada's vulnerability to US protectionism. At the same time, there was a growing number of firms which were confident of their ability to compete in the larger North American market but felt threatened by the US protectionist surge. There were also a number of key voices of opposition which enlivened the debate and kept the proponents honest. Their views were also recorded and duly reflected in reports to ministers.

The Views of Business

Many members of the business community were by this time ahead of the government.[26] At first cautiously but with increasing confidence, they had begun to speak in favour. In response to the discussion paper and the Quebec trade declaration, key national business associations, including the Chamber of Commerce, the Quebec Chamber of Commerce, the Canadian Manufacturers Association, the Business Council on National Issues, the Canadian Export Association, the Consumers Association of Canada, the Retail Council of Canada, and the Canadian Federation of Small Business called for serious consideration of a comprehensive trade agreement with the United States. At the end of a *Financial Post* conference on free trade, its Washington correspondent, Giles Gherson, concluded that: 'Among businessmen there's a cautious enthusiasm afoot. It's making for an increasingly clear sense of direction where there was mainly confusion only a few months back. Coming out of the conference, the chief issue appears no longer to be whether to press for freer trade or not, but what kind of package Canada should be seeking from the U.S.'[27]

This view was particularly strong among Quebecers whose dreams of political independence had been transformed into self-confident and hard-headed plans for economic growth. In 1986, these changed attitudes were exemplified in Robert Bourassa's triumphant return as premier and his growing support for free trade.

A thoughtful speech by Ted Newall, then chairman of Dupont Canada, summed up how the views and attitudes of all Canadian business had changed in the previous years:

> We, manufacturers, are caught in a catch 22 situation. On one hand, the tariffs in Canada are no longer high enough to offset the higher costs of producing solely for the Canadian market. On the other hand, even modest tariffs into the U.S. can make it difficult, if not impossible, to set up production in Canada to export into that market. When dealing on the location of a new production facility, why locate it on the small market side of the border especially when it's dependent on exports and faces the problems of the Non-Tariff Barriers. We need to be inside those safeguards.
>
> Unless we can negotiate increased and assured access to the U.S. market, Canadian industry will be unable to take the risks involved in making the substantial investments required to operate on a North American basis. Whether the strategy chosen to take advantage of the U.S. potential is specialization, rationalization, or whatever, secure access to the American market is mandatory.[28]

A gathering typical of the many business discussions of the issue took place on 2-3 May at the semi-annual meeting of the Canada-US relations committee of the two Chambers of Commerce on Amelia Island off the coast of Florida. In the conference centre of the resort, graced by the palms and warm breezes of Florida, senior executives from both sides of the border spent the better part of two days examining the rationale and prospects of a free-trade deal. They were in favour and agreed to send a joint letter to the president and the prime minister announcing their support. The letter urged that the negotiations be comprehensive and provide a viable and effective dispute resolution mechanism in which the private sector would be involved. In their view, the time for action had come.

The views of business, however, were not unanimous. On 28 May, in Cambridge, Ontario, the heart of the national policy's legacy of small-scale, increasingly uncompetitive, American-owned manufacturing branch plants, the Southwest Ontario Council of Chief Executive Officers met to discuss the implications of free trade for them. Following a boilerplate government presentation (the government was considering options for trade liberalization; no decisions had been taken; now was the time for business to make its views known), the initial reaction was a cold blast of protectionist fervour. Their firms were half as efficient as the parent; their costs were too high; their equipment was outdated; they could not export to the US; they would be closed down or turned into warehousing operations. Then other voices spoke out. Some had begun to rationalize; a longer term was needed; new investment was proving to be more profitable than the parent operations; the exchange rate and business environment gave them an advantage. A lively discussion ensued. While there was no consensus, the CEOs agreed the world was moving on and they had to move with it. With adequate time to adjust to a free-trade market, they could indeed prosper.

The pace of debate had by then begun to quicken and shift from general consideration of the benefits of free trade to a call for negotiations. The C.D. Howe Institute, through its Canadian-American Committee and other high-level business groups, had long advocated a more open trade relationship with the United States. In May, it released a detailed study urging the government to proceed rapidly with the negotiation of a comprehensive trade agreement. That study concluded:

> The time has come for Canada to take the initiative in launching negotiations for a CAFTA [Canadian-American Free Trade Agreement]. By liberalizing trade now, with all its positive consequences for the Canadian economy, Canada would take a decisive step into the future. By doing so now, Canada might also be able to preempt protectionist actions in the United States.
>
> This Canadian initiative would not be an act of desperation but of confidence. A CAFTA offers the most promising opportunity to create a more efficient and adaptive, and outward-looking Canadian – and U.S. – economy that would provide rising living standards and expanding employment opportunities for the great majority of people. Its success would demonstrate to the rest of the world that trade liberalization, rather than rising protectionism, remains – as it has since World War II – the practical key to prosperity.[29]

In case the government had not gotten the point, its chief author, Richard Lipsey, accompanied by the institute's president, Wendy Dobson, made a pilgrimage to Ottawa to buttonhole ministers and senior officials. They were pleasantly surprised to learn that ministers and senior officials had indeed gotten the message and had been busy for nearly a year giving it greater depth and shape.

One-Stop Shopping

As the ministerial consultations progressed, other consultative mechanisms were introduced. In May, Tom Burns was appointed as Special Coordinator for Market Access Consultations to meet privately with all interested groups and firms who wished to make representations. Burns brought a rich record of experience to the consultations. A former senior assistant deputy minister in the Department of Industry, Trade and Commerce, he had served for almost ten years as president of the Canadian Exporters' Association and had recently retired and joined the government relations firm of Public Affairs International. Well-known to the Canadian business community, he would complement Kelleher's general consultations by determining the nature of the type of agreement sought by Canadian business. The minister's press release announced that Mr. Burns would provide 'one-stop shopping for business, labour, and other interested parties. In this way, all those seeking to convey their views on either multilateral or Canada-US trade issues can do so through one central point in the Government.'[30]

Burns provided the perfect setting for this level of consultations. Eager to listen, he put his clients at ease and made them the centre of attention. Unlike so many government-business consultations, bureaucrats here did the listening and the probing and business people the talking and explaining. Burns was prepared to clarify points of confusion, but he saw his mission as essentially one of feeling the pulse of business on the future of Canadian trade policy. And business came, some with glossy charts or slick overheads, others with a lot of anxiety and questions. Burns convinced them that their views were important and that he was there to hear them and record them.

Each session started with a presentation by the company or organization being consulted, followed by questions and answers. Burns studiously avoided any presentation of his own, taking as his text the government's discussion paper. The quality of these presentations varied. Some provided a detailed and cogent case for or against free trade; others revealed only a vague understanding of what a comprehensive trade agreement might cover. By the end of the session, however, both sides had usually reached a clear understanding of each other's concerns and interests. The accumulation of briefs, presentations, and notes on each session further added to the dossier underpinning the negotiations to come.

Some ninety-one groups, organizations, and individual companies responded to Burns' invitation. The consultations provided extensive coverage of many goods-producing sectors. As well, a number of service-oriented companies and groups came forward with their views. While conducted in an informal atmosphere, the consultations provided the government with the next layer of information and a better basis for analysis. While Burns chaired each session, he was accompanied by various officials from concerned departments and a secretary provided by the Burney task force.

Of those consulted, fifty-two groups were clearly in favour of the negotiation of a comprehensive trade agreement with the United States, twenty-seven were opposed, and twelve were in an intermediate position (the latter included some which had not yet adopted a firm position, others which saw some benefits on individual issues, but were not prepared to support a comprehensive agreement, others which represented groups in which some members were in favour and others opposed). There was no obvious correlation between the position adopted and the size and/or location or ownership of those consulted.

In the absence of a clearly articulated position by the government, discussion was not always focused. The concept of phasing-in trade agreement provisions over a significant period of time, the likelihood that such issues as contingency protection measures and non-tariff barriers might be included, and the possibility that the government might be prepared to consider adjustment assistance measures in the context of a broad-ranging agreement were not always understood. During the discussions, a number of those who were opposed to a Canadian initiative appeared to be somewhat less concerned about the perceived adverse impact on their particular industries in light of these considerations.

The points of view expressed by those in favour included the following:

- For those with existing large stakes in and favourable terms of access to the US market, including subsidiaries of US corporations that already were, or were in the process of specializing and rationalizing on a North American basis, the principal concern was to avoid more adverse terms of access flowing from the sharply increasing protectionist mood in the United States as illustrated by the more aggressive application of US contingency protection measures.
- Those in favour were characterized by confidence in their competitive ability, by comparable unit labour costs, by world-class technology, and in some cases by easy access to raw materials. Their concern about the Canadian scene was not about these elements, but about the need for macro-economic policies in Canada that would underpin the competitive nature of the Canadian economy overall.
- Some saw substantial opportunity to increase sales to the US and wanted improved as well as more secure access to that market.
- Most favoured a phased elimination of the tariff; there was no consensus on whether the period should be long, short, or intermediate or whether asymmetrical phasing was important.

• In addition to tariffs and contingency protection measures, most were prepared for an extensive reduction or elimination of non-tariff obstacles to trade, especially government procurement practices at the federal, state, and provincial levels. Overall, they saw the objective to be the maximum degree of consistency between Canadian and US practices.

• Some expressed concern about restrictions in the transfer of technology to Canadian firms, particularly in the defence-related industries, and wanted to see this problem addressed in a Canada-US agreement.

• For many, bilateral trade liberalization with the United States was judged a forerunner for the required economies of scale without which Canadian industries could not aggressively and successfully pursue export opportunities in offshore markets.

Those groups that were opposed to a comprehensive agreement with the United States, or that wished to see themselves excluded from any such agreement, also expressed a number of common themes:

• Some pointed to the great disparity in industry and plant size between Canada and the United States, which put Canadian operations at a substantial competitive disadvantage. Their productivity and unit labour costs were not considered competitive with US counterparts, particularly those established in the US South.

• Those representing subsidiaries of US parent companies indicated that their operations were typically small mirror images of the US plants, and that relative costs were such that substantial investment would have to be made to bring Canadian plants up to standards competitive with those in the United States. These operations were generally aimed at satisfying the Canadian domestic market, and suffered from the resulting short runs of a large number of products. They had done little to move in the direction of specialization and rationalization with their parent companies.

• Those representing smaller Canadian-owned businesses tended to emphasize the relative under-capitalization of their current business, typically oriented towards the Canadian market only, and indicated they were comfortable with the existing situation in which US tariffs were usually significantly lower than the corresponding Canadian tariffs.

• Some tended to be sceptical that a comprehensive agreement could be successfully negotiated with adequate provisions to make Canadians confident that its elements would not be compromised in the future.

The overall orientation of the confidential consultations was positive. They provided invaluable insight into the particular concerns of the Canadian private sector and helped to confirm for the government the type of further analytical work required to prepare for negotiations. It also underlined for federal bureaucrats attending the consultations that the scepticism and cynicism about bilateral free trade rife in Ottawa were not generally shared by the business community.[31]

Let the People Speak
In July, a special parliamentary committee was set up to hold public hearings on a possible Canada-US trade agreement. An April green paper issued by Secretary of State for External Affairs Joe Clark, *Competitiveness and Security: Directions for Canada's International Relations*, raised a number of contentious issues, including free trade and Canadian participation in the American Strategic Defense Initiative. Clark asked the committee to provide him with advice on these two critical issues by the end of the summer. Over the course of a month of public hearings across the country, the committee replicated the earlier efforts by Kelleher, as well as the Macdonald Commission, in taking the public pulse. Again, groups for and against girded their loins, prepared briefs, and provided advice. Another five inches of testimony were added to the growing pile of views. The presence of opposition critics on the committee added spice to the questioning and news coverage. Throughout the hearings, however, Tom Hockin maintained an even-handed gavel. Opposition skirmishing that sought to undo what had initially been a unanimous interim report bolstered his credibility and the value of the report.

The broad outlines of the differing views of Canadians were evident from the opening hearing on 15 July in the ballroom of the Sheraton Hotel in Halifax. One of the grand old men of Canadian nationalism, George Grant, told the members that it is 'easier to maintain some kind of indigenous real life in the smaller context of Canada. In a continental community, it is harder to know your own. Canada's trading relationship with the United States is its biggest economic question, but some of Canada's political leaders are guilty of not thinking through all of the ramifications.' On the other hand, one of the biggest employers in the Atlantic region, National Sea Products, said it 'firmly believed that if Canada was willing to accept a free market approach to business and conclude a free trade agreement with the U.S. that the possibility for long-term growth and prosperity exists for Canadians, including those in the Atlantic fisheries.' Its views were echoed by various business organizations.

But in Halifax as well, business did not speak with one voice. Spokespeople for the brewing and textile industries warned of the negative consequences of more open trading conditions for their industries. Their views were echoed by the representatives of organized labour. CLC Vice President

Richard Martin suggested that 'there was a price to be paid for any "trade enhancement" agreement with the U.S. What guarantee was there that such enhancement would not mean shutdown of Canadian branches of U.S. companies? Or a slowdown in the rate at which new companies in Canada open? What guarantees were there that Canadian firms would not move their facilities to the U.S. in the medium and longer term as they are faced with decisions about where to put new investment?'[32] Opponents were not confined solely to nationalists and multilateralists, there was also a strong strain of fear and protectionism.

Similar discussions took place in Montreal, Ottawa, Toronto, Winnipeg, Calgary, and Vancouver over the next four weeks. Canadians from all walks of life appeared before the committee and expressed their hopes and fears for the future of Canada-US trade relations. Any who doubted that there was not enough discussion of the issues and the options in the months prior to the government's decision in September did not follow the work of the parliamentary committee or that of similar exercises.

In its interim report tabled on 23 August, the committee concluded that the health of Canada's trade relationship with the United States was of great importance and that this trade relationship was deteriorating, with the rise of protectionist sentiment in the United States Congress, with calls to impose import quotas on goods, and with a growing number of countervailing duty requests being filed with the US International Trade Commission and the US Department of Commerce. The committee, therefore, recommended that the government act swiftly and decisively to implement a multidimensional initiative in trade to secure access to traditional markets, to actively develop new markets, and to encourage Canadian industry to adapt to an increasingly competitive trade environment. The dimensions of such a strategy should include both bilateral and multilateral negotiations. Bilateral trade negotiations with the United States were not viewed as a substitute for multilateral trade talks but as a complementary, near-term action to deal with immediate problems. The multilateral mechanism was considered, by its very nature, to be a much longer-term process.

The committee did not believe that a bilateral trade agreement between Canada and the United States would result in exclusive concentration on the American market. It could parallel and co-exist with multilateral trade agreements and would not preclude other bilateral initiatives for trade liberalization directed at the European Community, Japan, and the Pacific Rim or developing countries. A series of new bilateral initiatives could serve to stimulate movement towards a new round of multilateral trade negotiations.[33]

The Provinces: Are They Onside?

The Mulroney government came to office with the restoration of national reconciliation between the federal and provincial governments as a major plank in its program. Consultations with the provinces on an initiative with the United States of this magnitude were, therefore, a *sine qua non*. If a majority of the provinces were to oppose, any initiative would bite the dust.

The Regina first ministers' conference in February, two weeks after the appearance of the Kelleher discussion paper, provoked a discussion on the prospects of negotiating bilaterally with the United States. While the discussion was tentative, there was clear support from virtually all the premiers for at least examining the prospects of negotiating a new Canada-United States trade agreement. The conclusion drawn by the prime minister was that he could proceed to explore the attitude of the US government, but with prudence. Views began to crystallize quickly thereafter in light of the results of the Quebec summit and its trade declaration.

At their annual spring meeting, the four western premiers joined in supporting a proposal to examine the benefits and disadvantages of a comprehensive Canada-US agreement, provided that there was full provincial participation in all stages of negotiations and that adequate adjustment measures were put in place for adversely affected workers and industrial sectors. The consensus position of the four premiers followed the advice of the respected Canada-West foundation which, in a number of briefs and position papers, had clearly laid out the benefits to the West expected to flow from a bilateral trade agreement.[34] The strong leadership of two of Canada's most experienced politicians, Bill Bennett of British Columbia and Peter Lougheed of Alberta, proved more than sufficient to overcome the reticence of NDP premier Howard Pawley of Manitoba. Pawley found himself in an uncomfortable position. Disposed by geography to favour an agreement and by political philosophy to oppose it, he started in favour, dithered, and finally jumped over the fence. His uncertainty gained him few friends from either camp. In 1985, however, he was still within the pro camp.

The four premiers also reaffirmed their interest in a new round of multilateral negotiations, and outlined their objectives, emphasizing the importance of both the United States and the Asia-Pacific area. In early May, Lougheed visited Washington and provided a first-hand report to the prime minister in a letter of 14 May in which he urged the federal government 'to initiate a new and comprehensive bilateral free-trade agreement with the United States' and signal its intention to the US to do so by mid-September, or 'the opportunity will probably be lost for many years.'[35]

At a federal-provincial trade ministers' meeting held in Vancouver on 28

May, there was unanimous agreement on the urgency of reaching a comprehensive trade agreement with the United States. All provinces also strongly supported an early round of multilateral trade negotiations with active Canadian participation. Beneath this harmony of view, there were differences. Whereas the western and Atlantic provinces wanted to see the federal government proceed with negotiations on a comprehensive agreement as soon as possible, the Ontario and Manitoba governments were more cautious in their approach. Ontario was in the midst of an election campaign and new Conservative leader Frank Miller was not keen to stake out a position on the issue. His trade minister, Andy Brandt, while not prepared to break the consensus, voiced a litany of Ontario concerns – the danger of import surges in high technology, possible disinvestment in Canadian industry, a potential negative employment impact, and US pressures for harmonization in other areas of economic and social policy. Manitoba Trade Minister Eugene Kostyra, helping his premier crawl to the fence, made his support for exploration of a comprehensive agreement 'conditional upon an extensive period of adjustment being provided for industry sectors and workers adversely affected.'[36]

Buttressing the political will to consult was the reality of the importance and interest of the provinces as partners in any trade negotiation. Their interest was intense because security and conditions of market access are critical to provincial industrial and agricultural development programs and policies. The importance of provincial participation in recent trade negotiations was a product of the success of previous rounds of trade negotiations. These had laid bare the range of non-tariff barriers employed by both federal and provincial governments that had by the 1970s become the main focus of international negotiations. Beyond substance, there was process. The provincial appetite for involvement in trade negotiations had been whetted by the experience of provincial officials during the Tokyo Round of GATT negotiations when the Canadian delegation in Geneva and the headquarters team in Ottawa had gone to great lengths to keep the provinces abreast of developments and to solicit their views. The development of a cadre of provincial officials trained to deal with Ottawa on international trade policy now gave them the means to press their interests in the looming discussions with the United States.[37]

The desire of many provinces to be closely associated with both the preparation and eventually the negotiations was very clear at the May federal-provincial trade ministers' meeting. This was particularly the case in regard to those matters under provincial jurisdiction that could be subject to negotiations such as provincial government purchasing preferences. To keep the provinces closely in touch as the initiative developed, it was agreed to establish single focal points in Ottawa as well as in the provinces to ensure ongoing two-way communication, to organize meetings of federal and provincial officials in June, July, and September, and to set up meetings with individual provinces on request. The question of provincial involvement in any negotiations was set aside until the necessary decisions had been taken to actually initiate them.

As consultations continued and a consensus was built for a decision to move towards negotiations, the government did its internal homework, consulted with the Americans, and paved the way for a formal decision already foreshadowed by the January discussion paper and the March trade declaration.

5

REACHING A DECISION

> All political decisions are taken under great
> pressure, and if a treaty serves its turn for ten or
> twenty years, the wisdom of its framers is
> sufficiently confirmed.
> – Herbert Fisher, *Political Prophecies*

B y late June, the initial preparatory work had been concluded and the
results reported to cabinet. The time had come to move towards a decision. Officials now needed a green light to continue work on the comprehensive trade agreement option and to undertake informal soundings
with US officials over the course of the summer. Among papers prepared to
help ministers reach a decision was a discussion paper which set out the elements of a possible comprehensive bilateral trade agreement.[1] It noted that
such an agreement, for the sake of ongoing analysis, was being interpreted to
refer to an agreement compatible with Canada's obligations under the
GATT, as laid out in Article XXIV. It then described the various substantive
elements of an agreement and the negotiating issues involved. From the outset, therefore, the government had a clear idea of what was involved in a
decision to proceed with negotiations.

The road to decision was traversed amidst growing cynicism. The auguries
were not propitious. Parliament had risen with the government in full retreat
over the issue of old-age pension indexing. In April, in a wide-ranging interview with the *Globe and Mail*'s Jeffrey Simpson, the prime minister had been
upbeat and positive about the initiative. He declared that 'we're going to be
ready to make a move in the late summer ... I wanted to move quickly [at
Quebec] to get a pretty strong declaration of intent as to where we were
going, and the public commitment from President Reagan to veto moves
that could be inimical to Canada's interests ... I've got until early autumn to
make this deal, whatever it is.' He went on to indicate that in May the government would consider a report from Kelleher on his consultations and
take the next step in the decision path.[2] But by the end of May, ministers
were in an apprehensive mood and were cautious in their endorsement of a
work program leading to another politically controversial decision. Scare

stories in the *Toronto Star* ('Would 125,000 auto jobs survive free trade?' – 11 May; 'Full free trade with US could cost 1 million Canadian jobs, labor warns' – 28 May; and 'Would US pact erode our sovereignty? Free trade: salvation or sell-out?' – 9 June) added to their anxieties and uncertainty.

Evidence from the Polls

That there were doubts about the ambitious project was evident as the debate on the subject gathered steam during the spring and summer of 1985. A Decima poll taken during July for External Affairs revealed that while a majority continued to believe it was a good idea, the traditional regional differences remained, with Ontarians still being the least comfortable with the concept and those in the Atlantic and Prairie provinces the most relaxed. Men tended to like the idea the most; students, the least. When asked whether a trade relationship implied too great a risk to Canada's political and economic independence, 60 per cent said no. A series of questions along this line led Decima to conclude that 'at the time the survey was taken, most people were relatively unconcerned about threats to Canada's independence, especially in the face of potential growth opportunities.' The survey showed that Canadians were less sure what form benefits from free trade would take and believed that the United States raised more tariff barriers against Canadian goods than Canada raised against US goods.

Table 5

Results of Decima poll on whether Canadians believe trade pact is an urgent need, 9-16 July 1985 (%)

All Canadians	49		
Men	54	Women	44
18-24 years of age	41	35-54 years of age	54
Students	35	Younger than high school age	56
Rural residents	53	Urban residents	47

The poll also revealed a growing awareness of the threat of US protectionism, a theme that the Trudeau government had begun to develop and that had been increasingly emphasized by Prime Minister Mulroney and his ministers. The notion of a special Canada-US relationship lingered, with respondents believing that Canada would not be treated as harshly as other US trading partners. Sixty-two per cent gave the government an excellent or good rating on 'managing our relations with the US,' with francophones scoring the government higher on this question than anglophones.

Although the poll did not show much unhappiness with the government's conduct of foreign policy, it clearly indicated that Canadians placed less emphasis on trade issues than did the government. Concern for global security, relieving hunger and poverty, and promoting world peace out-ranked concern for enhanced trade opportunities. The survey tested for differences in perception of the Liberal and Conservative governments in foreign policy, but Decima concluded that these differences were in style rather than substance, although 40 per cent recognized a difference in approach to the United States that they interpreted as positive. Nonetheless, only 10 per cent said the ideal Canada-US relationship should be 'warmest and closest of friends,' the kind of characterization most often expressed by the prime minister; 47 per cent wanted to keep the relationship on a 'business-like but neighbourly basis'; a scant 5 per cent preferred Canada to be 'cool and independent.'

Table 6

Results of Decima poll on whether Canada would benefit or lose from freer trade with US, 9-16 July 1985 (%)

	Benefit Great deal	Neither Benefit nor lose	Lose Great deal
Atlantic	60	12	28
Prairies	59	10	31
Quebec	50	16	32
Ontario (outside Metro)	54	10	35
Metro Toronto	45	8	47
British Columbia	42	22	35

The Happy Few

Thus the work continued for the small group of officials dedicated to the idea of a free-trade agreement with the United States. The country as a whole remained interested in free trade, but the government had shown signs of being averse to taking a risk. For those working on the initiative, these were factors that needed to be weighed in preparing material for ministerial consideration. The decision would be one taken by ministers, but it was up to these officials to ensure that the issues were sufficiently analyzed and considered so that ministers could reach an informed judgment.

When a great government initiative is undertaken, it is a honey pot to the bureaucracy. Everybody wants a piece of the action, and the choice of talent and offers of cooperation are abundant. Honey pots, however, are not always recognized from the outset, especially when they tilt against conventional wisdom; sometimes a great deal of hostility must be overcome first.

From the inception of the sectoral trade initiative in September 1983 until the decision to proceed to full-scale negotiations in September 1985, the exercise was carried by a few ministers supported by a handful of officials. By September 1984, sufficient resources had been extracted from External to establish a task force of five officers and two secretaries. While still pursuing the sectoral trade initiative, attention increasingly focused on the review of options and the writing of the discussion paper released at the end of January 1985. The Kelleher consultations, the follow-up to the Quebec summit, and the Burns consultations with business each added more personnel.[3]

The day-to-day supervision fell to the assistant deputy minister for United States Affairs, Derek Burney, who had also successfully coordinated the preparation of the Quebec summit. By the summer of 1985, he could call on the members of a task force of a dozen officials. Their task, however, was hampered by indifference and even hostility from their departmental and interdepartmental colleagues. Many felt that to embark on a bilateral initiative was quixotic at best and irresponsible at worst because it would generate expectations that could not be met. Officials who laboured in this vineyard were warned by their colleagues that sooner or later, ministers would run for cover.

The multilateralists had by now become seriously alarmed. In the early days of the sectoral trade initiative, they had regarded it as a bothersome diversion that would shortly go away. With the growing intensity of public discussion of the free-trade option and the short shrift being given to the multilateral trade negotiations, they argued strenuously that a free-trade agreement with the United States would betray Canada's multilateral tradition. If a bilateral arrangement had any rationale at all, it should be subordinated to Canada's main objective, a new round of multilateral trade negotiations, and should be conducted as a subsidiary operation in Geneva. From this point of view, the Burney task force, as a first step, should be folded into the coordinating unit set up for the multilateral exercise.

Bob Richardson, the trade deputy, finally decreed a stop to the infighting. On 10 May 1985, in a small sixth floor boardroom in the Pearson Building, Burney met with the competitors and read them the riot act. The department was damaging itself by unnecessary hostility between two government priorities – exploration of a bilateral deal and preparations for multilateral trade negotiations. They were complementary, not contradictory, initiatives. Burney was not an advocate of either approach; he was there to deliver the government's program which indisputably was to explore the scope and management of a possible free-trade negotiation. There should be cooperation. Information should be shared and overlap avoided since the basic trade policy issues confronting Canada were the same. The two initiatives should coexist. Henceforth, the relationship between the two groups was never easy, but the sharp edge of personal competition was blunted.

PUTTING A STRAIN ON THE OLD MACHINE

Arch Dale, *Winnipeg Free Press*, 1 March 1933

The economic and cultural nationalists also mounted stout opposition. They insisted that Canadian identity and sovereignty were at risk if trade barriers were eliminated. Traditionalists in the Department of External Affairs, clinging to their view of the legacy of the Pearson years, worried about maintaining a distinct Canadian foreign policy or indeed retaining the room to criticize the United States on everything from arms control with the Russians to US policy in Central America.[4] The outlet for the articulation of these views was the Department's executive committee.

On 19 June, that committee met in the eighth floor board room to review the results of Kelleher's consultations and the studies in progress. There was much concern about the very notion of a free-trade agreement. How would Canadian identity be maintained? Could the Americans be trusted? Was the multilateral route not the traditional Canadian way? Were ministers being told that they would be sailing the ship of state into uncharted waters with incalculable consequences for the country's future and their own political fate? There was little discussion of the results of the consultations which had shown scant concern about such issues. Richardson had to remind the meeting that ministers clearly wanted the free-trade option to be fully explored and that there was a distinctly different point of view outside of official Ottawa. Reluctantly, the executive committee had to accept these changing circumstances and the report on the consultations went forward.

Cooperation outside of External Affairs was also slow to develop. Most officials kept their distance. Officials in the Department of Regional Industrial

Expansion (DRIE) all but flatly refused to contribute detailed sectoral studies until well into the summer. They continued to be imbued with the traditional protectionism of industry department bureaucrats all over the world, and saw free trade both as complicating their lives and forcing many of their clients out of business. Key officials in Finance kept their own counsel, developing their own assessments and refusing to share them. The main trade policy units got involved, but their efforts were aimed at diverting the consideration of options for trade relations with the United States towards a plan of action which focused on the new round of multilateral trade negotiations. There was constant sniping from those who believed that any bilateral initiative with the United States would be selling Canada's birthright.[5]

In these circumstances, the political leadership of key ministers was critical, especially the secretary of state for external affairs, the minister for international trade and the minister of finance. All came to office free of the historical baggage that had sunk previous bilateral initiatives. All saw broad support in the private sector and the public at large for a bold new approach to the Canada-US trade and economic relationship. It was equally apparent that the sectoral trade initiative undertaken by the previous government had triggered a lively debate in the public about the merits of free trade. The question for the new government was whether to take part in the public debate and attempt to shape it or to let it roll on without a firm government position. Once the debate was under way, getting out would be as hard as proceeding with it. In the face of bureaucratic carping, key ministers had thus encouraged the small band of officials involved to press onward and bring forward a considered proposition on which to base a sober decision whether to proceed with negotiations.

Once the resolve of ministers was clear, however, there was a marked shift in bureaucratic attitudes. Suddenly, the negotiation of a comprehensive trade agreement with the United States turned out to be a topic in which every department had an interest and/or a view. All ministers, officials, provinces, and elements of the private sector cherished a role. The challenge then became one of harnessing the right minds and talents to the preparatory task without being overwhelmed by competitive as well as legitimate jurisdictional concerns. Many needed to be involved in order to ensure a solid consensus prior to, during, and after any negotiations, but the scope and degree of involvement that was required differed. The challenge of managing this process soon became painfully obvious.

In the early summer of 1985, despite an increasingly vocal opposition, a hostile bureaucracy, and a cabinet beginning to feel the sting of constant media attack and opposition criticism, the initiative was not without resources. The Burns' consultations were in full swing, and the federal-provincial contact points were functioning well with preparations in progress for a meeting of trade deputies in July. Work would proceed and a recommendation be brought forward at the end of the summer on whether or not to launch negotiations. But the high level of public attention that had prevailed over the first six months of the year had been replaced with invisibility.

To assist the government in reaching a decision, analysis and consultations concentrated on:
- further clarifying the specific objectives to be served
- outlining the basic elements of an agreement and the manner in which the negotiation of each element would affect Canadian interests
- assessing the implications for economic growth in Canada
- shoring up support among the provinces, the private sector, labour, and consumer groups.

Outside of External Affairs, the Departments of Finance, Regional Industrial Expansion, Agriculture, Fisheries and Oceans, Energy, Mines and Resources, Communications, Labour, Supply and Services, Transport, and Consumer and Corporate Affairs all began to contribute to the work, and their senior officials huddled together more frequently in a steering committee chaired by Richardson. They began to develop competitiveness profiles for the goods-producing sectors of the economy so that ministers would have a basis for assessing the potential impact of an agreement. Additionally, various departments contributed to policy papers on a range of possible negotiating issues including: government procurement, safeguards, contingency protection (anti-dumping and countervailing duties), trade in services, investment, adjustment measures, and consumer interests.

Outside experts were engaged to prepare papers on a number of issues, including a survey of studies of the impact of a comprehensive agreement on the Canadian economy by the Institute for Research on Public Policy, studies of the problems that might be encountered in coming to grips with the US system of contingency protection by the Washington law firm of Arnold and Porter and by retired Tokyo Round negotiator Rodney Grey, an analysis of the European experience with economic integration by retired bureaucrat Alec Lane, an examination of institutional issues by GATT expert Frank Stone, and a study of the implications for the autopact by Ottawa consultant Doug Arthur.[6] The work proceeded on the basis of achieving the following general negotiating objectives:
- greater security of access to the US market, particularly by reducing the risks inherent in the US system of contingency protection and limiting the

constitutional powers of the US Congress to initiate and implement legislative changes designed to restrict imports
- improvement in access to the US market in order to provide Canadian industry with a sufficiently large market base to realize economies of scale and specialization and to find niches for specialty products
- a stable North American trading system that would induce substantial but orderly adjustment in Canada towards a more competitive economy.[7]

By the end of the summer, the analysis, briefs, and memoranda were beginning to mount up. Much of it was based on academic work of long standing that was now bolstered by the additional knowledge and insight available in government and business. The work was of uneven quality. Some was very good; some would need to be redone before it could be used in any negotiation. What was important was that a considerable body of knowledge and analysis was being stored up and a core group of ministers and their officials were gaining the necessary experience and insight to carry the issue further.

Is There a Basis for Negotiation?

As part of the preparatory process, several meetings with US administration and congressional officials were held to explore American attitudes and approaches to possible bilateral trade negotiations. US officials were kept informed of the preparatory process and of the fact that a formal decision would not be taken until the fall. Nevertheless, officials were authorized to explore informally and without prejudice the prospects for and modalities of a bilateral trade negotiation. Additionally, ministers and other parliamentarians met with their counterparts to gauge the mood and degree of commitment.

On 12 June, Bill Dymond and Michael Hart, jointly responsible for the preparatory work, travelled to Washington to gauge the Washington mood. They called on Bill Merkin and his immediate boss, Jon Rosenbaum, as well as the senior majority counsels of the two congressional committees with immediate responsibility for trade issues. On the House side, in a small crowded office in the Longworth block, just off the main entrance, they talked for over an hour with Rufus Yerxa, Democratic counsel to the trade subcommittee of the Ways and Means Committee. On the Senate side, in an even smaller and more crowded anteroom, they briefed Len Santos, Republican trade counsel to the Finance Committee. Both were reserved in their views. If Canada was interested in a trade deal, Canada should propose it and they were sure the administration would welcome such a proposal. The Congress would at this point be indifferent but would likely welcome it later, once the dismal trade picture began to turn around. The indifference was grounded less in a hostile attitude towards Canada than in congressional dissatisfaction with the administration's trade policy and the trade policies of America's other trading partners.

Back at the embassy, the Canadian group considered the day well spent. They had lunched with Bob Herzstein of the law firm of Arnold and Porter, discussed the climate and possibilities with him, and commissioned a study of the problems and negotiating challenges in trade remedy law. They could report back to Ottawa that the mood in Washington was sufficiently favourable to continue the preparatory work. At USTR, preparations were set in train for Burney and Deputy USTR Mike Smith to get together later in the summer to discuss the state of preparations. Late July was considered a good time.

On 31 July, Burney travelled to Washington to meet with Smith. After an early morning start from a Washington hotel, Burney, accompanied by Michael Hart and Bob Martin from the Department of Finance, arrived in the shadow of the Chesapeake Bay Bridge to join Smith, his wife, and Bill Merkin, for a leisurely cruise on Smith's thirty-foot sailboat. The sky was blue, the temperature scorching, and the wind still as they slipped out of the moorings and headed for the Bay. By 10:30 they were gliding past James Michener's house and saw Annapolis off in the distance. Then over coffee and danish supplied by Mrs. Smith, they set to work to explore the full gamut of preparations for the Canada-US initiative and the feasibility of possible full-scale trade negotiations. The atmosphere was relaxed; good progress was made. The results of this meeting did much to shape the Canadian and US governments' attitudes over the next few months. At the end of the day, sunburned and tired, all five concluded that indeed there was a basis for negotiations.

The administration's general attitude was positive and upbeat. US officials were excited about the prospect of a trade negotiation with Canada, for both tactical and substantive reasons. The conclusion of a recent administration review of US trade policy was that the United States must take a more diversified and aggressive approach with its trading partners in order to deflect congressional protectionism and assert administration leadership. While the administration would continue to push hard for a new round of multilateral trade negotiations, it had concluded that any positive results were some way off and would not meet a number of US trade objectives because of the inevitable trade-offs leading to a lowest common denominator result. It regarded a negotiation with Canada as a first test of this alternative approach. It saw a bilateral agreement to be of interest in its own right as well as its potential for providing leverage for furthering US global interests.

The 1984 agreement with Israel did not satisfy the test because it was largely politically motivated and did not engage major US economic interests. The US Cabinet had given the USTR authority to continue exploratory discussions with Canada; other initiatives reported in the press, such as with ASEAN, remained strictly notional.

Smith reported that on the basis of early soundings on the Hill, Congress appeared to be equally well disposed towards Canada, despite its continuing emphasis on such irritants as lumber and the ugly mood on trade policy in general. This was confirmed later, for example, by Representative Sam Gibbons, chair of the trade subcommittee of the powerful House Ways and Means Committee, during a public hearing in Vancouver on the lumber issue, when he expressed broad support for negotiations. Other congressional leaders meeting with ministers also expressed admiration for a government prepared to take the long view and negotiate a new, liberalizing agreement. A good, hard negotiation, they felt, would capture imagination on the Hill as long as it was clear that such a negotiation would deal with the interests of both countries and provide a basis for resolving specific irritants. From a congressional point of view, a properly prepared initiative with Canada could demonstrate that the administration was not stuck on a multilateral treadmill.

Smith indicated that the administration had in mind a broad, comprehensive agreement and strongly urged that neither side come to the table with prior commitments to exclude sectors and issues; it was preferable that exclusions result only from the give and take of negotiations. In his view, an agreement with Canada would have to satisfy Canada's need for security and predictability by coming to terms with the effect on Canada of the US system of contingency protection. Equally, the United States needed to be seen to be making progress on the so-called new issues: investment, services, and intellectual property.

Smith believed it should be possible to negotiate a separate Canada-US regime that would address contingency protection measures by, for example, establishing higher thresholds and discipline and thus reducing the scope for harassment. He did not rule out exemptions for Canada from some aspects of US trade remedy law in return for tougher disciplines on subsidy practices. He believed reaching a common understanding on subsidies would be key to gaining congressional and private sector support. But he also warned that Congress would be less sanguine about coming to grips with US trade law, and that some would dismiss the possibility outright.

US priority objectives included tariffs and investment. Smith saw the phased elimination of the Canadian tariff as a major concession by Canada, but cautioned that slower phasing by Canada would be very difficult for the United States to accept. The administration would expect both sides to reach full duty elimination at the same time. On investment, the basic objectives would involve national treatment and right of establishment; this would be necessary to demonstrate that an agreement would be balanced.

Other elements of an agreement Smith saw as largely neutral, that is, of interest to both countries and with scope to make useful progress beyond what had been or was likely to be achieved multilaterally. These would include such issues as standards, intellectual property, and services. Regarding services, the US side had an interest in reaching a broad agreement over time, but its more immediate objective would be a declaration of principles that could be put to the test by negotiating a number of sectoral agreements as building blocks towards a broader agreement. Of immediate interest would be informatics, insurance, aviation, and certain professional services.

Smith concurred that any agreement would require strong and binding institutional provisions that would clearly indicate that the agreement would be between co-equal partners and that disputes would be settled on an equitable basis. The effect of the agreement should be to commit both the administration and Congress. From that perspective it might be best to conclude a treaty, both for its positive psychological impact and for its capacity to bind the states.

Smith concluded that the reports that Kelleher and Yeutter would be making to the prime minister and president in September (as called for by the Quebec trade declaration) would be the opportunity for a signal of intent with respect to any negotiation. Should the reports indicate that the negotiation of a comprehensive agreement would be the best way to reduce and eliminate barriers to trade, they could be used to trigger the US requirement to notify Congress and initiate the mandatory studies by the International Trade Commission and the ISAC (Industry Sector Advisory Committees) consultations. The United States would then be ready to enter formally into negotiations late in 1985 or early 1986. This process, however, would not preclude useful contacts among officials preparing for negotiations.

Burney was satisfied. From his perspective, Smith had indicated a clear willingness to engage on the Canadian priorities of secure and enhanced access. Burney could report back to ministers that the administration had not dismissed the possibility of addressing the thorny problem of trade remedy law. At the same time, Smith had indicated a sensitivity to the difficulties posed for Canada in negotiating contractual commitments on investment and the delicate issue of cultural sovereignty.

Based on these and other conversations with administration and congressional staffers, it was clear in the summer of 1985 that there was the potential for a big agreement. The key issues from Canada's perspective (contingency protection, procurement, and dispute settlement) were in the US view amenable to a meaningful negotiation as long as Canada was prepared to meet US preoccupations on investment, tariffs, and services. It was equally clear that of these six key issues, the most difficult would be contingency protection and investment.

US readiness to proceed was not only suggested in private bilateral discussions, but was also demonstrated in the readiness of US officials to appear on platforms in the United States and Canada to speak on the issues. Throughout 1984 and 1985, there was a lively debate on the pros and cons of free trade between Canada and the United States and many business and academic groups sought the participation of US and Canadian government officials to explain the issues and participate in the discussions. US officials readily complied with these requests. Both Smith and Merkin travelled frequently to Canada and learned to appreciate Canadian concerns and interests.

Much of the discussion during this period, however, concentrated on process. This was not a period of pre-negotiation. It was a period of probing and testing. The response was positive and geared to the, by then, well-established convention that Canada would set the pace and provide the vision. US officials would follow where Canada led. The administration felt confident that its broad ideological commitment to free enterprise could meet any negotiating challenge Canada was prepared to set. There was neither a need nor a desire for the United States to engage in the kind of detailed consultations and analysis taking place in Canada. Activity of this kind would be misinterpreted in both capitals – in Ottawa, as thinly disguised economic imperialism and in Washington as being at odds with the general thrust in Congress towards more protection. With hindsight, this complacency should have sown some seeds of concern among those responsible for the initiative in Ottawa.

Canada Is Ready

In mid-August, the pace began to pick up. The cabinet priorities and planning committee was to meet in Vancouver and was expecting a status report on the work at hand. The reaction of ministers would determine the next steps. The prime minister told the *Vancouver Sun*, when pressed on how he and his key ministers would fill three days of meetings at the Hotel Vancouver: 'We are going to be very busy here. We are dealing with preparations for the fall session and particularly with some major initiatives as well, which we hope will be beneficial to Western Canada and British Columbia.'[8]

The prime minister was relaxed and eager to get ready for the fall session. Instead of a government Challenger, he arrived first class on CP 967 (Air Canada flight attendants were on strike and Mulroney, the former labour negotiator, decided not to cross the picket lines), chatting with passengers on the way.

The problems of May and June had disappeared with the summer sun. A minor cabinet tune-up had helped to project a more positive image. The gloom and doom evident earlier in the summer were gone by the time ministers arrived in Vancouver. Kelleher's report to his colleagues caught the mood. Heavy on process, on the work accomplished, on the work near completion, on the results of the Chesapeake Bay discussions, the report indicated that all would be ready for a decision in September.[9] Momentum was restored. As ministers left at the end of the week, sceptical Vancouver-based pundits changed their tune. Full of sarcasm and cynicism about the motives behind the western cabinet meeting early in the week, they expressed grudging admiration at the end. *Vancouver Sun* columnist Jamie Lamb was particularly pleased with the prime minister's upbeat briefing of Vancouver business heavies on the prospect of a bilateral negotiation:

> As to trade relations with the United States, he [Mulroney] left no doubt that he favored and will shortly make moves toward more open trade with the United States. The moves would have to be made gradually, he said, because political factors such as Liberal David Peterson in Ontario had to be considered. He indicated that more open trade and more secure trading arrangements with the United States are necessary, but politics prevents a wild-eyed rush to the bargaining table. He said he knows what they know: that better trading arrangements with the U.S. are vital but that politics demands that each move be made slowly and with great care given to public relations.[10]

While the federal priorities and planning committee met at one end of the country, the premiers convened at the other end. Under the leadership of the mercurial Brian Peckford, they assembled in St. John's for their annual meeting. Free trade was at the top of the agenda. Present for his first meeting was Ontario's David Peterson. Present for their last meeting were Alberta's Peter Lougheed and Quebec's René Levesque. At the meeting, the consensus of the ten provinces evident at the May meeting of trade ministers began to erode. Peterson expressed the caution and scepticism, but not opposition, that would become his trade mark. The Quebec heir apparent, the absent Robert Bourassa, not yet certain of how federal-provincial games were being played in the 1980s, criticized the PQ for their support for this federal initiative. Pawley of Manitoba, still in accord with his western colleagues, was beginning to feel less sure about his support.

On a more positive note, Tom Hockin, chair of the special parliamentary committee examining free trade, had carefully crafted an all-party consensus and tabled his interim report on 23 August. The withdrawal of the NDP and Liberals at the last moment made them look like they were playing politics and not taking the issue seriously.

For the bureaucrats, the time for decision was fast approaching. In the last week of August, a plan was developed to bring the issue to decision in three stages. The first stage was to bring the sectoral analysis to a conclusion satisfactory to sectoral departments and ministers. The second was to report on the results of analysis and consultations. The third was the presentation of options: to proceed with its implications or not to proceed with the alternative strategy that would be required to manage trade relations with the United States.

September started with a final preliminary meeting between Smith and Burney in Toronto at the Four Seasons Hotel in Yorkville to discuss the state of preparations for the Yeutter and Kelleher reports. Both were happy with the Kelleher draft report which suggested that the two senior trade officials had agreed that the best way for Canada and the United States to meet the challenge of reducing barriers to trade and investment would be to enter into comprehensive trade negotiations. The draft report set out the rationale for the decision and outlined the objectives Canada would be pursuing. It was agreed that Yeutter would make a similar report.

While the formal end of the six-month deadline established in the Quebec trade declaration was 17 September, both sides agreed that there might be some slippage, but that a decision should be taken before the middle of October. Burney wanted to ensure that ministers would have the necessary time to discuss the issues and provide instructions and not be stampeded by any artificial timetable. Smith was somewhat surprised at the positive mood, having concluded from newspaper reports that opposition was too strong and that the government was consequently losing interest.[11] Nevertheless, he was clearly pleased and mused that a major policy address by the president scheduled for the third week of September might provide an opportune time to signal US interest. In the end, they agreed that a get-tough-with-trade speech might not be the best time to signal the beginning of free-trade negotiations with Canada.

After taking in a baseball game at CNE Stadium (won by the visiting Cleveland Indians) and a late supper in Chinatown, the two sides went their separate ways. The next morning, after a comedy of errors trying to return on City Express, Burney and his team arrived back at Uplands close to noon to be greeted by his brand new car and driver, complete with phone, the symbols of power in Ottawa. In late August, the prime minister had appointed Burney as associate undersecretary at External Affairs; at the same time naming Si Taylor to the top post of undersecretary. With Taylor and Burney now at the pinnacle of External Affairs, the problem of priorities was much attenuated. They would now chair the executive and management committees and guarantee greater interdepartmental cooperation. The initiative would from then on be less hampered by bureaucratic gamesmanship.

The next day, 5 September, the Macdonald Commission released its long-awaited report. While its conclusions and recommendations had been an open secret for months, the detailed rationale and argumentation still made news. Media coverage was overwhelmingly positive. Reporters across the country were favourably impressed with the quality of the report, and particularly with the sections dealing with free trade. In the next few days, columnists and

Donald Macdonald explains free trade to the press with all the passion at his command.
(Ottawa, 5 September 1985)

editorialists alike took the opportunity to chide those against free trade by pointing to the persuasive argumentation of the Commission report. The *Globe and Mail*'s lead editorial on 6 September, 'A Case for Free Trade,' was typical:

> There is vision in the report of the Royal Commission on the Economic Union and Development Prospects for Canada that almost justifies the length of its title. Better, there is substance to the vision, coherence among its parts, intellectual courage, and, even emotional force.
>
> If there is a 'leap of faith' in this major recommendation, the authors argue it is from a familiar but weakening ledge to a strange but stronger one. The Commission would turn the tables in this seminal debate: if you favor job creation, higher incomes, social justice, more multilateral economic relations, a stronger sense of national identity and Canadian unity, you must support a shrewd agreement on North American free trade.

The same day, the *Winnipeg Free Press* was more sober but no less supportive in its assessment:

> Leaps of faith can be left to theologians. Belief in the value of pursuing a free trade area with the United States is not a matter of faith; it is the result of rational judg-

ment about the kind of trading environment which is most likely to ensure a growth in investment, employment and prosperity in Canada. No economic policy carries an absolute guarantee but there is overwhelming evidence, confirmed again and again by serious studies, that the course most likely to ensure those results is free trade, with the world if possible and with the United States at least.

The Commission report buoyed the prime minister's confidence. September had already started off well for him. On 4 September he had celebrated his electoral landslide of a year earlier as well as the birth of a new son, Nicholas. Most pundits had not been kind to him in their first-year report cards, but he must have been bemused by Richard Gwyn's analysis of his decision-making style. Wrote Gwyn:

> His process of decision-making is not exactly intellectually elegant. It is not intellectual at all in fact, but is wholly pragmatic and political ... On free trade, Mulroney ... late this month will announce that he has decided to begin trade talks with the U.S. These talks have long been inevitable. What matters about them is whether they end up with a free-trade pact ... Canadians will not know Mulroney's real decision until the end of the talks, probably some two years away. Until then, he will have all the time he needs to listen to Canadians express their hopes and fears about cross-border trade ... By his style of leadership, Mulroney is forcing us to become democrats, that is, to actively involve ourselves in the national government process.[12]

Neither Gwyn, ministers, nor officials, however, were ready for the confident and decisive tone adopted by the prime minister at a Meech Lake meeting with his ministers on Friday, 6 September. Kelleher was scheduled to make a short state-of-play report on the initiative; no decisions were expected. But the prime minister, without preamble, had decided to proceed. He took the view that the time for discussion and study had been completed. Now was the time for leadership. The issue before the government now was not whether but when and how to announce and implement the decision.

A frenzied three-week period now began. Officials met with Clark and Kelleher on their return from Meech Lake for a quick review of what had to be done and who would be needed to help. The meeting resumed Saturday morning at 8:00 in Finance Minister Wilson's Centre Block office. At 2:00 that afternoon the first meeting of a special task force took place in the operations room of the Pearson building.

For three weeks, the task force met among the maps and world-time clocks of a room accustomed to frenetic activity. Two weeks before it had been used to plan Canadian assistance to Mexico following the devastating earthquake in that country and to respond to anxious calls from Canadian relatives of victims. Several months earlier, it had been used to plan the Quebec summit. Now another task force set about to:

- provide a vehicle for considering the issues that now had to be pursued, including the format of the Kelleher report called for by the Quebec Trade Declaration
- draw up a communications plan for the decision, including the best way to maintain and build on the momentum favouring trade negotiations
- draft a statement for the prime minister announcing the decision
- prepare a strategy for dealing with the provinces
- develop information kits and speech modules (set speeches easily adapted as required) for ministers, members of Parliament, and journalists
- devise a strategy for formally notifying the Americans.

After a hectic three weeks, all was ready for a Thursday, 26 September announcement. During those weeks, the patience of all involved had been severely tested. Three factors had made the task somewhat different from the routine. The heavy involvement of the Prime Minister's Office (PMO), political staff, and various Conservative party advisors added a complication with which most public servants were not familiar. Not used to the way public servants go about their business and convinced that only they were dedicated to the well-being of the government, political staffers issued orders and counter-orders and added to an atmosphere of crisis and confusion.

During the second week, days before the announcement was to be made, *Maclean's* and several Toronto-area newspapers released a leaked draft communications strategy which bared for all to see a cynical and manipulative plan. The fact that the leaked document was a very preliminary, rough draft was lost in the ensuing uproar. The need for denials in the House soured the atmosphere and proved a major setback to the launching of the initiative.

A further disappointment was the attitude in Washington. Now that a decision was imminent, the small group of US officials with whom Canadian officials had become familiar expanded to include many more. These new officials, including White House Chief of Staff Donald Regan and Treasury Secretary James Baker, did not share the established convention that Canada would set the pace and the United States would follow. They could not conceive of a major policy development involving the United States in which the United States did not call the tune. They were convinced that September was a poor month to launch the initiative; October was not likely to be better. Baker suggested that a good time might well be the January state-of-the-union address. Major, top-level diplomatic efforts were unleashed to convince the administration that Canada could not wait. Too much had been invested to let the initiative linger on a back-burner for three or four months waiting for a propitious time in Washington. These efforts succeeded, but not without raising alarms as to how committed the administration was to the initiative.

To add to the confusion and to give Canada a foretaste of the strange world of Washington decision-making, the furious diplomatic manoeuvring took place against a backdrop of positive statements by senior US officials. On 1 September, the US ambassador to Canada, Paul Robinson, warned that the Canadian government should not delay its decision much longer. On 16 September, Commerce Secretary Malcolm Baldrige urged Canada to take a positive decision, and the president in his Saturday radio message painted a glowing picture of the benefits of free trade. Canada would learn over the next two years that even the president did not always speak definitively for the US government.[13]

Finally, the third week of September brought a double political disappointment for the government. On Monday, Fisheries Minister John Fraser resigned as a result of the tainted tuna scandal and on Thursday, Communications Minister Marcel Masse resigned in the face of the news that the RCMP was investigating alleged election spending irregularities in his riding. What had started out as a new beginning for the government was rapidly turning into a nightmare.

Despite these difficulties, 26 September went like clockwork. The sun shone. The Gatineau hills provided a colourful background to the Parliament buildings. The prime minister phoned all the premiers in the morning. He then spoke to President Reagan at noon and rose in the House at three to read a sober statement indicating that on the basis of the report provided by Minister Kelleher the week before, the government had concluded that it would pursue exploratory negotiations with the United States for a new trade agreement between the two countries, based on the theme developed over the previous year that Canada needed to enhance and secure its access to its major market. A trade agreement would, he said, set Canada's economic prospects on the right course as well as provide the 'jobs, jobs, jobs' that he had promised in his election campaign.

The following week, he formally wrote the president a short but historic letter proposing that the two governments 'pursue a new trade agreement involving the broadest possible package of mutually beneficial reductions in barriers to trade in goods and services. Such an agreement should secure and enhance access to each other's markets by reducing and eliminating tariff and non-tariff barriers and result in a better and more predictable set of rules whereby our trade is conducted.' The president responded the next day, welcoming the proposal: 'As you know, I am committed to the pursuit of free and fair trade and I believe our objective should be to achieve the broadest possible package of mutually beneficial trade barrier reductions. If history has taught us one thing, it is that the freer the flow of world trade, the stronger the tides for human progress and peace among nations.'[14] When reviewing a draft the week before, the president had balked at inclusion of the words 'fair trade,' as did Canadian officials. The president's White House handlers, however, were adamant. The letter had to serve not only the Canada-US trade initiative, but also symbolize the new get-tough-with-trade policy. Canada acquiesced. It was more important to launch the initiative than to insist on a single word.[15]

Jeffrey Simpson, who had throughout the previous twelve months chided the government for its caution and slowness, remained true to his theme. The prime minister's speech was too flat and muted and out of keeping with the historic occasion, but consistent with the apparently deliberate strategy of playing the issue down and treating Canadians as adolescents. Other pundits, however, were more positive. The *Winnipeg Free Press* declared that the prime minister had taken the right decision at the right time and its business columnist Joan Cohen added: 'Backing up the negotiating team will be a government-wide research effort that, officially, began last June and, according to one bureaucrat, will make the trade negotiations the most thoroughly researched project in Canada's history. This government is doing some things right.'[16]

The Communications Challenge

No matter how well prepared, the first challenge that had to be met was to ensure that the damage sustained from the leaked communications strategy was undone. The government had already learned from the pension indexing debacle in May that no matter how challenging the substance of a major issue of public policy, even more challenging is the task of explaining it to the public and of building broad understanding and support. All major initiatives, therefore, require a communications strategy that maps out how the media and other moulders of public opinion will be influenced to help get the government's message across. There is nothing sinister about this, although old timers regard it with distaste and the media piously complain of manipulation when they inadvertently obtain a copy of such a document. A good part of the strategy is devoted to anticipating the unexpected. In practical terms, this involves communicating the message to the media. The government had sought to develop such a communications strategy and a budget to implement it, but through the malfeasance of someone with access to the work of the task force, that effort had been discredited before it could be launched.

It was not the only embarrassing document leaked that September. A draft memorandum to cabinet on Arctic sovereignty as well as a candid letter from Ambassador Gotlieb to Sinclair Stevens about an impending Investment Canada decision involving the Gulf and Western takeover of Prentice-Hall also found their way to front pages across the country. Someone appeared determined to undermine the government's policy of refurbished relations with the United States.

THE FIRST CASUALTY OF WAR IS TRUTH INFORMATION

Alan King, *Ottawa Citizen*, 3 June 1986

The leaked communications document was rightly characterized as slick and manipulative – it had been recognized as such and rejected. Once leaked, however, it provided a perfect foil to be cynically exploited by media and opposition who probably knew perfectly well that the document did not represent government policy but was a typical early draft attempting to develop a communications strategy for a major government initiative. The strategy had been closely held within the task force preparing for the announcement, but any time up to fifty people circulate around an issue as interesting and controversial as this, there is ample room for mischief. The fact that a large number of political staff and outside consultants were brought in to help, further complicated normal security precautions. It is difficult for public servants to instill their particular cult of secrecy and secu-rity in political and outside staff trained in the art of communications and manipulation. What had been surprising was not the fact of the leak, but that there had been no previous leak of equally or more sensitive documents.

Despite the embarrassment, however, the task of communicating the issue remained. Over the course of the first year, ministers had projected a cautious image: they were prepared to enter into negotiations with the United States, but only if there was strong support within the country and among the business community. Through consultations and study, the government had clearly demonstrated that such support existed and that it could proceed. The next challenge, however, was to sustain that support in the face of continued criticism and very little in the way of concrete evidence of progress and results. The basic thrust of the leaked strategy, therefore, was correct. The initiative was far easier to attack than to defend. Given the fact that the drama of the negotiations would be played out over a period as long as two years, a low-key strategy made sense until it was clear that there was going to be a positive outcome. Meanwhile, the details of the negotiations would remain virtually unknown until a conclusion had been reached, while the lack of substantive information would force the media to concentrate on the process and the peripheral. But the cynical reasoning underlying this strategy, as found in the leaked document, was neither necessary nor widely shared and, once leaked, proved disastrous. It would take the government a year to recover from this inauspicious beginning.

Lips that Move

As always, the battle for the hearts and minds of Canadians would have to be waged through the national media. From the beginning, the government knew that it had natural allies and diehard opponents. In Toronto, the principal ally was the *Globe and Mail*. In keeping with the tradition established by its founder, George Brown, over a century ago, current editorial writer William Thorsell and financial page columnists Peter Cook and Ronald Anderson became articulate defenders of free trade. But the *Globe*'s dedication to the cause of free trade was more than matched by the fierce opposition of its cross-town rival, the *Toronto Star*. From its publisher, Beland Honderich, to its lead business writer, David Crane, to its reporters Martin Cohn and Joe O'Donnel in Ottawa and Bob Hepburn in Washington, the *Star* attacked the negotiations relentlessly.

Nothing else quite matched the editorial jousting between the *Star* and the *Globe and Mail*. The leading business papers, the *Financial Times of Canada* and the *Financial Post*, consistently supported the negotiations, if not some of the tactics employed. Among the rest of the nation's print media, free trade was certainly an important issue, but editorialists were inclined to be much more even-handed, generally acknowledging that free trade with the United

States would be good for Canada. Television coverage, on both the French and English networks, tended to be cryptic. Only CBC's *The Journal* had the time to go into detail, and usually preferred to cast the issue in negative terms.

Despite its importance to Canada's economic development, trade policy and its somewhat arcane language might well have been Greek to all but a handful of journalists. To this day, few understand trade policy or its language. This is in part a function of the nature of Canadian journalism; only the largest or one-discipline media such as the *Financial Post* can afford a specialist. While business journalism has become a growth industry, an understanding of the business and the financial world is only one part of trade policy.

Two non-business writers who made the effort to understand trade policy and usually succeeded were the *Globe*'s Jennifer Lewington in Washington and Christopher Waddell in Ottawa. Their partnership provided a generally accurate description of the talks and the main items of contention. Among feature writers and pundits, Southam's economic columnist John Ferguson and the *Post*'s Hy Solomon in Ottawa and Giles Gherson in Washington proved they could interpret the sometimes impenetrable jargon with understanding and insight. Over time, the *Financial Times*'s Deborah MacGregor also crossed into this inner circle. At Canadian Press, Allen Bass in Ottawa and Juliet O'Neill from Washington vied with Lewington and Waddell in providing almost daily coverage of the negotiations. Among the general columnists, it did not take long for Jeff Simpson to grasp the essentials of the issues. Marjorie Nichols, who had become almost as much of an institution to readers on the West Coast as Jack Webster is to those who rely on television and radio, uprooted herself and came to Ottawa as the *Citizen*'s political columnist midway through the negotiations. Her columns came to reflect the ambivalence that many Canadians felt on the trade issue. Enjoying the benefit of many years of experience in the economic field, Southam's political columnist Don McGillivray could have had a special voice but seemed to prefer the inconsequential and trivial aspects of the negotiations. Others, like the *Globe*'s Hugh Winsor or the *Star*'s Carol Goar occasionally reflected on the negotiations in the context of the current political scene.

Outside of Ottawa and Toronto, other newspapers tended to rely upon Canadian Press or Southam for daily coverage of the negotiations, with the occasional columns from Frances Russell and Joan Cohen in the *Winnipeg Free Press*, Nancy Russell in the Saskatoon *Star-Phoenix*, and Don Whitely and Jamie Lamb in the *Vancouver Sun*. In the French press, Pierre April of Presse Canadienne provided continuing daily coverage, with Michel Vastel of *Le Devoir* and Maurice Jannard of *La Presse* doing regular pieces. The Quebec press, from the early days of the debate, voiced strong support.

Unlike their English colleagues, they had a lot less difficulty putting the cultural issue into perspective.

If the *Globe* offered the most detailed insight in print on the negotiations, the CBC was first in television coverage. Its then Ottawa bureau chief, Elly Alboim, is unknown to most Canadians but is highly respected by his peers for his knowledge and insight of the Ottawa political scene. By nature and profession a sceptic, he could accept the intellectual appeal of free trade if not the message carried by some of its more overzealous defenders. His own intuitions were backed up by those reporters in the CBC Hill bureau who made free trade part of their beat: David Halton, Mike Duffy, and Wendy Mesley.

For CTV reporters Mark Sixstrom, Peter Murphy, and Allan Fryer, free trade was just another story in their continuing coverage of the Hill. The same principle applied at Global where Doug Small and Kevin Newman did the story as required. Peter Trueman provided the occasional trenchant commentary. Daniel Lessard of Radio Canada gave continuing coverage for the French networks.

For the proponents of free trade, there were only a handful of articulate commentators, mostly economists, who could appear on talk shows, panels, and at debates. Through his sheer number of performances, the University of Toronto's John Crispo came to occupy the lead position for the free trade side. Other economists like Richard Lipsey, who had devoted considerable energy to the study of free trade, as well as Murray Smith and Carl Beigie, who had done valuable work in the area for the C.D. Howe Institute, also took to the podium. Outside of Donald Macdonald, whose Royal Commission on Canada's Economic Prospects helped to launch the negotiations, there were surprisingly few from the legal community who could speak with any authority; while several were always available to offer their contribution, only Macdonald spoke regularly to more than specialist audiences.

Over the course of the debate, as the government first consulted, then pondered, and finally negotiated, some of its energies were directed to these moulders of public opinion. While the three-ring circus of negotiation, federal-provincial consensus building, and business and labour consultations took pride of place, this fourth ring also required attention. Ministers, bureaucrats, and negotiators alike kept a close eye on the media, not so much because of their role as moulders of public opinion, but as indicators of the public mood.

The Phoney War
During the seven months between the September announcement and the May start of negotiations, much of the government's energy was devoted to

defending an initiative coasting in neutral. From all sides, the government was assailed by a wide range of dissidents, many of whom had no interest in understanding the issues and how these would be pursued. They had their own axes to grind. Their concerns were largely red herrings, but red herrings that the government could not ignore.

The mischief makers fell into three broad types: nationalists, idealists, and protectionists. The first off the block with an issue that could attract the requisite media attention (opponents also need communications strategies; the media is the terrain for these battles) were the cultural nationalists. By October of 1985, the general line emanating from the high priests of nationalism had become stale and been relegated to the back pages of the newspapers. What was needed was a new cause. That cause proved to be cultural sovereignty, a phrase sufficiently vague to encompass a whole range of emotional reactions.

Throughout the fall, the government worked to defuse the concerns of cultural nationalists. Mindful of the tremendous influence cultural nationalists can exert on the media, the External Affairs Minister Joe Clark met with leading members of the Toronto-based cultural industries on 26 November, flanked by Kelleher and the interim Communications Minister Benoît Bouchard. A number of cultural heavyweights quickly realized that they had to mount a more sophisticated behind-the-scenes campaign. For others, nothing short of repudiating free trade could appease them and the meeting gave them publicity on which to bring their campaign to greater heights. For the next two years they, in concert with other opponents, would continue to pound away at their theme that the negotiations marked the end of Canada. Wrote David Frum in *Saturday Night*, commenting on a collection of essays by the cultural elite:

> The protectionists definitely have the fun side of the great free-trade debate. The agreement's defenders claim that free trade will raise Canada's standard of living and create jobs. Substantiating that claim requires much toilsome research, expressed in measured and even technical prose. The protectionists, on the other hand, can sit down at the typewriter and write any old thing that pops into their heads ... What's wrong with [their views] isn't that they are overwrought or vituperative; it's that their authors simply do not consider themselves bound by the customary standards of evidence expected in controversies over matters of urgent public policy.[17]

The daily question period in Parliament was filled with the venom that cultural issues often generate in Canada, because they deal less with the head than with the heart. In the first major speech by a Canadian minister outside the country after the decision to negotiate, Joe Clark told the New York chapter of the Foreign Policy Association that Canada's culture was not on the negotiating table. Aside from puzzling his audience, the speech, which received extensive coverage in Canada, kindled the fires lit by the cultural lobby. The prime minister also chose to follow this tack in a major speech to a Chicago audience in December. Kelleher, on the other hand, took to the offensive. Speaking in London, Ontario, in January, he roasted the opponents of free trade and sought to explode the myths. The media dubbed it the 'Rambo speech.' It was a welcome change from the preoccupation with culture.

But were Canadians really troubled by the critics' claims that Canada's cultural sovereignty was in peril? An Angus Reid poll conducted in January 1986 suggested not. Asked whether they considered gains in economic well-being more important in the negotiations than possible losses in Canadian culture, heritage, and identity, a majority of the respondents – 50 per cent – favoured economic gains. Only 39 per cent said they were more concerned about losses in culture.

'There, there, you poor, delicate little thing ... You'd never survive outside in those nasty Free Trade winds, would you?'

Alan King, *Ottawa Citizen*, 19 December 1987

The cultural nationalists, of course, mined a broader vein of concern among Canadians, that of Canadian economic independence. Throughout the 1960s and 1970s, as Canada became more and more integrated into the international economy, particularly the US economy, economic nationalists raised alarms about the danger of foreign investment, technology, and services crowding out Canadian investors, inventors, and providers. While most Canadians liked the benefits of economic integration, nationalists appealed to a widely shared worry about Canada's identity as a separate nation in charge of its own destiny. From their perspective, negotiating free trade with the United States would open the gates to the enemy and further sap the will of Canadians to resist the lure of foreign goodies, especially cultural goodies.

The second group to voice their concerns were the idealists, including radical feminists and church groups. While the focus of their interest was some distance removed from tariffs and trade remedies, they seized opportunities to link their cause with the major public policy issue of the day. Always quick with a press release, the feminists were convinced that the brunt of the adjustment burden would fall on single and poorer women. They insisted that the government's own studies showed that the major adjustment burden would be in the service, textile, and clothing and similar industries, all industries that employed women. They concluded that women would be the victims of free trade. A further blow to women would result from the fact that because women had been last hired by many firms, they would be the first out. It is a hard truth that many of the jobs at the lower end of the work force and in less competitive industries like textiles are occupied by women. As their work was the most vulnerable to change, these jobs could be the first to disappear. What these critics forgot was that in sectors like textiles and clothing, while the Canadian industry is perhaps not world-competitive, it is more than a match for its American counterparts.

Not to be outdone, church groups added their voices, equally convinced that closer economic relations with the United States would compromise achievement of their social objectives. Remi deRoo, Roman Catholic bishop of Victoria, told a meeting of the Confederation of Canadian Unions on 6 October that a free-trade pact would integrate the two economies and result in Canadians 'serving the market interests of the United States, including that of military production ... In effect, Canada's economy is being reorganized in such a way that transnational capital takes precedence over human labor and human needs.' He declared that anything which compelled Canadian workers to become more competitive was unethical and unChristian.[18] While extreme, his views were echoed across the religious spectrum, reflecting more church leaders' commitment to the social gospel than the views of their parishioners, many of whom had voted for the Conservatives in 1984 and would do so again in 1988, despite the call to arms from the pulpit.

In the months ahead, other idealists would contribute to the emotional debate: environmental groups feared that the fight against acid rain would be sacrificed on the altar of free trade; warriors on porn convinced themselves that free trade meant that Canada would give up all control over imports of pornography; and native leaders warned that any programs which discriminated in favour of native groups would be vetoed by the Americans. Other red herrings fished from the free-trade waters included accusations that free trade would force the federal government to repeal bilingualism and end social programs. Many of these fears were variations on the theme that Canada would lose its identity. They could be easily refuted as Simon Reisman proved in the last speech he gave before entering formal negotiations. The speech, in May 1986 to the Canadian Federation of Labour, observed for example that comparative studies of both nations' social welfare programs revealed that the share of GNP devoted to health, education, and pensions was about the same in both countries. The differences lay more in the funding of these programs, especially for Medicare. The Americans have opted for private schemes like Blue Cross which the worker pays out of his or her pay packet; the Canadian system is funded through tax revenues.

The third, and most traditional voice of dissent came from labour and others worried about increased competition and the threat of job losses. The jobs issue was tricky. The government had been elected in part on the promise of 'jobs, jobs, jobs.' Employment was increasing to such an extent that by October of 1987, the government could claim to have created over a million new jobs. Some of this electoral rhetoric was rolled over into the free trade debate and government apologists were unambiguous in their claim that free trade would create more jobs. Loose talk about more winners than losers also created its share of problems because it nurtured the person on the street's fear that he or she might be a loser.

Trade does create jobs and long-term winners, but not overnight. The kind of free-trade deal the government had in mind would inevitably cause some industry adjustment and force some workers to shift jobs. Most significant in all the studies of this issue was the conclusion that under free trade, jobs would be better and more secure. This was the message the politicians sought to deliver. It was a message more difficult to convey than the blanket statement of 'jobs, jobs, jobs.'

The constant pounding in question period on the issues raised by the various critics and echoed in the media convinced the government that the opposition was setting the agenda and that it needed to get out its own version of reality through the medium of a beefed-up information kit. Since October, work had been in progress on a booklet of basic documents, speeches, and other information that would place the government's position on many issues firmly on the record. Such a booklet, in the requisite Tory blue, was finally released in January under the title *Canadian Trade Negotiations*. While not a runaway bestseller, it quietly found its way into the hands of business people, academics, newspaper columnists, and students to the tune of over 40,000 copies by summer.

Despite these interim measures, however, the communications challenge remained. Something more coherent and more organized was needed. The initiative was beginning to look a little tattered in the face of the constant barrage of criticism.

6

FORGING AHEAD

> The negotiation of a new trade agreement will, of course, be extremely arduous. The challenge to succeed, however, and the fruits of success, are well worth the enormous effort and good faith required for this initiative.
> – Brian Mulroney, 1 October 1986

Once the two chief executives had formally exchanged specific proposals to negotiate, the next step was up to the United States. Canada had done its homework and signalled its readiness to proceed. What was needed now was for the United States to take the next steps and prepare for negotiations. In practical terms, this meant triggering the US fast-track negotiating authority, i.e., sending a formal notice to the Senate Finance Committee and the House Ways and Means Committee of the president's intent to negotiate a free-trade agreement with Canada, followed by a notice to the International Trade Commission (ITC) which would prepare a report on the likely economic impact of an agreement. The ITC would report within six months of receipt of this request. If the two committees did not object within ninety days, the two governments could proceed with all but tariff negotiations, which would have to await the ITC report. The opening of negotiations early in January, preparatory to the next meeting of the two leaders in March, was confidently planned for and alluded to in the letters exchanged on 1 and 2 October.

But this orderly progression to negotiations was not to be. For the next three months, the Canadian government stood by helplessly as the strange world of Washington decision-making toyed with when and how to trigger the fast-track procedure. Crossed and confused signals were exchanged. Cabinet officials contradicted each other. No one appeared to be in charge in Washington. There were veiled and not-so-veiled attempts to use the initiative to gain some mileage on US irritants with Canada.

Slow Progress to a Fast Track
When Canada launched the initiative for a trade agreement with the United States, it was doing so very much in response to a Canadian domestic policy

imperative. Unfortunately, once made, the proposal was left dangling in the US decision-making process, subject to US political dynamics.[1] There were some Americans who contended that an agreement with the United States would be very difficult to achieve. In fact, some suggested that in the sour political climate regarding trade questions in the United States, Canada would not be able to obtain a pact for the next several years or at least until such time as the prevailing political mood changed. This was, however, a minority view.

The majority view held that an agreement such as Canada was suggesting was a feasible proposition, but certainly not capable of accomplishment without some difficulty. Some proponents of this argument thought that the best approach to working out an agreement would be to hold off requesting fast-track authority from Congress, possibly until such time as an agreement was largely worked out. Their interpretation of American trade law led them to question the requirement to seek congressional authority to initiate the negotiations. Thus, they felt, why risk exposure in Congress at a time when protectionist fever was running high? Rather than do that, why not wait until an agreement was seen to be achievable or almost in hand so that the potential American winners from any such pact could then be mobilized to lobby strenuously and successfully for fast-track authority and subsequent concurrence in the agreement itself?

Their position may have been tactically attractive but it was politically impossible for both the Canadian government and the US administration. To follow that route would almost inevitably have led to charges in Congress that the negotiations were going forward without the requisite authority. From Canada's vantage point, that kind of scenario would have put a cloud over the whole exercise. The debate within the administration over this very point, however, dragged on, very much to Canada's frustration.

For some American officials, there was another reason why the administration did not go to Congress at this time. As we saw in Chapter 3, the administration, in responding to the protectionist outburst in Congress, had countered with a few specific steps including the initiation of a number of trade cases against Korea, Taiwan, Brazil, and others. Part of the White House response was, however, more intangible but nonetheless important: the phrase 'free trade,' a standard feature in the president's lexicon, had by this time been excised and replaced by the more acceptable 'fair trade.' In that light, the timing of Canada's proposal seemed problematic. While these officials believed strongly that the proposal was a most important and welcome idea, it was not one that the president could embrace at that particular time. As a result, the response to the Canadian initiative was postponed and not linked to the new presidential campaign to fight back against Congress on trade.

Finally, there was also an internal administration debate over the assignment of responsibility for the bilateral negotiations. Clayton Yeutter was successful in winning control over the negotiations and moved eventually to enlist Peter Murphy, then in Geneva, to head the American negotiating team. But it was an appointment that appears to have been resisted by others, who wished instead to have someone – an outsider – with more personal stature and more political clout on Capitol Hill. While they had nothing against the USTR nominee, who was regarded as highly competent, they appeared to be looking for a better known public personality. This difference of view had the effect of further hampering the administration's handling of the trade initiative.

Canada thus faced two problems. First was the pressing Canadian domestic political requirement to have rapid movement on the proposal. The longer the initiative was not formally engaged in Washington, the more it came to resemble an orphan and the easier a target it became for critics. Inaction by the administration would simply be viewed as disinterest on the US side.

The second problem was that the administration's principal managers of the initiative – the State Department and USTR – did not appear to be fully equipped to deal with the congressional dimensions of the issue. Yeutter seemed to have all the right credentials – administration experience in USTR and Agriculture; a background in Congress as a Senate aide; and, most recently, a high-profile private sector job. Likeable, bright, and fully cognizant of the importance of Canadian trade in the US scheme of things, he was probably the most industrious member of the Reagan cabinet, with a deserved reputation for working eighteen-hour days. But replacing a popular and highly regarded individual – Bill Brock – is always difficult. While the US merchandise trade deficit continued to rise at record rates, sparking, as it rose, the most vociferous expression of protectionist sentiment seen in Congress since the Smoot-Hawley Tariff Act, Yeutter's role was to carry the administration's message that Congress should not bow to demands for protection from foreign exports. It did not increase his credibility.

In an effort to ensure early notification to Congress and a start to the negotiations, Canada mounted sustained diplomatic pressure on the administration, both through the Canadian embassy in Washington and through meetings at the political level. On 25 October, the prime minister used the occasion of a meeting of the Summit Seven in New York called by President Reagan to prepare for his meeting with Soviet leader Mikhail Gorbachev in December, to impress on the president the need to move forward with the initiative. He told the House on his return that Reagan had assured him that no jobs would be lost as a result of congressional protectionism. The president intended to veto any such legislation.[2] At the end of the week, Joe Clark repeated the message about the languishing initiative to Secretary of State George Shultz at their quarterly meeting in Calgary. At the end of the session, Shultz told reporters that the United States was prepared to begin talks in early 1986 and insisted that administration soundings on Capitol Hill indicated that a free-trade agreement would be acceptable to American legislators.[3]

Alan King, *Ottawa Citizen*, 15 April 1986

Congressional signals earlier that month had been mixed. At the beginning of October, ten senators on the Finance Committee had written to the president urging him to solve the softwood lumber problem before he entered into negotiations. The following week, eighty-six Republican representatives joined Minority leader Bob Michel in sponsoring the Trade Partnership Act of 1985 as an antidote to more protectionist bills being considered. Its provisions included a requirement that the president move expeditiously to negotiate a free-trade pact with Canada.

It was not until 10 December, therefore, that the administration could be persuaded to send its notice to the two committees. Congress had long expected the notice and saw no need to pay any particular attention to it, particularly since it arrived just prior to the Christmas break. It was big news in Canada and at the USTR, but not on the Hill. The notice, while demonstrating the president's own commitment to the initiative, was flat and uninspiring. The tone was deliberate and may have been right for the occasion. There was no desire to excite Congress. This tone, however, also had the unintended effect of failing to inspire much momentum within the administration's own ranks. The president wrote:

> I welcomed the Prime Minister's proposal for trade talks as consistent with the efforts of both my Administration and the Congress to open foreign markets for US exporters. I am aware that some Members are concerned about pending trade disputes with Canada, and have suggested that negotiations be delayed until those matters are resolved. I firmly believe, however, that we should not delay. With the enormous volume of trade that flows between our two countries, some differences of opinion are bound to arise. We must not permit such transitory frustrations, important though they may be, to obstruct the improvement of our long term trade relationship – an issue, by the way, that will be of immense significance in the coming decades.
>
> The initiation of new bilateral trade negotiations may significantly enhance our efforts to eliminate current trade frictions with Canada. And in any event, I assure you and the other Members of your Committee that the Administration will do everything possible to resolve such disputes in a reasonable and timely manner.[4]

There was further confusion as to what was meant by the ninety-day provision in the fast-track authority. Initially, the view from Washington was that ninety days meant ninety calendar days. This was changed to ninety congressional days which in turn provided endless opportunity for the lawyers to determine how ninety congressional days compared to calendar days. By February, it was clear that the ninety days would not be up until well past Easter and possibly not until early May, that is, at least seven months following Canada's official notification to the United States. More disappointment came when these same lawyers determined that the ITC notice could not be served until after the initiative had passed this first congressional hurdle. Its report, therefore, would not be finished until more than a year after both sides had agreed to proceed on a negotiation that all concurred needed to be completed within the political mandates of the two leaders. As if more proof was needed, this delay once again demonstrated sloppy homework on the part of those officials responsible for the initiative in Washington, who all along had opined that ninety days were ninety calendar days and that the notice to the ITC would proceed simultaneously, not sequentially. The law appeared to be susceptible to a variety of constructions, leaving room for the most opportunistic political interpretations.

In early February, the Brookings Institution in Washington and the Institute for Research on Public Policy in Ottawa jointly organized a closed conference for congressional staffers, selected Canadian and US government officials, a few Washington trade lobbyists, and some think-tank trade policy experts. Phil Trezise and Frank Stone, the organizers of the meeting, wanted to give Canadian officials who had been involved in the initiative for the past few years an opportunity to explain the issues to the American guests. This they did. Among those in attendance were Susan Schwab from Senator Danforth's office and George Weiss from the House trade subcommittee. Both listened with interest and expressed some concern at the sweep of Canadian interests. In their view, now that the notice had been sent, the negotiations themselves could be anticlimactic; it would take a very bad agreement to draw congressional ire.

Who and How

Although the decision to proceed to negotiations was announced 26 September and the exchange of letters between the prime minister and the president took place 1 October, six weeks passed before the first steps were taken towards equipping the federal government with a negotiating structure. There were a number of reasons for the delay. Ministerial attention was almost exclusively preoccupied with gauging and responding to public reaction to the initiative. There seemed little need to move quickly to establish the structure necessary to conduct the negotiations.

Confusion and uncertainty emanating from Washington also contributed to the delay. It was questioned whether Canada would not appear too eager, too far in front, if a chief negotiator were named before it was known when the administration would seek the requisite authority from Congress and whether or not Congress would agree.

Task force officials argued strongly for the need to maintain momentum, particularly if there was going to be a delay on the US side. To do nothing until the US obtained congressional authority would leave the field open to the opposition and, by calling into question the commitment of the government to the negotiations, would risk losing strong provincial and private sector support. On 1 November, following meetings with Joe Clark and Jim Kelleher, a joint letter to the prime minister was prepared urging that the government proceed as soon as possible to the nomination of a chief negotiator, the development of a negotiating apparatus, and the establishment of a separate cabinet committee responsible for the trade negotiations.

Throughout this period there was rampant speculation in Ottawa and the press about who would be named chief negotiator. Broadly speaking, there were three categories of people considered eligible: senior officials within the government with a stake in the outcome as professional career people, i.e., people with not only a past, but also a future; retired public servants with trade negotiating experience who would inspire confidence in the business community and the provinces on the basis of past performance; and prominent Canadians outside the government, particularly in the business community, who would bring their reputation and prestige to the negotiations.

The prime minister, however, had already embarked on his own search for the right negotiator. Although rumours of various candidates circulated in Ottawa, the prime minister kept his own counsel. He had his own candidate in mind. Early in October he had interviewed and sought the advice of Simon Reisman, both on the substance and the conduct of negotiations. On 8 November 1985, the prime minister announced the appointment of Mr. Reisman to head the Canadian negotiating team. While Reisman had been mentioned, his age, ties to opposition leader John Turner, views on water exports, and involvement in various other private sector interests all appeared to keep him off everybody's short list. The appointment, however, should not have been a surprise. He was a leading and knowledgeable advocate of the issue. He had the kind of crusty reputation which could be sold domestically as exactly what was needed to deal with the Yanks. His success in negotiating the autopact had assumed legendary proportions as had his other dealings with the Americans, some of which were apocryphal. His ties with business and Turner could be turned into assets.

Simon Reisman, sixty-six years old, combative veteran of almost thirty years in government, had been counsellor to eight successive Canadian prime ministers. He had spent his formative years in the Department of Finance as a trade policy practitioner. At the beginning of his career, he had been part of the Canadian delegation to the Havana Conference which established the International Trade Organization, and had participated in the preparatory meetings that had spawned the General Agreement on Tariffs and Trade. Subsequently, he had been involved in the next five rounds of GATT negotiations. He had capped this phase of his career with the Canada-United States Automotive Products Trade Agreement, the autopact, of 1965. He had been successively deputy minister of the Department of Industry, secretary of the Treasury Board and deputy minister of Finance. Then followed ten years as a private consultant and denizen of Canadian corporate boardrooms. While no longer a public servant, he continued to serve government, first as a one-person commission into the Canadian auto industry and then as a negotiator to settle some of the native land claims in the Northwest Territories.

Short in stature and pugnacious in style, Reisman's trademark had long been a big cigar and tough talk. His style was direct and his language colourful – the reputation for expletives deserved, his mastery of language less well appreciated. He was known to dominate any room he entered, whether the cabinet room, a corporate boardroom, an international conference room, or a drawing room. Reisman also had a tenacious sense of purpose, a great memory for details, and an innate judgment for the essence of any matter. He knew his stuff and he loved to trot it out. He is one of the best raconteurs in Ottawa.

$1 A YEAR $ 1000 A DAY

Which one is overpriced?

Alan King, *Ottawa Citizen*, 25 January 1986

The appointment met with exactly the kind of response the government sought. The qualities which could be sold as assets in a politically risky negotiation took centre stage. Only his $1,000 a day fee excited any real public controversy, and then more in terms of grudging respect for his chutzpa than in terms of outrage. The initiative was seen to be in sound hands. Southam senior correspondent Chris Young caught the general mood:

> Prime Minister Brian Mulroney's choice of Reisman to head the team preparing for trade negotiations with the United States should reassure those who fear the government is ready to give away the Canadian store, perhaps even the Canadian soul ... as a negotiator in the economic field, he has no peer in Canada, and he has shown on a number of occasions that he has no fear of tough guys from below the border. It would not escape Mulroney's calculations that the Turner-Reisman friendship might help to draw the fangs of Liberal opposition to whatever deal is made. More important, Reisman is a man who deals in substance rather than packaging and he is candid to a fault.[5]

Marjorie Nichols, an early fan of the negotiations, added in her column in the *Vancouver Sun*: 'The most fascinating part of this appointment is that it has further alienated Liberal leader John Turner from the influential group of former Liberals and Liberal appointees who have now climbed aboard the free-trade bandwagon.'[6]

Ironically, during the weekend of Reisman's selection as chief negotiator, the Liberals met in Halifax at a policy convention, with the free-trade negotiations the hottest topic on the agenda. While the leader and other MPs had made the necessary critical noises in the House, the party was split on what stance to take on the issue, and the Halifax meeting provided an opportunity for debate. Star of the discussion was Donald Macdonald defending the recommendations of his report and the government's decision to proceed.

While party philosophers debated, the leader was across town telling students 'We believe we should enter formal discussions with the United States ... but we want a full national debate first.'[7] As expected by the pundits, the meeting showed that the party was hopelessly divided. According to Jeffrey Simpson:

> Some Liberals want to embrace comprehensive free trade but are afraid to say so because the Tories got there first. A handful prefer irritant-by-irritant negotiations, a kind of holding action against the protectionist tide. More still want nothing of free trade, preferring instead a government-directed industrial strategy which, in as yet undefined ways, will not recreate all the mistakes of past policy. The majority, however, does not know what it wants. With apologies to that great Liberal philosopher Mackenzie King, yesterday's debate showed that the Liberals want free trade if necessary, but not necessarily free trade.[8]

Reisman's appointment added to confusion within the ranks of the official opposition, especially in view of the praise the appointment elicited among business leaders and even in the United States. Tom d'Aquino, president of the influential Business Council on National Issues told the *Globe and Mail*: 'He's not the sort who is going to give anything away. I will probably go to bed and sleep more soundly at night knowing that Simon Reisman is in charge of our negotiating effort.'[9] Phil Trezise, his opposite number during the autopact negotiations in 1964, remembered him as 'a pretty tough character. He's an unusual person, very frank, very blunt, very outspoken and sometimes profane. But he is bright and quick in a negotiation and knows his business. I think the Canadian government made a very good choice.'[10]

Reisman's actual title pending the formal start of negotiations was ambassador and chair of the preparatory committee. He would have, affirmed the prime minister, the best and the brightest of the Canadian public service for his team. Reisman's own inclination was to 'put together a lean, efficient team by plucking high-level civil servants from government departments and bringing them together in their own quarters for the duration of the preparation and talks.'[11] Joe Clark added a few weeks later that the team would be representative of the character of Canada. With this auspicious beginning, Reisman set about drafting a negotiating mandate and organizing a group of officials to conduct the negotiations into what was shortly baptized the Trade Negotiations Office – the TNO.

Shortly after the prime minister's announcement, Reisman moved quickly to take control and bring to an end debate about how the trade negotiations would be organized. Making clear that in his view little of the preparatory work had any value and that few of the people hitherto involved could make an important contribution, he declared his intention to construct a small team, no larger than six to seven officials of deputy or assistant deputy rank plus a small number of support people. The senior people would be expected to draw upon their home departments for whatever expertise they required. From the senior group, Reisman would appoint one deputy negotiator for 'what we want from the US' and one deputy responsible for 'what we would have to pay.' The Department of External Affairs, heir to the trade mandate of the old Department of Trade and Commerce, would supply the first deputy and the Department of Finance, historically the guardian of the public purse, would supply the second.

Reisman's predilection for a small team was soundly based. This core group would be easily manageable, serve as a senior and influential sounding board, and limit security problems. It would, moreover, replicate the manner in which federal budgets – he had been involved in preparing a great many – had been done in his time with information strictly limited to a need-to-know basis. His desire to have two deputies echoed the conduct of trade negotiations of twenty to thirty years earlier on a request-offer basis. Reisman would arbitrate between the two.

His advisors, however, drawing on the experience of the preparatory period, recommended that his team be somewhat larger and as nearly self-contained as possible. Notwithstanding his mandate from the prime minister, relying upon other departments, even with some of their senior people ensconced in the team, would not be productive. These departments would continue to push their own agenda and cooperation would be grudging at best. He would thus require experienced officers for each of the main subject areas for negotiation, an officer to coordinate sectoral analysis and to serve as the principal point of contact with the business community, an officer responsible for federal-provincial liaison, an officer responsible for communications, plus the necessary support staff to make the whole task feasible.

Once the concept of a larger team was accepted, a different consideration arose. Some, seeing what they wanted to see, viewed the TNO, especially as it began to grow, as the embryo of a Canadian version of the USTR or even of a new department of trade. They were thus anxious to stake out and defend a set of far-reaching prerogatives for the TNO. Others, fearing what they wanted to fear, sought to stamp out such heresies wherever found. The solution was to make Reisman nominally a deputy of the Department of External Affairs and the TNO a unit of the department for administrative purposes. It was also emphasized that the regular management of the bilateral relationship with the United States would remain with the Department of External Affairs and the normal interdepartmental networks. The TNO's focus would be exclusively upon the trade negotiations.

Reisman's mandate was written to extend to the GATT negotiations, and the incorporation into the TNO of the existing unit coordinating preparations for the yet to be launched new round gave rise to long discussion. It was recognized that the bilateral initiative would in fact determine much of Canada's multilateral agenda and objectives. Discussions in Geneva over the following two years would be largely procedural and scene-setting, rather than results-oriented. During that same time-frame, bilateral negotiations would both start and end. The bulk of resources, therefore, were needed immediately for the bilateral effort, rather than for multilateral negotiations.

The existing GATT unit was a creation of Sylvia Ostry and she mounted a strong argument not only to retain it intact, even if nominally under the roof of the TNO, but also to expand it considerably to cover the main subject areas of the new round – in effect, to duplicate the structure for bilateral negotiations. Reisman would have none of this. To set up a parallel negotiating team would be to establish competing negotiating priorities and contradict the government's public position that it had an integrated trade policy to achieve improved and secure access to all markets. More importantly, from Reisman's perspective, such a structure would detach the GATT multilateral trade negotiations (MTN) from his control and sow confusion among members of the business community, the provinces, and ministers as to what Canada's negotiating strategy and objectives were. The result of this struggle was a victory for common sense. Within the TNO, Ostry would be named a deputy chief negotiator for the MTN, a small structure would be created for coordinating purposes only and the substantive elements of the MTN would be the responsibility of the officers covering the same areas in the bilateral negotiations.

The nature of Reisman's mandate was also not without its difficulties. Although the announcement of his appointment made it evident that Reisman's authority would derive from the prime minister and that he would report to the cabinet through a subcommittee chaired by the secretary of state for external affairs, Privy Council officials sought to interpose a deputy minister's committee to which he would report on a regular basis. This proposal provoked ridicule from Reisman, and the idea that he would have any formal reporting relationship to deputy ministers was hastily dropped. It took a few months for the mandarins of 1985 to catch up to the full reputation of the most formidable mandarin of the 1960s and 1970s. His were not the virtues of collegiality, hierarchy, and anonymity.

Once the general shape and direction of his office became clear, Reisman moved to recruit. First on board was Andrei Sulzenko, his assistant during his investigation of the auto industry and in 1985 a director in the Transportation Industries Branch of DRIE. Styled chief of staff, he would provide Reisman with a link to the present. While Reisman was well-known in Ottawa, he had not kept up with the new generation of officials. Derek Burney, for example, was an unknown quantity to him. Reisman's predilection was to find some survivors from his own era, but he found that few of these were still there or in a position to drop what they were doing and join him. Sulzenko's first task, therefore, was to scout new talent and see what kind of preparatory work had already been done.

To help him set up an office, Privy Council officials recommended Dick Levy, whose last assignment had been as chief administrator of the National Economic Summit in March. To help with federal-provincial relations, Reisman recruited Alan Nymark, who was busy winding up the secretariat at the Macdonald Commission where he had acted as director of policy. Before that, he had worked in the Federal-Provincial Relations Office. Next came Charles Stedman, Sulzenko's former boss at DRIE and DRIE Deputy Arthur Kroeger's nominee to take on the task of industry liaison. At the same time, Reisman recruited Bruce MacDonald to help him with the task of managing media relations. These officials soon joined Reisman in temporary quarters in the Jackson Building recently vacated by the defunct Ministry of State for Economic and Regional Development. It had the virtue of being in the same building as one of Reisman's favourite restaurants, Atlantic Pavillion, and a block from the Rideau Club and Hy's, his other regular choices for lunch. In November he had in no uncertain terms spurned the offer of a temporary office in the Pearson Building. Not only was it far from downtown, but he was still a Finance official at heart and External Affairs was enemy territory.

Most of his staff, however, would have to come from the two trade policy departments, External and Finance, including those in the two task forces set up to prepare for the bilateral and multilateral negotiations. Before Christmas, it had been agreed that the bulk of these resources, including their heads, Germain Denis, Bill Dymond, and Michael Hart, would join Reisman as soon as he moved into new quarters. Also part of this group was John Curtis, formerly director of the International Economics Program at the Institute for Research on Public Policy and more recently a key player on Sylvia Ostry's team. As well, Bob Martin, director of Finance's international economic relations division; Kevin Gore, director of the tariffs divisions in Finance; and Mike Gifford, director-general of international relations at Agriculture, had been recruited to the cause. This group of trade policy veterans would take on the technical work of preparing and negotiating an agreement. Each would bring with them one or two more junior officers to help them.

A Three-Ring Circus

In an earlier age, trade negotiations were the business of professional negotiators. With a mandate from one or two ministers, the Canadian negotiating team would take passage to Geneva, Annecy, or Torquay, spend three or four agreeable months with their peers working out an agreement – interrupted perhaps by a visiting minister or deputy minister – and make only the occasional report home. This style of negotiations had by the 1980s become a casualty of the growing importance of trade and of instant communications. Negotiators were now kept on very short leashes and embroiled in complicated consensus-building as a precondition to conducting trade negotiations. In the Canada-US trade negotiations, this phenomenon would reach new heights.

The second important task, therefore, following the appointment of a chief negotiator and the establishment of a negotiating apparatus, was to build upon the existing ad hoc consultative arrangements and devise a structure to convey both the perception and substance of consultation and intimate involvement with the provinces and the business community for the duration of the negotiations.

Eleven or One

For the provinces, the focus was preparations for the first ministers' meeting in Halifax at the end of November. From the federal perspective, arrangements were needed to serve two separate but closely linked purposes: the first concerned the refinement, pursuit, and delivery of Canadian objectives, the formulation and assessment of negotiating offers and requests, and the judgment on the final outcome of negotiations; the second was the management of issues falling under provincial jurisdiction, the extension of results to interprovincial trade barriers, and the means by which legal commitments on these matters could be executed.

At a 10 October meeting of trade ministers in Halifax, the interest in full involvement, including a presence on the negotiating team, was reiterated by a number of provinces. A complicated structure of ministers, deputies, senior officials, and interlocking relationships with the negotiating team was discussed. The decision and, indeed, a formal federal offer had been deferred pending the nomination of a negotiator and determination of his or her preferences. But the provinces continued to see a federal government determined to maintain peace and harmony in federal-provincial relations and thus this situation was clearly a prime target for a major provincial power grab. Whereas during the preparatory period the issue had been largely the preserve of provincial officials responsible for trade and industrial policy, intergovernmental affairs' officials and political aides now began to gravitate to the issue.

The potential harm in a provincial power grab had become apparent to the Federal-Provincial Relations Office, which now began to insert itself into the discussion through its responsibility for preparations for the first ministers' meeting. Something more concrete than peace and harmony was required. Unfortunately, there was no consensus at either the bureaucratic or political level as to what that would be. Trade policy veterans just wished the problem would go away and saw the whole federal-provincial game as a triumph of process over substance. Veterans of the federal-provincial constitutional discussions saw the trade experts as hopelessly naïve. While discussion continued, no agreed plan for provincial involvement in the negotiations emerged. The problem was not a shortage of plans, but a surfeit.

At the first ministers' conference at the World Trade Centre in Halifax on 27-8 November, the main issue was federal revenue sharing. Outside, the weather was cold and blustery. Inside, there was plenty of bluster as well while temperatures ran high. It was evident that the early promise of federal-provincial cooperation under the Tories had faded and it was back to business as usual, with the provinces attacking the federal government for sins of omission and commission.

Over lunch, the premiers and the prime minister discussed the issue of free trade. This time a majority, led by the western premiers and supported by Ontario (the Quebec premier Pierre-Marc Johnson, in office only a few weeks and fighting an election, made only a brief appearance), was determined to gain full participation in the negotiations. Following an amicable discussion over lunch, the prime minister and premiers agreed on 'the principle of full provincial participation.' Joe Clark and provincial trade ministers would work out the details.

The premiers interpreted this to mean that they had obtained agreement that the negotiator would derive his instructions from the federal and provincial governments and that provincial representatives would be present at the negotiating table. This was not the view of ministers and their senior advisors, nor was it acceptable to Reisman. He made it clear that he could not and would not negotiate with the provinces present and maintained this position throughout. He saw provincial demands as a potential breach of federal interest and prerogative. Hurriedly flown to Halifax from Ottawa, he made no bones about his position and symbolically spat in the eye of those provincial bureaucrats who thought that they had pulled a fast one, including Premier Bennett's advisor, Norman Spector, soon thereafter recruited to take over the Federal-Provincial Relations Office in Ottawa.[12] Into this hornet's nest stepped Joe Clark, who adroitly bought time for the negotiator to become established and to recommend how the relationship with the provinces should be managed. Jeffrey Simpson correctly predicted that 'the three little words – full provincial participation – mask what will become a fierce behind-the-scenes battle in Canada's preparation for free-trade talks.'[13]

The Light Brigade
In addition to the provinces, the business community and other special interests are also key to successful consensus building. These latter two groups also became accustomed to being consulted more frequently during the Tokyo Round and the years immediately thereafter. They too were impatient with ad hoc arrangements and sought regular, institutionalized channels of communication. The Canadian Business and Industry Advisory Council, which was set up in 1979 to provide such a channel as an umbrella group for various business organizations (the Chamber of Commerce, the Canadian Manufacturers Association, the Canadian Exporters Association), proved inadequate to the task and various business groups called for something more extensive.

Their pleas fell on fertile ground. The Mulroney government wanted to encourage broad consultations. Early in its mandate, therefore, quite apart from the pressures of trade negotiations, the government decided to establish a formal consultative mechanism for involving business and other private sector interests in trade issues. It took as its model the US international sectoral advisory committee structure, established in Washington during the Tokyo Round in response to the Trade Act of 1974.

Thus, concurrent with the government's decision to explore more directly with the United States the scope and prospects for a new trade agreement, Kelleher announced he was establishing an international trade advisory committee system. This system would provide a two-way flow of information and advice between the government and the private sector on international trade matters. The advisory committees would address international trade, access, and marketing issues which were being pursued on both a bilateral and multilateral basis.

Throughout the fall, consultations with industry continued on how the system should work and on 9 January 1986, the first component was unveiled: a thirty-eight-member group, the International Trade Advisory Committee (ITAC), was established to concern itself with broad national issues relating to international trade, access, and marketing matters. Plans had also been laid for a series of fifteen sectoral advisory groups on international trade (SAGITs), which would interact with government to ensure that sectoral views were fully taken into account on international trade matters. Walter Light, former chairman of Northern Telecom, was appointed first ITAC chair. On 25 April, the heads of the SAGITs were revealed.

Invited to participate (as in the United States), organized labour turned a deaf ear to institutionalized consultations. With the exception of the less ideologically oriented Canadian Federation of Labour, the labour movement took the view that discussing trade issues with government in concert with management would give the Canada-US trade initiative a legitimacy which it did not deserve. The government, however, continued to maintain that they were welcome to participate.

More Evidence from the Polls
While free trade had enjoyed strong support from Canadians throughout the preparatory period, the real proof of support would come once the government had decided to proceed and to change the issue from one of possibility to one of policy. Also important would be the effect of the government's own drop in popularity, as well as the impact of other events in Canada-US relations. The voyage of the US icebreaker, *Polar Sea*, through Canada's Arctic waters in August had reawakened latent anxieties of American encroachment on Canadian sovereignty. The media had seized on the issue and played it to the hilt. Soon after Parliament had resumed, Joe Clark sought to assuage Canadians with a strong statement in which he explicitly claimed the waters of the Arctic archipelago as Canadian and confidently challenged any nation to take the issue to the World Court. Sovereignty had become a real issue.

A Decima poll, taken on behalf of *Maclean's* between 30 October and 3 November (and released in its first issue of 1986) showed that 75 per cent of respondents supported a more open trading agreement with the United States, whether it was free or freer trade. Despite the overall approval, there remained concerns: 55 per cent said they would oppose it if it harmed their own province, and 37 per cent feared that Washington might prove better at negotiating a deal. Opinion-makers continued to support the initiative. A poll taken for the *Globe and Mail* by Environics and CROP confirmed these findings. Support was beginning to erode somewhat but remained strongly in favour: 58 per cent were for; 31 per cent opposed; and 11 per cent were undecided. Support remained strongest in the West (68 per cent) with opposition strongest in Ontario (36 per cent) and Quebec (35 per cent).[14]

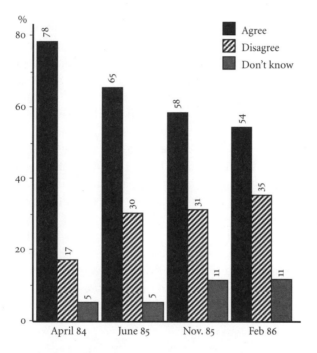

Chart 3: Support for free trade, February 1986 Environics poll

A survey of 217 of Canada's senior business leaders, federal and provincial officials, labour leaders, special interest groups, and the media taken at roughly the same time by Hay Management Consultants as part of their Opinion Leader Research Program showed that 68 per cent of the respondents felt that 'economic continentalism was Canada's most likely future,' with only labour leaders against this trend. The Hay analysis predicted that 'events surrounding the trade negotiations over the next year or two should not distract decision makers from the longer term trend towards a continental economy ... Most of the opinion leaders,' it concluded, 'do not believe that Canada will rely on Europe or the Pacific Rim for its prosperity. Canada's opinion leaders expect and prefer greater economic integration of the North American economy."[15]

Nevertheless, the general support for free trade continued to slip as the two countries prepared to enter into negotiations. A poll taken for the *Globe and Mail* between 19 February and 5 March by Environics showed that support had slipped a further four points from the level shown in December and was down to 54 per cent, while those opposed had risen to 35 per cent. More worrisome, those strongly in favour were losing faith. While 46 per cent were strongly in favour in April 1984, only 20 per cent were strongly in favour in February 1986. The greatest slippage had been in Ontario, where the issue was now supported and opposed by the same number, 45 per cent, suggesting that Premier Peterson's provincial government was having a greater influence than the prime minister and the federal government. Continued strong support in the West (65 per cent) and in Atlantic Canada (57 per cent) indicated growing polarization on the issue. The implication was clear: the government needed to get its message out and needed to be more convincing. And it was time negotiations got under way.

In the months following, there was a plethora of polls – all coming to roughly the same conclusion: as the government prepared to begin negotiations with the United States, support for the plan was slipping, although a majority continued to buy the idea. While a large proportion of Canadians felt the United States would gain more than Canada from a deal, a Gallup poll taken in February showed that on a personal basis, more Canadians felt they would gain than lose from any deal. The belief that the United States would be the big winner was particularly prevalent in Ontario and the Atlantic provinces, where 66 per cent said the United States would be the over-all winner.

Table 7

Results of Gallup poll on who would gain from free trade, February 1986 (%)

	National	Atlantic	Quebec	Ontario	Prairies	BC
Would gain most from deal:						
United States	59	66	54	66	55	50
Canada	17	16	13	18	19	25
Both equally	13	11	16	10	16	13
Can't say	11	8	17	7	10	11
Effect on family income:						
Positive effect	21	19	21	17	26	25
Negative effect	14	15	7	21	7	13
Not much at all	54	56	57	53	58	46
Can't say	12	10	15	9	9	16

7

GETTING READY

The picture of weak and timid Canadian negotiators being pushed around and browbeaten by
American representatives into settlements that
were 'sell-outs' is a false and distorted one. It is
often painted, however, by Canadians who think
that a sure way to get applause and support at
home is to exploit our anxieties and exaggerate
our suspicions over US power and policies.
– Lester Pearson, *Memoirs*

E arly in the new year, the Trade Negotiations Office began to take shape.
Its senior management would eventually consist of two deputy chief
negotiators and six assistant chief negotiators responsible for federal-
provincial relations, for industrial analysis and liaison with the private sector
advisory committees, for providing legal advice, for coordinating preparations for a new round of GATT negotiations, and for developing positions
on the major negotiating issues. Reisman also appointed a communications
chief and confirmed who would be the senior officers responsible for each of
the major areas to be negotiated: tariffs, customs matters, contingency protection, government procurement, intellectual property, services, investment,
autos, agriculture, and defence-related issues in the areas of subsidies and
procurement. Each of these senior officers would be allowed to bring with
them whomever they needed from their own or other departments to do the
jobs assigned.[1]

On 20-1 February 1986, the twenty-three senior officers of the TNO drove
the sixty kilometres down the Ottawa river to the stately Canadian Pacific
resort at Montebello. Reisman had convened his senior group to plan the
work ahead and to get to know one another. Also there as a special guest of
the chief negotiator was Derek Burney. The sessions were held in the
ground-floor meeting rooms of the resort's Seigniory Club, used for many of
the crucial autopact negotiating sessions in the fall of 1964. The symbolism
was intended. Intense discussions over the two-day period indicated that
substantial work had already been achieved and that the adoption of a basic
negotiating framework would help to define the issues more clearly and give
added purpose to the detailed analytical work that lay ahead.

Reisman declared that Canada's negotiating position would be built around the theme of national treatment, that is, Canada would seek an agreement that would ensure that Canadian and US goods would be treated the same in each country.[2] Whether US interests in negotiating trade in services and investment could be encompassed under the same theme remained an open question. To gain a sense of what this would mean for individual issues, each of the participants presented his view of how he saw his particular area and how he intended to proceed with the preparations in the weeks and months ahead. Although no firm decisions were reached, it was a first and useful meeting of the individuals who would carry the principal burden of negotiation both bilaterally with the United States and multilaterally at the GATT.

Alan King, *Ottawa Citizen*, 26 June 1986

By early April of 1986, nearly the full complement of officials was in place and it was an impressive number indeed, over one hundred, counting administrative and support staff. This was a self-contained team with a vengeance. The penthouse quarters in the new Metropolitan Life Tower were magnificent, well above public service standards for virtually all staff. All this cost money. Appearing before the Commons committee on external affairs and international trade, Derek Burney explained that the bill would amount to about $10 million annually. Treasury Board had allocated eighty-four person-years to the exercise and budgeted more than $5 million in salaries, including provision for more than thirty senior staff. The budget for the first year included $650,000 for the 'fit-up of facilities.' Chris Waddell of the *Globe and Mail* found all this to be somewhat at odds with Reisman's claim at his appointment that 'they'll give me anything I want, but I'm not asking for much. I'm very stingy with the taxpayers' money.'[3]

Reisman remained determined to acquire two deputies for the bilateral negotiations, but only one, Gordon Ritchie, originally brought in on a part-time basis to address adjustment issues, was eventually appointed to this task in April. Son of Ed Ritchie, former undersecretary of state for external affairs and like Reisman, present at the creation of GATT (as a United Nations official), Gordon Ritchie had enjoyed a meteoric rise through the ranks of the Department of Industry, Trade and Commerce and the Ministry of State for Economic Development to become associate deputy at DRIE. In the summer of 1985, he had been made federal economic coordinator for Ontario and initially commuted between Toronto and Ottawa to advise Reisman on adjustment and industrial policy issues. Once appointed deputy chief negotiator, he moved quickly to consolidate his position. Possessed of a precise and analytical mind, he assumed the role of running the office, leaving Reisman more time to concentrate on the negotiations. For ministers, fellow deputies, and the business elite, he became the main link to the negotiating process through his masterful briefing sessions. His arrogance and concern with hierarchy, however, put paid to any notion that the TNO would jell into a close-knit team. His abrasive managerial style was more likely to evoke grudging respect than abiding loyalty.

The establishment of the Trade Negotiations Office brought with it other teething pains. Stevie Cameron of the *Ottawa Citizen* described the leading players as the 'best and brightest' civil servants in Ottawa.[4] Anyone who had read David Halberstam's book of that title wondered if the characterization was used intentionally; for Halberstam, the best and the brightest had led America into the morass of Vietnam. There were also those who insisted that the team be representative of all Canadians. This caused a minor tempest in the House of Commons and Joe Clark made it clear that the choice of players did not reflect his requirements. Over the months, the TNO complement was gradually increased in an effort to reflect more adequately the realities of contemporary Canadian society.

Although building a team and an apparatus for the negotiations was important (as was deflecting criticism so that the government could keep its eye on the ball), even more important was preparing the ground for negotiations. There had developed a hiatus in the development of policy positions and background material. Much of the work achieved prior to the decision in September had been put on hold and not much new had been achieved as process assumed increasing importance. By late winter, however, with a team in place, the need to return to the central task was apparent.

The Canada-US task force had developed a solid core of material on which the negotiating team could build. But the members of the task force who had been incorporated into the team now constituted only a small proportion of the effort. With the exception of those officers in Finance who had worked closely on the project and of members of the GATT task force, most of the members of the negotiating team, and especially its senior members (with the notable exception of Simon Reisman), had little experience in preparing for or conducting trade negotiations. Many had not participated in the previous year of preparatory work. A 'not-invented-here' syndrome permeated the TNO in its early stages. Many wheels had to be reinvented and valuable momentum was lost.

A difficulty apparent from the outset was that twenty-three chefs could end up making a very complex and not necessarily tasty meal. Since many considered themselves to be executive chefs who would require sous-chefs and assistants of various kinds, the kitchen had the potential to become a confusing and messy place. The months of March through May were spent in arriving at a common understanding of the menu and the ingredients.

The management of issues reflected the dominating hands-on approach of Simon Reisman. He was his own principal advisor, abhorred large numbers of people offering advice, and preferred to deal directly with the officers responsible for individual issues. In contrast, the organization of work, including the flow of paper, operated within a structured hierarchical system akin to a regular government department and reflected the bureaucratic mindset of Gordon Ritchie, who sought to impose order on the management of the negotiations. Memos and papers addressed to Reisman had to be cleared through at least two layers; requests to meet with Reisman had to be passed through the same process; decisions on attendance at negotiating sessions and other meetings were made by the same method. The TNO thus became a hybrid between a single-issue task force and a full-fledged government department with layers of responsibility, structured methods of work, and inner and outer circles. The result was tension between Reisman's effort to mastermind the negotiations and Ritchie's effort to run an orderly office.

Within the TNO, two standing committees gradually emerged: an executive committee composed of Ritchie (with Reisman occasionally attending) and the assistant chief negotiators responsible for overall management, including administrative questions such as office allocation, personnel issues, and budget; and a policy committee originally composed of the management group and the heads of the individual negotiating areas, but open to most officers with an interest. The formal role of the latter was to assure coordination of all the substantive activities of the TNO and to serve as an internal clearing house for papers and memoranda.

While on the surface all appeared orderly, in reality the organization's neatly structured lines of authority and responsibility impeded rather than facilitated the negotiations. The rigid structure was irrelevant to the development of negotiating positions since these were established by Reisman and fleshed out by the responsible senior officers. It was their task to ensure adequate consultations with other departments as well as the provinces and the business community and to pursue negotiations with the United States through the working groups. While the plenary negotiating sessions that brought Reisman and Murphy together would set the tone and direction of the negotiations, the working groups would work out most of the detail.

The TNO might have functioned better if organized as a tight task force. Instead, it had been organized into tightly segmented units with little or no communication between them except through a rigid hierarchy. This stifled the creativity of many of the people who came on board and frustrated the need for everyone to have a solid appreciation of the negotiations as a whole. For all but the chosen few, there was insufficient opportunity to make contributions to broad strategy and tactics. In this respect, the office was too big. The TNO had some fifty professional staff but could have done the job with half that. The office was overly layered. It isolated Reisman and separated him from people who had the background and experience to make a serious contribution to the work of the negotiations.

Consultations with other government departments were strictly limited, given the security preoccupations of ministers as well as Reisman and Ritchie. Indeed, since Reisman had obtained his mandate directly from cabinet and had most of the resources at hand necessary to develop and deliver that mandate, the need for painstaking interdepartmental consensus building and the accompanying soul-destroying brokering could be ignored. Ritchie met frequently with the deputy ministers of key departments to report progress and to clear papers on their way to cabinet. By the time such papers reached deputies, however, the main policy issues had been resolved within the TNO and the scope of interdepartmental consultation even at this exalted level reflected more form than substance. As negotiations proceeded, few outside the TNO commanded the necessary range and depth of experience, analysis, and knowledge to criticize papers effectively and credibly.

The Provincial Conundrum
Reisman's style of management also brought light and colour, if not comfort, to the provinces. He took the view that he would consult to the fullest extent

possible with the provinces and would seek to negotiate an arrangement in which they would see it in their own interests to accept obligations in areas of provincial jurisdiction. In no circumstances, however, would he accept a provincial presence in the negotiations or on his team. To make his point, he moved quickly to invite the provinces to name provincial advisors to meet with him and discuss any and all aspects of the preparatory process. With a mischievous twinkle in his eye, he declared himself ready to meet just before or after Christmas if enough provincial representatives were ready to travel to Ottawa. A first meeting of what would become the Continuing Committee on Trade Negotiations was finally held 7 January. A second meeting took place 4 February. Reisman used these meetings to inform the provinces of his views, to give them an opportunity to express their concerns, and to impress upon them that trade was a federal responsibility.

To equip themselves to deal with Reisman, the provinces gradually moved to name senior representatives to these meetings. Ontario had in the fall hired Bob Latimer to advise it. A retired federal assistant deputy responsible for trade in both the former Department of Industry, Trade and Commerce and in the Department of External Affairs, he was now named Ontario's representative to these meetings. In March, Quebec hired former Tokyo Round chief negotiator Jake Warren, Alberta named consultant Harold Millican, and Nova Scotia appointed lawyer Fred Dixon. Other provinces were content to stick with established senior officials, such as Harry Nason for New Brunswick and Hal Stanley for Newfoundland. All came to meetings accompanied by a bevy of advisors, Ontario and Quebec at times bringing seven or eight officials.

Initial provincial attendance at these meetings was without prejudice to eventual provincial participation in the negotiations themselves. That was an issue that had been delegated to Joe Clark and would be resolved at the political level. In the spring, Clark toured the provinces to look for a solution short of a provincial presence at the table and short of the federal government being reduced to chair of a board of provincial premiers. Most of the provinces were unwilling to retreat an inch from what they regarded as an ironclad commitment from the prime minister to admit them to the inner temple.

Under the leadership of Alberta's new premier Don Getty and with the active support of Ontario's David Peterson and Quebec's rejuvenated Robert Bourassa, the premiers developed an eight-point plan for provincial participation. The centre-piece included one provincial representative each at the table, a full voice in the development of mandate and strategy, and a veto over anything that involved provincial jurisdiction. While the big provinces all agreed on this plan, the smaller provinces were less sure how this would serve their interests, and New Brunswick's Richard Hatfield went so far as to publicly disavow the provincial plan. It was also summarily rejected by the federal government.

As Clark's tour of provincial capitals continued, the premiers saw their only hope in another session with the prime minister and began to push their point of view. By the end of March, Clark was ready to concede that such a meeting might be necessary and fuelled speculation that the prime minister would use the opening of Expo 86 in Vancouver at the end of April as the occasion for bringing the issue to a conclusion. In the end, the meeting was postponed until June, but not before the prime minister wrote the premiers and firmly outlined the federal position: as much consultation as they wanted and a generous sharing of information, but no seat at the table and no formal role in the establishment of mandates or approval of the results of the negotiations.

The scene was thus set for the 2 June first ministers' conference. The stakes were high. Nine of the provinces had agreed to press on the principle of a joint mandate and direct participation; only New Brunswick took the public view that negotiations were a federal responsibility. It did not have the resources to play the kind of role sought by the larger provinces and it objected in principle to any arrangement that would make it a second-class citizen.

The auguries for settlement were not good. Many in Ottawa had become convinced that Ontario's Peterson was out to sink the negotiations and had seized on the issue of provincial participation as his first opportunity to make mischief. Reisman, however, would have none of this. He saw the provincial position as a matter of grand standing which, when countered, would collapse.

Building on the doubts of New Brunswick, the federal strategy became one of building support for a federalist position. The western provinces had to temper their enthusiasm for participation – which they saw as a way to counter the weight of Ontario and Quebec – with the realization that to entangle the negotiator in complicated procedures and accountabilities could well doom any prospect of success. Premier Getty, who was prepared to settle for a 'national figure' appointed as provincial representative, settled for process. Premier Bourassa came away convinced that this was the wrong issue on which to press. While he continued to harbour some doubts about the negotiations, the strength of support in the Quebec business community and the enthusiasm of his ministers and officials convinced him that a blocking alliance with Peterson was not in Quebec's interest.

The outcome satisfied Reisman. He would obtain his mandate from the federal cabinet and would consult closely with the provinces. The first ministers would meet each quarter to receive his report and consider any adjustments to the mandate which progress in the negotiations required. A committee of 'designated ministers' would provide continuing overview. The prime minister insisted that in any conflict between the provincial and the national interest, the national interest would prevail. As he told reporters: 'We're all Canadians and the government of Canada has its responsibilities and we'll fulfil those responsibilities.' As a token for the provinces he added: 'If the formula turned out to be inappropriate, we could re-examine it.' Getty agreed: 'We have agreed for the coming three months that we'll see whether the process of reporting is satisfactory to us. If it isn't, we'll change it.' Even Peterson declared himself satisfied: 'I'm satisfied that through these first ministers' meetings we're going to monitor everything.' In sum, the result was the addition of a political overlay to existing practice which had grown up since the Tokyo Round GATT negotiations, had proved workable, and had already been pursued in the Continuing Committee on Trade Negotiations. [5]

Communications and Communications Strategies

Given the difficulties that had been experienced so far in selling the initiative, Reisman established a small media unit in the TNO. Its task was to monitor the media, arrange meetings with reporters, organize press scrums at the end of negotiating sessions, and answer reporters' questions or point them in the right direction. Its job, however, was not to sell the initiative. That difficult task would remain the responsibility of the professional communicators in the Conservative party.

The Mulroney government's early distrust of bureaucrats has been well recorded; it had reached its apogee with the infamous gag order of November 1984 when civil servants were forbidden to have any contact with the media. While the atmosphere was no longer as strained, there was still a feeling among the politicians that they knew best when it came to getting the message across. They had, after all, waged an extraordinarily effective election campaign. And so it was that in the spring of 1986 the political wizards produced a short film extolling the merits of free trade. It was glitzy, well-produced, and unsullied by bureaucratic hands. It was also fatally flawed. The film was released to all members of Parliament in April and Ed Broadbent was among the first viewers. Unfortunately for the Tories, one of Broadbent's staff spotted a glaring geographical blunder. On the film's map of Canada, Prince Edward Island had apparently sunk into the Gulf of St. Lawrence, while Newfoundland was the same colour as the United States. The media were quickly invited to view the film and took great sport in making fun of it. One wit wondered whether Newfoundland was the price of free trade; another suggested Canada must have got the better deal. It did not create the impression the government had sought to achieve. All copies of the film, which had cost almost $200,000 to make, were quickly withdrawn. While the Toronto producers promised to issue a corrected version, it was never seen again.

A more successful effort involved the prime minister's taking to the national airwaves for the first time since his election to make the pitch for free trade. The speech provided the Canadian public with its first view of the direction the government would take in the negotiations. Canada would seek to enshrine the principle of national treatment so that, by the end of the century, the border would no longer play a significant role in commercial transactions and Canadian and American goods and services would be treated alike in each market. Short on detail, the speech tried to give the country a sense of the government's vision rather than its strategy. Unfortunately, the pundits insisted it was detail, tactics, and strategy they wanted. It was too hard to criticize vision.

Departing from the usual courtesy of furnishing a copy of the speech to the opposition leaders, the staff at the PMO only provided Turner and Broadbent with a further pretext for complaining about government secrecy. There was no malice aforethought in this so-called snub. Rather, it reflected the lack of experience at the PMO. The next day, the TNO received requests for copies of the speech from various ministers' offices, including that of Joe Clark.

The secrecy charge plagued the government throughout the talks and presented a special communications problem. It was virtually impossible to deal with this charge and the standard response, 'one never shows one's cards during play,' sounded more and more hollow with each repetition. The real problem was that the government's credibility, which had taken a beating on issues unrelated to free trade, inevitably affected the public perception of how it was handling the negotiations. In fact, there were literally volumes of material on free trade available for those who bothered to look for it. The blue booklet of documents issued early in 1986, *Canadian Trade Negotiations*, remained the best pocket guide. Other easily available guides to Canadian trade policy included the trade policy review of 1983 and the January 1985 discussion paper *How to Secure and Enhance Canadian Access to Export Markets*. At the end of May an access-to-information request secured the release of a series of twenty-six partially vetted studies which had been commissioned by the Department of External Affairs. While the studies concluded that a deal would leave Canada's economic, cultural, and social institutions unchanged, journalists found enough to warn of 'Big Tax Hikes After a Deal' (*Toronto Star*), 'Deal Is Unlikely to Spur Investment' (*Montreal Gazette*) and 'Pact Could Cut 131,000 Jobs' (*Ottawa Citizen*). Naturally, the fact of censorship also garnered its share of headlines.

Caution begets secrecy. There is no doubt that more information could have been shared with the public and the media without harm to the national interest. But would it have made any difference? Perhaps it would have prevented the 'secrecy' charges which would have been no small accomplishment. However, the journalists who took the time to plod through the vast amount of material available on free trade could be counted on the fingers of one hand. Unhappily, post-Watergate journalism thrives on sensation and few reporters feel they have accomplished their mission if they have not found an Achilles' heel. Most political reporters prefer 'gotcha' stories to analysis and explanation. Governments have as a result become extremely circumspect around the media; the Mulroney government was no exception.

Ambush

What the government needed in the spring was a shot in the arm to show that it was on the right track and that negotiations would soon indicate that a Canada-US trade agreement offered the best prospects for Canada. It did not get it. Rather, on Friday morning, 11 April, the US Senate Finance Committee ambushed the negotiations in a rancorous, ill-tempered display of unrestrained administration bashing. Over the next eleven days, until the Senate Finance Committee voted ten to ten on a motion to disapprove the negotiations and thus, through the back door, allowed them to proceed, the venture hung perilously in the balance.[6]

The vote was the final action in the complicated process of obtaining US fast-track authority before negotiations could be joined. By late winter of 1986, the administration was confident that the Senate Finance and House Ways and Means committees would present no problems to a clean launch. USTR Yeutter and his staff had met several times with committee members and staff and were convinced that approval was a mere formality. The administration had appointed its GATT ambassador, Peter Murphy, as its chief negotiator and he had arrived in Washington just before Easter to take up his new assignment.

The confidence of the administration was apparent during the prime minister's 18-19 March visit to Washington. With the trade initiative well launched, the focus of the visit was acid rain. There were, however, opportunities to make positive noises about the trade initiative in toasts at dinners and lunches and in meetings with congressional leaders. The prime minister and his advisors came home from the summit well satisfied that the initiative was in good hands and that when serious negotiations started in another two months, they would proceed on the basis of strong and broadly based political will on both sides of the border.

Neither the House Ways and Means Committee nor the Senate Finance Committee was obliged to act on the administration's notice of intent to negotiate; lack of action would mean approval and so the negotiations could proceed. Although each committee had sought written comments from American private sector interests, neither committee seemed inclined to convene hearings on the administration's request. Both committees had very large legislative agendas, especially the Senate, which seemed likely to be bogged down with tax reform until early in the summer. Members and staffers on both sides of Capitol Hill, as well as lobbyists and others, predicted that the administration's request would be approved by congressional inaction.

This predicted scenario was played out in the House. The chair of the trade subcommittee of the Ways and Means Committee, Sam Gibbons, had long favoured a bilateral trade agreement and had publicly stated that the fast-track approval would be granted, while the full committee's chair, Dan Rostenkowski, also supported the proposal. Their views were mirrored by the leading Republicans on the committee. The House committee had only a handful of members with a specific gripe against Canada and, even then, there was no opposition that could not be contained by the committee's leadership.

The Senate was different. Shortly after the prime minister's visit to Washington, the Finance Committee announced that it would hold a hearing on 11 April to review the administration's request for fast-track authority.

An immediate check with the committee staff revealed that the hearing was scheduled primarily for two purposes: to allow some senators to vent their unhappiness with Canada over specific trade irritants, notably lumber; and, more formally, to register the committee's jurisdiction in the fast-track process. On the latter, there was some concern in the Senate that allowing the negotiations to proceed without taking any action would, somehow, implicitly cede its authority to the administration.

Canadian complacency about congressional approval, however, was misplaced. In a prescient article in the *New York Times* on 10 April, columnist Flora Lewis warned from Ottawa:

> So far, the United States has been rather indifferent to the Canadian initiative. The Administration and Congress have other priorities just now. Canadian officials and politicians seem to be understanding, if disappointed, that their extraordinary gesture hasn't provoked more immediate interest. But they are pressing their point and Washington should bestir itself because this is an opportunity to move the world in the direction of U.S. principles and openness of many kinds.

On the eve of the hearing, a warning bell sounded. A group of senators meeting together in Senator Danforth's office realized just how deep their gripes with the administration ran and what an extraordinary opportunity the hearings offered to get that point across. There would in fact be a resolution; that resolution, to be introduced by Senator Packwood, the Republican chair of the committee, could well be to disapprove the negotiations; and there were sufficient votes to pass the resolution. Late that night Senator Daniel Patrick Moynihan from New York phoned Ambassador Gotlieb and warned him that something was afoot and that the easy passage expected was not to be. Gotlieb and his staff undertook an immediate canvas of the members and found that indeed there might be a resolution, although whether it would approve, disapprove, or grant a conditional go ahead remained unclear.

On the morning of 11 April, the committee gathered in its ornate, panelled hearing room. USTR Yeutter was the principal administration witness and, while prepared for sharp questions, he was confident of emerging with the authority without which negotiations would be doomed before they began. His confidence was misplaced. One senator after another castigated the administration's trade policy for inertia, ineptitude, and insufficient solicitude towards Congress. Of the twelve senators who attended, ten indicated opposition. Chairman Packwood concluded, 'it is my prediction that if we were voting today the committee would turn the Administration down' and then added 'I don't think there is much that can be done between now and that vote to turn the committee around.' Yeutter was in shock and warned the members, 'You must have no misunderstanding about the political implications and the reverberations that this will bring about.' The leader of the recalcitrant senators, Jack Danforth, shot back: 'I don't understand the train wreck idea. We've gone 210 years without a free trade agreement with Canada.'[7]

What had gone wrong? The fact that there was opposition in the committee was no revelation. What was disturbing, rather, was the extent of that opposition and, in some cases, the vehemence with which it was expressed. Two senators – Bentsen of Texas and Mitchell of Maine – had only recently indicated that they would be supportive, while Danforth of Missouri had no reason to oppose the request on the basis of any bilateral grudge. The outcome of the hearing, moreover, was surprising not only for the administration but even for a number of the senators on the committee and their staffs. No one had predicted that this would transpire – not the administration, not the senators themselves, not their staffs, and not any other informed followers of Capitol Hill. No one had guessed that the last-minute dynamics of the committee would have played out the way they did. As one Senate staffer ruefully remarked, 'there are rare occasions, and fortunately so, where Senators collectively rise up and try to run the place.'

The fire that broke out in the hearing room had been smoldering, unnoticed by the administration, for many months. The administration had dealt handily with small outbreaks, such as in 1985 when the Japanese were everybody's favourite targets. However, having put out the flames, the administration then reverted to what was seen in Congress as a continuation of its previous disregard of congressional demands for stronger action on trade.

The committee's consideration of the administration's request thus demonstrated the extraordinary tension that had developed between the administration and Congress on the objectives and conduct of US trade policy. Also demonstrated was the increasingly perverse way in which decisions are made in Washington. A number of factors were involved:

- Dissatisfaction with US trade policy; US legislators were profoundly unhappy with the administration's seeming reluctance to tackle the trade deficit by taking a tough stance against violators of US economic interests. The many trade bills before Congress were efforts to strengthen US trade remedy laws, make them more automatic, and generally reduce the flexibility available to the administration in its execution of US trade policy. Finance Committee members believed that the State Department was too ready to sacrifice US trade interests to US foreign policy interests.
- Dissatisfaction with administration tax and economic policy; both Houses

were unhappy with the strength of the administration's commitment to the market, its reluctance to tackle the deficit through reduced defence spending and an increase in taxes, and its refusal to alter monetary policy to reduce the US trade deficit. They saw the measures taken by Secretary Baker in the fall of 1985 to lower the value of the US dollar as too little, too late.

- Tension between committee members, especially between chairman Packwood and trade subcommittee chairman Danforth. Senate committees are made up of individuals who have their own constituencies, and thus, their own axes to grind. The inability of the committee to develop a common agenda had severely weakened its effectiveness and had led to charges and countercharges. Danforth was particularly unhappy with Packwood's unwillingness to give him hearing days to pursue his administration-bashing on trade issues.
- Party politics leading to the 1986 congressional election. The nine Democrats on the committee saw the Republicans as vulnerable on the trade issue and were keen to defeat a number of Republican senators that fall so that they could regain control of the Senate.

There were also a number of members who had serious political problems with Canada because of specific trade irritants, especially regarding softwood lumber. In this regard, the committee's chair, Bob Packwood of Oregon, was the most prominent and most obvious problem senator. As well, Senator Long, the most senior Democrat on the committee, plus Senators Symms, Baucus, and Pryor, all had serious constituency problems because of softwood lumber exports. John Heinz of Pennsylvania, chair of the Senate Steel Caucus, had been a persistent critic of Canada's exclusion from the president's steel program and was considered a potential opponent. Similarly, Charles Grassley of Iowa had been unhappy for some time because of Canadian agricultural exports to the United States, especially those which were particularly competitive with Iowa commodities, such as hogs and pork products.

To exacerbate the situation further, three of these senators (Grassley, Symms, and Packwood) were facing re-election in the fall and all of them had reason to be concerned about their electoral campaigns: Iowa had not returned an incumbent senator since 1966; Symms faced a strong challenge from Idaho governor John Evans after having won his 1980 election by less than one percentage point; and Packwood had never won an election by a significant majority and would be facing a Democratic challenger, Representative James Weaver, who promised to make Canadian lumber imports a central theme in his campaign.

Alan King, *Ottawa Citizen*, 25 April 1986

In the immediate aftermath of the 11 April disaster, there was stunned silence. But congressional rebellions, if disagreeable, are not unknown in Washington and the administration behaved like a family departing the gravesite after the sorrow of internment, but ready to turn to other things. Unless Canada was prepared to negotiate without fast-track authority, the negotiations could be regarded as terminated or at least delayed until after the November elections. Taking up the bloodied banner and resuming the fight seemed to carry unacceptable risks of either a major administration defeat if the matter were pressed to a vote, or of administration concessions to the Senate in return for a favourable decision.

In Ottawa, the opposition parties immediately jumped in and advised the government to quit while it was ahead and predicted that the government would have to pay with a cave-in on a sensitive issue such as lumber or pharmaceuticals.[8] Some pundits concluded that a Senate defeat might prove a boon to the Tories, many of whom, in the face of mounting opposition, were getting cold feet about the initiative.[9] The government, however, was determined to fight this possible setback with every weapon at its disposal. Trade Minister Kelleher told the *Toronto Star*: 'We've abandoned the traditional Canadian approach. We are not pursuing the traditional, hands-off approach – I can tell you that much. It's important that the Canadian people know that.'[10] The prime minister steadfastly maintained that President Reagan would prevail.

To ensure that the president would do just that and that Canada had done everything at its disposal, a special task force was set up in the PMO to monitor developments and implement strategy. A familiar face was brought in to coordinate the effort: External Affairs Associate Undersecretary Derek Burney. For the next week, he maintained a constant vigil and a calming influence on the cacophony of voices in and around the PMO.[11] While there were many advisors milling about at the beginning of the crisis, by the end Burney could count only on Don Campbell, his successor as assistant deputy minister for United States Affairs at External Affairs and Bill Fox, the PMO director of communications; the rest of the entourage had evaporated, only to reappear to join in the ultimate celebration of victory as the crisis of senate disapproval of fast-track authority was narrowly avoided.

A frequent visitor and advisor to Burney was Simon Reisman, who was astounded by the number of people who felt qualified to render assistance during the time of crisis. Walking down the Sparks Street Mall with Burney and Campbell at the end of a particularly raucous session with ministerial and prime ministerial aides, he complained bitterly about the lack of discipline and professionalism. He jested that perhaps the circle of advisors could be made even wider by inviting the man in the street to join them. At this point, he walked up to a saffron-robed Hare Krishna priest and asked if he had any opinion to offer on the crisis in Washington. Reisman took his astonished silence for an undecided vote.

The Canadian embassy in Washington, accused by the press of being asleep at the switch, had also swung into action. Not for the last time in the negotiations, Gotlieb was full of fight. The administration should do everything possible to gain the votes necessary to defeat disapproval. It should pull out all the stops. Negotiating without fast-track authority was a non-starter. Ottawa was fully on board. The only way to negotiate was through a clean launch.[12]

Slowly the administration recovered its morale and mobilized its forces. It realized that, like it or not, administration prestige was on the line and that relations with Canada would be severely damaged by a rebuff. President Reagan, Treasury Secretary Baker, Secretary of State Shultz, and USTR Yeutter were all directly engaged. Gotlieb was tireless in his contacts with senators, power brokers, and anyone with influence. Hard-core supporters, opponents, and waverers were tallied and retallied. Canada's consuls in the United States were recruited to the cause and they contacted governors, business leaders, and newspaper editors, all in an effort to save the negotiations from being still-born.

The situation began to turn around. Packwood, who had originally scheduled a vote on a motion to disapprove on 14 April, agreed to delay the vote until 22 April. The number of negative votes seemed to be between twelve and fourteen. More time was needed. On 15 April, Shultz issued a strong statement on behalf of the administration promising full consultation with the Congress in the course of negotiations. It was more and more evident that Canada was not the object of the Senate's wrath. Senators wanted to be players in US trade policy and the administration was seeking to accommodate them. Twelve senators issued a letter to the president proposing that the request for fast-track authority be withdrawn and resubmitted as evidence of the administration's reformed attitude towards dealing constructively with Congress.

Over the weekend from Friday, 18 April to Monday the 21st, the day before the vote, the number of positive votes crept up to nine, one short of what was needed. Favourable editorial comment in the *New York Times* and an article in the *Wall Street Journal* added to the momentum. The president responded to the twelve senators with a statement confirming his commitment to the negotiations and to working with the Congress:

> The Nation faces an historic opportunity with Canada. Opening the United States-Canadian borders will dramatically expand American exports, thereby creating thousands of new jobs. Furthermore, opening borders will make the firms and industries of both countries more competitive internationally.
>
> I am concerned, however, by your request that I withdraw the proposal for the use of accelerated implementing authority ... As Prime Minister Mulroney made abundantly clear, Canada will not enter into these negotiations without the fast-track authority. Accordingly, I believe that this authority is essential to the success of the enterprise. I have directed our negotiators to work with the Congress so that your views, as well as the views of the private sector, will be heard through the negotiations.
>
> Failure to initiate these negotiations would adversely color the tone of our political and economic relationships with Canada for many years to come. Allowing such Administration opportunity to pass could jeopardize progress in liberalizing the U.S.-Canadian trade relationship, the largest in the world. Further, Canada has been very supportive of U.S. international initiatives, particularly in combatting terrorism and maintaining a solid unity on major East-West and arms control issues.
>
> A denial of fast-track authority will also adversely affect our efforts to resolve current trade differences. Indeed, several issues – particularly lumber – have already been set back as a result of the Finance Committee hearing last Friday. I remain committed to obtaining resolutions of the lumber and other issues so that American industries will have fair opportunities to compete ...
>
> You can be assured that we will consult with you and your colleagues on the

Committee at every step throughout these comprehensive negotiations. Your assistance in this regard is welcomed and helpful in view of the role of Congress in the development and implementation of trade policy.[13]

By Monday the 21st, the number of negative votes remained at eleven. Most were Democrats, hoping to make trade a major campaign issue in the fall elections. The Republicans on the committee, with the notable exception of Danforth, had been turned around. It had been brought home to them that the chances of solving some of their individual complaints with Canada were infinitely better within the context of a negotiation than after the defeat of the most important initiative of the Mulroney government. One more vote was required. Efforts zeroed in on Senator Spark Matsunaga of Hawaii, who found himself at the receiving end of many phone calls, including ones from the president and from Governor Ariyoshi of Hawaii. The latter had been urged to call by Canada's consul general in San Francisco, Jim McCardle. To Matsunaga, the issue was not free trade with Canada, which he thought was a good idea, but congressional politics. The key issue for him was whether the Democratic leadership wanted a defeat for the administration or a narrow victory. The president's call helped to convince him that the message of congressional dissatisfaction had gotten through.

On the morning of 23 April, three resolutions were introduced into the committee. The first was a motion to disapprove fast-track authority. In introducing the motion, the chair, Packwood, said he would vote against it. The second resolution, introduced by Senator Danforth, denied fast-track authority but invited the administration to resubmit its request immediately and committed the Senate to vote on it within thirty days. The third, proposed by Senators Dole and Symms, would grant fast-track authority but set out a number of objectives for the negotiations.

The Dole resolution was withdrawn at the outset of the committee meeting. The first to be voted on was the Danforth proposal, and it was defeated by a tied ten to ten vote. The Packwood motion to disapprove was similarly defeated by a voice vote, thus allowing the negotiations to proceed. A defiant Senator Danforth declared: 'We'll be watching these Canadian negotiations like eagles. We will watch very, very carefully what is being done.'[14]

It appeared to some observers that the whole process had been carefully orchestrated. The negotiations had been approved by the narrowest of possible margins; the administration, and especially the president, had been forced to pay close attention to the issue; concessions had apparently been wrung out of the administration; and the committee had declared its close interest in the negotiations. Negotiations could now proceed, but not without a clear appreciation on both sides of the border that the final agreement would need to satisfy the Congress on its own merits. Many Canadians saw this drama as congressional rejection in advance of the initiative and as a strong negative signal to Canada. This was far from the case, as a number of senators who voted negatively were at pains to point out in subsequent months. The agreement would not be approved merely on the strength of neighbourly relations or its demonstration effect for multilateral negotiations. It would have to offer clear commercial advantages to the United States.

More ominous and less well appreciated was the fact that administration officials had once again mishandled a difficult situation and that a major and personal intervention by the president had been necessary to rescue the initiative. Without his involvement, the tied vote could not have been achieved. While not opposed to the negotiations, most senators were not convinced that the negotiations required fast-track authority. They saw no reason why negotiations could not proceed under the administration's general authority. Only a few were prepared to concede that America's trading partners were no longer prepared to negotiate twice: once with the administration and a second time with the Congress. The fast-track procedure has been devised to avoid such a development. To make it work, however, the administration needs to be able to read Congress carefully and work closely with the two principal committees of jurisdiction to develop their confidence. This it had failed to do prior to the April hearings. Only time would tell whether the administration had learned its lesson. Whatever the difficulties, the negotiations proper could now be launched.

PART TWO

NEGOTIATING AN AGREEMENT

8

THE SUMMER OF
INNOCENCE

To everything there is a season, and a time to
every purpose under heaven.
— Ecclesiastes 3:1

With the sound of one hand clapping, the Senate's failure to disagree to the administration's notice of intent permitted the negotiations to begin in earnest with a first get-acquainted session held in Ottawa on 21-2 May. The preface had been a visit to Washington on 10 April by Reisman and Ritchie to meet Yeutter and Murphy. They had talked in Yeutter's office and lunched together at the Maison Blanche on F Street, around the corner from the offices of the USTR. Reisman, with forty years of dreams about free trade under his belt and Murphy, with four weeks of briefings to back him up, were there to take each other's measure and set the tone for the challenge ahead. Reisman talked about a big agreement between Canada and the United States, ambitious in scope and imaginative in design. He boldly aimed for an agreement that would, by the end of the century, create a barrier-free North American market. He saw their task as challenging and exciting but realistic. Yeutter agreed that only a big agreement would attract the coalition necessary to gain congressional support. Murphy, on the other hand, was a little more circumspect, raising concerns about technical issues. The results of this first, if informal encounter, were declared gratifying by mutual consent, but a nagging doubt about Murphy's capacity to think big had already been raised.[1]

Reisman's views were no mystery. In his view, 'freer trade would allow us to overcome our deficiencies by having access to a bigger market and being able to use more up-to-date technology and having longer production runs and getting greater volume. That's the bottom line. The major benefit you expect to get from a free-trade arrangement will be to increase our productivity.'[2] This he would pursue with his unique blend of vigour and arrogance. His protagonist's views were less well known. One thing was certain, he could not have been more different. More than a foot taller, with a shock of red hair and a gangling gait, there was not much of a book on Peter Murphy. Taciturn, careful, and a survivor, he was initially in awe of his more experienced antagonist. He was, however, not a totally unknown quantity in Washington. He had, after all, been appointed by the president of the United States to undertake a negotiation to remake the largest trading relationship in the world.

Murphy had made his reputation in the tough, mean world of international textile negotiations. As a young economics graduate, he had joined the Special Trade Representative's Office and eventually found himself attached to the office of chief textile negotiator Mike Smith. He had earned a reputation for being thorough, discreet, and tenacious. Increasingly, Smith had relied on him as his principal adviser. When Smith was promoted to deputy USTR[3] and permanent representative to the GATT in Geneva in 1980, Murphy provided continuity for his successor. The new chief textile negotiator, a veteran of the US Foreign Agriculture Service, turned out to have one fatal flaw: he could not earn the confidence of the formidable US textile lobby and their congressional supporters. He lasted only a few months. When he left, Murphy kept the office going and gradually convinced his political masters that he was the man for the job. Only thirty years old, his quiet, unassuming style proved to be just what the doctor ordered. With veterans Bob Shepherd and Mike Smith backing him up in Geneva, Murphy took on the task of managing the negotiation of a new Multifibre Agreement and renewing the network of some thirty bilateral agreements between the United States and low-cost suppliers of textiles and clothing around the world. A major part of his task was working with the textile industry and Congress, a double-barrelled challenge which his predecessor could not meet but which is essential to successful trade negotiations in Washington. He could proudly claim that he knew his way around the Hill and had earned its respect.[4]

Three years later, when Bill Brock recalled Smith from Geneva to become his principal deputy, Murphy was off to Geneva to become permanent representative to the GATT. There he honed his multilateral negotiating skills and broadened his trade policy knowledge. Geneva in the period 1983-6 was a good place for a patient man. There was no major negotiation to manage; instead, there was the steady work of building coalitions for negotiations to come and managing the myriad of disputes GATT seeks to settle or keep from boiling over.

When new USTR Clayton Yeutter was looking for the right person to head the Canada-US negotiations, his instinct was to stick with existing resources. He rejected the advice of some, including that of Secretary of State George Shultz, that the United States should appoint a high-profile outsider. These views proliferated with the appointment of Simon Reisman in Canada. Yeutter was convinced, however, that given the prevailing mood in Congress, a high-profile candidate would prove counterproductive. Instead, he had a simple swap in mind. He wanted to appoint his own man, Mike Samuels, to the job of GATT ambassador. This would make Peter Murphy available for assignment in Washington. Why not make him the Canada-US negotiator? Rumours to this effect began to swirl late in 1985 and in late February, the US ambassador to Canada Tom Niles confirmed that Murphy would be the US champion.[5]

As a warm-up to the negotiations, Murphy granted a number of interviews and displayed some of the mischief he found levelled the playing field between him and his veteran opponent. He decreed that everything was on the table, including social programs. As a result, he occasioned a political uproar in Canada and media comments suggesting that while Reisman might be a sly old fox, Murphy appeared to be a young one.[6]

Between May and September of that summer of innocence, Reisman and Murphy would hold five negotiating sessions, dubbed plenaries, one in Ottawa, one in Mont Tremblant, one at Meech Lake, and two in Washington. They were billed as exploratory meetings intended to allow each side to establish more firmly the parameters of the negotiations and to set the stage for the detailed negotiations to follow. It was a time for Reisman to flesh out his concept of a free-trade agreement and lay on the table the major issues of importance to Canada, and for the Americans to begin to come to grips with the vastness of the vision and ambition which gave the Canadian conception form and direction.

A Lesson in Canadian Political Economy and GATT Rules
The first session took place in the penthouse suite of the Metropolitan Life Centre occupied by the TNO. The main conference room next to Reisman's office housed a twenty-five-foot conference table of walnut veneer, surrounded by twenty-four comfortable leather chairs. One of the chairs had been specially doctored to put Reisman at a level with the rest of his delegation. A Canadian and American flag at one end of the room symbolized its single purpose; a picture on the wall of a boy hugging a huge circus elephant suggested the formidable task ahead; and the door to the kitchen at the other end hinted at the liberal hospitality available.[7]

The principal focus of the first session in May was a slide show depicting Canada's economic history and structure.[8] The presentation was intended by Reisman to serve two distinct purposes. He wished to dispel any notion the US side might harbour that the two countries came to the table with the same cards. The Canadian economy was small, heavily dependent upon trade, and regionally diverse. He also intended to prepare the ground for a position that, given the enormous adjustment that free trade would require in the Canadian economy, secure and expanded access to the US market should be made available immediately upon implementation of any agreement, while Canada should have an extended period to lower barriers to US goods. The Americans were bewildered and bemused by the presentation, but not convinced.

Reisman also repeated his grand design of an agreement providing for barrier-free trade by the end of the century. Backing up his design for an agreement was his conception of Canadian and US obligations under GATT Article XXIV, an article which he had been involved in drafting as a young member of the Canadian delegation to the 1947-8 Havana Conference. This article allows for free-trade areas consisting of two or more countries between which 'duties and other restrictive regulations of commerce ... are eliminated on substantially all the trade' (8(b)). To substantiate his claim that a GATT free-trade agreement should aim at eliminating virtually all barriers between Canada and the United States, he had commissioned a substantial amount of preparatory work.

A staff paper on the issue had concluded that a free-trade area denies most-favoured-nation treatment to the non-partners and establishes new preferences coupled with more exacting obligations between the partners.[9] The basic principle is laid out in paragraph four of Article XXIV, which states that free-trade areas and customs unions are desirable if they facilitate trade between the constituent territories and do not raise barriers to the trade of other contracting parties. Paragraphs five to ten then spell out the specific requirements that must be satisfied:

- There must be no increase in trade barriers against third countries that are members of GATT.
- The parties to an FTA must remove duties and 'other restrictive regulations of commerce,' on substantially all trade between them.
- Some restrictive regulations may be maintained if they are permitted by specified articles of the GATT: XI and XIII (certain quantitative restrictions), XII, XIV, XV (balance-of-payments and exchange restrictions), and XX (general exceptions).
- Where elimination of trade barriers is not achieved immediately, the relevant agreement should contain a 'plan and schedule' for the completion of a free-trade area 'within a reasonable length of time.'
- The parties to an agreement are enjoined to notify the GATT of any agreement before it is implemented. GATT members acting collectively can make recommendations for changes in the agreement, and the parties

must not implement their agreement unless they act on these recommendations.

The drafters had intended to establish a set of rules that would provide sufficient flexibility to the negotiating parties to develop dynamic arrangements that would meet their individual needs as well as the general test of creating trade rather than diverting it. All postwar free-trade area agreements involving GATT members have been examined by the GATT. These agreements have varied substantially in their content and trade coverage. Specific aspects of the agreements have been questioned, but all the agreements have been implemented. The content of these agreements and their handling by the GATT provide some indication of the approach of the contracting parties to the formation of free-trade areas.

All notified agreements, such as the 1958 Treaty of Rome establishing the European Economic Community (EC) and the 1960 Treaty of Stockholm setting up the European Free Trade Association (EFTA), have been examined by GATT working parties. At times discussions in working parties are heated. Consideration generally concentrates on the broad requirements of paragraph four: a free-trade agreement should on the whole be trade-creating rather than trade-restricting or trade-diverting. That judgment and the questions which flow therefrom are based on a frank assessment of a country's commercial policy interest: will the agreement being examined affect its trade positively or negatively, or not at all. Thus discussion focuses not on the precise rules of article XXIV, but on rules of origin, the establishment of new preferences for agriculture and fishery products, and the application of temporary safeguard and balance-of-payment measures. Reaching a commercial judgment on the overall balance of advantage that should flow from an agreement is a familiar concept to many GATT participants. This attitude also explains the preference for the non-committal conclusions adopted by working parties. There is no advantage in placing the stamp of approval on any agreement. The trade practitioners who participate in these working parties prefer to leave some doubt as to the consistency of the agreement being examined with the requirements of the General Agreement in order to be able to press particular claims of disadvantage at some later stage.

Thus while the language of Article XXIV suggests that parties to a free-trade area agreement must eliminate all duties and other restrictive regulations of commerce between them, practice has not borne out this dictum. A range of regulatory barriers have remained in effect between free-trade partners, such as barriers to government procurement and trade in agricultural products, as well as the instruments of contingency protection. Despite the fact that few free-trade area agreements have eliminated all restrictive regulations of commerce, this does not appear to have stirred much criticism. The reason for this lies in the fact that the more restrictive regulations are removed, the more an agreement becomes preferential and discriminates against non-members. Working parties reviewing various agreements, therefore, have not been motivated to search for these kinds of deficiencies. On the contrary, they have been interested in limiting the scope of each agreement.

At the opening negotiating session, Reisman declared that Canada and the United States should not be deterred by the rather chequered application of article XXIV in various free-trade agreements. Canada and the United States had always taken their GATT obligations more seriously than others, and these negotiations would provide an opportunity to negotiate the best free-trade agreement ever conceived, a model for other GATT members. Not similarly steeped in such GATT lore, the US delegation was as bewildered by these assertions as they had been by the lesson in Canadian political economy. One US member commented that they were sure learning a lot about Canada and the GATT, but when were they going to get into the meat of the matter?

Reisman was also frustrated by this first session. He had expected Murphy to reply with his own broad conception of the agreement and the negotiations to get there. He had made no secret of the fact that this first session would be devoted to broad conceptual discussions. What he got was a portent of things to come: a litany of irritants and grievances such as lumber, border broadcasting, pharmaceuticals, magazine postal rates, and cable retransmission. Murphy had no broad framework or conception of his own to offer.[10]

At the conclusion of the session, Reisman and Murphy agreed upon a modus operandi for the negotiating sessions. There would be monthly meetings alternating between Canada and the United States. Each side would have a core negotiating team augmented, as necessary, by functional and sectoral experts for particular issues as they arose. The issues to be dealt with at each meeting would be decided in advance to allow for adequate preparation. Working groups would be established once the main table had agreed on the direction of the work.

The first session attracted a horde of Canadian journalists determined to make it a media event. Initially finding little that was newsworthy on the Canadian side, they besieged Murphy as he arrived with his delegation at the TNO in a small, modest blue van supplied by the US embassy. They hoped to extract a statement from him that Canadian social programs, Canadian cultural policies, and the autopact would have to go in any free-trade agreement. Murphy, as much numbed by the mob scene as shrewd, would not be drawn and proved an adept broken field runner. It was his first taste of an experience wholly new to him: celebrity status. Virtually unknown in

Washington, let alone in the United States, he would become a household name in Canada, and was stopped on the street by complete strangers eager to give him some advice.

For what turned out to be the first and last time, Reisman appeared together with Murphy for a formal press conference at the end of the session. In the absence of much hard news, stories were written on the contrast between the grizzled, tough old warrior Simon Reisman and the gangling, boyish, engaging Peter Murphy, thirty years his junior. Reisman lived up to his billing by bristling that 'this is not a news conference.'

Simon Reisman growls 'this is not a press conference' as he and Peter Murphy meet the press together for the first and last time at the conclusion of their first formal negotiating session. (Ottawa, 22 May 1986)

Canada and the US Go to War

Also in the absence of hard news, the media filled their pages with material that would at other times have had difficulty making the business pages. In addition to the public relations disaster of the release of twenty-six External Affairs studies replete with deletions, the continuing feud on the composition of the negotiating team, and the free-trade video with its original geography, the US administration decided to make Canada a target in its strange war of fighting protectionism with protectionism. To add insult to injury, Murphy gave no hint at the opening session of actions the United States was poised to take, despite his responsibility for Canada-US trade relations.[11]

In Washington, the president led off on 21 May by imposing a 35 per cent duty on Canadian shakes and shingles without so much as a fair warning to his friend Brian Mulroney. The prime minister reacted with rage, calling the decision 'unfair and unjustified,' adding 'actions like this make it extremely difficult for anyone, including Canadians, to be friends with the Americans.' An angry letter expressing 'profound disappointment' at an action that was 'pure protectionism, the precise thing you and I pledged, in Quebec and Washington, we would seek to avoid,' was dispatched to the president. Retaliatory measures, including a tax on imported books, tea bags, and Christmas trees, were introduced early in June.[12]

As if the tax on shingles was not enough, the US lumber lobby simultaneously filed a new countervailing duty petition, seeking a billion dollars in penalties on annual sales of four billion dollars of softwood lumber from

Canada. They had lost a similar suit in 1983 but now claimed that changed circumstances, including a recent decision by the Court of International Trade,[13] justified a new investigation. Canada's lumber barons, who had already spent over $5 million to fight the last petition, girded their loins for a new fight.

Also on 21 May, the US House of Representatives passed its version of what had become known as the 'ominous' trade bill by a whopping margin of 295 to 115, well over the two-thirds majority required to override any veto. In case there should be any illusions in Canada about the protectionist threat in Washington, the legislators offered a number of frankly protectionist solutions to America's trade problems, including a provision that would penalize Canadian resource exports by making any differential pricing practices subject to countervailing duties. Even if US lumber producers were to lose their countervail petition under the current law, they could count on a new law for a third try.

Finally, in a further display of insensitivity, Treasury Secretary James Baker told a Senate committee that he supported an increase in the value of the Canadian dollar and mused that that would be an appropriate entry fee for Canada to pay in return for its inclusion in the consultations of the G-5 group (the group of major industrialized countries that shape international monetary policy). It did not take long for Canadian commentators to decide that the United States would next demand that the Canadian dollar become part of the trade negotiations, as had already been suggested

In the House of Commons, the prime minister reacts with outrage to the barrage of punitive US trade actions that marred the opening of negotiations. (Ottawa, 23 May 1986)

by the US National Association of Manufacturers. Finance Minister Michael Wilson had to do some fancy arm-twisting to convince Baker that the Canadian dollar floated freely and did not need a boost. Baker backed down, but not before giving the opposition in Canada more ammunition.

It seemed as if the critics were right. The cost of free trade was going to be one disaster after another. Opposition cries that Canada should end the negotiations while it was ahead had more than a hollow ring. Meanwhile, the government had not yet solved the problem of provincial participation nor of how to communicate the issues effectively.

For the next three weeks, the negotiations played second fiddle to what appeared in the media to be a burgeoning trade war. While Canada's retaliatory tariff on books, Christmas trees, and tea bags created more pain in Canada than in the United States, the Americans were not happy either. Charges and countercharges and an exchange of correspondence between the president and the prime minister finally led to George Bush being dispatched to Ottawa as a symbolic gesture that the differences between the two countries were no more than a 'tiff.' After a discussion with the prime minister and his ministers and a pleasant lunch at 24 Sussex, he declared the war over.[14]

Alan King, *Ottawa Citizen*, 6 June 1986

The US government's handling of the long period between the announcement to enter into negotiations and the actual start of negotiations did not instill confidence in Canadians. An Environics survey taken during the period showed that only 27 per cent of Canadians liked the way the government was approaching the talks; 46 per cent disapproved of their handling. As disturbing was that only 40 per cent of those who supported the initiative approved of the way the federal government was handling the negotiations; 36 per cent disapproved; the rest had no opinion.[15]

From now on, the negotiations could only make things better. The May session had been billed as a preliminary get-acquainted session. The first formal meeting would take place in Washington in mid-June.

Learning Some Home Truths

Room 403 in the Winder Building on 17th Street in Washington is one of the most unprepossessing of conference rooms. Its narrow arborite table, its uncomfortable chairs, its mouldy ceiling, and its stale air unwittingly symbolized the just-another-day attitude of the US side. There was no door to a kitchen; an urn of coffee and plastic cups were the extent of any hospitality. Yesterday the Japanese, tomorrow the Europeans, today the Canadians; all are provided the same democratic and shabby treatment at the seat of world power. Room 403 would be the scene for the second session on 17-19 June and for many more to come.

The preliminaries to the meeting had been impressive. Two big issues were to be tackled: contingency protection and government procurement. The delivery was pedestrian: the Americans were not ready to address such critical matters; more time was needed for preparation. Customs procedures, the essential plumbing of any tariff agreement, and intellectual property occupied centre stage. The Americans proved to be no more ready on these marginal issues than they were on the main issues. On customs matters, further work was declared to be necessary while intellectual property, which neither side appeared to understand, was consigned to a working group with instructions that the chief negotiators should not be detained further on it until a text was ready for their consideration.

The desire to talk about customs matters rather than the tariff was occasioned by a quirk in US law. Under the fast-track procedures, the administration had no authority to consider any cuts in tariff levels until the International Trade Commission had concluded a confidential assessment of the likely impact of such tariff cuts. This study would not be ready until early 1987. Meanwhile, the US side was authorized to enter into discussion on tariff-related matters such as rules of origin, duty waivers, and remissions as well as other border-type measures such as quotas, licensing, and technical barriers. These were discussed alongside customs matters. Both sides, however, knew that the real issue for this aspect of the negotiations would be tariffs and that the sooner they could get at it, the better.

Intellectual property, that is patents, copyright, trade marks, and trade secrets, was a weighty matter for the United States.[16] Its discussion was based on the changing nature of commercial policy and broke new ground in free-trade negotiations. Specialized knowledge is one of the main building blocks for future economic growth. Barriers to access to that knowledge could, therefore, be just as detrimental to the development of advanced technology industries and modern service industries as barriers to market access. In addition, barriers to the latest, most efficient technology can have an impact on the competitiveness of potential users in the resource processing and traditional manufacturing industries.

Most countries grant exclusive intellectual property rights to individuals and companies with the aim of stimulating creative activity. Such rights are an important legal element in many commercial transactions, including those involving international trade. The pattern and volume of goods and services moving across international frontiers are thus influenced by the ownership and use of these rights. Intellectual property rights also confer economic benefits on those who hold them. The returns to owners of intellectual property manifest themselves in many ways, from increased profits, investment, and employment to higher levels of technology. Consumers can choose from a wider and more technologically advanced range of goods and services, although sometimes at higher prices than might otherwise be the case.

Trade-related intellectual property matters thus involve issues relating to the movement of goods and services in national and international markets and to the access and use of technology. They touch on some of the most deeply rooted and least tangible aspects of society such as culture and commercial reputations, as well as on the most dynamic and future-oriented elements of the economy.

Since US citizens and corporations are collectively the largest holders of intellectual property rights in the world, the United States has a natural interest in seeking to raise the level of intellectual property protection in other countries, including Canada. Its prime targets are the newly industrialized countries which, in its view, provide little or no effective protection to intellectual property owners. The bilateral trade negotiations provided an opportunity to tackle these issues. In the area of patents, the United States had long sought resolution of its concerns with respect to compulsory licensing of pharmaceutical patents. In the copyright domain, the United States had several outstanding concerns with Canadian law, including the lack of explicitly legislated protection for computer programs, semi-conductor computer chips, and cable retransmission rights. In the trademark area, the United States wanted to have the name 'American Bourbon' protected by regulation under the Canadian Food and Drugs Act. With respect to both copyright and trademarks, the Americans sought stiffer criminal sanctions for the infringement of rights. A common legal framework governing trade secrets (confidential information held within a firm) was a further American objective. US interests, therefore, were driven both by general goals and also by specific irritants.

Canada, of course, had its own interests. Under free-trade conditions with the United States, Canada required an environment in which inventors could obtain appropriate rewards from the market place for their work. Similarly,

Canadian industry needed to be assured that knowledge and technology would flow as freely as possible within North America to underpin increased investment and production. Of immediate concern, therefore, were the following US laws and practices:

- Section 337 of the US Trade and Tariff Act of 1930 which discriminates between imported products and US products. This provision had been used primarily to deal with patent infringing imports from countries that do not provide strong court systems, but Canada had also been a casualty. Resort to Section 337 had increased sharply in the 1980s. The most frequent result from proceedings under this section had been outright prohibition of imports of allegedly infringing goods.
- Section 301 of the US Trade Act of 1974 as amended in 1984 mandated the president to take trade retaliatory action against any country not providing adequate intellectual property protection. It thus represented a continuing threat to Canadian exports and could also prejudice investment decisions away from Canadian locations.
- US Customs authorities enjoy substantial discretionary power to determine the validity of imports of goods protected by trademarks and/or copyrights. In any case other than clear counterfeit, this discretionary authority represented an uncertainty for Canadian exporters as well as potential delays in shipments while determinations are rendered. In Canada, determinations as to validity/infringement for both imported and domestic goods could only be made by the courts. In the United States, this held true only with respect to US-origin goods.

The obverse of the intellectual property issue is access to technology. Canada's interest in seeking improved access to critical and sensitive United States technology thus raised questions regarding the application of export controls. The intellectual property discussions were to be largely driven by US interests, but Canada had its own interests to pursue and was not averse to a balanced package covering intellectual property matters. At this first discussion, however, little was accomplished either in setting the agenda or organizing collective spadework.

On the steps outside the Winder Building at the end of the session, reporters tried to see if they could get better answers than they had received in Ottawa three weeks earlier. Perhaps an impertinent question or two might set off the famous Reisman temper or trap the innocent Murphy. On the way in and out on Tuesday, 17 June, Reisman had been expansive:

> I think things are going well. I think the meeting [augurs] well for the prospects of eventually getting an agreement. What I like especially is that we view the whole

enterprise not as a sort of contest between us, but as a co-operative enterprise in which we're going to try to make a bigger pie out of which both countries can benefit ... We'll be planning at these meetings for our work for the ensuing meetings in July, August and September. That will enable us to have a first run at all the issues. Where need be, we'll establish some working parties and things of that sort.[17]

But this was pretty tame stuff and obviously not vintage Reisman. On the way out on Wednesday, together with Murphy, the questioning became more pressing. What of the alleged foul and unnatural designs of the Americans on Canadian social programs and how about the autopact? When Reisman volunteered that 'social programs are not negotiable,' the *Toronto Star* reporter snapped that the question was addressed to Murphy, not Reisman. Murphy, in his engaging if offhand manner, said that Canadian social programs per se were not of interest to the United States but in areas in which they had trade effects, the US side would, of course, want to examine them as part of the negotiations. As far as the autopact was concerned, Reisman insisted that 'if it ain't broke, why fix it.' But Murphy had a better answer: 'U.S. negotiators have a right to look at the Auto Pact and if we feel it's not perfect – and I think you could make a very strong argument that there are a number of points in that agreement that could be improved – then that's what we're going to look at.'[18] The journalist had his story, the headline writer his key words, and Reisman was left fuming and pledging never again to appear jointly with Murphy.

Further Developments on the Home Front
Parallel to the preparation for this second session, there had been important domestic events. First, detailed mandates had been obtained from cabinet. In a remarkable feat of engineering, broad mandates on all the issues, save the new ones of services and investment, were brought forward by way of memoranda to cabinet and slide shows. Specific proposals on all the major issues were approved by the end of June. Reisman could fairly say that he had both his general mandate and specific cabinet direction on individual issues so that he could enter the negotiations with confidence. He had ministerial backing on the central body of the concessions he proposed to obtain and those he was prepared to give. It soon became apparent that Murphy was not similarly equipped.

The second big event had been the resolution of the issue of provincial involvement in the negotiations. The question, would the provinces have a place at the table, had a short answer: No! A welcome development at the end of the tussle on provincial participation was the notable change in the public stance of Quebec premier Robert Bourassa. From a sceptic who needed a seat at the table to protect Quebec interests before the 2 June meeting, he had become a warm supporter, ready to speak out in favour and criticize the naysayers.[19]

Also of some comfort to the government was the continued floundering of the official opposition. While the position of the NDP was clear and leader Ed Broadbent and his trade critic Steven Langdon pressed it at every opportunity, sometimes even with an excess of zeal (Broadbent was expelled from the Commons early in June for calling the prime minister a liar), the Liberals still did not know where they stood. On 16 June, Hugh Winsor confidently told readers of the *Globe and Mail* that Turner would be making an important speech to the Ottawa Board of Trade in which he would make clear that he would take a nationalist direction. Winsor had obviously been briefed by someone from the Lloyd Axworthy camp. By the time it was delivered on 19 June, Don Johnston's wing of the party had worked on a redraft. Turner's strong suit continued to be the process of negotiations, rather than their substance, on which his political instinct seemed to point in one direction, and his heart and mind in another.[20]

Throughout the summer, the pundits continued to have fun at Turner's expense. Deborah MacGregor took him to task in the *Financial Times of Canada* and wanted to know where the real John Turner was. Jamie Lamb struck a similar theme in the *Vancouver Sun*:

> Somewhere on the road to his personal Damascus, John Turner converted from economic realism to economic nationalism ... Whatever else may lie behind this creeping process of conversion, it raises one telling possibility. Turner has failed to capture the Canadian imagination on his own terms, in his own right, as his own man.[21]

Meanwhile, the Axworthy and Johnston wings of the party continued to fight it out at policy seminars across the country, each occasioning more fun for the press.

Reisman for his part continued to provide good copy for the media mob. At a session with a parliamentary committee considering his appointment, he allowed that Murphy was not as ignorant as some people might believe. He also said that Murphy had to appear tough to appease the Congress, leaving the suggestion that in private he was a marshmallow. Murphy called to complain and drew the response that, as long as he continued to talk about social programs, he should not expect much consideration from his Canadian counterpart.[22] To prove that there was more to life than trade negotiations, Reisman went to New Brunswick to go salmon fishing and regale his fellow anglers with tales of yesterday and today. Murphy's ears must have burned! Reisman came back relaxed and ready to return to the fray and take on the serious parts of the negotiations.

Mont Tremblant

The third session took place at Mont Tremblant, north of Montreal. After two sessions in the sterile settings of Ottawa and Washington, Reisman wanted to capture some of the fun and grandeur of earlier negotiations. His first choice had been the Seigniory Club at Montebello, scene of a number of sessions during the autopact negotiations, but it was booked. Reisman also had fond memories of the old lodge at Mont Tremblant and there the two teams assembled on 29-31 July. But times and attitudes had changed. The good facilities of the 1950s and 1960s no longer met the standards of the 1980s. The cabins close to the lodge, in which Reisman and Murphy were housed, were beginning to show their age. The meeting room on the second floor of the lodge was huge, the acoustics horrible, and the air conditioning non-existent. Three large and noisy fans fortunately cancelled security concerns about open windows. There was a smaller room at one end for caucus sessions. Walks in the woods were complicated by the presence of reporters with boom mikes. To compensate for the poor meeting room, however, the food and recreational facilities were excellent.

While Reisman bubbled over with optimism to the press about a wonderful meeting, about the progress being made, about being on schedule, and about the naysayers finding no comfort in events to date, there remained profound misgivings about the readiness of the US side to engage in serious negotiations. There was little sign that the Americans had done their homework or in fact were contemplating doing any. Reisman came away convinced that Murphy was not connected to anybody of consequence in Washington.

Part of the opening session was spent with Reisman and Murphy complaining to each other that somebody was not honouring the deal not to reveal the agenda of each session to the press. While the ordinary hacks who specialize in sticking mikes under people's noses had been kept in ignorance (indeed, their presence made Mont Tremblant a little less than the idyllic, peaceful setting that had been promised), the stars who were more adept at building rapport with the lesser mortals on each team seemed to have no trouble getting information. The week before, Jennifer Lewington had had a detailed background piece on the agenda for Mont Tremblant and Giles Gherson did her one better the following week with the details of agendas past and present. Over the months to come, complaints and countercomplaints over leaks would become part of the negotiating ritual.[23] Both Lewington and Gherson correctly identified the main topics for Mont

Tremblant to be contingency protection and agriculture.

For Canada, so-called contingency protection measures (anti-dumping and countervailing duties to offset unfairly priced or subsidized goods, and safeguard measures to counter surges in imports)[24] posed a growing threat to many Canadian exports and were thus at the heart of the negotiations. Canadian companies doing business in the United States found themselves increasingly compelled to hire expensive Washington law firms as their US competitors resorted to the full array of US trade remedy laws in an effort to obtain relief from foreign competition.

The United States, however, appeared to have no similar concerns. Only a small proportion of US production is ever threatened by Canadian measures whereas Canada's dependence on the US market translated into the sobering fact that up to 90 per cent of a Canadian plant's production can be so affected. Of the Canadian trade remedy laws, US producers are more concerned with anti-dumping procedures than safeguard and countervail procedures. Nevertheless, they see the possibility of an anti-dumping investigation as a normal part of doing business in Canada.

Both countries, of course, use trade remedy instruments to restrict imports from the other country. While the overall incidence of final remedies has been relatively modest, averaging less than three a year for each country since 1980, US investigations, covering a wide range of alleged offenses, averaged more than twice the rate in Canada (more than ten a year) and involved a much wider range of remedies and products. This harassment has a chilling effect on investment and can be more damaging than the final remedy. Most cases initiated by Canada involve anti-dumping procedures, which can easily be countered by a change in pricing practice.

Given the importance of the United States market for Canadian producers, the elaborate US contingency protection system can have a profound impact on Canadian government policymaking and on the business activities of Canadian exporters. The widely shared belief in the United States that the country is being victimized by its major trading partners and constrained by multilateral trade obligations which favour foreign competitors, has led to demands for greater access to foreign markets and efforts to strengthen and extend trade remedy legislation. The instruments of contingency protection are perceived as the only means available to redress the imbalance by attacking 'unfair' imports and persuading other countries to open their markets to US exports.

Canada – and the United States's other trading partners for that matter – does not share the US assessment that the United States is being victimized and inundated by a flood of unfair imports.[25] Canada, for example, does not consider its regional development policies to be either unfair or responsible for increased exports to the United States. Knowledgeable observers in the United States agree that the real problems are often very different, such as exchange rate misalignments, budget deficits, failure to adjust, or the slipping comparative advantage of basic US industries. Nevertheless, in a broadly based trade negotiation, both real and perceived problems need to be addressed.

Since the US administration and Congress shared the view that subsidy practices in Canada distort trade to the disadvantage of US economic interests, the US side sought the elimination of Canadian industrial and regional subsidy practices. The depth of US commitment to eliminating foreign subsidy practices is demonstrated both by the broad US view as to what constitutes a subsidy, e.g., Canadian forestry management practices, and also by the strong commitment of the US to countervail procedures. It is based on a somewhat naïve perception that there are no or few subsidies in the United States, either at the state or federal level. This perception has been reinforced by the fact that until 1986, no United States export had ever been subjected to countervailing duties.[26] The fact that only the United States exacts countervailing duties in any significant way is not broadly appreciated by US politicians and industrialists. Addressing contingency protection, therefore, required a discussion of US subsidy practices in order to come to a common understanding of which practices seriously distort trade and which do not, and in order to find appropriate remedies to deal with the former.[27]

In the negotiations, Canada's interest was to establish a new regime which would eliminate or reduce the scope for US industry to use US trade remedy legislation to harass Canadian competitors. Such a regime would have to provide Canadian producers with greater certainty and predictability of access to the US market. Without this security, Canadians would not be able to take full advantage of other provisions of the agreement. At the same time, such a regime would have to address and discipline genuinely unfair trade practices. For example, it would require agreement on the permissible use of domestic subsidies to achieve legitimate socioeconomic, regional, and cultural goals and to reduce or eliminate cross-border, interprovincial, and interstate competitive subsidization to attract investment. Similarly, it would have to establish agreed rules on predatory pricing and other restrictive business practices.

Developing such a regime constituted one of the biggest challenges of the negotiations. The negotiators would try to establish new and more modern standards of what are acceptable and unacceptable governmental and industry practices and what are appropriate counter-remedies. Most importantly, they would try to curb the US penchant for litigation and unilateral decision-making and replace these with mandatory consultations and, ultimately, bilateral decision-making.

At Mont Tremblant, while the United States had been persuaded that addressing Canadian objectives in contingency protection could no longer be delayed, the American attitude varied between cautious interest and stony silence. The US team listened politely to a presentation of the rationale for an agreement that would deal root and branch with the issues that give rise to trade law remedies, but appeared uninspired by the suggestion that existing trade remedies should be relegated to the dustbin of history and hostile when US subsidy practices were laid out in exquisite detail. They could not agree to set up a working group, nor could they admit anything beyond the blindingly obvious point that contingency protection would be an exceedingly difficult area to manage. Their solution to the conundrum of contingency protection was neither imaginative nor helpful: delay dealing with it until the end of the negotiations. Both sides knew that this was no more than a delaying tactic; the issue was too complex and important to be left to the end of negotiations.

Agriculture turned out to be a better discussion.[28] The US side had brought Agriculture Undersecretary Dan Amstutz to see whether these negotiations were sufficiently serious to warrant the attention of his department. While most of the talk focused on events in Geneva, Murphy and Amstutz stated that something should be possible bilaterally – such as eliminating tariffs and harmonizing standards – and neither mounted a big attack on the sensitive issue of marketing boards. The follow-up was distinctly pallid: work on technical barriers could go ahead with tariffs and the other aspects to wait.

US resolve to discipline subsidies and liberalize world trade in agriculture sounded somewhat hollow and came under strong media attack when it was learned in Washington that the administration had agreed to help a beleaguered Senate majority leader Bob Dole in his re-election campaign in Kansas by subsidizing grain sales to the Soviet Union, depressing prices of traditional Canadian sales there. To add insult to injury, they pointed the finger at Canada and said they were just evening the score for Canada's having taken advantage of the grain embargo earlier in the decade, despite the fact that Canada was a long-term and reliable supplier of grain to the Soviet Union.

The direction of the negotiations was beginning to become worrisome. The US negotiators had obviously indulged in little strategic planning. Their agenda appeared to be no more than a compilation of the ongoing bilateral irritants list supplemented by any matter raised the previous week or two by any member of Congress. There seemed to be no conceptual framework guiding their approach nor did they appear to have a clear notion of what was involved in a free-trade agreement except that at the end of the day it would have to be a big deal. They seemed to expect the Canadian side to show all its cards before giving the least indication of any readiness to negotiate seriously on issues of importance to Canada. The most optimistic view was that if Canada was prepared to yield on investment, services, procurement, subsidies, and a whole range of individual issues, the United States would be prepared to sell a deal to Congress that looked like a free-trade agreement. This could be a good deal for Canada. But the process would be a string of infinite length unless a way could be found to cut it at some point and force the US to make some concrete proposals of its own.

To provide comic relief and feed the media some innocent fluff, the two sides played a game of softball. To allay fears by the government's media handlers that a badly played game might provide the media with too much critical material, each team was composed of Yanks and Canucks. Reisman and Murphy proved good sports, taking their turns pitching and batting, each with aplomb and success, thus providing great footage to fill otherwise dead air time.

Simon and Peter play ball at Mont Tremblant, Quebec, 31 July 1987, during a break in the negotiations.

Who Is Still on Board?

In the face of setbacks at the negotiating table, it was important that the government's main body of support remain steadfast. Two polls of business taken in June and July of 1986 showed that business was still committed to the venture. A July poll of corporate leaders showed 47 per cent of CEOs supported free trade in some sectors but not others, while 51 per cent favoured the principle of unrestricted free trade. This was a turnaround from a December 1984 survey which showed 59 per cent favouring the sectoral approach. Resource sector executives tended to be stronger in their support for full free trade, while those in manufacturing and the service industries tended to favour the sectoral approach. Regardless of their vantage point, respondents were considerably more confident that they would gain from free trade than be hurt by it – 52 per cent to 19 per cent. Those polled were twice as likely to say their company would be helped rather than hurt. About half saw protectionism as a very serious threat for Canada; another 40 per cent saw it as serious; only 10 per cent were unconcerned. Should no agreement result, the CEOs were inclined to think that trade would remain unchanged; only 27 per cent saw a decline while 24 per cent predicted an increase in trade. Fully 88 per cent of those polled thought the government had done the 'right thing' in launching the talks, but there were doubts about the government's ability to forge a deal that would be best for Canada. While 59 per cent were either fully or quite confident in the government's ability, 39 per cent were not.[29]

More than 22,000 members of the Canadian Federation of Small Business were surveyed and, on a national basis, 35.4 per cent felt an agreement would have a positive effect; 32.5 per cent indicated no effect would be felt; only 13.9 per cent feared the consequences. Export-oriented industries like oil, gas, and mining were particularly keen on an agreement.[30]

Table 8

Results of CFSB poll on the attitude of small business towards free trade, spring 1986 (%)

	Canada	BC	AB	SK	MB	ON	PQ	ATL
Positive	35.4	45.4	42.7	38.7	32.5	33.2	33.2	34.2
Negative	13.9	9.2	6.4	6.0	9.4	17.1	15.2	12.1
No impact	32.5	25.5	33.1	29.1	34.2	32.2	33.8	39.8
Undecided	18.3	19.9	17.8	26.1	23.9	17.4	17.8	13.8

Source: La Presse, 10 September 1986

One effect of the trade negotiations had been to give the commercial aspects of Canada's relations with the United States increased media attention. Trade news had moved from the business section to the front page, and every trade dispute received sustained scrutiny from the media. This coverage during a period when US protectionism was ascendant took the bloom off earlier euphoria over relations with the United States and made trade disputes appear larger than they in fact were. By July 1986 Canadians felt that the trend towards closer relations with the United States, which had begun with the election of the Conservatives, was ending. A Gallup poll, taken in July 1986, showed that 41 per cent of Canadians felt the two countries were pulling apart, compared with just 17 per cent in December 1985. Only one-third of those surveyed felt that the countries were drawing closer together; one-half held this belief in December 1985.[31]

Aside from conducting negotiations, therefore, the government believed it had to communicate its agenda more effectively and inspire more confidence that it could get the job done and protect Canadian interests. Particularly frustrating was the perception that the government was mishandling the negotiations when the only public basis for that perception was not what happened at the negotiating table, but how ministers fielded the daily pounding of question period and handled the growing number of trade disputes. Neither had much to do with the conduct of the negotiations. There was not much precedent for dealing with highly technical issues in the guerilla political theatre of the House of Commons and daily press scrums. In the age of television, image and perception are everything and the media projected an image of a government frustrated in its efforts to gain the hearts and minds of Canadians.

At the beginning of July, the prime minister shuffled his cabinet. Pat Carney, the energy minister, was thrown the free-trade ball and the PM told Canadians to 'watch her run!' Her appointment elicited much favourable comment in the media and there was speculation that the government would now take a more aggressive attitude to selling free trade. Her immediate energies, however, were diverted towards resolving the dispute with the United States over Canada's softwood lumber exports.

The pundits had become more and more strident in their criticisms of the government's perceived lax attachment to free trade, and comments by Donald Macdonald to a congressional committee in August that the Canadian government appeared to be treating this major initiative like an orphan elicited even more criticism. Wrote Bill Wilson in the *Calgary Herald*: 'The decision to seek a free-trade agreement with the United States is potentially the most far-reaching policy decision taken by a Canadian government since the Second World War, yet it has been left entirely without ministerial or other political support.'[32] At a summer cabinet meeting in Saskatoon, the prime minister vowed to turn the situation around. Relaxing at a backyard barbecue for ministers and press at the home of Ray Hnatyshyn, he complained: 'We lived six months of negatives – spurious arguments, contrived situations designed to debilitate the initiative ... everybody had a real run at this because we had to wait for approval from the United States Senate.'[33]

The basic problem, however, could not be solved. It is impossible to explain the detail of negotiations in progress without compromising the negotiations or to sell an agreement that remains to be negotiated. There could thus be no real change in the government's public relations campaign. If anything, the government continued its low-profile approach to dampen expectations. In a speech at Brandon University on 16 September, the prime minister showed his frustration with both the negotiating process and the public relations impasse when he told a student audience that if he 'were a betting man, you'd have to say there's going to be no deal – the Americans are going to shoot it down' because of the hostility of protectionist forces in the US Congress.[34] There was no question of his commitment to the initiative; the frustration lay in failed efforts to control the public agenda and to demonstrate that the government was on top of the issues.

Serious Talk at Meech Lake

Right after Labour Day, negotiations resumed, beginning in the downtown boardroom of the TNO, continuing at Meech Lake in the Gatineau Hills just outside Ottawa, and terminating back at the TNO. The main items were a return engagement on intellectual property, and an introduction to services and government procurement.

The US side led off on services with a long, rambling outline of a framework agreement that would set out some general principles. To it would be added some specific binding agreements in certain sectors, such as insurance, tourism, and transportation, and, as an indication of the determination on both sides to move to freer trade in services, a services chapter in the agreement would include provisions aimed at resolving specific irritants. Murphy was careful to stress that the indication of specific sectors was purely personal and did not reflect a considered US position. Indeed, it became clear that the United States had yet to think out how principles would relate to binding arrangements on specific sectors. For example, would the principles be binding on individual sectors or constitute no more than general guidelines? Such an offhand presentation of an issue of such central importance to the US trade agenda, bilaterally and multilaterally, provoked questions about seriousness and credibility. Canadian bewilderment was accompanied by the uneasy feeling that unless there was a big deal on services, notwithstanding the apparent incapacity of the US side to imagine what it might be, let alone to negotiate it, the US side might find the whole package insufficient. Certainly US service industries were to date the biggest boosters of a comprehensive agreement.

Trade in services represented the frontier of international commercial policy in the 1980s as industrialized economies were becoming increasingly dependent on the wealth generated by service transactions.[35] As a consequence, the United States gave high priority to the negotiation of a framework of principles to cover traded services. It was thought that such a framework would establish a number of general principles analogous to those established in GATT for trade in goods, and would provide a basis for the subsequent negotiation of more specific commitments in particular service sectors such as banking, transportation, consulting, insurance, and engineering. In a bilateral context, the US interest in negotiating such a framework agreement related not only to the specific issues to be negotiated, but also to the demonstration effect such a negotiation with a major trading partner would offer for multilateral or other bilateral negotiations. All this the US side confirmed at the fourth session. But there was no indication that they had thought much beyond these general propositions. Particularly, they had not considered that Canada, a net importer of services, might have some concerns and interests of its own.

Although the United States maintained that its market was open to foreign firms and responsive to market forces, in fact many Canadian service industries were restricted in their access to a variety of US markets. These restrictions ranged from problems related to professional accreditation, difficulty in obtaining short-term work permits, the ban on the sale of foreign commodity options, regional interstate banking compacts, restrictive access to US government procurement, and restrictions governing maritime and air cabotage trade. The impact of these measures varied, but in many cases they affected the ability of Canadian firms to compete and to gain the benefits of economies of scale. In addition to the redirection of investment which might occur as a result of these trade barriers, there were US restrictions on direct investment in specific service industries of interest to Canadian companies (such as marine transport and telecommunications).

The issue, however, was more than a matter of opening up service markets. It is no longer possible to talk about freer trade in goods without talking about freer trade in services because trade in services is increasingly 'co-mingled' with the production and trade of goods. Companies today rely on advanced communications systems to coordinate planning, production, and distribution of products. Computer software helps to design new products and to run the robots that produce them. Some firms engage in-house lawyers, accountants, and engineers; some have 'captive' subsidiaries to handle their insurance and finance needs. In other words, services are both inputs for the production of manufactured goods (from engineering design to data processing) and necessary complements for organizing trade (from financing and insuring the transaction to providing after-sales maintenance, especially critical for large capital goods).

The basic economic efficiency and competitiveness gains expected from the removal of barriers to trade in goods between Canada and the United States largely apply to the services sector. The key differences between trade in goods and trade in services lie in the nature of government intervention. The prime instruments favoured by governments to intervene in goods trade have been border measures to raise the price of imports competing against domestic goods. For services, the principal instruments have been domestic regulation. Usually this intervention has non-trade motivations which, for example, assure a certain standard of service, such as in medicine, or to apply stringent rules to its provision, such as in banking. It has proven to be but a short step to apply regulation in a manner to prevent or severely restrict the capacity of foreigners to provide the same service, as illustrated by asset limitations in banking.

Thus the negotiating agenda for services, but not the objective, is different from the negotiating agenda for goods. To achieve the economic gains from liberalizing trade in goods, border measures – tariffs, quotas, subsidies, trade remedy laws – occupy centre stage with the fundamental objective of expanding trade and underwriting the result through observance of the principle of non-discrimination. To achieve the same economic gains in services, the target is regulations that constitute trade barriers. In some cases, the focus is the right of establishment, such as for real estate brokers. In other cases, it will be professional standards, such as for consulting engineering. The fact that the barrier – regulations – are more differentiated according to the nature of the service than is the case for goods should not obscure the fundamental objective of expanding trade in pursuit of higher efficiency and the consequent income gains.

In principle, there should be no obstacle and every advantage to negotiating a set of rights and obligations governing trade in services based on the principle of non-discrimination. As with the elaboration of the principle of non-discrimination to goods trade in the GATT as a precondition to negotiating tariff reductions, the initial challenge would be to construct a framework of binding obligations based on non-discrimination and subsequently to negotiate the reduction of barriers in individual service sectors. This might in turn require gaining some negotiating experience applying general principles of non-discrimination to a few specific sectors.

Negotiating general rules for trade in services would be a trail-blazing effort and could lay the foundation for further work multilaterally. Because it would be pioneering, however, expectations were modest. From the outset, it had been clear that negotiating one set of rules covering all service sectors would be an ambitious project. Efforts, therefore, would concentrate on achieving an agreement on general principles and their application to a number of discrete sectors as a basis for more far-reaching negotiations at a later stage. Even such a modest result would constitute a major step towards open and competitive trade in services between the two countries. Given the fact that trade in services was an important part of the US trade agenda, Canada was prepared to let the United States take the lead. It was a disappointment, therefore, to see that the initial US position did not match the promise of early rhetoric. It would take some effort to keep Canada's more developed thinking in check and give the Americans a chance to catch up.

Murphy's suggestion that services be sent to a working group provoked Reisman to assault Murphy on his unwillingness to establish a working group on contingency protection. A group on services without one on contingency protection would make things very difficult for Reisman. Ministers might even cut his pay.

The next morning, the fearless negotiators decamped for Willson House at Meech Lake. The scene was breathtaking with the first autumn colours reflecting in the blue waters of the lake and the special softness of Indian summer creeping languidly in the air. There were lots of walks in the woods with the cameras of the ever-present horde of journalists poking out from behind trees.

The morning began with a confused and ill-tempered discussion on intellectual property. The principal US interest was to hammer the Canadian side on pharmaceuticals, notably the failure to deliver on the oft-made promises of ministers to provide better patent protection from the ravages of the generic drug manufacturers; the inadequacy of draft legislation; and the importance of meeting US expectations. Reisman responded with a long speech on the treatment of intellectual property within a free-trade agreement, indicating that the US appeared to approach the negotiations in this area as no more than an irritants-resolution exercise. It was again decided that the working group should continue to meet and try to devise a draft text on intellectual property.

This exchange was followed by a presentation of the Canadian proposal for a comprehensive government procurement agreement extending to all levels of government and to all goods and services, including defence. The Americans were reminded that this was a long-standing Canadian interest. The presentation laid out again the Canadian rationale for government procurement liberalization, warned of the pressures in both Canada and the United States for even more restrictive government procurement preferences, and described the principal elements of an agreement in this area, including national security provisions.

Canada had for more than a decade sought a more open US procurement system. GATT rules exempt purchases by governments for their own use from national treatment requirements. In other words, GATT allows governments to discriminate in a manner that is not tolerated for private sector transactions. This was originally not considered a major breach of GATT principles. Over the years, however, as government activity and, consequently, government purchasing, have grown, most governments have found that they can use their purchasing as a tool for industrial development or as an instrument for placating special interests or currying political support.

Efforts to introduce GATT principles to government purchasing began in the late 1960s and resulted in the 1979 GATT Procurement Agreement of which both Canada and the United States are members. This agreement opened a limited amount of government purchasing to international competition – amounting in 1984 to some $500 million of Canadian purchases and about $25 billion in the United States. The agreement does not cover all federal procurement and excludes the provinces or states, federally funded programs, set asides for small and minority businesses, crown corporations, research and development, and service contracts. The trade impact of the agreement had been, accordingly, modest. In 1984, Canadian exports to the United States under this agreement amounted to $249 million while US exports to Canada were $34 million. The GATT agreement thus provided only a modest start towards introducing the principle of non-discrimination to government purchasing. Within a free-trade area agreement, however, Canada took the view that it should be possible to go much farther and place government procurement between the partners on a fully competitive basis as far as North American suppliers were concerned. This position had been staked out by the Canadian government for more than a year as central to its market access objectives.

The US procurement market is ten times the size of the Canadian market. US government purchases in 1985 of goods and services at the federal, state, and local levels totalled approximately C$750 billion, almost twice the size of

Canada's gross national product. Defence procurement alone was valued at almost C$280 billion. By contrast, Canadian government procurement at all levels in 1985, including crown corporations, was estimated at C$75 billion. Few of these procurements, however, benefited from non-discriminatory or fully competitive procedures. Canadian companies, for example, enjoyed fully competitive access to less than 5 per cent of the US market and were confident that, under more open conditions, they could successfully compete for more.

Opening the US procurement market would constitute an important gain in new market access for Canadian producers and could stimulate investment and rationalization to achieve economies of scale and specialization. The elimination of Canadian preferences which induce small-scale, high-cost manufacturing for the Canadian procurement market would force restructuring to a more competitive base. For governments and crown corporations, more competitive purchasing policies would achieve significant savings in overall procurement costs – up to $500 million annually in federal spending alone.

There was abundant evidence of the negative impact these restrictions had on Canadian firms. The 'Buy America' rider on federally funded state procurement, for example, had disposed manufacturers like Bombardier to establish manufacturing or assembly facilities in the United States (in the case of Bombardier, in Vermont). Exports of cement and steel for federally financed roads and bridges were virtually blocked. Set asides were arbitrarily administered. After obtaining a contract for hospital beds, an Ontario company retooled its plant to meet subsequent orders only to have the next order 'set aside' for US small business. Canadian textile and clothing and food industries were shut out of the lucrative US military market. A New Brunswick firm had a subcontract from a US naval yard cancelled because of the prohibition on foreign content in US naval vessels.

Any concessions in this area, of course, needed to be reciprocal. The United States would seek fully competitive access to Canadian federal and provincial procurements, including to crown corporations and funded programs, and would ask for an end to the Canadian practice of seeking offsets in the award of major purchases. Given relative market size, however, the United States would not regard access to Canadian government procurement alone as compensating for similar access to US procurement and would expect Canadian concessions in other areas. US procurement barriers, particularly those restricting access to defence programs, play a major role in stimulating US industrial and regional development, and the United States would be reluctant to forgo the political and economic advantages its programs offered without compensating benefits.

The negotiation on government procurement was one of the major areas involving provincial jurisdiction and hence an important challenge for fed-eral-provincial cooperation. Provincial procurement, including by provincial crown corporations, amounted to over 40 per cent of the total Canadian public sector market in 1985. Some provinces attach considerable importance to procurement preferences as an instrument for promoting industrial development and employment. The instruments employed are similar to those used by the federal government: limited bidding opportunities, restricted source lists, directed procurement, and premiums for Canadian or provincial content. Provincial crown corporations are the single largest pur-chasers in the Canadian public sector, with purchases concentrated in heavy electrical, telecommunications, and urban transit equipment. Some provin-cial crown corporations give preference to local suppliers; in some instances, major procurements are directed to provincial sources.

In market access terms, Ontario and Quebec firms would enjoy significant benefits from new access to the US procurement market, but would also bear the brunt of additional US competition. In relative terms, it was the Atlantic region which depended most upon Canadian government purchasing poli-cies including offsets. Opening provincial markets for US competition would be a highly sensitive issue since procurement preferences are perceived as one of the few economic development tools available to the provincial governments. But negotiations with the US could also be an important catalyst for the removal of interprovincial procurement barriers. While there was a growing consensus among provinces that such barriers should be eliminated, the linkage with the trade negotiations required sensitive management.[36]

From Canada's perspective, a comprehensive government procurement agreement would require the override or amendment of all relevant US fed-eral and state procurement legislation, including federally funded programs; the extension of the 'Buy America' provisions to Canadian goods and ser-vices; the extension of set-aside programs for small business to Canadian businesses under the same conditions as defined in US law; the exemption of Canadian goods from import prohibitions; an agreement to accord to quali-fied Canadian firms the same access as US firms in respect to national security restrictions and export licensing requirements; and a new deal on defence procurement to give Canadian firms full access to compete for US defence purchases. Furthermore, a comprehensive procurement agreement would have two critical operating features: a high degree of transparency in all phases of the bidding system, and effective provisions to allow bidders alleg-ing a breach of the agreement to protest contract awards and obtain redress.

All this was set out in the initial Canadian presentation at Meech Lake. It was a stark contrast to the US presentation of the previous day on services and required a substantive response. Murphy confined his initial remarks to some rather technical observations, such as that any deal would have to be strictly bilateral and that a working group should be set up. After lunch and more walks in the woods, the temperature heated up.

Murphy led off with the blindingly obvious: given the ten to one market disparity, any broad deal would be extremely hard to sell since the benefits would be perceived to be overwhelmingly on the Canadian side. This remark was a red flag to the bull and Reisman came charging out, head down, horns pointed menacingly at Murphy and foot pawing the ground. In the voice he uses for innocents mouthing nonsense, he bellowed that he was confident that should idiotic ideas be put out, reasoned argument would quickly put them to rest. Of course, if that were not the case, maybe procurement should not be discussed at all. He should take it off the table. Or maybe he should go for a deal confined to the federal governments and to civilian purchases only.

In face of this charge, Murphy backed away somewhat. He was not rejecting anything. Nothing should be rejected at this stage. He found the Canadian proposal interesting, even appealing. All he was doing was telling the truth. This would be a hard sell and he wanted Reisman to know the reality. After some further exchanges which in increasingly acrimonious terms repeated the same arguments, Reisman proposed a recess and a very sober Canadian group retired to the upper room to consider strategy.

There was consensus on the Canadian side that the ten to one argument applied to the whole of the negotiations. The US economy is more than ten times the size of the Canadian economy. As a consequence, Canadian producers would gain access to a market ten times the size of their own but at the same time face ten times as many competitors. If this issue was not settled, it could well be asked whether the US side was serious about a big deal, its protestations notwithstanding. Murphy should be tested with a proposal that a procurement working group be established with a mandate to negotiate a national treatment agreement. No one suggested that Murphy's bluff be called at this meeting.

The Canadian side filed back into the room and discussion quickly concluded with a decision to strike a working group. Reisman did not press on the mandate. To the press, Reisman reported progress. Seven of the nine major issues had been addressed and so far no obstacle had been discovered that would prevent an agreement.

This optimistic tone stirred a response from Murphy the following morning. He did not detect any progress. On the contrary, the Canadian side had made no serious proposal to date to meet US interests. These observations provoked Reisman into a repeat of the previous day's discussion on procurement. When would the US be ready to negotiate? What did they intend to negotiate? What did they mean by a big deal?

When the dust settled, the discussions moved on to a desultory consideration of telecommunications and energy. On the former, the US side made a pitch that the relationship between Bell Canada and Northern Telecom was privileged and constituted denial of access to US suppliers. This allegation was rejected but it was agreed that any issues which arose in telecommunications could be addressed in the government procurement group. It was generally agreed on the Canadian side that the Americans were engaging in issue management and wanted to be able to reassure domestic interests that their concerns had been raised.

Reisman had by now mastered the art of dealing with the media mob. Coming in and out of negotiating sessions, he would utter sufficient inanities to keep them satisfied. The transcript for one of these scrums at Meech Lake ran to seven pages, another to five. He was living up to his reputation, captured nowhere better than by Dalton Camp: 'There are those who say that when the good Lord installed Reisman's tongue, He had in mind providing the world with its first example of perpetual motion.'[37]

Mopping Up

The final exploratory session took place in Washington on 27-8 September. It was billed as the conclusion of the first phase and a large number of unconnected items were addressed: autos, fisheries, general state and provincial barriers, and customs issues.

Investment was addressed for the first time.[38] Murphy laid out in general terms US investment objectives covering performance requirements, national treatment, right of establishment, repatriation of profits, and more. Reisman recalled that in the exchange of letters between the prime minister and the president launching these negotiations, there had been no mention of investment and, accordingly, he had no mandate to negotiate on investment (apart from TRIMs – trade-related investment measures). If the United States wanted to negotiate on this matter, a formal proposal to Canada at the appropriate political level should be made. The US side should be aware, however, that investment would be an extremely sensitive area. Canada had never before accepted any binding obligations on investment policy. Such obligations could only be contemplated in the context of a comprehensive agreement that accommodated Canada's fundamental interests, and negotiations to this end would need to be fully engaged before Reisman would be prepared to raise the issue with cabinet to determine what kind of negotiating mandate might be granted.[39]

The conclusion of this fifth session was largely devoted to process. Eight working groups were confirmed: intellectual property, customs and related matters, government procurement, subsidies and related issues, agricultural subsidies, agricultural technical barriers, services, and miscellaneous non-tariff barriers. In addition, two fact-finding groups were established on energy and automotive trade. The mandate of these groups was to explore the possibility of negotiating issues in these areas and report to a plenary negotiating session how they should be treated.

The mandate of the working groups was, in the Canadian view, to negotiate the details of an agreement for each of these areas, seeking additional instructions from a plenary session as necessary. At the first meeting of some of the groups, however, it became evident that in the US view, the mandate was restricted to exchanges of information as a basis for negotiations and was well short of any commitment to negotiate. It remained unclear whether the US position was a tactical manoeuvre or hid a more fundamental strategic view: the Americans were wary of Canadian ambition and wished to reduce their appetite before engaging seriously on any issue. Pessimists remained convinced that the American side had neither the mandate nor the resources to negotiate a substantive agreement. To date they had shown no understanding of the difference between negotiating a comprehensive free-trade agreement and resolving irritants. On that unsure note, the summer of innocence had come to an end. The two sides would now take stock and see where the negotiations were headed.

9

THE FALL OF IMPATIENCE

It will be a long and arduous negotiation, but one that may have a potential of having more to say about the United States trading relationship generally than any single thing that has happened or will happen in this century. [A trade agreement with Canada] truly has historic potential. We can essentially open the doors between Canada and the United States. The economic benefits of that are just awesome to contemplate as we move into the next century.

– Clayton Yeutter

Rain on the Parade

In the run-up to the negotiations, it had been claimed that their launch would dampen protectionist pressures in the United States explicitly directed against Canada. This turned out to be naïve. While the main objective was clearly and unambiguously shared – a new Canada-United States trade agreement – the process of negotiating an agreement would contain pressures for restrictive action by the United States which would require adroit handling by both sides.

That the optimistic hope of dampening protectionist pressure in the United States might be dashed was not totally unexpected. That it happened so suddenly and brutally was a surprise. The denouement of the ten to ten Senate decision to permit negotiations to proceed was not a good sign. Many in the media believed that the president had bought negotiating authority at Canada's expense. Letters from the president to key senators promising early action on lumber and giving assurances that the full rigour of US trade remedy laws would remain unimpaired lent substance to the pessimists' worries. Equally, the flurry of protectionist actions at the end of May seemed timed to coincide with the opening of negotiations to prove that the United States was going to be a tough partner.

By mid-summer, the accumulating straws in the wind suggesting that the negotiations were beginning to stagger could no longer be ignored. The softwood lumber issue presented real hazards. A bad result on lumber could well generate enormous pressures on the whole exercise as the resources of the Canadian government were irrevocably committed to saving the industry. If that effort failed, courage for the bigger deal could well flag. Even a victory could be a Pyrrhic one if the Americans made their first priority vis-à-vis Canada the reduction of Canadian lumber sales and found other means if the countervailing duty petition failed. Increasingly Pat Carney, appointed trade minister in July in order to give the negotiations a more prominent and positive public profile, found her energies being sapped by the complications of softwood lumber.

Lumber trade between Canada and the United States has always created friction. Canada's abundance of lumber and other forestry products has resulted in a considerable volume of exports. Until the growth in auto trade, forestry products were Canada's largest export to the United States. In the 1980s, they had been growing prodigiously, particularly from British Columbia. A diminishing resource in the US Northwest combined with rising costs and a lower valued dollar had made Canadian lumber competitive anywhere in the United States. By the mid-1980s, Canadians held more than 30 per cent of the US market.

US lumber interests did not take this invasion with equanimity. They fought back, using every device US trade law put at their disposal, as well as fierce lobbying on Capitol Hill for new laws. While Japanese exports might be a more familiar bogey for most Americans, for members of Congress from lumber states, Canadian lumber exports were responsible for the economic downturn facing many of their constituents. In 1983, the Canadian industry had narrowly escaped a countervailing duty. In 1986 the US industry tried again. The issue was Canadian stumpage practice, which the US industry and its supporters in Congress condemned as a blatant subsidy. In the United States, most lumber is cut on private lands and cutting rights are sold at auction. In Canada, most lumber is cut on public lands and the cutting rights are made available on the basis of complicated formulas. In the late 1970s, US lumber interests had bid high and in the 1980s found themselves competing with a more efficient Canadian industry that had access to more, if less desirable resources which, due to the different Canadian stumpage practice, cost a fraction of what US producers were paying. They demanded that the US government impose a duty to offset the advantage of the lower cost resource.

Normally, such battles between foreign and domestic producers are relegated to the business pages of the daily press, even though the stakes are sometimes enormous. During the period 1981-3, when the issues had been as fierce and significant as they were in 1986, there were no front-page headlines in Canada. Due to the interest in Canada-US trade relations generated by the negotiations, however, the issue became not only front-page news, but also a test of the Canadian government's ability to deal with the United States. An added complication for Pat Carney was that as senior minister for British Columbia she needed to demonstrate that a Conservative government could deliver for her part of the country. While any trade minister would have devoted considerable energy to the issue, for Pat Carney the issue assumed monumental proportions. At times in the fall, it appeared that there was no other issue.[1]

The second straw was the US unreadiness, unwillingness, or inability to engage in substantive negotiations. The US protested that they could not be seen to be discussing Canadian objectives in limiting contingency protection or in opening up government procurement markets given the supercharged, protectionist atmosphere in the Congress. This US reluctance was clearly a transparent excuse for the absence of a plan and the failure to articulate objectives. By mid-July, the specialized business press had picked this up:

> Washington has been exasperatingly slow to get its act together, including stating the U.S. position. Ambassador Murphy has given every impression of mostly relying on a lengthy shopping list of allegedly unfair Canadian trade practices that Congress wants ended. Lacking a broader vision of the community of interest that stands to benefit from lower Canada-U.S. trade barriers and clearer rules for settling trade disputes – what Reisman calls 'making a bigger pie' – Murphy's approach has been disquietingly adversarial and narrow.[2]

One well-connected Washington trade lawyer and former official was quoted as saying that 'at the moment, I'm not very optimistic about the negotiations. The resources being devoted to them by the administration in terms of numbers of people and top-level attention just don't seem adequate.'[3]

Within the administration, trade had assumed a new importance in 1986. Where once Commerce vied with USTR for the spotlight, new actors had now taken centre stage. The creation of the cabinet-level economic policy council with jurisdiction over trade enabled the White House – notably Chief of Staff Donald Regan, who had retreated from the hands-off approach to trade he had advocated as treasury secretary – to manage trade issues. Many observers had concluded that USTR Clayton Yeutter did not enjoy the influence of his predecessor. Treasury Secretary James Baker played a key role as chair of the economic policy council. Other heavyweights included Commerce Secretary Malcolm Baldrige, Secretary of State George Shultz, Labor Secretary Bill Brock and Baker's deputy, Richard Darman. But there was no indication where these people wanted to go. According to a former USTR official:

There is no centre of gravity in the Reagan Administration in the conduct of foreign economic policy. To the extent the White House and the President have gotten involved, it has been with a view toward short-term management of political problems – a once-over lightly so we can get over the next 60 days. As a result this pudding has no theme.[4]

Canada had proposed negotiations in September 1985 against the background of a consistent and long-standing message from the administration that the United States wanted to negotiate a new trade agreement. Canada had, from the start, a clear view of what it wanted to achieve. The prime minister, ministers, many senior officials, and the negotiators agreed that Canada would benefit from a far-reaching agreement. The political will to pursue such an agreement was there. A plan for the conduct of the negotiations had been developed. The same did not appear to be true in the United States. The administration had insisted that it could sell a balanced trade agreement to the Congress. Senior members of the Congress generally echoed the administration in indicating that they would welcome a Canada-United States trade agreement. They considered that, notwithstanding the strength of protectionist forces in the United States, an agreement that could be seen to convey real commercial benefits to US industry would be accepted by the Congress.

But over the first few months of negotiations, confidence in the capacity of the administration to manage US trade policy and work constructively with the Congress to that end had been substantially eroded. The near failure of the administration to obtain fast-track authority, the shakes and shingles decision, the softwood lumber investigation, the House trade bill, the relentless hammering of the Japanese and the Europeans, and failed attempts to get the multilateral trade negotiations started, among other problems, were all clear signs that protectionist forces were driving US trade policy and were being only feebly resisted by the administration. The imminence of congressional elections and the prospect that the Republicans could lose control of the Senate virtually paralyzed US trade policy except when it pandered to protectionism. Whatever the results of the elections, there was nothing to suggest that protectionist forces would falter or that the capacity or readiness of the administration to take risks for a Canada-US trade agreement would be significantly strengthened.

In the bilateral negotiations with Canada, USTR was responsible for the day-to-day operations, with key staff support supplied by Commerce, State, and Treasury. But USTR was a small agency with a small staff and even smaller budget, and there was growing evidence that it was having trouble juggling its many responsibilities, including a new round of global trade talks, bilateral negotiations with Canada and Mexico, a trade war with Europe, textile negotiations with the LDCs, and Japan-bashing, all the while keeping an eye on Congress and its penchant for ever more protectionist legislation. The influential *National Journal* charged that

> there are too many pots on the trade policy front burners, not enough chefs and no coherent menu ... USTR is understaffed and overworked ... The demands of the growing number of items on the trade agenda have cut into planning and liaison work with Congress and the business community. And Yeutter's lack of political clout, trade experts maintain, has hampered the formulation of a coherent trade policy.[5]

Peter Murphy was an integral part of the USTR staff, reporting directly to Clayton Yeutter, with only Deputy USTRs Mike Smith and Alan Woods senior to him. He had been appointed to head a negotiation that appeared to be increasingly peripheral to the main players in Washington. To date, he had received only the thinnest of resources, as compared to the bottomless pit in Canada. Congress appeared to be hostile. Without the active support and interest of cabinet-level officials, Murphy had to rely on his instincts. A natural lone wolf, his inclination was to divine what might prove acceptable to Congress, but to do so initially at a distance. His strategy appeared to be one of playing out the string. He would see what Canada was prepared to offer and at the last possible moment take this to Congress and see what they were prepared to pay in return. Meanwhile, he would make as few promises as possible. In this approach, he had the natural support of his team members. All jealous of their prerogatives, they saw no advantage for themselves or their agencies in a big deal, but they could see some advantage in solving long-standing irritants. Thus the US strategy appeared to be forged not of design or vision but of default and absence of leadership.

The results of the Punta del Este Conference in September 1986, which launched an eighth round of GATT multilateral trade negotiations, offered scant comfort. While failure was averted by narrow margins the compromises reached to secure the launch were so paper thin that the prospects of an early and substantive engagement on the major issues in Geneva were also rated to be slim. The Canada-US negotiators could take little comfort from the vision and leadership offered by the United States in Uruguay. Traditional US leadership of the multilateral trade agenda appeared to have foundered. Murphy was not unique.

For Canada, the key objectives of the bilateral negotiations were to serve domestic economic interests by achieving secure and unimpeded access to the US market through a new approach to contingency protection measures and free access to US government procurement markets. For the United States, the key objectives were to serve global economic interests by achieving national treatment for investment, a new regime for intellectual property protection, and stringent disciplines on Canadian subsidy practices. There were also common interests, including trade in services, some improvements in the conditions of agriculture trade, the elimination of tariffs, and a binding international agreement to encompass the results of the negotiations.

There were both unique and shared constraints. On the Canadian side, the principal constraints were the need to ensure policy room for culture-related measures and regional development programs. Any issues perceived to touch Canadian sovereignty would also remain sensitive items. On the US side, a protectionist Congress, determined to reduce access to the US market and distrustful of the administration, was perceived as a serious constraint to any agreement. In addition, the US team would have a hard sell in persuading its constituencies that given the disparities in relative market size, a free-trade agreement would not be overwhelmingly to Canada's advantage.

Despite these constraints, both sides had expressed confidence that there could be Canadian and US concessions in all areas of the negotiations if they made sound economic sense. Only the Canadian side, however, had a clear vision of how the various parts fitted together. Canada's secure and free access objectives in the US market could not be paid for by giving reciprocal access to the Canadian market, one-tenth the size of the US market. US objectives regarding Canadian investment, services, subsidy, and intellectual property practices and policies were considerably greater than Canada's interests in US practices and policies in these areas. But none of these areas provided, individually, the scope for a self-balancing package.

Strategically, the challenge was to negotiate an overall package acceptable to both Canada and the United States. Tactically, the challenge on the Canadian side was to deploy negotiating positions in a manner that would extract maximum value for each accommodation Canada was prepared to make to US interests. The timetable imposed by the legislative requirements of the US fast-track authority meant that the president had to notify his intention to sign an agreement with Canada no later than the beginning of October 1987. Since Congress would demand to be consulted before the president signified his intention to enter into an agreement, the two sides had concluded that the negotiations had, for all practical purposes, to be finished in all their essentials by late-summer of 1987 at the latest.

The third summit meeting between the prime minister and the president, scheduled for April 1987, had particular importance in light of this timetable. The summit would generate expectations that a clear signal would be given on the prospects of arriving at an agreement. The first summit had launched the initiative; the second had laid the basis for starting negotiations by reminding the president of his commitments, which he in turn used to gain fast-track authority. Some weeks before the third summit, it would be necessary to delineate the areas that were obstacles so that attempts could be made to find solutions. If the judgment was that an agreement satisfactory to both parties could not be concluded, it would be of the highest importance to lay the ground for a successful and constructive disengagement.

'Hear somethin'? . . . No, I didn't hear somethin' . . . Why, did YOU hear somethin', Simon?'

Review

With these solemn considerations to cheer their deliberations, the Canadian team set aside October for sober stock-taking. Reisman presided over two lengthy sessions of the TNO trade policy committee, convened to reach a collective judgment on the progress achieved and the steps ahead. Some care went into the shaping of the agenda. It sought to provide a general impression of the stage that had been reached, an assessment of where the two sides stood on the full range of issues being negotiated, and a prognosis of where the negotiations were headed.

Reisman led off by declaring that he intended to listen and on that basis determine whether his views were the same as those of others. If not, one side would have to adjust. He would, however, say one thing: although he had declared publicly that the first round of negotiations had now been concluded, the negotiations were in fact still at a very early stage. He would not be satisfied that the first stage had been concluded until he could determine what were Murphy's terms of reference and who was in charge of the US negotiating effort. While he, Reisman, had a fairly complete mandate from cabinet, Murphy seemed to be on his own. Canada had laid out in some detail Canadian interests and objectives but, in contrast, had learned very little about US interests and objectives. This meant that Murphy was either on a very long leash or on no leash at all. The best guess was that his instructions envisaged a large agreement but one which would not cause problems for the administration in the Congress. Clearly, in the initial sessions, Murphy had been concerned, no doubt excessively, by the congressional elections and had been anxious to avoid any impression that he was negotiating changes to trade remedy law or any other sensitive subject.

Reisman then declared that the principal Canadian objectives were contingency protection, government procurement, and the tariff, in that order, and progress on each was reviewed.

On contingency protection, the message to the United States had been crystal clear: this was a deal-breaker for Canada. The US side had acknowledged the importance of the issue to Canada but believed that this had been overstated. The US Department of Commerce's position was particularly derisory – if Canada wished to avoid trade remedies, it should cease engaging in unfair trade practices. More seriously, it was evident that Congress was taking aim at foreign trade practices and intended a major tightening up of trade remedy laws. Negotiating a significant deal in contingency protection would therefore be extremely difficult.

Canadian objectives were to maximize constraints on US contingency protection laws. That meant shifting the focus of remedies to deal with fair and unfair disruptive trade away from trade restrictive measures. The key to the US interest was discipline on real and perceived Canadian subsidy practices. This would imply an end to direct industrial subsidies and disciplines on other types. It would be necessary to work out lists of acceptable and unacceptable practices and provide for a dispute settlement mechanism to resolve questions of interpretation.

As to Murphy's game plan on contingency protection, there appeared to be three possibilities. One was that the US side did not know what might be possible and was waiting for further elaboration of Canada's ideas. A second was that they knew that nothing or very little was possible and would wait until the maximum possible had been extracted from Canada. The third was that they had a plan but were uncertain how it would fly in Congress. Until the Americans actually engaged on contingency protection, the Canadian team could do little more than speculate.

On government procurement, the readiness of the US side to envisage an agreement of any type could not be determined. The main US procurement trade interests were with Europe and Japan. If the Americans felt that market disparity was a serious obstacle to a big deal in a bilateral agreement, they would be led to an entity by entity approach such as that which underpinned the GATT Procurement Code. The prospects of doing a deal that would seriously open up government procurement trade by that approach were minimal.

In circumstances in which the United States did not appear to have a real interest in improving access to the Canadian government procurement market, the fate of the procurement negotiations lay elsewhere. If the agreement broke the back of the contingency protection issue, the difficult decisions required by politicians on both sides for such an arrangement would make procurement seem easy. If there were no such deal on contingency protection, it was unlikely that there could be significant results on government procurement either.

On tariffs and customs matters, while most of the issues had been engaged, the United States was precluded from commencing tariff negotiations pending receipt of a report from the International Trade Commission at the end of the year analyzing the likely impact of tariff elimination. The main issues were rules of origin and tariff-related matters concerning duty drawback and remissions. Without opening tariff negotiations themselves, however, discussions on customs matters were limited to technical considerations.

Agriculture presented three sets of issues: MTN-related matters such as trade in grains on which little progress in the bilateral negotiations could be expected; market access issues including tariffs and supply management schemes; and technical barriers to trade. The United States had made it clear that domestic programs such as those for dairy and sugar would not be open for discussion. They were prepared to talk about tariff elimination and would be very interested in obtaining concessions from Canada on wine and beer. The Canadian interest was a big deal, and if big enough, Reisman was even prepared to make the case that ministers should consider some changes in supply management on which a range of possibilities could be examined – a long phase-out, adjustments, prohibiting trade-distorting subsidies on cross-border trade, and ensuring that agriculture was covered by the contingency protection deal. It was already clear at this stage that the possibility of anything big on agriculture was remote. This was not unexpected. The agriculture sector had a long track record of resistance to trade liberalization. Additionally, with the Meech Lake meeting of the Cairns Group – a group of fourteen like-minded agricultural exporters seeking to develop a common approach to agriculture in the multilateral negotiations which had met in Ottawa in September to plot GATT strategies – emphasis had begun to shift to Geneva as the more likely venue for any breakthrough in agriculture.

Intellectual property discussions had begun to move towards developing specific rights and obligations for incorporation into a trade agreement. This approach would, in the Canadian view, focus on market access issues, national treatment on enforcement, elimination of trade restrictions as a remedy, and enhancement of the balance between exclusive rights and competition. On the US side, the emphasis was more on rewards to inventors, increasing the level of protection for rights holders, and improvement of cooperation in enforcement, including third-country enforcement on, for example, counterfeit goods.

Services discussions were concentrating on the three-part approach proposed by the United States: a framework, sectoral agreements, and resolution of specific irritants. There was much groundwork to be done, for example, on the choice of sectors, and not much sign that the US side had any clear idea of the implications of its proposal or how to proceed with it. The appropriate forum for treating financial services and their relationship to an overall free-trade agreement was the subject of sharp interagency disagreement, with the Treasury continuing to insist that negotiations in this area should be separate from the free-trade agreement. This was a US problem so long as it was understood that for Canada, agreements on financial services would be part of the overall package for which appropriate payment would be made by the United States.

Discussions on miscellaneous non-tariff barriers such as licensing requirements, trade in alcoholic beverages, the restrictive maritime regulations in the United States Jones Act, standards, exceptions, and extraterritoriality had yet to begin. No one, however, expected these to present any real difficulty or any major opportunities.

Investment loomed large as the deal breaker for the United States. But it was the collective judgment of the Canadian team that ministers would not be willing to engage this issue until it could be said that negotiations on contingency protection had seriously begun and were making real progress. Some weeks would go by before this determination could be made.

These were sobering conclusions. To some at the TNO failure seemed preordained. Others, however, especially those with previous trade negotiating experience, felt that the negotiations were about to turn the corner. Nothing happens until something has to happen. They were convinced that the period of drift would soon be over. There would need to be either engagement or disengagement, and the moment of decision would shortly be at hand. Only time would tell whether the pessimists or the optimists were the realists.

Developments on the Domestic Front

It had now been more than a year since the Canadian government had formally sought negotiations with the United States. To date, it had very little to show for them except for some new protectionist actions. While this may have bolstered the argument that an agreement was necessary, critics countered that all that the government had done was make Canada more visible in Washington, the result of which was more protectionist trade actions. The instinct to soft-pedal the negotiations thus continued. The 1 October 1986 throne speech contained only muted reference to the negotiations – the government, it said, would seek to secure a 'mutually advantageous trade agreement' with the United States. In the throne speech debate, government members appeared to put the emphasis on the GATT negotiations and on opening new trade links with Japan and the Pacific Rim.

US actions on trade continued to affect directly Canadian trade. Before the Congress adjourned to prepare for the 4 November mid-term elections, it passed a number of measures including a .22 per cent customs' user levy on all imports to the United States (expected to cost Canadian exporters about $200 million annually) and a 3.5 per cent surtax on imported crude oil, product, and liquid petroleum gases to help finance the $9.5 billion, five-year Superfund to clean up the environment. As the biggest source of US energy imports – 720,000 barrels of oil per day – Canadian producers would bear the largest share of the surtax. But the biggest blow came not from Congress but from the administration. On 16 October, the US International Trade Administration in the Department of Commerce assessed a 15 per cent preliminary countervailing duty on imports of Canadian softwood lumber. The decision was not unexpected but the media and the opposition had made it a litmus test of US good faith in the negotiations. Small matter that the other two decisions were very much a breach of the declarations made at Quebec (and Punta del Este) on the importance of free and unimpaired trade; for Canadians the softwood lumber issue had come to characterize the state of the free-trade negotiations.

The efforts to reach a negotiated settlement by seeking a postponement of the US announcement and then by presenting a compromise were fully covered by the media. When this attempt failed, the opposition made full use of this fact to cast into doubt the government's handling not just of this issue but of the free-trade talks as well. Their attack was aided by the contrived and strained nature of the American decision to determine stumpage practices to be a subsidy. In the 1983 decision it had found exactly the opposite. It raised further public doubts about American sincerity in the talks and the ability of Canada to get a good deal.

The government's reaction to the countervail decision was much more muted than to the shakes and shingles tariff. Appearing on PBS's *McNeil-Lehrer Newshour*, the prime minister told Americans that they, as consumers, would be the principal victims of protectionism. In the House of Commons, Pat Carney suggested that the US action was exactly the reason that Canada was seeking a free-trade agreement – to prevent such actions in the future. Speaking to the New England-Canada Business Council in Boston on 22 October, she repeated the prime minister's homily about protectionism hurting the consumer and condemned the 'use of existing rules to advance narrow interests over broader national interests.'

In what seemed to the press as a tit-for-tat move,[6] the Department of National Revenue finished its preliminary investigation of imports of US corn early in November, concluding that corn producers in the United States benefited from a wide range of subsidies and from slapping on a preliminary duty of 67 per cent. Canadian corn growers had launched their complaint the previous July in a little noticed action. The preliminary decision was noticed in Canada and in Washington. No one had ever before imposed such duties on American products and both USTR Yeutter and Agriculture Secretary Dick Lyng reacted with outrage. Apparently they felt that countervail was exclusively an American game. The professionals in Washington tried to smooth the troubled waters but, unwittingly, Canada seemed to have scored a point.

The polls continued to show a majority of Canadians favouring the trade initiative and willing to take the gamble, mindful of whatever adverse effects it might have initially on employment and Canadian independence. While support for the government declined from an election high of around 50 per cent to the low 30s, support for free trade remained about where it had been for the previous quarter century – around 55 per cent. The economy was only starting to reflect the benefits of the post-recession recovery and the solution of closer economic relations with the United States had always been more attractive when times were tough. As Canadians learned more about the issue, it was only natural that doubts would creep into the equation – and the opposition was certainly being allowed to play out the debate on its own terms. In spite of its best efforts, however, support for the idea remained strong.

Inevitably the media, especially the print side, continued to play an essen-

tially pernicious role in the debate. If headlines were all that mattered, readers would draw the conclusion that few, if any, Canadians supported free
trade. Consistently, stories took as their cue leads that emphasized the negative: support for the initiative is dwindling; the PM is untrustworthy;
Canadians would lose the most from an agreement. Conveniently buried in
the text of the stories was the fact that a majority of Canadians still supported a free-trade agreement and believed it would enhance their economic
prosperity. As negotiations continued, the gradual turnabout in the perspective of the pundits who interpret the news proved rather ominous. Columnists
and editorial writers, generally supportive at first, were becoming critical of
the initiative. While many continued to favour free trade in principle, they
had decided that this particular negotiation would not be successful.

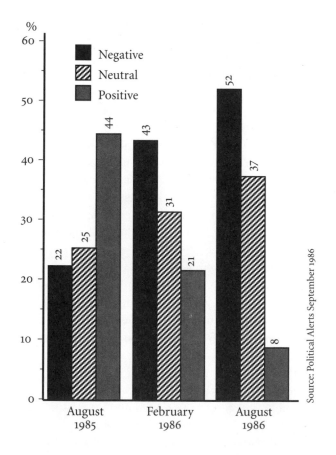

Chart 4: Free trade: Columnist and editorial opinion

Getting Tough

The Americans were called to account for their lacklustre performance at the sixth session held on 12-14 November in Ottawa. The United States had weathered the mid-term elections. The administration now faced a Democratic Senate as well as a Democratic House. As far as the negotiations were concerned, the spectre of wrongly influencing the elections could no longer be raised. It was time to take the gloves off.[7]

Alan King, *Ottawa Citizen*, 6 November 1986

Given the six-week break, all the working groups had managed to meet at least once. The one single theme to emerge was that there was no evidence that the United States had a position or was doing the homework necessary to get one. The consensus was that the negotiations appeared headed for stalemate and might soon need to be dynamited or disengaged. The key would be Murphy's readiness to agree to equip the working groups with mandates to search for solutions, rather than to establish whether or not there was an issue.

The result was a stormy session that avoided the main issue but left the negotiations in business for a few more weeks. Reisman reminded Murphy in the manner of a bank manager drawing attention to a long overdue note that he, Murphy, had continually emphasized the objective of a big deal but to date had not said what, in his view, constituted the said big deal. Canada, on the other hand, had made comprehensive proposals, had agreed to work on issues of importance to the US side like intellectual property and services, but had heard nothing in return. The Canadian side had gradually unclothed itself like an anxious maiden and was worried that it would soon be completely bared before it knew whether American intentions were honourable. The Canadian side was no longer willing to play that game. What, for example, was Murphy's mandate on contingency protection? If he had none, it would be better to go home. The two sides would part sadder but wiser and still be friends.

Yes, affirmed Murphy, the United States was interested in a big deal and a deep deal, concluded within the current fast-track authority. He did not share Yeutter's recently stated view that an extension could be obtained for the fast-track authority if negotiations were not concluded in time. Although Congress would be easier to handle, since there now seemed to be a more positive bipartisan spirit on trade, it was premature to start working out specific solutions. He was fully aware of Canadian interests on contingency protection, but what was the Canadian mandate on investment? If there was no such mandate forthcoming, both sides could go home. Throughout the meeting, Reisman and Murphy played hound and hare, stopping periodically to look into the abyss and each deciding that he liked the game after all. While this game had its entertaining moments, lesser mortals on both sides of the table were beginning to grow weary of it. Canadians and Americans alike, experienced or inexperienced, thought the time had come for Murphy to engage. Murphy, however, continued to demur.

The main outcome was a measurable step forward, at least in process. The US side agreed that the Canadian side should prepare a fleshed-out working hypothesis on government procurement for discussion at the next meeting of the working group. It was settled that the subsidies group would pursue only the subsidies issue while Murphy would undertake to negotiate contingency protection himself and would propose to Reisman at the next plenary a process for dealing with it. On services, the US tabled a draft set of principles for discussion in the working group. The energy fact-finding group reported that trade was mostly free and fair. Considerable progress had been made on both sides of the border in removing government intervention from the industry. It would be important to reflect the principle of the free play of market forces in an agreement. There was, however, a problem of export controls, and it was agreed that this problem should be considered not sectorally but horizontally.

Murphy pressed on investment, drawing the response from Reisman that the absence of investment from the president's October 1985 letter continued to make it a very difficult issue to deal with unless there was a formal proposal from the US side. He did undertake to seek such authority once he was convinced that negotiations were seriously engaged on a broad front.

Given the continuing poverty of Murphy's replies to his probing, Reisman decided to up the ante and give the media mob something to chew on. If Murphy was having trouble understanding what Reisman was getting at, perhaps he would have less trouble reading it in the press. There was also the off-chance that someone else, higher up in Washington, might get a copy of a clipping. This time, therefore, his fifteen-minute scrum contained some substance: 'I, the chief negotiator, would never recommend an agreement to the government that didn't make substantial progress – very considerable progress – in limiting and constraining the U.S. unilateral right to use these measures [contingency protection].' He even gave them the standard Peter Murphy response: 'Simon, I know where you're coming from, I know what you want, I know what you need, and we're still talking.' He also acknowledged that in return, the United States could legitimately seek to place limits on Canadian subsidy programs, including some regional development programs. Peter agreed and decided to return the favour by telling the press that Canada would have to make very meaningful concessions – 'the more progress we can make on subsidies, the more likely it will be that maybe we'll have some latitude [on countervail].'[8]

An interesting subplot running through the meeting was a duel at a distance between Reisman and NDP leader Ed Broadbent. A few days earlier, the thrust of a memorandum to cabinet on the autopact had been leaked. Broadbent had made a great play of this in the House, accusing the government of having misled the Canadian people in declaring that the autopact would not be on the negotiating table. Reisman canvassed views on how he should handle the inevitable media questions and received unanimous advice that officials always lose in public arguments with politicians. This advice was rejected; Reisman accused Broadbent of being immoral in leaking government secrets and playing into the hands of the US negotiators, called into question his integrity, and demanded that Broadbent apologize. Broadbent decided enough was enough and refrained from further public comment. The minister, for her part, was mightily annoyed and instructed Reisman not to speak further to the media. The result was that Reisman gave a twenty-minute scrum the following day.

Whatever the views of the opposition, the auto issue could not be ignored. The industry is the linchpin of Canadian manufacturing, and the trade flow between Canada and the United States is enormous. Auto workers on both sides of the border have been beneficiaries of what had been the most important bilateral deal between the two countries – the autopact. The spectacular impact of the agreement on production, employment, and consumers provided an early example of the benefits of freer trade. No wonder the future of the autopact became an early and enduring concern in the negotiations.

'If it ain't broke, don't fix it' was Reisman's reply to the worriers. But the issues in automotive trade could not be swept under the rug that easily. At a minimum, the two governments had to decide whether to leave it intact and separate, incorporate it into the new agreement, or negotiate a replacement regime. And the key public policy issue was what should be done about the safeguards attached to the autopact, i.e., the agreements with the auto companies to maintain certain minimum production levels in Canada. Under the pact, the companies were required to assemble as many cars in Canada as they sold, and the value of the materials and labour in those cars had to reach at least 60 per cent of the value of the cars they sold in Canada. If these minimum requirements were not met, the agreement provided for the application of the regular tariff of 9.2 per cent.

These conditions were established in 1965, at a time when the Canadian auto industry was small, inefficient, and disorganized and when jobs in the industry were rapidly declining. The industry hid behind a 25 per cent tariff wall. Canadian consumers paid significantly more for their cars than their US neighbours and had fewer models from which to choose.

But since then costs had fallen and efficiency had improved. In 1986, Canadian consumers paid roughly the same price as Americans and there was a wide range of models available. Both the companies and auto workers had prospered. Employment had increased tenfold. Investment had grown far beyond the minimums attached to the agreement, and the Big Three continued to invest in Canada. General Motors, for example, had invested $7 billion in Canada between 1980 and 1986; Ford had invested $2 billion over the previous decade. With the brief exception of Chrysler during its troubles in the 1981 recession, the minimum thresholds in the autopact had been exceeded every year since 1968.

With respect to the tariff, the operative assumption in the negotiations would be that all tariffs between Canada and the United States would be phased out over ten years. Could Canada seek to exclude tariffs on a third of its total trade? Could it do so without inviting American requests for exceptions in areas of interest to Canada? In petrochemicals? In forest products? In steel? Would an exemption of this size not undermine the GATT requirement to remove barriers on substantially all bilateral trade?

Reisman had a ready reply. He argued that the automotive tariff between Canada and the United States was a red herring! It was a tariff that had not been collected for over 20 years. He maintained that if production were to decline to a level that brought the safeguards into play, the government would have to scramble to find another solution. The real issue, of course, was the participation of offshore auto makers in the North American market. A substantial and increasing portion of North American automotive trade was taking place outside the autopact. It was a pressing problem with or without bilateral negotiations. The real question, therefore, was whether anything could be done through the negotiations to improve the third-country threat – or opportunity – other than the red herring of the tariff.

In 1965, most North Americans bought domestically produced cars. By 1985, about a third of the cars sold in Canada were made overseas. Even the Big Three sold cars made offshore. The negotiations were necessarily considering imports from third countries, duty remission programs, foreign trade zones, subsidies, and potential overcapacity in the auto industry and in other industries. For the auto sector, the problems of overcapacity and the challenge of new producers were caused by forces that were not contemplated in 1965 and that the autopact was not designed to address. They had led to tensions between Canada and the United States on automotive trade as the states and provinces, with the help of the federal governments, sought to attract offshore investment. These automotive trade issues had to be discussed. A fact-finding group had been established in September to prepare the ground for possible negotiations of the issue. Meanwhile, Reisman and Murphy would continue to play cat and mouse with the autopact conundrum, to the delight of the media and to the chagrin of the government.

In the succeeding weeks, the first snows of winter smothered the late autumn optimism that felt Murphy was on the verge of engaging. The results of the next series of working groups were no better than those of the first. No progress was made on contingency protection or procurement. On no subject had the US side a coherent proposal to put forward. Even on services, for which there was a US draft, there was still no evidence that the US side had thought through its implications, nor did it command any interagency support. Reisman's concern was that the negotiations had reached a crisis point much too early: the United States was not organized for this negotiation and Murphy seemed ill-equipped for the job, a problem that Canada could do little to resolve.

The Mid-Term Elections: A New Mood
Despite the shortcomings in the bilateral discussions, the trade policy scene in Washington had become more optimistic. A year earlier, despair about the US protectionist mood was widespread. Following the mid-term elections, there appeared to be a subtle shift towards a more positive attitude derived

from an assessment that there was a need to foster competitiveness rather than protectionism, that there was a need for an offensive strategy based on a better export performance rather than for a defensive strategy based on curbing imports. Related to this shift was the continuing desire of the Democrats in Congress (with the help of a sufficient number of frustrated Republicans) to outflank the administration and show that they could exert constructive leadership on the trade issue. With careful planning and execution, this was a mood Canada could exploit to its advantage in pursuing and selling a new trade agreement. Perversely, the key to success lay in using the Congress to goad the administration into devoting the necessary energy, resources, and creativity to the negotiations to carry them to a successful conclusion.

There was consensus that Senator Bentsen, the new chair of the Senate Finance Committee, would take an active interest and shepherd a trade bill through Congress. While the Senate Finance Committee would look at the House version developed during the last Congress, it was more likely to begin anew and develop a bill that would be more outward-looking and less protectionist. The major players in the committee on trade were judged to be Senators Bentsen, Bradley, and Baucus for the Democrats and Heinz and Danforth for the Republicans.

This more upbeat mood was predicated on a number of developments and sub-themes: relief that the issue of control of the Senate was history and that Congress could now tackle the trade issue with renewed and less electorally driven vigour; some comfort that the trade deficit was shrinking following three months of reduced imports and one month of increased exports; appreciation that protectionism does not build strong and lasting coalitions; and realization that the economic recovery was fragile and that the challenge was to sustain real adjustment and restructuring instead of protection.

On 9 December, Senator Bentsen, accompanied by Senators Baucus, Matsunaga, and Chafee visited Ottawa at the initiative of Trade Minister Carney. There had been great consternation that such a visit had been organized without consulting the Trade Negotiations Office, followed by prognostications that the visit would be a disaster. Pat Carney was determined to demonstrate that she was in charge of the agenda and had a contribution to make. The visit proved a resounding success, surpassing the wildest expectations both publicly and privately. Bentsen demonstrated that he was a consummate statesman. He declared that the administration had to put the necessary resources behind the negotiations and that, on contingency protection, he was prepared to contemplate negotiations that resulted in new disciplines and a separate regime. Murphy had been outflanked. Public diplomacy and political discussions appeared to hold more promise than the stalled discussions between the negotiators. If they continued to stall, a new direction had become clear.

The proof for all this renewed optimism would be the next plenary to be held in Washington in mid-December. The agenda showed promise: contingency protection, government procurement, services, and dispute settlement as well as a review of progress in other working groups. An examination of the mandates for each of the working groups convinced the Canadian side that with the exception of services, where the mandate was to explore, and of investment, where there was no mandate, the Canadian side was fully equipped to negotiate. It remained to be seen whether the US side was ready to come similarly equipped.

Christmas Cheer in Washington

As a step to a successful negotiation, the 16-18 December plenary in Washington turned out to be slim but positive. The consensus on the Canadian side was that a step forward had been made and the pace accelerated but little of substance had been agreed. The first session began with most of the delegation sitting around in the horribly stuffy and cramped facilities offered by Room 403 in the Winder Building, while Reisman and Ritchie lunched elsewhere with Murphy and Merkin on sandwiches which, like the room, were terrible. They reappeared two hours later full of optimism. Murphy was ready to negotiate; he had a plan which seemed to make sense.

Murphy's plan was to negotiate a complete agreement and take it directly to the US cabinet. He could not obtain a mandate now because he would be dragged down by the third and fourth-tier people comprising his team. It was, therefore, essential that nothing be agreed until everything was agreed. No text should be finalized in any formal sense because it would quickly leak and attract the unhelpful attention of special interest groups and their friends in the Congress, the bureaucracy protective of its turf, and the lobbyists. Instead, as agreements were reached, they would be put aside and only at the end drawn together into a whole.

There seemed, however, a serious gap in this strategic architecture. Accepting that Murphy's collaborators were ducks with bills nibbling away at him, how did the negotiations get from here to there? Was Murphy going to do it all by himself? The bumps in the road ahead emerged quickly enough.

Events moved along smartly the first afternoon with a useful if tedious discussion on customs issues followed by a running of the videotape of Senator Bentsen's press conference in Ottawa the week before. There was general consensus that here was a true pro. Some wags were even prepared to trade large numbers of Canadian politicians for Bentsen.

In the meantime, the softwood lumber battle was coming to a climax and the gods of irony reigned. While the free-trade delegations met in one room to remove all barriers to trade, the softwood delegations met in another to erect new barriers. For once, the media horde deserted the Reisman-Murphy show, preferring the high drama of the here and now discussions.

The following day began with a delegation breakfast and a long discussion of softwood lumber on which negotiations were going from bad to worse. Once at USTR, the meeting started with procurement. As during the fourth session, the procurement exchange reflected the basic issue confronting the negotiators: big deal or small deal.

The US side gave an upbeat account of the working group's progress by explaining that the Canadian working hypothesis could neither be accepted, rejected, nor countered. This brought Reisman charging out of his corner in the first of the day's theatrical events. You have no policy, he bellowed at Murphy, and when you have one, let us know but in the meantime let's not fool around. Replied Murphy, it is true that we have no policy, but the only way to get one is to acquire more information. Reisman countered that no information had been held back and further information exchanges would be pointless in the absence of direction and purpose. After further acrimonious discussion, a three-line mandate was agreed upon, providing for the group to draft a text, thus clearing the way for the main event.

The Canadian proposal on contingency protection was introduced. Reisman proposed that the best way of approaching the question was to strike a working group to consider trade-distorting practices and rules to address them. Murphy contented himself with technical comments combined with assurances that the Canadian proposal would receive close study. So far, so good. Then the wheels fell off. No working group was possible, opined, or rather, moaned Murphy, as if he knew that he was about to face a blast. The subject was extremely difficult and striking a working group could blow the whole thing out of the water.

Reisman once again flabbered his gast all over Murphy. If the US was not prepared to negotiate, they had better say so. Contingency protection was central to the agreement. He, Reisman, was badly exposed in front of Canadian ministers. How could he say that the United States was prepared to negotiate if they would not accept a working group? How could he seek negotiating authority on investment, when the United States had put nothing on the table? The US contingency protection system had become totally corrupt as softwood lumber showed. It amounted to an unbinding of all the tariff bindings Canada had bought over many years of GATT negotiations.

He would recommend that the Canadian tariff be unbound. The proposed working group mandate was so anodyne that refusal to accept it would call into question the whole point of continuing with negotiations.

Only the street noise interrupted the silence that followed. At last Murphy replied in a shaky voice. He was addressing the Canadian interest; he had asked questions; he had undertaken to study the document and he would return to it. Was this not enough to report progress to ministers? What he was proposing was that contingency protection be considered by the two chief negotiators themselves. Surely this was better than a mere working group.

After more of the same, the session broke. Breakfast the following morning was a dark and gloomy affair. The dismal, rainy weather conformed to the mood of the delegation, the optimism of the previous day but a fleeting memory. Reisman concluded that a crisis should not be provoked at this point. Washington was in disarray over Irangate and its conduct on the softwood lumber issues demonstrated the administration's inability to deal with serious matters.

The concluding session was devoid of passion – all had been spent the day before. Reisman accepted without further bombast Murphy's proposal to treat contingency protection as a head of delegation issue. There followed a brisk presentation of the Canadian proposal to incorporate binding dispute settlement mechanisms into a comprehensive agreement, a brief discussion on services, and a sandwich lunch offered together with wine, champagne, speeches, and a present for Reisman's first grandchild. A short, desultory discussion on agriculture, and Murphy's proposal for fewer plenaries of a general nature and more concentrated discussions on key issues concluded this session and 1986.

While brief, the Canadian presentation on dispute settlement opened an issue that would assume increasing importance in the months to come.[9] From the start, Canadian business had intimated that a suitable dispute settlement mechanism would go a long way towards satisfying its concern about security of access. The insistence of the negotiators that dispute settlement without rules was a fool's paradise did not bother them. Indeed, the conventional trade policy view was that little could be done on dispute settlement until the shape of the agreement as a whole had become clearer. As the prospect of good rules for contingency protection became increasingly remote, however, dispute settlement began to take on a new importance to the negotiators.

Agreement on each of the main aspects of a new bilateral arrangement continued, of course, to constitute the heart of the negotiations. Consensus on all these elements would count for little, however, without the establish-

ment of effective institutional mechanisms to guarantee their terms and conditions, that is, institutional arrangements to manage the agreement and
procedures for the avoidance and settlement of disputes.

As the smaller of the two countries and more liable to be affected by the
exercise of power by the other, Canada had a relatively greater interest in
effective dispute-settlement. Only through the development of procedures and
institutions based on jointly agreed principles and rules would the power
disparity be attenuated. This was all the more important since the elimination of barriers would involve significantly greater adjustment and commitment to the changed circumstances by Canada than by the United States.

A number of objectives were identified which could provide a regime that
maintained the integrity of the agreement and that met the interests of both
countries. First, to respond to the disparity in size between the two countries, resolution of disputes should be pursued on the basis of the rules of
the agreement being negotiated, rather than through the exercise of economic power or other leverage.

Second, dispute settlement and institutional arrangements should provide
certainty and predictability, and thereby respect the expectations of the two
governments and private parties as to the rules that would govern bilateral
trade. Avenues for redress should not be susceptible to use or abuse solely for
harassment, but should result in binding decisions that would ensure correc-
tive action for governments and private parties affected adversely by unau-
thorized or unforeseen conduct. Only binding dispute settlement would adequately respect the significant financial and other commitments made in
anticipation of the benefits of the agreement.

Third, the dispute settlement and institutional arrangements would have
to support and promote the objectives of a free-trade area. Remedies should
not have the effect of unravelling the agreement. Having made a significant
adjustment and eliminated tariffs and other barriers to trade, Canada and
the United States should have a basis on which to seek compensation from
each other by way of tariff or other concessions in response to improper
conduct. Conversely, a dispute-settlement procedure that provided only for the
right of one country to take retaliatory action against the products or producers of the other would do little to restore the legitimate competitive position of the industry affected, would undermine the adjustments already made
on the basis of tariff-free access, and would invite the erection of a new barrier
to bilateral trade. Both countries had an interest, therefore, in dispute avoidance
arrangements that would minimize or eliminate the use of border measures.

Fourth, to ensure the effectiveness of any dispute settlement regime, the
mechanisms developed would have to respond to a wide variety of possible

disputes. Pricing decisions, border crossings, and business planning are daily activities. Governments are faced with questions of trade policy almost as frequently; administrative decisions on matters ranging from customs procedures to procurement represent the business of entire departments or agencies. The rules of any agreement would, in effect, be tested constantly in a number of areas. Thus mechanisms would need to be developed to avoid disputes and resolve as many issues as possible through normal domestic procedures or at the technical level.

Finally, dispute settlement and institutional arrangements would need to respect the sovereign prerogatives of both governments. Overall supervision and management of the relationship would be a political responsibility. Consultation to alert each government to the potential impact on the other of actions proposed or taken would respect this responsibility. It would also support the desire of both governments to avoid disputes in the first place, as would government-to-government surveillance and review.

The diversity of disputes and the frequency with which they might arise, combined with the fact that not every incident involving failure to apply the agreement would seriously jeopardize the relationship, suggested that any regime should provide procedures for government-to-government consultation at the request of either government. These avenues could be pursued in the first instance at the officials' level, whether through ad hoc consultations or through standing committees, prior to any consultations at the political level.

A key element of the dispute settlement system would provide that, failing a mutually satisfactory solution through consultations, either government could seek a binding ruling before an independent bilateral tribunal or panel. Binding procedures would compensate for disparity in power, respect the need for certainty, predictability, and fairness, avoid remedies that might unravel the agreement, and condition the future conduct of governments and private parties. Such rulings could be made by either standing or ad hoc bodies; whatever body made such rulings would have to be seen to be fair and independent and capable of giving effective and final direction in difficult cases.

A final institutional arrangement, meeting the objectives of dispute avoidance and political responsibility, could involve a bilateral entity responsible for overall, political supervision of the agreement, such as a Canada-US Trade Commission at the ministerial level. Consultations at the officials' level concerning specific disputes or more general difficulties in administration, whether ad hoc or through standing committees, would fall under the umbrella of such a commission. Periodic meetings could include a review of reports of the various committees of officials established.

The commission could seek or provide fact-finding, technical analyses or other studies in support of any issue before the two governments. In addition, either government could refer a question for investigation, study, or review to experts of both governments under the wing of the commission, whether these experts were seconded by the two governments or resided in the respective bureaucracies. Reports to the commission could be limited to facts and technical information or could include non-binding recommendations to both governments, on a public or confidential basis. The commission might also be supported by a private sector advisory panel or some other group of independent, eminent persons.

These were the principles along which satisfactory institutional provisions could be designed. The details, however, could not take shape until the substantive rules in each of the functional areas were much further along. Two points, however, were overriding: any dispute settlement mechanism would have to be tied to substantive rules and would have to replace unilateralism with bilateralism. The US listened politely to a presentation along these lines and agreed that the lawyers could strike a working group to begin a more detailed assessment of the elements. Murphy agreed that only binding dispute settlement made much sense. And on that hopeful note, the two groups parted to enjoy the Christmas holidays.

THE WINTER OF
DISCONTENT

Now is the winter of our discontent
Made glorious summer by this sun of York.
— Shakespeare, *Richard III*

The new year started with alarms and excursions. Eight months of negotiations had produced little in the way of tangible progress towards a comprehensive agreement. On all the major issues save tariffs and investment, clear and detailed Canadian positions and proposals had been laid on the table. All were animated by the same overall philosophy: Canada and the United States would treat each other's goods and services as they treated their own. There had been little in the way of US response, acceptance, counterproposals, or rejection. Murphy's position was summed up in a constantly repeated litany, 'I hear you; I know where you are coming from; we are still talking.' The negotiating imbalance was striking and profoundly worrisome. Canada had provided a feast; the United States had brought only thin and watery gruel.

To add to the pervasive gloom, the three-year imbroglio on softwood lumber came to an ignominious end. Over the Christmas break, negotiations for a settlement hurtled along to reach a conclusion minutes before the US government brought down a final determination imposing a sizeable countervailing duty on lumber. The settlement whereby Canada agreed to impose an export tax drew scathing criticism from the opposition, the media, and the industry. Only the lumber provinces, whose treasuries would be enriched, were supportive. Jeff Simpson summed up the media's view: 'Absolutely nobody comes away from the softwood lumber negotiation with the United States with an enhanced reputation for competence.'[1]

The effect of the lumber deal upon the negotiations seemed ominous and obvious. In the view of the critics enjoying the government's discomfort, the softwood settlement was proof that Canada would offer anything to get a comprehensive agreement. In their view, waiting Canada out until the last possible moment would prove a profitable US enterprise. They were convinced that the government had neither the will nor the capacity to stand up to the Americans. Editorialized the *Montreal Gazette*: 'It is a bad deal. We would have been better off with no deal at all ... If anything, the softwood case shows that Washington would expect to oversee Canada's economy, in the interest of compliance, under a free-trade deal. It is a bitter foretaste.'[2] The *Financial Post*, however, while also critical of the lumber settlement, came to the opposite conclusion: 'This sorry episode provides yet more evidence of the need for a wider Canada-U.S. trade agreement.'[3]

Alan King, *Ottawa Citizen*, 6 January 1987

To add disaster to misery, the government became mired once again in scandal. On a cold Sunday morning, 18 January, the minister for small business, André Bissonette, was summoned to the prime minister's office and sacked for conflict of interest. No matter that he was subsequently vindicated in the courts; with critics on his trail, the government had to endure a long and painful political torture. In the Gallup poll taken in the immediate aftermath of the lumber settlement, the government slipped below 30 per cent in the polls; no modern government had ever suffered such a reversal of fortunes in such a short period.

The government appeared unable to sell itself to the public. Everything it touched turned to ashes. On the other hand, in the first parliamentary session, over 100 bills were passed, many important. The economy was in good shape and improving, with growth at over 3 per cent, unemployment below 10 per cent, inflation hovering about 4 per cent, and the deficit down without the cutting of any programs.

What did this atmosphere mean for the negotiations? On many fronts, the government deserved high marks: first, for its courage in launching the initiative; second, for its perseverance; and third, for giving Reisman the broadest mandate any trade negotiator has had in modern times. But the government could be faulted for its anemic communications program. Since the beginning of 1986, there had been only spasmodic attempts to lead the debate on the issues, and the field had been left to the opposition. In spite of the communications gap, public support for free trade had remained remarkably high at over 50 per cent.

Within the TNO, the elements of a draft agreement were beginning to be cobbled together in a slide show for cabinet and individual showings to ministers. For the first time, the outline of a possible agreement was beginning to take shape. Those working on individual issues could begin to connect the specific to the general and see where their mission lay.

The Half-Way Point

The eighth plenary session took place in Washington, 13-14 January, with a heads-of-delegation discussion on contingency protection scheduled for dinner, and a plenary review of customs matters, with a view to concluding on that set of issues before the opening of tariff negotiations and the beginning of discussions on financial services. Based on the fast-track clock, half the allotted time had now elapsed. The first seven plenary negotiating sessions had taken almost nine months. Fewer than nine months remained before the US negotiating authority ran out. Reisman reminded everyone, however, that wondrous miracles could be wrought in nine months.

Preparations for the session had not been without drama. Reisman made clear that at this session there would need to be a clear indication that Murphy was prepared to engage on Canadian issues or there would be no more meetings until Murphy was ready, willing, and able to negotiate. Reports from New York that Murphy had been misrepresenting the Canadian position by telling American business groups that Canada was seeking an exemption from US contingency protection laws was a further source of intense irritation.

To add some warmth to the cold winter air, the autopact began increasingly to find its way into the negotiations. In a question and answer session following a speech at a Washington conference sponsored by the *Financial*

Post, Murphy, in his offhand, ingenuous manner, first hinted then demurred that the autopact would need to be renegotiated. Speaking without a prepared text, his indiscretion provoked cries of alarm from Premier Peterson of Ontario and expressions of anger from Reisman on two counts. First, Murphy had to date made no formal offers or requests regarding the autopact. If, in fact, he had proposals to make on the autopact, it was common courtesy that they be made to Reisman before being aired publicly. Second, for Ontario to whine about the fate of the autopact in the hands of its founder and principal defender could not be tolerated.

The political uproar at home appeared out of all proportion to what had in fact been said by Murphy.[4] But his timing had been less than sublime. The week before, Linda Diebel had spread a story across the front page of the *Montreal Gazette*, based on an inspired leak from an Ontario official, that the negotiators did not believe the safeguards in the autopact made sense any more. Dave Barrows had been part of a group of provincial officials who had been briefed on automotive issues by assistant chief negotiator Charles Stedman. His negative views on the autopact were well known by the industry and the provinces. Barrows faithfully recorded these in a memo to file and added a few embellishments. This memo had found its way to Diebel's desk and from there to front pages across the country. The NDP, Liberals, and Ontario all had a new twist for an old cause. Furious denials by the government that the memo represented the views of Reisman had now been undermined by Murphy's indiscretion.

The response was vintage Reisman. In several media interviews he indignantly denied that the autopact was in any danger. The Canadian position enunciated by ministers was clear. The pact was working; there was no need to address it in the negotiations, but if the United States had proposals to make that would increase Canadian automotive production and employment, Canada would listen to them. He could only conclude that the Ontario premier was deliberately sowing alarm and confusion. As for Murphy: 'I think the result of what he did is mischievous and I don't like it ... I don't know whether he's being foolish or being a knave ... But I intend to find out ... I'm going to have very frank words with him, I'm going to let my hair hang down. We're going to talk a little about things.'[5] Murphy for his part smiled. He was beginning to learn how to get under Reisman's skin and would use this in the future as part of his negotiating technique.[6]

In the negotiating room, after an initial temper tantrum, there was calm. Reisman again took Murphy through the Canadian proposal on contingency protection point by point, and it was agreed that the subsidies group would pursue discussions. On that basis, Reisman decided that he could go to the ministers on investment and establish a working group on financial services. While the US side continued to suffer from internal bickering as to whether or not financial services were part of the negotiations, Murphy had reached the point that he was prepared to have Treasury officials negotiate separately with Reisman. To carry this burden, Reisman had brought in Bill Hood, one of his successors as deputy at Finance. Hood's task had been made considerably tougher at the beginning of December when the Ontario government announced that it would make sweeping reforms in the financial services sector and throw it open to foreigners. Not to be outdone, Junior Finance Minister Tom Hockin hinted that the federal government would follow suit. Any incentives for the Americans to pay for access to the Canadian financial market had been severely compromised. Reisman complained 'I'd like to have that in my poke to bargain with but it's gone.'[7] Also at this session, there was agreement to complete the drafting of a bracketed text by June in order to leave the summer for the hard bargaining to follow. This may have been small beer but it was better than the vinegar the US side had been spewing out to date.

More important, further progress had been made on customs issues and the way cleared for discussion on the tariff. The US side had by now received the ITC report. By 1986, the tariff had been on the wane as a trade policy instrument in both Canada and the United States.[8] Since the establishment of the GATT in 1947, the two countries had participated in successive rounds of trade negotiations in which they had agreed to reduce tariffs in return for improved access to foreign markets. For Canada, however, high US tariffs – 15 per cent and more on petrochemicals, rolling stock, clothing, and many other products – continued to raise barriers to the US market and prevent Canadian firms from achieving the economies of scale on which increased competitiveness and employment in Canadian industry depends. Removal of remaining tariff barriers could thus assist competitive Canadian companies in penetrating the US market. Additionally, the existence of Canadian tariffs on imports from the United States is often costly to Canadian industrial users because Canadian producers typically charge their Canadian customers the US price plus the Canadian tariff.

The US similarly sought elimination of Canadian tariffs. The incidence of the Canadian tariff on dutiable imports from the United States by the mid-1980s was in the order of 10 per cent with some products attracting rates as high as 25 per cent. Elimination, especially of the high tariffs, would increase the ability of US producers to compete in Canada, particularly against third-country suppliers.

Related to tariff elimination were other customs issues such as rules of origin (i.e., rules to prevent transshipment of third-country goods through one country to the other by establishing how a product qualifies under the terms of the agreement as a United States or Canadian product rather than as an imported product), marks of origin, and customs clearance procedures. On each of these, significant progress had already been made.

Eliminating the tariff on a wide range of finished products would, of course, result in more direct competition. Consequently, tariff elimination would need to be phased in over a period of time sufficient to allow industries sensitive to import competition the necessary breathing space to adjust to the new competition.

Tokyo Round tariff cuts had generally been phased in over seven years. Up to eight or ten years were recommended both by the Economic Council in its study on free trade in 1975 and also by the Senate Committee on Foreign Affairs in its report on Canada-US relations in 1982. This conservative approach was in line with earlier free-trade agreements such as EFTA and the Australia-New Zealand agreement. In addition, it would be possible to negotiate individual variations. Some reductions could be implemented more quickly than the general rule, while for others, more time might be required for affected companies to adjust to the reductions they would face.

In line with these various proposals, Canada suggested that the two countries seek to eliminate all tariffs by the end of seven years. The US side, however, despite the fact that its tariffs were generally lower, believed a seven-year phase-out was inadequate and indicated that it would prefer ten years. Canada reluctantly agreed to accept this more cautious approach. Reisman had at the beginning of the negotiations suggested that, given the greater adjustment burden on Canada, the US tariff should be eliminated immediately while the Canadian tariff be eliminated in the final year of the transition period. A less transparent variant on this proposal, that all tariffs below 5 per cent be eliminated immediately while the rest be phased in over ten years, was also put forward. Murphy insisted that any differential phasing of this nature was impossible and Reisman finally agreed. Instead, they agreed that they would apply a more neutral differential phasing formula. All tariffs would be eliminated at the end of ten years on the basis of ten annual cuts but, in addition, wherever there was industry consensus, tariffs would either be eliminated immediately or in five annual steps. On the basis of this formula, the tariff specialists set to work.[9]

While phased tariff elimination would address the concerns of some producers, others continued to seek exemptions. A number of industries, for example, stated their opposition to the removal of their tariff protection in the context of the consultations held by Tom Burns in 1985. In some cases this opposition was based on a belief that real and secure access is not possible. Without a doubt, a number preferred to maintain their tariff protection on the assumption that they would not be able to compete in a tariff-free environment. The US International Trade Commission had heard similar representations from US producers. Both governments, however, were mindful that in a GATT Article XXIV free-trade area agreement there is only limited scope for exceptions. Exempting whole sectors from tariff elimination, for example, would bring into question whether the agreement liberalized substantially all the trade between the partners. Murphy and Reisman decided to proceed on the basis of no exemptions.

Canada-US duty elimination, however, would leave intact each country's MFN tariffs on third-country imports. The concerns of many producers on both sides of the border were often driven by the misconception that they would lose tariff protection against third-country suppliers. This was a concern raised, for example, by US textile producers who saw the bilateral agreement as the thin edge of the wedge eroding their protection from first Mexican and then Asian competitors. They feared that bilateral concessions might have to be applied multilaterally. Both governments, however, were participating in the new round of multilateral trade negotiations (MTN) which could result in reductions or elimination of many MFN rates. Such reductions would, of course, form part of a larger package that would involve improved market access to the European Community, Japan, and other developed, as well as developing, countries. Reductions on an MFN basis would thus be addressed on their own merits, wholly separate from considerations influencing the bilateral discussions.

Canada and the United States maintained a number of tariff-related programs which were also being addressed in the customs group. Canada, for example, made extensive use of duty drawbacks and duty remissions to encourage manufacturing in Canada using foreign inputs where these were not available in Canada. The machinery program provided for a tariff if the equipment was available from a Canadian manufacturer and duty-free treatment if it was not. A number of these programs were tied to specific performance requirements which had raised concerns in the United States and prompted allegations that some acted as subsidies. The United States had similar programs, such as free-trade zones and outward processing regulations which also used the technique of tariff forgiveness to encourage domestic manufacturing. Once the tariff was eliminated, the scope for such measures would be limited to third-country trade. Nevertheless, rules were required to ensure that such programs could not be used to the detriment of the trade interests of the other country.

Canada had traditionally made relatively greater use of the tariff and related programs than had the United States. Consequently, Canada's position on tariffs had been carefully coordinated with its stance on other issues. There were many areas where non-tariff measures were the real barriers to the US or Canadian market. In such cases, tariff elimination alone would not improve access. Major non-tariff measures that restricted Canadian access to the US market included federal, state, and local government procurement requirements, as well as a number of practices that restricted entry of particular products, such as the Jones Act in regard to ships, and trade barriers disguised as technical regulations in the agricultural sector. For its part, the United States would expect Canada to make reciprocal moves on procurement, both federally and provincially, and had its own list of Canadian non-tariff measures it wanted to pursue.

For Canada, the key issue, however, continued to be security and predictability of access. Investment which would be either partially or largely dependent on access to the US market would be less likely to take place in Canada if there were a possibility that tariff-free access would be impaired by new or existing US protective measures. The use or threat of these measures would have a significant impact on the location of new investment and/or the profitability of existing investment. In essence, this meant that a satisfactory new regime on contingency protection remained key to a satisfactory agreement. Little progress had been made on this front. From now on, at least part of each session would be devoted to this critical issue, and public diplomacy would increasingly focus on it.

Vice Presidential Reassurances

As part of that public diplomacy, 22 January saw Vice President George Bush, accompanied by Treasury Secretary Jim Baker, in Ottawa for a tongue

Welcome to Ottawa: Prime Minister Mulroney greets US Vice President George Bush, Treasury Secretary James Baker, and US Ambassador Tom Niles in the snow and sleet of a typical Ottawa winter, while Finance Minister Michael Wilson looks on. (24 Sussex Dr., Ottawa, 21 January 1987)

lashing by the prime minister. The vice president was visiting for the second time in less than a year, having made a similar pilgrimage the previous summer. Two items headed the agenda: acid rain and the trade negotiations. On the first item there was palpable Canadian anger that the administration's budget omitted funding for programs that had been agreed to at both the 1984 and 1985 summits. There was little cause for hope from this meeting on acid rain, but on the second item, the vice president reassured the prime minister of the importance of a comprehensive agreement to the United States, concurred that the negotiations should have higher priority in the administration, and pronounced that the economic policy council of the US cabinet, chaired by Secretary Baker, would begin to review progress at an early date.

A few days later, there was tangible evidence that the prime minister's conversation with the vice president had not been in vain. In his state-of-the-union address, Reagan renewed his commitment to a comprehensive agreement with Canada: 'We will work to expand our opportunities in international markets through the Uruguay Round of trade negotiations and to complete a historic free-trade arrangement between the world's two largest trading partners – Canada and the United States.'[10] To make sure that Mulroney would be aware, he had the White House switchboard track down the prime minister in Zimbabwe at a Commonwealth meeting to inform him of this fact.

The significance of this short passage in Reagan's speech was apparent even to the *Toronto Star*: the administration's priority had been established and US officials, if not the Congress, could be expected to act accordingly.[11] A new, if false, euphoria set in at the TNO. To be mentioned in the state-of-the-union address appeared to be its own reward. But the pundits also pointed out that this was an administration whose clout was definitely waning. While it is normal in the United States for an administration to lose some of its influence with the Congress and opinion-moulders in the final two years of its second mandate, Reagan's influence had taken an even sharper dip than usual as a result of the growing scandal over the clandestine arms sale to Iran and the secret funnelling of funds to the Contras in Nicaragua.

The euphoria did not last long. The next day former House Speaker Tip O'Neill told a Toronto audience that while he was all for an agreement, Canadians appeared to be awfully thin-skinned on this issue. 'You can't be selfish. You can't be protective. You have to give just like everybody else.'[12] On 2 February, USTR Yeutter would demonstrate just how thick Canadian skins had to be. At a conference on free trade jointly sponsored by the Institute for Research on Public Policy and the Brookings Institution, which in all respects had been a huge success, he told the closing dinner that 'I'm prepared to have America's culture on the table and take the risk of having it damaged by Canadian influence after a free-trade arrangement. I hope that Canada is prepared to run that risk too.' Efforts by Donald Macdonald and others present to help him extract his foot from his mouth had the opposite effect: he stuck the other one in too and told an embarrassed audience that some of his best friends were Canadians and that he had spent his honey-moon in Canada.[13]

The ensuing storm was predictable. While Murphy may have been shrewdly trying to undermine Reisman's confidence, Yeutter's remarks were plainly insensitive and once again brought to the fore a difficult issue that to date the negotiators had managed to keep off the front pages. The prime minister rose to the challenge by pulling out all the rhetorical stops and referred to Yeutter's stunning ignorance. The *Montreal Gazette* called Yeutter a hoser as editorial writers across the country tried to outdo each other with verbal pyrotechnics. Yeutter, however, refused to back down and thought it all a tempest in a teapot. To confirm this view, Bob Hepburn, Washington correspondent for the *Toronto Star* wrote a humorous piece on the discomfiture of White House press-briefer Marlin Fitzwater trying to assure Canadian Press, amid gales of laughter from the front row US media stars, that the administration did take the negotiations seriously.[14] It seemed the Canadian government could not win. Even its friends seemed determined to undermine the negotiations.

A Working Dinner

Reisman and Murphy next met in New York on 10 February. Murphy was scheduled to meet with a group of US business executives in New York, and the two negotiators decided to see if a quiet working dinner away from the capitals could bring results.[15] From the beginning, Reisman had dined privately with Murphy during the course of most plenary sessions. They used these occasions to get to know one another, build confidence away from the pressure of full delegations, and prepare the ground for the business of the day. Such private sessions are a normal part of any major negotiation. In December, however, Reisman admitted to his team that the Murphy he dined with seemed unrelated to the Murphy he met the next day across the conference table. Deals struck over the port and cigars evaporated with the morning sun. In future, Reisman would not dine alone with Murphy. Gordon Ritchie would accompany him, and Bill Merkin would be Murphy's partner.

The four used the occasion in New York to initiate informal discussions on a possible package on investment. The meeting was to become a source of confusion and mutual charges of bad faith that would bedevil the negotiations on this sensitive but central issue. The investment issue proved to be as difficult for Canada as contingency protection for the United States. Indeed, the United States made not-so-veiled attempts to link the two issues, a linkage Canada was not eager to concede. Canada wanted to keep investment as a separate issue to be measured on its own merits.

At the negotiating table, Reisman had continued to maintain that investment had not been contemplated in the exchange of letters between the president and the prime minister in October 1985, and that US interests extended well beyond trade-related investment issues such as performance requirements to the politically sensitive matter of national treatment and right of establishment.[16] Murphy, on the other hand, continued to insist that without investment there could be no deal and that this had been made clear in the discussions leading up to the October exchange of letters. Its lack of specific mention in the letter was an oversight, an oversight that could be rectified if Reisman insisted but should not be necessary if Canada was interested in making a mutually acceptable and beneficial deal. He could not see how a new exchange of letters between the president and the prime minister, expanding the scope of the negotiations, would be helpful in the public management of the issue at this stage.

Of course, the US investment position was not without some merit.[17] Should Canada's objectives be met, the elimination of existing US tariffs, import quotas, and other barriers such as 'Buy America' restrictions would give Canadian industry unimpeded access to a market of some 250 million people. It would make Canada a more attractive place to invest, not only for Canadians but also for Americans, Europeans, Japanese, and others who regard open access to a large market as a prerequisite to profitable, employment-creating enterprises. Some of this investment from abroad would be influenced by the rules on foreign investment. The Tories had already welcomed foreign investment, but since their Grit predecessors had introduced screening, Canada continued to be perceived by some Americans to be hostile to foreign investment. As a result, foreign investors continued to be wary of major investments in Canada, and Americans especially continued to press their government to seek a more secure climate in Canada for both existing and future investments. Their anxieties were similar to those of Canadians worried about security of access to the United States market.

In order to achieve its broad economic development objectives, Canada has historically recognized the need for foreign capital to supplement Canadian savings in developing the economy. But the high level of foreign investment in Canada had become a matter of concern. Rapidly increasing levels of direct investment, its concentration in secondary manufacturing and resource industries, and its predominance in some of these industries had provoked considerable public debate about the costs and benefits of foreign ownership in the 1960s and 1970s. As a result, Canada had adopted measures to ensure Canadian control or a Canadian presence in certain key sectors as well as measures to encourage the growth of strong Canadian-controlled enterprises and the investment of Canadian savings in Canada. The most important measure, however, had been the creation of the Foreign Investment Review Agency (FIRA) in 1974 to review the acquisition of control of a Canadian business enterprise and the establishment of a new business in Canada either by a person or corporation not already having a business in Canada or by a foreigner with an existing business in Canada.

But things had changed since 1974, especially Canadian and US foreign investment patterns. The early 1980s had witnessed a switch in the traditional roles of Canada and the United States as importer and exporter of capital, respectively. Both countries retained their net traditional host and home positions towards foreign direct investment, but their ratio of assets held abroad to domestic assets held by foreigners changed significantly (from 4.5 to 1.5 in the case of the United States and from 0.28 to 0.50 in the case of Canada over the 1975-84 period). Nevertheless, the importance of foreign direct investment in the economies of the two countries remained disproportionately greater in Canada (with 26 per cent of the equity capital employed in the non-financial sectors effectively foreign-controlled) than in the United States (with a corresponding 2 per cent level of foreign control).

By 1984 a number of factors, including economic performance and increased competition for foreign direct investment, led to a reassessment of the Foreign Investment Review Act. It was widely perceived to have contributed to creating an inhospitable investment climate in Canada. Increasing concern was expressed that FIRA ran counter to the desire to increase Canadian competitiveness, particularly as it affected new, direct investment. This was a theme struck repeatedly by the private sector. There were allegations that FIRA had been used to shield existing Canadian enterprises from the competition of prospective new investors. There was concern that FIRA operated on the assumption that significant Canadian benefit was not necessarily coincident with the best business judgment of the investor. There was the matter of trying to persuade foreign firms to settle in locations that were not the most efficient or economical for long-term competitiveness. Finally, there was concern that the FIRA process itself discouraged promising firms from establishing in Canada.

The new government met these concerns by turning FIRA's mandate on its head. Instead of screening new investment, FIRA officials were told to promote and search out investment, and the agency's name was changed to Investment Canada. These changes were welcomed in the United States and elsewhere, but did not alter the perception that Canadian foreign investment policy was capricious. Thus the United States had an interest in changing existing practices into contractual commitments.

The United States sought acceptance of a contractual commitment not only regarding the right of establishment and acquisition, but also regarding extension of the same treatment to US investors once established in Canada as is afforded to Canadian investors once established in the United States. US officials appreciated that national treatment for investment would be a difficult proposition for Canada and that there might be need for special provision for some sectors, such as cultural industries. Again, there was a naïve perception on the part of some that there are no or few barriers to investment in the United States. Indeed, wholesale national treatment would be as difficult for the United States to apply as for Canada. The United States would, therefore, also have to seek special treatment for sectors barred to foreign investors and which it would presumably wish to continue to exclude, such as transportation and communications industries.

The combined effect of the changing foreign investment pattern of both Canada and the United States, as well as the more receptive attitude to foreign investment in Canada demonstrated in the changes in government policy, made the investment issue an important, if delicate concern. Changing the laws in Canada to welcome foreign investment in Canada's own economic interests was one thing; entering into a contractual commitment to maintain open investment policies was quite another.

National treatment (even if circumscribed by exceptions) touches the sensitive nerve of national sovereignty. Attitudes towards the international regulation of investment demonstrate this sensitivity. Smaller countries like Canada, which have traditionally been major importers of capital, could be expected to welcome foreign investment on a non-discriminatory basis. Such countries, however, often depend on trade with the same larger countries which are the sources of much of that capital, and chafe at the fact that foreign investment can limit their ability to influence the terms on which trade takes place. Consequently, they frequently resort to discriminatory policies for reasons of national self-determination. A decision to enter into contractual commitments, therefore, would need to be weighed carefully against the benefits in other aspects of the agreement. Only in the context of an agreement that provided Canadians with full and secure access to the US market for Canadian goods and services as well as non-discriminatory access to US technology, could any Canadian government sell a contractual commitment to maintain an open foreign investment regime. This was a point not always appreciated by American policymakers.

The United States would thus need to be careful in formulating its position in this area. Canadian ministers understood that a comprehensive agreement that would meet Canada's principal objectives would need to address US investment concerns. If the United States was interested in a package which would ensure that some future government could not revert to hostile investment policies without endangering Canadian access to the US market, there might be scope for negotiating a set of commitments that would go far beyond anything that the United States had achieved or could hope to achieve with any major industrial country. Pat Carney made this clear in an appearance on CTV's *Question Period* in January, a statement not picked up by the rest of the media, but not missed by the negotiators. Reisman, while this was the direction he wanted to go, had not been ready to have his hand tipped so clearly. In New York, Murphy indicated he wanted to go further and Reisman told him to forget it.

The trip to New York later created some controversy of its own. Reisman had accepted a ride in the Bank of Nova Scotia's corporate jet and his secretary, in preparing his travel claim, had made a note of this. When the claim was made available to the press on a routine access-to-information request bent on determining just how carefully Reisman was handling the public purse, a howl of protest was raised about conflict of interest. All this, however, was far in the future.[18]

Back to Washington

Reisman and Murphy next met formally in Washington on 19-20 February. This ninth plenary marked the fourth meeting in a row on US soil and made up for the fact that four of the first six meetings had taken place in Canada. The two teams had agreed to take advantage of the weather: summers in Canada, winters in the USA. A rough balance thus prevailed for the plenary sessions; not so for the meetings of working groups. Most of these took place in Washington. Since the United States had opted for a decentralized negotiating team, individual agency budgets and priorities dictated both the availability of US negotiators and their disposition to travel to Ottawa. The subsidies group, for example, rarely met in Canada. That it was difficult for the rich United States to fund the logistics of this negotiation proved a ready source for cheap shots. That it was not the top priority for most of the US negotiators was a source of constant frustration and largely explained the lamentable level of preparation of US team members.

This ninth meeting would focus on services and intellectual property, two issues placed on the negotiating agenda by the US side. Canada would have been prepared to leave them alone, but recognized that progress in these new areas was critical to gaining support from influential US sources. On services, there had been agreement to proceed on a three-track plan: a code of binding principles on future policies, legislation, and regulation for all services; specific agreements on certain service sectors, for example, financial services, and business/professional services; and the resolution of specific irritants, notably those related to the cultural industries. But the discussion revealed once again that even when the US side was the instigator, it did not do its homework.

Intellectual property continued to be unfamiliar terrain for the two chief negotiators. Highly technical and out of step with the general theme of opening up and securing each other's markets, discussions were desultory and confused. The US side seemed unprepared to recognize the difference between a multilateral negotiation in Geneva and a bilateral negotiation with its largest trading partner. No connections were drawn between the US multilateral agenda of gaining better protection for US owners of intellectual property in developing countries and the negotiation of a free-trade agreement. The prospects for reaching a sensible result seemed remote. At a minimum, the Americans would have to recognize that protecting intellectual property went hand in hand with a more open attitude towards sharing it. Canada was prepared to extend more stringent levels of protection to US owners of intellectual property in Canada, but in return wanted to ensure that the US government would not resort to national security or other devices to deny Canadian producers access to the latest technologies. Discussion to date suggested that the US side was unprepared to make this necessary connection.

Outside, on the steps of USTR, culture was the hot issue of the week. The combined effect of Yeutter's comments of a few weeks earlier and stories about an impending new film distribution policy made it the natural subject for pressing questions. Reisman decided to send a message of his own. Since the November press scrum when he had decided that they could serve a useful purpose, he had never failed to take the opportunity to make a point related either to the day's negotiating calendar or to the public issue of the day. His comments were often shrewdly aimed at a variety of audiences: the Americans, the Canadian public, the provinces, or Canadian ministers. He told the press on 19 February:

> Canada will need a great deal of freedom, a great deal of flexibility when it comes to looking after our cultural needs and our cultural interests. There are measures that we will need to take in the cultural areas which we believe are perfectly reasonable and legitimate measures for Canada. Culture is a very special preoccupation of Canadians, has always been, probably always will be. That's the syndrome of a small country living alongside a large country.[19]

An Inspired Leak

In late February, a light breeze began to fill the limp sails of the negotiating ship. The first sign of movement was a Canadian Press story revealing Canada's negotiating objectives in considerable and informed detail. The source proved to be none other than Reisman himself. He had consented to provide some background information on the autopact to an earnest, if somewhat impressionable, journalist, Allen Bass from Canadian Press, and went on to explain the whole of the negotiations. In effect, Reisman took over the public debate in a message aimed both at domestic and US audiences.

Reisman was convinced that it would be helpful if the government explained in more detail what it was doing. This would ease the constant pounding the government was taking in question period and from the media. It was time to lay the cards on the table to the greatest extent possible without compromising Canadian negotiating positions. It would at the same time reassure the United States of Canada's seriousness, allow for more informed national debate, expose the Grits for their lack of policy, and confirm the NDP as fundamentally and irreversibly opposed to the negotiations.

Leaking material to the media is a time-honoured method of communications. How it will play, of course, depends on how it is written, how many other stories are in play, and how much prominence the editor decides to give the story. The parliamentary break during the third week of February was a particularly dull period. The public appetite for scandal had reached satiation. Thus, what could have been just another routine story on the trade talks citing an unnamed official achieved national prominence and, in the process, served to put the communications campaign on track for the first time.

The story was extensively reported on the evening news of 25 February and featured on front pages across the country the next day. The *Globe and Mail* added to its impact with a scare headline: 'Weak Industries and the Auto Pact Reported Abandoned in Trade Talks.' The story went on to claim that the negotiators were seeking an agreement that would remove all tariffs between Canada and the United States by the end of the century, with no exceptions to protect weak industries or the autopact. Both the Liberals and the NDP called press conferences in which they used their strongest hyperbole to proclaim that here was proof that the autopact, marketing boards, and culture were about to be auctioned off to the Americans. Pat Carney was furious. Reisman had breached their understanding that he would negotiate while she communicated. She was learning that there were bureaucrats and then there was Simon. Pundits were beginning to remark on changing attitudes towards Reisman. Said Doug Fisher: 'There's now a bittersweet feeling about Reisman among the ministers and mandarins of Ottawa. His rudeness and arrogance with them are insufferable. But they suffer, consoled that he treats the Americans the same way.'[20] But the event forced the government to take stock of its position on free trade. Just after Parliament resumed its sitting, Joe Clark announced that a full day's debate on the negotiations would be held within weeks.

There was even a slight puff of wind from the US side. Richard Darman, deputy secretary of the Treasury, told a group of visiting Canadians that the administration had concluded that in view of the growing scandal over Iran and Nicaragua, a foreign policy success was needed. A trade agreement with Canada would qualify and to that end, the administration would put its whole weight behind the negotiations and actively work with Congress.

The Premiers Come to Town

For more than a year, Reisman had honoured his arrangement with the provincial trade representatives. Every month, he met with them and reviewed progress to date. He took one or two key issues at each meeting and discussed them in detail. As part of the ritual, he would hector Bob Latimer for his (or Ontario's) lack of faith and try to demonstrate to Jake Warren (representing Quebec) that he, Reisman, was more on top of the issues. Jake, after all, had never served in Finance and was thus by definition a lesser man (he had only been deputy at Trade and Commerce, high commissioner to London, ambassador to Washington and coordinator for the Tokyo Round GATT negotiations and, after retirement from government, vice-chairman of the Bank of Montreal). The other mortals around the table were all given a chance but were obviously of a different order. Occasionally some complained that perhaps this 1960s reunion could be brought to an end and the rest allowed to join the discussion.[21]

In addition to the monthly Simon, Jake, and Bobby show, Alan Nymark provided a detailed debriefing at the end of each negotiating session through the vehicle of a pre-arranged conference call. All the provinces took copious notes and some were known to make verbatim transcripts. It was not unusual for the premier of Ontario to be informed of the details of a negotiating session before any ministers and deputies in Ottawa had been debriefed, often in less detail.

The provinces had also been buried under an avalanche of paper

The Simon, Jake, and Bobby Show: Reisman and provincial representatives meet in one of the monthly sessions of the Federal-Provincial Continuing Committee on Trade Negotiations. (Ottawa, 7 January 1986)

and working level consultations. Before the negotiations concluded, the TNO shared more than 700 different documents with them and engaged in numerous exchanges of letters and phone conversations. All the senior officers were available to provincial officials at any time to explain the issues. Most of them arranged for regular consultations at the working level. Bill Dymond, for example, visited every province to consult on the government procurement issue. Alan Nymark and his staff made regular liaison visits.

The crowning touch to all this consultation and information sharing was the quarterly meeting of the prime minister and premiers agreed to in June 1986. In September, the premiers had dined with the prime minister and in the course of four and a half hours, received a detailed briefing from the prime minister, Pat Carney, and Simon Reisman. The November annual meeting in Vancouver had been dominated by lumber, but the premiers had also received a briefing from Reisman as well as a homily from Allan Gotlieb on the dangers of US protectionism.

The third in this series of meetings was held on 11 March. Because no meeting can take place without an issue, Peterson, Pawley, and Bourassa let it be known that they thought the time had come to solve the matter of provincial ratification. By this time the other western premiers had lost their appetite for this particular rendition of the federal-provincial wars and indicated that they saw no need for agreement on either a process or a principle. They were in town to get a first-hand report on how the negotiations were going. And that is what they got. Through the medium of the ubiquitous slide show, the prime minister, Carney, and Reisman took them through the issues. All three demonstrated that they were on top of the situation and pursuing the Canadian interest, even if the Americans were continuing to be obstinate and unimaginative.

Outside again after five hours, the dissidents avowed they had given the prime minister a run for his money on the ratification question and were disappointed the issue had not been settled. Pawley was particularly bitter and, like Peterson, could be relied on to mouth cynical concern at every opportunity. Joe Ghiz also began to show he was more comfortable on the negative side. Bourassa, on the other hand, was now clearly in the pro-free-trade camp and did not dwell on the ratification issue.

Parliament Debates the Issues
Energies now turned to the House debate. Considerable effort was going into the preparations. To give the prime minister an opportunity to become comfortable with his material, he agreed that the trade talks would be the central theme of a scheduled speech in Longueuil on 12 March. To show that she was

the quarterback, Pat Carney appeared on that Sunday's *Question Period* on CTV, the day before the House debate. TNO was assigned responsibility for preparing the speech texts for the debate as well as for the prime minister's Longueuil speech for approval by the PMO, which would then pass them on to ministers. Their staffs could do some final polishing but they were asked to stick with the thrust of the supplied texts.

The debate was held on 16 March. While the television age has focused almost total media attention on the drama of the forty-five minutes of question period, the main business of Parliament is accomplished in the morning and afternoon debates. It is during this time that all sides are given the chance to put forward their positions around a specific motion. The speeches average a little over fifteen minutes after which other members ask questions. These debates continue to have public value; they are almost the only opportunity for the public to watch politicians thoroughly testing their arguments.

From the government's perspective, the day-long focus on free trade was a grand success. The government motion: 'that this House supports the negotiation of a bilateral trading arrangement with the US, as part of the government's multilateral trade policy, while protecting our political sovereignty, social programs, agricultural marketing systems, the auto industry, and our unique cultural identity' was carefully crafted to give the opposition maximum discomfort.[22] The Liberal amendment to the motion was a monstrosity of verbiage that came close to being disallowed by the Speaker.

The prime minister led off for the government side. His Longueuil speech had gone well, and he was still buoyed by his performance the previous week at the first ministers' meeting. For three-quarters of an hour he demonstrated that he had become a master of this brief. While the pundits may not have liked his flights of oratory, there was no question he had a clear vision of where he wanted to go. Pat Carney took his basic theme of a richer and more confident Canada and used it to lay out the negotiating agenda in some detail. Agriculture Minister John Wise dismissed the fears over abandonment of marketing boards; he could be forgiven the obvious falsehood that 'any deal which is a good deal for Canadian farmers is a good deal for Canadians generally.' Treasury Board president Robert de Cotret spoke about the benefits for Quebec. Finance Minister Michael Wilson addressed Ontario's concerns and spoke of the autopact. In his usual dazzling display of verbal pyrotechnics, Minister of Justice John Crosbie mocked the little Canadians of the opposition and pointed out the advantages of free trade for the Atlantic provinces. Communications Minister Flora MacDonald kept to the party line on culture. Her officials were unhappy; they had been particularly incensed at having to stick with the TNO-prepared and PMO-sanctioned text. Health Minister Jake Epp rounded out the debate by summarizing the government arguments, drawing attention to the benefits of free trade for the West and putting to rest, once more, any fears about the loss of social benefits.

For the Liberals, Messrs Turner, Axworthy, and Johnston were the principal speakers. All three spoke at length. All three recognized the problem of US protectionism and the challenge of economic renewal, but offered no concrete alternative to the government's approach. Their stance was characterized by one Tory back-bencher as 'free trade if necessary but not necessarily free trade.' The main thrust of their attack was not directed against substantive issues, but against the government's management of the negotiations.

For the NDP, Messrs Broadbent and Langdon led the debate. They rejected a comprehensive trade agreement outright and offered as alternatives the multilateral GATT negotiations complemented by bilateral sectoral deals with appropriate safeguards as well as an agreement establishing a dispute settlement mechanism.

The House debate received full coverage from all the media. In the days leading up to the debate, there had been expectations that the government would lift the veil and reveal what the negotiations were all about. Having anticipated the impossible, pundits and reporters alike declared themselves disappointed that their expectations were not fulfilled and criticized the government for failing to reveal more of its hand as well as for resorting to displays of partisanship. The opposition was castigated for neglecting to offer any realistic alternative. The basic CP story, repeated by most papers, highlighted the prime minister's 'passionate appeal for support' for a free-trade deal that would cause 'jobs and wealth [to] flow to the poorer regions,' an appeal that 'did not convince sceptical opposition leaders' who did not feel the PM could get a good deal from President Reagan 'without sacrificing Canadian jobs and independence.'[23] Charles Lynch did the only mood piece. He pointed out that very few members were present in the House except as audience fodder for the TV cameras when a minister or leader was speaking. 'Today,' he lamented, 'there are no major events, and in terms of reverberations, nothing done or said in the Commons has the impact of a single public opinion poll, or a structured circus like a political convention.'[24]

The *Toronto Star* predictably claimed that 'the only thing Mulroney demonstrated ... is that, as long as he keeps Canadians in the dark, there really can be no meaningful debate.' Equally predictably, the *Globe and Mail* thought that the talks had 'suddenly ... assumed an air of reality' and that 'if a good deal could be struck, a consensus will probably be found within Canada to support it.' It assailed the Opposition, suggesting that 'the Liberals remain the party for all seasons on trade ... the NDP speak clearly but carry a complex brief.' The *Montreal Gazette* felt that the debate had failed to address the concerns of average Canadians and said that while Pat Carney's remarks 'shed some welcome light' on the talks, they raised as many questions as they answered.[25]

Whatever the views of the media, the government had successfully seized the public initiative and breathed new life into its principal economic policy. It had demonstrated it was on top of the issues and prepared to follow through. Reisman could ask for no more. Ministers now had speeches with which they were comfortable and which they could use time and again across the country. In the following months, while debate continued to rage, the government felt it had put its position solidly to the public. It had taken command of the agenda. And with that command the government became confident in its vision of the Canada that would result from free trade.

Agriculture Once Again

Agriculture took pride of place at the tenth plenary in Ottawa, 16-17 March, coincident with the parliamentary debate. This was the third time around on agriculture for the two chief negotiators. The negotiating group had not been making much progress. On both sides, the technicians came from within the agricultural establishment and had a strong disinclination to negotiate a deal that would truly open up agricultural markets. They saw no domestic constituency for such a deal and the potential for bitter opposition. Their role was to ensure that farmers were protected in any agreement.

Reisman's inclination as a good economist was to treat all sectors of the economy equally. Nevertheless, pragmatic political considerations suggested that this might not be realistic for agriculture. In forty years of multilateral trade negotiations, trade in farm commodities had always been treated along sectoral lines. The European free-trade agreements had all treated agricultural issues separately. Indeed, some commentators have concluded that the decision to treat agriculture differently in international negotiations is one of the reasons that barriers to agricultural trade have proven so intractable. That is not to suggest that there had not been progress in eliminating some barriers. Over half of Canada-US agricultural trade was already free of duties by the mid-1980s and the average trade-weighted tariff on the dutiable remainder was down to about 6 per cent. Moreover, in many instances the Canadian and US tariffs had been harmonized at the same rate. The one major area where there remained significant tariff disparities and peaks was fresh and processed fruits and vegetables.

The real issues in agriculture, however, involved non-tariff measures, which in most cases were linked directly to domestic agricultural income support and marketing policies. Both Canada and the United States maintained import quotas to protect domestic price support mechanisms. While there were differences, they were matters of technique and commodity coverage rather than philosophy. In the United States, import quotas were used to protect the sugar, dairy, and other price support programs. In Canada, import quotas were used to support the national supply management programs for dairy, poultry, and eggs. For both governments, therefore, the issue was whether the trade expansion resulting from a significant liberalization of non-tariff restrictions would be sufficient to outweigh the social and political dislocations associated with substantially altering related domestic policies and programs. In addition, both countries would have to determine the extent to which they could liberalize processed products if they insisted on maintaining non-tariff barriers for primary products.

A further issue was competition between Canadian and US farmers in third markets and the techniques used to support export sales. This discussion was taking place against a background of considerable uncertainty and instability in global agricultural markets caused by excess capacity in developed countries resulting from domestic support programs and improvements in technology. Structural surpluses were likely to persist for at least the balance of the 1980s and possibly well into the 1990s. As long as surpluses persisted, export markets would remain highly competitive, particularly for cereals, dairy products, beef, and sugar.

In contrast to this relatively sombre global outlook, the potential for agricultural trade expansion between Canada and the United States appeared promising. Close proximity, relatively high economic growth rates, and similar grading and distribution systems for a very wide range of products suggested that bilateral agricultural trade could continue to grow. But this would require a relatively open trade environment. Like many other sectors of the economy, the value of a bilateral trade agreement to Canadian agriculture would be measured by the extent to which access could be made both more open and more secure. It could be made more open by reducing existing barriers such as the tariff, end-use certificates for seed potatoes, excessive 'spot checks' for conformity with US grading and health regulations, and periodic restrictions on meat imports. It would be more secure if a better contingency protection regime was negotiated. The latter would require at least an examination of how the two governments support farm incomes.

Alas, as a function of the House debate, marketing boards were now clearly sacrosanct. Well-organized farm lobbies, such as the chicken and dairy farmers, had convinced the minister to take supply management off the table and had thus doomed any prospect for a serious breakthrough on bilateral trade in agriculture.

It would take some subtle bargaining to find a smaller mutually acceptable package of reductions in barriers to farm products. Both governments from long experience had learned that for the farm sector, unlike for other sectors, the deal would have to be self-balancing. No deal could be sold to farmers on the basis of benefits to the economy in general. Each concession in the farm sector would have to be related directly to a benefit for farmers. Thus, while the desire for a big deal was initially there, pragmatic factors gradually narrowed the scope.

But as long as there was a chance, Reisman wanted to ensure that he had examined the outer limits of an acceptable farm package. He did not give up as easily as the specialists. He was prepared to push the Americans very hard on their meat import restrictions, their sugar quotas, their grading and sanitary regulations, and other barriers. In return, he was prepared to phase out the tariff on fresh fruits and vegetables, adjust import quotas, and deal with the vexing problems of beer and wine. He was even prepared, in a big deal, to address some aspects of the supply management system. But as in other aspects of the negotiations, the Americans were better at requests than at offers. By the end of the session, it looked like agricultural protectionism would not be greatly compromised.

Shamrock Three

Concurrently, preparations for the 6-7 April summit meeting between the prime minister and the president began. The meeting offered both opportunities and risks. It had been the first summit in Quebec two years earlier that had set in motion the events leading to the negotiations. The second summit in 1986 had had no perceptible effect. This third summit was crucial not for the issues that it could resolve but for the momentum and the message it could generate.

The agenda for the summit comprised the usual array of irritants and problems: acid rain, the trade negotiations and trade irritants, defence issues and arms control, Arctic sovereignty, and broad foreign policy questions, such as the problems of Central America and South Africa. The key Canadian objective was to secure a concrete action program for the reduction of acid rain emissions.

In the initial preparations, the United States, in contrast to earlier summits, seemed better organized and made an effort to show that serious planning and thought were being put into the meeting. Given the president's problems with the Iran-Contra scandal, the United States was hoping for a 'foreign policy' success from the visit. On the trade negotiations, however, Murphy claimed that there was no particular negotiating issue that required attention during the visit. Giving prominence to the negotiations could be counterproductive if it produced a knee-jerk reaction in the Congress. In Murphy's view, the less public attention drawn to the trade negotiations at this time, the better.

The TNO view was the opposite. The two sides had agreed to complete a draft text of the whole agreement by June or July. To get there, it was imperative that both negotiators have the mandate to cut a deal meeting the fundamental interests of the other side.

This was the last summit before the scheduled conclusion of the negotiations. The visits by Senator Bentsen and colleagues, by Vice President Bush and Secretary Baker, the president's state-of-the-union address, and the House of Commons debate had contributed to a public perception that the negotiations were on course. It was important to maintain this momentum.

On the US side, the administration's support at the highest levels for a comprehensive agreement had been consistent, but this had yet to be translated into progress at the table. On a range of key issues, such as trade remedy law, services, dispute settlement, and government procurement, the US side continued to be either unprepared or unwilling to spell out how it envisaged meeting Canadian or US requirements.

Support at senior congressional levels, notably Senate Finance Committee chairman Bentsen and House Ways and Means chairman Rostenkowski, had been similarly strong on the general idea of a comprehensive agreement. At the same time, Congress was preparing to pass highly protectionist legislation that, in the absence of a comprehensive trade agreement, would be severely damaging to Canada. It was clear that the administration would have a major task in securing congressional approval of a comprehensive trade agreement.

Reisman argued that a clear message on the negotiations had to emerge from the visit, given the prime minister's recent reaffirmation of their importance to Canada and the president's state-of-the-union address. Anything less would be seen as a retreat. The trade negotiations were as important, if not more important, than acid rain and defence issues and should be played that way. An opportunity should be sought to inform Howard Baker, the president's new chief of staff, on the objectives and scope of the negotiations, and to remind him of the short timetable available for the hard decisions which needed to be taken.

In this light, the Canadian objective during the summit was to secure the president's reaffirmation of his undertaking in the state-of-the-union address to 'complete a historic free-trade agreement with Canada.' This would require his commitment to equip US negotiators with the mandate necessary to ensure the successful conclusion of the negotiations within the fast-track timeframe. Additionally, he would need to recognize that an agreement would have to meet Canada's basic security of access requirements involving new rules to control trade-distorting measures, binational binding dispute settlement, and no trade restrictions. In short, the new trade agreement should underpin the unique relationship between Canada and the United States. At the same time, the prime minister wanted to indicate that he understood that investment was a critical issue for the United States and that he was prepared to be receptive.

The Canadian script for the summit went forward without a misstep. The president declared his unequivocal support for the negotiations and committed the full resources of his administration to that end. In his speech to the combined houses of Parliament, he poured praise on the prime minister for his vision and boldness and declared the negotiations an example to the world. Additionally, during their private sessions, the prime minister forcefully pressed the Canadian trade remedy case. Although there was no concrete response from the American side, there could be no risk of surprise as the negotiations on this critical issue proceeded.

One familiar face at the summit was there in a new role. Derek Burney, veteran of both the annual economic summits and bilateral summits as a senior official at External Affairs, had joined the PMO at the beginning of March as chief of staff. Mulroney had finally decided that some of his political woes had originated with his own staff. To change things around he needed a professional manager with a sure sense of the issues and a steady hand in dealing with political staff and the bureaucracy. In February he had recruited Burney to this task and given him wide latitude. As part of the reform, Burney had organized the prime minister's agenda in order to ensure more efficient concentration on the major issues. As such, he was in an excellent position to influence priorities and participate in the unfolding of those issues that mattered. His knowledge of free trade added to his influence. This had already been evident in the House debate. The bilateral summit was another such event and Burney was there, front but not centre. As a bureaucrat he had learned the art of influencing without being seen. At the summit, he quietly gave advice and spent some time with his opposite number, Howard Baker, impressing upon him the importance of making progress in the bilateral negotiations.

Following the summit, there was a pleasant afterglow. Unlike the previous year's meeting, which had passed into history with hardly a trace in both countries, and the 1985 meeting which, despite the Canadian hoopla, represented no more than business as usual in the United States, Canada remained on the US agenda. In his next regular Saturday morning radio address, the president referred in glowing and positive terms to his visit and to the negotiations. The same week he met with the Advisory Committee on Trade Negotiations – the senior US private sector group – and confirmed in strong terms his administration's commitment to a deal: 'Canadians are concerned that, while this negotiation is their most important economic issue, some in the United States are not paying attention to it. Well, it has been a top priority for me and my administration.'[26] Word also filtered out from a meeting of the economic policy council chaired by Secretary Baker that the administration considered that a free-trade agreement with Canada would be a major achievement of the Reagan presidency confirming what Deputy Treasury Secretary Richard Darman had indicated earlier.

Investment Hits the Table

The eleventh plenary, held in Washington on 9-10 April, provided the first test of US commitment. The main event was the presentation of the formal US position on investment which, it was fully anticipated, would reflect the months of private discussions that had laid the ground for the treatment of this critical and sensitive issue. This was a Treasury issue and presenting the script was Bob Cornell, the senior Treasury member of Murphy's team. Murphy was there largely in the role of moderator.

The US presentation was both sanctimonious and patronizing. The US proposal was cast as one which went beyond what had been achieved with various developing countries, but which was entirely in accord with Canadian interests. In addition to the anticipated requests for national treatment on new investment, divestiture, repatriation, and expropriation, it sought to abolish the Canadian capacity to review direct and indirect takeovers, to roll back existing commitments undertaken by investors under existing and previous legislation, and demanded ironclad guarantees against the reintroduction of investment reviews or takeover legislation.

The US proposal was in Reisman's view nothing less than a draft license to take over the country. Canada was open for business but not for sale. If this proposal were pressed, it would awaken the worst Canadian fears and would probably prevent inclusion of investment in the agreement, perhaps even proving fatal to the negotiations as a whole. More than that, in Reisman's view the proposal was evidence of bad faith. On the basis of numerous private conversations with Murphy, Reisman had been entitled to draw the conclusion that the US request, while far reaching, could be accommodated. Now there was a proposal that went far beyond anything that had been discussed privately and well beyond any realistic view of the possible or the desirable.

Reisman recalled once again that the prime minister and the president, in launching the negotiations, had not included investment beyond trade-related investment measures. He, Reisman, had pressed for a formal US proposal to cover investment in all its respects but this had not been forthcoming. There had been, however, many informal discussions as well as visits by Bentsen, Bush, Baker, and the president which had made clear US interest in all aspects of investment. He had made a commitment that if negotiations were going reasonably well, he would seek a negotiating mandate based on an approach that he could recommend. To do so, he would need to have a clear idea of US interests. He regretted that the US proposal did not provide such a basis. On the contrary, it would arouse alarmist reactions and indeed could doom prospects for a sensible agreement overall. In the circumstances, he would not dignify the US proposal with even a flat rejection. He would refuse to accept the proposal as having been made and so, with ceremony and courtesy and a small smile playing at the corners of his lips, he handed the paper on which the outrage was inscribed back to Murphy.

Murphy seemed unsurprised but persisted for a while. The Canadian side had many proposals that were very difficult for the United States; none of these had been rejected or handed back; all were part of the negotiations. If the US proposal was too difficult for Canada, then Reisman should make a counter-proposal. Reisman declined and proposed that investment be treated as a heads-of-delegation question where he would explain once again what was possible. He assured Murphy that the final result on investment would go far beyond anything the United States could have dreamed of having with Canada or any other industrialized country. And with that, Murphy had to be satisfied.

Alan King, *Ottawa Citizen*, 16 January 1987

More Shadow-Boxing

How quickly the summit glow faded. The twelfth plenary took place in Ottawa on 28-9 April with a Canadian side determined to corner Murphy. It was agreed that if no progress was made, the charade should be called off. Unless Murphy showed a readiness to engage, there would be no more plenaries and no more working groups. But at dinner the preceding evening, Murphy escaped again. In response to probing, Murphy countered that there was substantial engagement on all issues. On procurement, Murphy confirmed US interest in a big deal; on contingency protection, the US side was negotiating on the basis of a Canadian paper; and on dispute settlement, they stood ready to negotiate on the basis of binding arbitration. In view of these assurances, notwithstanding all the doubts about Murphy's credibility that past performance fully justified, it was decided that the negotiations should continue and indeed that Reisman should proceed to obtain a negotiating mandate on investment.

That any optimism flowing from the dinner was misplaced was rapidly confirmed in the plenary session. The first day was devoted to customs issues and intellectual property with little progress being made. Murphy arrived expressing extreme irritation with Reisman's public comments on the observations of US Commerce Undersecretary Bruce Smart that the Amoco takeover of Dome petroleum had better be accepted or negotiations would be badly affected. Reisman had provided the press with a field day by calling these remarks unfortunate, unwise, and imprudent. This led to a long mutual harangue on the negotiations. The real source of Murphy's irritation, however, was that he had received a tongue-lashing from Smart for publicly responding to Reisman and suggesting that he was the negotiator and that the comments of other US officials were unhelpful. To goad Reisman further, Murphy raised again the US investment proposal, leading Reisman to declare that he had lost confidence in their ability to conclude an agreement. After a two-hour heads of delegation meeting, it was agreed that no progress could be made and that the day should be written off. The two delegations hung about fearing that if the US side left earlier, the press would fall upon them like hungry vultures drawing the conclusion that the negotiations had been suspended.

Reisman had given the press little fodder in Washington at the beginning of the month. Jennifer Lewington's story for that session showed how difficult it had become to write a story without a little outrage from Reisman. He gave her colleague Chris Waddell what he needed in Ottawa. Reisman had opened with his comments about Smart. In addition to criticizing Smart's comments about Amoco, he dismissed the view that a smaller, tariff-only deal would be easier to negotiate. He also did not like Smart's comment that a big deal had to address investment. Reisman was not interested in a small deal and if the United States wanted something on investment, they had better be more forthcoming on contingency protection. The link he had sought to avoid was now made publicly. Nevertheless, he bubbled over with enthusiasm, insisting that progress was being made and that an agreement would emerge. Asked whether the talks were getting easier or more difficult, Murphy gave an enigmatic answer: 'You deal with Mr. Reisman. You tell me. From my perspective, life never changes.'[27]

An Impasse?

What did all this portend? Had negotiations reached an impasse? Mercifully, the winter of discontent was over. Spring and summer promised little better, but at least the weather would be an improvement. The rationale for a comprehensive Canada-United States trade agreement remained compelling. Despite its public commitment, circumstances in the United States appeared to have sapped the strength and willingness of the administration to take the necessary risks to permit the successful conclusion of the negotiations within the timetable established. Murphy appeared to lack the skill and experience to put forward proposals and stick with them. He appeared to have no vision and no compelling philosophy. He appeared to be driven by a desire simply to survive and resolve as many irritants as possible. There remained, however, the possibility of achieving Canadian objectives if the US administration and senior members of Congress threw their full weight behind the negotiations. Nothing less would suffice.

The time to determine the readiness of the United States to proceed and to provide its negotiating team with the necessary mandate would be the summer. To this end, an approach would have to be made once again to the most senior members of the administration. If it was determined that an agreement was not possible, an early decision would need to be taken on a program of constructive disengagement. Steps were taken to test US commitment once again using the spring round of senior multilateral meetings: the OECD Ministerial Meeting in Paris, the NATO Ministerial Meeting in Iceland, and the Economic Summit in Venice.

11

Spring Again: Moving Rocks

We've got some pretty big rocks to move.
— Simon Reisman

While the disappearing snow and spring flowers should have brought renewed energy and optimism, there was nothing but gloom in the air. By this time, early perceptions of US tactics had been confirmed in spades: get Canada to lay out the whole of its negotiating position without giving anything in return. Another view, scarcely more comforting, was that the US side had not thought out its position and had no clear idea of either Canadian needs or US interests.

The senior members of the US team encountered thus far had the bureaucratic reverence for safety and caution.[1] They were interested in resolving irritants and thus satisfying individual congressional concerns and, more generally, securing disciplines on Canada, while avoiding any new disciplines on the United States or any need to change US law and procedure. They were of the view, for example, that there should be no disciplines on purely domestic subsidies. They contended that only subsidies with an export effect should be subject to disciplines. This was a convenient point of departure for a country possessing a large continental market. There appeared to be no hope that they would agree to any discipline on domestic subsidies displacing imports.

By this time, it could have been expected that the core of the US delegation would have jelled into a team, working to a common purpose based on an agreed strategy and a clear mandate. While the US negotiators had come from at least eight different agencies, they had worked together for a year. Unfortunately, they remained a collection of individuals, seemingly drawing their authority from their agency position rather than from Murphy, and their mandate from their immediate superiors rather than from the US cabinet. Murphy appeared to have neither the capacity nor the will to impose a single view on his team. Even more aggravating, all considered themselves experts on Congress and never tired of indicating that everything Canada proposed would be very difficult if not impossible for Congress to contemplate. The administration appeared to have no comprehensive view of its own. Even senior US team members recognized the problem. Bill Merkin, Murphy's deputy, complained that 'in general ... it is safe to say that the senior policy makers in Washington had very little idea of what was actually taking place in the negotiations.'[2]

Each US core member was responsible for one or two working groups, each of which appeared to be drawn together from an ever-changing cast of junior interagency individuals. Like the main team, they too seemed to derive their inspiration from their immediate superiors and their reading of Congress rather than from their team leader. There appeared to be no general vision that held these disparate views together. It was all a far cry from the tightly disciplined and centrally led TNO team.

While Reisman was responsible for the negotiations, he had delegated responsibility for running the office and the team to his deputy, Gordon Ritchie. Ritchie ran a tight ship. He met regularly with concerned deputy ministers from around town, and senior members of the team kept their colleagues in other departments informed of the issues in order to avoid nasty surprises. But essentially the negotiations were a TNO effort. Each senior team member could count on two or three specialists to help. None was dependent on the resources of other departments. Thus virtually all those working on the project came under the single-minded leadership of Ritchie and worked on the basis of the vision and philosophy supplied by Reisman. While not everyone thrived under Ritchie's highly disciplined approach and many chafed at the arrogance of the senior members of the team, there was nevertheless a strong sense of purpose.

In addition to his periodic meetings with Murphy, Reisman also met regularly with senior provincial representatives in the Continuing Committee on Trade Negotiations. Ritchie and the senior officers also maintained a regular schedule of consultations with business through the ITAC and SAGIT system. These duties were necessary but essentially secondary to the main event. Reisman's job was to negotiate a comprehensive trade agreement with the United States. For this he had been given the best resources available and a free hand in how to deploy them. He had a general mandate from the government as well as specific mandates on individual issues. His broad approach had been endorsed by the premiers. All he needed was someone on the other side of the table with an analogous mandate and a shared vision, if not philosophy.

After nearly a year of negotiations, what progress could Reisman report in his regular sessions with the committee of ministers chaired by Pat Carney? What could he tell the premiers? There was nothing to show on the whole range of issues. In the meantime, the government was finding the battle for the hearts and minds of Canadians a tough slog as it fought steady rearguard actions on issues such as film distribution, agriculture, and regional subsidies and continued to be handicapped by the fact that the details of the negotiations had to be kept confidential. Reisman found meetings with ministers and the provinces to be increasingly sharp. The strain sapped his energy and he lapsed more frequently into his famous temper tantrums. Few appreciated the difficulty of dealing with a protagonist who had no clear mandate or framework for prosecuting the negotiations. While the United States appeared not to take this initiative seriously enough, it remained a very serious matter in Canada. The pressure on Reisman was immense.

There was, of course, a different US perspective. The administration was trying to come to terms with the most virulent outbreak of congressional protectionism since the depression of the 1930s. It seemed resistant to all the usual arguments. Protectionism was the most important issue on the trade agenda and that was the issue that required the best resources. Editorialized *Newsday:* 'Protectionism will gain greater and greater respectability not because it makes any more sense than it ever did, not because it will protect U.S. living standards or American competitiveness but because the credibility of its enemies will be exhausted.'[3] The House was considering its version of a protectionist trade bill for the second time. The Senate was working on its own draft. No amount of testimony on trade issues by secretaries and other senior officials appeared to have any impact. Since the fall, USTR had worked flat out on an administration version of a trade bill. It had devoted considerable resources to this effort, resources which Canadian negotiators felt could have been better devoted to the bilateral negotiations, but which the administration felt had been well used. The draft bill was tabled on 20 February and then disappeared, never to be heard of again. No one in Congress was interested. Perhaps Canada had been right, but no one was going to admit it.

Similarly, the administration felt beleaguered on other fronts. The Uruguay Round of multilateral trade negotiations seemed to be stuck in neutral; the Japanese continued to export and not to import; the Europeans did not seem to appreciate that the Americans had problems; and the Brazilians and other advanced developing countries were, in the view of their embattled US competitors, dumping and subsidizing their way into the US market, adding to congressional anger. And then there were the Canadians, swimming upstream, equipped with a huge negotiating team headed by the brassiest negotiator the Americans had ever seen. And every time things did not look good enough for the Canadians, they upped the ante and forced secretaries and even the president to spend valuable time mollifying them. Why could these Canadians not accept that in its proper time, the issue would be resolved and meanwhile, the task of the negotiators was to clear away the technical underbrush?

Peter Murphy was an experienced negotiator going about his job in a very difficult environment. He had the confidence of the president and the administration. His style was just different from that of Reisman. In fact, not all on the US side were enamoured of the Reisman style. Said one anonymous source to the *Globe and Mail*'s Jennifer Lewington: 'It's just part of the game. He clearly knows the issues in detail and we respect his vision for Canada, even if we don't always appreciate his tactics.' She went on: 'Some of those tactics are dismissed as histrionics, designed to spark a reaction or shed light on U.S. thinking. The result, U.S. officials sometimes complain, is time-wasting tangents that side-track the main discussion for hours. They also bristle at Mr. Reisman's habit of talking down to chief U.S. negotiator Peter Murphy ... Some of the most rancorous moments at the negotiating table occur between Mr. Reisman and senior U.S. commerce department officials.'[4]

The Canada-US negotiations were also not of the same order in Washington as they were in Ottawa. Everyone could agree with Bob Strauss, Jimmy Carter's special trade representative, that the negotiations were like chicken soup. 'Of course one is in favour. People aren't negative about it. They simply haven't given it a thought.'[5] Even Congress was seen to be pleasantly disposed, 'in a pleasantly unfocussed sort of way.'[6] But no one was prepared to invest the negotiations with a lot of political capital.

Even more germane, while the administration had been very supportive of the initiative from the beginning and had encouraged Canada to proceed, it was only now getting serious about the substance of the exercise. It wanted to prove to Congress that it could drive a hard trade bargain, thereby gaining a renewed mandate to take to the Uruguay Round of talks. But, according to *Business Week*:

> Unfortunately for Reagan, the talks never really got off the ground. The White House is only now deciding what it wants. And as time has passed, the political position of Canadian Prime Minister Brian Mulroney has deteriorated, making it difficult for him to cut a deal. U.S. negotiators are trying to save the talks, confident that they can reach a substantial agreement before the President's negotiating authority expires in September ... But any accord will fall far short of the complete free-trade agreement Reagan once envisioned.[7]

And that was the point.[8] From Washington's perspective, much of the whining seemed to be coming from a government that had taken a disastrous tumble in the polls and was desperately trying to regain votes with a coup in the trade policy area. If the Canadians were desperate, let them make a deal. If this government did not survive, the United States would have to deal with a government made up of one of the other two parties, both of which were hostile to the idea. This was a time for caution. Caught between a Congress indifferent to the Canadian negotiations but hostile to any deal that would compromise US ability to deal with unfair trade, and a Canadian government mired at the bottom of the polls, the US side saw no advantage in being visionary. Leave that to the Canadians.

All of this might have been true, but it did not help break the log-jam. The Canadian team could, of course, present the US team with a draft agreement and not meet again until the US side was prepared to deal on that basis. Some had argued for months that the only way to deal with an opposing team that had no vision and no discernible plan was to provide a complete Canadian proposal presented in treaty language and take it from there. One drawback to this step was that there remained some gaps in Canada's own positions. Reisman wanted to be sure that he knew how to press the Canadian case regarding special treatment on such key issues as regional development, culture, and food processing, before tabling a complete document. The more telling argument, however, was that to advance such a draft agreement at this stage would run the risk of a leak to the media complicating the public management of the negotiations. If the United States was not prepared to put all its cards on the table and show clearly where it was coming from on such central issues as contingency protection and dispute settlement, Canada should not make it easy by giving the full Canadian position in exquisite detail.

Could Canada have tabled a complete draft treaty at this time? With a little work, yes. Starting in January, members of the team had made steady progress on a detailed outline. A slide show of this outline had been shared with ministers as well as provincial representatives. Individual ministers had been taken through it in detail so that they could appreciate what a deal along the lines suggested by the outline would mean for their portfolios. Individual working groups had been beavering away for more than six months and some had developed the beginning of a draft text. In addition, inspiration was available from a number of existing agreements such as the Treaty of Rome establishing the European Economic Community and the Treaty of Stockholm establishing the European Free Trade Association. While somewhat dated, they showed how a comprehensive agreement could be constructed. The more recent US-Israel agreement did not provide much guidance, given its limited coverage and unambitious approach. Finally, a number of draft agreements had been prepared in the period leading up to the negotiations.[9] Putting a draft text together was not an impossible task. It would be easier, however, if there was more input from the US side to give it a necessary air of reality.

The U.S. position on...

FREE TRADE   ACID RAIN   SANCTIONS ON SOUTH AFRICA

Alan King, *Ottawa Citizen*, 3 February 1987

The Alliance Lends a Hand

But all was not bleak. Support from business continued to be strong, although it lacked cohesion. This situation began to change. With the active encouragement of the government, an independent and non-partisan alliance to promote free trade began to coalesce early in 1987 and was formally announced on 19 March. Co-chaired by Donald Macdonald, former Liberal cabinet minister, royal commissioner, and establishment lawyer in Toronto, and Peter Lougheed, former Conservative premier of Alberta, it took as its name the Canadian Alliance for Jobs and Trade Opportunities (CAJTO).

David Culver gave its secretariat a home in the Montreal offices of Alcan. In Ottawa, Tom d'Aquino and his BCNI staff handled fundraising and set up a stable of around thirty speakers including Macdonald, Lougheed, Culver, John Crispo, the peripatetic free-trade crusader from the University of Toronto business school, and Darcy McKeough, former treasurer of Ontario and chairman of Union Gas. In the months that followed, the group raised a budget of around $3 million, ran a series of newspaper ads promoting free trade, and spoke up at every opportunity. In early July, members of the group, led by Lougheed and Macdonald, met with US business executives and congressional leaders in Washington. At the end of the meeting, US business leaders expressed strong support for the talks as the best way to expand two-way trade and create jobs.

Great expectations were held out for the Alliance. However, its value lay less in proselytizing the general public than in talking up the benefits of free trade at Rotary Clubs and chambers of commerce across the country. Business had proven masterful in quietly lobbying government to achieve changes in tax and fiscal policy. But when it came to placard-waving and marching on Parliament Hill, they were clearly outdone by the spider's web of groups from the arts, churches, farms, labour, native communities, and feminist organizations which opposed free trade. Shirley Carr and the Canadian Federation of Labour had earlier proclaimed labour's opposition to free trade and set aside over a million dollars to be used effectively in radio, television, and newspaper advertising and large billboards. Bob White, the charismatic president of the Canadian Autoworkers, and Edmonton publisher Mel Hurtig could always be counted on to appear at any rally.

By the late spring of 1987, the opposition, led by Maude Barlow and John Trent, had also unified into a group calling itself the Pro-Canada Network. Barlow had been previously employed as an advocate for women's rights during the days when Marion Dewar (by then the NDP member of Parliament from Hamilton) was mayor of Ottawa. Barlow had then become a policy advisor to the Liberal party. Trent is a University of Ottawa political scientist active in the NDP party. The Network drew its strength from Hurtig's Council of Canadians and organized labour, as well as the NDP and anti-free traders in the Liberal party. With its headquarters in Ottawa, the Network drew further support from regional alliances in Quebec, Ontario, Prince Edward Island, Manitoba, and Saskatchewan, mostly based in the provincial labour federations.

As negotiations entered the home stretch, two organized groups thus stood ready to cheer and jeer, whatever the results. Both sought solace in the polls. For the Alliance, an Angus Reid poll in February showed that support was remaining steadfast above 50 per cent (57 per cent for and 32 per cent against, confirmed by a Globe-Environics poll in March that placed support at 57 per cent and opposition at 27 per cent). Even more gratifying was Reid's determination that a plurality of supporters of all three political parties favoured an agreement. Among Conservatives, 74 per cent were in favour; Liberals favoured an agreement 55 to 34; and even more New Democrats were for (48 per cent) than against (42 per cent). Most Canadians (53 per cent) placed economic gains ahead of any potential losses in cultural identity or heritage, compared to 34 per cent who thought the opposite.[10]

The Pro-Canada Network, however, took comfort in the fact that Reid also found that an increasing number of Canadians expressed concern about the government's handling of the negotiations. Fifty-eight per cent did not believe that the prime minister could represent their interests in the negotiations, up from 52 per cent in June of 1986 and 45 per cent in January 1986. Reid concluded that 'the Prime Minister's popularity is perhaps the biggest political obstacle to the free-trade initiative.'[11] In a shrewd move, the Network increasingly began to refer to the initiative as the Mulroney-Reagan agreement or negotiations.[12]

Five months remained and the road ahead was strewn with heavy rocks. Was there time enough to move these barriers and build a comprehensive agreement? Could the will be found to clear away the obstacles?

A Return to Meech Lake

For the thirteenth plenary, 18-20 May, the negotiations returned to the peaceful setting of Meech Lake. Reisman and Murphy and large delegations on both sides met around the rectangular conference table on the second floor of Willson House where a few weeks before the Meech Lake Accord on the constitution had been hammered out. A large press contingent followed them. While the negotiators growled and spat at each other inside, the reporters chewed the fat, started rumours, and provided a feast for the black flies. They accompanied Reisman on several walks around the grounds. Reisman, inspired by the scenery and a print in Willson House of some big rocks being removed from the Ottawa river, told them the negotiations were proceeding on schedule. The two sides had by now exposed the big rocks and were preparing to move them. The cartoonists had another bonanza. Given the sylvan setting, the press were again given some new softball footage, including a nice shot of a US team member taking a ball on the nose. At last there was some proof that the Americans were prepared to bleed a little for these negotiations.

This meeting had been billed as a complete review of the major issues. Reisman's purpose was to take Murphy firmly by the hand, lead him through the issues, and force him to respond. In his view, the negotiations on various issues should have proceeded in lock step, balancing conflicting Canadian and US priorities. The US response had, at a minimum, been inadequate. Canada was prepared to make real concessions to secure a good agreement that met its requirements. The key would be the rules on subsidies and dispute settlement.

'Trouble is, they're in a rather awkward place.'

Alan King, *Ottawa Citizen*, 12 May 1987

On subsidies the real problem was quickly exposed. It was indeed a central US objective to negotiate subsidies rules applying to Canada. It was a far different question whether such rules would eliminate countervailing duties from the US arsenal. Would subsidy rules be administered bilaterally or unilaterally? If the former, both sides would have a keen interest in a good and binding dispute settlement process. If the latter, the United States would continue to rely on countervail and would have little interest in binding dispute settlements.

Reisman's response was a calm and lucid presentation of Canada's reasons for entering these negotiations and Canada's basic requirements for an agreement:

- The Canadian interest was secure access to the US market so that businesses could take decisions in the knowledge that their market access would not be unilaterally interrupted on either side.
- This meant that Canada needed an agreed set of rules covering all its bilateral trade in goods and services as well as investment flows. Such rules had to be clear, easily interpreted, and enshrined in a trade agreement that would govern the relationship.
- If there emerged a difference on those rules which could not be resolved through consultation, fact finding, or good faith efforts, then there should be binding arbitration. Both governments should forgo the right to a unilateral interpretation of the rules.
- The United States could offer only one thing of real value that Canada would pay for and that was to give up the right to unilateral determina-

tions of the rules; without that concession no agreement was worthwhile. Otherwise there would be no reason for Canada to give up the tariff or to accept binding obligations on services, investment, and intellectual property. There were no circumstances under which Reisman would recommend, and no possibility that the government would accept, such an agreement.

- Was it possible for the US side to envisage an agreement that had a clear set of rules for which interpretation would be binding and joint and not unilateral? Without an answer, the US side would not be negotiating in good faith, and he would not be prepared to continue.
- Canada was entitled to a clear exposition of the US view. If the US position was that, once Canada had agreed to rules that were tight and met US interests, the Americans would retain the unilateral right to decide whether or not Canada was adhering to those rules, then Murphy should tell him that.[13]

Murphy responded with his classic bob and weave. The US negotiators were not without their own grievances; on services, investment, and intellectual property, in Murphy's view they had not obtained satisfaction. This negotiation was very difficult; no one had said it would be easy. If Canada was looking for a total exemption from US trade law, this would place a tremendous strain on the negotiations. Nevertheless, the two sides had worked together for a year and should keep on working. He believed that an agreement acceptable to Congress was still possible. But he was not prepared to work on the basis of any preconditions.

Reisman made short shrift of this response. Answers were needed. Murphy should assume that there would be good rules on subsidies, and deals on services, investment, and intellectual property where none existed before, rules going well beyond what the United States could even dream of accomplishing with others. Murphy dipped, dived, and ducked again but committed himself to preparing proposals on subsidies and dispute settlement. The thirteenth plenary ended.

Concurrent with the meeting, Reisman had had to travel downtown to meet with ministers and consider investment. While the two teams played softball, he played hardball. Not satisfied with the discussion, he used the press scrum at the end of the day to talk about investment. The investment issue had finally hit public consciousness and had become a subject of controversy in the press and of hyperbole in the House. Reisman's sermon on the difficulties of the investment issues did not fool Jeffrey Simpson. He knew that the issue was before ministers and concluded that ministers had been Reisman's audience. Simpson and other pundits were not impressed by the Opposition hype: 'This is what the negotiations are about – give and take within the investment area and, more broadly, between those sorts of

American priorities and Canadian concerns. Not much of this was reflected in the unreality that pervaded Ottawa all week.'[14] Hy Solomon, whose weekly column was usually based on meticulous interviews with some of the best sources in Ottawa, took a different tack:

> [There is] plenty of room for a deal on foreign investment as part of the Canada-U.S. free-trade package, providing, of course, both sides can agree on some ground rules, and then exercise a little restraint and sensitivity in the negotiating exercise ... The recent parliamentary debate on investment – shrill, emotional, and full of cheap scare tactics – missed the point. It's not whether we're ready, but whether the Americans are.[15]

The Venice Card

Following the thirteenth plenary, it was blindingly evident that the US team was either unable or unwilling to negotiate. Time was running short. There was a serious risk that not for lack of agreement, but rather for lack of engagement, the negotiations would fail. Urgent preparations were launched to make the negotiations the centrepiece of the prime minister's meeting with the president on the margins of the Venice summit of the western industrialized countries.

This would be the fourth time since the negotiations began that the Canadian side had tried to kick-start the US side into serious engagement on Canadian issues. On each of the three previous occasions – the visit of Senator Bentsen and colleagues in December 1986, the visit of Vice President Bush in January 1987, and Shamrock Three in April – Peter Murphy and his troops had been considerably discomfited, expressing grave disquiet about losing control of a delicate and difficult process. The result each time had been the same: a momentary flurry of life lapsing into lassitude a short time after.

It was important to clear the decks to ensure that this meeting would have the maximum effect. The vehicle was a letter from Reisman to Murphy declaring the Canadian side to be fully equipped to negotiate on all issues and expressing disappointment that he had not, contrary to previous under-takings, engaged on the issues which for Canada would make or break the negotiations. The answer from Murphy was the written version of the bob and weave, urging Canada not to press too soon for answers on difficult issues, that the United States was interested in a large agreement and that negotiations should continue. Reisman immediately responded that this sit-uation was wholly unsatisfactory and that the prime minister would be fully briefed in advance of his meeting with the president prior to the Venice summit.

The signals out of Washington, however, had once again been confused. Murphy did not like Canada again upping the ante. Said one senior official, 'Simon Reisman may be trying to elevate it to the political level. But we don't want to go along with it. We want to back up Peter Murphy.'[16] Treasury Secretary James Baker, however, in briefing reporters from the seven summit partners, had gone out of his way to point to the Canada-US negotiations as an outstanding example of where the world should be headed, a theme Reagan would repeat at the summit: 'There are still some major hurdles along the way. We have always said – and I think the Government of Canada recognizes – that no agreement is going to be approved that is not good for Canada and good for the United States.'[17]

At the conclusion of the Venice summit, the prime minister and the president met in the garden of the US villa. The prime minister laid out the Canadian case in strong and unambiguous terms. The Canadian team had all the authority it required to negotiate a far-reaching agreement. The key to such an agreement for Canada was dispute settlement. There had to be agreement that problems of interpretation would not be resolved unilaterally. Rather, such problems should be resolved through impartial, binding arbitration committing both sides to the decision. If the United States could not under any circumstances accept binding arbitration, it should let Canada know at the earliest moment so that the process of disengagement could begin in an orderly fashion to limit the damage that would inevitably flow from failure.

The president was accompanied by Howard Baker, his chief of staff, Frank Carlucci, his national security advisor, and George Shultz, his secretary of state. The Americans for the most part listened. On process, they agreed that they had to take hold of the negotiations and guide them to a successful conclusion. The economic policy council of the US cabinet would begin to play a more direct role. Howard and Jim Baker, Shultz and Commerce Secretary Baldrige would form a small committee to address the negotiations. On substance, the president undertook to respond to the prime minister on the key issue as soon as possible.[18]

Venice was long-distance adrenalin. Would its strength survive the passage home? Time had become both the ally and the enemy of success. Without the imperative imposed by US law to conclude the negotiations by October 1987, no serious negotiation could take place; in other words, no pressure, no deal. Both delegations had been united from the beginning in their resolve to suppress ruthlessly any suggestion that the time limits could be extended. But was there enough time to conclude? No one knew for sure, but on the Canadian side, everyone felt that if the political will to do a deal appeared in Washington, then the negotiators would be up to the task.

Preparing an Integrated Text

The two sides had now, over the course of a year, met formally fifteen times. They had established more than a dozen working, fact-finding, and technical groups to carry on the more detailed negotiations. Despite the fact that a number of very major issues still required significant input from the US side and that a range of issues remained to be engaged, Reisman finally concluded that the negotiations had reached such a stage that it was possible to develop a comprehensive, integrated text of a final agreement. To this end he established an internal drafting committee.

If nothing else, the process of preparing an integrated text provided useful insight into the stages reached on the various issues. For all areas there remained significant work to be done, especially on the detailed provisions that would make up the annexes to the main agreement, but there were clear differences in the progress that had been made on individual issues. The text also showed the interrelationships among the various parts, a clear benefit for those heads of working groups who had had little previous trade policy or negotiating experience. It demonstrated how the major and lesser issues reinforced one another. It provided a framework within which decisions on the hard points could be taken later.

Despite the continued cynicism inside and outside the negotiations, the task of preparing an integrated text proved that there was room for cautious optimism. The work of the individual groups had obviously been more productive than the plenary sessions. Some cynics even suggested that there should be a moratorium on meetings at the heads-of-delegation level so that the negotiations in the working groups could move the two sides closer together.

After the preparation of an initial complete draft of an integrated text, it was possible to come to a better assessment of the status of the negotiations on individual issues and to divide progress into four categories. The first comprised issues where there had been significant progress, where there was likely to be agreement, and where the nature of that final agreement was beginning to take shape. Characteristic of the first category of issues was that, with few exceptions, they covered the familiar terrain of previous trade negotiations. They reflected largely shared interests that were neither deal-making nor deal-breaking, such as the tariff and rules of origin, customs matters, technical standards, and emergency safeguards. They also included issues that had been engaged early on, for which the remaining differences were clear, but which could only be resolved pending progress elsewhere in the agreement, such as in government procurement, intellectual property, and business travel.

The second category was composed of issues on which, with the exception of services, it was not yet possible to draft even preliminary texts due to continued disagreement as to what the issues were and how they were to be approached.

Further work was required either in terms of basic policy development or in bridging significant gaps between the two sides. Essentially involving sectoral matters, the points at issue either blazed new trails or required sensitive political compromises. None could be considered make-or-break issues, but politically satisfactory solutions would add to support for the agreement or neutralize potential opposition. These included agriculture, services, energy, automotive trade, and cultural irritants. On the latter two, Canadian nationalists had raised their profile to such a level that the Americans knew they could drive a hard bargain for the kind of special treatment that Canada had to seek.

The third category of issues involved the make-or-break issues that had now been fully engaged. Here the policy issues were clear but the shape of any final agreement remained difficult to surmise. Characteristic of this third set of issues was that they broke new ground and were key to reaching a satisfactory agreement. This third set included subsidies and countervailing duties, dispute settlement, and investment.

Finally, there was a range of issues that had yet to be joined. They had at most been raised tangentially in the context of other issues. Some needed to be discussed immediately; others would fall into place once agreement was reached on other issues. The need for addressing them and an initial approach became clear in the context of the integrated text. They included dumping and other anti-competitive practices, exceptions, national security, export controls, extra-territoriality, balance of payments, government enterprises and monopolies, the scope of state and provincial obligations, and administration and enforcement of the agreement.

Progress on individual issues was thus very uneven, but the overall impression was that the negotiations were more advanced in reaching a working consensus on approach and even policy than had appeared to some to be the case. Fourteen weeks, however, was not a long time to reach final policy consensus and draft a final text. The Canadian side could meet this challenge; it was less clear that the US side could. The US delegation's internal work would benefit from the discipline and overview of the framework provided by an integrated text. The sooner the Canadian side shared it with them, the sooner they would benefit. Unfortunately, there was no consensus on this point.

Nevertheless, there was room for some optimism. The make-or-break issues, identified as such from the start, now stood out in sharper relief. Agreement was not likely to be reached on these until the eleventh hour; to reach this point would require clearer thinking and more input on the part of the Americans. There had been significant progress on a range of smaller, and some major, issues. The US side was beginning to involve more senior and creative people. A lawyers' group had been established to begin to mould the overall US approach into a coherent framework.

Building a US Consensus

While the main negotiating challenge was inside the negotiating room, some of what would be required to turn things around lay elsewhere in Washington and even outside Washington. From the outset, there was divided counsel among officials on the role Canada should assume in selling the initiative in the United States. On the one hand, there were those who suggested that that was an American problem. On the other, there were those who said that if free trade was an important initiative, Canada had to make its voice heard; lobbying Congress was what politics in Washington was all about.

Both sides argued persuasively. Those for a passive approach saw potential downsides: it could expose Canada to being seen as caught between the administration and the Congress on a subject – trade – that had developed a high political profile. It could give the appearance of making Canada seem overly anxious and could be embarrassing if, after launching such an effort, it proved impossible to proceed to the conclusion of an agreement with the administration (or, alternatively, if the agreement were rejected by Congress). It could anger the administration and its negotiators by implying less than full confidence in its capacity to deliver any agreement in Congress. It might give the issue a higher profile in the United States, thereby providing a greater opportunity for otherwise submerged American special interests to make difficult demands as a pre-condition for entering into such an agreement. Finally, the effort and resources required to pursue such a campaign effectively might be beyond Canada's capacities. Canadian energies, this school concluded, were best spent on the home front.

On the other side were those who felt that if the initiative was that important to Canada, the American dimension could not be ignored. The lesson of the failed East Coast Fisheries Agreement of 1979-80 was that the administration could no longer be counted on to deliver Congress.[19] Even with the fast-track authority, it was vital to monitor the pulse of Congress and intervene actively when appropriate. Policy in the United States, much more so than in Canada, is determined less by grand design than by coalition building. This is what the American division of powers is all about. Lobbying, both at the federal and state level, is in essence a matter of building coalitions; its sophistication can be illustrated by a glance at the Washington telephone book's long list of lobby groups. The Canadian government had already recognized the importance of hiring political consultants and legal advisors on issues like acid rain as well as individual trade issues like lumber and pork. Surely, the same logic extended to free trade?[20]

There were also the realities of American politics. The Reagan Administration was in its last two years in office and would be hard pressed on all fronts on Capitol Hill, especially after the mid-term elections had given the Democrats control of both the Senate and the House. Would it have the capacity to deliver on its own? Would not the marginal advantage of a Canadian promotion effort give the initiative the extra boost needed? Peter Murphy had limited political visibility or clout on Capitol Hill. It was accepted by all observers that the US Trade Representative's Office as a whole was overworked, understaffed, and unimaginative. Finally, American opponents of an agreement would be lobbying Congress; how better to respond than to enter the fray right away.

This division in approach was never wholly resolved. As a result, a long-term strategy was not developed to meet the Washington challenge. Nevertheless, in the wake of the near stillbirth of the initiative, a paper on a US strategy began to be cobbled together. It argued that sustained negative pressure from protectionist elements could be expected to continue unabated throughout the negotiations. It would be more difficult to generate similar positive support. The strategy paper argued further that the lesson of the ten to ten Senate vote was to identify and bring to the initiative's side industry, labour, consumer, and other domestic US groups who had weight with US legislators. Americans had to hear from Americans on the virtues of free trade, but Canadians could lend a helping hand. The cultivation of influential 'back-home' opinion-makers was an important part of this strategy. The message from the Canadian consulates in the United States was clear: they required instruction and information if they were to wage an effective campaign. There was little awareness of the initiative in the United States outside of Washington and New York and even there it was confined to small circles. Inasmuch as there was interest, it was in the effect the agreement would have on the fisheries, agriculture, lumber, potatoes, beer and wine, oil and gas supply, exchange rates, transportation, and the auto trade. The US-Israel Agreement was not held in high regard and there was worry, especially in the southwest, that an agreement with Canada would be the precursor of an agreement with Mexico.

Throughout the months that followed, the consulates warned of the need for a policy to meet the lobbying challenge. They wanted a campaign that trumpeted that Canada was a bright spot on the US trade front. They wanted to tell their contacts that an agreement would bring benefits to both countries and could serve as a model for other trade agreements. They buttressed their arguments with the claim that a campaign would have potentially broad benefits for Canadian interests in the United States – especially at a time when protectionist threats in the Congress appeared greater than ever before.

The behaviour of Peter Murphy throughout the negotiations only confirmed this view. He claimed at almost every meeting that this or that would be unacceptable to Congress. Cleverly, he extracted a promise early on from the Canadian side that Congress be left to him. But there was a suspicion that Murphy was painting too bleak a picture of congressional intransigence for negotiating purposes. Proof that Murphy's assessment of Congress was not entirely accurate had come with the visit of Senator Bentsen to Ottawa in early December 1986 when he made it clear that he favoured an agreement, understood the Canadian requirements, and thought that the differences could be resolved. This more balanced congressional point of view had been confirmed by the Canadian embassy in Washington and by various team members who had made use of their own contacts on the Hill to help gauge the congressional mood.

But the kind of grand and concerted congressional relations strategy that might have been introduced was never achieved. The embarrassment caused by the hiring of former White House senior aide, Michael Deaver, chilled the idea of hiring a phalanx of consultants. Instead, the Canadian embassy decided to work closely with the American Coalition on Trade Expansion with Canada (ACTEC) which had been created to promote the negotiations within the US, especially with members of Congress. Its chair, James Robinson of American Express, was also chair of the President's Advisory Committee on Trade Negotiations. The 500-member coalition read like a who's who of American industry. Many were members of the influential US Business Roundtable. ACTEC also included a number of business organizations such as the American Business Conference, National Retail Federation, Computer and Business Equipment Manufacturers Association, and the National Federation of Independent Business.

The coalition had an impressive brain trust including former USTR Bob Strauss, now a Washington lobbyist, who coordinated the overall effort while former Carter aide Jody Powell handled media work. It targeted its initial activities on three states: California, Michigan, and Pennsylvania. In the fall, it widened its efforts to include Missouri, Illinois, Texas, West Virginia, Oregon, Oklahoma, and Ohio. All were the home states of members of Congress whose voices would count.

For their part, the Canadian embassy and the US branch at External Affairs set to work to prepare a glossy pamphlet, *Partners in Prosperity*, for distribution throughout the United States. Ambassador Gotlieb continued to make speeches about the trade initiative to American audiences. The consuls general continued to press the case for a trade agreement to local industry, the media, and opinion-makers. Would their efforts be enough? Could the mood be turned around? Only the summer months remained.

THE SUMMER OF DESPAIR

A comprehensive agreement can improve the
standard of living of all of our people on both
sides of the border. If we in North America can
lead the way with a truly comprehensive, ground-
breaking bilateral trade agreement, then our
chance for opening up trade for the rest of the
world is much improved.
— Senator Lloyd Bentsen

Spitting Bullets in Washington
The fourteenth plenary took place in the heat of mid-June with Washington
masquerading as an urban steam-bath. Murphy had promised proposals on
subsidies, dispute settlement, and procurement. On the agenda for the first
time was the question of an integrated text of an agreement, that is, how and
when to start the drafting and on what basis. The watch word on the
Canadian side was to be calm, even if the proposals fell short of the promise.
Temper and decorum would be maintained. On the way in, Reisman told
reporters he was not very confident. 'I'm a betting man. I love to gamble a
little bit now and then, but I wouldn't be gambling on this one.'[1]

Murphy led off at the opening session on 15 June by indicating that he had
proposals on dispute settlement and subsidies but, as a result of the Venice
meeting, he could not share them with Reisman until after he had reported
to the president. Murphy pronounced himself confident that the president
would approve these proposals, which he said were imaginative and consistent with the objective of a comprehensive agreement. But until the economic policy council had met and the president had approved its recommendations, no proposals could be made. He noted that some on the US
delegation had been prepared to go further than some at the political level,
aware that there was a danger in going to the political level too soon. He was
sorry it had to be this way, but it was Canada that had decided to up the ante
by raising specific issues at the political level and these might, as a result,
now have to be solved at the political level. The question for the administration in these deliberations remained what it had always been: how was it
going to pull off a good agreement? Murphy continued to be caught between

the danger of overshooting if Congress rejected the deal and of undershooting if he was too cautious.

Reisman responded calmly. This was extremely disappointing. The Canadian delegation had come to Washington expecting to make progress on some key issues. Murphy's refusal to divulge positions made this a non-meeting. But if Murphy and his team were not in a position to negotiate, so be it. He then proceeded to deliver a homily.

There were not many weeks left. It was vital that the economic policy council have a clear understanding of the bottom lines. The two sides had in fact reached the point of bottom lines, not negotiating positions. These bottom-line positions had an economic foundation, but they were driven by political imperatives. Canada needed to know US positions as soon as possible so that, if necessary, the process of disengagement could begin and damage resulting from a failure minimized. If it would help, he was prepared to review the bottom line with Murphy once again so that he could brief the economic policy council accurately.

Responding to a Murphy defensive sortie about the provinces and a non sequitur about the implications of the current debate in the Congress on a trade bill, Reisman stressed that he was very close to bringing all the provinces on board for a big deal. But like everyone else, the provincial premiers wanted to know where the United States stood on subsidies and dispute settlement. Reisman agreed the trade bill could be a problem. Canada was prepared to have Congress say whatever it needed to say regarding US global trade problems, but the situation with Canada was different because Canada wanted a comprehensive agreement that would set a shining example for the rest of the world. It was his understanding that this was well understood in Congress. If not, he, Reisman, was prepared to accompany Murphy and brief congressional figures.

Murphy demurred on this last point, confident that the problem of Congress could be left to the administration. Nor did he need to have the Canadian bottom line spelled out once again. He knew what Canada wanted and could explain it to his political masters. While he could not proceed on dispute settlement and subsidies, he was prepared to talk on other issues.

At that point, the small rocks began to move. Murphy laid out a comprehensive procurement offer – all goods and services, all levels of government – after a recitation, mercifully brief, about difficulties, and then proposed negotiations to this end whenever and wherever Canada chose. He emphasized that procurement was possible only in an overall deal. He followed with a sensible and far-reaching proposal on the easing of restrictions on business travel. The plenary ended with the handing over of a detailed index of the contents of an integrated text prepared by Canada and with an agreement to return to this question at the next meeting.

What conclusions could be drawn from this plenary? The most charitable was that Venice had yet to play fully through the system. The gloom remained. By not advising the Canadian delegation that US proposals would not be ready, the US side had shown arrogance, insensitivity, and discourtesy. However there was no alternative but to carry on, if only for the benefit of the media.

On the steps outside, the usual guerilla warfare was played out. Reisman indicated that 'we've had some very concrete proposals on some critical issues. But ... there's still a far distance to go. We [Canada] have bitten most of the bullets. They've got a few more to go.' Asked for his comments later, Murphy retorted: 'I could make some comments, but I'll refrain. ... He's biting bullets? Did he spit any at you?'[2]

'Remember the good ol' days when it was easier to negotiate trade deals than arms deals?'

Alan King, *Ottawa Citizen*, 15 September 1987

Back to Ottawa

On 22 June, the scene shifted to Ottawa and the negotiations moved another inch, though not without some drama and morbid pessimism. The backdrop was Murphy's promise of positions on subsidies and dispute settlement following review by the economic policy council and his meeting with the president on 19 June. Murphy arrived with a letter from the president to the prime minister confirming that Murphy was the US negotiator and that he was authorized to put forward a proposal on dispute settlement that should go a long way towards satisfying Canada. Between the lines the message read that Canada should not try to seek more. Independently, however, other messages conveyed through various back-channels hinted at exactly the opposite. The strange world of Washington decision-making had struck again, and the Canadian team could only draw the conclusion that whatever Murphy presented should be taken as negotiating positions and not as final offers.

The meeting began with the much-heralded US proposal on subsidies which proved to be a vague concept piece wandering in confusion along the highways and byways of the issue and limping towards an unstated but obvious conclusion that here was a real crusher of a problem. In presenting the paper, Murphy admitted that he was at a loss as to what to do. What was feasible – what was doable? The United States was interested in increased disciplines on Canadian subsidy practices but professed indifference to Canadian trade remedy law. Warming to his theme, Murphy allowed that the Canadian interest was the opposite: little interest in US subsidy practices, but an abiding preoccupation with US trade remedy law. The price for Canada of any concessions on US trade remedy law would be severe disciplines on Canadian subsidies, particularly regional development subsidies. How on earth could Canada accept such disciplines and live up to them?

Reisman pounced. Through all this 'bafflegab,' the heart of the problem was clear and he laid it before the assembled troops in unmistakable terms. The United States could not accept the disciplines which its own countervail law sought to have others accept; it wanted Canada to accept increased disciplines while retaining the right to countervail any subsidies that it did not like. Its loud protests about the recent Canadian corn countervail decision showed the intellectual poverty of its position. If imagination and creativity in subsidy disciplines proved necessary, Canada stood ready to do a lot of hard work. If the United States could in no circumstances cede the right of unilateral determination of the rules, then no agreement was possible. It was also apparent that Murphy was not in charge of the issue. He was being hamstrung by officials in the Commerce Department who were determined to keep their rice bowls intact.

It seemed wise at this point to move on to dispute settlement. Here the US proposal was more serious. The president's letter spoke of a step forward in meeting Canadian interests. The proposal was the first genuine attempt to come to grips with the fundamental character of a free-trade agreement, but it fell short. Binding dispute settlement would be possible only if the two parties agreed in advance to send a particular issue to a binding arbitration panel; otherwise, ad hoc panels, whose conclusions could be accepted or ignored, would be normal and, indeed, the preferred route.

Reisman's observations were short and to the point. The US proposal was typical of a big-country approach to dealing with a small country. It meant that whatever the merits of a case, the United States would retain the right to take action against Canada in any circumstances where, in the US judgment, Canada was in violation of the rules. Of course, Canada would have the same rights but the fundamental reality was that small countries, as a matter of habit, regard retaliating against big countries as blood sport. The US side had to understand that Canada would not agree to obligations on investment, intellectual property, or services, nor dismantle its tariff to secure such a scheme which, though it might deal with nine out of ten problems, would still leave the risk of unilateral application of trade restrictions. If the United States could go no further, then there was little point in continuing.

Murphy's spirited response kept the plug in a little longer. He could not obtain new instructions until there were real results on matters important to the United States, for example, investment, services, and alcoholic beverages. These things must be laid out and then his political masters would have another look. In the meantime, we should keep on negotiating.

Murphy was tight-lipped on his way out. Reisman, on the other hand, took the elevator down to the foyer to feed the media mob. It was always fun to see which of the many Reismans would step out of the elevator: the cocky, brash negotiator; the father confessor figure; the elder statesman; the much sinned against professional; the pessimist; the optimist; or the pragmatist. One of those condemned to await his appearances, Jane Taber of Southam News, compared his ever-changing moods to a ride on a roller coaster.[3] The previous week, it had been first the pessimist and then the brash negotiator. On 24 June, it was the optimistic elder statesman who confronted the mikes:

> We've stepped up the pace. We are now engaged on every issue of critical importance to Canada and we are in fact exchanging proposals. This was an occasion on which they made written proposals to us. We made oral responses and asked a lot of questions for clarity and we will be following up with written responses ... on the U.S. side I can see a much more lively participation than we've had on earlier occasions.[4]

Trying to Make Sense of Agriculture

The sixteenth plenary, held in Ottawa on 29 June, was devoted to agriculture. The meeting began with some churlish exchanges on leaks to the press. Murphy complained that the president's letter to the prime minister about dispute settlement had appeared in the Canadian media. This could only complicate his life. Moreover, the Canadian press knew that Canada had prepared an integrated text, together with a slide show for showing to the first ministers. This news prompted suspicion in the Congress that Murphy was holding back. Why could not Congress be entitled to the same courtesies as the Canadian provinces?

Reisman pointed out that all the serious leaks in these negotiations had come out of Washington, either from the Congress or the administration. If Congress was unaware of the state of negotiations, this spoke volumes about Murphy's relationship with it. If Murphy wanted to pursue the discussion on leaks, the day would be lost and there were too few days remaining to lose them on pointless discussion. The good sense of this observation was appreciated and the meeting turned to agriculture.

This discussion, lasting most of the day, demonstrated that agriculture continued to be resistant to good sense on both sides of the border. On the crucial political issue of subsidized grain sales to third markets, the United States could agree to no more than consultations, but whether before or after a subsidy had been paid or announced, could not yet be determined. The heart of the problem – an agreement to stop subsidizing – could not be settled by Canada and the United States alone; the United States could only move bilaterally lock-step with progress in the Uruguay Round of GATT negotiations. A commitment could be made to work together in the multilateral negotiations on agricultural export subsidies and to eliminate export subsidies on bilateral trade. A significant agreement on red meats might be feasible, but beyond that there were slim pickings on border trade restrictions. For the United States, sugar and sugar-containing product barriers were, though senseless (as freely admitted by the US side), nevertheless immovable objects. For Canada, the removal of seasonal tariffs on fresh fruits and vegetables would only be possible if it retained the capacity to impose barriers if US competition became too stiff. Poultry and dairy quotas were similarly barren fields for trade negotiations. The irony was that no one knew whether the farmers would be pleased or enraged by these results.

The consideration of domestic agricultural subsidies mirrored the impasse on subsidies generally. Here, the Canadian proposal was that since neither country could eliminate subsidies, the two governments should undertake to operate them in a manner that would not damage the interests of the other country and to change them if they were damaging. The US side collectively gagged on this proposal. They had gained the impression that, while Canada sought the elimination of countervailing duties combined with severe subsidy disciplines on industrial products, it was ready to submit to the continuation of the countervail lash in agriculture. To be told that this was not the case produced alarm and consternation and the subject was not pursued.

The discussion on agriculture was followed by a run-through of the slide presentation on the Canadian version of an integrated text and by an agreement to set up a working group with a somewhat unspecified mandate. Murphy continued to be leery of what Canada was trying to do with its insistence on moving towards an integrated text, but realized that with less than three months to go, the time to press ahead had arrived. He made clear, however, that he did not necessarily share the Canadian view of the contents as presented in the slide show. He had his own views which, in good time, he would share. Earlier public comments by senior US negotiators that such a text would be ready by June appeared to have been forgotten.

Reisman then concluded with some plain but measured speaking on investment. In the working group, the US side had repeated its earlier outrageous proposal on investment, with the US representatives swearing that Murphy had seen it and approved it line by line. Reisman said that he had not seen the US proposal; he had, however, heard about it and this proposal was contrary to what he had been led to believe would make an acceptable deal with the United States. Such a proposal could not and would not be a basis for negotiations. The US side had to understand that he was only going to deal with investment when a realistic proposal offered a chance for settlement. He would propose no such text himself.

As the plenary rose, the ticking of the clock became louder. The prime minister had replied to the president that the US proposal on dispute settlement, while a good start, did not meet Canada's requirements and could not be the basis for settlement. To date, however, the US side had not changed its position and nothing new could be expected until well into August. On investment, the US side was pressing very hard for more than the simple incorporation into the agreement of the status quo in Canadian investment policy. These were extreme positions. Since Canada was pressing very hard on something unacceptable for the moment to the Americans, it could well be that the US side was testing Canada on issues as sensitive and difficult for Canada as dispute settlement, subsidies, and contingency protection were for the United States.

The prime minister had agreed with Reisman that he should remain unwavering in his determination that a binding dispute settlement regime was necessary to reach an agreement. He wanted this issue to be negotiated right until the end; in other words, a mid-summer crisis would not be welcome. He was, however, prepared to walk away if this fundamental requirement was not met.

Canada had problems of its own, starting with the autopact. Over the past few months not a week had gone by without a new leak or charge about the impending disasters if the autopact were to be abandoned. The latest had been a memo written by an unnamed congressional staffer reporting on a briefing given by US Deputy Chief Negotiator Bill Merkin that the United States intended to press a position that would make a hollow shell of the autopact. Here was an issue where the cold hard logic of the national interest had to navigate a narrow and treacherous course between the self-interest of the big three automakers and the paranoia of Ontario politicians. The logic was unassailable. The United States wanted to eliminate the safeguards in the autopact but was unable to make such a proposal because the big three wanted them maintained. Ontario professed to believe that the autopact safeguards were the holy of holies even though they were no longer operative and, should production ever fall to a level where they would be operative, the Ontario economy would be in grave difficulty requiring much more than the triggering of the safeguards would provide. The debate, however, continued to be framed in terms of whether or not the autopact was on the table.

On another front, the Canadian side had not yet defined a realistic position on culture. Beyond repeating the litany that Canadian culture was sacrosanct and not part of these negotiations, Canada had not clarified what would be an acceptable outcome. Again, there had been no shortage of scare stories in the media to keep both politicians and negotiators wary of the issue. Small in economic terms, the issue continued to loom large in political terms. It was such a hot potato that most of the political pundits tended to shy away from it, leaving the field open to extremists. Any suggestions for a reasonable settlement brought out the most virulent opposition to the agree-

Trade Minister Pat Carney meets with US trade representative Clayton Yeutter in her office to discuss progress in the negotiations. (Ottawa, 3 June 1987)

ment from the culture mafia. To keep a sense of proportion on such a ticklish issue, the government could count only occasionally on someone saying something sensible, such as Mordecai Richler's dig at the cultural nationalists: 'Nationalists are lobbying for the imposition of Canadian content quotas in our bookshops and theatres ... In a word, largely second-rate writers are demanding from Ottawa what talent has denied them, an audience.'[5]

The Premiers Again

The July national holidays and a first ministers' meeting on 7 July filled the two-week gap before the next plenary in Washington held on 13-14 July. The mood in Ottawa had become one of quiet desperation, with the frustration breaking through more and more often. On the last day of June, the prime minister publicly admitted that there was a lot of tension between Reisman and his political boss, Trade Minister Pat Carney. She had dropped her guard in Vancouver the week before and told reporters that Reisman was going nuts with only three months to go and an agreement nowhere in sight. As a result, he was straining at the leash while she was determined to keep him under a tight rein. Jeffery Simpson wrote that 'Ms. Carney finds Mr. Reisman abrasive, arrogant, insufficiently respectful of her ministerial prerogative. Mr. Reisman believes his mandate runs directly to the cabinet committee over-seeing the free-trade negotiations. He also thinks he knows more about negotiating than the minister.'[6]

Reisman's tiffs with ministers and other senior mandarins had, of course, been the stuff of legend in Ottawa for decades, with reporters and bureau-crats alike eager to add an anecdote about how Reisman had bested this min-ister or that mandarin. The pundits were betting on Reisman once again. There were others, however, who insisted that in Carney, Reisman might have met his match. Carney and Murphy were not Reisman's only targets that sum-mer. His other favourite was the premier of Ontario who was continuing to take delight in playing the sceptic and posing as the protector of Canadian identity. In this role, Peterson and his senior officials wrote a series of letters to the prime minister, Pat Carney, and Reisman over the course of the sum-mer. Each raised a different problem and seemed designed less to elicit infor-mation or assurances than to create a paper trail for eventual distribution in a Pontius Pilate campaign to ensure that no blame for any disaster could be attached to Ontario. Since Peterson was not always available, Reisman used Ontario officials attending his monthly briefings as proxies. Whined one: 'Reisman heaps abuse on us all the time. The brow-beating is constant.'[7]

Given little room for speculation on substance, the media decided to con-centrate on form. They opined that at their quarterly meeting with the prime minister in July, the premiers intended to demand that they be given the time to consider the details of an agreement before endorsing it and autho-rizing Reisman to initial it for Canada. Peterson and Pawley, the leading scoffers, publicly agreed with this media prompting and set the stage for the impending dust-up. To further goad the premiers, the *Toronto Star* ran a series of editorials outlining what specific issues they should raise.

As often happens, media speculation and reality were some distance apart. The first ministers were treated to a seven-hour slide show by the prime minister presenting the outline of a possible agreement based on the Canadian integrated text. The ensuing discussions were serious and support-ive. Only Ontario seemed upset because, whatever the length of the show, there was little about what the United States was prepared to do on the critically important Canadian issues. Said Peterson, 'If I were asked for my agreement in principle on what I have seen today, I would say no!'[8] Others were more optimistic. Thus, the negotiations lurched through another federal-provincial encounter.

The media now changed tack and concluded that Mulroney's tactic had been brilliant. By meeting the premiers regularly and taking them into his confidence, he was co-opting them into a supportive position, whether they liked it or not. July was the last meeting for them to back out. Any later, and they would be accused of treachery, back-stabbing, and lack of patriotism.[9] Again, the reporters missed the mark. From the beginning, all but Ontario and, to a lesser extent, Manitoba, had been more convinced of the benefits of an agreement than the federal government. Their mission at these quarterly meetings was to play federal-provincial politics and to ensure that the type of agreement they had sought remained in the offing. These meetings also proved educational. The premiers understood the political importance of an agreement, but they were not trade specialists. Each meeting provided an opportunity for the prime minister, Carney, and Reisman to take them through another series of hard facts. In March, they had learned that discipline on US countervail could only be bought with discipline on Canadian subsidy practices, including provincial industrial and agricultural support programs. In July, they learned about investment and dispute settlement. They proved good students and the prime minister and his team good teachers. All remained on board. The question still needing an answer was if the United States was on board.

The continuing media pounding on the autopact, investment, and dispute settlement prompted John Turner to write to the prime minister and advise him to withdraw from the negotiations before it was too late. The media termed this piece of advice fatuous, a characterization with which Steven Langdon of the NDP could agree when he told the press that his party had concluded that the talks had reached such a point that they should now continue to a conclusion. This, in turn, provided more grist for the pundits commenting on the NDP flip flop. The next day, Langdon flipped back to the orthodox NDP position and joined Turner in calling for an end to the negotiations. Burned by the happy savagery of pundits and editorialists with little else to fill their summer pages, both opposition parties decided the following month that they really did not want to know more about the negotiations and declined Carney's offer of a confidential briefing by the negotiators.

Marjorie Nichols drew the conclusion from this strange episode that the negotiations were proceeding to a successful conclusion, reasoning that

Langdon would never have made his statement without a briefing from Pawley, reporting the consensus of the negotiators and premiers at the 7 July meeting of first ministers that negotiations should continue to a conclusion.[10] Ministers and negotiators were not the only ones frustrated by the drawn-out and confusing process. Nichols too was having trouble putting her allotted number of words on paper. Given the NDP's position, Langdon's behaviour had simply been bizarre, regardless of what he had heard from Pawley.

The US Backpedals on Services

The next plenary on 14-15 July took place in a Washington awash with the Ollie North hearings. The street merchants had available not only Ollie North T-shirts and sweatshirts, but also videos and colouring books. It provided welcome comic relief from the continuing rhetoric of protectionism, the more common theme in Washington. Jeffrey Simpson was prompted to write:

> Three weeks vacationing in the United States reconfirmed the obvious – the free trade talks don't cause a ripple in the public consciousness. Worse, they face a strong current of protectionism. The summer figures for the U.S. trade deficit were bad, even desperate. The Congress, sweltering through a Washington summer, worked away on an ominously protectionist trade bill. A preliminary ruling from the Commerce Department proposed massive duties on Canadian potash; a court ruling, which may yet be appealed, threatens exports of Canadian uranium.
>
> Protectionism in the United States should sweeten the arguments for free trade in Canada, since a case-by-case fight against trade harassment will lead to endless frustration and irritation. But that very protectionism calls into question American good faith and makes the argument more, not less, difficult for Canadian free traders. And, of course, the forces of protectionism create a political climate on Capitol Hill that runs directly counter to considering more liberalized trade.[11]

Inside the negotiations, the American negotiators' perceptions of that protectionist mood added to their caution. This seventeenth plenary focused on services but concluded with a drama on dispute settlement. On services, the US side demonstrated once and for all that whatever the boldness of its rhetoric on services, it was not ready to do a serious deal. A code of conduct for the future seemed likely, but US negotiators now wanted to exclude basic telecommunications and transportation, without which the code would have little effect on the development of service industries or on the right of either government to regulate the sectors, irrespective of the effect on trade. With that outcome, few would be interested in a services deal. The irony was the apparent US satisfaction with such a thin and insubstantial result on an issue that was at the heart of US trade objectives in the multilateral trade negotiations.

Ever since the failed GATT Ministerial Meeting of 1982, US officials had beaten the drum worldwide that they wanted to expand international trade rules to trade in services. They wanted a code of conduct that would introduce general rules of non-discrimination to the industries of the future. They had insisted on work programs at the GATT and the OECD to prove that their rhetoric on services was both credible and in the interest of all trading nations. They had fought hard at Punta del Este to include services on the multilateral trade negotiating agenda against the strong opposition of countries like Brazil and India. They had gained the active support of the EC, Japan, and Canada and overcome the opposition of many developing countries. Canada and the UK especially had responded to the US call with detailed national studies. For many, the bilateral negotiations would prove that it was feasible to negotiate a services code.

Now came the truth. These same US officials had not tested their position widely at home. It had the general support of USTR, State, and the Treasury, but such important regulatory departments as Transportation seemed not to share in the enthusiasm to introduce principles of non-discrimination. Neither did the industries they regulated. Such a lackadaisical approach never ceased to astound the Canadian side. For Canadian officials, it would have been inconceivable to mount a major international initiative without solid support at home. But for US officials, working in a city where unanimity is so rare as to be regarded with suspicion, international initiatives can be used to build coalitions at home. The fact that there was opposition within the administration, the Congress, and the private sector had nothing to do with the legitimacy of the issue. That in the end it might prove unacceptable was a fact of negotiating life. After all, the GATT was the result of such an initiative and it had served US and world interests well.

Whatever the deficiencies of the US decision-making process, Canada had done its homework and had concluded that if the United States were truly interested, a broad deal on services held promise. It came, therefore, as both a shock and a disappointment to learn that the US side was not able to deliver. Even a deal limited to a commitment not to introduce new forms of discrimination was too rich, let alone a rollback on existing forms of discrimination. Attempts to blame Canada for this lamentable state of affairs appeared hollow and self-serving and were not carried very far. Most members of the US team realized that they had blown this one and blown it badly.

The drama on dispute settlement came at the end. In order to recover some self-esteem, the US side complained that Canada had made no counterproposal to their latest and only proposal and that the ball was thus in Canada's court. Reisman responded that if the US delegation expected

Canada to back away from a fundamental Canadian need, they had no business negotiating. They had the Canadian proposal and when they were ready to negotiate on the basis of that proposal, they would find him ready. With that, another plenary concluded.

For the media, Reisman introduced a new wrinkle. He had now concluded that the press scrums were not helpful and that for the final weeks of negotiations, mum was the word. He would no longer provide them with scraps and tidbits on the way in and out. The negotiations were at too delicate a stage to risk any negative repercussions from an unguarded word. All he would say was that the negotiations were now all business, with no time out for posturing and frivolity.

A Non-Meeting
The eighteenth plenary convened in Ottawa on 20 July with small hopes and even smaller results. The scheduled agenda included some hard issues: dispute settlement, subsidies, and government procurement. None seemed ready for serious discussion.

These prognostications were confirmed when the US team arrived. Following an hour's stale exchange on dispute settlement, Murphy was cornered into saying that he did not think that Congress would accept binding dispute settlement at the demand of either party. Even an arrangement of narrower scope, in which binding dispute settlement would apply to the subsidies/countervailing duty package only, would have little prospect for success in the Congress. A fundamental Canadian need to replace unilateralism with bilateral dispute settlement remained unthinkable. Murphy was not even prepared to test it out with his contacts in Congress.

The subsidies discussion was equally unproductive. The US team wanted to focus on a 'red list' of specific programs that Canada would agree to abandon, but was not interested in addressing the rules that would determine the kinds of programs that would be permissible or prohibited. Reisman made clear that while Canada was prepared to undertake serious and binding disciplines on subsidies, it would only do so on the basis of clearly defined rules, bilaterally agreed and administered, and never on the basis of any unilaterally determined 'red list.'

On government procurement, the US negotiators were still bereft of ideas. They no longer believed that a comprehensive package could be sold to the Congress, nor did they think that any package of concessions on the Canadian side would be sufficiently convincing to persuade the Congress to open up US procurements. They hauled out the old argument that with a procurement market ten times as big as that of Canada, they would need an awful lot of other concessions to make any balanced package on procurement saleable. Reisman was too tired of this old saw to respond with more than a token protest.

When substance is lacking, turn to process and so the two sides turned. The working groups were to continue and complete their drafting by 15 August when the integrated text group would be mandated to produce a first complete draft representing the accumulated work of the plenaries and working groups. Based on progress at this eighteenth plenary, however, the chances of concocting a joint text appeared slim. If anything, the Americans were now marching backwards.

Putting in More Time
The nineteenth plenary took place in Washington on 5-6 August, more because it was scheduled than because the time had come to leap forward. Taking a government executive jet to Andrews Air Force Base added some spice to the life of the Canadian delegation. Reisman was getting tired of the unreliable service provided by commercial air carriers and had gained permission to use a government aircraft. With most ministers on vacation, the fleet of Canadair Challengers was idle. Ritchie had also become convinced that it was cheaper. It saved the cost of at least eight return air fares and hotel rooms for one night. As a result, the team arrived refreshed in time for a leisurely delegation lunch and joined the Americans early in the afternoon.

That morning the action had been in the Senate. The Finance Committee had summoned Yeutter and Murphy to hear a lecture on the responsibilities of Congress in matters of trade negotiations. There had been great trepidation in Ottawa over the encounter. On the one hand, it was feared that Yeutter and Murphy would fumble the event. The consensus was that Murphy had obstinately refused through more than a year of negotiation to show that he understood either what was involved in a free-trade agreement or what was the Canadian position; on the other hand, there was a distinct risk that the senators would declare themselves opposed to an agreement, draw linkages with the trade bill (passed by an authoritative vote of seventy-one to twenty-seven the week before), or otherwise seriously compromise any possibility of success.

By this time, the Canadian side had learned that many of Murphy's consultations with Congress were confined to discussions with Jeff Lang, counsel to chairman Lloyd Bentsen. Murphy and Lang were birds of a feather. They were reticent to a fault. To those who knew both, the idea of the two of them engaged in animated conversation strained credulity. In fact, however, a warm relationship had developed between the two and they spoke to each other frequently. Murphy's sense of Congress, therefore, was largely Lang's sense of Congress supplemented by conversations Bill Merkin had with other staffers such as Sue Schwab of Senator Danforth's staff and George Weiss from the House trade subcommittee staff. Neither Murphy nor Merkin had the kind of access that allowed them to talk directly to members of Congress.

Earlier in the summer, efforts by some members of the Canadian team to use their contacts on Capitol Hill to brief some of these all-important staffers on Canadian perspectives had resulted in a bellow of rage from Murphy. Sue Schwab had phoned to tell him that she had learned more over breakfast with a Canadian negotiator than she had learned from the US side over a period of months. And she did not like what she had learned. Murphy had insisted that he should be the only conduit to these people. Any interference from the Canadian side would severely compromise his ability to cut a deal with them later. Reisman had acquiesced and from then on, Canadian presence on the Hill was limited to Ambassador Gotlieb and his staff.[12]

Murphy's command performance before the senators, therefore, was an opportunity to determine whether his approach was the right one. Would the senators have been sufficiently briefed by Lang to keep a lid on unhelpful statements? Again, disaster was avoided and the negotiations remained in business. Murphy characterized the committee meeting not as an opportunity for the administration to explain the negotiations, but rather as an occasion for a lecture. The main message was that the Senate expected to be consulted, that the agreement would have to be an economic agreement in the interests of the United States, that the agreement would need to be comprehensive, and that matters of key importance to the United States would have to be dealt with. It appeared that Murphy and Lang had cooked up the occasion to give weight to Murphy's strategic point that Congress was in a fractious mood and not disposed to accept the kind of concessions Canada was seeking.

Just as the session began, a press statement appeared declaring these points to be the view of the Finance Committee. In addition, the senators stated their assumption and expectation that the negotiations would be completed within the time-frame of the fast-track authority and that the administration would bring forward, on 4 October, the complete text of the agreement, a statement of administrative intent, and any necessary implementing legislation.

The press conference took place in a small, high-ceilinged committee room with panelled walls, a carved dais for the senators, the seal of the United States over the door, and the flag in the corner. The senators emerged from a small door at the end and the horde of mostly Canadian journalists turned away from the buzz of conversation and gossip. There were two principal questions: Would the United States agree to binding dispute settlement and exempt Canada from trade remedy laws? Were the negotiations on track? The answers were predictable: This would be very difficult. The United States could not treat Canada differently from other countries and remain 'GATT legal.' No one should expect final positions to be put on the table until the eleventh hour. The current time was judged to be at least a half hour before that.

After the report from the battlefront in the Senate had been sifted, analyzed, and evaluated, the plenary proceeded to its agenda. As usual, the US side was not ready on any of the issues and the discussion was mostly around and about the negotiations. The main question concerned the time frame for developing an integrated text. Murphy promised to have an integrated text ready by 19 August. Canada promised one by 15 August. An integrated text group would meet once drafts were exchanged to ensure that the two sides had a clear understanding of each other's approach, followed by a plenary the week of 24 August to begin the drafting of a single text. Reisman and Murphy agreed that the whole week should be set aside. Meanwhile, Murphy sought Reisman's indulgence. He would be very busy over the next two weeks consulting Congress and ensuring that an integrated text would be ready. While the working groups should continue to meet, he would not be available. He failed to mention that for part of that period he would be in Mexico City putting the finishing touches on a consultative arrangement with the Mexicans. It remained a sore point with Canada that even the US chief negotiator did not devote all his energy to the negotiations; he continued to have other responsibilities.

It was evident that the starting points for preparing the integrated texts would be poles apart. Murphy viewed the drafting of an integrated text as essentially a matter of stapling the product of the working groups together. To the extent that a coherent position could be perceived, the United States seemed to be starting with a GATT-plus approach with no overriding or residual obligations. The danger in such an agreement was that the day after it was signed, a new restriction not explicitly covered could be imposed and Canada would have no recourse under the agreement to have it removed. This prospect alarmed Reisman and he attacked Murphy unsuccessfully, attempting to get him to lay out the underlying concept of the US approach to an agreement. Murphy would not be drawn and resorted to his familiar obfuscation.

Reisman was frustrated and annoyed. Insistence on a residual clause, in effect asking Congress to bind itself against the unknown, could well be asking too much. He was not prepared to risk a good agreement for an obscure legal point. On the other hand, he did not want to run the risk that Congress or the administration might rapidly find other ways to restrict Canada's trade as soon as the ink was dry. The idea continued to haunt him in the weeks to come and strengthened his resolve that there had to be good dispute settlement provisions.

The remainder of the plenary was devoted to aimless meandering around some of the key issues, but nothing could be done until the US draft appeared. While the Canadian drafting team had already reached draft six of its text, the Americans were still at the starting gate. To drive the point home, Reisman waved the text at Murphy, who obstinately maintained that they were hard at it. But to help the US side prepare a text that bore at least some resemblance to the work his own team had done, Reisman agreed to hand over the latest table of contents.

Concocting a Sales Pitch

While the prognosis for reaching an agreement did not look good, efforts still had to be set in train to sell an agreement should the situation turn around. In early July, the communications group, under the direction of Pat Carney's deputy, Gerry Shannon, met at External Affairs to discuss the preparation of a strategy paper.

The best suggestions on how to handle the communications side came from Peter Daniel, the communications expert at Finance. Drawing on the lessons learned during the launch of the tax reform package in the spring, he advised that a small group of officials, with first-hand knowledge of the agreement, should begin privately to brief key members of the media. Unhappily, the requirement for secrecy within the TNO and the general fear and loathing of the media by officials and political aides alike scuttled this sensible suggestion. The absence of any authoritative and recognized source had already forced the media to speculate and hypothesize on what was happening. Inevitably, it aimed at the sensational and played up the possible costs of free trade. Such reporting only increased the contempt of the negotiators for the media. The consequences were acrimonious allegations of leaking and orders that contact with the media be curtailed.

Over the course of the summer, indeed since the 16 March House debate, the government had been more open and had spelled out its bottom line in a strategy aimed at both the US negotiators and the Canadian public. The prime minister and ministers were much more visibly in charge of the agenda and more confident about their approach. The government wanted US negotiators and politicians to know the elements that had to form part of any successful conclusion to the negotiations and it wanted the public to know that the government was pursuing the Canadian interest. For both audiences, the message was the same: without these elements, there would be no agreement. But this strategy had opened up its own dilemma. Said Jennifer Lewington and Chris Waddell in the *Globe and Mail*: 'The more fully Canada's main objectives are met, the harder it will be to sell on Capitol Hill; the less clearly the well-publicized Canadian "bottom line" is met, the more difficult the sales job at home.'[13] The media handlers shared this perception and were acutely aware of the pitfalls of preparing the ground too early.

The meeting also looked at the accumulated baggage of poor press relations from the beginning: the autopact, culture, investment, farm marketing boards, and so on. All needed badly to be explained properly to a sceptical public; all seemed capable of creating the kind of negative reaction that could sink the agreement; yet none was likely to be affected negatively by the agreement. If an opportunity to reverse the bad press on these issues needed to be found, the impending election in Ontario stood out as a possible candidate.

'Bye, Larry ...'

Alan King, *Ottawa Citizen*, 21 August 1987

The federal government had no interest in making free trade an issue in the Ontario election (it appeared clear that David Peterson would win and that there would be little point in making him take a stand which could later come back to haunt the negotiators), and Conservative leader Larry Grossman initially seemed inclined to stay away from the issue. Nevertheless, the provincial Tories needed an issue that would distinguish them from the other two parties. Going slow on bilingualism and full speed ahead on free trade thus became the rallying cry as they charged to oblivion in the 10 September election. To the federal government's media handlers, this was not the opportunity they were seeking to get the government's message out.

In the end, little was accomplished. Until it was clearer what kind of agreement was likely to emerge from the negotiations, concocting a strategy appeared impossible. With negotiations in the doldrums, enthusiasm for such a task was not very high either.

Breakthrough at Cornwall?

The fourth week of August saw the two delegations camped out at the Transport Canada Training Centre on the banks of the St. Lawrence River near Cornwall, Ontario. Billed as a make-or-break session, the chief negotiators intended to work with the heads of each working group and their legal advisers and thus develop a joint integrated text with a minimum of items left unresolved. The stage would then be set for intense negotiations on the three or four main issues required to conclude a deal.

Prior to meeting in Cornwall, the two sides had completed their own perceptions of what the complete text of an agreement should look like and the status of the negotiations as they understood them. The two texts were exchanged in Washington on 20 August. The Canadian version of the integrated text comprised eighty-three articles, thirty-five annexes and explanatory notes, and totalled 179 pages. It was comprehensive and far-reaching, based on a single philosophy and intended to stand alone as a new charter to govern Canada-US trade and economic relations for the foreseeable future. The Canadian drafters had taken the raw material produced by the working groups, reduced it to its essential components and then knitted a complete text together, fitting in new material where the existing text was not sufficient. All duplication had been removed. Material had been rearranged so that the agreement as a whole would proceed logically from general objectives and principles through precise and detailed rights and obligations to the steps and procedures necessary to implement and administer the agreement and resolve disputes. Based on the experience and language of the past, it had been written in a style and format that would be intelligible to the informed reader. International trade agreements, such as the GATT or the Treaty of Rome, remain abstruse and difficult to read. If possible, the Canada-US agreement would be an exception.

Reisman had presided over a final drafting session that had examined the text line by line and declared it to be both elegant and precise, a document the whole team could be proud of. He concluded that if the final agreement bore any resemblance to this text, the team would have accomplished a great thing. He rated chances of that happening as slim, but he also thought the time had come to make the Canadian position crystal clear by laying this detailed proposal on the table. His military training, however, warned him that even at this late stage, he needed something in reserve. He, therefore, had the text stripped of all but the headings for three elements of particular interest to the United States: the investment chapter, a few paragraphs relating to subsidies, and an annex dealing with alcoholic beverages. The text for these three areas would only be made available if the United States showed a willingness to make real progress on the subsidies issue and was prepared to bend on others. To add to their value as carrots, the Americans were informed that Canada had good offers to make in these areas. For the rest, he was no longer prepared to play tactical games. He wanted the text as it had been prepared. It was clear and represented a good outcome.

The United States version was not of the same calibre. While the Canadian version was the product of three months of intense work by a team of lawyers and policy experts under the careful scrutiny of Reisman and his closest advisors, the Americans appeared not to have started producing an integrated text of their own until after the last plenary in early August. The product exchanged with the Canadians on 20 August totalled some seventy-three pages in length. The text had been divided into six parts, some of which were further broken down into chapters and articles. Major issues remained unaddressed, others contained a variety of square brackets reflecting not only differences between the United States and Canada, but also issues that had not yet been resolved within the American delegation. It included duplication and inconsistencies. The US lawyers had taken complete texts and inserted them wherever they seemed to fit, cutting out only those articles and paragraphs that were obviously redundant or out of place. It would need a lot more work before it could be declared an integrated text.

In two respects, however, the United States had taken a major step forward. For the first time the US side tabled, albeit separately, a complete proposal dealing with subsidies and countervailing duties. As expected, it suggested greater discipline on Canadian subsidy practices while maintaining the US right to determine unilaterally what constituted an offensive subsidy through domestic countervail proceedings. Nevertheless, it did constitute a written proposal. Second, the US advanced a written proposal on investment, putting on paper a position that had been presented orally months before and rejected by the Canadian team. Both proposals were disappointing; they did, however, represent the greatest gap between the American position and the Canadian, and made the size of the gap measurable. In most other areas, the size of the gap was well known and suggestions for bridging them known to the team leaders of both sides.

What was not known was whether the Americans would have both the capacity to deal with the issues necessary for a stand-alone, integrated agreement as provided in the Canadian text, and also the will to include a strong, bilateral dispute resolution mechanism. The institutional provisions, which had only recently begun to be addressed in a serious way, would be the glue which would hold any deal together. Without them, agreement on various functional issues would be no more than temporary resolutions of outstanding irritants.

Arrangements had initially been made for some dozen members of each team to meet near Cornwall, Ontario, to try to mould these two texts into a single negotiating text which clearly set out the major differences between the two sides. The task appeared daunting. Not only were the two texts very different in style and organization, but they proceeded from wholly different philosophies. The Canadian text sought to establish a stand-alone agreement that would evolve into a charter providing for the eventual free movement of goods and services and most capital as well as the unfettered movement of people for business reasons. While building on past agreements such as the GATT, it was not dependent on them. Its philosophy was clearly stated in the opening chapter: national treatment and no new restrictions. The US text, on the other hand, proceeded from the philosophy that the two sides would affirm existing rights and obligations, particularly those in the GATT, and add to or clarify those that had proved wanting. The primary aim was to find a basis for resolving as many irritants as possible.

Even before the delegations arrived, it had become clear that the tight and disciplined sessions foreseen at the beginning of August were not to be. The various US team heads all insisted that they needed their advisors with them. The US core group of a dozen had thus swollen to nearly five dozen. US fears about budget restraints were easily overcome when news spread that the facilities near Cornwall would cost a mere $32 US per day for meals and lodging. Canadian team heads responded by indicating that if their US counterparts were going to have help, they should also be allowed to bring their advisors. Fortunately, summer is a slow time at the Training Centre. Built to house 640 mature students, it easily accommodated the almost eighty negotiators and their support staffs who showed up on Monday, 24 August. By the end of the week, more than 120 Canadians and Americans had passed through the front door.

Three miles east of downtown Cornwall, the Transport Canada Training Institute (TCTI) was built in the early 1970s to provide a modern training centre for the various specialists necessary to ensure the smooth operation of

Canada's transportation system, including Great Lakes pilots, air traffic controllers, airport managers, flight instructors, and inspectors. While the Institute is dedicated to the needs of Transport Canada, a whole wing is devoted to the requirements of military air traffic controllers. Additionally, transportation courses are offered for students from other countries. Groups from the Caribbean and China were in residence that fourth week of August. The centre is also available to other federal government departments looking for a quiet and inexpensive place to hold a seminar or think-tank session. Many of the Canadians present that week had been there before.

The facilities are very good. Since some students are in residence for up to nine months with little opportunity of going home, great care had been taken to provide recreational facilities, including a 25-metre pool, sauna, gym, weight rooms, tennis courts, archery facilities, pistol range, pool and table tennis, as well as access to a nearby golf course. All the equipment one might want is freely available. The rooms are comfortable if somewhat small – similar to modern university residence accommodation. The cafeteria and bar are also more reminiscent of university than home. The food is copious but unimaginative and both teams throughout the week sought a break, the best food in the area being offered at Violi's in Massena across the river. The architect appeared to have had more experience in designing prisons than hotels or university dormitories. There are hundreds of doors. Each corridor and section is divided and subdivided. The effect is disconcerting and confusing. For a week-long session, however, the facilities were ideal. Each group had a permanent conference room assigned to it and got on with its work without the distraction of phones and other business, and there was plenty of opportunity for informal chats.

The main contingents of both groups arrived early Monday afternoon to be greeted by the usual gaggle of reporters hoping to catch an unguarded word or new insight. By now trained to smile and say nothing, both sides disappointed the press which had to be satisfied with a few banalities from Reisman and Murphy and then had to make up the rest. They were encouraged to go home and come back for Friday noon so that they could catch everybody leaving and be fed closing non-comments. The mum's the word rule was still in effect.

After lunch, work commenced in four working groups: subsidies, investment, agriculture, and government procurement. Unemployed working group heads were encouraged to find their counterparts and pursue their issues informally. Reisman and Murphy, accompanied by their sidekicks, Ritchie and Merkin, went for a walk on the grounds to discuss grand strategy. They soon discovered an isolated picnic table close to the horseshoe pitch, not too far from an entrance to their dormitory, and made it their headquarters. Except for a single transport student interested in practising his pitch, they enjoyed privacy and sunshine for the rest of the week. Bill Merkin proved to be the best athlete in the group, scoring more than 40 per cent ringers. All improved their tans.

After breakfast on Tuesday, the plan of attack was laid out in the private delegation caucus: the working groups were ordered to proceed in preparing a common text, closing as many gaps as possible, leaving a minimum of issues between square brackets. They would by turns be hauled to the horseshoe pitch to get their marching orders as to how to bridge remaining differences. If differences could not be bridged on some issues, they would be removed from the agreement. Reisman insisted he would push very hard and get as close as possible to a complete text by the end of the week.

American intransigence and lack of preparation, however, were enough to thwart even Reisman's determination. As had been evident in reviewing the two texts, Canada had, in integrating the disparate pieces and supplying missing elements, moved beyond the stage reached in individual negotiating groups; the American text had returned to positions dismissed months earlier. Working group heads found that their first task was to return to the stage reached at their last meeting.

Work proceeded apace with the agriculture and procurement groups, honoured as the first two to be hauled in for head-of-delegation cross-examination. Rumours spread. A deal had been struck on agriculture and procurement was out of the agreement. The two sides were very close on investment. Procurement was down to one issue. Alas, it was all sham. Murphy would not be cornered. Alternating between affability and surliness, he refused to make any final commitments on any issue. Even when there appeared to be gaps in his armour, the US delegation could count on individual group heads balking at concessions made by their head of delegation and undoing them. No amount of shouting and abuse from Reisman could change this pattern.

Reisman despaired. Who was in charge? Was it Ann Hughes from the Commerce Department who sat Buddha-like in the chair for the US side of the subsidies group? Was it Bob Cornell from Treasury, the smooth-talking head of the investment group? Was it Charles (Chip) Roh, responsible for dispute settlement and integrating the US text? Reisman wanted results and there was no one there who could stand and deliver. On Tuesday, Murphy affirmed that he was in charge and that he and Reisman would agree on a complete text by the end of the week which Murphy would then try to sell in Washington. By the next morning, this deal was off. On Wednesday afternoon, Reisman, Murphy, Merkin, and Ritchie went fishing on Lake Francis and again an attempt was made to gain some sense as to where they should end up. Now there was agreement to go as far as possible but leave contentious issues in brackets. And so the week went.

Meanwhile, the working groups toiled away. For the first time, they had the luxury and the pressure to continue in session for a week. Contact could not be avoided. Both delegations were in one place, eating in the same place, running into each other in the corridors and at the bar. Even long internal caucuses could not undo the pressure of proximity. There had to be some progress. Despite rumours that their issue had fallen off the table, the government procurement people concluded the outline of an agreement. The services group, while no longer addressing anything of real substance, declared itself close to agreement. Intellectual property was virtually there. The gap even narrowed for investment. On three issues, however, there had been little progress: contingency protection or trade remedies, dispute settlement, and the production of a single text. The subsidies group met in almost continuous session and produced a single text representing the very disparate positions of the two sides. Alas, it was like an integrated text of the Koran and the New Testament: the subject matter may have suggested a superficial similarity, but the approach was wholly different. Putting it all side by side only made the differences stand out in sharper relief. Other trade remedy issues, such as dumping and competition policy, remained equally far apart. There was no meeting of the dispute settlement group, and the integrated text group met only to catalogue the differences between the two texts.

Attempts were made to continue work through the weekend and into the following week if necessary. By Thursday evening, however, the Americans declared that they were exhausted and needed to go home to recharge their batteries. They would be prepared to meet again in two weeks. Meanwhile, some of the working groups could make their own arrangements and continue their efforts. By Friday afternoon, all had gone home. Reisman told the press that progress had been made but that the negotiations would go down to the wire and, with a twinkle in his eye, declared that it might be necessary to have the president and the prime minister conclude the negotiations at a minute to midnight.

Had something been accomplished at Cornwall? Had there been a breakthrough? Yes and No. Reisman declared himself satisfied despite the frustrations of the week. He had found Murphy as obstructionist as usual, but it had been possible to keep the American noses to the grindstone for a whole week. For the first time, many of the American working group heads and their advisors had been confronted by the totality of the negotiations and the implications of what they were doing. For the first time they were beginning to see the interconnections and the real problems. There had been less shadow-boxing at the working group level and some real progress had been made. While it was late in the day, there had never been a negotiation that did not go down to the wire or that saw either side prepared to compromise on major issues only a month before the end. An agreement remained possible, if difficult.

Not everyone shared in this optimistic assessment. Those Canadian team members responsible for crafting the agreement as a whole had seen or heard little to be optimistic about. There continued to be wide gaps to be bridged and major holes to be plugged. Even if all the contentious issues could be resolved, there still remained the formidable task of drafting an agreement that would stand the scrutiny of the teams of lawyers and special interest groups who stood ready to criticize anything the negotiators produced. What was needed was an agreement that could be sold. That would take time. The real deadline for agreement on substance was, in their view, 15 September, not 4 October. Without having at least two weeks available after substantive agreement was reached, crafting a final text would be an impossible task.

Midway through the week, Reisman had gone home. He needed a good dinner with his wife Connie and a good night's sleep. With Reisman on the way home, Ritchie had spent time on the phone reporting progress. On the basis of his assessment, the prime minister formally invited the premiers to join him on 14 September for a discussion of the text of the agreement. While they had not seen a promised text at their 7 July session, Ritchie concluded that such a text should be available for their September session. Although a meeting had been tentatively scheduled for 8 September, the Ontario election of 10 September had required a week's delay. At the same time, serious thought was being given to the end game. If Reisman and Murphy continued their gamesmanship, were alternative routes to agreement available? Was an agreement slipping out of reach? Should ministers step in? In the weeks that followed, as Reisman continued in his titanic struggle with Murphy, answers had to be found to these questions.

13

IMPASSE IN SEPTEMBER

Boast not of what thou would'st have done, but do
What then thou would'st.
– John Milton, *Samson Agonistes*

September was the make-or-break month. The 4 October deadline meant that the agreement had to be reached sometime in September or there would be no agreement. Indeed, Reisman and Murphy had agreed at Cornwall that they should work towards a 15 September deadline in order to give each side time to clean up the text, consult their political masters, and complete the task by the time the fast-track deadline expired. The Americans continued to maintain that an agreement would have to be reached by 4 October in order for them to be able to notify Congress of the president's intent to enter into the agreement ninety days before the fast-track authority ran out on 3 January 1988.

On returning home from Cornwall, every working group head was encouraged to hold at least one working group meeting to consolidate what had been achieved at Cornwall and to ensure that as firm as possible a basis was laid for the next plenary meeting, scheduled for Washington 10-11 September. Most working group heads met this challenge, ensuring that Labour Day weekend marked the fourth summer holiday weekend in a row which passed like a blur. But little progress had been made in these working group meetings. The Americans seemed to have exhausted their collective imagination at Cornwall and now appeared to wait for Canada to see the light and appreciate that it was the American offer or nothing.

By this time, the prime minister had begun increasingly to play a central role in the management of the issue. Ever since the March parliamentary debate, the government had succeeded in projecting a more confident image. The PM in particular had remained steadfast in indicating what Canada had to have and what it could not live with. He had monitored events closely from spring on. He had written and spoken to the president on several occasions. In August he had established a trade executive committee which he chaired. While Pat Carney continued to be responsible for day-to-day management of the issue, he had taken charge of grand strategy. The continued media and opposition pounding no longer troubled the government as it had earlier. Steven Langdon's double flip-flop in August was in large measure occasioned by his frustration with the government's self-confident determination to carry the issue through to a conclusion.

What was not clear was what that conclusion would be. While success was what was wanted, the government would not accept success at any price. Ministers and their senior advisors had by now begun to harbour an uneasy feeling about the negotiations. Where were these negotiations headed and what would be the fall-out? On the central issues, the two sides were so far apart that the ultimate shape of the agreement could not be surmised. Indeed, the text of the agreement had not yet reached such a stage that ministers could be asked to make hard choices. Fewer than three weeks remained. The time had come to think of alternative strategies. Reisman had been given full scope to negotiate a good agreement. Every few months, the government had sought to inject new political momentum into the negotiations and force the Americans to play a more constructive role. Yet the negotiations remained stalemated. Perhaps other means would have to be found or the stage set for disengagement.

There was now growing concern in the country about the conduct of the negotiations, at least that was the impression gained if one relied strictly on the Toronto media and its coverage of the Ontario provincial election. A Goldfarb poll for the *Toronto Star* said that 67 per cent of Ontarians were not happy with the way the trade talks were going, and outright opposition had grown to 49 per cent, with only 36 per cent continuing to support an agreement.[1]

For the media, the Ontario election had proved a godsend. There was little new to report on the negotiations and with Parliament in recess, they could not count on question period to provide a daily fix. Ontario Conservative leader Larry Grossman, in the absence of any other issue, had zeroed in on free trade and was defending it to the teeth. Liberal Premier David Peterson, whose impending electoral triumph appeared assured, did not need free trade, but was prepared to give Grossman battle. The election helped to keep the issue before the public, at least in central Canada.

With Grossman defending the federal government's trade initiative and NDP leader Bob Rae equally adamant that the bilateral negotiations had to be stopped and that it was the moral duty of the Ontario government to insist on this, Peterson had changed his sceptical ambivalence to more open opposition. He was prepared to acknowledge that free trade with the United States had its merits, but he was not convinced that the negotiations in progress were sensitive to Canada's real needs. He then outlined his own bottom line. He would oppose any agreement that would:

- weaken the autopact
- threaten Canada's cultural identity
- not provide safeguards for agriculture
- allow unrestricted foreign investment in Canada
- not allow for the reduction of regional economic disparities within Canada
- not include a binding dispute settlement mechanism.

Peterson couched his six points in sufficiently vague terms to give him the room to move in either direction depending on the results of the negotiations. From the TNO's perspective, it looked like Ontario had moved into the plus column. These were all conditions with which the Canadian negotiators could agree. They made sense and echoed the government's own bottom line. But that was not the view of the pundits. They saw Peterson as opposed but not prepared to say so.

Whatever the merits of the position of the three leaders, enough doubt had been sown among the voters of Ontario to ensure that a pro-free-trade position would not help any candidate. Peterson was returned with an overwhelming majority and, from his point of view, moral superiority in his continuing battle with the federal government over free trade. It was not a good omen for the final phase of the negotiations.

Is Anyone There?

Before the plenary sessions could resume, the Canadian side raised the stakes once again. Reisman was of two minds: the process had been moved along and the difficult issues more clearly drawn, but prospects for an agreement remained slim. He firmly believed that without more political momentum on the US side, little could be achieved. This struck a responsive chord with ministers and the prime minister. The Americans had to understand clearly that Canada very much wanted an agreement, but not at any price. Accordingly, Derek Burney, the prime minister's chief of staff, was asked to write to his US opposite, Howard Baker, reminding him of the president's June commitment in Venice to indicate whether the key Canadian demand on binding dispute settlement could be met. More importantly, Burney used the occasion to outline the Canadian bottom line and the need for some movement on the part of the United States to meet Canada's position. A basis was being prepared for elevating the issue to the political level or for an honourable disengagement if that proved necessary. An unstated part of the message was that Burney would be Canada's designated hitter should the negotiations be elevated.

The reply was like a kiss from a sister: correct, with some perfunctory warmth, but not very satisfactory. Howard Baker reminded Burney that Jim Baker was the president's point man on this; the president had full confidence in him and was sure that a mutually satisfactory result was still possible. The Canadian side did not share this optimism and interpreted the letter as further evidence that, even at this late stage, there was not sufficient political interest in the US capital to ensure a breakthrough in the remaining three weeks. The next plenary would tell whether satisfactory progress could still be made between the two chief negotiators. If not, further effort to open a second front would be needed.

The twenty-first meeting in Washington 10-11 September was organized around a familiar agenda with dispute settlement and trade remedy law again occupying centre stage. The result was equally familiar. The Americans seemed to have but one agenda: shake the Canadian tree until every piece of fruit and every leaf had fallen and only then decide whether there was a basis for meeting any of Canada's basic requirements.

The focus was further discussion of the subsidy issue. Murphy began by reporting results of the previous day's discussions at the economic policy council. He had described the Canadian proposal for new, strict, and jointly agreed rules, but was promptly sandbagged with the accusation that Canada was not prepared to accept serious disciplines on its subsidy practices. Until there was clear evidence of Canadian flexibility on subsidies, there could be no question of the US contemplating any changes in its trade remedy laws. Obviously, members of his team had taken a different point of departure in briefing their principals. Murphy had based his report on conversations with Reisman. Others had prepared their briefings on the basis of discussions in the working group. Rather than opening the gate to progress, discussion in the economic policy council had thrown up new roadblocks. A late night meeting served to clear up some of the confusion and the United States came up with a proposal that for the first time showed a willingness to consider reduced Canadian exposure to countervail procedures in return for increased discipline on subsidy practices. What precisely the US side would be prepared to do and within what time frame remained unclear. There was still some way to go.

The United States was in retreat on procurement. Earlier in the summer, Murphy had been convinced that he could deliver a full procurement deal. This had evaporated at Cornwall, but Murphy had insisted that he could develop a smaller but still interesting package. Now the USTR procurement specialist, Bev Vaughn, put forward a US proposal that could only be described as miniscule: in return for Canada lowering its thresholds subject to the GATT code and adding all federal crown agencies and service contracts to the code coverage list, the US would be prepared to lower its procurement threshold and add services. The deal would be strictly federal-federal. Reisman agreed that it would be possible to craft a federal-federal only procurement deal but rejected the US offer out of hand as unbalanced and derisory. Nevertheless, he was prepared for the working group heads to explore it further to see whether it could be improved.

There was also some discussion of the tariff schedules, with the US negotiators seeking to add products to the list of items that would face immediate or five-year tariff elimination. Murphy claimed that the tariff package as it stood was unbalanced and would not play well in Congress. Reisman threw the request back at Murphy, reminding him that it was the US side that had insisted on a long transition period – ten years – and that had suggested that only those industrial sectors, for which a clear consensus favoured an accelerated schedule, should face faster duty elimination. Canada had already worked diligently to increase the number of volunteers and the result was a rough balance. At this late stage any further arm twisting would be counterproductive. The package could not be improved. The US side appeared to be engaged either in positioning to justify a failure or in wringing further advantage out of Canada.

What seemed on offer following the plenary would be a very small agreement and with three weeks to go, the prospects of concluding the deal by 4 October looked slim. Those who believed in an agreement at that late stage, had to have faith in the old cliché that it is indeed darkest before the dawn. A weary Reisman, however, insisted to reporters that 'it's possible that we can meet our objective in time ... Sure, I think 50-50's a good nice round number.'[2]

There were, amidst the gathering darkness in Washington, some hopeful glimmers. Senator Richard Lugar, the ranking Republican on the Foreign Affairs Committee, had come on board, following a call from Ambassador Gotlieb. At a hearing on Central American policy, Lugar grilled Secretary of State George Shultz as to why the administration was not putting a greater effort into ensuring the success of these very important trade negotiations: 'If we're unable to work out an agreement with our closest friends ... I think this would be a very very serious deficiency.'[3]

Shultz insisted that that was exactly what the administration was trying to do and agreed that the negotiations were very important. He insisted that an agreement would be 'a really major economic advance that would be an example in the world.' The tricky part was dispute settlement. 'From our point of view, we want that process, whatever it is, to be consistent with our basic laws of countervailing and dumping. From the Canadian point of view, they want to have an assured method of dealing with the problems that inevitably arise in such a huge trading relationship.'[4] Recognizing the problem was one thing, proposing solutions was quite another. To date, the Americans had yet to make any realistic proposal to address this conundrum.

On the other side of Congress, a number of Senate staffers briefed by embassy officials finally seemed to seize the importance of binding dispute settlement, accepting that non-binding dispute settlement made little sense. They would reflect this revelation in their briefing notes for their principals and in their conversations with the negotiating team. This information came back to the Canadian team through one of the frequently used indirect conduits. Jennifer Lewington, by now a confidante of some senior US negotiators, reported on 15 September that 'U.S. negotiators appeared to be backing away from opposition in principle to the establishment of a bilateral panel to settle trade disputes. Sources said yesterday they "can envision" a panel that issues binding decisions in certain cases.'[5]

The First Ministers Get Cold Feet

On returning home, Reisman had to meet the first ministers. Various efforts to postpone the meeting further had not succeeded. Initially scheduled for 8 September, it had been delayed a week on account of the Ontario election. Mulroney would now need to deal with a Premier Peterson flush with a victory as impressive as his own three years earlier. Peterson would put this to the test at the meeting. In his view, the negotiations were all but over and the prime minister should have the courage to recognize this and bring them to an end. He adopted a statesmanlike mien, telling reporters, 'I don't believe there's one bit of disgrace in standing up and saying, "I did my best, and I couldn't make a good enough deal, and therefore, we're out."'[6] But if there was going to be an agreement, he insisted that the provinces be given a chance to study it. 'We're not going to do anything until we have three months of rigorous analysis.'[7]

If nothing else, this eighth meeting of first ministers on 14 September made it clear that Canada had precious little to show for sixteen months of negotiations. The prime minister allowed that an agreement might still be possible, but appeared definitely intent on lowering expectations. In an interview with Carol Goar of the *Toronto Star* on the third anniversary of his swearing in, he set the stage for a possible unsuccessful end to the negotiations.[8]

The meeting was tough. With the ambitious free-trade package that was originally envisioned now seemingly beyond Canada's grasp and the need to consider a smaller package clear, premiers showed that they were politicians first and statesmen second. All, including Peterson, insisted that they were prepared to think big if the agreement was to be big. With a smaller agreement now in prospect, they had a different bottom line: be sure to solve my problems and do not create any new ones for me. Peterson took particular exception to the news that the Americans had officially asked to include discussion of the autopact at the next meeting.

It was a sober group that met the press on the steps of the Langevin Block. The prime minister set the tone. 'An acceptable agreement remains achievable, but Canadian concerns have not been, in our judgment, appropriately addressed in some important areas.'[9] Premier Peterson was more voluble and pessimistic: 'I'm not at all sure it's attainable ... we're not making much progress ... huge decisions have to be made in the next three weeks and we're a very, very long way from a big deal ... If a deal is made it won't be as big as originally contemplated. They were originally contemplating a huge deal; now a number of things have been taken off the table.'[10] Newfoundland's Brian Peckford, however, showed the frustration of the rest of the premiers with their Ontario colleague and with the slim prospects for an agreement: 'Mr. Peterson is the least of my worries. All of the kinds of things Mr. Peterson has been saying, we've been saying for months ... behind closed doors. We just don't wash our dirty linen in public, election or no election.'[11]

Alan King, *Ottawa Citizen*, 6 October 1987

Alternative Strategies

In reality, the stage had now been set for a new end-game. Since the previous December, the American tactic had been to negotiate on all items of interest to the United Sattes without making commitments or concessions of their own. Meanwhile, Murphy and his colleagues had probed on every issue of interest to them. Murphy had indicated he would not go to the Hill until he could present the whole package. In the weeks leading to Cornwall, he had begun to take pieces to the Hill and to seek specific instructions from the economic policy council of cabinet. Reisman had acquiesced to this strategy, hoping it would help build a package that would sell on the Hill. By now, the poverty of the strategy had become evident, and the time to move to alternative strategies was pressing. There was little time left.

Derek Burney's attempt to open a second front by writing to Howard Baker in the first week of September had been rebuffed. At the conclusion of the first ministers' meeting, the government was even more convinced that a second front was required. The likelihood of Reisman and Murphy successfully concluding an agreement was now considered remote. Hy Solomon and Giles Gherson of the *Financial Post* had come to the same conclusion based on their probings in Ottawa and Washington: 'A breakthrough in the impasse is likely only if top-level political pressure is exerted from the White House. Canada is counting on the powerful Economic Policy Committee, headed by Treasury Secretary James Baker, and the National Security Council, headed by Frank Carlucci, to produce that pressure – and soon.'[12]

The crunch issues would be subsidies and dispute settlement; the specific question was whether the Americans were prepared to accept binding determinations regarding the conformity of national subsidies with agreed rules, and whether subsidies could be defined in a manner to leave adequate room for regional development. Rumours suggested that a more complete US proposal would be considerably less attractive than the outline presented on 11 September, and past performance suggested that, on the rare occasions when the US side did have ideas, they were quickly rendered dull and unimaginative when committed to paper or when revisited in follow-up discussions. The time had come to get some real answers.

To get action rolling on this second front, the prime minister directed Burney and Finance Minister Michael Wilson to meet with Treasury Secretary James Baker. On Saturday, 19 September, they flew to Washington on a government Challenger and, accompanied by Gotlieb, called on Baker. Burney and Wilson presented five bottom-line conditions that had been rehearsed in various ministerial speeches:

• Rules applying to fair and unfair trade such as dumping, countervail, and subsidies had to be spelled out in the clearest possible terms and in the event of a disagreement, had to be subject to an impartial, binational, and definitive resolution.

- There had to be clear, general rules covering all trade with everything in the agreement subject to clear and expeditious dispute settlement procedures, commensurate with the nature of the commitments undertaken.
- There should be a balanced widening of access for each country's agricultural and food products in the other's market.
- Changes to the automotive trade rules were only possible if they held the potential for more trade, production, and employment in both countries.
- The agreement should provide for a ten year phase-in during which all barriers would be eliminated or reduced and no new barriers could be introduced.

Burney's underlying message to Baker and Yeutter was clear: if the United States would not or could not respond to these requirements, the game was over. Burney thus laid the basis for pulling the plug later if an agreement along these lines did not prove negotiable.

Canadian embassy probing in Washington had established that Baker wanted a deal and believed one was possible, but not if Canada continued to insist on binding dispute settlement as its bottom line. This Baker confirmed. He appeared well briefed but not hugely receptive to Canadian positions; nor did he seem to grasp the urgency. He thought that any talk of extending the 4 October deadline for completion of the negotiations should be suppressed, but that the next plenary should meet to clear away the underbrush so as to isolate the main issues. Burney and Wilson argued that this plenary had to be the decisive one. Canada had to know whether the deal was there or not. The time for tactical games was past and Baker should ensure that Murphy had the necessary instructions to conclude an agreement. Baker made no commitments.

By Sunday, 20 September, the strategy had become clear. The negotiators were far apart. The premiers were getting restless. Efforts to engage senior politicians in Washington in the detail of the negotiations had not borne fruit. The Americans continued to be complacent. Time was pressing. If the negotiators could not engage the Americans during this final three-day session, Reisman was to suspend negotiations and return home. This would then provide a clear path to the end-game. Either the Americans would come through with an acceptable basis for concluding an agreement, or the groundwork had been laid for an honourable and decisive termination.

The Final Plenary

The twenty-second and final plenary 21-3 September, originally scheduled for Ottawa, had been moved to Washington to allow the Americans easier access to their political masters. Its purpose was to determine once and for all whether the Americans could meet Canada's needs on trade remedy law. If not, Reisman had specific instructions to break off negotiations Wednesday morning and return to Ottawa. To provide Reisman with the greatest flexibility to suspend negotiations, a government jet was once again put at his disposal. To demonstrate to the Americans that he was in a position to craft and close a deal, Reisman came equipped with all his senior staff, the whole panoply of legal advisors, support staff, four computers, and two printers. If an agreement could be reached, he was ready to put the finishing touches to it right then and there, with his initials if necessary.

Monday morning, 22 September, began with a delegation breakfast. Reisman declared his intention to force the issue on subsidies and dispute settlement or else break off. He would not agree to clear away the underbrush first. Whatever happened, the meeting promised to be filled with drama.

Most of the morning was spent waiting around while Reisman and Murphy sparred in private session. Murphy balked at starting the plenary session with a detailed examination of a new US proposal on subsidies and countervailing duties. He wanted the subsidies working group to consider the paper first. The US negotiators had for some time been of the view that plenary discussions were rarely constructive and that there would only be breakthroughs as a result of lower level technical discussions. While the working group studied the new US proposal, Murphy wanted to discuss issues of concern to the United States. He wanted to be able to report to the economic policy council that the two sides had engaged on the US subsidy paper, and that issues of concern to the United States were being resolved. Reisman was equally adamant. He would not let the working group meet unless he determined that there was a basis for their work. He was in no mood to delegate his responsibility. After two hours of fruitless wrangling, Murphy reluctantly agreed that he would introduce his proposal at the plenary.

Murphy's instinct, and that of the Commerce officials who had prepared the proposal, had been right. It stood little chance on its merits and even less if it had to pass Reisman's scrutiny first. It was drafted in such draconian terms that, if accepted, it would have taken the Canadian federal and provincial governments out of the subsidies business altogether. It was tantamount to saying that so long as Canada did not subsidize it would have no worries about countervail. It seemed to ignore the fact that for that kind of result, a negotiated agreement was unnecessary. However admirable an economic policy this might have been, it had no hope of leading to a settlement. Reisman declared that if it became public it would destroy any Canadian government. Reisman countered with a proposal that would severely constrain federal and provincial subsidy programs, but leave sufficient room to promote regional development as well as research and development. And there the matter stood. The working group was authorized to examine the issues further, but neither group of experts had much enthusiasm left for the project.

At the end of the day, Gordon Ritchie flew back to Ottawa and briefed ministers on the lack of any useful exchange. The decision hatched on Sunday to suspend the negotiations was confirmed.

The next day started with a brief discussion on anti-dumping. In effect the US side rejected Canada's earlier proposal for a regime leading ultimately to a reliance on domestic price discrimination law (competition law) as a substitute for protectionist international price discrimination law (anti-dumping law). Instead, the Americans offered a joint ten-year work program to study the issues involved. Agricultural matters were also addressed with similarly dismal results. Not so disappointing were signs of US movement on other issues, with some softening on their previously fixed positions, such as on alcoholic beverages. The Canadian team, however, interpreted these shifts as tactical attempts to compensate in peripheral areas in order to hang tough on the central core of the negotiations. Working groups, meanwhile, laboured away at investment, safeguards, and other issues. While the prospect for a successful conclusion was slim, no one could be accused of slacking off.

During a morning break, a frustrated and angry Reisman provided some comic relief for the media horde by calling the *Toronto Star*'s Bob Hepburn a 'hack' and his paper a 'rag.'[13] The rest of the media delighted in this contretemps. A garrulous Mike Duffy went so far as to call Reisman at 3:20 AM the next morning to offer him congratulations on a job well done. The call did not improve Reisman's mood, especially since Murphy had cancelled dinner at the last moment. The Americans sensed that something was afoot.

At breakfast on Wednesday morning, Ritchie confirmed that unless there was a major breakthrough in the discussions, Reisman would walk out sometime during the morning and go home. He designated who would be returning on the Challenger and suggested that other team members ensure that they had reservations for later in the day.

The team proceeded to USTR to await the denouement. While a plenary and several working groups had been scheduled, Reisman and Murphy met privately. All morning the two sides hovered like an extended family awaiting the death of the patriarch. There was much scurrying about while the discussion focused on subsidies. As their final negotiating challenge, Reisman and Murphy chose which draft subsidies paper they would work from. In the end, the US side could not agree to work from the Canadian draft while Canada saw little to be gained in pursuing the US proposal. Reisman repaired to Room 419, the Canadian delegation office, to consider his position. For several more hours, emissaries moved back and forth between Room 419 and Peter Murphy's fifth floor office. As a contingency measure, Ritchie consulted with the death watch committee in Ottawa advising the prime minister: Burney, Gerry Shannon, and Don Campbell from External

Affairs and Privy Council Clerk Paul Tellier and his assistant, Harry Swain. They agreed on a brief statement of 'suspension,' in both official languages, declaring the negotiations to be at an impasse on fundamental issues. Like the team in Washington, the Ottawa contingent nervously waited around in the Cabinet anteroom for the end. Everyone knew Reisman's instructions, but had no control over how they would be carried out.

A deeply disappointed Simon Reisman announces the suspension of negotiations on the steps of the Winder Building in Washington, DC. (23 September 1987)

The prime minister's press officials, meanwhile, had already begun background briefings for the media and by the end of the morning, Quebec government officials phoned the delegation in Washington seeking confirmation of what it was hearing from the French-language media that the negotiations were over. The prime minister was preparing to make a statement to the House of Commons and wanted to do so before the story broke fully. Frantic phone calls from Ottawa to Washington instructed Reisman to get on with it. With great reluctance, he finally proceeded to the door at 1:30, telling reporters that 'the US is not responding on elements fundamental to Canada's position. I have therefore suspended the negotiations.' He continued to his car and on to the airport. There was a mad scramble to gather up briefcases and computers and join him. There was only room for nine others on the Challenger. The rest of the crowd made it home on either Continental or Piedmont.

The bilateral trade negotiations between Canada and the United States appeared to be over. The government had reluctantly concluded that the United States, after sixteen months of negotiations and with only eleven days to go, would not or could not accommodate Canada's fundamental objectives. The prime minister told the House later that afternoon that 'Canada has tried vigorously, effectively and well to conclude this arrangement and the burden is now on the US to deliver on its end of the bargain.'[14]

The United States, in a hastily called press conference dominated by Canadian media, responded with a statement from USTR Clayton Yeutter saying 'We are prepared to resume talks and are ready to meet round the clock if necessary.'[15] What had gone wrong? Were the talks finished?

Alan King, *Ottawa Citizen*, 25 September 1987

PART THREE

The Real Thing

14

WHAT HAD GONE WRONG?

> Any featherhead can have confidence in times of
> victory, but the test is to have faith when things
> are going wrong, and when things happen which
> cannot be explained in public.
> – Sir Winston Churchill

nalysis of what had gone wrong began almost immediately. The media
had a field day, especially those who had opposed the initiative from
the start. It was a good game for Monday morning quarterbacks with
twenty-twenty hindsight. But it was also necessary. The government had
made good relations with the United States a central element of its foreign
policy and a comprehensive bilateral trade agreement the centrepiece of its
economic policy. Both policies seemed to have come up short. The country was
entitled to debate what had gone wrong and to consider alternative strategies.

When the government had started on this venture, it was with the strength
of conviction that it was on the right track. But it had never claimed that
success was certain. Indeed, it had repeatedly stated that success was far from
certain, but that the rewards would be worth the risk should the negotiations
succeed. As negotiations proceeded, it became evident that while the faith
was strong and the energy unflagging, the chances of success were receding.
Why? Had there ever been a chance? Had Canada misread the American
mood? Had the Americans negotiated in bad faith? Had the negotiators
fooled themselves? Could things have been done differently?

Where the Negotiations Stood at Suspension
The lack of progress reflected the seemingly irreconcilable differences of
approach between the two sides. Canada saw the purpose of the negotiations
to be the establishment of a wide-ranging and comprehensive free-trade
agreement that, by the end of the century, would provide for open and
secure movement of all goods and services as well as better rules for the
movement of investments and people between the two countries. The
United States saw the negotiations basically as an opportunity to resolve outstanding irritants and make a head start on its multilateral trade negotiating

agenda. Rather than envisioning a free-standing and comprehensive trade and investment agreement, US negotiators saw the agreement as an adjunct to the GATT. The vision of a big deal between the world's two largest trading partners seemed beyond the grasp of the US negotiating team. Interagency rivalry coupled with an apparent absence of firm leadership, at both the political and bureaucratic levels, had stymied the negotiations for months.

While the media focused on dispute settlement as the main stumbling block, the differences were wider and more profound. For example, it was by now clear that the United States was unwilling to consider anything more than minor adjustments on procurement and technical standards and was seeking only a small deal on trade in services. Their demands on issues like intellectual property, investment, and subsidies, especially as they related to culture and regional development, were unreasonable and betrayed a continuing ignorance of Canada. Reluctance to make any significant move on issues that required changes to existing US legislation demonstrated both a lack of commitment and of clout. On every issue that mattered, the gap was very wide indeed. Even relatively minor matters had not yet been resolved.[1]

Trade Remedy Law

From the beginning of the negotiations, Canada had flagged security of access as central to its whole approach. Achieving security of access would require a new regime to address the issues which give rise to trade remedies, such as countervailing and anti-dumping duties, safeguard actions, and similar measures taken at the border to control injurious imports.

Canada had sought to achieve secure access to the US market by proposing an agreement that would make the application of US trade remedy law more predictable and less capricious. This would involve bypassing existing procedures and establishing new rules to discipline the practices that give rise to complaints under US trade remedy law. Any breaches of these new rules or complaints would then be addressed through bilateral consultation and, if necessary, binding, bilateral dispute settlement by an objective and permanent tribunal.

Of the three principal trade remedy issues (subsidies and countervailing duties, dumping and anti-dumping duties, and safeguard measures), a new regime to discipline subsidy practices was perceived by both sides as key to any agreement. But the US side had proven to be unprepared to write precise rules into the agreement defining acceptable and unacceptable practices unless the rules were significantly tougher than current US trade law and applied more stringently to Canadian than to US practices. In addition, the US side was not prepared to subject any such rules to bilateral administration and interpretation. Rather, it insisted on the right to retain the full weight of US countervail law, i.e., the unilateral application and interpretation of what would and what would not be an acceptable trade practice. At the same time, Canada had made the task more difficult by insisting that it needed room to carry on practices the United States found offensive, such as regional development assistance programs, research and development grants, and resource pricing practices.

Throughout the negotiations, the US side had sought to have specific Canadian programs outlawed; American negotiators claimed that they had to have scalps on their pole which they could hold up to Congress as proof of their success. In contrast, the Canadian side had sought to establish principles that would have mutual application. The US final offer: a high 'bright line' and small 'safe harbours.' Canada was free to maintain subsidy programs generally available in law and practice to all sectors (the bright line); the only exception would be for those Canadian industries that exported less than 10 per cent of their goods to the United States – any subsidies to these industries would be of little concern to their US competitors. Specified programs, if they met certain conditions, would also be free of countervail (safe harbours). Additionally, the United States would consider phasing in a binding mechanism to resolve disputes concerned with whether programs fell above or below the bright line, or inside or outside a safe harbour, depending on Canadian behaviour over the years.

The difficulty of negotiating a new subsidy regime had been apparent since at least early summer when discussion changed from general to specific proposals and the lead US negotiator became the Commerce lawyer responsible for international trade law rather than the senior officer responsible for trade and economic relations with Canada. The US side was unprepared to contemplate a clear definition of what constitutes a subsidy and to subject the application of this definition to dispute settlement. US domestic law, unlike Canadian law, does not contain such a definition. Rather, it contains a non-exclusive list of types of practices that are countervailable. The problem of definition had bedeviled similar GATT negotiations for more than a generation and had, during the Tokyo Round, resulted in a code long on procedures dealing with the countermeasures, but short on disciplines dealing with the practice.[2]

Even if it had proved possible to negotiate tough new disciplines on subsidy practices, it would have been a tough sell in Canada. While the economic desirability of disciplining subsidy practices was evident, political desirability was quite another thing. Federal and provincial ministers and officials had become attached to various assistance programs and were reluctant to give them up – sometimes even more reluctant than the recipients. The extent of the discipline contemplated by the United States in its final offers went well beyond what would have been politically feasible and made even the existing gamble with US countervail law look attractive.

Dumping was a less intractable problem. At the suspension of negotiations, Canada had rejected a US proposal to set up a working group to examine the feasibility of relying on competition laws after the transition period as a substitute for anti-dumping law. In Canada's view, such a technical group had concluded its work over the course of the summer. It had considered all aspects of the problem and prepared a number of technical papers. Canadian experts were satisfied that it would be feasible to rely on competition policy at the end of the transition period and to implement a special regime based on competition principles during that transition. The 22 September US proposal was its first formal response. The United States was not prepared to commit itself to the development of a regime based on domestic competition law, it was only ready to explore the issue. The US proposal also did not address the possibility of changes in the existing anti-dumping regime for the duration of the transition period.[3]

Concerning safeguards (such as quotas or special duties on injurious but fairly traded goods), the two sides agreed that bilateral actions should be available only during the transition period and should be limited to a tariff snapback. The continued applicability of global actions under GATT Article XIX proved more difficult. On the final day, US negotiators agreed that the two parties would exclude each other from global actions unless imports from the other party were an 'important contributing cause of injury' or unless there was a subsequent surge in imports. Details remained to be worked out. The US side had also agreed that safeguard actions would be subject to binding dispute settlement.

Of the three trade remedy issues, therefore, only that of safeguards was close to resolution. A basis for resolving the other two issues, however, could be found. A starting point was to take existing US law, translate it into treaty obligations subject to binding dispute settlement, and use that as a basis for gradually moving towards a more acceptable regime along the lines sought by Canada.

Much of the existing gap between the two sides resulted from US concern that it could not move away from existing US law when the Congress was seeking to make that law even more restrictive, as well as from lack of trust that Canada was seriously prepared to discipline subsidy practices. Canada had been prepared to incorporate US legal concepts into the agreement so that the US would not have to depart from its law. Canadian concerns could be met by making these concepts subject to bilateral interpretation and dispute resolution. Such a regime would give Canada the incentive to adjust its programs and thus build credibility with US politicians and officials. Experience with both enhanced subsidy discipline and bilateral administration would provide a basis for eventually negotiating a new regime.

Key to an agreement along these lines was the commitment to establish such a regime. In the case of subsidies and countervailing duties, a new regime would require rules about acceptable and actionable subsidies, and in the case of dumping would rely on competition laws. Such an approach could be sold in the United States on the basis of continuity of current law and in Canada on the basis of bilateral interpretation and evolution towards a more rational economic regime. Could such a deal still be negotiated? The betting was that it could not. A return to the table depended on clear signals that the United States was prepared to negotiate along those lines.

Dispute Settlement

In the eyes of the media, the opposition parties, and the public, dispute settlement had come to symbolize the state of the entire negotiations. From the beginning, the prime minister had said that there must be a form of dispute settlement. More often than not, Canada had insisted that it be binding in application.

The US side had proposed a dispute settlement mechanism involving a pool of experts from which ad hoc panels would be drawn to give declaratory rulings on any disputes. Only if both parties agreed could these rulings be implemented. In addition, the United States was prepared to submit to binding arbitration with the prior approval of both parties. Behind the US proposal lay the following preoccupations: avoiding the creation of a new and unknown bureaucracy; limiting the scope for politically inspired appointees dominating the tribunal; preserving flexibility; avoiding the appearance that foreigners could tell the US government what to do; and retaining an unrestricted right to retaliate in cases of non-compliance.

Canada had insisted on the establishment of a permanent tribunal with power to make binding rulings and issue remedial orders. Behind the Canadian proposal lay the desire to ensure consistency and predictability. There was concern that any consensus approach would maintain disparity of power. There was also the need to establish symmetry: both sides would have to be equally bound by rulings, and Canada hoped to limit US ability to retaliate and maintain unwarranted pressure.

These two approaches were not irreconcilable, particularly if the primary concern was trade remedies. For example:

- Appointments could be made from existing bodies, such as the International Trade Commission and the Canadian International Trade Tribunal, on an ex officio basis, thereby avoiding the appearance of a new bureaucracy and limiting the scope for political abuse.
- Trade remedy findings would have to be final and determinative, that is, binding, but only where they ruled against the complaining party. If they were in favour of the complaining party (for instance, the United States in a subsidy case), the right to retaliate would in virtually all cases ensure compliance.
- The tribunal need not issue remedial orders; declaratory findings would be sufficient. It was not likely that a party would retaliate in excess of the harm done; in any event, retaliation could be avoided by compliance with a finding (such as, by Canada's amending a non-complying subsidy program).
- Binding arbitration by mutual consent, as proposed by the United States, could be retained. This would allow the parties to insulate themselves from politically difficult issues and solutions.
- Other issues were of a secondary order; for them non-binding, declaratory findings would suffice. In light of the non-binding nature of these findings, Canada could, if pushed, also live with a pool of experts and ad hoc panels for non-trade remedy disputes.
- A nullification and impairment provision (i.e., a right to seek a panel rul-

ing in circumstances where a particular trade measure did not violate a specific rule but did undermine achievement of agreed objectives) could substitute for the absence of clear rules in some areas.

Thus a basis did exist for a mutually satisfactory result on a regime for the settlement of disputes, particularly if there was a breakthrough on trade remedy law. Negotiations on dispute settlement, however, could only come to a conclusion once the substantive rules of the agreement had been agreed.[4]

Customs Matters

Tariff negotiations were virtually complete. Discussion in the tariffs working group had been based on agreement to eliminate all tariffs in ten equal steps beginning 1 January 1989, except where industry sectors were prepared to eliminate them either immediately or in five equal steps. Both sides were disappointed that certain sectors were in the five or ten-year categories (e.g., the US sought faster elimination of paper tariffs and Canada preferred earlier elimination of the tariff on beef). Details of the rules of origin regime remained to be resolved, although this was not perceived to be a make-or-break issue.

The two sides had also agreed that future import or export controls would be governed by the provisions of the GATT and would be available in limited circumstances, such as for health and safety reasons. Some existing provisions were to be eliminated, such as the Canadian embargo on used cars and aircraft. Others were to be grandfathered, such as the provisions in the Jones Act requiring that any coastal trade or shipment on the Great Lakes between US ports had to be carried in US owned and staffed ships (its elimination was an important Canadian objective). Outstanding issues included what to do about Canadian controls on log exports and on unprocessed fish.

Agreement had been reached on most other customs issues. There were some technical or relatively minor issues outstanding, such as the timing of the elimination of some remission programs. Unresolved was whether the United States would eliminate customs user fees under the FTA and whether Canada would either eliminate its machinery program or determine availability on a North American rather than Canadian basis only.

A text on technical barriers was virtually complete. The only specific irritant that remained to be resolved was Canadian plywood standards and the readiness of Canada to accommodate US interests by granting Canada Mortgage and Housing Corporation (CMHC) standards equivalency status to US standards. The US side had proved more forthcoming in agriculture for which a detailed annex of various standards and procedures providing for mutual recognition and harmonization had been agreed.

NEWS ITEM: REISMAN SAYS U.S. NEGOTIATORS WAITED FOR CANADA TO UNDRESS FIRST

Alan King, *Ottawa Citizen*, 19 September 1987

'I dunno about you, but the sound of tariffs comin' off just drives me wild.'

Government Procurement

From the beginning of the negotiations, Canada had identified free and open access to the huge US procurement market as a major element in gaining improved access. To achieve this objective, Canada had been prepared to eliminate all buy-national preferences in North America at the federal, provincial, and state levels. Failing this, Canada would have been satisfied with a deal limited to federal civilian procurements only, leaving state, provincial, and military coverage for another day.

Negotiations proceeded on the assumption that coverage would be determined by the quality of the agreement as a whole. But hopes for a big deal were dashed when all that the US side would consider was an additional US $20 billion in federal procurement. It was prepared to lower the threshold for access under the GATT procurement code and provide access to US service contracts. In return, the US sought a similar lowering of the threshold in Canada and access to Canadian service contracts and procurements by Canadian crown corporations. No state or provincial procurement would be involved.

Canada continued to insist on a comprehensive deal covering all goods and services, civil and defence, and all levels of government. The US side, notwithstanding its acceptance in principle to work towards a comprehensive agreement, indicated that only an arrangement based on rough balance of coverage would be saleable. Canada rejected this approach because it would remove all Canadian government procurement restrictions, while leaving many US restrictions in place. If the US preferred to negotiate on the basis of federal government procurement restrictions alone, leaving aside states and provinces, Canada was prepared to cooperate. The US side indicated that it was considering alternative scenarios, but none of these was brought forward.

The negotiation of the rules and procedures of government procurement was virtually completed. But rules and procedures were of limited value in the absence of an agreement on coverage.

Trade in Services

An agreement on services was a critical part of the US agenda. Canadian willingness to entertain a broad services agreement, plus a number of sectoral agreements, could thus help pay for US concessions in other areas. But as negotiations proceeded, it became evident that US rhetoric had far outrun reality. At the suspension of negotiations, the US remained willing to freeze the existing situation with the promise of improvements for new services only. Even in freezing the status quo, the US sought some room for manoeuvre. Little headway had been made in reaching any meaningful sectoral agreements. Application of the services chapter to transportation and communications, two of the biggest regulated service industries, remained to be worked out.

As part of a comprehensive agreement facilitating the free flow of goods and services, Canada sought provisions that would ensure that business travellers could move freely across the border to pursue legitimate commercial objectives such as sales and service. In essence, Canada sought an agreement that would ensure that immigration requirements would not frustrate achievement of the other objectives of the agreement.

The United States was prepared to see relatively easier access for managerial and professional travellers, but was reluctant to include general service and sales personnel, largely due to strong opposition from organized labour. Various texts were in play. As negotiations neared the end, the US side was toying with the creation of a separate visa category for Canada tied to activity under the agreement.

Intellectual Property

The second major issue on which the United States had sought progress with Canada as part of its broader trade policy agenda was a new regime to protect intellectual property. Again, while Canada's immediate interest was to maintain the status quo, an intellectual property chapter could serve the useful purpose of balancing other aspects of the agreement of greater interest to Canada. More indirectly, Canada could use the intellectual property discussions to advantage by tying it to better access to US technology, particularly technology developed for the US government under procurement contracts or protected under national security regulations. Additionally, Canada could exact exemption from section 337 proceedings (the expedited procedures by which US producers can obtain exclusion orders against foreign goods alleged to be tainted by patent infringements) in return for an enhanced intellectual property regime.

While US interest in intellectual property was driven by broad policy concerns and a desire to demonstrate to the world the feasibility of including intellectual property in a trade agreement, US negotiators were also concerned with a number of specific irritants. They wanted to resolve the long-standing pharmaceutical and cable retransmission issues in the context of an intellectual property package.

At the suspension of negotiations, a clean text had been agreed with two issues outstanding: the US team was not satisfied with the changes in Canadian patent legislation relating to pharmaceuticals and was consequently unprepared to exempt Canada from section 337 proceedings. Without such an exemption, Canada would be hard pressed to agree to an intellectual property chapter. Additionally, specific language to resolve the cable retransmission issue remained to be agreed.

Investment

From the US perspective, investment was the issue that would make any agreement worthwhile. On the other hand, from Canada's perspective, an investment chapter could be a potential minefield. In substantive terms, the issue had only just been addressed. The United States wanted national treatment in Canada with no government review of takeovers of new or foreign-owned establishments. Canada had sought to establish a regime that would freeze the status quo in both countries, leaving open the possibility of some improvements involving the right to review direct and indirect takeovers. Both countries were agreed that all future laws and policies would have to meet the national treatment test.

The issue gained increasing prominence in the negotiations as a result of Canada's refusal to engage the issue and the not so veiled attempts by both sides to link progress on this issue to progress on trade remedies. While they were not formally linked, both sides knew that failure to meet each other's needs in these two areas would doom the negotiations to failure. Canada had made this point directly by refusing to enter substantive negotiations until the United States had shown a willingness to engage the trade remedy issue.

Other Issues

A range of other horizontal issues, such as national treatment, exceptions, extraterritoriality, balance-of-payments provisions, and national security exceptions remained to be engaged in any substantive way. While they had been addressed in the context of other issues and language had been prepared in one or both of the draft integrated texts, no detailed policy discussions had been held on these issues. While these were not make-or-break issues, they were conceptually difficult and would need more than perfunctory attention.

Sectoral Issues

Although negotiations had been pursued largely along functional lines, a number of issues had been addressed sectorally. Progress on these matters was particularly important in ensuring broad support for an agreement or in avoiding erosion in support on both sides of the border. In some cases, sectoral discussions were necessary because the functional provisions were too broad in application; in others a special problem needed to be solved. Agriculture and energy were the most important sectoral discussions.

Some progress had been made on agriculture, but not enough. The US side refused even to consider a commitment to consult prior to the introduction of new subsidies to third markets or to contemplate any backdown on sugar quotas. There had been no progress on domestic price support issues. There was agreement on tariffs, although Canada was still seeking to ensure some freedom to protect horticulture trade from the fact that the earlier US growing season for perishable products made the Canadian crop vulnerable to price depression during a bumper crop year. There was some movement on removing bilateral use of quotas on red meat as well as on technical barriers, but this was relatively minor. The result looked like a very modest package that would find little favour with Western farmers but could be subjected to criticism from horticulture interests and Eastern producers. There appeared also little room for either side to try to enrich the package.

An energy fact-finding group had over the course of the year considered the special problems in energy trade and monitored work on various chapters with a view to determining whether their provisions would be appropriate to energy. The US position was somewhat schizophrenic. At some points they preferred a separate chapter; at other times they were content to rely on general provisions. Canada was prepared to enter into a broad agreement that would guarantee access to supply in return for secure access to the US market. At suspension, the US side was still not sure whether its interest was served by gaining enhanced access to supply or in protecting US suppliers.

Most of the work had been pursued at the technical level; there had been only sporadic references to energy at the main table. By pursuing individual issues, an acceptable package was beginning to emerge. Some progress had been made, for example, in addressing the threatened US embargo on imports of uranium.

The autopact had never been 'officially' discussed at the table. In effect, the autopact had never been 'on' the table, but everyone knew it was 'under' the table, waiting to emerge at any time. There were a variety of automotive issues that had to be addressed and some link had to be established between the autopact and the new agreement. If the deal was big enough, agreement could be reached on duty remission programs (Canada would have to phase them out), rules of origin (they would have to be based on North American manufacture), and the tariff (it could be bound at free, i.e., phased out, in 1999 after a ten-year transition).

A deal on alcoholic beverages which satisfied most US interests was gradually emerging. The goal would be to introduce national treatment but leave the provinces with the time to phase in its provisions. Discussion, however, was still at an exploratory stage and time was pressing.

Discussion of cultural issues continued to be uninformed and insensitive. Canada continued to insist that cultural issues had to be exempted from the agreement, and the United States insisted individual irritants had to be resolved.

Alan King, *Ottawa Citizen*, 17 November 1987

Could the Initiative Be Salvaged?

Given the fact that at suspension on 23 September fewer than two weeks remained to conclude a deal within the time frame imposed by the fast-track procedures, the two sides were remarkably far apart on a whole range of issues. It appeared virtually impossible to conclude an agreement in principle, let alone a final text for initialling. According to the position taken by the US side, by congressional staffers, and by most outside counsel in Washington, the fast-track procedures required the two sides to initial a final text by midnight 4 October. At most, they could fix obvious errors and omissions between then and 3 January, the day by which the president had to table the agreement in Congress. Given such an inflexible schedule, the situation looked hopeless. Little wonder that energy was being devoted to post-mortems and scenarios for a constructive disengagement.

A myriad of factors needed to be taken into account in understanding why an agreement appeared to be beyond the government's grasp. Some lay south of the border; others were to be found closer to home. A number were inter-related. Some were political; others economic. Some were tactical; others strategic. Together these factors appeared to be enough to thwart once again an idea that might be impeccably logical but impossible to implement.[5]

Troubled Times

The most fundamental factor was economic. Conditions for an agreement of the scope Canada was seeking had to be right. Conditions in Canada had to be such that business would support negotiations, either for negative or positive reasons. Those conditions included a fear of the consequences of US protectionism and a realization that Canada needed more than its domestic market to grow. Such conditions had existed in Canada throughout the negotiations and continued to exist. But conditions in the United States also had to be right. In good times, US politicians are magnanimous and outward-looking. In bad times, they are xenophobic and ugly. In 1984-5, as preparations for the initiative were launched, the mood was turning increasingly ugly but was expected to turn around once the US trade deficit improved. That was expected to happen during 1986. By the time negotiations were to conclude, both sides expected a more receptive congressional audience. In June 1985, for example, congressional staffers, including House Ways and Means counsel Rufus Yerxa and Senate Finance counsel Len Santos, had suggested that the kind of agreement in which Canada appeared to be interested would get a negative reception if brought to the Hill at that time. Two years from then, however, a different mood should prevail.

This message was repeated at a Brookings seminar in December 1985.

Congressional staffers at that seminar, including George Weiss from the Ways and Means Committee and Susan Schwab from Senator Danforth's office, were optimistic. They shared the view that it would be hard for either the administration or Congress to turn down a good agreement with Canada and there was every reason to proceed.

By December 1986, the new majority trade counsel to the Senate Finance Committee, Jeff Lang, had become more cautious. His view was echoed by Senator Bentsen and his colleagues when they visited Ottawa that month. A deal was possible but had to meet congressional concerns. Fears were beginning to be voiced that the administration might come forward with a politically motivated agreement rather than an agreement that was clearly in the commercial interest of the United States. There was consensus on the Hill that gaining congressional approval would require a better US trade performance and a new trade bill that would satisfy the myriad of special interests. At the same time, few on the Hill were convinced that the administration was putting the necessary resources and effort into the negotiations.

But the change in trade performance did not materialize and new legislation remained a threat rather than a reality. The trade and budget deficits continued to worsen and the mood had deteriorated accordingly. Hostility came not only from increasing xenophobia fuelled by the worsening trade deficit, but also from the unhappy relationship between the administration and Congress. The administration's continuing inability to address congressional frustration with the trade situation was of general concern; its failure to work closely with Congress in developing a position for the bilateral negotiations was of particular concern. Both anxieties spelled trouble for the initiative.

The administration's record in managing the Congress had never been good. Its most senior officials were uncomfortable with congressional log-rolling. Only Bill Brock had previously served in Congress; few had much experience from former administrations. The record had been particularly bad on trade, with Congress insisting that it was in charge and the administration no more than its executor. As long as Bill Brock, whose Washington career had started in Congress, was in charge of the trade portfolio, there remained a modicum of good relations. Once he had been replaced by Clayton Yeutter, Congress took the gloves off. To both Republicans and Democrats, the administration had little credibility on the Hill when it came to trade.

Events in Iran and Nicaragua culminating in Contragate conspired to make a bad situation into a no-win situation. The normal weaknesses of a lame duck administration were compounded by a scandal that demonstrated that the president was not in charge. The prestige and authority of the president evaporated steadily with every day of Contragate testimony. Canadian appeals to the administration to give the negotiations a higher profile were addressed to an executive branch that had increasingly limited prestige and authority to offer.

Differing Priorities

From the start of the negotiations, Canadians worried how they could negotiate with the United States without being mugged and left in the street. Cartoonists constantly played on the theme of the supplicant Canada beaten up by the big American bully. The apparent failure of the negotiations was seen as the inevitable result of the power imbalance. The truth was somewhat different.

For Canada, trade policy must always be close to the top of the national agenda, and trade relationships with any major trading partner a matter of high state policy. It had been thus at the time of the 1854-66 Elgin-Marcy Treaty in 1911 when the voters chose Empire over prosperity, and in 1947 when Mackenzie King felt that the political implications of tariff elimination with the United States were so grave and so poorly understood by the negotiators that he abruptly ended the discussions.

The United States, with a huge population and a continental economy, approaches trade negotiations from a different starting point. Up until the 1960s trade policy had been deployed as the handmaiden of broad US foreign policy interests. Only relatively recently had trade surfaced in any consideration of national priorities. Even in 1971, when the US closed the gold window and imposed a surtax of 10 per cent on dutiable imports, trade accounted for less than 5 per cent of its national income. In the 1980s, the trade account had grown to approximately 10 per cent as a share of the US national pie, and trade issues crept almost surreptitiously onto the front pages of the newspapers and onto the agendas of state visits to Washington. Beyond the Beltway, the huge expressway that encircles Washington, people could appreciate the complaint that their jobs were going to Taiwan and Singapore and that their children's opportunities would be reduced to flipping hamburgers at McDonald's. Still, the United States is a superpower and a super-economy and trade, even with its largest trading partners, must jostle for space with many other issues close to the hearts of the American people and its leaders.

The economic importance of the negotiations for Canada and their political, historical, indeed somewhat metaphysical, character (for Canadians if not Americans) demanded that the negotiating team appear to be composed of the best and the brightest. Simon Reisman was chosen because, said the prime minister, he was the best and most experienced negotiator available.

He would, moreover, have his pick for a delegation; nothing would be denied including the best office space that Ottawa had to offer. The delegation would for all practical purposes work full time on the negotiations, undistracted by the management of ongoing trade relations with the United States or any other country. It would have complete control of the negotiations with other government departments providing technical advice at the beck and call of Reisman and his team.

The US team enjoyed neither the luxury nor the burden of running an issue at the top of the country's agenda. An overworked, understaffed if talented United States Trade Representative's Office had to negotiate not only a free-trade agreement with the United States' most important trading partner, but co-ordinate trade relations with all other countries. Far from having undisputed control over the negotiations, the USTR had to share responsibility with Congress and the myriad of US agencies interested in trade. Moreover, in the management of trade negotiations, many other US interests would have to be brought to bear. While the United States had an advantage in that it could and did treat the negotiations as a commercial arrangement without an overlay of emotional nationalism, the United States could not escape its role as a global power with global interests and responsibilities. Hence, while the US side worried about precedent, the Canadian side took pride in the innovative and unprecedented character of the agreement. For a big country, absence of precedent can be a potential weakness; for a small country, it can be a source of strength.

An additional difference between the Canadian and US approach was the level of political control over the negotiations. From the very beginning, the free-trade negotiations engaged the attention of the prime minister, cabinet, Parliament, national business and labour organizations, the cultural lobby, and the media in Canada. In the United States, the level of political attention in the cabinet and the White House had to correspond to the place which trade held in the national agenda. That place had been steadily rising over many years, but it always competed for space with issues such as arms control negotiations with the Soviets, the administration's Central America policy, the fate of American hostages in the Middle East, the budget deficit, and trade relations with Japan and Europe, among others.

Despite Canada's appeals, the bilateral trade negotiations had yet to reach the top of the US political agenda. From the beginning of formal negotiations in June 1986 until they were suspended in September 1987, the negotiations had never gained the necessary political momentum in Washington to ensure success. The US negotiators never coalesced into a team with an acknowledged leader, a sense of purpose and direction, and a clear mandate.

Rather than taking direction from the US cabinet, every member looked to the interests of his or her agency and each individually kept a wary eye out for what Congress might or might not find acceptable. No one appeared to be in charge of a congressional strategy. Given the enormous importance that Congress plays in US decision-making and the constant allusions as to what would or would not fly in Congress, it was particularly galling to learn as late as July that senators and representatives and their staffers had only the faintest notion of what was being considered in the bilateral talks. The administration had yet to build a coalition of support in Congress, despite clear warnings in April 1986, at the time the administration gained approval to negotiate under the fast-track procedures, that failure to build such a coalition would doom the negotiations.

It had also been apparent for some time that the administration was long on ideology and rhetoric but very short on policy and execution. No administration had ever stated its faith in free trade more eloquently and then initiated more actions that put the lie to its commitment. Like its strong faith in balanced budgets, the gap between rhetoric and reality grew from year to year. The retreat from free trade was couched in terms of ensuring fair trade, but with the clear understanding that only America would determine what constituted fair trade. In the face of the highly protectionist legislation threatened in Congress, the administration dithered. Not until the spring of 1987 did it come up with draft legislation of its own. It was too little, too late. The administration bill found no sponsors and died soon after it was born. It had no influence on the Senate version of a new trade bill. The House had already passed its version, a slightly revised version of the bill that had died on the order paper in 1986 at the end of the 99th Congress.

There was a large gap between words and action. From the very beginning, the word from Washington at the highest levels of the Congress and administration was that the United States wanted a big, bold trade agreement; indeed, anything less would not fly. This message was checked and rechecked and never varied. The Canadian side acted under the government's instruction that it wanted a comprehensive trade agreement. It assumed that since the president and the prime minister agreed on the objective, the US side would have instructions to negotiate the boldest, most innovative trade agreement ever concluded. This would not mean that the negotiations would be easy, but it should have meant that the two teams had a single objective.

It was not sufficiently understood on the US side that in Canada when the prime minister decides, the bureaucracy swings into action and delivers. By contrast, in the United States, the president's voice is important, but it is not the only voice. The US team, operating in an entirely different political system, certainly knew what the president and his senior cabinet officers wanted in an agreement, but they also had a lively sense of what would be acceptable to the American business community and Congress. Tough, slow, nerve-wracking negotiations were the result, characterized by mutual doubts.

The third difference lay in the degree of public profile the negotiations attracted. The free-trade negotiations in Canada were virtually front-page news every day while in the United States they rarely surfaced on the national radar screen. In Canada, the negotiations became part of the public domain from the very beginning: journalists sought out the real story, staked out the negotiating sessions, solicited the opinions of every walk of life, explored the bizarre and the inane, and discussed the personalities, the regional dimension, and the influence on Canadian culture and life. In the United States, the negotiations made the news on infrequent occasions, such as when the Senate almost killed the enterprise and when the prime minister and the president met at Shamrock two and three. Canadian negotiators knew that their every move would attract a press horde. They laboured in a public vineyard. The American team worked in obscurity; few seemed interested in what they were doing yet they knew that they would eventually be called to account.

Trouble at the Table

But any negotiation that does not result in agreement must in part be the responsibility of the two chief negotiators. From the beginning it was apparent that it would have been hard to pick two individuals less well suited to each other. Simon Reisman is pugnacious, even bellicose in style. He lived up to his billing as a tough-talking, abrasive, and experienced negotiator with a quick grasp of the issues. Peter Murphy is a haggler. While he bargained over a point in the tariff, Reisman was reaching for a new economic constitution for North America. Murphy played these negotiations like the textile negotiator he was, low-balling every offer and waiting for the last day to trot out his real position. He could not understand a man who placed all his cards on the table from the beginning. Throughout the fifteen months, they sat opposite each other, neither making any real effort to adapt to the style and needs of the other. Increasingly, they were two ships passing in the night.

Where Simon was brutally frank, Peter was elliptical. When Simon bullied, Peter dissembled. When Peter explained, Simon misunderstood. When Simon shouted, Peter withdrew deeper into his shell. When Peter wanted to defer an issue to a working group, Simon insisted he wanted the issue resolved then and there. When Simon demanded that a working group be established to examine an issue, Peter insisted it would be best pursued at the heads-of-delegation level. Said one Washington wit: 'These negotiations are a set of talks between a man who can't talk and a man who won't listen.'

The two men never built the rapport so essential to a good negotiating relationship. Simon's charming and generous side was lost in bluster and bravado; Peter's shyness was mistaken for an unwillingness to engage. Their chemistry was negative. Rather than working towards a common goal, they saw each other as antagonists. While intellectually convinced that any worthwhile agreement had to be based on a win-win result, emotionally they saw every concession as a loss to be made up elsewhere.

As went the Simon-Peter relationship, so went the relationship between their two teams. Frequently, in major negotiations, the two teams soon make common cause and work towards an agreed goal, the enemy being not the person across the table, but the critics back home. There develops a chemistry peculiar to negotiations. Long-term negotiations build great friendships. The camaraderie of working closely together over a period of almost two years on a common project builds understanding and friendship. Little of that was evident between the Canadian and US teams. Too often, proximity built contempt. Discussions away from the table were superficial and even strained.

But the problems went deeper than the mismatch of negotiators and the small-country/large country phenomenon. Knowing the nature of the US decision-making system, Canada took a conscious decision not to build a US constituency to champion its cause. Canada chose to rely on the administration to carry its message to Congress. Belated efforts towards the end of the negotiations to help American business interests to influence Congress were too little too late. The Canadian initiative was thus at the mercy of an administration neither willing nor able to build and maintain a coalition. Too many in Ottawa remained convinced that the diplomacy and negotiating style of yesterday were still applicable. The full implications of the fragmented Washington decision-making process did not sink in.

Could the Canadian negotiators have taken the Americans more into their confidence and developed for them a vision of the possible by tabling the full text of an agreement much earlier? Some had advocated from the beginning that Canada should capture the American imagination with the text of an agreement that would have taken the discussion from the conceptual to the concrete. This could have been done as early as November 1986 and should have been done no later than May 1987. Concurrent with tabling a complete and far-reaching text at the negotiating table, Canada could then have mounted a full-court press with Congress and US business interests to counteract the natural antipathy in Washington to bold and visionary ideas. Instead, Canada accepted the US strategy of waiting until all the fruit had fallen off the tree and hoping that Congress would consider it enough.

Policy is not made on the basis of concepts, but is a quilt of competing pressures felt by governments. A big deal requires vision and statesmanship. It could be sold by appealing to representatives and senators as statesmen. The US negotiating team chose to appeal to them as the representatives of special interests. They thus sought to resolve individual irritants, to safeguard sensitive special interests, and to appeal to the needs of individual power brokers. This is how laws are passed in Congress. It is not the best way to craft pioneering international trade agreements.

And yet much had been accomplished. There had been two years of detailed preparation followed by a year and a half of intense negotiations. Never before had Canada examined trade policy issues in greater depth. For Canadians, the negotiations had developed a breadth of vision and understanding unmatched in modern trade policy history. But it had also developed a vociferous opposition with a competing and entirely different vision. Obviously all the warts in the government's vision and approach showed as the country faced the bitter end.

Opinion in Canada was divided as to whether the negotiations were over or whether the government had engaged in a tactical manoeuvre. Business and economic columnists lamented the end of the talks and urged a return to the table, with lowered expectations if necessary. Wrote Peter Cook in the *Globe and Mail*:

> So aggressive are the Americans about pursuing their own self-interest on trade, and so frightening are the implications of the latest raft of congressional legislation, including the U.S. Trade Bill, that it is true Canada does not have a strong negotiating position. For that reason, a less-than-perfect deal that still safeguards Canada's interests better should be an easier thing for the Mulroney Government to sell. It would also be a sensible thing for Canadians to accept.[6]

Political pundits opined that an agreement had never been in the cards and perhaps it was a good thing that negotiations had finally come to an end. The Southam stable of Don McGillivray, Marjorie Nichols, and Alan Fotheringham all steeped their comments in acid. Yet there was a tinge of regret. Wrote Bill Johnson: 'We are in a mess, that we know. What we don't know is how we'll get out of it. Free trade with the United States was our major policy for prosperity. Now, it seems, we don't have a policy.'[7] Editorial opinion, with the notable exception of the *Toronto Star*, expressed regret. Even the *Montreal Gazette*, which opposed the negotiations, felt that the denouement was regrettable.

Could the initiative still be rescued? As events unfolded, apparently it could. Pundits and officials alike had discounted too early what the Americans can do when they finally turn their energy to an issue and what new leadership can do when all the chips seem to be down. The Canadian side could count on a prime minister determined to conclude a good agreement and not prepared to be bested by a negotiating process that had deteriorated into gamesmanship. If it could be carried off, he had in Derek Burney a chief of staff who had the tenacity, skill, and knowledge to succeed. On the US side, there was determination not to fail. While not a constructive and imaginative motivator, it could in the end prove a powerful stimulus to positive action.

15

A NEAR RUN THING

> It has been a damned nice thing –
> the nearest run thing you ever saw in your life.
> – Sir Arthur Wellesley, Duke of Wellington

As the talks were suspended the third week of September, those betting in favour of success found the odds lengthening and the takers few. By the end of the week, the consensus among ministers and officials in Ottawa was that an agreement was not possible. The two sides were too far apart and the price for agreement was too steep. The Americans were not willing or able to meet Canada's bottom line. The job at hand was not to rescue the initiative, but to give it a decent burial.

That was not the view in Washington. As long as administration officials believed that Canadians were desperate for an agreement, they had given the negotiations short shrift, intent on ensuring that if these Canadians were going to get an agreement, they had better pay for it and not expect too much. Similarly, those members of Congress actually aware of the negotiations appeared to be lukewarm about an agreement. It was a good idea with clear benefits, but Canada was the demandeur so let Canada stand and deliver. But failure was another matter. It would mean that the prestige of the presidency had been squandered on a failure. While success might be of only marginal benefit, failure could have unfortunate consequences. While there had not been enough political will to conclude an agreement on its merits, these new considerations were a sufficient incentive to stave off failure.[1]

The initial American response to the suspension, however, was anger. Those crazy Canadians appeared not to know what they were doing. It was a tactic. They would be back. But by the end of the week, a different perspective began quietly to surface. The Canadians might be prepared to live without an agreement. They might indeed be serious. The negotiations might fail when the administration's political agenda needed a success. This had been clearly signalled earlier in the year when former Treasury Deputy Richard Darman had indicated that the Canada-US agreement was one of two remaining foreign policy priorities for the Reagan administration (the other being an arms treaty with the Soviets). Given the dearth of successes on other fronts, the administration needed a successful conclusion to the negotiations.

Failure could also complicate US objectives in the Uruguay Round of GATT multilateral trade negotiations. It would be difficult to maintain a leadership role, arguing for extensive new obligations in services, intellectual property, agriculture, and trade-related investment matters when it was impossible to reach agreement with Canada on the same agenda. If agreement with its closest ally and major trading partner was not possible, what hope was there for significant breakthroughs with the other members of GATT? In Congress, both senators and representatives began to express disappointment and to signal what they might be prepared to live with. A successful trade agreement might not have been part of Congress's political agenda, but many in Congress did not relish the idea of failure.

Absent for most of the negotiations, except at times of crisis, the American media joined in calling on the administration to show some flexibility and imagination and on the Congress to rise above the parochial. Opined the Los Angeles *Times*: 'Failure of the talks would be a loss for both the United States and Canada. As the world's largest trading partners, they have demonstrated the validity of cooperative agreements that already leave a majority of their trade unrestricted. Furthermore, the failure would have a chilling effect on the new round of world trade talks so vital to economic growth in the United States.'[2]

Jockeying for Position
In this new – essentially political – situation, the principal American broker became not Peter Murphy but Treasury Secretary James Baker. A tall, nononsense Texan, Baker was President Reagan's Mr. Fix-It. He had a reputation for energy and drive and for never touching a loser. As chair of the economic policy council of cabinet, he knew the issues. Appearing on the NBC *Today* show on 24 September, he suggested cautiously, 'I'm sure that there will be additional efforts to bring about a meeting of minds and I think these efforts will be at the highest levels of both governments.'

Mulroney's point man was Derek Burney, his energetic and determined chief of staff, who could count on the wisdom and sense of purpose of Finance Minister Michael Wilson and the political skills of Trade Minister Pat Carney in any effort to either rescue or bury the initiative. There was a certain irony in this situation. Two years earlier, when the government had decided to proceed with the initiative, it had been on the basis of Burney's advice and work prepared under his direction as assistant deputy minister for United States Affairs. Many had considered him the leading candidate for the job of chief negotiator. Instead, he had been appointed associate under-secretary in the Department of External Affairs. A year later, Mulroney had turned to him to reorganize his office and place it on a more professional footing in the intensely political job of chief of staff. He now turned to him to rescue the government's most important initiative.

Both as associate undersecretary and as chief of staff, Burney had contin-ued to play a major and influential role in the conduct of the negotiations. Tough, tenacious, but fair, he knew his brief and stood ready to take over. The prime minister wanted an agreement, but not at any price. If there was a deal available, Burney should get it. But if there was not a deal, the prime minister wanted him to bring the talks to an honourable end. Neither Canada nor the United States could afford to finish them on a note of acri-mony. The prime minister had thus given him a double-barrelled assign-ment: if there is a deal, get it; if there is not one, limit the damage.[3]

In view of External's responsibility for trade and foreign policy and Pat Carney's key role as trade minister, Burney turned to two of its senior offi-cials for help: Gerry Shannon, the experienced deputy for international trade, former senior ADM at Finance, and an expert on US affairs gained in eight years of assignments in Washington; and Don Campbell, Burney's suc-cessor as ADM for United States Affairs. Throughout the negotiations, Shannon and Campbell had provided Carney with independent advice. Like Carney, they had devoted most of their energy in 1986 and the beginning of 1987 to the swamp of softwood lumber. With that issue behind them, they had concentrated on the trade negotiations and had become part of the inner group of experienced advisors not only to Carney, but also to the prime minister and his other key ministers. They were now called on to help Burney bring the negotiations to either a successful or an honourable con-clusion. Their insight into Canada-US relations in general and their knowl-edge of the American political scene would be particularly important.

Alan King, *Ottawa Citizen*, 9 December 1987

Liaison with the TNO came largely through Gordon Ritchie. With Reisman's failure to bring the negotiations to a successful conclusion, his famous temper became harder to take. Ritchie now stepped into the vacuum. Reisman, meanwhile, showed up on CBC's *The Journal* and CTV's *Question Period*, bitter and disappointed. He was of the view that it would take a miracle to reach an agreement. The negotiations, he declared, were over. As he talked, he burned his bridges to the Americans, making the task of restarting the negotiations that much more difficult. He told Pamela Wallin, for example, 'They haven't really focused at the proper level until the last twenty-four, thirty-six hours and it's probably too late. There was nobody really in charge in the United States' and 'They kept leading us on on a few things.'[4]

It was clear that any initiative to restart negotiations would have to come from the Americans. And it did. As early as 24 September, White House chief of staff Howard Baker had telephoned Burney to say that the president would call the prime minister at noon. Burney called back and said that unless the president had serious proposals to make, there was no point in a call. There was no call. In the meantime, Congressman Sam Gibbons had called Ambassador Gotlieb. He was a tough, seasoned legislator from Florida, and the chair of the trade subcommittee of the House Ways and Means Committee. He had called to suggest a way to break the log-jam: this was a plan whereby both countries would keep their current trade remedy laws but submit the application of those laws to binding dispute settlement. Variously dubbed the Gibbons, Gotlieb, and Gibbons-Gotlieb proposal, it eventually took on great significance although it did not initially prove an acceptable basis for a return to negotiations. At USTR, Clayton Yeutter and his deputy, Mike Smith, were furiously reviewing the US position with Peter Murphy, looking for new proposals that could form a basis for reopening the talks. Rumour had it that Smith would take over the negotiations, thus suggesting that Burney and Smith, the two officials who had worked well together two years earlier to prepare for the negotiations, would now be called on to conclude them.

By Friday, Yeutter and Smith were confident that a basis could be found for returning to the table and suggested that Jim Baker call Burney. But there seemed little hope. Baker rejected the Gibbons approach, considering that it had no future in Congress, but instead offered special treatment for Canada reminiscent of the safe harbours and bright lines already rejected. The important thing in his view was to get back to negotiations so that the United States could explain what it had to offer and clear away the underbrush in a normal negotiating setting. The significance of the Canadian decision to suspend, and the width of the gap, had not yet sunk in in Washington.

Gotlieb too was pressing for a return to the table. He continued to insist that every avenue be explored before failure was admitted. He worried about the repercussions on the Canada-United States relationship of a failed negotiation. Ottawa would have to decide what was acceptable, but he now urged Burney to come down to see Baker and determine what was politically feasible. Burney was dubious, but the idea was not rejected. Canada would not be accused of refusing to walk the extra mile. No reasonable American proposal would be rejected. But neither would Canada return to the table for anything less than a major breakthrough. Now that the initiative was stalled, the more politically difficult aspects of any potential agreement stood out in sharp relief and any appetite for a big deal was rapidly waning. While the prime minister preferred a successful conclusion to the negotiation, he was prepared to give Burney the tactical room to decide how to play overtures from Washington. The prime minister instructed Burney to resist until the prospects of doing serious business became more promising.

That same day, in a speech in Vancouver, Trade Minister Pat Carney warned that if the trade talks collapsed and the US passed punitive trade legislation, Washington could expect a similar response from Canada. She said that talks would resume if the US side responded to Canada's key demands. She warned that the United States could expect its trading partners to 'enact mirror legislation to protect their own interests. Congress should remember that it plays a leadership role in the world economy and that what it does may well be copied elsewhere.'[5] The gloves were off. If Washington wanted a deal, they had better be prepared to compromise and show a little more imagination. Meanwhile, Finance Minister Wilson left for Washington to attend the annual IMF and World Bank talks and, if possible, to buttonhole Baker.

Saturday afternoon, 26 September, a two-page US proposal to restart talks arrived in Ottawa. It built on the concept of a subsidies code based on safe harbours and dispute settlement procedures. It also reiterated longstanding US demands on investment and on a list of specific irritants. Preliminary analysis by ministers and senior officials suggested there had been very little movement. Nevertheless, there had to be a response. The mood was to resist US overtures and reach a clear and final disengagement, but no US proposal could be summarily rejected. The response was, therefore, a cautious 'no' – there had to be more. The US had to address other Canadian concerns, particularly regional development and culture.[6]

That was the view in Ottawa, a view not shared by the embassy in Washington. Continuing to press for a more constructive attitude, Ambassador Allan Gotlieb was working feverishly to build bridges. From his perspective, the US paper was constructive in that it finally showed the US political side involved; it was the Canadian response that was unpromising. Finance Minister Michael Wilson agreed and recommended that Burney soften the tone of the letter. Gotlieb and Wilson then met with Baker for thirty minutes and agreed that the two political teams should meet on Monday to explore the prospects for restarting negotiations.

Thus on Monday afternoon, 28 September, Burney, accompanied by Wilson and Carney, met with Baker and Yeutter for almost eight hours, first in the secretary's office and then in his small conference room in a slightly larger group with the addition of Baker's deputy, Peter McPherson, Ambassador Gotlieb, and Don Campbell. The Treasury Building, unlike the ratty quarters at USTR, retains its old grandeur. High ceilings, marbled floors, and a sweeping staircase lead up to the secretary's third-floor suite. The period furniture fits the setting and provides a non-institutional flavour – more like the offices of a successful Washington lawyer than those of a politician. If nothing more, the backdrop for the negotiations had at least reached a higher tone.

At first, steady progress was made; both sides wanted to do business and the discussion was direct, agreeable, and productive; both sides were looking to see if a basis could be found for returning to the negotiating table. After three hours, they started to draft a guidance paper and the oral progress began to lose meaning in the written translation. A secretary called in to take notes asked to be excused after a while; she did not return; she had found the dictation to be too confusing and someone else had to be found. Still, they persevered and emerged to tell the press that there had been progress. Pat Carney indicated that there had been 'sufficient movement on the American side to justify further consultation at the political level.' At the White House, presidential press secretary Marlin Fitzwater was equally hopeful, noting that President Reagan was 'very anxious that these negotiations continue and that we be able to conduct and hopefully reach a conclusion.'[8]

The debriefing at the Canadian embassy revealed a less optimistic consensus. To the question of whether negotiations should be resumed came the response that prospects were marginal. The outcome on subsidies and dispute settlement was seen as too vague to offer real progress while the long-standing US target list of beer, wine, autos, postal rates, cable retransmission, and pharmaceuticals continued to represent political dynamite unless Canada's fundamental requirements were met. Gotlieb contended that the point was not whether Canada would succeed, but rather how the next few days were played. In his view, it was essential to persevere. There was only a faint hope but the Canadian team did not want the Americans to say that they were ready to continue but Canada had broken off without determining the final US offer. No one disagreed. The game had to be played to the end. But the Ottawa group also had a clear perception of the bottom line. The agreement had to represent a substantial improvement on the status quo and be clear of political minefields. Otherwise, the prime minister had told them, he would be prepared to talk to the president and bring the negotiations to a dignified if unsuccessful conclusion. Over the previous few weeks, the PM had made it clear that this was his agenda and either this view would prevail or there would be no agreement.

The following day another document was prepared clarifying the Canadian position on rules that would have to apply in any subsidies code and dispute settlement provisions. The sour mood in Ottawa persisted. Enthusiasm for any return to the table was minimal. Most ministers were ready to clear the decks of this issue and move on to something more positive. As media attention had focused more and more on dispute settlement and discipline on subsidies, the negotiations had become an albatross around their necks rather than a bright hope for the future. The negotiations did not appear to be doing the government any good as support for the initiative continued to slide and support for the government remained in the doldrums. They agreed with Hugh Winsor, writing in the *Globe and Mail*, that 'a quiet but honorable death of the free-trade negotiations may not be all bad.'[9] Appearing on CBC's *The Journal*, Joe Clark noted that 'we're not very optimistic about this leading to anything but it might,' while the prime minister told the House of Commons that 'the bottom line remained the same. This deal shall be in the national interest of Canada or there shall be no deal at all.'

On Parliament Hill, Cabinet appeared to be in permanent session.[10] Once again, with the prime minister in the chair, the trade executive committee reviewed the options. At the same time, Washington and Ottawa were linked by a constant stream of phone calls between cabinet officers and senior officials. Any Canadian response to the latest US proposal had to tread a delicate line. It was not acceptable and the response had to make this clear. In its place, ministers had to devise a reasonable Canadian alternative in the knowledge that it might not prove acceptable. If not, so be it. By the end of Tuesday, ministers had developed the policy position. It took until well into the evening to translate it into a detailed negotiating proposal. An exhausted Burney approved it in his tiny Parliament Hill office next to that of the prime minister and then discussed it over the phone with Baker, who was attending one of Washington's interminable dinners. It took some effort. By this time, after hours of arguing with ministers and officials, Burney's voice was beginning to wear out. Canadian enthusiasm for American demands was wearing equally thin. Despite their desire to restart negotiations and avoid failure, the Americans were not showing much in the way of compromise or imagination. They seemed incapable of understanding why Canada had sought these negotiations in the first place and why it was insisting that it had to have something substantive on trade remedy law and dispute settlement. The new Canadian proposal might not fly, but at least Canada had tried. The prime minister told reporters in Quebec the next day that if the United States 'persist in their refusal, it looks bad. But I think that we had to try, because it is in the interests of Canada and Quebec.'[11]

The last day of September was a quiet day, like the calm before the storm. The next few days would tell the tale. USTR Clayton Yeutter called for the resumption of face-to-face talks, saying that they could no longer negotiate by telephone. Some members of the US Senate Finance Committee, meanwhile, dampened his enthusiasm by warning against any deal that would affect congressional ability to make trade law while others pointed in the other direction, suggesting that an extension of the fast-track timetable should not be excluded.[12] Phone calls continued to be fast and furious between cabinet officers and their advisors in both capitals as both sides reviewed their options and examined and re-examined their bottom lines. After weighing the pros and cons, the prime minister decided to send a team once again to Washington.

The Americans were confident that with only a few days left to go, the Canadians would come to their senses and be prepared to finish the negotiations. Senior US politicians continued to be oblivious to the seriousness of Canada's intentions in breaking off negotiations.

Alan King, *Ottawa Citizen*, 7 October 1987

The view in Ottawa, however, was sombre. Burney had concluded that the negotiations were finished. He had rated chances early in the week as marginal. He now rated them as nil. The task was to ensure that the Americans knew this and would accept failure and part friends. He had to be satisfied that he had put the Canadian position squarely and convincingly before the Americans. There should be no room left for recriminations to sour the relationship. He worked and reworked his notes and early the next morning he and Campbell laboured over them again. He was convinced that the Americans had never understood what Canada wanted and what had driven Canada to the negotiating table in the first place. He was not sure that the American politicians understood what it was like for a small country, dependent on trade with a big country, to see that big country turn protectionist and indifferent. It would be up to him to make them understand so that there would be no doubt about the Canadian position. He would have to convince the most powerful cabinet official of the most powerful nation on earth that doing it the US way, irritant by irritant, had been a recipe for failure. He had to ensure that Baker and Yeutter understood why Canada did not want the kind of deal the United States appeared prepared to offer.

In the Billy Bishop lounge on the military side of Uplands airport, the prime minister, on his way to Toronto to give a speech, conferred again with his ministers and chief of staff. He endorsed the approach. If there could not be an agreement that was clearly in Canada's interests, there would be no agreement. He would use the meeting to be held the next day with the premiers to begin the process of changing the government's agenda.

The team arrived at the Treasury at 1:30 in the afternoon. Too late for lunch, they proceeded directly to the meeting from Andrews Airforce Base. In the same classic setting as three days earlier, Burney, Wilson, and Carney met with Baker and Yeutter for three hours. They found a dejected US team. It had been prepared for a full-scale negotiating session, with all the senior members of the US team standing ready, and it was a surprise to see only Burney and the two ministers. The message had not yet penetrated.

Burney put on the performance of his life. The light dawned. The talks had failed. There was no basis for an agreement. All the work of the past three years had been for nought. Baker and Yeutter retired to Baker's office to reconsider their position. They had no bright new ideas. When they returned, they had no more to offer than a face-saving salvage proposal. The Americans had been putting together a package which was now proposed to the ministers. It was not a worthwhile package. Without the inclusion of measures to address trade remedy law, there was no basis for an agreement. Burney, Wilson, and Carney agreed they would confirm their negative response later after conferring with their colleagues and with the prime minister in Ottawa, but they did not hold out much hope.[13] It was all but over and so the Canadian media reported. The ministerial delegation went home and set up shop in the Langevin Block to confirm the decision and prepare for the negative announcement.

Meanwhile, Secretary Baker met with members of the Senate Finance Committee to apprise them of the latest developments and to indicate to them what it would take to get an agreement. He and Burney may not have parted in hope, but Baker now knew Canada's bottom line and related that to the senators. Baker came away disappointed and pessimistic. There was no basis for a deal. Whatever he offered would be rejected either by Canada or by the Senate. Most of the senators had been silent during the meeting, letting Jack Danforth, the Savonarola of the committee, denounce the Canadian bottom line as unacceptable. Only Senator Bradley of New Jersey spoke in favour. The negotiations were over and arrangements had better be put in place for the president and prime minister to bring this farce to a conclusion.

This was not the interpretation of the meeting perceived by Senator Bradley. Former basketball star, Rhodes scholar, committed free trader, member of a blue-ribbon international panel that two years earlier had prepared recommendations for a new round of GATT negotiations, he was disappointed at the impending failure but not convinced that all was lost. Hearing that Baker had concluded that the negotiations were over, he roused his colleagues to action and within the space of a few hours, USTR Yeutter received a series of phone calls urging him to have a close look at the possible. Rather than agreeing with Danforth, Bradley's silent colleagues had agreed with him and thought this had been clear to Baker.[14] Bradley also found a receptive Gotlieb, who urged him to press on. On the phone to Ottawa, Gotlieb urged a change of heart and a willingness to consider once again the Gibbons proposal. In Gotlieb's view, Ottawa was determined on failure and needed to be drawn out for a fresh try.

While not convinced, Canada would give it one last effort. Briefing notes of a week earlier describing what various specialists thought was meant by the Gibbons's proposal were quickly dusted off. It appeared to involve enshrining US trade law in the agreement, but making its application to Canada subject to bilateral dispute settlement. This was the last chance for a resolution of the key issue. Late in the evening, Baker, buoyed by the unexpected support from Congress, called Burney and confirmed that they were now prepared to work on the Gibbons approach. Ministers agreed that on that basis, a final attempt could be made. Burney and Wilson rushed to brief the prime minister. He too agreed. The bottom line, however, remained the same: the agreement had to mark a substantial improvement over the status quo and not compromise fundamental Canadian requirements on such delicate issues as culture.

At a midnight meeting at the TNO, preparations were hastily set in motion for an early departure. The whole team would go. If there was a chance, Canada would be equipped for all contingencies. With Burney and the ministers now in charge, the whole negotiating apparatus was to be at their disposal.

Working Out a Deal
In the dark, still tired after at best four hours sleep, the negotiators gathered at Uplands to take Piedmont to Washington at 6:15 AM. The political team, this time accompanied by Reisman and Ritchie, would take a government Challenger later in the morning. Meanwhile, the negotiators were to proceed to USTR, set up their equipment, and await instructions.

A testy and tired political team arrived by mid-morning. In the plane, they had worked out a modus operandi. Burney, the two ministers, and their senior advisors, including Finance Deputy Stanley Hartt, Don Campbell from External, and Ambassador Gotlieb, would proceed to Treasury and engage the US political team.

At 10:30 the ministerial group disappeared into the Treasury building. The drama would be played out in the secretary's main conference room where the political teams would meet in a plenary session, in Baker's office where he and Burney would meet frequently one on one, and in meeting rooms and offices in Treasury and USTR where the details would be hammered out in a setting that suited the drama of the moment. The secretary's main conference room is a large and beautiful room decorated with framed miniatures of long-dead American worthies and old currency, and furnished with an imposing table and comfortable chairs. The secretary's own office, as well as the small conference room to which the Canadian team repaired for caucuses and telephone conversations with the prime minister, are equally sumptuous. Hollywood could not have constructed a better set.

The working groups were instructed not to meet until the political teams had worked out what role the negotiators would play. Meanwhile, efforts were set in train to translate the Gibbons idea into a detailed negotiating proposal for review at a later stage. By early afternoon, new instructions came. Given the late hour, the two political teams would work out the elements of what the agreement would contain. In effect, they would prepare a memorandum of instructions for the two legal teams to translate into the actual text over the ensuing two or three weeks. To that end, the working groups were to meet and produce an agreed document of no more than a page each indicating areas of agreement and disagreement.[15]

The 'command centre' for the Canadian side was the reception area of Baker's suite. All day, the meetings continued. To keep the numbers in the main room down to manageable proportions, a core of Burney, Wilson, and Carney were supplemented as required by Reisman, Ritchie, Hartt, Gotlieb, or Campbell and the head of the particular working group whose issue was under discussion. Burney's role was to forge a consensus out of this remarkable group. As the time for hard decisions came, the Canadians disappeared into their caucus room to consider their position and consult the prime minister in Ottawa. The debate was lively; differences were sharp, as befit the difficulty of the issues and the varying experiences and perspectives each brought to the table. All made their contributions and, before any decision was communicated to the Americans, all agreed. Burney was not prepared to negotiate unless his team was clearly on board. Allan Gotlieb, a key member of the team, remarked: 'In the end, he [Burney] was the spokesman for the political team. There was a massive agenda and many unresolved issues and his demonstrated qualities of forcefulness, directness and organization were all paramount. It was a very, very fine performance – his finest hour.'[16]

On the US side, Baker relied on Peter McPherson and Clayton Yeutter and, as required, Murphy or Merkin and other senior members of the US team, as well as USTR General Counsel Alan Holmer. Baker's office served as the US caucus room. In the main negotiating room, the atmosphere was extremely businesslike. The tones hushed. Neither the room nor the substance lent themselves to informality or frivolity. The negotiations were under the gun. It was now or never.

Throughout the afternoon, a growing number of working group heads were summoned to the room and then told to wait further instructions. As they waited, they took turns pacing the long stately halls of the Treasury building, alternating between admiring glances at the walls festooned with large portraits of all the secretaries of the treasury since independence, and speculations on whether a deal was still doable. One office was marked with a plaque indicating that it had housed Union cavalry during the Civil War. Up and down they marched between long periods of sitting, awaiting developments, and exchanging gossip. News of agreement and disagreement filtered out of the room as the package began to be put together. Progress was being made.

Meanwhile, over at USTR, the working groups laboured away, first considering areas of agreement and disagreement and, following a summons and fresh instructions, the actual elements of agreement. The difficult issues, which the political teams had deferred until later, were, as expected, subsidies and dispute settlement. After an initial sparring session, it was clear that the two sides were miles apart even in agreeing on what constituted the Gibbons proposal. Outside counsel was brought in to give on-the-spot advice. Throughout the afternoon and evening, drafts were prepared which explored what the Gibbons proposal meant. Its author not being a party to the negotiations and not available for explanation, it was in many ways a moot question. The issue was on what basis the agreement would cover countervailing and anti-dumping procedures. Key factors were whether any deal would freeze the countervailing and anti-dumping statutes as they stood and what would be the basis for settling disputes. The question of disciplining subsidies had disappeared. The focus was no longer on the offensive practice but on rules governing application of the countermeasure.

As midnight neared, everyone agreed that it had been a long day at the end of a trying ten days, and that little would be gained by testing physical stamina much further. A good night's sleep might dispel some of the gloom. By midnight, the Treasury building was dark and closed. Word took longer to reach those still working away at USTR. The troops there did not disperse until the wee hours of the morning. They would not be getting their money's worth at the Madison and Georgetown that night.

Saturday was a rainy and gloomy day, especially for the media mob which staked out the Treasury and waited for scraps of news. On Friday, Mike Duffy had bought a rather theatrical floppy hat to keep the sun from burning his exposed pate. By Saturday, he needed a large umbrella and a warm parka. On Friday, those summoned to the scene took the pleasant walk along either Pennsylvania or the Ellipse to get from USTR to Treasury. By Saturday, the embassy organized a fleet of cars to drive team members the short two blocks.

As usual, USTR again overlooked the necessities of life. On Saturdays, downtown Washington is like a morgue and finding a simple sandwich is a major challenge. Short on sleep, without even coffee to sustain them, the intrepid negotiators needed food. Finally, around two in the afternoon, one of the many helpful people from the embassy, property manager Glen Bullard, took matters in hand, went out in his car to a more civilized part of the city and picked up $450 worth of sandwiches and cold drinks for the Canadian troops paying for it all with his credit card. Luckily, Canadian team members grabbed them quickly. A USTR staffer, spying the rich array, bundled up what had not been consumed and took it over to Treasury to feed the mob over there. Even the ministerial group had been left out of the planning. No one had budgetary authority to feed them. Later in the evening, Karen Kolodny, one of the young TNO lawyers, looked after the evening's requirements by ordering enough Popeye's fried chicken for everyone. Again, the embassy paid.

All day, the focus of discussion was dispute settlement and trade remedies and things were not going well. At USTR, the working group persevered under the pressure of constantly changing deadlines. Early in the afternoon, they were told that Baker was scheduled to meet the president at Camp David at four to report progress and wanted to thrash out the remaining issues at the political level before he left. The Canadian group of experts stuck to their guns. It was no use proceeding with a paper for the ministers that no one could understand. What the experts could agree on and what they could not needed to be clear. It required the advice of outside counsel. The afternoon dragged on. The presidential appointment disappeared. Finally, late in the afternoon, the Canadian experts were satisfied that they had developed a basis for discussion.

Their caution had been well advised. The US experts had by then prepared their own version of the Gibbons proposal and could not concur with the Canadian version. The issues were arcane, not easily understood, and subject to a myriad of interpretations. The challenge was now taken up by Burney and Baker. While the two sides were far apart, discussion among the experts had at least clarified what were the real issues within the general framework provided by the Gibbons proposal: would the agreement freeze US and Canadian law, either as of October 1987 or January 1988 – the distinction being important given the threat of the Omnibus Trade Bill? Could the administration agree to revoke existing judicial review and vest it in a binational tribunal? What standards would the binational panel apply? On what basis should trade remedy issues continue to be negotiated?

Discussion by the two political teams, first separately and then together, did not clarify matters. The central issue of dispute settlement applying to trade remedy law did not appear resolvable. Without it, there could be no agreement. The tension was palpable. The pressure that had propelled the two teams forward began to mount. Burney told Baker that if the US could not respond, they had reached the final impasse. Baker was equally adamant and told Burney not to push; Congress would not buy Canada's insistence that it have a voice in the application of US law. Burney's counter: 'The U.S. administration is going to have to take a risk for Canada with Congress.' Canada could live with a rejection by Congress; what was not tolerable was an administration that would not fight for a good agreement. Either Baker came through, or there would be no deal.[17]

Meanwhile, good progress had been made in the less contentious areas of the negotiations. Most of the working group heads had been summoned and were now preparing the one-page statements summarizing the elements of agreement. Some had already made a second appearance. Ministers had reviewed their work and issued final instructions. Group heads were now revising their statements and preparing to sign off. The elements of agreement, largely based on the hard work of the previous months, reflected in each case a pragmatic political judgment on what was doable and what was not. Baker and his crew changed the balance on the US side by indicating a clear desire to conclude a well-rounded package. He had a sure political feel for what he could sell to Congress – he would deal with senators and representatives, not their aides. Burney and the two ministers, for their part, were prepared to close. They might not know the fine details of each issue, but they had a solid grasp of what to insist on and what to give up. They had confidence in their mandate which was hammered out over the previous two weeks in drawn-out sessions chaired either by the prime minister or by Deputy PM Don Mazankowski. In addition, issues of detail had been discussed even further with individual ministers. If the main issues could be resolved, the Canadian side had the mandate to close a good deal.

Throughout the late afternoon and evening, those standing around stole glances at another drama unfolding on a flickering black and white television in Baker's reception area. The Toronto Blue Jays, who had entered the final week of the season with a commanding lead, choked and handed the American League East pennant to the Detroit Tigers. Members of both teams hoped the negotiations, in which so much had been invested, would not suffer the same ignominious fate.

By early evening, the discussions had reached a strange fork in the road. While one team of officials prepared texts for initialling later that evening, Burney called the prime minister to tell him the negotiations were virtually completed, with only the final page left to be turned. A satisfactory compromise on trade remedies and dispute settlement, however, continued to elude the two sides. The prime minister agreed with Burney's assessment: without a good result on trade remedy law, it did not look promising and would not be politically credible in Canada. Throughout the day, they had consulted frequently. While not physically present, the prime minister was clearly in the driver's seat. Burney returned to tell Baker that the prime minister wanted to call the president and Baker disappeared into his office with his team to try again. He returned to say that the president was at Camp David and that it might be better to delay the call for a little while yet. He suggested the call be made after ten. Baker was playing for time. The call was never made.

At the other end of Baker's suite, teams of officials had gathered to begin the process of initialling at the level of the heads of working groups the one-page summaries containing the elements of agreement. Each set of initials brought a round of applause. Two floors below, huddled in his parka, Mike

Duffy took the applause to be cheers for a final agreement and concluded that he had enough to report in. On his radiophone he told Peter Mansbridge, reading *The National*, that it appeared that the two sides had reached agreement. He was a little premature. There was no agreement. No more than some elements of the agreement had been concluded. Indeed, one of the initialled pages would later prove embarrassing.[18]

Time marched on. The deadline was midnight and had been revised to 3 October rather than 4 October. The president never sent letters to Congress on a Sunday. By midnight on Saturday the president would have to sign letters to the chairs of the Senate Finance Committee and the House Ways and Means Committee indicating his intention to enter into an agreement with Canada. Negotiations were no longer continuing in the main conference room. The Americans were in Baker's office; the Canadians, in his anteroom. The mood was dark. There was talk that midnight meant anywhere in the United States. Midnight would not arrive in Hawaii until six hours after Washington time. A long night stared the two teams in the face, without even the Blue Jays to provide entertainment and diversion.

Finally, shortly after 10:00 PM, Washington time, Baker emerged and walked across with a new proposal. If Canada agreed, the president would send his message to Congress and the deadline could be met. He caught Burney on the phone to the prime minister. Mulroney had come into Ottawa from his summer residence on Harrington Lake, resigned to the fact that he would probably have to make a negative announcement. Burney was now explaining that there appeared to be some movement, but he was not sure if it would be enough.

Baker had used the intervening two hours to forge a consensus on the US side. As throughout the negotiations, representatives from the various agencies around Washington had their own view of matters and Jean Anderson, the senior representative from Commerce responsible for trade law, was concerned that the Gibbons proposal might raise more problems than it solved – some senior Justice officials, for example, were of the view that it was unconstitutional. She shared the secretary's desire for a positive outcome, but she saw problems and technical obstacles that needed to be resolved. To complicate her task, she could not call on her secretary for advice; Mac Baldrige, killed in a tragic rodeo accident the previous summer, had not yet been replaced. But Baker had persevered and in the end the US side had put together a proposal that he felt the Canadians could accept and that met various US concerns. The proposal contained three key elements:

• Canadian and US trade law would continue to apply and both sides would be free to change their laws, but they would have to specify that the changed law applied to the other and any such changes would be subject to bilateral review for consistency with the agreement and with the GATT – the issue of whether or not the law was frozen, either immediately or as of 1 January 1988, was thus neatly sidestepped.

• Existing judicial review as to whether the law had been applied fairly and properly would be replaced with review by a binational panel on the basis of whatever standard would have prevailed in the domestic tribunal.

• Negotiations would continue for five years (with the possibility of a two-year extension) to negotiate a wholly new regime to replace the existing one.

Burney reviewed the offer and concluded that he could now see the basis for a deal. His colleagues unanimously agreed and so advised the prime minister. He agreed that on the basis of this proposal, Canada should be prepared to give a conditional green light for the Americans to proceed with their notification. Baker and Burney shook hands. The final hurdle appeared to have been passed.[19]

The moment was critical to the United States side. Canada was not operating under a deadline. It was the US side that had to determine whether it was close enough to proceed with the notification to Congress. Baker and his advisors believed they were. Burney and his team did not demur. On that basis, Baker phoned the president at Camp David and issued instructions to the White House to dispatch two very short and simple letters to the chairs of the two congressional committees. Minutes before midnight, 3 October, dispatch of the letters was registered in the White House log, thus meeting the formal timetable. Up until the end, Canadian officials thought that the president had physically to sign the document. There was even a rumour that Baker and Yeutter would have to leave by helicopter to fly to Camp David by 9:00 PM to ensure that the signature was obtained. It turned out that three different versions of the letters had already been prepared and signed. The issue was which ones to register and send.[20]

For Canada, a critical test had been met. Canada's goal of a new regime on trade remedies that would ultimately obviate the need for countervailing and anti-dumping duties had proven unattainable. It would remain the goal of continued negotiations for the next five years. But with the temporary regime regulating the application of existing remedies, the United States could not continually change the rules unilaterally, either through legislation or application. The deal offered by Baker met this test by giving Canada a voice both in determining whether legislative changes were consistent with the intent and purpose of the agreement, and by giving Canadians a voice in determining whether the law was being properly applied. In short, the United States had recognized that within a free-trade area, its penchant for unilateralism had to give way to bilateral review. It was this recognition that buoyed the confidence of Burney and his advisors and of the prime minister that a deal consistent with Canada's basic requirements could now be concluded; it was on that basis that they agreed that the Americans should proceed with their notification.

But all was not done. A considerable risk had been taken. The notice spoke of an ad referendum agreement on the elements, but in fact there was much that remained to be settled and the next day would prove a further test of everyone's stamina. Shortly after midnight, the Canadian team was told to gather in the hallway to await an an-

An exhausted political team is all smiles in the wee hours of Sunday morning at the Treasury in Washington, DC. Left to right: Allan Gotlieb, Stanley Hartt, Don Campbell, Derek Burney, Pat Carney, Gordon Ritchie, Michael Wilson, and Simon Reisman. (4 October 1987)

nouncement by Michael Wilson, who soon emerged from the caucus room to indicate that the two political teams had just shaken hands and that the Americans, for their own internal reasons, had decided sufficient progress had been made to release their letters. Much work remained to be done, but in essence the final turning point had been reached. The road home was clear. In effect, Canada was now in the driver's seat. Everyone who had worked so hard on the issue was to be congratulated and should now get a reasonable night's sleep because the next day could again be gruelling.

Wilson was right. There followed another marathon with breakdown threatening on financial services, dispute settlement, pharmaceuticals, culture, and that perennial favourite, softwood lumber. Tension remained high as did the drama; people were emotionally and physically drained, and consequently testy – things were said within and between delegations that might better have been left unsaid. Talks continued until 9:40 in the evening. The tone, however, had changed dramatically. Faces no longer wore hangdog expressions. Steps were more purposeful. After so many months of frustration, a final product was at hand. The form of the agreement consisted of twenty 'element papers' covering all the subjects agreed, arranged in no particular order. Major legal drafting remained to be done and the legal boiler plate at the beginning and the end was not even touched. But the main job was finished.

The focus of activity at USTR had changed from dispute resolution to public relations. The two Macintosh computers and the Laserwriter printer brought along in the Challenger were now pressed into service to write press statements rather than negotiating proposals. While Michael Wilson and Jim Baker worked on financial services, Burney joined other team members on the fourth floor of USTR to set the tone for public statements. The Ottawa team would do the detailed work, but the Washington team would prepare the editorial material. He dictated the essential points Michael Wilson and Pat Carney would make in a press statement later that afternoon. A detailed synopsis of the agreement, in plain language, would also need to be ready by that time.

The US side might be laggard when it came to providing sandwiches, but they wasted no time in preparing press material. At 10:00 Sunday morning, with a number of issues remaining to be settled, they handed Canadian officials their version of a press synopsis for comment. The US synopsis looked as if it had been written a few days earlier and hastily updated.[21] It contained errors and a very strong political spin. Canadian officials decided to prepare a much more neutral, factually correct summary of the agreement and leave the spin for later. Because so much remained to be settled, it was not finished until 6:00 that evening, despite threats from Ottawa that it was going to lose the media battle. To help officials in Ottawa, as much material as possible was faxed as it became available in order to give them time for translation and to prepare other explanatory material, all of it clearly marked draft. From this material the embassy stapled together the elements of an agreement to hand to the media after a Wilson-Baker press conference later that afternoon. Included in this package was a reference to Bill C-22, the controversial pharmaceutical legislation then stalled in the Senate, which, when it had been passed to the ministerial group for clearance, had been deleted. This small faux pas would give endless joy to the media and opposition in the weeks to come.[22]

Meanwhile, Back at the Ranch

While almost the entire trade negotiations team was in Washington for the last effort at a deal, planning the communications for success or failure had to be done in Ottawa. A detailed plan on how the final days would be handled had been worked out in early September, but most of what had been decided had to go by the boards. Instead, the weekend became an exercise in flying by the seat of one's pants.

In Ottawa, the weather was as cold as the motley crew assembled in the prime minister's cosy boardroom on the second floor of the Langevin Block. They took their direction from Gerry Shannon. As there was no indication at this point of which way the talks would go, the only useful exercise the group could do was prepare material to be used in case of failure. There was no point in preparing material in the event of success for that would have to come out of Washington, depending on the final trade-offs. There was an inconclusive debate on how failure would be announced, but it was generally agreed that the prime minister would make a perfunctory statement of regret and leave Pat Carney to carry the ball.

By evening it appeared that the buffet dinner laid out by the uniformed waiters would mark the wake of the trade talks. There was the gallows humour associated with defeat. The bureaucrats shuffled about uneasily and the political staff joked about their own futures. Meanwhile, upstairs in the cabinet room, Lowell Murray, Joe Clark, Don Mazankowski, and Robert de Cotret had assembled to hear the latest news from Washington. The downstairs crew began to drift home with only a few waiting to hear the final words. Then, just after 10:00, came word that, like Lazarus, the trade talks might rise again. The televisions were tuned and shortly thereafter the beaming face of Mike Duffy announced from Washington that a deal had been struck. He was a little premature, but luck was with him; after midnight, with a deal now in the cards, a visibly overjoyed Duffy grabbed the now familiar Peter Murphy for an on-the-spot interview. Murphy confirmed the deal was done and then excused himself saying they still had a lot of work ahead of them. Despite the months of planning, Canadians were informed by an American that there was an agreement. It was well after midnight when Pat Carney appeared and told the media: 'It is an historic agreement, it is balanced and it benefits all Canadians in all regions.'[23] While the networks promised to come back for the prime minister, the delay proved too much for them.

Back at the Langevin Block, the prime minister and his ministers were being briefed by phone on the outline of the deal by Derek Burney, Michael Wilson, and Pat Carney. At about 1:30 AM, the PM and his ministers walked midway down the main flight of stairs and Mulroney told the lingering aides and the assembled press, many of whom had huddled outside in the cold wind for eight hours, that the main elements of a deal had been done. They had made a contribution to history. 'A hundred years from now, what will be remembered was that it was done. And the naysayers will long have been forgotten.'[24] But what were the elements and how could the government be expected to make it public in time for Monday? Most of the communications team had dispersed earlier when it looked like it was all over. The survivors decided to reassemble at nine the next morning and take stock.

The officials held a preliminary meeting in the undersecretary's boardroom at the Pearson building. An exhausted Shannon announced that the PM had decided to release the elements on Monday. Plans for a press lockup had been cancelled on Friday as had plane reservations to be used to deliver the documents to the premiers. The team would just have to improvise. Those who had gone to bed consoling themselves they had fought the good fight, were summoned to action.

At the PMO, all was chaos. Information from Washington was the key to direction; most of the day was spent on telephones trying to find out what was happening and when more documents could be expected. The entire resources of the government printing establishment had been put on standby; now it would have to perform.

The first word came from TNO staffer Colin Robertson. Trying to contact the Canadian team, he was put through to the US Trade Representative's Office. Who should pick up the telephone but Clayton Yeutter himself. Ever the cornpone politician, he told Robertson that 'we all got a good deal ... you Canadians should be proud of yourselves,' and then the call was passed to Peter Murphy's office. Murphy was less ebullient. He did not know where the Canadian team was and as he clearly did not want to prolong the conversation, he passed Robertson on to one of his staff, Tim Skud, who promised to have Roger Bolton, the USTR media director, or one of his staff, get in touch within the half hour.

Bolton indicated that the Americans were aiming to release the elements at 2:00 that afternoon. This put the Canadians in an impossible position. There was no way that Canada could simultaneously release the material in Ottawa at that time; the whole text was still not available! The Canadians pressed for a twenty-four hour delay; but the Americans were adamant. This was the main event of the day. For the first time the trade talks had a chance of being news in the United States. Tomorrow would be too late as the media returned to their deathwatch on the nomination of Robert Bork to the Supreme Court. Besides, Clayton Yeutter had already started to telephone key members of Congress; it would only be a matter of hours before Jennifer Lewington and Mike Duffy got versions from them. Again, it was the American drum setting the pace. But a 2:00 PM press conference was too early. Material would not be ready. Shannon telephoned Burney. He, in turn tracked down Baker, who was lunching at a popular Washington restaurant, and gained a precious two hours.

Finally at 4:00, the two teams took a break and met the press. Baker and Wilson, flanked by Carney, Yeutter, Reisman, and Murphy, each read a statement, introduced the other members of their teams and answered queries.[25] With the press conference, the deal tentatively reached near midnight on Saturday now became fact. Whatever details remained had better be worked out. There could be no turning back.

Reaction to Triumph

The next morning broke bright and sunny. The ministerial return home, however, had been a comedy of errors. Their Challenger jet had developed mechanical trouble soon after takeoff and had had to return to Andrews Air Force Base. Two options were available. Wait for another Challenger or delay return until repairs were completed the next morning. They opted for repairs and started off again three hours later. All showed signs of wear in the House the next morning.

Senior bureaucrats and ministers' staffs had started the day in the old rail-road station, now the Government Conference Centre, with an 8:00 AM briefing by Gerry Shannon and Don Campbell. Just before they broke at 9:00, the final pieces of the information kit arrived from Supply and Services.

It was a minor miracle, as the final translation had not arrived until just before 6:00 that morning. They were soon joined by Simon Reisman and Gordon Ritchie. This was Reisman's hour. He began the briefing with a paean of praise for the prime minister as the architect of the agreement. He was in good form and enjoyed sparring with the media. After answering their questions for another thirty minutes, Reisman excused himself saying he had an appointment with the prime minister. An hour later he joined Burney in the prime minister's gallery in the House of Commons to accept the prime minister's accolades.

The prime minister gives Simon Reisman the thumbs up sign in the gallery of the House of Commons, while Derek Burney smiles enigmatically. (Ottawa, 5 October 1987)

In the afternoon, the opposition leaders spoke in reply to the prime minister's speech with predictable criticisms. Theirs was a hard row to hoe. They had had little time to absorb the enormous achievement of the previous forty-eight hours. In question period, it was Brian Mulroney and Michael Wilson who took most of the questions. In the evening, the government communications blitz continued with the prime minister's speech to the Canadian Export Association. Simon Reisman gave interviews to both Barbara Frum on *The Journal* and Pamela Wallin of CTV.

The papers were circumspect in their opinion of the elements text. The *Globe and Mail* headline over the story by Lewington and Waddell proclaimed that Canada and the United States had signed a continental energy accord. Most papers wondered about the dispute settlement mechanism and whether it would be adequate. All asked for more details. To the chagrin of the Canadian communications contingent, the *Globe and Mail* published excerpts from the American explanatory document which was written for Americans and contained some serious errors. When asked to explain, the *Globe* said it required something for its early print deadline and the Canadian document was unavailable. The *Citizen* printed the Canadian summary version. It was essential that a new and more comprehensive document be prepared. Work began immediately but it was two weeks before it was released.

The overall mood, however, was generous. TNO and Reisman would take the glory. Reisman had had the courage to walk out and the grace to make way for Burney and the final push. Clayton Yeutter created some discomfort by suggesting in an unguarded moment that the deal would have been available six months earlier without Reisman. He apologized the next day but the damage had been done or, as some suggested, Reisman paid back for his comments of the previous two weeks. He told the media that he took the comment as a compliment.

Further reaction was as might have been expected. In the United States, debate developed quickly around the transfer of final decisions on the application of US trade law from US courts to a bilateral panel. In Canada, attention continued to focus on political issues such as Canadian absorption into the United States, cultural sovereignty, and a continental energy deal. The real point was missed – the radical restructuring of the Canadian economy into a world class competitor, the final destruction of the National Policy, and reliance on market forces for future economic development.

What Had Made the Difference

Canada had an agreement. Despite the conviction only a few days earlier that it could not be done, the government had succeeded. US determination not to fail and Canadian adherence to the bottom line had paid dividends. It took a while to sink in. For the previous six weeks, ever since Cornwall, the negotiators had seen their initial enthusiasm and conviction gradually sapped and destroyed. All bets had been off. Yet Canada had in the end succeeded. What had happened?

In the first place, it was clear that the US attitude had changed dramatically. Driven by the desire not to fail, US officials became prepared to make compromises in areas in which previously they had only reluctantly considered Canadian demands. While the focus of hard bargaining over the course of the weekend had been on trade remedies and dispute settlement, many other intransigent issues had been settled. Intellectual property, a key US interest, had been dropped from the agreement when Canada was unprepared to go further than the provisions of Bill C-22 dealing with pharmaceuticals. The US reasoned that no loaf was better than half a loaf. A very small government procurement package, a key Canadian demand, remained. A package had been hammered out on alcoholic beverages by excluding beer. The automotive issue had been settled by agreeing on a new rule of origin. Investment and financial services, key US requirements, had been met with provisions that would open up these aspects of the economy on a reciprocal but cautious basis.

Balancing the US desire not to fail was Canada's determination that it had to have an agreement that made economic sense and would stand the test of time. Asked to give an assessment of the final package at the end of the day on Sunday, the experienced trade policy practitioners milling around Baker's suite concurred that the agreement was strong economically, but might face some tough sledding politically. Canada had compromised on the short-term issues on which the United States needed to be seen to be making progress while insisting that the basic agreement be sound. The tariff would be eliminated over ten years and most other access issues had been resolved to the mutual benefit of both countries. The security of access issue, so important politically, had been only partly resolved, but a good basis had been laid for making things better. Canadian sovereignty had been protected by the establishment of a good general dispute settlement mechanism which placed Canada and the United States on an equal footing in administering and interpreting jointly agreed rules. A start had been made on services trade, access by Canadian business people to the US market had been eased, and balanced commitments had been concluded on investment.

More importantly, over the course of the final two weeks, both sides had been led by individuals who could decide and close a deal. They had been prepared both to listen and to explain, and both were operating on the basis of a shared political commitment.[26] They had substituted political will for gamesmanship. Rather than strangers passing in the night, they were people determined to conclude a good deal based on mutual trust and advantage. In that they had succeeded. The substance of the package was sound, although many details remained to be worked out. It was not at all clear that this would be a simple matter.

Given the role of members of Congress in bringing the two sides back to the table, chances of success in Congress had also been strengthened. The failure of both sides to deal adequately with Congress throughout the course of the negotiations had in many ways been neutralized by the strange course of events at the end of the negotiations. Indeed, critics in Congress over the ensuing few weeks expressed their concerns in muted terms. If anything, the fact that they found little to criticize did not help the Canadian public relations battle, which would have been buoyed by some vigorous comments from senators claiming that the US side had given the store away.

The business at hand, however, remained to be concluded. The government now had to sell the deal, the details of which remained to be worked out, to Canadians.

16

THE LAWYERS TAKE OVER

They have no lawyers among them, for they consider them as a sort of people whose profession it
is to disguise matters.

– Sir Thomas More, *Utopia*

O nce an agreement in principle had been reached, the government
faced two challenges: to explain and sell the agreement and to translate the principles contained in the elements of the agreement into a
precise legal text. Both tasks were critical. The positive momentum gained
over the course of 2 to 4 October in Washington and Ottawa could not be
lost. The strange turn of events, however, had severely complicated the two
tasks. No one had anticipated the situation the government now faced.

After two years of debate, critics of the initiative were not content to take
the bare outline of an agreement as sufficient. They pointed out that the elements did not take them very far. Supporters were equally sceptical if less
vocal in their views. In order to come to some judgment about the deal, both
sides needed the detail that only a legal text could supply. At its simplest
level, individual companies needed to know what tariff concessions had been
agreed and how the rules of origin would operate before they could make
any assessment of how they would be affected. Without such detail, therefore, the debate continued to be based on general views as to whether any
agreement was desirable.

The government, having indicated that it had reached an agreement in
principle with the United States, took the stand that sufficient detail was now
known for the debate to move into a new phase and geared its public relations effort accordingly. To mute any criticism, it indicated that the final text
would be available in a matter of a few weeks.

Preparing a legal text, however, was more than a matter of a few lawyers
sitting down and expanding on the text agreed to in Washington. It required
a further round of negotiations and more than the two or three weeks opti-
mistically promised.[1] In effect, the ever-changing rules on the fast-track procedures had been given a new twist. It seemed that no more was needed than

a firm statement from the president indicating his intent to enter into the agreement. The next real deadline was 2 January by which time he would have to sign the agreement and submit the text to Congress. US lawyers had originally indicated that the agreement had to be finished on 4 October. They said they would require the period from 4 October to 2 January for consultations with Congress on preparing legislation for submission with the text of the agreement on 3 January. They now insisted that consultations could take place while the two sides worked on the final text and legislation did not need to be submitted until some time after 2 January. Only one thing was certain: no one in Canada or in the United States would ever again speak with authority on the Washington decision-making and legislative process or take pronouncements on these matters from US officials as the definitive word.

The period from 4 October to 11 December thus took on a surreal quality. Canada had an agreement and it did not; the government could finally explain what it had done and it could not; it could take the country into its confidence and it could not. Deadlines came and went. Days became nights and weekends evaporated into the following week. For a group that had finished its main task, the negotiators appeared to have a lot of work to do. The drama was played out against the background of an increasingly sceptical audience, while the battle for the hearts and minds of Canadians appeared to be going to the opposition. The delay in producing the final text did not help the cause.

Alan King, *Ottawa Citizen*, 19 December 1987

Reactions

Initial Canadian media reaction was mixed. Business writers such as Southam columnist John Ferguson, the *Globe and Mail*'s Peter Cook, *Montreal Gazette* columnist Peter Hadekel, *Toronto Sun* writer Diane Francis, and the *Financial Post*'s Hy Solomon all described the agreement as a balanced and positive achievement that made economic sense and would help Canadian business increase sales to the United States. Political columnists were more sceptical. Outside of the unreserved praise of Doug Fisher and Laura Sabia in the *Toronto Sun* (balanced by the usual vitriolic comments from the pen of Claire Hoy), most were critical and sceptical. Jeffrey Simpson, in a full-page analysis for the *Globe and Mail*, came to a cautiously positive conclusion, but Southam columnists Alan Fotheringham and Don McGillivray provided their usual sour scepticism. All political columnists repeated the basic worry that the agreement would over time erode Canada's independence. The process by which this would happen was never described with any precision, but the result was declared inevitable.

Editorial reaction was equally mixed. As usual, the *Toronto Star* and its whole coterie of writers maintained their negative tone. To disprove charges of bias, the occasional guest was given a few column inches. Balance was provided in Toronto, however, by glowingly positive editorials in the *Globe and Mail*. In its view, the 'free trade deal with the United States looks stronger as we get to know it ... We believe in liberalized trade, consistent with national sovereignty. This deal appears to have achieved it.'[2] Editorial writers for the *Ottawa Citizen* and the *Montreal Gazette*, however, were not so positive. Said the *Citizen*: 'Some argue that the better we get to know this deal, the stronger it looks. On the contrary. The more we see of it, the scarier it looks.'[3] Two months later, however, having looked at it some more, the *Citizen* changed its mind and in a series of three editorials, came to the same conclusion as the *Globe and Mail*. By that time, the *Star* and the *Gazette* remained the only major Canadian newspapers editorially opposed to the deal.[4]

For the media, the main problem areas revolved around energy and dispute settlement. While the oil and gas industry reacted positively to the energy chapter, others took exception not only to the commitments in the chapter to maintain American access to energy resources in the event of a shortage, but also to the obligation to end government-imposed price discrimination. In the view of central Canadian critics, Canada should keep its energy resources for itself and ensure that its abundance translated into cheap energy for Canadian consumers and a competitive advantage for Canadian industrial users. It sounded like a repeat of the energy debates of the 1970s. The debate on dispute settlement pitted protectionists and perfectionists against those who saw the provisions as a welcome step in the right direction, if not exactly the provisions that Canada would like to have achieved. The government's rhetoric insisting on binding dispute settlement had hinted at the desirability of an exemption from trade remedy law. Critics now insisted exemption had been the government's position. Critical comments on the investment and financial services chapter, on the other hand, were much more muted and suggested that the passion that these issues had once roused had been largely dissipated.

Canadian business leaders appeared at first to be slow in warming up to the deal. While the main business organizations were all quoted in the media as generally pleased with the agreement (such as Robert McIntosh for the Canadian Bankers Association, Roger Hamel for the Canadian Chamber of Commerce, Larry Thibeault for the Canadian Manufacturers Association, Brien Gray for the Canadian Federation of Independent Business, and Tom d'Aquino for the Business Council on National Issues), it took a few days before interviews with individual business people indicated that the most direct beneficiaries of the agreement were satisfied.[5] Many waited until they had had a chance to look at the preliminary text and to benefit from briefings of the International Trade Advisory Committee and the individual sectoral advisory groups. Once they had had a chance to review the agreement and had been debriefed, they were not reticent in their support.[6] Not all businesses, however, were pleased. Farmers continued to be sceptical, as did food processors such as Quaker Oats's Jon Grant.[7] Roger Phillips of Saskatchewan-based Ipsco expressed extreme disappointment that the negotiators had not been able to achieve a better deal on anti-dumping, but other steel producers expressed satisfaction.[8] Among bankers, the Bank of Nova Scotia's Ced Ritchie expressed profound unease in a letter to BCNI's Tom d'Aquino, a letter eventually displayed with glee in the *Star*.[9]

Reaction in the United States was largely positive. On Monday and Tuesday, for the first and only time, the initiative enjoyed extensive coverage in the US print media. On Monday, the *New York Times* alone had seven separate stories detailing the process, the contents, business attitudes, and Canadian reaction. The *Washington Post*, the *Wall Street Journal*, and the *Journal of Commerce* also provided detailed coverage, basing their comments on the Sunday press conference given by Secretary Baker, USTR Yeutter, and Ministers Carney and Wilson, as well as the media package prepared by USTR. The coverage was on the whole constructive, reflecting the positive editorial coverage the issue had consistently enjoyed in the United States. Over the course of two years, while coverage had been infrequent, it had occasionally elicited editorials praising the Mulroney government for its courage in pursuing the initiative and in effect swimming upstream against the tide of protectionism in Congress.

US business reaction was also generally positive, as were the comments of members of Congress. Senators Bentsen, Packwood, Chafee, Bradley, Moynihan, and Matsunaga all spoke in glowing terms of the agreement. Indeed, their strong endorsements convinced Canadian critics that Canada had been suckered. Over the ensuing weeks, however, a number of US industries would criticize aspects of the agreement and the US maritime industries would mount an active lobby to ensure that their interests would not in any way be affected by the agreement.

First Ministers Again
For the ninth time in less than two years, Canada's ten premiers returned to Ottawa on 7 October to get the latest details. Seven of them had hardly reached home from their Friday meeting when they had to turn around for a return engagement. As some columnists suggested, the prime minister had no trouble controlling the frequent meetings with the premiers. They came whenever he beckoned and over time, whether they liked it or not – and most of them did – they became active participants in moving Canada towards an agreement. Criticism sounded increasingly hollow.

This time they met for eight and a half hours. Whatever was discussed, the only issue of public interest was how many would speak in favour and how many would oppose. In an effort to dampen expectations, the prime minister took a tough line, suggesting that these meetings were largely a courtesy. The federal government was responsible for trade and commerce and for international treaties. As it was, little under provincial jurisdiction was affected by the agreement and he expected no difficulty in ensuring provincial compliance in implementing those few provisions that fell within provincial jurisdiction.

The line-up going into the meeting was identical to that coming out. The three westernmost premiers were strongly supportive, as they had been throughout the process. Quebec's Bourassa also strongly endorsed the pact as did New Brunswick's Hatfield. The latter's view, however, carried little weight. In the middle of a gruelling election campaign that he was given no chance of winning (and indeed would lose by the most convincing of margins: no seats), Hatfield's presence was his last hurrah as the longest serving premier and consistent booster of federalism. Strongly opposed was Pawley of Manitoba whose earlier flirting with support had led to severe chastisement from the national NDP caucus; his criticisms continued to sound unconvincing, as if he were reading a script he did not believe in. Equally opposed and unconvincing was Ontario's Peterson who sounded like someone who knew he was supposed to oppose but was having trouble remembering why. The other three Atlantic premiers, as is their tradition, sat on the fence, with Ghiz leaning towards opposition and Peckford and Buchanan favourably disposed. In their view, this might be a good or bad agreement, but it was a federal issue and if the federal government thought their support was important, the federal government might be prepared to do something for them. Such an attitude had paid dividends in the past; it should work now. Certainly there was no reason to come out strongly in favour until they had had an opportunity to be courted.

The Selling of Free Trade

Given the mixed reaction, the government saw its first and primary task to be the selling of free trade and the full resources of TNO, PMO, and External Affairs were bent to that effort. Preparations were made for brochures explaining the agreement, hearings before House and Senate committees, speeches by ministers and senior officials, and briefings of the ITAC and the SAGITs. The theme was the unfortunate 'what you see is what you get'; the main act in the drama, the daily pounding in question period; the result, growing impatience as delays in the production of the final text suggested that the government had something to hide.

٬ A telephone hot-line to field inquiries was set up at External Affairs and the lines were covered from early morning until early evening. Over the next six weeks, dragooned telephone sitters, armed with an orange-covered volume of basic questions and answers, dealt with the public calls. For some, it was a fascinating study in Canadian sociology, especially on Friday evenings as lonely hearts from the Atlantic would phone around six Ottawa time just to chat. There were also the regular afternoon callers, looking for someone with whom to pass the time. The cost for the line was over a quarter of a million dollars – all for just over 500 calls.

The government urged ministers and MPs to accept as many speaking engagements as they could in order to get the message out. The principal spokesman, however, turned out to be salesman Simon. In the first few weeks, he became amenable to every media request for interviews. Reporters from the *Star*, Southam, the *Financial Times*, *Maclean's* and more found him available. Repeat performances were sought on *The Journal* and *Question Period*. Peter Gzowski sparred with him for an hour on *Morningside*. He accepted speaking engagements for the first time in sixteen months. Between a May 1986 speech to the Canadian Federation of Labour and his appearance before a combined audience of the Empire and Canadian Clubs on 16

October in Toronto, Reisman had confined his public remarks to media scrums and appearances on *The Journal* and *Question Period*. He was now available for audiences anywhere in the country.[10]

On *Morningside* he launched an attack on the *Toronto Star*, singling out one of its many negative editorials as particularly scurrilous and suggesting that the government would be well advised to investigate the ethics of a rich man owning a newspaper and using it to foist his extreme opinions on the country. The media had a new story. He added to the new story the following week by suggesting at a conference in Toronto sponsored by the Institute for Research on Public Policy that the opponents of free trade were practicing the same tactics as Joseph Goebbels, the Nazi minister of propaganda and inventor of the Big Lie.[11] During an appearance before a parliamentary committee, Sheila Copps wanted to know if he was comparing her to Goebbels because she was opposed to the agreement. Reisman beat a hasty retreat.[12] He may have had a point about some of free trade's critics, but in the politically charged atmosphere of the public debate, his approach was too uncompromising; a less direct advocate was required to explain the agreement. Screamed a *Montreal Gazette* headline: 'Canada's Chief Negotiator Is No Diplomat.' The story went on: 'Reisman's style now is the same as in the bargaining process, when his Napoleonic manner – he is a diminutive but blustery man who indulges in profanity – irked the Americans across the table.'[13] The qualities which the fickle press had considered assets only two years earlier were by now described as liabilities. By the third week, Reisman's appearances became less frequent[14] and attention turned increasingly to the issue of preparing a final text.

Preparing the Text
While the government sought to maintain control of its public relations agenda, the TNO returned to the other task at hand, the preparation of the legal text. In charge on each side was the chief legal counsel: Charles 'Chip' Roh for the United States and Konrad von Finckenstein for Canada. Each relied on a battery of lawyers who had participated in the working groups. It would be their task to translate the elements of the agreement reached on 4 October into a tight and unambiguous legal text.

Preparation of the legal text, however, had by now been placed in the straight jacket of time pressure and been hampered further by the ongoing debate which sought to interpret the elements text in particular ways, thus limiting the scope for imaginative drafting. In normal circumstances, the lawyers would have been given six months or more to translate such a complicated and detailed 'agreement in principle' into precise legal language, and they would have been allowed to pursue their task in confidence. What they faced in October and November was the whole country with views as to what the elements meant or did not mean.

The task was supposed to take two to three weeks. Working flat out, it took ten weeks. Translating 35 pages of text into an agreement of some 250 pages divided into 21 chapters and some 150 articles and annexes was more than a mechanical process. It was no less than a second round of negotiations with the main difference being that both sides agreed on the objective and could work in a more constructive atmosphere.

Before the task was wholly delegated to the lawyers, however, each working group was instructed to finish, in the light of the elements of agreement reached on 4 October, the text they had been working on prior to suspension. This presented a different challenge to different groups. For those working on tariff and customs matters, there was a good basic text to work on. For the investment group, a lot of work remained. For the dispute settlement group, while the general provisions had been largely agreed upon and were spelled out in the elements text, the separate chapter on countervailing and anti-dumping dispute settlement represented virgin territory, with only the language in the elements text as a guide. Rather than reporting to a plenary session, the working groups now reported to the lawyers group.

The first meeting of the lawyers' group was held at the Ottawa Congress Centre 19 and 20 October and continued at the TNO 21 October. The lawyers wanted to start their work in some isolation from the policy people and agree on how they were going to tackle the job before returning to the TNO. Each side came armed with a complete text. Each had taken the elements text and the various draft texts in play before suspension and created a complete text. After some preliminary sparring and comparison of the texts, it became clear that the group would make the greatest progress if they worked from the Canadian text. There were two reasons. The Canadian draft was more complete and better organized and thus easier to work with. More importantly, however, it had been prepared on an Apple Macintosh computer. As a result, it looked much more professional and finished than anything the Americans were able to prepare and, even more importantly, the Macintosh's portability made it possible to work with the computer at hand. In the weeks prior to suspension, the Integrated Text Group had already seen the benefits of having the computer in the room and the advantages of entering text into the computer as various alternatives were considered.

A working pattern was thus established for preparing the text. At the end of each week, Canada would prepare a complete printout of the text for both delegations. It would incorporate the state of the text as agreed in each working group. Agreed text was printed in plain type, US text in bold and Canadian in italics. In the lawyers' group meetings, Michael Hart would operate the computer and enter any agreed changes with his two index fingers the instant they were agreed, in effect acting as secretary for both delegations.

Use of the Macintosh had not been without controversy. When the TNO had been established, computer experts had been brought in and had designed an elaborate network of desktop terminals linked to a mainframe computer and a word processing centre. The system turned out to have two major flaws. It could not handle more than about a dozen users at a time and computer novices found it hard to use. Many terminals sat idle. Elaborate plans to do everything electronically fell by the wayside. Consultants were brought in and a whole new system was designed and installed. It was an improvement on the old system, but was prone to frequent breakdowns and remained a challenge to the uninitiated.

One group stubbornly refused to join this system. The task force at External Affairs that had originally been responsible for preparing the initiative had, prior to the formation of the TNO, been equipped with Macintosh computers and a laser printer. Everyone had become very attached to these little wonders and refused to change to anything else. They had found them very easy to use, even for beginners. To the chagrin of the computer specialists, the output from the Macintosh group outpaced that of everyone else and looked more professional. What's more, the group never needed any help from either the technicians or the word processing unit. Most frustrating of all, Gordon Ritchie also had one of these machines and refused to order the heretics to conform to the office norm. Indeed, he kept ordering new programs and upgrading equipment. Finally, to add insult to injury, the much reviled Macintosh group now appeared to be in charge of preparing the final text and had convinced the Americans to go along with them. The system proved its value. Not only was the Canadian side in full control of the preparation of the text, it was also able to produce a finished text for printing within forty-eight hours of initialling the final text.

After a first run through the text on 19-21 October in Ottawa, the lawyers continued the task in Washington on 28-9 October. By that time, various parts of the text were beginning to look like the final product. The lawyers had agreed on a format and style. They were able to let the working groups know where they needed further policy work. They had cleared away much of the legal boilerplate. They were making progress, but they were far from finished.

A third session back at the TNO on 4-5 November finished the basic task and clearly identified the problem areas that could not be solved without policy guidance. This session was attended by Warren Dean, a lawyer from the US Department of Transportation. His performance gave new meaning to the word intransigence. Given a brief to ensure that any transportation annex to the services chapter would make application of the obligations in that chapter virtually meaningless, he had done his job and defended it to the chagrin of the lawyers from the other US agencies. Almost a whole day was spent on this thorny issue without any progress towards agreement.

The lawyers soldiered on and met again in Washington from 10 to 13 November. Tuesday and Wednesday were spent trying to make further progress on the dispute settlement chapter while Thursday and Friday were devoted to honing the text. Wednesday was a statutory holiday in the United States (Veterans Day). The weather, however, brought a holiday of a different sort. Washingtonians, not used to much snow even in January and February, were greeted with a freak snowstorm that dumped up to 15 inches of wet snow on Washington and its suburbs. Everything ground to a halt, including the heating systems. Rather than progress, Wednesday brought a very cold day to the Commerce Department and a wet walk back to the hotel. On Thursday and Friday, the lawyers were joined by agriculture, customs, services, and business travel experts, while in Ottawa the investment working group was wrestling with its remaining policy issues. All working group heads had been told that anything they had not concluded by midnight 13 November would be solved at a more senior level. This would be the last chance for the experts.

The Parliamentary Committee: Democracy at Work

The lawyers had now been at their task for six weeks, already twice as long as the process was supposed to take. Their political masters were becoming impatient and were leaning on Reisman who in turn leaned on von Finckenstein. The government was not happy with the progress in the debate and needed the text to breathe new life into it. The consistent answer from the TNO, however, was soon, very soon. By mid-November that line had begun to wear thin.

Faced with a barrage of accusations in question period every day, the government sought to deflect criticism by mandating the parliamentary committee on External Affairs and International Trade to delve into the text. It was scheduled to hold cross-country hearings and present its final report by the middle of December in order to allow for a parliamentary debate before the prime minister and president signed the text on 2 January. In the face of continued criticism, the government maintained that the elements text provided all the answers and that the final text would not in any way deviate from it.

The opposition would have none of it and complained that it could not ask experts to testify and come to an informed opinion in the absence of a final text.

The first meeting of the parliamentary committee on 29 October saw Pat Carney, Simon Reisman, and Gordon Ritchie all assured that the final text would be faithful to the preliminary text. The opposition members of the committee again balked and found their views echoed by the columnists and editorial writers. They insisted that in the absence of a final text, the hearings were a farce. In fact, they were not. The committee heard from a wide spectrum of witnesses, a number of whom returned after the full text and detailed implementing legislation were available without in any way changing their testimony, whether positive or negative. The Senate Committee on Foreign Affairs similarly held hearings, similarly delved into the details of the agreement and its negotiation, and similarly complained about the absence of a final text. The House hearings especially were intensely political and reflected competing views of the country rather than of the agreement.[15]

Gordon Ritchie had by this time stepped into the vacuum created by Reisman's frequent absences from Ottawa. Ritchie had already gained a reputation with ministers as a consummate and knowledgeable briefer. The prime minister was heard to say that Ritchie 'spoke in paragraphs.' Examples of this essential bureaucratic skill were now put on public display before the House and Senate Standing Committees, each of which he treated to a three-hour slide show and question and answer session.[16] He returned to the House Committee throughout the fall and winter, demonstrating his mastery of the agreement and raising opposition anxieties about an official so capably explaining a government initiative. At the TNO and around town, Ritchie came into his own, organizing and keeping on track the myriad of activities required during this delicate stage in the negotiations. But even his masterful briefing and organizational skills did not conceal the fact that the government was trying to explain an agreement while the lawyers were still working on the fine print.[17]

One of the more amusing opposition charges revolved around pharmaceuticals. The pharmaceutical bill had been bogged down for months in the Senate. One of the opponents' arguments had been that its passage was part of the pay-off for free trade. The government vehemently denied this claim. Some government apologists, probably confusing their lines with those provided for autopact questions, had even gone so far as to suggest the subject had not been raised in the trade talks. This was not the case. Indeed, the Americans had raised the issue and it had even got so far as to be included in the elements of agreement paper on miscellaneous issues. In the chaos of the

Saturday and Sunday negotiation, it had been signed off by the joint working heads, Germain Denis for the Canadians and Bill Merkin for the Americans, and then passed up to the ministers for approval. This version had been summarily rejected and a new one prepared. Unhappily, in the haste to get the elements documents out to the media, the first version had been included and passed out to the press. The eagle eyes of Allan Gotlieb had noted the error and John Fieldhouse, the embassy press officer, had asked reporters to return the documents just distributed as they were inaccurate. Several canny reporters, including Jennifer Lewington, tucked the document into their other papers. It had not caused a problem in Ottawa; the amended version was sent late in the evening and corrected before the material was printed and distributed on the Monday morning. But rumours that the pharmaceutical package had been included began to circulate. Washington reporters checked their documents and voilà: instant headline! While the explanation was reasonable, the perception was left of a government sleight of hand. It gave credence to opposition claims that there would be secret side letters on some issues.[18]

What was missing from all this political and journalistic jousting was some recognition of what is involved in the give and take of a negotiation. International negotiations involve at least two sets of objectives and political imperatives. What counts in the end is the extent to which these objectives and imperatives are met. To get there, however, both sides have to be prepared to listen to and weigh the views of the other side. In this instance, for example, the United States had a strong desire to address intellectual property issues and a compelling need to advance the interests of its pharmaceutical manufacturers. Canada was not averse to exploring the parameters of an intellectual property chapter, but was allergic to any chapter that fully satisfied the US pharmaceutical manufacturers, particularly in the absence of any movement by the US side on the elimination of section 337 (the section that provides for discriminatory, expedited procedures in foreign patent infringement cases) and on better access to US technology. In the political and journalistic discussion, however, Canada's willingness to explore was too frequently equated with a willingness to accommodate. The same critics, however, would have proven equally indignant at any signs that the US side was not prepared to explore Canadian concerns about access to procurement markets or to address trade remedy laws. It is this lack of seriousness in the public debate that disposes officials to maintain their penchant for secrecy which, in turn, feeds more of this kind of uninformed discussion and charges of 'secret' negotiations and side deals.

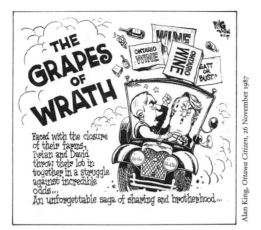

Alan King, *Ottawa Citizen*, 26 November 1987

Return to the Negotiating Table

With the failure of the working groups and the lawyers to deliver a finished text within the anticipated time, Gordon Ritchie stepped in to clear away the problem areas. He organized a meeting at Meech Lake for 16 through 18 November to resolve all the remaining issues. He had hoped that Peter McPherson, the treasury deputy, would lead the US delegation, but had been told in no uncertain terms that McPherson would only step in at such time as all the underbrush had been cleared away.

The threat of the meeting quickly solved a number of problems and reduced the difficult issues down to no more than two or three per chapter. To that end, a complete text was printed out on Saturday, 14 November and the following Monday morning, the two sides made a good start. But that was all. The Americans appeared more interested in taking measure of the problems than in resolving them. They wanted to go back to Washington to consult before agreeing to any deviations from the elements text or to changes in suggested US language in the draft text.

There was no shortage of sticky issues. In addition to continuing problems in the autos and dispute settlement chapters, the two sides had yet to conclude on yarns and fabrics and a number of related rules of origin issues, on the treatment of fish, cable retransmission, and postal rates, on the energy chapter, and on the application of global safeguards. They still needed to decide whether transportation was included in the services chapter and how to treat telecommunications monopolies. The tricky issues of whether or not to have a specific exemption for water,[19] whether or not to include beer in the chapter on alcoholic beverages, and whether or not to have a nullification and impairment provision in the dispute settlement chapter remained outstanding. All these were resolvable problems, but they could not be settled through legal drafting. They required policy decisions and political compromises.

To continue the work, Reisman and Ritchie agreed to come to Washington on 20 November and conclude the task. Murphy declared that he would be in a position to close on many of the issues and it should be possible to finish the task before the American Thanksgiving on 26 November. Thus negotiators and lawyers once again climbed into a Challenger, packing their trusty Macintosh, and prepared to wrap up. To the question of whether or not to pack for the weekend, the answer was a categorical no. This would be a one-day task. Everyone would be needed in Ottawa over the weekend to prepare the final text for public release.

Once at USTR, the team divided into two groups. While Reisman and Ritchie met with Murphy and Merkin to conclude the final issues, the lawyers' group would continue cleaning up the text and incorporating the results of the policy discussion. The latter had started the previous week on a detailed, line-by-line clean-up of the text, ensuring internal consistency in style and format as well as substance. Good progress had been made, but the job was tedious and slow going. Rushing it was counterproductive. By the end of the day, more than half the text was in excellent shape.

But no input had been received from upstairs. That group had made little progress, spending most of the day on the auto question. At internal TNO meetings over the previous year, whenever autos came up, it had resulted in endless discussion. It fascinated Reisman and, as the doting father of the autopact, he never tired of it. By now everyone knew all the stories as well as he did. This performance was now being visited once again upon Murphy and company. The autopact may not have been on the table, but it was always present.

To the astonishment of Murphy and his colleagues, Reisman declared that he planned to go home that night. Murphy was under the impression that Reisman had come to finish the task, no matter how long it took, before the Thanksgiving break. No, declared Reisman, he was going home, but the Americans were welcome to come to Ottawa on Monday to continue. Feeling betrayed and now sure that a text could not be concluded by Thanksgiving, the Americans refused. With the exception of four of the lawyers who stayed behind for the weekend to continue on the clean-up of the text, the rest of the Canadian delegation went home. Those who stayed rushed out to purchase toilet kits and a change of underwear and to find a hotel.

While the Canadian government had felt time pressing on it throughout the previous six weeks, so had the US government. Soundings on Capitol Hill found that members of Congress were as reluctant as NDP and Liberal politicians to come to any conclusions on the agreement in the absence of a final text. They declared Thanksgiving to be the last date for the receipt of any text if the administration held out any hope for early consideration of any agreement. If the negotiators could deliver the text, preferably in confidence, before Thanksgiving, administration and congressional officials could work together between then and the end of the year and prepare a statement as to what would be required in the way of implementing legislation before making the agreement public. Both the agreement and such a statement would then be released at the time of signature, paving the way for early congressional consideration.

But now it was clear that the final text would not be finished by Thanksgiving and that the Canadians intended to release the text as soon as it was concluded. US time pressure thus disappeared and no member of the US side was prepared to sacrifice his or her Thanksgiving break. If Reisman was not prepared to work over this weekend, the task would have to be continued after Thanksgiving and congressional consideration delayed until further into 1988.

The week off turned out to be a blessing in disguise. It provided a respite from negotiations and an opportunity to stand back and assess where things stood. While the text of the agreement was in good shape, with some dozen difficult issues requiring policy resolution, there were ways it could be improved. The text also needed to be explained and the intervening week was used to write up the basic notes that would accompany the text at the time of release. Other deficiencies in the text became apparent as this commentary was being prepared, and these problems were added to the inventory of issues that needed to be addressed in the lawyers' group.

A rested US delegation returned to Ottawa to finish the job on 2 December. As in Washington the week before, the work was divided between policy discussion between Reisman and Murphy and technical discussion in the lawyers' group. Again, as in Washington, the second group made good progress but received very little in the way of instructions on how to incorporate the remaining outstanding issues. No issue was resolved. Murphy decided to return to Washington and his colleagues followed the next day. Only some members of the lawyers' group stayed behind to continue the task of line-by-line clean-up.

An Agreement at Last

Back in Washington, Murphy sought to convince his superiors that it would take another meeting at the political level to conclude negotiations. If Peter McPherson was prepared to come to Ottawa, Derek Burney would be available on the Canadian side. Otherwise, a deal could not be concluded before the end of the year. McPherson was available. The Americans spent Thursday and

Alan King, *Ottawa Citizen*, 15 December 1987

'So much for mining and hewing . . .Now it's cars and computers, right, Simon?'

Friday, 3-4 December, briefing him and getting him ready for the final push.

In Ottawa, Reisman and his senior advisors were bent to the same task. For the second time Derek Burney had been called in to close the deal. All day Thursday briefing notes were prepared, and Reisman, Ritchie, and the core group spent all day Friday closeted with Burney giving him the benefit of their advice. As two months earlier, Burney again called on Gerry Shannon and Don Campbell to help him prepare for a weekend session and to join him in the briefing. On Friday, the order went out to the rest of the TNO: everyone was to be in attendance and lend assistance Saturday and Sunday.

The US side arrived promptly at 9:00 Saturday morning. Led by Peter McPherson and Alan Holmer (elevated from general counsel to deputy USTR in the interval) and accompanied by Ambassadors Murphy and Niles and assorted specialists, they were provided with offices and a meeting room and told that the Canadians were ready any time they were. It took them a while to sort out where they were and who was going to do what. By early afternoon a familiar pattern had been established. Working group heads were to examine where they stood and what they could do to resolve the issues. When they had made progress, they were to report to the political group which would provide final instructions.

By the end of the day, Burney and McPherson had developed an interesting twist to the routine. They saw no need for a large meeting attended by a horde of advisors. It would be better if individual issues were thrashed out in the Canadian and US caucuses before the two principals met to discuss them. Then, accompanied by one advisor each, they could see if they agreed.

Thus all day Sunday, Burney, accompanied by Ritchie, and McPherson, accompanied by Holmer, shuttled back and forth between their respective delegations and the office set aside for Burney's use.

Ottawa, unlike Washington, did not shirk on the needs of the body. All weekend David Dunlop and his helpers did yeoman duty to find a variety of food for nearly 200 assorted negotiators, lawyers, translators, and support staff. In addition to the fifty or sixty Americans, he had to feed the whole of the TNO as well as the extra help brought in by Burney and the two dozen translators standing by to translate all agreed text instantly into French. They had been at this for some months already and by now knew the text as well as the negotiators. The translators, as is their wont, wanted to improve the text and had to be dissuaded; their task was to prepare a faithful rendering, not an improved text.

The lawyers had set up shop, appropriately, in the library of Osler, Hoskins, and Harcourt, a law firm three floors below. TNO facilities were very good but not spacious enough to accommodate the mob that had descended on it that weekend. Fourteen floors below, the media set up their equipment and waited. Unlike in Washington in October, they were invited into the building and spent most of the weekend lounging on the marble floors of the entry hall. The negotiators were virtually captive in their own den. Any attempt to step outside for fresh air required running the media gauntlet. The previous Wednesday, Reisman had escaped by using the freight elevator.

The issues were the same as those at Meech Lake three weeks earlier. Little of substance had been resolved in the interval. Indeed, issues had been added to the list. The crunch issues were dispute settlement for countervail and anti-dumping and the rules of origin for autos. But there were still lots of other tricky issues such as the treatment of yarns and fabrics, the export rules in the energy chapter, obligations on postal rates,[20] the treatment of fish, coverage of beer, and so on. And then there was the nasty issue as to whether or not maritime transportation would be covered in the services chapter.

In the auto chapter, the two sides had both sought to move beyond what had been achieved at Washington two months earlier. The US wanted to move the rule of origin from 50 to 60 per cent combined US and Canadian content for non-autopact auto trade. Canada was not averse to this change if in return the US was prepared to give Canada more time to phase out duty remission programs. The US was not. As a result, the two sides decided to stick with what had been agreed at Washington.

In the trade remedy chapter, the sticky issues included the composition of panels, the right to appeal decisions made by a panel which in some way had been tainted by the malfeasance or corruption of its members, the scope for panel review (i.e., which decisions could be appealed to a panel), and the degree of symmetry in the issues that could be brought before a panel from Canadian and US decisions. The solutions lay in:

- prescribing that only three of the five panelists had to be lawyers
- allowing appeal from a binational panel decision to a binational panel of ex-judges, but only in very limited circumstances, such as an occasion of conflict of interest by one of the panelists
- extending the jurisdiction of the panel to all decisions that terminate domestic proceedings, such as a finding of injury and the imposition of a countervailing duty
- ensuring that the types of issues subject to review were roughly similar in the two jurisdictions. Under existing law and practice, more issues were reviewable by the courts in the United States than in Canada. Determinations of dumping and subsidization by the deputy minister of National Revenue, for example, were not subject to judicial review but would be subject to bilateral review by a panel.

By the end of the weekend all but one issue had been resolved and incorporated into the final text. It had been agreed, for example to exclude transportation from the services chapter; to drop the issue of postal rates from the agreement; to include a provision on nullification and impairment; to revisit at some point in the future the quota on fabric made up from imported yarns; to grandfather current beer marketing practices but keep them subject to GATT obligations; and to grandfather current restrictions on the export of unprocessed fish caught off the East Coast. The only remaining issue was cable retransmission. On it, the two sides needed to consult some more with the experts and resolve it over the phone as quickly as possible.[21]

Just before 2:00 in the morning, Burney, Reisman, McPherson, and Murphy repaired to the lobby to tell the media mob that the two sides had concluded a final text. Reisman did all the talking. The two sides would take the time to put together and proofread what had been agreed, but by the end of the week a final legal text would be available. By 3:00 AM a final text of the agreement had been printed for the Americans and the last stragglers headed home. Another exhausting, but, this time, fruitful weekend had come to an end.

Proofreading

Monday was spent proofreading and preparing the text for public release. On Tuesday, the government placed an old Cosmos at the disposal of the lawyers and they flew down to Washington for their final meeting. In the conference room at the Sheridan complex of the Canadian embassy, they spent another long day poring over the text. Despite the care of the previous three weeks, they were still able to find inconsistencies and small errors. As they worked, they were treated to the sound of sirens escorting Mikhail Gorbachev and his advisors up and down Massachusetts Avenue. The administration's other major foreign policy initiative also appeared to be paying dividends. It took until the wee hours of the following morning, but finally shortly before 3:00 in the morning of 9 December, Konrad von Finckenstein and Chip Roh finished initialling the final text – except for two pages on cable retransmission. As a symbol of the age of new technology, Chip Roh and Michael Hart also initialled copies of the computer disks containing the text of the agreement. Cable retransmission remained unresolved and was the subject of a separate meeting in Ottawa and continuing phone calls between Burney and McPherson. It would not be resolved until 4:00 PM on 10 December. Ironically, it was one of the specific issues the president and the prime minister had agreed to resolve at the Shamrock Summit in Quebec that had started the process almost three years earlier.

At 4:30 PM on Thursday, 11 December, Reisman walked across to Parliament Hill and in a small ceremony handed the prime minister a copy of the final agreement in English and French – a total of six looseleaf books full of material. The negotiations were over. The next day the prime minister tabled the text in the House. The job was finished. Canada and the United States had concluded a comprehensive trade agreement.

The prime minister poses with three of the key players in the negotiations – Gordon Ritchie, Derek Burney, and Simon Reisman – to celebrate the conclusion of negotiations. (11 December 1987)

Simon Reisman presents Trade Minister Carney and the prime minister the first copy of the final text of the Free Trade Agreement. Don Campbell, Gerry Shannon, John McDermid, Gordon Ritchie, and Derek Burney look on. (11 December 1987)

Launching the Final Text

As the October launch had not been exactly propitious, the completion of the final text provided an occasion to try again. The first task for the new launch was the preparation of detailed notes and annotations for the agreement. A separate document detailing the deviations in the final text from the elements of the agreement was also prepared. While von Finckenstein and his small team of lawyers finished the final clean-up of the text, the rest of the team went through the explanatory notes and annotations before passing them on for translation and production. On Wednesday, with the return of the lawyers, further changes were made and a series of questions and answers prepared. At 3:00 in the morning, everyone called it quits.

The next morning, the final changes were made and by early evening every document had been translated and printed and sent to the printing plant in Hull. The triumph of modern technology had made it possible to conclude negotiations at 4:30 on Wednesday afternoon and be in a position to hand the press a complete text with annotations – over two thousand pages of text, in English and in French – by 9:00 the following Friday morning. It called for a minor celebration. For the past week the staff had been putting in seventeen-hour days. A case of Mumms, borrowed from Don Campbell's private cellar for the previous weekend but never opened because of the late hour, was finally cracked open. Ritchie made a graceful speech of gratitude for the team's efforts. Reisman told the group that when the prime minister had asked what he could now do for the group he replied, 'Find us new jobs.' This set off a chorus of 'What do we want ... Jobs, Jobs, Jobs.'

The next morning a press lock-up was held from 9:00 to 12:00. At noon, the final text was tabled in the House. Simon Reisman appeared on *The Journal* to express his satisfaction with the agreement. At the morning press conference, Reisman paid Clayton Yeutter back for his gratuitous comments of two months earlier. He crowed that the Canadian negotiators had thoroughly outnegotiated the Americans. He described American lack of preparation and awareness of the issues as akin to that of a Third World country, in one phrase insulting both the United States and the Third World. The next day he picked another fight with Ontario Premier Peterson by calling him old-fashioned, triggering a column from Bill Fox suggesting he should do the wise thing and fade into the woodwork.[22] His job was done and his salesmanship left something to be desired.

Columnists throughout the negotiations had found Reisman an endless source of material. He fascinated them. He had come out of retirement the acknowledged dean of Canadian trade negotiators. Tough, assertive, brash, uncompromising, visionary, and dedicated, he had sought to negotiate the best possible agreement Canada could get. But Ottawa had changed, as had Washington. He had had to rely on people he did not know. Instead of a compact team, he had found himself in charge of a small army. Instead of facing a wily old veteran like himself, he found himself sitting opposite a beardless youth. Instead of butting heads on real issues, he had found that much of the time he was dealing with phantoms. Thoroughly prepared and confident of his goals, he had to deal with a US team with an uncertain bottom line, while operating in a charged Washington trade policy environment.

The negotiating world had changed. Expecting to concentrate on negotiations, he had had to expend enormous energy on the crucial tasks of building provincial consensus, keeping the business community warm and toasty, and developing a mandate with ministers. In Washington, cabinet officials had been indifferent and members of Congress had played Washington politics with the negotiations. As the months slipped by without any clear indication of where the two sides would end up, he had become increasingly frustrated.

His no-nonsense and direct style had been admired at the start. But his high public profile now became subject to critical commentary from journalists who had forgotten the praise they had heaped on him only two years earlier at his appointment. All that frustration showed in his public comments over the closing months.

In Washington, Congress demonstrated its displeasure at the late arrival of the text. In a joint letter to Secretary Baker and USTR Yeutter, Senate Finance Committee chairman Bentsen and House Ways and Means Committee chairman Rostenkowski thanked them for the final text and suggested that, due to the charged congressional calendar, they might not be able to begin consideration of implementing legislation until June. Meanwhile, every opportunity should be taken for Congress and the administration to work together in preparing that legislation.[23] This warning shot across the administration's bow contained the not-so-veiled threat that Congress saw some connection between passage of its Omnibus Trade Bill and implementing legislation for the trade agreement. A veto of its trade program might lead to defeat of the administration's trade agreement. The battle lines were drawn for the next stage in the US version of the drama.

Reactions Again

In Canada, the battlelines had been in place for so long that reaction to the legal text proved low-key and anti-climactic. Now that the debate could proceed on the basis of an actual agreement rather than speculation, the country was sated with the subject of free trade. Everything that could be written had been written. Even opponents had lost their appetite for more criticism. Wrote Orland French in the *Globe and Mail*: 'I ... entered the free trade debate totally opposed to any deal and now ... grudgingly concede that maybe, just maybe, Canada has no other realistic choice.'[24]

In Parliament, Pat Carney introduced an anodyne resolution concluding that the agreement was in the national interest and opened the debate with a stalwart defence. The opposition tried its best to indicate that it represented a sell-out and that the government should call an election. The debate, however, lacked the emotion and urgency of the last debate on 16 March. Even leaders' day was predictable and lacklustre. The House remained largely empty as MPs prepared to leave for the Christmas break. The media gave the debate only scant attention.

The public debate had by now begun to explore some of the more out of the way highways and byways. Keith Spicer, editor of the *Ottawa Citizen*, gave a new twist when he wrote a lighthearted commentary – 'Tammy Baker and Pals on Free Trade' – criticizing the churches for their bizarre stance on the issue.[25] Other columnists joined in, debating whether the critical views of the churches and their divines had any legitimacy. William Johnson in the *Montreal Gazette* had already pointed out that their position – that the agreement responded to a corporate agenda at the expense of ordinary people – was based on left-wing populism and prejudices rather than on any serious analysis or theology and said more about the credibility of the church than about free trade or the agreement.[26]

By now, the country had made up its mind and rational debate was unlikely to change the opinions of very many. The government could take comfort in the fact that a majority of those polled continued to support the concept of free trade and many of these, despite their reservations about the credibility of the government, were prepared to concede that the agreement was good and, on balance, did more to help the country than hurt it. The debate had demonstrated, however, that the issue was not so much about free trade as such but about differing visions of the country. Terrance Wills concluded in his summary of the parliamentary committee hearings for the *Montreal Gazette:* 'Everywhere the theme was the same: the central choice is between a nationalist east-west Canada versus a continentalist north-south Canada. That core argument underlies the whole range of debate about the Canada of the future – whether it is to be a "caring," government-interventionist liberal-socialist Canada or a competitive, market-oriented conservative Canada.'[27]

The debate was really about the operation of the market and the appropriate role of government; the line-ups for and against reflected people's attitudes on that central question. That question had also been the main economic issue in the 1984 election and had led to a strong Conservative mandate. To add some spice, the opposition threw in arguments about patriotism, Canadian identity, independence, and sovereignty, many of them betraying an underlying anti-Americanism. Most Canadians, however, were not buying these views.

Among the premiers, the score settled at seven to three when John Buchanan agreed to back the agreement on receipt of a letter from the prime minister assuring him that regional development remained a government priority and would not be sacrificed. Ontario's opposition was undercut somewhat when provincial treasurer Bob Nixon released a report indicating that the Ontario economy would benefit from the agreement. A near consensus for the agreement had emerged from the business community with a similar consensus against among labour leaders. Most of Canada's major newspapers were in favour, with the exception of the *Toronto Star* and the *Montreal Gazette*. Political columnists were unhappy while business columnists liked it. The mainstream churches were against and consumer groups were for, both pleading concern for the poor. Canada's glitterati (those who had not migrated to the United States to make their fortunes) were generally against, expressing concern about Canada's identity. Professional economists were generally for the agreement, while their political science colleagues were more sceptical. Professional feminist groups had decided they were against, but women in business and the professions were generally in favour.

Given these line-ups and attitudes, it did not matter all that much what brochures the government produced and what speeches ministers gave. The real issue was not what was in the agreement. Few Canadians would take the trouble to read the text. Most would have trouble understanding it. It was not written for laypeople. The issue was one of trust and credibility. Whose word were people prepared to take – that of the government or of the opposition, that of editorial writers or columnists, business leaders or labour leaders, the glitterati or the analysts, the churches or consumer groups? For the government, therefore, the real challenge was to bolster its credibility and provide good government. The trade agreement would help, but, in the end, people would vote for the government on its overall record and not on free trade. To implement the agreement, the government had to be re-elected. It now turned to that task. And that is another story.

Final Text and Signature

The drama, however, was not quite over for the negotiators. They still needed a signature and a final text. The lawyers devoted the last few weeks of the year to that task. The text released was that initialled at the level of negotiators. The text to be signed would be one carefully scrutinized by the treaty lawyers, printed on 100 per cent cotton, acid-free paper, and bound in special treaty binders. To the lawyers' chagrin, there were still errors. Longitude had been misspelled, as had government. In a number of places, punctuation was declared to be inconsistent. In the rules of origin, the policy people wanted to fix a last-minute glitch. By 21 December everyone agreed that the text as it sat in the computer was the absolute final text. All that was needed now was paper. There was enough Canadian treaty paper, but the Americans, unable to find the equipment to print their own, had entrusted the Canadian team with the final printing job and to that end had sent a box of US treaty paper to the US embassy in Ottawa. It had not arrived and would not arrive until after Christmas. Reluctantly, the US treaty lawyers agreed that both copies of the text, in English and French, could be printed on Canadian treaty paper.[28] By the end of the day, the job was done.

The next morning the text was delivered to the Langevin Block in order to obtain the prime minister's signature on the American version of the text.[29] Around noon Burney telephoned that the prime minister had signed and that it could now be transmitted to Washington for the president's signature. At the American embassy, a young officer returning to Washington for the Christmas holidays had been pressed into service as a courier. Overwhelmed by the sheer volume of the material, she asked if she could please borrow the huge briefcase used to carry it over to the embassy. Of course, if she agreed not to let it out of her sight until she handed it over to the treaty lawyers at the State Department, who would pick her up at Dulles airport in suburban Virginia that evening.

The president signed the Canadian version of the text the next morning and the US version was packed to go to California with him for signature at the ranch on 2 January. At the Canadian embassy, another returning officer was pressed into service as courier and by Christmas eve, the Canadian version, complete with presidential signature, was safely locked up in the Langevin Block for final signature on 2 January.

On 2 January, the prime minister came in from Harrington Lake and in a brief ceremony signed the agreement. Simultaneously at the ranch in Santa Barbara, California, the president signed the American version and later that day copies were officially registered as received by the Senate Finance Committee and the House Ways and Means Committee. The task was finally complete. Canada had an agreement, and it had been done within the window of opportunity provided by the US fast-track authority. The rest was out of the negotiators' hands.

The prime minister in his Parliament Hill office and the president at the ranch in Santa Barbara sign the final text of the Canada-United States Free Trade Agreement. (2 January 1988)

17

CONCLUSIONS:
A GOOD AGREEMENT[1]

> Canada and the United States have negotiated ... a
> timely, historic, and mutually beneficial treaty ... it
> will encourage a process of industrial adaptation,
> resource allocation, and investment in infrastruc-
> ture that will not easily be reversed ... [its provi-
> sions] remove nationally imposed trade barriers
> that segment markets, shelter inefficient produc-
> ers, and distort or impede investment decisions ...
> with the agreement in place, the opportunities
> made available by the larger market will hasten
> the transformation to a high-value-added
> [Canadian] economy.
> – Economic Council of Canada, *Venturing Forth*

It took five years, a royal commission, task forces, a full-fledged negotiating team, a bevy of lawyers, crisis management galore, false starts, dashed
hopes, courage, vision, and dedication, but Canada's negotiations with
the United States were finally crowned with success. The government's tenacity had paid dividends. At first tentatively and then with increasing confidence, it had embraced the vision of a free-trade agreement with the United
States. The prime minister had steadfastly stuck with it, even when political
wisdom seemed at times to make retreat a compelling option. Had it been
worthwhile? Was it a good agreement? Did it measure up to the goals and
objectives the government had set? Was it an agreement that could stand the
test of time? Had it been worth the political risk?

What no one could have predicted was that the agreement would be
superseded within five years by a more comprehensive agreement involving
not only Canada and the United States, but also Mexico and potentially
other countries. Within two years of its entry into force, Canadians were
once again debating the merits of free trade, this time focusing on its extension to Mexico.[2] Trilateral negotiations dominated the trade agenda in 1991
and 1992 and resulted in the replacement of the FTA by a new North
American Free Trade Agreement (NAFTA). While the policy intent of the
FTA and the NAFTA are identical, the NAFTA in effect subsumes the FTA
into a more modern trade agreement.[3] Additionally, before the NAFTA could

enter into force, Canadians had to absorb the impact of the successful conclusion of the drawn-out Uruguay Round of GATT negotiations. By the end of 1993, therefore, Canadians had witnessed an extraordinarily charged decade of trade negotiations. Divining the impact of these three agreements on the Canadian economy is no easy task, particularly since all three agreements aimed at long-term structural changes rather than immediate results.

Nevertheless, an assessment of the Canada-US negotiations and of the resulting agreement can and should be undertaken. This can be approached at two levels: in political terms and in terms of public policy. Much of the debate in Canada during the negotiations and immediately after took place at the political level. It involved competing views of the country, engaged different perceptions of the national interest, and concentrated on the process rather than on the substance of the negotiations. In the final analysis, political judgment is put to the test during an election. The return of the government in 1988 in effect vindicated its political judgment. Politically, the agreement marked a success.

A second level of analysis needs to focus on whether the agreement constitutes good public policy. The 1983-8 political debate obscured many of the issues at play in the negotiations and made it difficult to come to a sensible judgment about the agreement as public policy. As such, the agreement sought to ensure that Canada would prosper through more open trading conditions by removing barriers that retard growth and nurture inefficiency. It is based on one of the most established of economic concepts: that freer trade leads to prosperity while protection undermines it. The agreement thus sought to provide a better and improved bilateral framework of rules within which to pursue freer trade while maintaining Canada's ability to chart its path as a free and independent nation. As public policy, the agreement can be assessed in terms of the objectives sought and achieved, as well as in terms of the impact intended and realized.

Analysis at this level, of course, proceeds on the basis of a particular set of values and assumptions that may not be shared by all Canadians. From our perspective, we proceed on the basis that Canada is a relatively small power in a global political and economic system dominated by more powerful players. Canada is also critically dependent on the global economy for its continued prosperity and is vulnerable to capricious, power-based actions by others which may undermine the ability of Canadians to benefit from the international exchange of goods, services, capital, and technology.

These two facts of life translate into two sets of interrelated objectives that can be achieved through the negotiation of international agreements. The first is the economic objective of nurturing open, market-based, international economic exchanges, and the second the political objective of establishing rules, procedures, and institutions aimed at reducing the disparities in power among international actors. By achieving these two objectives, Canadian governments can assure Canadian-based firms and individuals that they can participate in the international economy with some certainty that their investments and efforts will be more than a gambler's throw. By competing internationally, at home and abroad, such firms and individuals steadily contribute to the prosperity of all Canadians.

In effect, therefore, our analysis proceeds from the assumptions that (1) trade is beneficial to growth, (2) politically unencumbered trade grows faster than managed trade, (3) trade governed by markets is more efficient in the aggregate sense than other, more interventionist regimes commonly employed, and (4) trade governed by rules is more likely to grow and benefit both parties than trade that is subject to discretionary political management.

Trade agreements are primarily about economics, commerce, and business. Their purpose is to make the world better off economically and they involve rules governing the movement of goods, services, technology, and capital between countries. Governments have engaged in such negotiations since time immemorial. They have found that in return for agreeing to do things in a certain way, their own citizens get treated much better and the world is much better off. Such agreements have proved particularly important to smaller countries dependent on trade with larger countries.

Any agreement, therefore, constrains the freedom of governments to act. Under the GATT, for example, to which Canada and the United States have been signatories since 1947, governments are not free to impose new duties or quotas or other barriers except in very limited circumstances. Under the International Energy Agreement, governments are committed to sharing their petroleum resources in time of world shortage. Under the North Atlantic Alliance, members are committed to go to war in defence of their allies. The UN Security Council can compel member states to impose sanctions. Each constrains the ability of governments to act arbitrarily and indifferently.

True freedom requires structure. Without a framework to define the rules, there are no rules. Without rules, there is anarchy. In international relations, anarchy becomes a matter of might makes right. Large powers convince smaller powers that consent is in their interest. In such a system there is no accountability and no responsibility. In reaching agreement, therefore, delicate compromises have to be reached between the freedom to act and a sensible framework of rules within which to act.[4]

Perfectionists and Protectionists
A credible assessment of any agreement must be made against real goals and

objectives and involve an analysis of the extent to which these objectives were compromised in reaching an agreement. The agreement was the result of two negotiating partners seeking to meet competing interests within a single document that satisfied the political and public policy requirements of both parties. To get there required compromises consistent with a realistic bottom line: it had to mark a significant improvement over the status quo, it had to make economic sense, and it had to leave the negotiating governments room for manoeuvre in sensitive political areas, such as, in Canada's case, culture and agriculture. The process by which the parties reached the agreement, of course, had some bearing on the outcome, but should not be exaggerated. In effect, the question of whether Canada was or was not out-negotiated by the United States can only be answered by looking at the results and evaluating the extent to which Canadian and US objectives were met.[5]

Good agreements require compromises. Such compromises, however, are largely among interests within a country. In the case of the Canada-US FTA, many were wholly within Canada or wholly within the United States, rather than between Canada and the United States. Every barrier removed by Canada was of benefit to both Canada and the United States and every barrier removed by the United States was similarly of benefit to both countries. Much of the debate about the virtues or deficiencies of the agreement thus reflected competing interests within Canada representing different views of the country. Such debate was healthy and necessary but threw little light on whether individual elements of the agreement were consistent with Canadian interests. It was directed more to the question of whether *any* bilateral trade agreement with the United States would serve Canadian interests.

Unfortunately, too many people have been taken in by the rhetoric of traditional mercantilist bargaining at GATT. For political, not economic, reasons, the GATT was conceived as a 'balance of concessions' and every new negotiation had to achieve a new balance. Thus every concession made (in terms of lowering one's own barriers) had to be matched by concessions gained (in terms of the reduction of foreign barriers). As a result, countries aggressively sought concessions and grudgingly paid for them. The most successful agreements were perceived to be those in which much was gained and little was paid. For smaller countries like Canada, the multilateral exchange of rights made it possible to gain much and pay little, because much of the payment came from bargaining among the major powers. Such victories, however, were political rather than economic. They maintained barriers that shielded inefficiency and prevented adjustment to a more productive and efficient economy. The Canadian economy was the long-term loser from this process of mercantilist bargaining.[6]

Alan King, *Ottawa Citizen*, 19 December 1987

Mercantilist score-keeping also reflects old-fashioned tariff negotiations; it is much more difficult to keep score when the main thrust of negotiations is rule making. Rules are mutually beneficial, even where one country is making the demands. In the FTA negotiations, Canada placed much greater emphasis on new rules to deal with trade remedies while the United States pursued new rules on investment. Neither got the kind of rules sought, but both would benefit from rules that increase certainty and reduce the ability of either government to act arbitrarily and unfairly.

A balanced assessment of the agreement needs also to consider concessions made to both Canadian and US goals and interests. An agreement that is more responsive to the interests and priorities of one side than the other will not be perceived as a balanced agreement and is not likely to stand the test of time. That kind of agreement would not have been in the interest of either country. Neither Canada nor the United States achieved all of its objectives. Compromise was necessary.

Score-keeping is further complicated by the very different negotiating strategies used by Canadians and Americans. The Canadian parliamentary system, in which all authority emanates from a single source, cabinet, lends itself to a coherent, first-principles approach. In the United States, where power is dispersed, checked, and balanced among a large number of political actors, an issue-by-issue approach is preferred. Canadian negotiators work from the top down, starting with general principles and translating these into specific negotiating objectives. US negotiators proceed from the bottom up, seeking to resolve individual irritants in order to build support among as many special interests as possible. In order to come to an intelligent assessment of the agreement as a whole, therefore, it is necessary to step back from the give and take of the negotiating process and focus on longer term objectives.

Objectives

Fortunately, Canadian interests and objectives in the free-trade negotiations were well publicized. There is a clearly marked public paper trail of five years or more spelling out what the government had in mind, what its private sector advisors suggested, what a royal commission recommended, what a parliamentary committee concluded, and what Canada and the United States thought jointly.

The general objectives of Canadian trade policy were summarized in the government's trade policy review of 1982-3. They are the more credible because they were set out in a policy document adopted by a previous government. These broad objectives of Canadian trade policy bear repeating: 'The development of a stronger, more efficient, productive, competitive, growing and non-inflationary domestic economy, the increased per capita wealth of which is shared by Canadians from all regions of the country; and the promotion of a more stable and open international trading environment within which competitive Canadian and foreign firms alike are encouraged to plan, invest and grow with confidence.'[7] Among the means suggested for attaining these objectives was the negotiation of sectoral agreements with the United States that would remove particular problems experienced in those sectors, such as government procurement restrictions or tariffs.

Two years later in *How to Secure and Enhance Canadian Access to Export Markets*, the new Conservative government, in stimulating debate about whether to move beyond the by then stalled sectoral initiative, indicated that any agreement with the United States would have to secure and enhance Canadian access by addressing specific barriers, including tariffs, non-tariff barriers, countervailing and anti-dumping duties, emergency measures, balance-of-payment restrictions, government procurement preferences, quantitative import restrictions, and other measures. As well, any agreement would need to include appropriate institutional provisions and a dispute settlement mechanism.[8]

Two months later, in the Quebec Trade Declaration, the prime minister and US president agreed that they 'wanted to establish a climate of greater predictability and confidence for Canadians and Americans alike to plan, invest, grow and compete more effectively with one another and in the global market.' This they would achieve by giving the 'highest priority to finding mutually acceptable means to reduce and eliminate existing barriers to trade in order to secure and facilitate trade and investment flows.'⁹

The Macdonald Commission, writing at about the same time, recommended that Canada negotiate a legal arrangement with the United States that would incorporate strong safeguards to protect culture and defence coupled with a more aggressive policy of support for indigenous cultural expression. Such a legal arrangement, it went on, should attempt to regulate three general types of barriers that restrict trade between the two countries:

• Tariffs should be phased down to zero over a period of ten years and provision made for effective rules of origin.
• Enforcement of measures of contingent protection (safeguards, dumping, and countervailing duties) should be shifted from national administrative tribunals to a new Canada-US intergovernmental body.
• Detailed codes of national conduct should be developed to govern resort to other non-tariff measures such as procurement practices, product standards and customs classification, and administrative procedures.¹⁰

A government discussion paper, prepared in the summer of 1985, suggested that free trade between Canada and the United States would always be less than what the economists have traditionally envisaged, but that it should mean more than the removal of tariff barriers. Additionally, in order to gain something of value, it concluded that Canada would have to give something of value. Canada would have to face hard choices and be prepared to make trade-offs. For the United States market, Canada's objectives would be to encourage a trade and investment climate that could contribute directly and positively to the creation of more and better employment opportunities. This would involve:

• security of access to that market particularly by reducing the risks inherent in the U.S. system of contingency protection;
• better access to world-class technology;
• unimpeded access to the U.S. market in order to provide Canadian industry with a sufficiently large market base to realize economies of scale and specialization and to carve out niches for specialty products; and
• a stable North American trading system which would induce a substantial but orderly adjustment in Canada towards a more competitive economy, providing an increased incentive for investment from all sources.¹¹

These were echoed a few months later in a report prepared for the prime minister by the minister for international trade, James Kelleher. A companion piece prepared for President Reagan by USTR Clayton Yeutter provided a clear public statement of US objectives:

From preliminary, informal discussions which my staff and I have held with representatives of the private sector and Members of Congress, I believe that a number of U.S. industries have an interest in expanding their access to a prosperous and proximate Canadian market. Canada takes nearly one-fifth of our total exports, and there exist significant barriers to U.S. exports of goods and services in a number of sectors. In particular, these include:

- high Canadian tariffs across a wide spectrum of products which act as major impediments to U.S. exports;
- non-tariff barriers at both the federal and provincial level which effectively preclude many U.S. exports from entering the Canadian market;
- obstacles to U.S. investment; and
- federal and provincial regulations which impede U.S. exports of services.

In addition, a great many U.S. industries and Members of Congress have expressed concern over a number of governmental assistance programs, both federal and provincial, which allegedly result in subsidized competition. I have been urged to obtain in any bilateral discussions agreement on procedures to limit the use of subsidies.[12]

All these statements represent unambiguous and conventional statements of the objectives of any major trade negotiation. Over the course of the negotiations, however, more ambitious goals and objectives came from two fronts: the vision, ambition, and drive of Canada's chief negotiator, Simon Reisman, and the rhetoric of politicians. Judged against the general objectives outlined above, there is no question that the agreement achieved most of Canada's objectives. Judged against the more ambitious objectives of Simon Reisman and against the government's rhetoric, the agreement may have fallen somewhat short. These latter two, however, must be placed in context.

The government chose Simon Reisman to conduct the negotiations because of his track record, tenacity, and sense of purpose. The choice was widely praised. He said he would be uncompromising and zealous in his approach. Canadians felt more comfortable with the negotiations knowing that they were in the hands of a man who was unlikely to take no for an answer, who would not have the wool pulled over his eyes, and who could teach the Americans a lesson or two.

What he brought to the negotiations was a vision of what the agreement should be and a principle around which to organize the negotiations, that being national treatment. He wanted an agreement that would, at the end of the day, establish rules that would end discrimination in the treatment of Canadian goods and services in the United States. For tariffs and other traditional restrictions applied at the border, it meant their removal; for government procurement, it meant a single standard for all transactions within Canada and the United States; for trade remedy law, it meant jointly administered codes of conduct and reliance on domestic procedures; for immigration, it meant free movement for business travellers; and for services and investment, it meant a code to end discrimination. Where Canadian interests were concerned, he pursued this vision with a dogged single-mindedness. Where US interests were concerned, he was prepared to go very far if Canadian interests

A proud and happy Simon Reisman leafs through the Free Trade Agreement at the press lock-up on 12 December 1987.

were met. There was never any ambiguity about what he wanted and was prepared to pay. That the Americans may have chosen not to believe him was another matter; his statements were unambiguous, at the table, and in public.[13]

As a means of organizing the preparation of position papers and for informing ministers, premiers, provincial officials, and private sector advisors, his single objective made matters simple and direct. Without it, the conduct of the negotiations would have been more defuse and Canada might have been driven to fallback positions much earlier. The result would have been a smaller and less effective agreement. A less determined man would not have been able to keep the negotiations on track for two years in the face of unrelenting opposition and American indifference.

The government's rhetoric during the conduct of negotiations is easily explained and revolves largely around the curious institution of question period. A new government made up of ministers more used to asking questions than answering them, had to stand up daily to answer hostile questions about its biggest public policy initiative and do so without compromising the conduct of the negotiations. Resort to hyperbole, subterfuge, and misdirection when the real answer was not available, too sensitive, or too complicated, at times proved counterproductive. With the help of a largely critical media, which fed the credibility problem daily, a much more experienced opposition had a relatively easy time exposing the cracks in the government's armour.

What the government did have was a sense of purpose and vision and a determination to stick it out. It gave Simon Reisman all the resources he required. It gave him a superb mandate and all the room he needed to manoeuvre. As the deadline for concluding negotiations loomed, on his own advice, the government decided to pull the plug. The decision was not a decision to pull back, but a recognition that the Americans had proved incapable of delivering an agreement sensitive to Canada's needs, both economic and political. In the end, such an agreement did prove negotiable in a dramatic series of events that no one had predicted and that involved a remarkable group of people on both sides of the table. While this final phase of the negotiations seemed to have an air of desperation about it, in fact it built on two years of preparations and another two years of negotiations. At suspension, the two sides were far apart on the main issues, but these differences were more tactical than real. Both sides knew what was required to bridge the gap and, once equipped with new, political-level negotiators, they quickly cut through the underbrush and agreed on the essential elements of a mutually beneficial deal. The careful translation of these elements into a legal text gave both sides the opportunity to make sure the agreement was consistent with their objectives.

Results

The agreement that finally emerged in December 1987 largely met the general objectives outlined above. As recommended by the Macdonald Commission, for example, Canada achieved a legal arrangement which eliminated all tariffs and some other barriers to trade over a period of ten years; codes of conduct were negotiated to deal with barriers that by their nature cannot be eliminated; and the pursuit of trade remedies was constrained by binational dispute settlement. The agreement left intact Canadian ability to pursue cultural policies, regional development, and farm marketing boards. The rules in the agreement were made enforceable through the establishment of joint institutions and a dispute settlement mechanism. As a result, access to the United States market was made more open and more secure and the Canada-US economic relationship placed on a stronger, mutually beneficial foundation. The agreement thus marked a major step forward from the status quo. It met the economic objective of providing an incentive to restructure and become more competitive, and the business objective of setting up a shield against the excesses of US protectionism.

The agreement built on fifty years or more of experience in Canada and around the world in cutting barriers to trade. In putting the agreement together, inspiration was sought from similar agreements reached across the Atlantic in Europe and across the Pacific between New Zealand and Australia. It was influenced by previous trade agreements between the

United States and Canada dating back to 1935, including the autopact and the defence production sharing arrangements. And it elaborated on the commitments of the two governments to each other under the GATT, the OECD, the International Energy Agreement, and more. The habit of cooperation between Canada and the United States was not new; the two countries share the longest and most open border in the world and there is more commerce between Ontario and the United States than between any two nations other than Canada and the United States. Compared to other free-trade agreements negotiated under GATT, the Canada-United States agreement was more comprehensive, covered more trade, and addressed more barriers than any previous agreement.

So much for the general. Looked at more specifically, there were objectives wholly achieved, some only partially achieved, and some not achieved at all. For both Canada and the United States, the gradual elimination of the tariff on all products was a major, if conventional, objective. That was achieved, with the pace of elimination largely based on the views of affected industries. The general rule was ten years; immediate and five-year elimination was based on the affected industries agreeing to faster elimination. The Macdonald Commission and others had suggested that since the burden of adjustment would fall heavier on Canada, the US tariff should be eliminated immediately and the Canadian tariff over ten years. That proved neither negotiable nor necessary from the point of view of many Canadian industries that were prepared to meet full competition immediately.

The rules of origin in the agreement did not fully meet Canadian expectations and must be viewed as an objective only partially met. Canada wanted rules that would be simple to understand and administer and that would allow Canadian companies to source inputs from all over the world and still meet the rules. The United States insisted on much tighter and more complicated rules involving not only a change in tariff heading, but in many cases also 50 per cent value added. It took some time for Canadian industry to become fully familiar with these rules; they imposed an administrative burden that could have been avoided; and they resulted in more trade deflection than would have occurred under less stringent rules. Nevertheless, it was a price worth paying for an agreement that met many of Canada's objectives. Similar rules have been incorporated into the NAFTA, but with important improvements and safeguards. More fundamentally, however, as tariffs are reduced and eliminated on an MFN basis, the need for such rules will gradually wither away.[14]

Related to the tariff and rules of origin were the revised rules covering trade in automotive products. Settlement of auto issues was needlessly complicated by the emotional attachment of the CAW and the NDP to the letter of the autopact, an agreement both had criticized only five years earlier when the balance of trade was in the US favour, and by the US political desire to phase out the Canadian safeguards. Reisman's own attachment to the autopact did not simplify matters. The final package represented a pragmatic compromise. Canada retained the safeguards, which continue to have some bearing on the ability of autopact producers to import offshore imports on a duty-free basis, and phased out various duty remission programs, while the United States introduced a new and more stringent rule of origin for non-autopact imports from Canada. As free-trade policy, the package represented a retrograde step. But for those who believe in industrial policy and managed trade, it retains the essential features of the autopact and extends them to trade not previously covered by the pact.

A much better compromise was achieved on energy. Canada had long sought secure access for its energy products (oil, gas, uranium, and electricity) to the United States. The United States had long sought assurances that Canada would be a reliable supplier and not cut supplies arbitrarily. The agreement enshrined commitments that met both objectives. That was a victory for free trade and a defeat for nationalism and xenophobia. There is, however, no obligation on either party to buy or sell any energy commodity. The agreement requires no more than the commitment that when an energy commodity is traded, neither government can arbitrarily cut off either access to its market or the supply of available energy; in times of short supply, the producing country agrees to make a proportion of its supply available for export at prevailing prices on the basis of the historical level of exports.

Canada also sought to enhance security of access by limiting the ability of US producers to invoke US escape clause (safeguard) procedures when imports from Canada increase too rapidly or reach intolerable levels. This was achieved. Under the terms of the agreement, no Canadian industry would ever again see its shipments reduced as a result of a safeguard action. Canadian exporters to the US could for a temporary period of ten years have faced a return to the MFN tariff (not much of a burden for most Canadian industries) or, when the US imposed restrictions on imports from all sources and if they were a major participant in the US market, have had growth in their shipments held for a limited period to the trend line of the previous few years. Again, this chapter represented a major step in the right direction.

The government procurement chapter was a disappointment and must at best be seen as an objective partially achieved. For years, Canadian manufacturers of steel and transportation, power generating, and telecommunications equipment had seen their access to the large US government market virtually blocked by discriminatory procurement laws. That situation was only marginally improved and remains as part of the unfinished business in Canada-US trade. Rules governing procurement were improved and a commitment reached on future negotiations, but the amount of trade actually covered by the rules remains small.

The provisions on agriculture and wine and distilled spirits were a mixed blessing. For too long, agriculture had been treated differently from other products in international trade and the problems had multiplied. Most other free-trade agreements completely exempted agriculture. The Canada-US agreement at least did include trade in agricultural products, in itself a major achievement. Tariffs were eliminated and other non-tariff barriers ameliorated through tighter rules. It cannot be said, however, that these chapters were at odds with Canadian objectives. Neither Canada nor the United States was prepared to move to true free trade in these products, although their views on the instruments used to protect farm income and regulate imports may have differed. Canada wanted to leave its marketing boards and supply management programs intact. This was agreed. The United States was not prepared to do anything about its restrictive marketing orders, import quotas under its 1933 Agriculture Adjustment Act, or extensive farm subsidies, and nothing was done. Canada was reluctant to do anything about its discriminatory beer brewing and marketing practices and agreed to live with the result of any GATT findings. These chapters, therefore, marked a victory for pragmatic politics if not for free trade, and left the real issues for resolution later, either through multilateral or bilateral negotiations or as a result of dispute settlement proceedings.

The result on trade remedies can be described as a qualified success. Canada was prepared to enter into far-reaching commitments that would have put the rules covering so-called unfair trade on a much more equitable and predictable footing. This objective proved too rich for the United States, at least in 1987. The door, however, was left open to further discussions. In the meantime, Canada agreed to live with a halfway house of special dispute settlement provisions that could be invoked to challenge both changes in the law and the application of existing law. Both aspects promised to go some way towards meeting Canada's desire for greater predictability and security, but not all the way. Again, the vexing problem of trade remedies was left as part of the unfinished agenda, but with the hope that experience with dispute settlement would create a better climate for future negotiations.

Real security, of course, could only have been achieved if Canadians were to have become immune from the application of American trade law. That may never be achieved. These are laws sanctioned by GATT and widely used in Canada, the United States, and elsewhere in the world to respond to perceived unfair trade practices. In the negotiations, Canada never sought exemption from US trade laws. What it sought was some means of controlling or influencing their interpretation and application. It sought to end unilateralism and the ease with which the US Congress could change the rules if it did not like the way they were applied. On that agenda, Canada made some progress and can expect to make more progress in future negotiations. If Canada wants to obtain significant improvements, however, it will have to be prepared to pay the price, and that price might include very stringent controls on its ability to use subsidies as a tool for regional and industrial development. That was a price Canada was not prepared to pay in 1987 and might have equal difficulty paying at some point in the future.[15]

Related to trade remedies was Canada's desire for binding dispute settlement. Much was made during the negotiations of this objective. Subsequent criticism rightly pointed out that the Canadian government did not achieve this objective except as regards safeguards. But perhaps too much was made of this point. At the beginning of the negotiations, some proponents argued that all that was needed was a dispute settlement mechanism. The negotiators responded that dispute settlement in the absence of rules was of little use, akin to a vehicle without an engine to move it. Canada's objective, therefore, was to establish good, substantive rules with sound institutional provisions to manage the agreement and to settle disputes. In this context, Canada sought recognition that the findings of a dispute settlement panel would be · final and determinative unless the two governments jointly agreed otherwise. Indeed, Canada would have been very pleased if it had achieved one small change in the dispute settlement text. As finally agreed, either country remains free to accept or reject a panel finding and to take retaliatory action, even should a panel find it in the wrong. In Canada's view, retaliatory action is only appropriate where a panel vindicates a complaint, but the other party refuses to change its policy or make amends. Acceptance of this point would have satisfied concerns about 'bindingness.'

Despite this shortcoming, the institutional provisions, in general, constituted a very important step in the right direction. For the smaller partner, more heavily dependent on bilateral trade than the United States, however, Canada would have benefited from even stronger and more independent institutions. That was not the official view on both sides of the border. Both governments were content with as little permanent apparatus as possible and preferred that the principal institution be a commission jointly chaired by the minister for international trade and the United States trade representative. The establishment of a small secretariat to act as a post office for requests for panels to review anti-dumping or countervailing duty findings was a last-minute addition.

Finally, the chapter on business travel was a major advance and went a long way towards solving what had become a vexatious problem. While not a traditional part of trade negotiations, the fact that Canada and the United States are neighbours, share a border some five thousand miles long, and enjoy very close business ties had made US immigration rules an increasingly irksome non-tariff barrier. As a result of the agreement, harassment of legitimate business travellers could now become a problem of the past and ease achievement of some of the other objectives of the agreement.

Derek Burney looks on as the prime minister signs the American copy of the Free Trade Agreement. (Ottawa, 22 December 1987)

On balance, therefore, both in general and specific terms, Canadian free-trade proponents could claim that their objectives as regarded enhanced and secure access to the United States market were either wholly or partly met. For two of those only partly met – government procurement and trade remedies – work programs were established to continue the negotiations with a view to meeting the objectives in the long run.

And what of US goals and Canada's defensive objectives? The United States achieved most of its traditional trade policy objectives, including the elimination of the tariff and other barriers at the border, as well as the development or improvement of codes of conduct for a range of non-tariff barriers. It gained much better rules on export restrictions, a long-standing US objective of particular significance for trade in energy. During the Tokyo Round, under a Liberal government, Canada had been prepared to meet US requests for more secure access to resources in return for open and secure access to its market for such resources and their downstream products. The FTA honoured that pledge. The United States also made major progress on new issues, with the agreement on financial services being the most significant achievement in terms of its domestic economic interests.

The chapters on services and investment met some US objectives but not all. The United States pursued these issues both in their own right and for their demonstration effect for multilateral trade negotiations. The second objective was wholly met while the first only partially. In the case of services, the problem lay largely in the United States. US services trade objectives at the beginning of the negotiations far outran what the United States was prepared to do itself. Once it became clear to US negotiators that any commitments would have to be reciprocal, a much less ambitious chapter became their goal. The result was a cautious but important beginning as it brought the principles of non-discrimination to an area of economic activity that, while not burdened with barriers such as those that fettered trade in goods fifty years ago, had remained largely outside the bounds of international rules. The agreement stated that the two governments would treat providers of a specific list of services on an equivalent basis. This commitment was prospective. It left intact all existing rules and regulations. Only new rules and regulations were affected. Room was left, however, to improve the coverage of the chapter later. The only major disappointment for Canada involved air transportation. A more open and equitable air transportation system would have been a major achievement for Canada. In the end, however, pressure from the US maritime lobby as well as the aviation industry removed all transportation from the agreement. Again, this was a triumph for protectionism and xenophobia, not for rational economic policy.

The investment chapter was a similar mixed blessing for the United States. The goal was very ambitious if not wholly appropriate to the Canada-US relationship. The United States sought unfettered access for its investors to the Canadian market, along the lines of its bilateral investment agreements with developing countries. It did not get it. The investment chapter is a lot less ambitious. American investors achieved more predictability, but access is not unfettered. Major takeovers, covering about two-thirds of all corporate assets in Canada other than financial institutions, would continue to be subject to review. Sectors that were barred to foreign ownership or required review – particularly transportation, energy, and communications – would continue to be treated this way. Once established in Canada, US firms became entitled to national treatment. Any controls that any future government might wish to impose on investment practices would have to be applied to both Canadian and American investors. Like everything in the agreement, this is a reciprocal commitment. Canadian investors in the United States – Canadians have invested more per capita in the United States than vice versa – would benefit from the same clear framework of rules.

There were some important US objectives that were not achieved at all. The United States had sought a major chapter that would significantly improve the protection of US intellectual property in Canada and establish a general body of rules that could act as a starting point in developing a multilateral code of conduct for the protection of intellectual property rights. No such chapter was agreed upon. In the end, the United States was not prepared to compromise on its demand that Canada dismantle compulsory licensing of pharmaceuticals. Canada was similarly not prepared to give in to the United States on this issue and insisted that the price of any chapter was US willingness to give up its section 337 proceedings for Canadian products. This the United States was not prepared to do. As a result, the whole chapter disappeared. Canada was not unhappy to see the end of the intellectual property chapter. Stronger protection of intellectual property was not a high priority, although the government would have been prepared to live with it in return for greater and more secure access to advanced technology, another concession the United States found difficult.

A second high priority for the Americans was much greater discipline on Canadian subsidy practices, a concern somewhat overstated due to an exaggerated notion of the extent of subsidies in the Canadian economy. Nevertheless, it was a concern Canada was prepared to address as part of a package dealing with trade remedies. For Canada, the goal was to develop a code of conduct that would delineate acceptable and unacceptable practices. Having developed such a code, Canada was prepared to phase out all programs that fell afoul of the code and let bilateral panels determine any future breaches of the code. Such a code would have obviated the need for countervailing duties.

The Americans were eager to develop such a code if it would outlaw programs in Canada that they found offensive or that had run afoul of US countervail law. They were less zealous about applying such a code to US practices and unprepared to accept that certain practices would not be countervailable.

In consideration of a possible subsidy code, there was much discussion of regional development programs. Canada took the view that certain types of programs could be proscribed, but that it could not live with an agreement that seriously compromised the government's ability to promote regional development. Additionally, Canada wanted to safeguard research and development programs and reach clear rules on resource pricing. As a quid pro quo, it was prepared to accommodate US interests in safeguarding defence spending.

Since the Americans had countervailed some regional development and research and development programs, as well as resource pricing practices, Canada wanted a better regime. Little would have been gained, however, if such rules had outlawed all programs aimed at promoting regional development or research and development. Canadian governments do not need a new regime to do that. They can do that unilaterally. What Canada wanted was clear rules establishing which kinds of programs would be susceptible to US countervail procedures and which would not. Governments could then pursue regional development or research and development on a much more secure basis.[16]

Social and similar universal programs were never at issue. Universal programs aimed at people rather than regions, sectors, or firms had never been the subject of US countervail. While there had been dark mutterings by US industrialists and even some legislators about the unfairness of such programs, these were about as serious as the anxieties of Canadians that they would be sacrificed on the altar of free trade. The US political process may encourage such statements, but they are rarely taken seriously. The agreement ensured that they would never be taken seriously. By freezing US law, which includes the requirement that countervail can only apply to programs that are specific, the possibility of a countervail complaint involving, for example, health care or unemployment insurance, became even more remote. It would require an amendment in US law that would be at odds with the agreement. The equilibriating effect of the exchange rate is also not well understood by those who claimed that once the agreement took effect there would be efforts to reduce the cost of such universal programs. Should costs in the Canadian economy be far out of line with costs in the US economy, this would eventually be reflected in the exchange rate, thus neutralizing any advantage or disadvantage.

Finally, the United States entered the negotiations with a long list of irritants in the cultural sector. In its view, a good agreement would have resolved these issues. In the end, the agreement resolved very few of them. The two sides agreed that activities of the cultural industries (film, video, audio, broadcasting, and publishing) would be exempt from the provisions of the agreement, but should any action by one side harm the other, the other could seek consultation and take offsetting action under the dispute settlement provisions. Canada remained free to do as it pleased, but in the knowledge that the United States could claim that a particular program or policy harmed its interests and that it had a right to seek to balance the matter. This marked a distinct improvement over the status quo which had seen various cultural issues sour Canada-US relations in the absence of procedures for resolving them. The border broadcasting issue, for example, festered for years because there was no domestic basis for the US government to declare the issue closed as a result of an international settlement, as existed in the case of anti-dumping and countervailing duty procedures. The article establishing the cultural exemption provided a basis for closing off domestic complaints.

In general terms, therefore, the balance of advantage in the agreement probably lay with Canada. In pure economic terms, Canada was the principal beneficiary. By gaining open and secure access to a market more than ten times as large, Canadian industry could restructure and become more competitive and productive. In terms of objectives gained or partially gained, Canada did better than the United States. This is not to suggest that the United States lost in the negotiations. Rather, both countries gained, but Canada probably gained a little more. Canada also had more to lose. It would need to invest more in adjustment and restructuring. If those investments were not made, Canada would not be able to realize the benefits offered by the agreement. Overall, therefore, the agreement can be judged to be balanced and mutually advantageous.

Impact

The agreement came into effect on 1 January 1989. On that day about a third of the remaining tariffs on trade between Canada and the United States were reduced to zero, while other tariffs were reduced in their first scheduled step towards elimination. Government procurement thresholds came down, business travel became easier, and governments on both sides of the border became subject to a variety of new constraints on their regulation of economic behaviour. For firms on both sides of the border, these changes were important but not dramatic. Many had already begun to make adjustments to the new, more open and more competitive conditions; others calculated that they could delay adjustment until later in the implementation of the agreement. Over time, however, firms on both sides of the border, but particularly in Canada, had to take account of the changes and make appropriate modifications. Similarly, governments had to take account of the rights and obligations of the agreement in their approach to the regulation of economic activity and the management of bilateral relations.

How much difference has the agreement made in changing business and government behaviour? Outside of the political arena, few would be prepared to make any precise claims. When Canada set out to negotiate the agreement, it sought three basic objectives. The most important was to affect domestic economic reform by eliminating, at least for trade with the United States, the last vestiges of the National Policy and to constrain the more subtle new instruments of protection. By exposing the Canadian economy to greater international competition, while simultaneously improving access to the large market to the south, Canadian firms would be given an incentive to restructure and modernize and become more efficient and productive. The second was to create a bulwark against US protectionism. By gaining more secure and open access to the large, contiguous US market, Canadian business could plan and grow with greater confidence. Finally, the agreement would provide an improved and more modern basis for managing the Canada-US relationship. New and enforceable rules, combined with more sophisticated institutional machinery, would place the relationship on a predictable and less confrontational footing.

The FTA largely achieved these objectives. Nevertheless, it has been a disappointment to many Canadians in that nothing dramatic has happened in the first few years. The achievement of free trade proved to be remarkably dull. There is understandable disappointment that five years of thrilling debate turned out to be a prelude to routine. Some Canadians appear to be waiting for Promethean signs of splendour. They may be looking for the wrong things. Bombarded with the inanities of political debate and the sensationalism of the front page, they may have become too conditioned to the allure of statistics and immediate results.

Free trade is too complex a policy to produce significant gains immediately, especially when tariff cuts are to be phased in over ten years. There are simply too many other variables at play. Monetary and fiscal policies – real or anticipated – have, for example, had a much larger impact on business decisions over the past few years than the FTA, in some instances wiping out its influence, in other cases reinforcing it. Similarly, changes in the technology and organization of production have led to a much more integrated and more competitive global economy, again producing larger impacts than the FTA.

Trade policy seeks to directly influence the extent and nature of a country's foreign trade and indirectly affect a country's economic development. Generally speaking, minor changes in the deployment of trade policy instruments will lead to minor changes in exports or imports or industrial activity, while major changes encourage conditions which can lead to more substantial changes. Over the years, most changes have been incremental, despite claims to the contrary. The ability of the FTA to effect major changes was and continues to be exaggerated, both by its defenders and detractors.

At the beginning, the FTA's impact was more psychological than real. Gradually, however, fundamental changes began to take place. The result is a country that is painfully rejecting its past attachment to the false comfort of protectionism. Convinced by the success of the resource sector that Canadians were international traders, few appreciated how few companies and how limited a range of products were traditionally involved in exporting.[17] The National Policy succeeded in establishing an uncompetitive manufacturing sector in central Canada. Forty years of chipping away at that policy under GATT had some impact, but not enough. The 1981-2 recession showed that more needed to be done. The FTA succeeded in getting that more fundamental process started. The 1991-3 recession accelerated the process.[18]

Canadian business is thus reacting steadily to the challenge to adjust to the demands of global competition. More and more Canadian companies are developing international strategies comprising not only exports, but also joint ventures, licensing arrangements, investment packages, mergers, and distribution networks. The free-trade debate alerted many companies to the changing realities of international business and the FTA gave them the incentive to get started or move faster. They are proceeding to take advantage of the latest technologies; to develop markets beyond their traditional territories; to source inputs from all over the world; and to enter into joint ventures and other cooperative arrangements with partners in far-flung places. These strategies all assume more competition at home and abroad.

Successful companies have concluded that strategies based on protection are recipes for short-term gain and long-term pain. Open borders and free competition, on the other hand, are a recipe that involves short-term pain for long-term gain. Such a change in attitude is hard to capture with numbers. The results may take a few years. The first steps may hurt, requiring the closing of antiquated plants and uncompetitive product lines. But from such painful decisions will emerge companies able to take on the world, not just in Canada but also in the United States, Latin America, the Pacific, and Europe. These are the companies that will provide the good jobs of the future. The ones that close are those that supplied the jobs of the past.[19]

That progress has been slow, however, should not be surprising. The GATT experience was similar. It is almost conventional wisdom now that the stability and trade liberalization fostered by GATT were major factors in underwriting the spectacular growth in trade and production over GATT's first twenty-five years. This rosy assessment was not evident in Canada in the first few years. The aborted 1947-8 free-trade negotiations with the United States were an indication of a government having trouble adjusting to the new policy framework that it had itself helped to promote. For the next ten years, Canadian participation in GATT was one long litany of complaints.[20] Not until the 1960s did the payoff become clear.

In one respect – in dispute settlement – the impact of the agreement has been clearly beneficial. Both Canada and the United States have been able to use the procedures of chapters eighteen (general dispute settlement) and nineteen (panel procedures for anti-dumping and countervailing duties cases) to resolve a number of tricky irritants and prevent others from getting out of hand. The temperature in cross-border economic relations is significantly lower than it was in the years before the FTA, thanks largely to the highly professional approach of the two governments to the management and resolution of actual or potential disputes. While it would be desirable not to have any disputes at all, such an expectation is not realistic. In a trade and investment relationship within which more than $300 billion in goods and services is exchanged annually and billions more are invested in each other's markets, it would be naïve to expect an absence of conflict. Rather, one should consider whether disputes that do arise are handled quickly, equitably, and satisfactorily.

The early warning afforded by the formal requirement to notify and consult has avoided potentially nasty issues from boiling over into full-scale disputes. A number of issues have proven complex enough to require panel proceedings which have succeeded in helping the two governments resolve difficult issues ranging from restrictions on the export of Canadian salmon and herring to US interpretations of the rules of origin in automotive trade. In a number of cases since the implementation of the FTA, either Canada or the United States or both determined that the issues involved in a dispute were better addressed within the broader context of the GATT.

Of interest here are not the details of individual cases, some of which were resolved in Canada's favour, some in the US's favour, some on the basis of a mutually acceptable compromise, and some remain to be resolved. Rather, it is the absence of the deeply controverted rancour that marked trade relations between the two countries in the first half of the 1980s. The system is working to address and resolve problems on the basis of clear rules and procedures and it is keeping the temperature down.

A lower temperature is even more evident in the area of trade remedies (anti-dumping and countervailing duties and safeguards). By the end of 1993, some forty-six panels had been established to consider a range of appeals, involving both US and Canadian cases on a wide range of products. In most cases, panels composed of US and Canadian lawyers and trade experts ruled on whether US or Canadian laws had been properly applied. In some cases, they determined that they had been; in others, they remanded the cases back to the original tribunals for reconsideration. In such cases, panels interpreted the law differently than the original tribunals and ordered the International Trade Commission and the Department of Commerce in the United States, or the Department of National Revenue or the Canadian International Trade Tribunal in Canada to change their methods. In a number of cases, the results were significantly different, even lifting the penalty that had been imposed. These cases succeeded in establishing the authority of the panel procedure and placed national decision-makers on notice that panels expect a very high standard to be pursued in the application of US and Canadian laws. They have achieved these results more quickly than would have been possible in domestic courts and they have impressed legal observers on both sides of the border with the thoroughness and quality of their reviews. Noted US trade lawyer Gary Horlick: 'Based on the panels' track record, Canadian companies are getting a fair, impartial hearing. The FTA panels are off to a good start. They are doing exactly what they were intended to do in a speedy, impartial manner. In short, they are living up to their advance billing.'[21]

The US system of government encourages private sector groups to pursue their interests vigorously and to convince the US government to champion their concerns. US procedures make such efforts very transparent, requiring Canadian private interests as well as governments to plead their cases before US administrative tribunals, often at considerable expense. The result at times is a noisy and fractious debate. What counts, however, is not the process but the outcome. Efforts by Canada over the past few years have proven the value of clear rules and objective decision-making and the danger of power-based dispute settlement. Whenever there has been scope for the United States government to exercise discretion, it has exercised that discretion in favour of domestic interests at the expense of Canadian interests, even where the case was weak and where doing so would undermine confidence in international rulemaking. Objective panels, however, have consistently overturned these decisions. While the immediate cost may appear high, the end result is the highly prized objective of gradually strengthening the rule of law and enhancing stability and predictability.

From a Canada-US FTA to a North American FTA

The most telling vote of confidence in the FTA, however, did not come from Canada, but from Mexico. Within two years of the conclusion of the FTA, Mexican officials began to make cautious soundings in Washington and Ottawa to determine the extent to which the US and Canadian governments were prepared to extend the same rules and obligations to Mexico. By June of 1991, the US administration was prepared to enter into negotiations to test Mexican resolve, and by the following February the three countries had agreed that they would try to negotiate a trilateral agreement.

Over the course of the following eighteen months, while the primary focus of negotiations was the extension of the FTA regime to Mexico, Canada and the United States agreed that they would apply the lessons learned in three years of living with the FTA to make improvements. The result is an agreement that in all respects continues the policy regime ushered in by the FTA, but one that significantly improves upon it. The rules are more precise, the coverage more extensive, and the procedures more transparent. As well, by successfully extending these rules to a developing country in an agreement that includes an explicit commitment to welcome other countries prepared to live with its rules, the NAFTA clearly establishes that it is forward-looking and open-ended. The story of the negotiations and the details of the NAFTA are sufficiently complex and interesting to warrant a study of their own. What is important for our purposes is that the NAFTA demonstrates the extent to which the FTA was, and the NAFTA is, the foundation of a dynamic regime dedicated to ensuring a more open and outward-looking economy.[22]

A New Beginning

With the conclusion of the FTA, Canadian trade policy finally achieved one of its longest standing and most enduring objectives. From pre-Confederation days, the quest for free trade with the United States has been a dominant theme in Canadian history. The practical details of that quest may have changed over the years, reflecting the changing nature of the Canadian economy, the increasing sophistication of international economic transactions, and the vagaries of Canada-US economic relations, but the basic objective has always been the same: free and secure access to the giant market to the south.

The FTA achieved that objective by removing almost all barriers to trade in goods and many obstacles to trade in services, investment, and business travel, and providing a code of conduct for the two governments to follow in their regulation of private firm behaviour and their pursuit of their own economic policies. In many ways it changed the relationship between government and society in North America, particularly in Canada, and stimulated market-based adjustment to the economic challenges of the next century.

At the same time, the FTA also put paid to a second, contradictory theme in Canadian economic history. While Canadians may long have sought free access to the US market, particularly for resource-based products, they have also wanted to protect the less competitive sectors of the economy from foreign competition, secure in the knowledge that the wealth generated by our resources would absorb the costs that came from sheltering the weaker sectors of the economy. In the more integrated and competitive global economy of the 1980s, such a strategy was no longer judged to be tenable.

The agreement thus stood at a divide in Canadian economic history. It recognized the end of an era during which Canada could sell its surplus of resource and agricultural products on world markets while protecting its manufacturing and services sector from too much competition. It appreciated that the economic structures and trading conditions that underpinned our development as the second most prosperous economy in the world have given way to a much more open global economy in which every economic activity must be prepared to take on global competitors at home and abroad. As a relatively small but active participant in the global economy, Canada has learned that in a world of much larger economic powers, its ability to compete is critically dependent on rules that reduce disparities in power between large and small countries. The FTA provided such a set of rules, and did so on a basis that allowed Canada to continue to develop as a strong and viable independent nation. In short, despite the problems posed by an often indifferent and difficult United States, Canada succeeded in negotiating a good agreement.

NOTES

Preface
1 The course was co-taught with Brian Tomlin of the Norman Paterson School of International Affairs and Bruce Doern of the School of Public Administration. It offered an ideal setting in which to think issues through and subject them to discussion and challenge. For Doern and Tomlin, the course provided the essential raw material for their own book on the negotiations, *Faith and Fear: The Free Trade Story* (Toronto: Stoddart 1991). Theirs is a different treatment than ours, based on extensive interviews with many of the principles and broader coverage of the issues. The two books, however, are complementary; the differences are those of coverage and judgment rather than detail. The notes below suggest where we differ significantly from their analysis and conclusions.

Chapter 1: The Fork in the Road
1 The authors attended the debate at Ryerson on 19 September 1985 and many others like it across the country. They would not, however, wish the reader to think that their report on the debate captures in detail the views expressed that evening. Rather, they have used that evening to dramatize the two opposing views held by Lipsey and Crane (and views of others who favour or oppose free trade with the United States) which, on the whole, corresponded with the main political and economic arguments for and against a Canada-United States bilateral trade agreement presented during the early phases of public discussion. Many of these were in fact made by either Lipsey or Crane during the course of the evening, but we have taken some liberties in presenting and organizing the arguments, relying as much on their writings for and against the idea of a bilateral trade agreement as on what the two protagonists actually said that night.
2 (Toronto: C.D. Howe Institute 1985). Shorter versions of the Lipsey argument can be found in 'The Economics of a Canadian-American Free-Trade Association,' in Michael D. Henderson, ed., *The Future on the Table: Canada and the Free Trade Issue* (North York, ON: Masterpress 1987) and 'Canada's Trade Options,' in A.R. Riggs and Tom Velk, eds., *Canadian-American Free Trade: Historical, Political and Economic Dimensions* (Montreal: Institute for Research on Public Policy 1987). Lipsey has continued to write on the issue and has become one of the most articulate defenders of a policy of steady trade liberalization by whatever means are likely to benefit the Canadian economy. He has passionately defended the FTA to audiences around the world. He was a strong advocate of Canadian participation in the NAFTA negotiations and has written about the benefits and drawbacks of expanding the NAFTA beyond North America. He has equally advocated Canadian participation in multilateral trade negotiations.
3 'Free-trade: salvation or sell-out?' *Toronto Star*, 8-12 June 1985; and 'Canada's threatened identity,' *Toronto Star*, 2-5 August 1986. Over the course of the subsequent seven years, Crane continued to be one of the most articulate and reasoned opponents of bilateral free trade, staunchly defending his deep conviction that Canada should liberalize its economy, but multilaterally in concert with others and at a slower pace, rather than bilaterally or trilaterally and at the expense of opening up fragile sectors of the economy to foreign competition. At the conclusion of the Uruguay Round of GATT negotiations, for example, he wrote a series of articles setting out why Canada should have waited because the GATT negotiations provided Canada with what it needed without having to pay for it to the same extent as required under the bilateral negotiations. He continued to see GATT multilateral trade negotiations and bilateral trade negotiations with the United States as competing alternatives rather than as complementary strategies to reach the same objectives. See 'GATT far better for Canada than US free trade deal,' and 'Trail of broken promises,' *Toronto Star*, 18 December 1993 and 1 January 1994.

4   They were finally launched at Punta del Este, Uruguay, in September 1986 and concluded in Marrakesh, Morocco, in April 1994.

Chapter 2: Policy Origins

1   See particularly volume three, Senate Standing Committee on Foreign Affairs, *Canada's Trade Relations with the United States* (Ottawa: Supply and Services 1982).
2   Economic Council of Canada, *Looking Outward* (Ottawa: Queen's Printer 1975).
3   Among the most important contributors to this work in Canada were John Young, *Canadian Commercial Policy* (Ottawa: Queen's Printer 1957); Ronald and Paul Wonnacott, *Free Trade between the United States and Canada: The Potential Economic Effects* (Cambridge, MA: Harvard University Press 1967); Ronald A. Shearer, John H. Young, and Gordon R. Munro, *Trade Liberalization and a Regional Economy: Studies of the Impact of Free Trade on British Columbia* (Toronto: University of Toronto Press for the Private Planning Association 1971); James R. Williams, *The Canadian-United States Tariff and Canadian Industry: A Multisectoral Analysis* (Toronto: University of Toronto Press 1978); Roma Dauphin, *The Impact of Free Trade in Canada* (Ottawa: Supply and Services 1978); and Richard G. Harris and David Cox, *Trade, Industrial Policy and Canadian Manufacturing* (Toronto: Ontario Economic Council 1983).
4   John Young, *Canadian Commercial Policy*, 160.
5   Mitchell Sharp, *Canada-U.S. Relations: Options for the Future*, special issue of *International Perspectives* (Ottawa: Department of External Affairs 1972). Sharp's position has not changed. See, for example, his testimony before the Standing Committee on External Affairs on 3 November 1987, or his exchanges with Anthony Westell in the pages of *International Perspectives* in 1985. See Mitchell Sharp, 'Sharp on Westell,' *International Perspectives* (January/February 1985): 3-4 and Westell's reply in *International Perspectives* (May/June 1985):32. See also Mitchell Sharp, 'Canada's Independence and U.S. Domination,' in Edward R. Fried and Philip H. Trezise, eds., *U.S.-Canadian Economic Relations: Next Steps?* (Washington, DC: Brookings Institution 1984), 11-20.
6   Canadian Chamber of Commerce press release, April 1985, in the files of the Chamber of Commerce.
7   Department of External Affairs, *A Review of Canadian Trade Policy* and *Canadian Trade Policy for the 1980s: A Discussion Paper* (Ottawa: Supply and Services 1983).
8   While Burney provided overall management and direction, he appointed Michael Hart to coordinate the interdepartmental research, analysis, and consultations and to take charge of preparing the background documents.
9   Toronto *Globe and Mail*, 26 March 1983.
10   See Lyndon Watkins, 'Lumley seeks trade pacts with U.S.' Toronto *Globe and Mail*, 19 October 1982, B1.
11   The minister's personal views can be found, for example, in testimony he presented to a parliamentary committee four years later and reproduced in Earle Gray, ed., *Free Trade Free Canada* (Woodville, ON: Canadian Speeches 1988).
12   The continuing dominance of the third option in official thinking is well illustrated by an article prepared by Allan Gotlieb and Jeremy Kinsman, 'Reviving the Third Option,' *International Perspectives* (January/February 1981):2-5. At the time, Gotlieb was undersecretary at External Affairs and Kinsmen was head of the policy planning unit.
13   For a veteran journalist's jaundiced view of the relationship between the ministry and the bureaucracy, see Dave McIntosh, *Ottawa Unbuttoned: Or Who's Running This Country Anyway* (Toronto: Stoddart 1987).
14   The minister remained true to his convictions. He believed in free trade. Two years later, in an article for the *Ottawa Citizen*, he bucked the politics of his party and wrote a strong endorsement of the newly released trade agreement. Several months later he told a parliamentary committee: 'When I was minister of trade in Mr. Trudeau's government, I recognized the importance of obtaining better guarantees of access to the vital American market to which we send

the lion's share of our exports. I sought to move in that direction by initiating free trade talks with the United States on a sector-by-sector basis. The defeat of the Liberals ended that effort, but I have come to the conclusion that the present free trade project is a more meaningful, more courageous, and an important undertaking – more important than our limited negotiations.' Quoted by Earle Gray, *Free Trade Free Canada*, 81. In 1988, upon the appointment of Donald Macdonald as high commissioner to the UK, he became co-chair of the Alliance for Trade and Job Opportunities, the pro-free-trade business lobby group.

15 *Ottawa Citizen*, Toronto *Globe and Mail*, and *Toronto Star* of 1 September 1983; Halifax *Chronicle-Herald* of 2 September and *Winnipeg Free Press* of 10 September 1983.

16 7 September 1983.

17 Quoted by Hyman Solomon, *Financial Post*, 22 October 1983.

18 As explained in the previous chapter, Canada's wealth derives from its ability to produce goods and services that the world wants to buy at prices the world is prepared to pay. Without access to a large market, it is difficult to achieve the economies of scale to be competitive in world markets. It is also difficult to attract world-class investors and the management skills, technology, and sales networks they command to an economy of only 26 million people without secure access to a much larger market.

19 The issue of national treatment and non-discrimination is considered in Michael Hart, 'The Mercantilist's Lament: National Treatment and Modern Trade Negotiations,' *Journal of World Trade Law* 21, no. 6 (December 1987):37-61; see also Hart, *Canadian Economic Development and the International Trading System*, vol. 53 of the research studies of the Royal Commission on the Economic Union and Development Prospects for Canada (Toronto: University of Toronto Press 1986); and Frank Stone, *Canada, the GATT and the International Trading System* (Montreal: Institute for Research on Public Policy 1984).

20 For a discussion of the pitfalls of industrial policy or managed trade, see Michael Hart, 'The Chimera of Industrial Policy: Yesterday, Today and Tomorrow,' *Canada-United States Law Journal* 19 (1993):19-48.

21 A spirited defence of mercantilism can be found in Edmund Dell, 'Of Free Trade and Reciprocity,' *The World Economy* 9, no. 2 (June 1986):128. Dell was trade minister in Harold Wilson's last Labour government in the UK. A good antidote to Dell can be found in Martin Wolf, 'Fiddling while the GATT Burns,' *The World Economy* 9, no. 1 (March 1986):1-18.

22 A good synopsis of the views of leading world experts on trade policy problems in the early 1980s can be found in William R. Cline, ed., *Trade Policy in the 1980s* (Washington, DC: Institute for International Economics 1983).

23 The United Nations Conference on Trade and Development (UNCTAD), set up in 1964 in response to developing country concerns about the unequal distribution of global economic benefits, pursues its discussion on the basis of resolutions sponsored by various regional groups. Most of its activity is devoted to debate on detailed resolutions and future agendas. Unlike the GATT, these resolutions have a moral or political rather than contractual impact on members' policies.

24 For an appreciation of GATT's trials and tribulations in the 1980s, see Patrick Low, *Trading Free: The GATT and US Trade Policy* (New York: Twentieth Century Fund 1993).

25 Royal Commission on the Economic Union and Development Prospects for Canada, *Final Report* (Ottawa: Supply and Services 1985).

26 *Ottawa Citizen*, 7 December 1983.

27 Volumes 9-14 and 68 of the Collected Research Studies of the commission. The seventy-one volumes are a gold mine of material that remains to be fully exploited by students of the free trade issue. The charge that little homework was done before the government proceeded with negotiations is refuted by these studies alone. What the critics mean, of course, is that there is an insufficient number of studies with which they agree or which predict with sufficient accuracy what the results of a negotiation would involve. Such studies are not possible. This section

has benefited from a talk delivered at a 1985 conference at McMaster University by Professor J. R. Williams setting out the economic arguments for and against free trade. Professor Williams kindly made a copy of his notes available to us to help us sharpen our economic arguments.

28 For a discussion of the economic literature on the size of gains from a Canada-US free-trade agreement available by the mid-1980s, see Andrew R. Moroz and Gregory J. Meredith, *The Economic Effects of Trade Liberalization with the USA: Evidence and Questions* (Montreal: Institute for Research on Public Policy 1986).

29 See Richard Harris, *Trade, Industrial Policy and International Competition*, vol. 13 of the research studies of the Royal Commission on the Economic Union and Development Prospects for Canada (Toronto: University of Toronto Press 1986); and Andrew R. Moroz and Gregory J. Meredith, *The Economic Effects of Trade Liberalization.*

30 Over the course of the summer of 1985, Gil Winham and a group of students worked diligently to assess the likely sectoral economic impact of free trade with the United States through detailed interviews with business executives, government officials, and other experts. While the results of that study were not included in the collected research studies of the commission, it was made available in mimeo form to interested reporters and others.

31 The introduction to John Whalley, *Canada-United States Free Trade*, vol. 11 of the research studies of the Royal Commission on the Economic Union and Development Prospects for Canada (Toronto: University of Toronto Press 1986), sums up the various views of economists.

32 The proceedings of that conference were edited by Charles F. Doran and John Sigler and published as *Canada and the United States: Enduring Friendship, Persistent Stress* (Englewood Cliffs, NJ: Prentice-Hall 1985).

33 Toronto *Globe and Mail*, 19 November 1984.

34 Michael Hart was one of those collaborators. He had originally authored one of the Commission's research studies (Volume 53: *Canadian Economic Development and the International Trading System*) and had participated in some of the seminars and colloquia organized by Whalley, Winham, and Quinn. In the fall of 1983, he joined the staff of the Commission on a part-time basis as a policy advisor and in that capacity participated in the Commission's deliberations and helped to put together its final report.

35 Simon Reisman, 'The Issue of Free Trade,' in Edward R. Fried and Philip H. Trezise, eds., *U.S.-Canadian Economic Relations: Next Steps* (Washington, DC: Brookings Institution 1984), 50-1.

36 See Chapter 6, p.121.

Chapter 3: No Anchor, No Rudder, No Compass

1 For an introduction to the making of US trade policy in the 1980s, see Harold Koh, 'A Legal Perspective,' in Robert M. Stern, Philip H. Trezise, and John Whalley, eds. *Perspectives on a U.S. Canadian Free Trade Agreement* (Washington, DC: Brookings Institution 1987); Robert E. Baldwin, *The Political Economy of U.S. Import Policy* (Cambridge, MA: MIT Press 1985); William R. Cline, ed., *Trade Policy in the 1980s* (Washington, DC: MIT Press for the Institute for International Economics 1983); Stanley Metzger, *Lowering Non-Tariff Barriers: U.S. Law, Practice, and Negotiating Objectives* (Washington, DC: Brookings Institution 1974); I. M. Destler, *American Trade Politics: System Under Stress* (Washington, DC: Institute for International Economics 1986); and Robert A. Pastor, *Congress and the Politics of U.S. Foreign Economic Policy 1929-1976* (Berkeley: University of California Press 1980).

2 See Joseph M. Dobson, *Two Centuries of Tariffs: The Background and the Emergence of the United States International Trade Commission* (Washington, DC: USITC 1976).

3 See William Diebold, Jr., *The End of the ITO*, Essays in International Finance, no. 16 (Princeton, NJ: Princeton University Press 1952).

4 Charles Ritchie, *Storm Signals: More Undiplomatic Diaries* (Toronto: Macmillan 1983), 79-80.

5 Changes in US perceptions and attitudes are also reflected in the literature. Between the founding of the GATT and the Kennedy Round, little was written about United States trade policy

and participation in the GATT outside of general treatments of US diplomatic history. Soon after the Kennedy Round, US scholars discovered the GATT and became fascinated with US participation in trade policy. At least four major studies were completed between 1969 and 1971: John H. Jackson, *World Trade and The Law of GATT* (Charlottesville, VA: Michie Co. 1969); Kenneth W. Dam, *The GATT: Law and International Economic Organization* (Chicago: University of Chicago Press 1970); Ernest H. Preeg, *Traders and Diplomats: An Analysis of the Kennedy Round of Negotiations under the General Agreement on Tariffs and Trade* (Washington, DC: Brookings Institution 1970); and J. W. Evans, *The Kennedy Round in American Trade Policy: The Twilight of the GATT* (Cambridge, MA: Harvard University Press 1971).

6   See Martin Wolff, 'A European Perspective,' and Harold Koh, 'A Legal Perspective,' in Robert M. Stern et al., *Perspectives on a U.S. Canadian Free Trade Agreement*.

7   See David Leyton-Brown, 'The Domestic Policy-Making Process in the United States,' in D.H. Flaherty and W.R. McKercher, eds., *Southern Exposure: Canadian Perspectives on the United States* (Toronto: McGraw-Hill Ryerson 1986); and Allan E. Gotlieb, *I'll be with you in a minute, Mr. Ambassador: The Education of a Canadian Diplomat in Washington* (Toronto: University of Toronto Press 1991).

8   David Leyton-Brown, 'The Domestic Policy-Making Process in the United States,' 35.

9   25 January 1983. In *Public Papers of the Presidents of the United States: Ronald Reagan, 1983*, Book I (Washington, DC: US Government Printing Office 1984), 106.

10 For the 1984 Trade and Tariff Act, see Stephen L. Lande and Craig VanGrasstek, *The Trade and Tariff Act of 1984: Trade Policy in the Reagan Administration* (Lexington, MA: D.C. Heath 1986).

11 State of the Union Address, in *Public Papers of the Presidents of the United States: Ronald Reagan 1983*, Book 1, 108.

12 Speech by USTR Bill Brock, Washington, DC, February 1984, available in mimeo form.

13 Gary C. Hufbauer, Diane T. Berliner, and Kimberly Ann Elliott, *Trade Protection in the United States* (Washington, DC: Institute for International Economics 1986).

14 Reported by Hyman Solomon in the *Financial Post*, 4 February 1984.

15 *Ottawa Citizen*, 8 May 1984.

16 See, for example, Sir Roy Denman, *European Community-United States Relations: Twisting the Dragon's Tail*, speech to the United States Chamber of Commerce, 15 September 1982, available in mimeo form.

17 See Jennifer Lewington in the Toronto *Globe and Mail*, 8 April 1985.

18 For an overview of the postwar Canada-US relationship, see Robert Bothwell, *Canada and the United States: The Politics of Partnership* (Toronto: University of Toronto Press 1992). The early years of the Reagan administration in Canada-US relations are told from different perspectives in Stephen Clarkson, *Canada and the Reagan Challenge: Crisis in the Canadian-American Relationship* (Toronto: Canadian Institute for Economic Policy 1982); and David Leyton-Brown, *Weathering the Storm: Canadian-U.S. Relations 1980-83* (Toronto: C.D. Howe Institute 1985). For US attitudes regarding Canada-US relations and the bilateral negotiations, see Willis C. Armstrong, Louise S. Armstrong, and Francis O. Wilcox, *US Policy Towards Canada: The Neighbour We Cannot Take for Granted* (Washington, DC: The Atlantic Council of the United States 1981); Willis C. Armstrong and Louise S. Armstrong, *US Policy Towards Canada: Guidelines for the Next Decade* (Washington, DC: The Atlantic Council of the United States 1987); and Charles F. Doran, *Forgotten Partnership: U.S.-Canada Relations Today* (Toronto: Fitzhenry & Whiteside 1984).

19 See Richard G. Lipsey and Murray G. Smith, *Global Imbalances and U.S. Policy Responses: A Canadian Perspective* (Toronto: C.D. Howe Institute 1987).

20 I.M. Destler, *American Trade Politics: System Under Stress* (Washington, DC: Institute for International Economics 1986) and Gilbert R. Winham, *International Trade and the Tokyo Round Negotiation* (Princeton, NJ: Princeton University Press 1986) both argue that Congress's

new assertiveness was as much an effort to protect itself from the criticism of constituents as it was protectionism per se.

21 Not all commentators would agree that the Smoot-Hawley Tariff Act of 1930 marked a triumph of congressional ability to manage a coalition of diverse interests. The classic study of the Smoot-Hawley Tariff – E.E. Schattschneider, *Politics, Pressures and the Tariff* (New York: Prentice-Hall 1935) – argues precisely the opposite. Nevertheless, while the protectionist coalition of the early 1930s soon fell apart, it was a marked characteristic of the 1980s that Congress increasingly managed to forge new, if temporary, coalitions on trade issues capable of imposing their will on the administration in a manner unthinkable a generation earlier.

22 The extent of US ambivalence towards the virtues of trade liberalization is well illustrated by the review of US trade policy and practice conducted under the auspices of the GATT Trade Policy Review Mechanism in 1989. It provides good insight into the deeply ingrained view in Washington that what the United States does to protect its industries is necessary for good reasons while the actions of other governments are often dismissed as frivolous. See GATT, *Trade Policy Review: United States* (Geneva: GATT 1990).

Chapter 4: Preparing the Way

1 For a discussion of the Elgin-Marcy Treaty, see Colin Robertson, '1854: Plus ca change plus c'est la même chose,' *bout de papier* 5, no. 2 (July 1987), 18-22; and Donald C. Masters, *The Reciprocity Treaty of 1854* (Toronto: McClelland and Stewart 1963).

2 For earlier Canadian efforts at negotiating free trade with the United States and the adoption of the National Policy, see J.L. Granatstein, 'The Issue That Will Not Go Away,' in Denis Stairs and Gilbert R. Winham, eds., *The Politics of Canada's Economic Relationship with the United States* (Toronto: University of Toronto Press 1985).

3 For a discussion of the 1911 free-trade episode, see W.A. Dymond, 'Free Trade and All That,' *bout de papier*, 5, no. 2 (July 1987), 22-5; and Paul Stevens, 'Reciprocity 1911: The Canadian Perspective,' and A.R. Riggs and Tom Velk, 'Reciprocity 1911: Through American Eyes,' both in A.R. Riggs and T. Velk, eds., *Canadian-American Free Trade: Historical, Political and Economic Dimensions* (Montreal: Institute for Research on Public Policy 1987), 9-31.

4 L.D. Wilgress, *Canada's Approach to Trade Negotiations* (Montreal: Private Planning Association of Canada 1963), 13.

5 A detailed account of the 1947-8 negotiations drawn from archival sources can be found in Michael Hart, 'Almost But Not Quite: The 1947-48 Bilateral Canada-U.S. Negotiations,' *American Review of Canadian Studies* 19, no. 1 (Spring 1989):25-58.

6 For a discussion of the bilateral initiative, see Michael Hart, *Some Thoughts on Canada-United States Sectoral Free Trade* (Montreal: Institute for Research on Public Policy 1985); and W.A. Dymond, 'Canada-U.S. Trade Options: A View from the Canadian Side,' *Canada-United States Law Journal* 10 (1985):27-34.

7 Toronto *Globe and Mail*, 13 September 1983.

8 Quoted by Hyman Solomon in the *Financial Post*, 7 April 1984.

9 *Ottawa Citizen*, 21 February 1984.

10 Toronto *Globe and Mail*, 16 March 1984.

11 Toronto *Globe and Mail*, 16 March 1984.

12 Toronto *Globe and Mail*, 26 September 1984.

13 *A New Direction for Canada: An Agenda for Economic Renewal* (Ottawa: Department of Finance, 8 November 1984).

14 Toronto *Globe and Mail*, 1 November 1984.

15 Speech by the Right Honourable Joe Clark to the Strategic Planning Forum, Ottawa, 25 October 1984, p. 5.

16 The same concerns had already been raised by the foreign policy traditionalists in the context of the sectoral initiative and were dismissed by Prime Minister Trudeau in a May 1984 Chicago

speech. The best antidote to the sovereignty worries remains an essay prepared for the Economic Council by Peyton Lyon, *Canada-United States Free Trade and Canadian Independence* (Ottawa: Economic Council of Canada 1975).

17 Toronto *Globe and Mail*, 31 January 1985.

18 Toronto *Globe and Mail*, 31 January 1985.

19 The *Canadian Forum* had a headstart on many of the opponents of free trade by identifying the sectoral initiative as a threat to its preference for industrial strategy and as a precursor of a more far-reaching initiative. See, for example, the March 1985 issue.

20 For an appreciation of the emotionalism that marked the opposition at this stage, see the collection of essays by Canada's glitterati: Laurier Lapierre, ed., *If You Love this Country* (Toronto: McClelland and Stewart 1987) as well as the comic book produced by the Action Canada Network as a paid insert in Canadian newspapers during the 1988 election.

21 In the fall of 1987, the opposition to free trade published two booklets long on passion and short on analysis: LaPierre, ed., *If You Love this Country*; and Keith Davey, ed., *Canada Not For Sale* (Toronto: General Paperbacks 1987). A first-class review of the first by David Frum can be found in *Saturday Night* (April 1988):61-3. In 1990 and 1991, Mel Hurtig and Maude Barlow, who had risen to prominence as leader of the Hurtig-inspired Pro-Canada Network, each published an account of the negotiations and their impact on Canada. See Maude Barlow, *Parcel of Rogues: How Free Trade is Failing Canada* (Toronto: Key Porter 1990); and Mel Hurtig, *The Betrayal of Canada* (Toronto: Stoddart 1991). Michael Hart reviewed both in 'Nationalist Gobbledegook,' *bout de papier* 9, no. 2 (Spring 1992):13-16. Hurtig went on to test the political appeal of his views by founding the National Party. In the 1993 election, all but a few Canadians indicated that they did not share his views sufficiently to vote for candidates from his party.

22 The Declaration is reproduced in Department of External Affairs, *Canadian Trade Negotiations: Introduction, Selected Documents, Further Reading* (Ottawa: Supply and Services 1986), 13-14.

23 Toronto *Globe and Mail*, 6 March 1985.

24 'Time to Talk Free Trade,' *Winnipeg Free Press*, 21 May 1985.

25 Toronto *Globe and Mail*, 27 March 1985.

26 Bruce Doern and Brian Tomlin in *Faith and Fear: The Free Trade Story* (Toronto: Stoddart 1991) provide a good account of business interests and influence, but leave the impression that business leaders were even further ahead of the government than in fact they were. In the period leading up to the summer of 1985, large firms that had active interests in export markets had become strongly supportive of the idea of a free-trade agreement, without having given much thought to what such an agreement would involve. More generally, Canadian businesses had come to appreciate the need to become more integrated into a North American market, but had not given a lot of thought to what an agreement to achieve that objective would entail, including the degree of adjustment that would be required in Canada to meet US competition both in Canada and in the United States. Business supported the idea of an agreement, therefore, but there was a strong need to consult in order to deepen and widen this support.

27 *Financial Post*, 4 May 1985.

28 In an address to a Conference Board of Canada International Conference, Toronto, 6 February 1985, pp. 10-11, available in mimeo form.

29 Richard G. Lipsey and Murray G. Smith, *Taking the Initiative: Canada's Trade Options in a Turbulent World* (Toronto: C.D. Howe Institute 1987), 183.

30 Department of External Affairs and International Trade, No. 85/57, 3 May 1985.

31 Mr. Burns's report is reproduced in Department of External Affairs, *Canadian Trade Negotiations*, 57-64.

32 The hearings and activities of the Committee over the course of the summer are summarized in Appendix E of its Interim Report of 23 August 1985. Special Joint Committee on Canada's International Relations, *Interim Report Pertaining to Bilateral Trade with the United States and*

Canada's Participation in Research on the Strategic Defensive Initiative, Canada, House of Commons, 23 August 1985. The Halifax portion of the hearings is summarized on pages E-4 to E-20.

33 The conclusions of the Committee's report are reproduced in Department of External Affairs, *Canadian Trade Negotiations*, 43-8.

34 For example, in briefs prepared for the parliamentary committee, in pamphlets such as *International Trade: The Western Perspective*, and in its newsletter *Western Perspectives*.

35 His trip and letter were extensively covered by the media. See, for example, the *Calgary Herald* and Toronto *Globe and Mail* of 14 May 1985. The quotation is from the letter to the prime minister.

36 The meeting attracted little media attention, but see the *Ottawa Citizen* and *Toronto Star* of 29 May 1985, and *Montreal Gazette* of 30 May 1985.

37 For a provincial point of view, see David Barrows and Mark Boudreau, 'The Evolving Role of the Provinces in International Trade Negotiations,' in Allan M. Maslove and Stanley L. Winer, eds., *Knocking on the Back Door: Canadian Perspectives on the Political Economy of Freer Trade with the United States* (Montreal: Institute for Research on Public Policy 1987). See also Douglas M. Brown, 'The Evolving Role of the Provinces in Canadian Trade Policy,' in Brown and Murray G. Smith, eds., *Canadian Federalism: Meeting Global Economic Challenges* (Montreal and Kingston: Institute for Research on Public Policy and Institute of Intergovernmental Relations 1991).

Chapter 5: Reaching a Decision

1 A slightly revised version of that paper was subsequently published in a booklet released by the government in January 1986 containing most of the key documents leading up to the decision to negotiate an agreement. Department of External Affairs, *Canadian Trade Negotiations* (Ottawa: Supply and Services 1986), 19-35.

2 Jeffrey Simpson, 'The timing of a deal,' Toronto *Globe and Mail*, 17 April 1985.

3 The leadership of the task force had also changed. In the summer of 1984, Tony Halliday began preparations to take up new duties as Canada's consul general in Chicago and Bill Dymond had assumed his responsibilities. Michael Hart joined him in the spring of 1985, following a stint on the task force set up to prepare for the Quebec Summit.

4 This traditional view of Canadian foreign policy and its hostility to bilateral Canada-US trade negotiations are best exemplified by the fact that four senior departmental veterans all lent their considerable talent to the non-parliamentary opposition: John Holmes, John Halstead, Ken Wardroper, and George Ignatieff all wrote op-ed and other articles opposing an agreement on the ground that it would erode Canada's sovereignty and ability to pursue an independent foreign policy. Wardroper accepted a senior position in the Pro-Canada Network while Ignatieff contributed to Laurier LaPierre, ed., *If You Love this Country* (Toronto: McClelland and Stewart 1987). Another veteran, Michel Dupuy, joined the office of Senator Allan MacEachen and ran as a Liberal candidate in Montreal, dedicated to the defeat of the free-trade agreement. Surprisingly, Pearson himself had been a strong supporter of a free-trade agreement in 1947-8 and scorned those who believed that Canadians could not negotiate successfully with the Americans. See, for example, Pearson's memoirs, Lester Pearson, *Mike: The Memoirs of the Right Honourable Lester B. Pearson* (Toronto: University of Toronto Press 1972), vol. I, 72. Michael Hart discusses the diminishing relevance of Canada's Atlanticist tradition in 'Canada Discovers its Vocation as a Nation of the Americas,' in Fen Osler Hampson and Christopher J. Maule, eds., *After the Cold War: Canada Among Nations 1990-91* (Ottawa: Carleton University Press 1991).

5 See the Toronto *Globe and Mail*, 11 January 1986; and *Toronto Star*, 1 February 1986.

6 All these studies were eventually released as a result of access-to-information requests, although some aspects were deleted; a new request would probably yield the full version.

7 These objectives and related considerations were set out in a paper subsequently published in

Department of External Affairs, *Canadian Trade Negotiations: Introduction, Selected Documents, Further Reading* (Ottawa: Supply and Services 1986), 21.

8   *Vancouver Sun,* 21 August 1985.

9   Like all references to cabinet discussions throughout this account, this reference is limited to the information that ministers shared publicly in their debriefings of business contacts and journalists.

10 *Vancouver Sun,* 24 August 1985.

11 US officials frequently conclude that what they read in Canadian newspapers bears some resemblance to government thinking, assuming that the artful leaking that is an essential part of the Washington policymaking process, must also take place in all other capitals. While some leaking does take place in Ottawa, journalists tend to be sceptical and seem to prefer their own, often more fanciful constructions of official thinking in Ottawa.

12 *Toronto Star,* 4 September 1985.

13 David Leyton Brown, in 'The Domestic Policy-Making Process in the United States' in D.H. Flaherty and W.R. McKercher, eds., *Southern Exposure: Canadian Perspectives on the United States* (Toronto: McGraw-Hill Ryerson 1986), 35-6, tells how the president changed his mind publicly on several occasions as his budget director and energy secretary sought his support on a gasoline tax.

14 The president's and the prime minister's letters, as well as the Kelleher and Yeutter reports and the prime minister's statement in the House of Commons on 26 September, are reproduced in Department of External Affairs, *Canadian Trade Negotiations,* 65-78.

15 For insight into the decision-making process in the Reagan White House, see Peggy Noonan, *What I Saw at the Revolution: A Political Life in the Reagan Era* (New York: Random House 1990).

16 *Winnipeg Free Press,* 27 September 1985.

17 David Frum, 'Free for All,' *Saturday Night* (April 1988), 61.

18 Toronto *Globe and Mail,* 7 October 1985, A13.

Chapter 6: Forging Ahead

1   See Allan Gotlieb, *'I'll be with you in a minute, Mr. Ambassador:' The Education of a Canadian Diplomat in Washington* (Toronto: University of Toronto Press 1991), 102-7.

2   Toronto *Globe and Mail,* 26 October 1985.

3   *Calgary Herald,* 28 October 1985; and Toronto *Globe and Mail,* 29 October 1985.

4   See White House press statement in *Public Papers of the Presidents of the United States: Ronald Reagan, 1985,* Book II (Washington, DC: US Government Printing Office 1987), 1465.

5   *Montreal Gazette,* 9 November 1985.

6   *Vancouver Sun,* 12 November 1985.

7   Geoff White, *Calgary Herald,* 9 November 1985.

8   Toronto *Globe and Mail,* 9 November 1985.

9   Toronto *Globe and Mail,* 9 November 1985.

10 *Montreal Gazette,* 14 November 1985.

11 Toronto *Globe and Mail,* 9 November 1985.

12 Reisman's own description of his role in this meeting can be found in an account of the negotiations he gave to Deborah McGregor, of the *Financial Times of Canada,* published in the 25-31 July 1988 issue.

13 Toronto *Globe and Mail,* 30 November 1985.

14 Toronto *Globe and Mail,* 23 December 1985.

15 Quoted with permission from Hay Management Consultants' Opinion Leaders Research Program, *Canada's Future: Competitiveness and Technology Issues* (Toronto: Hay Management Consultants 1987).

Chapter 7: Getting Ready

1   See the Toronto *Globe and Mail*, 11 January 1986; the *Toronto Star*, 1 February 1986; the *Ottawa Citizen*, 26 April 1986; and the *Toronto Star*, 18 May 1986 for media profiles of the TNO.

2   For a more detailed exposition of this theme, see Michael Hart, 'The Mercantilist's Lament: National Treatment and Modern Trade Negotiations,' *Journal of World Trade Law* 21, no. 6 (December 1987); and Michael Hart, 'GATT Article XXIV and Canada-US Trade Negotiations,' *The Review of International Business Law* 1, no. 3 (December 1987). Both articles are based on staff papers prepared at Reisman's request with a view to exploring the details of his vision.

3   Toronto *Globe and Mail*, 25 April 1986.

4   Stevie Cameron, 'Reisman's trade team: future stars of public service,' *Ottawa Citizen*, 1 February 1986. See also Martin Cohn, 'Best and brightest on Canada's free-trade team,' *Toronto Star*, 18 May 1986.

5   *Ottawa Citizen*, 3 June 1986.

6   In 1987 Harvard (Kennedy School of Government) graduate student Glenn Tobin prepared a detailed case study of the events and elements that went into the dramatic events in Washington in April 1986, 'U.S.-Canada Free Trade Negotiations: Gaining Approval From Congress to Begin.' The paper, based on extensive interviews with US sources, suggests the extraordinary nature of the Senate's actions and how senatorial displeasure was largely unrelated to the actual issue in question. The research was later summarized in Raymond Vernon, Deborah L. Spar, and Glen Tobin, *Iron Triangles and Revolving Doors: Cases in U.S. Foreign Economic Policymaking* (New York: Praeger 1991), 21-53.

7   Toronto *Globe and Mail*, 12 April 1986.

8   For more than a year already lumber and pharmaceuticals had been at the top of the bilateral irritants list. For an explanation of the lumber issue, see pp. 186-8 and 211-12. In the case of pharmaceuticals, multinational firms had long pressured the Canadian government to give them a longer period of patent protection in Canada in return for which they indicated they would do more research in Canada; without more protection, they were pulling their labs out of Canada. The short period of patent protection in Canada provided generic drug manufacturers, mostly Canadian owned, the opportunity to supply the Canadian market with lower priced generic substitutes for name brands. The Canadian government had earlier asked economist Harry Eastman to study the question, but had not yet brought in legislation. The delays pleased no one, least of all the multinationals, who put pressure on the US government to use its section 301 powers as well as the impending trade negotiations to put pressure on the Canadian government. A complicating factor was that Ed Pratt, the chair of the US Advisory Committee on Trade Negotiations, the principal private sector advisory body to the USTR, was also the chief executive of Pfizer, a major pharmaceutical manufacturer.

9   See, for example, Peter Cowan in the *Ottawa Citizen*, 12 April 1986.

10 *Toronto Star*, 15 April 1986.

11 See the postmortem by Carol Goar in the *Toronto Star*, 26 April 1986.

12 See Allan Gotlieb, *'I'll be with you in a minute, Mr. Ambassador:' The Education of a Canadian Diplomat in Washington* (Toronto: University of Toronto Press 1991), 105-8.

13 Reproduced in Glenn Tobin, *U.S.-Canada Free Trade Negotiations (B)*, Appendix B, Case Program, Kennedy School of Government, Harvard University, Case #C96-87-786.0.

14 *Montreal Gazette*, 24 April 1986.

Chapter 8: The Summer of Innocence

1   Reisman refers to this meeting in the account of the negotiations he gave to Deborah McGregor, of the *Financial Times of Canada*, published in the 25-31 July 1988 issue. In this same article, he also discusses an earlier encounter with Yeutter and his deputy, Mike Smith, in Trade Minister Kelleher's parliamentary office the previous winter, a meeting he would refer to many times later as proof positive that the Americans were prepared to think big, even in the face of

potential congressional problems. At that meeting, Smith had in effect confirmed what he had told Burney on the placid waters of Chesapeake Bay in July of 1985: if Canada was prepared to address the full range of US concerns, the United States would be able to match the vision and address Canada's concerns.

2   See Alexander Ross, 'Free Trade's Mr. Tough Guy,' *Canadian Business* (March 1986):22-9, 101-2.

3   In 1979, the Special Trade Representative, created in 1962 to pursue the Kennedy Round negotiations, was put on a more permanent footing and renamed the United States Trade Representative. Both the incumbent and the office are referred to as USTR.

4   *Ottawa Citizen*, 14 June 1986.

5   The *Financial Times* of Canada had already sent a man to Geneva at Christmas to interview the unnamed ambassador and ran a story at the beginning of January comparing him to Simon Reisman. See also *New York Times*, 13 December 1985.

6   See, for example, the *Montreal Gazette* of 26 April and the *Toronto Star* of 18 May 1986.

7   Reisman's description of this first meeting can be found in the account of the negotiations he gave to Deborah McGregor, of the *Financial Times of Canada*, 25-31 July 1988. *Maclean's* of 2 June 1986 gives very complete coverage, with extensive colour commentary.

8   Reisman had already told the press the previous week that he intended to start off with a broad economic discussion. See *Toronto Star*, 15 May 1986.

9   Prepared by Michael Hart and subsequently published as 'GATT Article XXIV and the Canada-United States Trade Negotiations,' *Review of International Business Law* 1, no. 3 (December 1987):317-55.

10   See Reisman's comments in the 25-31 July 1988 *Financial Times of Canada*. Bill Merkin, Murphy's deputy, later wrote: 'The U.S. side, on the other hand, had clearly not engaged in that type of conceptual thinking. Instead, we proceeded to run through a litany of long-standing problems. The difference in approach lasted throughout the entire course of the negotiations.' See William S. Merkin, 'Negotiation of the U.S.-Canada Free Trade Agreement,' in Judith H. Bello and Alan F. Holmer, eds., *Guide to the U.S.-Canada Free-Trade Agreement* (Englewood Cliffs, NJ: Prentice-Hall Law & Business 1990), 26.

11   Reisman indicates in the 25-31 July 1988 *Financial Times of Canada* that Murphy gave no hint of these pending decisions during the course of their meeting or in their private sessions.

12   See the Toronto *Globe and Mail* and *Ottawa Citizen* of 22 May 1987.

13   The US Court of International Trade, the special court in New York responsible for judicial oversight of trade law cases, had held in a case involving carbon black from Mexico that the US doctrine of specificity required that a benefit made generally available in law was still a specific subsidy if in practice only one or two plants or only one industry could benefit from the program. Subsequent cases refined this landmark decision and led to a change in US law in the 1988 Trade and Competitiveness Act, making this issue clear.

14   *Ottawa Citizen*, 13 and 14 June 1986.

15   Toronto *Globe and Mail*, 2 July 1986.

16   On intellectual property generally, see Economic Council of Canada, *Report on Intellectual and Industrial Property* (Ottawa: Queen's Printer 1971); and D.G. McFetridge, ed., *Technological Change in Canadian Industry* (Toronto: University of Toronto Press 1986). For a US view, see Harvey E. Bale, 'The Links between Investment, Intellectual Property, and Trade,' *Economic Impact*, no. 55 (1986):30-5; and United States Trade Representative, *Administrative Statement on the Protection of U.S. Intellectual Property Rights Abroad* (Washington, DC: USTR, 17 April 1986).

17   *Ottawa Citizen*, 18 June 1986. Reisman said 'augurs well,' but Brian Butters of Southam News transcribed it as 'argues well.'

18   *Montreal Gazette*, 19 June 1986.

19   See, for example, stories in the *Ottawa Citizen* of 21 June 1986 and the *Montreal Gazette* of 26 June 1986. For an amusing and iconoclastic account of the differing aproaches of Premiers

Peterson and Bourassa, see the testimony of John Crispo before the House Standing Committee on External Affairs and International Trade, 17 November 1987, in Issue No. 38 of its proceedings.

20 Chris Young commenting on the same speech in the *Ottawa Citizen*, 20 June 1986.

21 Deborah McGregor in the *Financial Times of Canada* of 23 June 1986 and Jamie Lamb in the *Vancouver Sun* of 24 June 1986.

22 Toronto *Globe and Mail*, 27 June 1986.

23 Jennifer Lewington in the Toronto *Globe and Mail*, 25 July 1986 and Giles Gherson in the *Financial Post*, 2 August 1986. Given the number of people involved in Ottawa, Washington, and the provinces, the preoccupation with containing leaks was neither necessary nor productive.

24 Rodney Grey has coined this phrase to refer to the various devices available to governments to restrict trade on a contingent or administrative rather than regular basis. These devices include anti-dumping and countervailing duties, safeguard procedures, and measures to deal with unfair trade. In all these cases, trade continues to flow unless it can be proven that the goods are tainted by unfairness or injury calling for either exclusion orders or offsetting penalties. Grey has argued that this form of administered protection is inherently discriminatory and only suitable for larger countries capable of devoting the necessary investigative resources to make it work. See Rodney deC. Grey, *United States Trade Policy Legislation: A Canadian View* (Montreal: The Institute for Research on Public Policy 1982). Because of the growing importance of these remedies in US trade policy, there is now a large and growing specialist literature, including John H. Jackson and Edwin Vermulst, eds., *Antidumping Law and Practice* (Ann Arbor, MI: University of Michigan Press 1989); Richard Boltuck and Robert E. Litan, eds., *Down in the Dumps: Administration of the Unfair Trade Laws* (Washington, DC: Brookings Institution 1991); James Bovard, *The Fair Trade Fraud* (New York: St. Martin's Press 1991); Pietro S. Nivola, *Regulating Unfair Trade* (Washington, DC: Brookings Institution 1992); and J. Michael Finger, ed., *Antidumping: How It Works and Who Gets Hurt* (Ann Arbor, MI: University of Michigan Press 1993).

25 See, for example, the speeches of Sir Roy Denman, the witty and articulate EC envoy to the United States in the early 1980s, such as *European Community-United States Relations: Twisting the Dragon's Tail*, an address to the United States Chamber of Commerce, 15 September 1982 in Washington, DC, or his letter to Senate Finance Committee chair Lloyd Bentsen of 8 April 1987.

26 In July 1986, the Canadian Department of National Revenue accepted a petition by the Ontario Corn Growers' Association alleging that US agricultural price support programs and other farm subsidies had injuriously depressed prices of Ontario corn. The Department agreed and the Canadian Import Tribunal subsequently found injury. US corn imports were penalized with a 65 per cent countervailing duty. The US complained bitterly about the unfairness of the procedures used, which in effect ruled that the threat of imports at lower prices depressed prices in Canada, requiring higher subsidies, and launched a complaint in the GATT. The US was particularly concerned that the Canadian case might encourage European farmers to lodge complaints with the commission in Brussels regarding a range of subsidized imports from the United States. The perception created was that only the United States was entitled to launch countervail suits.

27 US commentators frequently suggest that subsidization is largely a foreign problem; see, for example, Gary Hufbauer and Joanna Shelton Erb, *Subsidies in International Trade* (Washington, DC: Institute for International Economics 1984). In the early 1980s, there was no shortage of public sources which demonstrated the opposite. Among the most important were various studies by the Congressional Research Service (e.g., *The Subsidization of Natural Resources in the United States*, 5 February 1985) and the Congressional Budget Office (e.g., *Federal Support of U.S. Business*, January 1984). A handy overview is provided by Beryl Frank, ed., *Encyclopedia of U.S. Government Benefits*, 11th edition (New York: Dodd, Mead & Company 1985). As a guide to

US subsidy practices, the Trade Negotiations Office commissioned a survey conducted by the Institute for Research on Public Policy and the Government Research Corporation, *An Annotated Inventory of Federal Business Subsidy Prgrams in the United States*. The main growth in US subsidies had been at the state level, for which see, *Directory of Incentives for Business Investment and Development in the United States*, prepared by the National Association of State Development Agencies, 2nd edition (Washington, DC: Urban Institute Press 1986); James Moses, *State Investment Incentives in the USA*, Economist Intelligence Unit Special Report no. 187 (London: Economist 1985); *Industrial Development and Site Selection Handbook* 31, no. 5 (October 1986); John M. Kline, *State Government Influence in U.S. International Economic Policy* (Lexington, MA: D.C. Heath 1983). Equally, there were various sources of information on Canadian subsidy practices, such as J. Peter Johnson, *Government Financial Assistance Programs in Canada*, 3rd edition (Toronto: Price Waterhouse 1985); Government of Canada, *Services and Subsidies to Business: Giving with Both Hands*, A Study Team Report to the Task Force on Program Review (Ottawa: Supply and Services 1986); Federal-Provincial Relations Office, *Federal-Provincial Programs and Activities: A Descriptive Inventory* (Ottawa: Supply and Services 1986). Older analytical accounts can be found in Peter Morici and Laura L. Megna, *U.S. Economic Policies Affecting Industrial Trade: A Quantitative Assessment* (Washington, DC: National Planning Association 1981); and Peter Morici, Arthur J.R. Smith, and Sperry Lea, *Canadian Industrial Policy* (Washington, DC: National Planning Association 1982). Again, the FTA stimulated more work which helped to lay the foundation for the breakthrough on this issue in the Uruguay Round of GATT negotiations. See Michael Hart, *The Canada-United States Working Group on Subsidies: Problem, Opportunity or Solution?* Occasional Paper (Ottawa: Centre for Trade Policy and Law), 89-3.

28 The issues concerning agriculture are discussed in Chapter 10, pp. 231-3.

29 Results of the poll were published in the September 1986 *Globe and Mail, Report on Business*.

30 *La Presse*, 10 September 1986.

31 *Ottawa Citizen*, 11 August 1986.

32 *Calgary Herald*, 9 July 1986. See also an editorial in the Toronto *Globe and Mail*, 4 July 1986.

33 Toronto *Globe and Mail*, 3 July 1986.

34 Geoffrey York, 'U.S. Has Stacked the Deck against Free Trade, PM Says,' Toronto *Globe and Mail*, 17 September 1986, A1.

35 For a discussion of the role of services in the international economy and the agenda for international negotiations, see M.G. Clark, *The GATT and Trade in Services*, IRPP Discussion Paper (Montreal: Institute for Research on Public Policy 1985); Ronald K. Shelp, 'Trade in Services,' *Foreign Policy* 65 (Winter 1986-7):64-84; Helena Stalson, *U.S. Service Exports and Foreign Barriers: An Agenda for Negotiations* (Washington, DC: National Planning Association 1985); Raymond J. Krommenacker, *World-Traded Services: The Challenge for the Eighties* (Dedham, MA: Artech House 1984); Janette Mark, *Trade and Investment in Services: An Issue for the 1980s* (Ottawa: North-South Institute 1984); Rodney deC. Grey, *Concepts of Trade Diplomacy and Trade in Services* (London, UK: Harvester Wheatsheaf for the Trade Policy Research Centre 1990); and Rodney deC. Grey, *The Services Agenda* (Montreal: Institute for Research on Public Policy 1990).

36 The problem of discriminatory interprovincial trade barriers has long been recognized in Canada. Some argue that their removal should have taken precedence over any further efforts to liberalize external trade in the belief that by thus achieving a true economic union, Canada would be more capable of reaping the advantages of trade liberalization. Concurrent with the bilateral negotiations with the US, the federal minister of regional industrial expansion launched yet another effort with his provincial counterparts to create an internal common market, beginning with procurement preferences. The federal government hired Jim Grande, consultant partner to Simon Reisman, to chair a federal-provincial task force charged with negotiating an end to internal discrimination. In 1994, after many tries and changes in person-

nel, these efforts were finally crowned with modest success during the summer of 1994, suggesting that those who insisted that the domestic issue should be tackled before the international were in fact providing a counsel of continued protectionism. The problems of interprovincial barriers are discussed in: A.E. Safarian, *Canadian Federalism and Economic Integration* (Ottawa: Information Canada 1974); Michael Jenkin, *The Challenge of Diversity: Industrial Policy in the Canadian Federation* (Ottawa: Supply and Services 1983); M.J. Trebilcock, J.R.S. Pritchard, T.J. Courchene, and J. Whalley, *Federalism and the Canadian Economic Union* (Toronto: Ontario Economic Council 1983); F.R. Flatters and R.G. Lipsey, *Common Ground for the Canadian Common Market* (Montreal: Institute for Research on Public Policy 1983); and Kenneth Norrie, Richard Simeon, and Mark Krasnick, *Federalism and the Economic Union in Canada* (Toronto: University of Toronto Press 1986).

37 *Toronto Star*, 8 July 1986.

38 The possibility that investment might be part of the negotiations was first picked up by the *Ottawa Citizen* of 12 September 1986 ('U.S. Wants Investment Included in Trade Talks), but elicited little comment in other newspapers for months to come.

39 In his article in the *Financial Times of Canada* (25-31 July 1988), Reisman suggests that Murphy first raised the issue at their very first meeting. At that meeting, he raised investment concerns in general as part of his long litany of irritants and complaints. At Meech Lake he specifically complained that he wanted to get on with negotiating an investment chapter and received what for months became the standard litany – 'the president should have thought of that in his 1 October letter,' 'if you want to add it, have the president send another letter.'

Chapter 9: The Fall of Impatience

1 The trials of the Canadian softwood lumber industry are described in Michael B. Percy and Christian Yoder, *The Softwood Lumber Dispute & Canada-U.S. Trade in Natural Resources* (Montreal: Institute for Research on Public Policy 1987).

2 Editorial in the *Financial Post*, 26 July 1986.

3 Quoted in the *Financial Post*, 2 August 1986.

4 Quoted in the *National Journal*, 19 July 1986.

5 *National Journal*, 19 July 1986.

6 Countervailing duty investigations, whether conducted in Canada or the United States, take considerable planning and evidence-gathering by the complaining industry. Once the industry is satisfied it has a substantial claim, it launches a complaint. Once such a complaint is accepted, the procedures follow strict time deadlines with virtually no opportunity for administrative discretion. It was in fact a coincidence that the corn decision came down within days of the softwood lumber decision.

7 Jennifer Lewington reported on the new Canadian mood from Washington in the Toronto *Globe and Mail* on 12 November 1986.

8 *Toronto Star* and *Montreal Gazette*, 13 November 1986.

9 For informed opinion on dispute settlement in the mid-1980s, see Louis B. Sohn, 'Dispute Resolution under a North American Free Trade Agreement,' *Canada-United States Law Journal* 12 (1987):319-27; C.F. Teese, 'A View from the Dress Circle in the Theatre of Trade Disputes,' *The World Economy* 5, no. 1 (March 1982):43-60; Robert E. Hudec, *The GATT Legal System and World Trade Diplomacy* (New York: Praeger 1975); Hudec, *Adjudication of International Trade Disputes* (London: Trade Policy Research Centre 1978); Erik B. Wang, 'Adjudication of Canada-United States Disputes,' *The Canadian Yearbook of International Law* XIX (1981):159; Maxwell Cohen, 'Canada and the US – new approaches to undeadly quarrels,' *International Perspectives* (March/April 1985); and Frank Stone, *Institutional Provisions and Form of the Proposed Canada-United States Trade Agreement* (Montreal: Institute for Research on Public Policy, mimeo 1985). Following conclusion of the FTA, dispute settlement became the focus of a torrent of literature, largely by lawyers speaking at conferences and contributing to legal periodicals. See Michael

Hart, 'Dispute Settlement and the Canada-United States Free Trade Agreement,' in Fakhari Siddiqui, ed., *The Economic Impact and Implications of the Canada-U.S. Free Trade Agreement* (Lewiston, ME: Edwin Mellen Press 1991).

Chapter 10: The Winter of Discontent

1   Toronto *Globe and Mail,* 3 January 1987.
2   *Montreal Gazette,* editorials of 2 and 3 January 1987.
3   *Financial Post,* editorial of 5 January 1987.
4   A transcript of Murphy's remarks is reproduced in the *Financial Post* of 19 January 1987.
5   Toronto *Globe and Mail,* 16 January 1987.
6   Bill Merkin told an audience of lawyers in Washington, 31 January 1988 that Peter enjoyed needling Reisman this way – Canadian Press wire service of 31 January 1988. He repeated this for the amusement of a Baylor University audience in October 1989. See Glen E. Lich and Joseph A. McKinney, *Region North America* (Waco, TX: Baylor University Press 1990), 47-50.
7   The Ontario decision was given extensive coverage by the media on 5-7 December 1985. For Reisman's complaint, see *Toronto Star,* 17 January 1987.
8   There is currently no modern study of the Canadian tariff. The classic study is Orville John McDiarmid, *Commercial Policy in the Canadian Economy* (Cambridge, MA: Harvard University Press 1948). Chapter V of Department of External Affairs, *A Review of Canadian Trade Policy* (Ottawa: Supply and Services 1983), and Chapter 2 of Robert K. Paterson, *Canadian Regulation of International Trade and Investment* (Toronto: Carswell 1986) provide more modern descriptions of the tariff and tariff policy. Older studies include: John H. Young, *Canadian Commercial Policy* (Ottawa: Queen's Printer 1957); J.H. Dales, *The Protective Tariff in Canada's Economic Development* (Toronto: University of Toronto Press 1966); G.A. Elliott, *Tariff Procedures and Trade Barriers: A Study of Indirect Protection and Trade Barriers* (Toronto: University of Toronto Press 1955); James R. Williams, *The Canadian-United States Tariff and Canadian Industry* (Toronto: University of Toronto Press 1978); and Hugh McA. Pinchin, *The Regional Impact of the Canadian Tariff* (Ottawa: Supply and Services 1979). The classic study of the US tariff is F.W. Taussig, *Tariff History of the United States* (New York: Putnam 1931). A more modern treatment can be found in Joseph M. Dobson, *Two Centuries of Tariffs: The Background and the Emergence of the United States International Trade Commission* (Washington, DC: USITC 1976).
9   See Reisman interview in the *Financial Times of Canada,* 25-31 July 1988.
10 State-of-the-union address, 27 January 1987, *Public Papers of the Presidents of the United States, Ronald Reagan, 1987,* Book I (Washington, DC: US Government Printing Office 1989), 58.
11 Bob Hepburn, 'A Canada-U.S. Trade Deal Now Seems Likely,' *Toronto Star,* 29 January 1987, A19.
12 *Toronto Star,* 30 January 1987.
13 The proceedings of the conference, including Yeutter's statement and the subsequent question and answer session are contained in Edward R. Fried, Frank Stone, and Philip H. Trezise, eds., *Building a Canadian-American Free Trade Area* (Washington, DC: Brookings Institution 1987).
14 *Toronto Star,* 12 February 1987.
15 See the *Toronto Star,* 11 December 1987.
16 See Reisman interview in the *Financial Times of Canada* of 25-31 July 1988.
17 For a general discussion of discrimination and foreign investment, see OECD, *Report on the National Treatment Instrument* (Paris: OECD 1985). A good summary of the United States position is found in Harvey Bale, 'The United States Policy Towards Inward Foreign Direct Investment,' *Vanderbilt Journal of Transnational Law* 18 (1985):199-222.
18 See the *Toronto Star,* 11 December 1987. The story broke as a result of a routine access-to-information request on Reisman's expense accounts and involved a quite proper accounting of the trip. The sensational *Star* story illustrates why public servants are not fond of access-to-information requests.

19   *Toronto Star,* 20 February 1987.
20   *Toronto Sun,* 6 March 1987.
21   See Charlotte Gray, 'The Simon, Jake and Bobby Show,' *Saturday Night* (September 1986):9-12. One Ontario official is quoted in the *Financial Post* of 4 May 1987 as saying 'Reisman heaps abuse on us all the time. The browbeating is constant.' See also Reisman's own characterization of these meetings in the *Financial Times of Canada,* 25-31 July 1988.
22   The debate, including the resolution, can be found in *House of Commons Debates* (Hansard), vol. 129, no. 87, 2d session, 33rd Parliament, 16 March 1987, 4144-64 and 4176-231.
23   See, for example, the *Ottawa Citizen,* 17 March 1987.
24   *Ottawa Citizen,* 17 March 1987.
25   *Toronto Star,* Toronto *Globe and Mail,* and *Montreal Gazette,* 17 March 1987.
26   *Toronto Star,* 9 April 1987.
27   Toronto *Globe and Mail,* 30 April 1987.

Chapter 11: Spring Again

1   For Reisman's characterization of the senior members of the US team, see his interview in the *Financial Times of Canada* of 25-31 July 1988.
2   William S. Merkin, 'Negotiation of the U.S.-Canada Free Trade Agreement,' in Judith H. Bello and Alan F. Holmer, eds., *Guide to the U.S.-Canada Free-Trade Agreement* (Englewood Cliffs, NJ: Prentice-Hall Law & Business 1990), 24. Merkin notes further that with the exception of Murphy, Merkin, and one other USTR staffer, all other US team members had other, unrelated responsibilities. Ralph Johnson from the State Department, for example, could not always attend meetings because of obligations to attend OECD meetings in Paris.
3   Reproduced in the *Ottawa Citizen,* 8 January 1987.
4   Toronto *Globe and Mail,* 19 February 1987. These comments and others had long convinced Canadian negotiators that Lewington's best sources were senior Commerce officials with an agenda of their own.
5   Quoted by Jeffrey Simpson in the Toronto *Globe and Mail,* 2 April 1987.
6   Former USTR official Harald Malmgren speaking to Jennifer Lewington, Toronto *Globe and Mail,* 2 May 1987.
7   *Business Week,* 2 March 1987.
8   In the lead up to the bilateral summit, both the *New York Times,* 5 April 1987, and the *Wall Street Journal,* 2 April 1987, had focused on the slide in popularity of the Mulroney government and what this might portend for the negotiations.
9   Chris Thomas and Jock Finlayson prepared a draft text and annotations for BCNI, part of which was subsequently published as 'The Elements of a Comprehensive Canada-United States Trade Agreement,' *The International Lawyer* 20, no. 4 (Fall 1986):1307-34. Twenty years earlier, the Canadian-American Committee of the National and Private Planning Associations had sponsored a series of studies including one by Sperry Lea, *A Canada-U.S. Free Trade Arrangement: Survey of Possible Characteristics* (Washington and Montreal: Canadian-American Committee 1963); and a staff report, *A Possible Plan for a Canada-U.S. Free Trade Area* (Washington and Montreal: Canadian-American Committee 1963). The pre-negotiations task force had used these and previous free-trade area agreements to develop a composite text for the preparatory work. Tabling a text at a much earlier stage in the negotiations, therefore, would not have presented insuperable technical difficulties.
10   Toronto *Globe and Mail,* 6 April 1987 (Globe-Environics poll) and 21 April 1987 (Decima poll).
11   Toronto *Globe and Mail,* 21 April 1987.
12   We do not spend much space in this book discussing the views and attitudes of either the Pro-Canada Network or the Canadian Alliance for Job and Trade Opportunities. Both groups came into their own during the 1988 election, i.e., well after the period covered by this book. The prominence of their role in the election – CAJTO campaigned vigorously for the agreement

while PCN campaigned with equal vigour against it – may have given some the impression that their role was also critical to the negotiations. That is not the case. Their main contribution was political; neither had much influence on the course or content of the negotiations. The views and contributions of both groups are treated extensively by Bruce Doern and Brian Tomlin, *Faith and Fear* (Toronto: Stoddart 1989).

13 Later that summer, Reisman repeated this little homily for the benefit of reporters. See Toronto *Globe and Mail*, 30 June 1987.

14 Toronto *Globe and Mail*, 25 May 1987. Marjorie Nichols struck a similar theme in her column for Southam (*Ottawa Citizen*, 21 May 1987).

15 *Financial Post*, 1 June 1987.

16 Toronto *Globe and Mail*, 10 June 1987.

17 *Ottawa Citizen*, 4 June 1987.

18 Interview with Derek Burney.

19 The East Coast Fisheries Treaty did not gain the necessary two-thirds ratification vote in the Senate largely because two senators, Claiborne Pell of Rhode Island and Edward Kennedy of Massachusetts, opposed it in response to the complaints of fishing interests in their states. They succeeded in convincing enough of their colleagues to vote against ratifying the treaty on the basis of the well-worn practice of senatorial courtesy. Senators without strong substantive or constituency reasons to vote either for or against the treaty, were prepared to extend a courtesy to their colleagues in the expectation that they would be extended similar courtesies in the future. Part of any administration's congressional strategy is to give such senators a reason to vote for its legislative proposals. In the case of the East Coast Fisheries Treaty, the Carter administration failed to meet this test and Canadian officials drew the obvious conclusion that, in future, relying on the administration alone would not be a sufficient strategy. Soon thereafter, the embassy bolstered its congressional liaison program. See the discussion of this issue in Allan Gotlieb, *'I'll be with you in a minute, Mr. Ambassador': The Education of a Canadian Diplomat in Washington* (Toronto: University of Toronto Press 1991), 18-21 and *passim*.

20 This was the view increasingly adopted by Ambassador Gotlieb, a view which he explains in *'I'll be with you in a minute, Mr. Ambassador.'*

Chapter 12: The Summer of Despair

1 *Toronto Star*, 16 June 1987.

2 Toronto *Globe and Mail*, 17 June 1987.

3 *Ottawa Citizen*, 27 June 1987.

4 Toronto *Globe and Mail*, 24 June 1987.

5 Quoted by Seymour Friedland in the *Montreal Gazette*, 7 July 1987.

6 Toronto *Globe and Mail*, 4 July 1987.

7 *Financial Post*, 4 May 1987.

8 Toronto *Globe and Mail*, 8 July 1987.

9 See, for example, Marjorie Nichols, *Ottawa Citizen*, 8 July 1987.

10 Marjorie Nichols, *Ottawa Citizen*, 11 July 1987.

11 Toronto *Globe and Mail*, 25 August 1987.

12 Sue Schwab was not the only person on the Hill who expressed some frustration at the quality of Murphy's briefings. Senator Max Baucus later wrote: 'The Reagan Administration's consultations with Congress concerning the FTA were reminiscent of the academic strategy of the average college student. During the term, important assignments were ignored or half-heartedly carried out. But with failure close at hand, they were able to study all night and pass the final.' See 'Trade Agreement Retrospective: The Views of Three Senators,' in Judith H. Bello and Alan F. Holmer, eds., *Guide to the U.S.-Canada Free-Trade Agreement* (Englewood Cliffs, NJ: Prentice-Hall Law & Business 1990), 88.

13 Toronto *Globe and Mail*, 15 August 1987.

Chapter 13: Impasse in September

1   *Toronto Star*, 20 August 1987.
2   Toronto *Globe and Mail*, 12 September 1987.
3   Toronto *Globe and Mail*, 12 September 1987.
4   Toronto *Globe and Mail*, 12 September 1987.
5   Toronto *Globe and Mail*, 15 September 1987.
6   *Ottawa Citizen*, 14 September 1987.
7   *Montreal Gazette*, 14 September 1987.
8   *Toronto Star*, 18 September 1987.
9   *Ottawa Citizen*, 15 September 1987.
10 *Ottawa Citizen*, 15 September 1987.
11 *Toronto Sun*, 15 September 1987.
12 *Financial Post*, 14 September 1987.
13 See Hepburn's indignant column in the *Toronto Star*, 24 September 1987.
14 Toronto *Globe and Mail*, 24 September 1987.
15 Toronto *Globe and Mail*, 24 September 1987.

Chapter 14: What Had Gone Wrong?

1   Although the details of the negotiations continued to be shrouded in mystery, good analytical reporting by Giles Gherson and Hy Solomon in the *Financial Post*, Deborah McGregor in the *Financial Times of Canada*, as well as the day-to-day analysis of Jennifer Lewington in Washington and Chris Waddell in Ottawa for the *Globe and Mail*, covered more than the events – they also had a handle on the issues and showed it in their post-suspension reportage.
2   For a detailed discussion of the subsidy issue, see Michael Hart, *The Canada-US Working Group on Subsidies: Problem, Solution or Opportunity?* Occasional Paper No. 3 (Ottawa: Centre for Trade Policy and Law 1989).
3   For a more detailed discussion of the anti-dumping issue, see Michael Hart, 'Dumping and Free Trade Areas,' in John H. Jackson and Edwin A. Vermulst, eds., *Antidumping Law and Practice* (Ann Arbor, MI: University of Michigan Press 1989), 326-42.
4   For a more general discussion of dispute settlement and the Canada-US negotiations, see Michael Hart, 'Dispute Settlement and the Canada-U.S. Free Trade Negotiations,' in Fakhari Siddiqui, ed., *The Economic Impact and Implications of the Canada-U.S. Free Trade Agreement* (Lewiston, ME: Edwin Mellen Press 1991), 113-46.
5   Both Reisman and Ritchie have on several occasions hinted that they intend to write their own books on the negotiations. Their preliminary views, however, are already in print. Reisman, while concentrating on the final results in his speeches and in a number of op-ed pieces (see, for example, articles in the *Globe and Mail* of 4 October 1988 and the *Ottawa Citizen* of 18 October 1988, as well as the transcript of a speech he gave to an IRPP conference in Murray Smith and Frank Stone, eds., *Assessing the Canada-U.S. Free Trade Agreement* [Montreal: Institute for Research on Public Policy 1987]), has also provided his insight on the process. In a 25 July interview in the *Financial Times of Canada* he describes the process and frustrations and places the onus for the near failure of the negotiations squarely on the Americans. Ritchie, in a chapter in John Crispo's *Free trade: the real story* (Toronto: Gage 1987), takes a different tack, minimizing the differences between the two sides and suggesting that the final political drama was a normal step for any major negotiation, necessary to square away a few remaining issues.
6   Toronto *Globe and Mail*, 24 September 1987.
7   *Montreal Gazette*, 24 September 1987.

Chapter 15: A Near Run Thing

1   Reisman's analysis of the need for shock treatment is along similar lines. He notes: 'You know what I think happened there? I think that from the top down the Americans had the view that

we wanted and needed an agreement very badly and that in the end we would take an agreement that suited them and that wouldn't have the features that were so important to us. They believed that. And I think they made a serious error. When it became evident to me that they would not make their move without delivery of a shock, I proceeded down that path.' The *Financial Times of Canada*, 25-31 July 1988.

2   Los Angeles *Times*, 26 September 1987.

3   In an interview with Carol Goar, Burney explained the tough assignment he had received from the prime minister and other details of the remarkable ten days between suspension and the conclusion of the elements of agreement. See the *Toronto Star*, 6 October 1987. Once in Washington as ambassador, and thus charged with ensuring that the agreement worked as it was designed to work, he also provided extensive interviews to journalists like Lawrence Martin and Jeffrey Simpson in an effort to explain what he had sought and why. Martin seemed to have listened with only half an ear; his *Pledge of Allegiance* (Toronto: McClelland and Stewart 1993) paints a caricature of Burney that tells us more about Martin's views than Burney's. The chapter devoted to Burney in Simpson's *Faultlines* (Toronto: HarperCollins 1993), however, captures the essential nature of the man, including his passionate devotion to the free-trade issue. Simpson indicates, for example, the extent to which Burney's convictions were shaped by experience and pragmatic considerations rather than ideology.

4   On CTV's *Question Period*, aired 27 September 1987.

5   Honourable Pat Carney, speech to the National Conference of Editorial Writers, Vancouver, 25 September 1987 (DEA 87/51).

6   Reisman characterizes the various US proposals as 'anything they had to offer was derisory! So they kept coming up with formulae, none of which was acceptable.' *Financial Times of Canada*, 25-31 July 1981. Derisory is one of Reisman's favourite words; during a lighter moment in the negotiations, he asked his staff to prepare a lexicon of alternate words he could use for some of the American proposals, ranging from excellent to derisory, and then showed the list to Murphy and challenged him to learn the words at the top of the list rather than the bottom.

7   Toronto *Globe and Mail*, 29 September 1987.

8   *Ottawa Citizen*, 29 September 1987.

9   Toronto *Globe and Mail*, 28 September 1987.

10 The drama of these tense days is well captured in a *Maclean's* story: 'Free Trade: A Historic Midnight Deal,' 12 October 1987.

11 Toronto *Globe and Mail*, 29 and 30 September 1987.

12 For insight into the role of the members of the US Senate Finance Committee in bringing the negotiations to a successful conclusion, see the account by Senator Bill Bradley in 'Trade Agreement Retrospective: The Views of Three Senators,' in Judith H. Bello and Alan F. Holmer, eds., *Guide to the U.S.-Canada Free-Trade Agreement* (Englewood Cliffs, NJ: Prentice-Hall Law & Business 1990), 92-5.

13 For a US perspective on these discussions, see William S. Merkin, 'Negotiation of the U.S.-Canadian Free-Trade Agreement,' in Bello and Holmer, eds., *Guide to the U.S.-Canada Free-Trade Agreement*, 30-2. Merkin acted as note taker at the meeting.

14 See Senator Bradley's account in Bello and Holmer, eds., *Guide to the U.S.-Canada Free-Trade Agreement*, 94.

15 For another description of some of the negotiating dynamics, see testimony by Gordon Ritchie before the Senate Standing Committee on Foreign Affairs, 17 November 1987. See Issue No. 30 of its proceedings.

16 As told to Warren Caragata of Canadian Press in the *Ottawa Citizen*, 11 March 1988.

17 See Burney interview with Carol Goar, *Toronto Star*, 6 October 1987.

18 See p. 336 of this text for an explanation of the confusion on pharmaceuticals, Canada's Bill C-22, and the discussion on intellectual property.

19 Bruce Doern and Brian Tomlin in their account of these dramatic hours in *Faith and Fear: The*

Free Trade Story (Toronto: Stoddart 1991), 190-4, suggest that investment was a critical part of the final equation. While important to the Americans, it had not assumed the same apocalyptic proportions as trade remedy law for the Canadian side, and thus did not not figure as dramatically in these final political discussions. That it was important to the Canadian and US lead negotiators, the source for this impression, is unquestionable; similarly, as we have seen, Reisman sought to gain the maximum strategic advantage out of US interest and set up the potential for a quid pro quo. In the end, it did not materialize because neither Baker nor Burney saw investment in these terms. Like many other issues, it contributed its share to the tension, as did financial services, intellectual property, government procurement, and other issues, none of which were easy. The issue that determined success or failure was trade remedy law and no other.

20 For a US participant's account of these dramatic events, see Peter McPherson, 'Political Perspectives,' in Jeffrey J. Schott and Murray G. Smith, eds., *The Canada-United States Trade Agreement: The Global Impact* (Montreal: Institute for Research on Public Policy 1988), 187-95.

21 Apparently the US synopsis had been prepared quickly. While patrolling the halls the previous evening, embassy First Secretary John Fried, posted to Washington from the TNO to take on responsibility for congressional liaison, spied a table with two stacks of documents. One contained a press release expressing Clayton Yeutter's regret that the negotiations had failed; the other expressed Yeutter's pleasure that they had succeeded. To both were appended detailed background notes spelling out the details of what had been agreed or could not be agreed. The Americans might have been slow in developing their bottom line, but they were always ready with the requisite press releases.

22 Both senators and MPs took after Gordon Ritchie on this point, with the senators scoring the best hits. Ritchie's Senate testimony can be found in the 17 November 1987 Proceedings of the Standing Committee on Foreign Affairs, while his less detailed House testimony can be found in the 2 November 1987 Proceedings of the Standing Committee on External Affairs and International Trade.

23 *Maclean's*, 12 October 1987, 22.

24 *Maclean's*, 12 October 1987, 23.

25 Derek Burney was not among the officials on the dais. He had been at USTR working on some of the details of the final package and was astounded to learn on his return to Treasury that Wilson and Carney had acquiesced in Baker's demand to meet the press. In Burney's view, there were still too many details to be ironed out, a process which would be complicated once the press had been briefed.

26 US Deputy Negotiator Bill Merkin makes essentially the same point. He wrote: 'If there is a lesson to be learned from this, it is that in any negotiation, both sides must be prepared to apply equivalent priority and resources to a negotiation in order for it to fully succeed with a minimum of disruption. Both sides must have the full support and mandate from the political process in order to ensure serious progress at the negotiating table. Were it not for the last-minute intervention at the political level in this negotiation, and the belated recognition both in the Administration and in the U.S. Congress that this negotiation had to succeed both for the good of the bilateral relationship as well as for the welfare of the global trading system, this negotiation quite likely would have failed, and failed miserably. That it succeeded despite all the obstacles which faced us could almost be considered a minor miracle.' William S. Merkin, 'Negotiation of the U.S.-Canadian Free-Trade Agreement,' in Bello and Holmer, eds., *Guide to the U.S.-Canada Free-Trade Agreement*, 36. Merkin's lesson was apparently learned at USTR. In 1991-2, when the United States, together with Canada, pursued a trilateral agreement with Mexico, the US side assigned Deputy USTR Julius Katz to the task and gave him the resources and mandate to pursue a major deal. The result was a much better prepared and more constructive US approach to the conduct of the North American free-trade negotiations.

Chapter 16: The Lawyers Take Over

1   By 29 October, Reisman and Ritchie had already become a little more cautious in their predictions. Reisman told the House Committee: 'We all know that lawyers are very methodical people and are inclined to be cautious in completing the fine print. They do not like to be hurried. In this case, we have to deal with two groups of lawyers. The result is that this process is taking a little longer than was anticipated.' Proceedings of the Standing Committee on External Affairs and International Trade, 29 October 1987.

2   Toronto *Globe and Mail,* 7 October 1987.

3   *Ottawa Citizen,* 16 October 1987.

4   *Ottawa Citizen,* 15-17 December 1987, backed up by a personal column by editor Keith Spicer on 15 December. See also the *Citizen*'s survey of the editorial stance of Canada's major papers on 16 December 1987.

5   All the major newspapers carried quotes from these men during the week following 4 October.

6   See, for example, the testimony of Alf Powis and Tom d'Aquino of the Business Council on National Issues before the House Standing Committee on External Affairs and International Trade on 5 November 1987. The Committee hearings, as well as those of the Senate Standing Committee on Foreign Affairs, are a gold mine of material on the differing views of Canadians on the agreement and the assumptions they have about Canada and its place in the world. D'Aquino, as well as Donald Macdonald (until his appointment as high commissioner to London), and Peter Lougheed criss-crossed the country over the next twelve months giving speeches and participating in debates, many of their presentations concentrating on debunking the myths.

7   Grant's views can be found in Laurier LaPierre, ed., *If You Love this Country* (Toronto: McClelland and Stewart 1987), 110-13.

8   See his testimony before the House Standing Committee on External Affairs and International Trade on 5 November 1987 where he explained his disappointment but refused to be drawn into a denunciation of the agreement as a whole.

9   See the *Toronto Star* of 9 December 1987.

10 Once released from government service in the summer of 1988, Reisman used these speeches as the basis for op-ed articles, especially during the course of the federal election, such as one in the *Globe and Mail* of 4 October 1988 and the *Ottawa Citizen* of 18 October 1988.

11 The speech as well as the consequent questions and answers and Reisman's participation in discussion of other presentations can be found in Murray G. Smith and Frank Stone, eds., *Assessing the Canada-U.S. Trade Agreement* (Montreal: Institute for Research on Public Policy 1987).

12 The exchange can be found in the 29 October proceedings of the House Standing Committee on External Affairs and International Trade. Copps, who was not a member of the committee, appeared to be there in the absence of Lloyd Axworthy.

13 *Montreal Gazette,* 10 October 1987.

14 Reisman appeared at the second sitting of the House Standing Committee on 29 October, accompanied by Ritchie, and promised to return. At its third sitting, on 2 November, Ritchie turned up without Reisman, causing Steven Langdon to complain that Reisman was showing contempt for the Committee. Reisman never returned, nor did he appear before the Senate Standing Committee. Other members of the TNO did, however, spend many hours being grilled by the two committees, thus adding to the available public information and explanations. See also the *Toronto Star* article by Joe O'Donnell of 6 November 1987 on Reisman's lower public profile.

15 Christopher Waddell prepared an interesting analysis of the two solitudes in the debate, including a quote from Donald Macdonald commenting on the fact that he and former colleague Mitchell Sharp both testified, but from diametrically opposed points of view: 'He used to be the free-trader and I was the nationalist,' *Globe and Mail,* 9 November 1987.

16 Sessions were held on 29 October and 2 November before the House Standing Committee on

External Affairs and International Trade and on 17 November before the Senate Standing Committee on Foreign Affairs. The Senate record is both more entertaining and more informative, in part because the senators have the time to become more informed on the technical details of the issues and are thus able to pursue their questioning with more astuteness than their more political counterparts in the House.

17 Ritchie's higher profile inevitably led to press interest and on 1 December 1987, the *Ottawa Citizen* finally ran a sympathetic half-page profile of the deputy negotiator. Wrote Elizabeth Thompson: 'During the negotiations and in the heady days after the Oct. 3 tentative pact, the free-trade spotlight shone on outspoken chief negotiator Simon Reisman. But recently, its beam has shifted to Ritchie, leaving Reisman in the shadows.'

18 Both parliamentary committees grilled Ritchie on Bill C-22, the senators being particularly skillful in their cross-examination on 17 November 1987. See *Proceedings of the Senate Standing Committee on Foreign Affairs*, Issue no. 8. Throughout November and into December, Ritchie, accompanied by various members of the TNO senior staff, also appeared before the House of Commons Standing Committee on External Affairs and International Trade. See its *Proceedings* for the second session of the 33rd Parliament starting with Issue no. 30.

19 No issue created more confusion and nonsense than that of water. There was no question that there was discussion during the drafting – as opposed to the negotiating – stage whether or not to include a specific provision exempting water from the agreement. There were strong arguments on both sides. Water is, of course, included in the Harmonized Tariff Schedule in the chapter dealing with beverages. Water in bottles, therefore, is covered by the agreement. A larger and essentially political problem, however, was raised by Reisman's association before being appointed chief negotiator with the Grand Canal project for the diversion of water from the James Bay basin to the United States. He had added to concerns with his musings at a *Financial Post* conference in 1985 that a willingness to include negotiations about supplying water on a large scale to the United States might make an agreement more attractive to the Americans. Throughout the negotiations, therefore, the opposition insisted that he was giving away water. In fact, the issue of water was not considered until the drafting stage and then only in the context of this political dimension – would it be wise to include a specific exemption for water, other than as a bottled beverage, in Chapter XII? The final consensus was that it was better not to have such a provision since the inclusion of an exemption for an issue that had nothing to do with international trade – water diversion projects are not part of international trade agreements – would later raise legal questions about other non-trade issues that were not specifically excluded. On a personal note, Michael Hart was quoted in the House of Commons in March 1988 as the source of a statement that a 'good legal case' could be made that water was included. What was not included was the rest of the conversation to the effect that an even stronger case could be made to the contrary and would likely be upheld should the issue ever go as far as a dispute settlement panel. The winning case, however, would make clear that the FTA nowhere requires that anything be sold to anyone. The rules only come into effect once a commodity has been commercialized – as bottled water has – and would require Canadian federal and provincial governments to allow such commercialization pursuant to environmental and other considerations. The remoteness of such a development made the whole argument about the inclusion of water silly.

20 At issue was whether restrictions would apply to all US-origin general circulation magazines or only to such major publications as *Time* and *Reader's Digest*.

21 As an indication of how well plugged in they had become, Christopher Waddell and Jennifer Lewington were able to write an accurate story in the *Globe and Mail* on 8 December 1987, outlining the details of the still secret bargain struck over the previous weekend but not yet released.

22 Bill Fox in the *Toronto Star*, 20 December 1987. A similar, less charitable article was penned by Allan Fotheringham in the *Ottawa Citizen*, 16 December 1987.

23 Letter jointly signed by House Ways and Means Committee chairman Dan Rostenkowski and Senate Finance Committee chairman Lloyd Bentsen to Treasury Secretary Baker and USTR Yeutter, Washington, 4 December 1987, reproduced in Bello and Holmer, eds., *Guide to the U.S. Canada Free Trade Agreement*, 114-15

24 Toronto *Globe and Mail*, 8 December 1987.

25 *Ottawa Citizen*, 9 December 1987.

26 *Montreal Gazette*, 16 and 17 July 1987.

27 *Montreal Gazette*, 12 December 1987. A similar theme is struck in a *Globe and Mail* editorial of 26 November 1987 and by Richard Anderson in a guest column in the *Globe and Mail* of 3 December 1987. Even the *Star*'s Martin Cohn was prepared to write: 'For all the emotion, rhetoric and economic debate raging across the country, the arguments for and against free trade appear to be based largely on the political beliefs of the two sides – rather than on the elements of the deal itself,' *Toronto Star*, 23 November 1987.

28 Treaty paper has a distinctive water mark, thus distinguishing the Canadian from the American brand.

29 On 2 January, the prime minister and president separately but simultaneously signed an original text presigned by the other. It had not been possible to arrange for a more elaborate signing ceremony. A month earlier there had been talk of jointly signing the agreement on the border under the Peace Arch at White Rock, British Columbia and Blaine, Washington. Reluctantly, these plans had been scrapped. The agreement had to be signed on 2 January. Both leaders had long-standing plans to be at home, Reagan at the ranch, Mulroney at Harrington Lake. Reagan was scheduled to attend a charity event honouring Bob Hope that evening and could not leave California before the next day. Mulroney was unwilling to go to California, preferring a neutral border site. It could not be done earlier because Reagan had to wait ninety days after his notification to Congress of 4 October; it could not be done later because the Act giving Reagan authority to enter into this agreement ran out the next day. They thus had to satisfy themselves with individual low-key ceremonies and a phone conversation.

Chapter 17: Conclusions

1 An earlier version of this chapter appeared as 'A Good Agreement: The Results of the Canada-U.S. Free Trade Negotiations,' in Mark Charlton and Elizabeth Riddell-Dixon, eds., *Crosscurrents: International Relations in the Post-Cold War Era* (Scarborough, ON: Nelson Canada 1993), 249-64.

2 For a discussion of the issues involved in the trilateral negotiations see Michael Hart, *A North American Free Trade Agreement: The Strategic Implications for Canada* (Ottawa: Centre for Trade Policy and Law 1990).

3 The NAFTA is described in detail in Government of Canada, *NAFTA: What's it all about?* (Ottawa: External Affairs and International Trade Canada 1993).

4 Many of the left-wing critics of the FTA in Canada do not share these assumptions. Their value systems include a preference for more government planning and less private enterprise, for greater national self-sufficiency and less international economic interdependence, for greater economic government regulation and less reliance on market forces. There is, of course, a long intellectual tradition espousing such values. What they lack is a basis in Canadian experience. To pursue policies based on such values, therefore, would require a radical restructuring of the Canadian economy and society. For people who view the FTA from this perspective, the details of either the agreement or the negotiating process are of little consequence; the whole agreement is suspect and criticism of the details has a hollow ring. For a good introduction to Canadian policy analysis based on these alternative assumptions and values, see Daniel Drache and Meric S. Gertler, eds., *The New Era of Global Competition: State Policy and Market Power* (Montreal and Kingston: McGill-Queen's University Press 1991). A critical assessment of these views can be found in Michael Hart, 'The Chimera of Industrial Policy: Yesterday, Today and

Tomorrow,' *Canada-United States Law Journal* 19 (1993):19-48.
5   Bruce Doern and Brian Tomlin, in their assessment of the negotiations in *Faith and Fear: The Free Trade Story* (Toronto: Stoddart 1991), concentrate more on the process than on the substance and conclude that the United States politically out-negotiated Canada. They reach this curious conclusion by concentrating on the tactics adopted by the two teams: Murphy's determination not to play his cards until the last possible moment and Reisman's equal determination to dream big, push hard, and lay his cards on the table from the outset. They conclude that Murphy's strategy of enticing Canada to show all its cards and frustrating its vision resulted in the United States being able to drive a hard bargain and gaining more from the negotiations. This analysis, in effect, elevates bargaining tactics over strategic objectives and sets up a score card on the basis of form rather than results. It assumes that Murphy's tactics were the result of careful calculation based upon a sure sense of the desired outcome. As we have shown, however, Murphy's approach was the result of fear, of avoiding mistakes, and of being able to shift blame elsewhere in the event of failure. While a satisfactory day-to-day strategy for a team with neither the vision nor the desire to conclude an agreement, it was more likely to lead to failure than success. It is like a football coach determined not to lose and therefore concentrating all his energies on defence but unable to win because he has developed no offense. In both football and trade negotiations, a zero-zero tie is not satisfactory. It may be a great tactical show, but it leaves the paying customers feeling cheated. Murphy adopted this tactic because he did not feel confident that the United States was committed to the negotiations to the same extent as Canada. It was a strategy that responded well to US interest group politics, but provided little room for introducing a positive vision based on US strategic objectives. It also meant that when the negotiations were finally elevated to the political level at the final hour, Murphy had left his political masters with a very difficult hand to play. It is hard to conclude that this amounted to a brilliant and winning strategy. While the process was important, provided important insight into the differing characterictics and political and economic structures of the two countries, and had an important bearing on the shape and content of the agreement, it is the results that count and which should be the basis for any assessment.
6   It is noteworthy that during the Uruguay Round of multilateral trade negotiations, this form of bargaining no longer proved productive. The emphasis on rule writing, rather than concession swapping, required a different approach, and partially explains why the Round took so long to complete. To symbolize the transition to a new, much more complex and more integrative global trade regime, the GATT regime will officially end on 1 January 1995, to be subsumed into the new, more comprehensive regime created by the establishment of a World Trade Organization. For more analysis of the new trade policy, see Michael Hart, 'The End of Trade Policy?' in Christopher J. Maule and Fen Osler Hampson, eds., *Global Jeopardy: Canada Among Nations 1993-94* (Ottawa: Carleton 1993); and Michael Hart, *What's Next: Canada, the Global Economy and the New Trade Policy* (Ottawa: Centre for Trade Policy and Law 1994). For an analysis of the Uruguay Round negotiations, see Fen Osler Hampson and Michael Hart, *Multilateral Negotiations: Lessons from Arms Control, Trade and the Environment* (Baltimore: Johns Hopkins University Press, 1995).
7   Department of External Affairs, *Canadian Trade Policy for the 1980s: A Discussion Paper* (Ottawa: Supply and Services 1983), 1. For a more recent general discussion of the aims and objectives of Canadian trade policy and the role of trade in the Canadian economy, see Michael Hart, *Trade – Why Bother?* (Ottawa: Centre for Trade Policy and Law 1992).
8   Department of External Affairs, *How to Secure and Enhance Canadian Access to Export Markets* (Ottawa: Supply and Services 1985).
9   The Quebec Trade Declaration is reproduced in Department of External Affairs, *Canadian Trade Negotiations: Introduction, Selected Documents, Further Reading* (Ottawa: Supply and Services 1986), 13-14.
10 Royal Commission on the Economic Union and Development Prospects for Canada, *Final*

Report (Ottawa: Supply and Services 1985), paraphrase of recommendations in vol. 1, pp. 382-3.

11 'Canada-U.S. Trade Negotiations: The Elements Involved,' in Department of External Affairs, *Canadian Trade Negotiations: Introduction, Selected Documents, Further Reading* (Ottawa: Supply and Services 1986), 21.

12 'Yeutter Report,' in Department of External Affairs, *Canadian Trade Negotiations*, 70-1.

13 See, for example, his article 'The Issue of Free Trade,' in Edward R. Fried and Philip H. Trezise, eds., *U.S.-Canadian Economic Relations: Next Steps?* (Washington, DC: Brookings Institution 1984); his interview in *Canadian Business* in the spring of 1986; and his comments during scrums at the end of negotiating sessions. His vision of a national treatment approach was developed into a staff paper by Michael Hart and subsequently published as 'The Mercantilist's Lament: National Treatment and Modern Trade Negotiations,' in the *Journal of World Trade* 21, no. 6 (December 1987): 37-61.

14 Experience in the administration of the agreement bore out the need to reconsider the rules of origin. They proved too complicated to administer and were thus easy prey for protectionist interests. The NAFTA negotiations provided an opportunity to fix some of the most egregious shortcomings and to put in place procedures requiring a greater degree of joint decision-making and interpretation.

15 As Derek Burney noted in a letter to the authors: 'Canada rejected several common definitions of "trade-distorting" subsidies in the FTA negotiations because they would have been too costly, politically and economically, particularly given the asymmetry of trade dependence between the two countries. Instead, Canada negotiated a comparatively cost-free binational mechanism to check abuses of trade law administration. Notwithstanding the laments of die hard anti-free traders, this unique instrument broke new ground in trade dispute resolution, is paying real dividends to Canadian exporters and is attracting widespread recognition from others seeking to check global protectionism.'

16 The Uruguay Round negotiations ultimately succeeded where bilateral negotiations could not. The Uruguay Round final results include a code on subsidies that bears striking resemblance to what Canada originally sought in its bilateral negotiations with the United States. This approach proved negotiable in Geneva because the number of players involved and their interests in the issue made the matter sufficiently important to the United States to make the necessary compromises.

17 Some five sectors of the Canadian economy accounted for more than 70 per cent of all exports by the late 1980s: transport equipment, forest products, basic metals, petrochemicals, and food products. More startling is the fact that some 70 per cent of Canada's manufacturing establishments still had no significant stake in international markets. At best, their involvement was as suppliers to internationally involved companies. By the mid-1990s, however, these numbers were beginning to change.

18 Recent assessments of the FTA by independent economic analysts have all emphasized that the adjustments of the past five years have laid the foundation for a strong take-off by the Canadian economy in the latter half of the decade. Daniel Schwanen, for example, wrote: 'there is no evidence that free trade has resulted in a net loss for the Canadian economy. There is, however, evidence that a restructuring with both winners and losers has taken place, and in all likelihood is continuing since the agreement is still being implemented. Virtually all of the losers are among Canada's traditional manufacturing industries. Many of the industries that have seen their exports to the United States grow strongly under free trade, however, are higher valued-added resource transformation, high-technology, or service industries. These industries are crucial to Canada's economic future.' See Daniel Schwanen, 'A Growing Success: Canada's Performance under Free Trade,' C.D. Howe Institute *Commentary* 52 (September 1993):15.

19 Other than the confident assertions by the opponents of free trade regarding job losses and plant closures, few studies have yet emerged tracking the economic impact of the FTA. Among early studies that suggest that the FTA is having the intended economic effect are Peter Pauly,

'Macroeconomic Effects of the Canada-U.S. Free Trade Agreement: An Interim Assessment,' mimeo (Toronto: Institute for Policy Analysis, November 1991); Daniel Schwanen, 'Were the Optimists Wrong on Free Trade? A Canadian Perspective,' C.D. Howe Institute *Commentary* 37 (October 1992); and Daniel Schwanen, 'A Growing Success: Canada's Performance under Free Trade,' C.D. Howe Institute *Commentary* 52 (September 1993). One of the reasons that trade economists did not pursue more of this kind of research is that their attention was diverted to studies of the potential impact of the NAFTA. Prospective studies are more fun than retrospective ones. More general considerations of the changing structure of the economy and its response to global competitive challenges can be found in Susan Goldenberg, *Global Pursuit: Canadian Business Strategies for Winning in the Borderless World* (Toronto: McGraw-Hill Ryerson 1991); and Dian Cohen and Guy Stanley, *No Small Change: Success in Canada's New Economy* (Toronto: Macmillan 1993).

20 See B.W. Muirhead, *The Development of Postwar Canadian Trade Policy: The Failure of the Anglo-European Option* (Montreal and Kingston: McGill-Queen's University Press 1992) for an account of the deep disappointment in Canada with the GATT in the 1950s.

21 Toronto *Globe and Mail*, 12 January 1991, B-4.

22 For a comprehensive overview of the NAFTA, see Department of External Affairs and International Trade, *NAFTA: What's it all about* (Ottawa: Supply and Services 1993).

CHRONOLOGY OF THE CANADA-US FREE-TRADE NEGOTIATIONS

1846	Britain repeals its Corn Laws and ends preferences enjoyed by Canadian producers in the British market.
1849	A US annexationist movement briefly flourishes in Montreal.
1854	Governor General Lord Elgin successfully negotiates a treaty – the Elgin-Marcy Reciprocity Agreement – between the Canadian colonies and the United States providing for free trade in a range of commodities of export interest to Canadians.
1866	US Congress abrogates the Elgin-Marcy treaty, claiming treaty favoured Canadian interests. Northern dominance of post-Civil War Congress and British support to South also factors in decision.
1866-7	Sir John A. Macdonald tries, unsuccessfully, to negotiate successor reciprocity agreement with USA.
1 July 1867	Ontario, Quebec, New Brunswick, and Nova Scotia form a new Confederation, in part in order to ease trade among themselves and offset the negative effects of the increased barriers to the US market.
1871	Liberal Prime Minister Alexander Mackenzie tries, also unsuccessfully, to negotiate a new reciprocity agreement with the USA.
1879	Conservatives under Macdonald adopt the National Policy of higher tariffs, increased immigration, and a railroad to the West in order to forge a stronger economic union, but only after another futile attempt at negotiating reciprocity with the Americans.
1891	Macdonald successfully campaigns against reciprocity in 1891 election, but only after checking in Washington that the Americans are as unreceptive to the idea as ever.
1896	Election of a Liberal government under Sir Wilfrid Laurier, pledged to reciprocity. Early overtures to Americans, however, are rejected in most jingoistic and uncertain terms, and, as alternative, government introduces preferences on British goods and, unsuccessfully, invites Britain to reciprocate.
1911	Laurier, and his finance minister, W.S. Fielding, successfully negotiate a reciprocity agreement with the Taft administration, only to be defeated at the polls in the subsequent election.
1912	Conservatives, under Sir Robert Borden, intensify efforts to expand imperial preferences.
1930	US Congress adopts Smoot-Hawley Tariff Act, raising tariffs to an average level of almost 60 per cent.
1931	Britain adopts across-the-board tariffs, ending almost a century of unilateral free trade.
1932	Imperial Economic Conference in Ottawa adopts policy of Empire-wide preferences; Canada negotiates series of bilateral preference agreements with other dominions.
1934	US Congress adopts Reciprocal Trade Agreements (RTA) Program, delegating trade policymaking to the president and thus providing a basis for reversing nearly a century of steadily mounting protectionism.
1935	Canada and the United States successfully negotiate a trade agreement under the RTA program, ushering in more free trade than under any previous agreement.

1938	Canada and the United States expand their trade agreement following trilateral negotiations between Canada, the USA, and the UK to release Canada from some of its preferential obligations to the UK and other commonwealth members.
1947	Canada and the United States, together with twenty-one other countries, successfully negotiate the General Agreement on Tariffs and Trade (GATT), a multilateral version of the earlier RTA agreements.
1947-8	Canada and the United States secretly work on a bilateral free-trade agreement, but end efforts when Prime Minister Mackenzie King changes his mind about the political consequences of such an agreement.
1949-56	Canada and the United States participate in four more 'rounds' of GATT negotiations which deepen tariff cuts among members and gradually consolidate GATT regime.
1957	John Young study for the Gordon Royal Commission warns about the high cost of protection to the Canadian economy.
1961-2	Dillon Round of GATT negotiations.
1963-7	Kennedy Round of GATT negotiations.
1965	Canada and the United States implement the autopact, providing for free trade in automotive products among automotive producers located in the two countries.
1967	Wonnacott brothers publish their pioneering study of the benefits of free trade between Canada and the United States.
1973-9	Tokyo Round of GATT negotiations.
1975	Economic Council of Canada recommends Canada negotiate free-trade agreement with the United States.
1982	Senate Foreign Affairs Committee recommends Canada negotiate free-trade agreement with the United States.
1982-3	Canadian business community organizes committee under the chairmanship of David Braide to lobby government to improve trade relations with the United States; most provincial governments echo their sentiments.
1983	Government establishes a royal commission chaired by former minister Donald Macdonald to examine Canada's economic prospects.
1983	Government releases *A Review of Canadian Trade Policy* and announces plan to negotiate sectoral free-trade agreements with the United States.

1984

	Sectoral initiative flounders while debate in Canada for a more far-reaching bilateral agreement intensifies.
4 September	Election of Progressive Conservatives under Brian Mulroney.
26 September	New prime minister visits with President Reagan and ushers in era of 'refurbished' Canada-US relations.
9 October	US Congress passes Trade and Tariff Act of 1984 authorizing, *inter alia,* bilateral negotiations with Canada to reduce and eliminate tariffs and other barriers.
6 November	Re-election of President Reagan and election of a Republican majority in the Senate.
8 November	Finance Minister Michael Wilson releases *A New Direction for Canada,* which sets the new government's economic agenda, including consideration of freer trade between Canada and the US.
18 November	Donald Macdonald tells Canadians they should be prepared to take a leap of faith to embrace free trade with the United States.

| 10 December | Prime Minister Mulroney, in a speech to the Economic Club of New York, announces that Canada is open for business. |

1985

29 January	Minister for International Trade James Kelleher releases discussion paper, *How to Secure and Enhance Canadian Access to Markets*, setting out the options for future trade relations with the United States.
14-15 February	The prime minister meets with his provincial counterparts and is urged to proceed with Canada-US free trade.
17-18 March	Prime Minister Mulroney and President Reagan meet in Quebec City and pledge to 'give highest priority to finding mutually acceptable means to reduce and eliminate existing barriers to trade in order to secure and facilitate trade and investment flows.'
19 March	Minister for International Trade Kelleher initiates a fifteen-city tour to consult Canadians on the pros and cons of free trade with the United States.
14 May	Alberta Premier Peter Lougheed warns that the 'window of opportunity' is closing, urging federal government to address Canada-US free trade with greater despatch.
28 May	Federal and provincial trade ministers meet in Vancouver and conclude that Canada should proceed with free-trade negotiations.
23 August	Following six weeks of cross-Canada hearings, a special joint committee of Parliament chaired by Tom Hockin recommends that Canada pursue bilateral free-trade negotiations with the United States.
2 September	Canadian-American Committee calls for negotiation of a comprehensive bilateral trade agreement.
5 September	The Macdonald Commission tables its final report and strongly recommends that Canada negotiate a free-trade agreement with the United States.
16 September	Tom Burns, appointed in June by Minister for International Trade Kelleher to hold hearings on the costs and benefits of bilateral free trade, reports strong support among Canadian businesses for free trade, but with important pockets of concern.
17 September	Minister for International Trade Kelleher and US Trade Representative Clayton Yeutter report that the best way to secure and enhance access to each other's market, is to negotiate a free-trade agreement.
26 September	Prime minister announces that Canada will seek a new trade agreement with the United States to secure and enhance Canada's access to the US market.
1-2 October	Prime Minister Mulroney and President Reagan exchange letters pledging to proceed with negotiations in the near future.
8 November	Prime minister appoints Simon Reisman as Canada's chief trade negotiator.
29 November	Prime Minister Mulroney at First Ministers' Meeting in Halifax, agrees to 'full provincial participation' in the negotiations and directs Secretary of State for External Affairs Joe Clark to work out the details.
10 December	President Reagan formally notifies Congress, under the fast-track procedures, of his intent to enter into negotiations with Canada.

1986

| 9 January | Minister for International Trade Kelleher appoints Walter Light to chair International Trade Advisory Committee set up to provide government with advice in the negotiation of trade agreements. In the months that follow, some fifteen sectoral advisory groups are also set up to provide the government with more detailed, industry-specific advice. |

18 March	Second bilateral summit held in Washington; President Reagan heralds trade agreement as a 'cornerstone for future prosperity.'
10 April	Simon Reisman and newly appointed US chief negotiator, Peter Murphy, meet in Washington for a first, get-acquainted session.
23 April	US Senate Finance Committee, in a 10-10 vote, agrees not to disapprove bilateral negotiations with Canada, thus clearing the way for the administration to enter negotiations pursuant to the fast-track approval procedures.
21-2 May	Simon Reisman and Peter Murphy, accompanied by their senior advisors, launch formal start of negotiations in Ottawa. US announces series of restrictive measures on shakes and shingles and softwood lumber setting off a war of words between the two governments.
2 June	First Ministers' Meeting in Ottawa agrees to modalities of federal-provincial cooperation and consultations during negotiations, including quarterly meetings of the prime minister and premiers and monthly meetings of officials in the Continuing Committee for Trade Negotiations.
13 June	Vice President George Bush visits Ottawa and declares end to mini-trade war.
16 June	Prime minister takes to the airwaves and outlines government's vision for an agreement.
17-19 June	Second plenary negotiating session in Washington.
30 June	Pat Carney appointed trade minister.
29-31 July	Third plenary negotiating session held in Mont Tremblant, Quebec.
3-5 September	Fourth plenary negotiating session held in Ottawa and at Meech Lake, Quebec.
8-11 September	US congressional hearings in Washington on trade talks raise concerns about everything from electricity to lumber.
27-8 September	Fifth plenary negotiating session held in Washington.
16 October	US Commerce Department imposes a preliminary duty of 15 per cent on Canadian softwood lumber imports.
5 November	US congressional elections give Democrats control of the Senate.
12-14 November	Sixth plenary negotiating session held in Ottawa.
20-21 November	Premiers meet with the prime minister in Vancouver for their quarterly debriefing.
9 December	US senators Bentsen, Chaffee, Matsunaga, and Baucus visit Ottawa and indicate strong support for an agreement.
16-18 December	Seventh plenary negotiating session held in Washington; concurrently discussions continue on a bilateral deal to head off a final US countervailing duty ruling on softwood lumber.
31 December	Canada and the United States conclude a softwood lumber agreement: Canada agrees to place a 15 per cent export tax on softwood lumber destined for the United States, while the US agrees to suspend the countervailing duty investigation.

1987

15-16 January	Eighth plenary negotiating session held in Washington.
21 January	Vice President Bush and Treasury Secretary Baker visit Ottawa to indicate continuing political importance of negotiations to the administration.
27 January	In his annual state-of-the-union speech to Congress, President Reagan commits his administration to conclude 'an historic free trade agreement' to cover the world's largest trade relationship.
10 February	Reisman and Murphy meet in New York to explore scope for including investment in the negotiations.
19-20 February	Ninth plenary negotiating session held in Washington.

24 February	An inspired leak – Reisman takes the gloves off and briefs the press on the details of the negotiations.
16 March	Parliament debates the pros and cons of the negotiations and of free trade.
16-17 March	Tenth plenary negotiating session held in Ottawa.
11 March	Premiers meet with the prime minister in Ottawa for a quarterly debriefing.
19 March	The Canadian-Alliance for Jobs and Trade Opportunities (CAJTO) established, with Donald Macdonald and Peter Lougheed as co-chairs.
1-3 April	The Canada-US Relations Committee of the Canadian and US Chambers of Commerce adopts a resolution to promote free trade in both countries.
5-6 April	Third bilateral summit held in Ottawa; President Reagan hails prospect of bilateral agreement as example to rest of world.
9-10 April	Eleventh plenary negotiating session held in Washington.
April	Founding of the Pro-Canada Network, co-chaired by Maude Barlow and John Trent.
13 April	A joint session of the US-based National Association of Manufacturers and the Canadian Manufacturers Association issues a statement of support for a balanced and comprehensive trade agreement.
27-30 April	Twelfth plenary negotiating session held in Ottawa.
18-20 May	Thirteenth plenary negotiating session held at Meech Lake.
8 June	American Coalition for Trade Expansion with Canada (ACTEC) established to lobby for a comprehensive agreement with Canada in the United States.
11 June	Prime Minister Mulroney and President Reagan meet at the conclusion of the Venice Economic Summit to add political momentum to the negotiations. PM impresses importance of binding dispute settlement on president.
15-16 June	Fourteenth plenary negotiating session held in Washington.
22-3 June	Fifteenth plenary negotiating session held in Ottawa.
29 June	Sixteenth plenary negotiating session held in Ottawa.
7 July	The prime minister and premiers meet in Ottawa for their fourth quarterly discussion of progress in the negotiations.
14-15 July	Seventeenth plenary negotiating session held in Washington.
20 July	Eighteenth plenary negotiating session held in Ottawa.
5 August	Senate Finance Committee chairman Bentsen, after receiving briefing from US negotiators, states he is confident agreement will fall into place, but warns that binding dispute settlement and exemption from US trade remedy laws would not pass congressional scrutiny.
5-6 August	Nineteenth plenary negotiating session held in Washington.
20 August	Two sides exchange 'integrated' texts of an agreement.
23-7 August	Twentieth plenary negotiating session held in Cornwall, Ontario; progress on issues is disappointingly small.
25 August	Economic Council of Canada releases study suggesting that a free-trade agreement would create 189,000 to 350,000 new jobs and would spread benefits across the country.
8 September	Ontario electorate gives Liberal Premier David Peterson a majority mandate, following a campaign in which he expresses scepticism about the benefits of an agreement.
9 September	Prime minister's chief of staff Derek Burney exchanges correspondence with White House chief of staff Howard Baker in an effort to lay basis for a second front and is informed that Treasury Secretary James Baker is the President's point man on free trade.
10-11 September	Twenty-first plenary negotiating session held in Washington; no progress achieved on any of the issues fundamental to Canada.

14 September	Prime minister and premiers meet in Ottawa, with doubts emerging about the negotiability of a good agreement.
19 September	Burney and Finance Minister Michael Wilson hold discussions with James Baker in Washington and are assured that Peter Murphy has the confidence of the president and that the administration believes that the negotiations are on track.
21-3 September	Twenty-second plenary negotiating session held in Washington.
23 September	Reisman reluctantly announces that he is suspending the negotiations because the United States is not responding to elements fundamental to Canada's position.
25 September	Trade Minister Carney tells a Vancouver audience that Canada will return to talks if US is prepared to respond to five fundamental Canadian demands: clear rules on what is fair or unfair trade; speedy, binding dispute resolution; balanced access to each other's markets for food and agriculture products; no changes to autopact unless these improve production and employment opportunities; and removal of all tariffs.
26 September	Reisman appears on television and disparages US negotiators.
28 September	Burney, Wilson, and Carney meet with Baker and Yeutter in Washington and report some progress in clearing way for return to table.
1 October	Burney, Wilson, and Carney meet again with Baker and Yeutter in Washington and report that there is no basis for a return to negotiations; Baker, prodded by Canadian Ambassador Gotlieb and various senators, finally agrees that US could return to table to meet fundamental Canadian requirements on trade remedies and dispute settlement. PM and cabinet agree and instruct Burney to make one more effort.
2-4 October	Burney and Baker, accompanied by senior political advisors and with the full support of both negotiating teams, hammer out the 'Elements of an Agreement' in Washington, allowing the United States to notify the Congress of its intent to enter into an agreement pursuant to the fast-track approval procedures.
5 October	Prime minister announces elements of agreement in Parliament.
7 October	Prime minister meets with the premiers to brief them on the outcome of the negotiations.
19-21 October	The lawyers begin the process of translating the elements of agreement into a detailed legal text.
29 October	House of Commons Committee on External Affairs and International Trade begins hearings on the agreement.
16-18 November	Simon Reisman and Peter Murphy meet at Meech Lake to unblock final negotiating issues standing in the way of completing text.
20 November	Simon Reisman and Peter Murphy continue their efforts in Washington.
3-4 December	Derek Burney and Deputy Treasury Secretary Peter Macpherson are brought in to put the finishing touches to the negotiations in Ottawa.
9 December	Lawyers conclude final negotiations and initial text of agreement on behalf of Canada and the United States.
11 December	Simon Reisman delivers final legal text of agreement to the prime minister.
12 December	Prime minister tables final text of agreement in House of Commons.

1988

2 January	President Reagan and Prime Minister Mulroney sign free-trade agreement.
21 November	Progressive Conservatives re-elected, pledged to implementing agreement.

1989

1 January	Canada-United States Free Trade Agreement enters into force.

GLOSSARY OF TRADE AND RELATED TERMS

International trade policy, like other specialized fields, has its own distinctive vocabulary which can be mystifying to non-experts – sometimes even to experts. This glossary provides a guide to many of the specialized terms, abbreviations, and acronyms used in international trade policy and negotiations.

Accession The process of becoming a contracting party to a multilateral agreement such as the GATT. Negotiations with established GATT contracting parties, for example, determine the trade liberalizing concessions or other specific obligations a non-member country must undertake before it is entitled to the full benefits of GATT membership.

Ad valorem tariff A tariff calculated as a percentage of the value of goods cleared through customs, e.g., 15 per cent ad valorem means 15 per cent of the value. *See also* Specific duty or tariff

Adjustment The ongoing process by which the economy declines or renews and adjusts to changing circumstances. Among the factors which influence the scope and pace of adjustment are changes in technology and productivity, trade liberalization, consumer taste, resource exhaustion, and the changing composition of the labour force.

Adjustment assistance Financial, training, technical, and other assistance to workers, firms, and industries to help them cope with adjustment difficulties arising from increased international competition.

Anti-dumping code A code of conduct negotiated under the auspices of GATT that establishes both substantive and procedural standards for national anti-dumping proceedings. *See also* Codes of conduct; Dumping

Anti-dumping duty A special duty imposed to offset the price effect of dumping that has been determined to be materially injuring to domestic producers. *See also* Dumping

Autarky *See* Economic nationalism

Autopact A sectoral trade agreement (Automotive Products Trade Agreement) entered into by the United States and Canada in 1965 in order to encourage the rationalization and growth of the North American auto industry. It provides for duty-free movement between the two countries of new automobiles and original equipment parts. In the case of Canada, only producers are allowed to import duty-free.

Balance of payments A tabulation of a country's credit and debit transactions with other countries and international institutions. These transactions are divided into two broad groups: current account and capital account. The current account includes exports and imports of goods, services (including investment income), and unilateral transfers. The capital account includes financial flows related to international direct investment, investment in government and private securities, international bank transactions, and changes in official gold holdings and foreign exchange reserves.

Balance of trade A component of the balance of payments, the surplus or deficit that results from comparing a country's expenditures on merchandise imports with receipts derived from its merchandise exports.

Binding Concept of agreeing to maintain a particular tariff level or other trade restriction, i.e., binding it against increase or change. In trade negotiations, binding a tariff is considered equivalent to a significant reduction in the level. The industrialized countries have bound virtually all their tariffs on industrial products in eight rounds of GATT negotiations while FTA Chapter IV binds all Canadian and US tariffs at free by the end of the transition period.

Binding arbitration Concept in dispute settlement where the parties to the dispute agree at the outset to abide by the results of dispute settlement procedures.

Buy-National Discriminatory government procurement policies, such as Buy-American or Buy-Canadian, which provide a margin of preference for local suppliers over foreign suppliers. The GATT does not require non-discrimination by governments in their purchasing policies. A modest code agreed upon during the Tokyo Round provides for non-discriminatory purchasing practices by specified government entities. FTA Chapter XIII provides a modest extension of the coverage of the GATT code. *See also* Government procurement

Canadian International Trade Tribunal *See* CITT

Certificate of origin *See* Rules of origin

CIF Abbreviation used to indicate the terms upon which goods are sold for export, i.e., the price includes the cost of the good plus insurance and freight charges. *See also* FOB

CIT US Court of International Trade is a special court set up to hear appeals from administrative and quasi-judicial trade decisions, e.g., from decisions of the ITC or ITA.

CITT Canadian International Trade Tribunal is a body responsible under Canadian legislation for findings of injury in anti-dumping and countervailing duty cases and the provision of advice to the government on other import issues.

Codes of conduct International instruments that indicate standards of behaviour by nation states or multinational corporations. *See also* Anti-dumping code; Subsidies code

Commercial presence Trade in services concept which reflects the presence that a national of one country must have in another country in order to complete a service transaction, such as a branch office staffed by local staff. Concept falls short of establishment.

Common market A more integrative version of a customs union in which the member countries agree to common policy measures affecting the internal operation of the market in order to promote the free movement of goods, capital, services, and people.

Comparative A central concept in international trade theory which holds that an advantage country or a region should specialize in the production and export of those goods and services that it can produce relatively more efficiently than other goods and services, and import those goods and services that it can produce relatively less efficiently.

Compensation Concept that reflects the withdrawal or amendment of a previously negotiated or bound concession, such as a tariff increase, change in quota level, temporary surtax, etc., requiring a new and equivalent concession.

Competition policy Set of policy measures which have the objective to protect the effective operation of the economy based on the premise that generally a market system will give better results in terms of economic and industrial performance than any alternative system of industrial organization. Canada's competition policy is founded in the Competition Act.

Contingency protection Collective term referring to trade remedies that may be imposed by a government contingent upon certain criteria being met, such as the importation of dumped or subsidized goods that cause material injury to domestic producers. *See also* Anti-dumping duties; Countervailing duties; Safeguards

Countervailing duties Additional duties imposed by an importing country to offset government subsidies in an exporting country when the subsidized imports cause material injury to domestic industry in the importing country.

Customs Act Canadian legislation which provides the basic framework for customs procedures in Canada.

Customs classification The particular category in a tariff nomenclature in which a product is classified for tariff purposes, or the procedure for determining the appropriate tariff category in a country's nomenclature system used for the classification, coding, and description of internationally traded goods. Most of the important trading nations have agreed to use a common classification system known as the Harmonized Commodity Coding and Description System (HS).

Customs duties *See* Tariff

Customs Tariff Act Canadian legislation which provides the legal framework for the collection of customs duties in Canada, including rules related to drawbacks, duty remission, valuation, etc.

Customs union A group of nations which have eliminated trade barriers among themselves and imposed a common tariff on all goods imported from all other countries.

Defence production sharing arrangements (DPSA) A set of administrative arrangements between the United States and Canada dating back to the 1941 Hyde Park arrangement providing for free trade in defence material and encouraging shared production of such material.

Deficiency payments Government payments to compensate farmers for all or part of the difference between domestic market price levels for a commodity and a higher target price. *See also* Variable levy

Dispute settlement mechanism Those institutional provisions in a trade agreement which provide the means by which differences of view between the parties can be settled.

Domestic content requirements A requirement that specifies that firms selling a particular product within a particular country must use, as a certain percentage of their inputs, goods produced within that country.

Drawback Import duties or taxes repaid by a government in whole or in part, when the imported goods are re-exported or used in the manufacture of exported goods.

Dumping The sale of an imported commodity at a price lower than that at which it is sold within the exporting country. Dumping is considered an actionable trade practice when it disrupts markets and injures producers of competitive products in the importing country. GATT Article VI permits the imposition of special anti-dumping duties against dumped goods equal to the difference between their export price and their normal value in the exporting country. *See also* Anti-dumping code; Anti-dumping duty

Duty *See* Tariff

Duty remission Import duties or taxes repaid by a government, in whole or in part, to a particular company or industry contingent upon exports, manufacture in the importing country, or similar performance requirements, usually on imports of components, parts, or products to complete a product line.

EC or EEC European Economic Community is a common market established by the Treaty of Rome in 1958 and which by 1986 included Belgium, Denmark, France, Germany, Greece, Ireland, Italy, Luxembourg, Netherlands, Portugal, Spain, and the UK. Since 1993, it is referred to as the European Union.

Economic nationalism A desire to make a nation as self-sufficient as possible in terms of trade, so that it requires few imports or exports for its economic well-being; also known as autarky or national self-sufficiency.

EEA European Economic Area is the term used to describe the end result of a series of negotiations between the EC and the EFTA countries aimed at creating greater market integration between the two groups.

EFTA European Free Trade Agreement, comprising Austria, Finland, Iceland, Norway, Sweden, and Switzerland.

Emergency restrictions *See* Escape clause; Safeguards

End-use tariff item Tariff classification where the rate of duty depends upon the use to which the imported product is put, e.g., cotton sheeting for medical use is taxed at a lower rate than all other cotton sheeting.

Escape clause A provision in a bilateral or multilateral commercial agreement permitting a signatory nation to suspend tariff or other concessions when imports threaten serious harm to the producers of competitive domestic goods. GATT Article XIX and FTA Chapter XI sanction such 'safeguard' provisions to help firms and workers adversely affected by a relatively sudden surge of imports adjust to the rising level of import competition. *See also* Safeguards

Establishment One of the basic principles which comprise national treatment for investors. Right of establishment involves providing foreign investors with the right to establish new businesses on the same basis as nationals.

European Economic Community *See* EC
European Free Trade Agreement *See* EFTA
EU *See* EC
Exceptions Provisions in a trade agreement that provide for rules to deal with special circum-stances, such as import or export controls for security reasons. GATT Articles XX and XXI pro-vide for the basic exceptions to the GATT. FTA Chapters XII and XX provide similar excep-tions.
Exchange rate The price (or rate) at which one currency is exchanged for another currency, gold, or Special Drawing Rights (SDRs).
Exemptions Provisions which exempt particular products or situations from a general rule, e.g., agriculture might be exempted in a free-trade area where all tariffs have been eliminated
Export and Import Permits Act Canadian legislation which provides the mechanism (licens-ing) by which exports from Canada and imports into Canada can be controlled. Three basic controlling lists are prescribed under the Act: an Import Control List, an Export Control List and an Area Control List. Any product listed on the first two lists or any exports to a country on the third list requires a permit, the conditions for which may be prescribed by Order-in-Council.
Export quotas Specific restrictions or ceilings which are imposed by an exporting country on the value or volume of certain exports to protect domestic producers and consumers from temporary shortages of the goods affected or to bolster their prices in world markets. Some International Commodity Agreements explicitly indicate when producers should apply such restraints. Export quotas are also often applied in Orderly Marketing Agreements and Voluntary Restraint Agreements, and to promote domestic processing of raw materials in countries that produce them.
Export restraints Quantitative restrictions imposed by an exporting country to limit exports to specified foreign markets, usually pursuant to a formal or informal agreement concluded at the request of the importing country.
Export subsidies Government payments or other financially quantifiable benefits provided to domestic producers or exporters contingent on the export of their goods or services.
Extraterritoriality The application of national laws, policies, and practices beyond the fron-tier. The United States actively practises the extraterritorial application of its laws, e.g., in the area of antitrust and strategic export controls through its influences over the head offices of US-owned multinational enterprises.
Fair trade *See* Unfair trade
Fast-track procedures US legislative procedures stipulating that once the president formally submits to Congress a bill implementing an agreement negotiated under the Act's authority, both houses must vote on the bill within 90 days. No amendments are permitted. The purpose of these procedures is to assure foreign governments that Congress will act expeditiously on an agreement they negotiate with the US government.
FIRA Foreign Investment Review Agency. *See* Investment Canada
FOB Free-On-Board is an abbreviation used to indicate the terms upon which goods are sold for export, i.e., the price does not include insurance and freight charges. *See also* CIF
Free trade An economic concept used for analytical purposes to denote trade unfettered by government-imposed trade restrictions. It is also used as a general term to denote the end result of a process of trade liberalization. Freer trade is the comparative term used to denote circumstances between current practice and the achievement of free trade.
Free-trade area An arrangement among two or more nations to remove substantially all tariff and non-tariff barriers to trade between them, while each maintains its differing schedule of tariff and other barriers applying to all other nations. GATT Article XXIV provides a frame-work of rules for the negotiation of free-trade areas such as the Canada-US FTA.
Free-trade zone An area within a country (a seaport, airport, warehouse, or any other desig-

nated area) regarded as being outside its customs territory. Importers may therefore bring goods of foreign origin into such an area without paying customs duties and taxes, pending their eventual processing, transshipment, or re-exportation. Free trade zones may also be known as free ports, free warehouses, and foreign trade zones.

FTA In North America, Free Trade Agreement usually refers to the Canada-US Free Trade Agreement that entered into force on 1 January 1989.

G-7 A group of seven of the most important industrialized countries (Canada, France, Germany, Italy, Japan, the UK, and the USA) that meet annually at an economic summit to discuss economic and, increasingly, political issues of common concern.

GATT General Agreement on Tariffs and Trade, a multilateral treaty which delineates rules for international trade, subscribed to by 120 countries which together account for more than four-fifths of world trade. The primary objective of GATT is to liberalize world trade and place it on a secure basis, thereby contributing to global economic growth and development.

GDE or GNE Gross domestic/national expenditure is the total of all domestic purchases by corporations, individuals, and governments.

GDP or GNP Gross domestic/national product is the total of goods and services produced by a country.

General Agreement on Tariffs and Trade *See* GATT

Government procurement Purchases of goods and services by official government agencies. Procurement preferences refer to discriminatory purchases from domestic suppliers, even when imported goods are more competitive and are a major non-tariff barrier to trade. *See also* Buy-National

Grandfather clause A GATT provision (the Protocol of Provisional Application) that allowed the original contracting parties to accept various GATT obligations despite the fact that some existing domestic legislation was otherwise inconsistent with GATT provisions. More generally, any clause in an agreement which provides that certain existing programs, practices, and policies are exempt from an obligation.

HS (Harmonized System) *See* Customs classification

IBRD (World Bank) International Bank for Reconstruction and Development which was established, together with the International Monetary Fund, at the Bretton Woods Conference in 1944. Its original purpose was to help countries to reconstruct their economies after the damage inflicted by the war, but it is now devoted to helping developing countries develop and strengthen their economies. Its headquarters are in Washington.

IMF International Monetary Fund which was established at Bretton Woods Conference in 1944. Its purpose was to restore and promote monetary and economic stability. Its headquarters are in Washington. All OECD and most developing countries are members.

Import quota *See* Quantitative restriction

Import substitution An attempt by a country to reduce imports, and hence foreign exchange expenditures, by encouraging the development of domestic industries.

Industrial policy Governmental actions affecting, or seeking to affect, the sectoral composition of the economy by influencing the development of particular industries.

Injury The term used in international commerce to describe the effect on domestic producers of decline in output, lost sales, decline in market share, reduced profits, reduced return on investment, reduced capacity utilization, etc., as a result of import competition. A distinction is often made between serious injury (required for emergency safeguard measures) and material injury (required for anti-dumping and countervailing duties).

Intellectual property A collective term used to refer to new ideas, inventions, designs, writings, films, etc., which are protected by copyright, patents, trademarks, etc.

International Monetary Fund *See* IMF

International Trade Commission *See* USITC

Investment Canada Agency established by the Canadian federal government in 1984 to promote and monitor incoming foreign direct investment with a view to ensuring that Canada benefits to the greatest extent possible from such investment. It replaced the Foreign Investment Review Agency (FIRA) which had a mandate to screen foreign direct investment and determine the extent to which each proposed investment would be of net benefit to Canada.

Investment performance requirements Special conditions imposed on direct foreign investment by recipient governments, sometimes requiring commitments to export a certain percentage of the output, to purchase given supplies locally, or to ensure the employment of a specified percentage of local labour and management.

ITA International Trade Administration is the branch of the US Department of Commerce responsible for investigating and determining the existence of dumping or subsidization in US trade remedy cases.

ITAC International Trade Advisory Committee is a committee of private sector leaders that advises the Canadian government on trade negotiations. *See also* SAGITs

ITO International Trade Organization is the still-born organization which was to do for trade what the IMF has done for the management of international monetary issues. GATT, the commercial policy chapter of the Havana Charter for an ITO, has gradually gained organizational status and now performs this function.

Kennedy Round The sixth in a series of GATT multilateral trade negotiations (1963-7).

Liberalization Reductions in tariff and other measures that restrict world trade unilaterally, bilaterally, or multilaterally. Trade liberalization has been the objective of all GATT trade negotiations as well as of the FTA and NAFTA negotiations.

Market access Availability of a national market to exporting countries, i.e., a reflection of a government's willingness to permit imports to compete relatively unimpeded with similar domestically produced goods.

Mercantilism A prominent economic philosophy in the 16th and 17th centuries which equated the accumulation and possession of gold and other international monetary assets, such as foreign currency reserves, with national wealth. Although this point of view is generally discredited among 20th-century economists and trade policy experts, some contemporary politicians still favour policies designed to create trade 'surpluses,' such as import substitution and tariff protection for domestic industries, and consider such policies essential to national economic strength.

MFA Multi-Fibre Agreement is a sectoral derogation from the GATT which allows countries to reach discriminatory agreements or to impose quotas restricting trade in low-cost textile and clothing products.

Most-Favoured-Nation treatment (MFN) A commitment that a country will extend to another country to offer the lowest tariff rates it applies to any third country. The MFN principle has become the foundation of the world trading system since the end of the Second World War. All contracting parties to GATT apply MFN treatment to one another under GATT Article I. Exceptions to this basic rule are allowed in the formation of regional trading arrangements, provided certain strict criteria are met. *See also* National treatment

Multilateral agreement An international compact involving three or more parties. For example, GATT has been, since its establishment in 1947, seeking to promote trade liberalization through multilateral negotiations.

Multilateral trade negotiations (MTN) Eight rounds of multilateral trade negotiations have been held under the auspices of GATT since 1947. Each round represents a discrete and lengthy series of interacting bargaining sessions among the participating countries in search of mutually beneficial agreements looking towards the reduction of barriers to world trade. The agreement reached at the conclusion of each round constitutes new GATT commitments and thus amounts to an important step in the evolution of the world trading system. The Uruguay Round of MTNs, launched in September 1986 at Punta del Este, Uruguay, and concluded in

Marakesh, Morocco, in April 1994, was the eighth such round. *See also* Round of trade negotiations

NAFTA North American Free Trade Agreement involving Canada, the United States, and Mexico, which entered into force on 1 January 1994.

National self-sufficiency *See* Economic nationalism

National treatment Extension to imported goods (services, investment, etc.) of treatment no less favourable than that accorded to domestic goods (services, investment, etc.) with respect to internal taxes, laws, regulations, and requirements. GATT members are obliged to accord to one another national treatment with respect to internal measures that can affect trade in goods. *See also* Most-Favoured-Nation treatment

Non-Tariff barriers or measures Government measures or policies other than tariffs that restrict or distort international trade. Examples include import quotas, discriminatory government procurement practices, measures to protect intellectual property. Such measures have begun to impede trade more conspicuously as tariffs have been reduced during the period since the Second World War.

OECD Organization for Economic Cooperation and Development is a Paris-based organization of industrialized countries responsible for the study of and cooperation on a broad range of economic, trade, scientific, and educational issues. Membership includes the US, Canada, Japan, Australia, New Zealand, France, Italy, Belgium, Germany, Netherlands, Luxembourg, Denmark, UK, Ireland, Greece, Spain, Portugal, Austria, Switzerland, Finland, Iceland, Norway, Sweden, Turkey, Yugoslavia, and Mexico.

Predatory pricing Business practice that involves the deliberate charging of prices at a level low enough to drive a competitor out of business or deter entry by new competitors. It is usually directed towards competitors at the same level of production or distribution as the offender. Both Canadian and US laws on competition consider predatory pricing an offence.

Price discrimination Business practice that involves charging different customers different prices for the same product by differentiating between groups of customers. It may be used to benefit the seller or the buyer of the product. Both Canadian and US laws on competition consider certain types of price discrimination as offences. Dumping is a form of international price discrimination.

Productivity A way of expressing changes in the value of economic activity: labour productivity measures the amount of production per unit of effort; capital productivity measures the amount of production per unit of capital; total factor productivity measures the amount of production obtained from combined units of effort, capital, and technology. For economists, growth in productivity is an important indicator that an economy is making the best use of available factors of production. Sustained increases in total factor productivity are an important determinant for a rising standard of living.

Protectionism The deliberate use or encouragement of restrictions on imports to enable relatively inefficient domestic producers to compete successfully with foreign producers.

Quantitative restriction (QR) Explicit limit, or quotas, on the physical amounts of particular products which can be imported or exported during a specified time period, usually measured by volume but sometimes by value. The quota may be applied on a 'selective' basis with varying limits set according to the country of origin or on a global basis which only specifies the total limit and thus tends to benefit more efficient suppliers. Quotas are frequently administered through a system of licensing.

Quasi-judicial procedures Procedures through which decisions are made by regulatory agencies applying general statutes to specific cases. On trade, procedures administered by the Canadian International Trade Tribunal (CITT) and the Department of National Revenue determine the eligibility of petitioners for import relief under safeguards, countervailing duty, anti-dumping, and other trade rules.

Quota *See* Quantitative restriction

Reciprocity   The practice by which governments extend similar concessions to each other, such as when one government lowers its tariffs or other barriers encouraging its imports in exchange for equivalent concessions from a trading partner on barriers affecting its exports (a balance of concessions). Reciprocity has traditionally been a principal objective of negotiators in GATT rounds. Reciprocity is also defined as mutuality of benefits, quid pro quo, and equivalence of advantages.

Reciprocity agreements   Historical term referring to trade agreements between Canada and the United States providing for reciprocal trade concessions, including the 1854 Elgin-Marcy Treaty and the aborted 1911 agreement.

Retaliation   Action taken by one country to restrain the imports from another country that has increased a tariff or imposed other measures that adversely affect the exports of the former country in a manner inconsistent with GATT. The GATT and the FTA, in certain circumstances, permit such reprisal, although this has very rarely been practised. The value of trade affected by such retaliatory measures should, in theory, approximately equal the value affected by the initial import restriction.

Right of establishment   *See* Establishment

Round of trade negotiations   A cycle of multilateral trade negotiations under the aegis of GATT leading to simultaneous trade agreements among participating countries to reduce tariff and non-tariff barriers to trade. Eight rounds have been completed thus far: Geneva, 1947-8; Annecy, France, 1949; Torquay, UK, 1950-1; Geneva, 1956; Geneva, 1960-2 (the Dillon Round); Geneva, 1963-7 (the Kennedy Round); Geneva, 1973-9 (the Tokyo Round); and Geneva, 1986-94 (the Uruguay Round). *See also* Multilateral trade negotiations

Rules of origin   A term which defines the set of measures used to differentiate between goods originating in one country and those originating in another for the purpose of the application of trade measures such as tariffs. For example, goods made up of components originating in various countries but which when assembled add 50 per cent to their overall value may be considered to be goods originating in one country, whereas the addition of 25 per cent in value would not qualify. Such rules are very important for countries which are members of a free-trade area. In the FTA, all exported goods require a certificate of origin to demonstrate to customs authorities that they qualify for FTA treatment.

Safeguards   Emergency actions in the form of additional duties or import quotas which are applied to fairly traded imports which nevertheless cause or threaten serious injury to domestic producers. *See also* Escape clause

SAGITs   Sectoral advisory groups on International Trade were established to provide the Canadian federal government with advice on trade negotiations from a sectoral perspective. *See also* ITAC

SDRs   *See* Special drawing rights

Section 301   Provision in US law that enables the president to withdraw concessions or restrict imports from countries that discriminate against US exports, subsidize their own exports to the United States, or engage in other unjustifiable or unreasonable practices that burden or discriminate against US trade. Canada enacted similar legislation in the Special Import Measures Act of 1984.

Services   Economic activities which result in the provision of services rather than goods. This includes such diverse activities as transportation, communications, insurance, banking, advertising, consulting, distribution, engineering, medicine, and education. It is the fastest growing area of economic activity in Canada. More than two-thirds of working Canadians are now employed in the service sector. Trade in services takes place when a service is exported from a supplier nation to another nation, such as an international air flight, the extension of credit, or the design of a bridge.

Special drawing rights (SDRs)   A reserve asset created by the IMF to replace gold and US dollars as the basic monetary unit in the management of the international monetary system.

Specific duty or tariff An import tax set at a fixed amount per unit or per unit of measure regardless of the value of the item imported. *See also* Ad valorem tariff

Special Import Measures Act (SIMA) Canadian legislation adopted in 1984 following four years of study and debate which incorporates Canadian rights and obligations flowing from the Tokyo Round in the area of anti-dumping and countervailing duties and safeguards procedures. It provides similar provisions covering anti-dumping and countervailing procedures including separate investigations of the existence of dumping and subsidization and their margin by the Department of National Revenue and of injury by the Canadian International Trade Tribunal.

Standards As defined by the GATT Agreement on Technical Barriers to Trade (standards code), a standard is a technical specification that lays down characteristics of a product such as levels of quality, performance, safety, or dimensions. It may include, or deal exclusively with, terminology, symbols, testing and test methods, packaging, marking, or labelling requirements as they apply to a product.

Subsidies code A code of conduct negotiated under the auspices of GATT during the Tokyo Round that expanded on Article VI by establishing both substantive and procedural standards for national countervailing duty proceedings as well as developing obligations under Articles XVI and XXIII regarding notification and dispute settlement in the area of subsidy practices. *See also* Codes of conduct; Subsidy

Subsidy An economic benefit granted by a government to producers of goods, often to strengthen their competitive position. The subsidy may be direct (a cash grant) or indirect (e.g., low-interest export credits guaranteed by a government agency). *See also* Subsidies code

Surcharge or surtax A tariff or tax on imports in addition to the existing tariff, often used as a safeguard measure. *See also* Safeguards

Tariff A duty (or tax) levied upon goods transported from one customs area to another. Tariffs raise the prices of imported goods, thus making them less competitive within the market of the importing country. After seven rounds of GATT trade negotiations that focused heavily on tariff reductions, tariffs are less important measures of protection than they used to be. The term tariff often refers to a comprehensive list or schedule of merchandise with the rate of duty to be paid to the government for importing products listed. The tariff rate is the rate at which imported goods are taxed.

Tariff escalation A situation in which tariffs on manufactured goods are relatively high, tariffs on semi-processed goods are moderate, and tariffs on raw materials are nonexistent or very low. Escalation which exists in the tariff schedules of most developed countries is said to discourage the development of manufacturing industries in resource-rich countries.

Tariff schedule A comprehensive list of the goods which a country imports and the import duties applicable to each product. Annex 401.2 to the FTA sets out the tariff schedules of the United States and Canada and the schedule for the elimination of tariffs.

Terms of trade The volume of exports that can be traded for a given volume of imports. Changes in the terms of trade are generally measured by comparing changes in the ratio of export prices to import prices. The terms of trade are considered to have improved when a given volume of exports can be exchanged for a larger volume of imports.

Third option Policy adopted by the federal government in the mid-1970s which sought to develop a more independent Canadian economy by strengthening Canadian economic ties to Europe and Japan, promoting Canadian ownership, and decreasing ties to the US economy.

Tokyo Round Seventh in a series of multilateral trade negotiations held under the auspices of GATT, launched in Tokyo in 1973 and concluded in 1979.

Trade diversion A shift in the source of imports which occurs as a result of altering a country's import policies or practices, without regard for any increase in importation of the item or items involved. For example, the establishment of a customs union will cause countries participating in the new economic unit to import goods from other countries in the union that previously were imported from countries outside the union.

Trade liberalization A general term used to denote the gradual process of removing tariff and non-tariff barriers. Seven rounds of negotiations under GATT since 1947 have resulted in a large measure of trade liberalization among industrialized countries.

Transfer of technology The movement of modern or scientific methods of production or distribution from one enterprise, institution, or country to another through foreign investment, international trade licensing of patent rights, technical assistance, or training.

Transitional measures Those measures, in place for a limited period of time, which enable a new trade agreement to be gradually implemented. The FTA tariff cuts, for example, are being phased in over a period of ten years. Other transitional measures could include, for example, the right to take certain temporary safeguard measures or apply adjustment assistance measures.

Transparency Visibility and clarity of laws and regulations. Some of the codes of conduct negotiated during the Tokyo Round sought to increase the transparency of non-tariff barriers that impede trade. Much of the FTA is predicated on the idea of improving transparency.

Unfair trade An American term used to describe trade in dumped, subsidized, or counterfeit goods; the application of the term has steadily widened as US trade remedy laws have defined new practices which are considered to harm the export and import interests of US companies.

Uruguay Round Eighth in a series of multilateral trade negotiations held under the auspices of GATT. This round was launched at Punta del Este, Uruguay, in September 1986 and concluded at Marrakesh, Morocco, in April 1994.

US Court of International Trade *See* CIT

USITC US International Trade Commission is an independent US fact-finding and regulatory agency whose six members make determinations of injury and recommendations for relief for industries or workers seeking relief from increasing import competition. In addition, upon the request of Congress or the president, or on its own initiative, the Commission conducts comprehensive studies of specific industries and trade problems as well as the probable impact on specific US industries of proposed reductions in US tariffs and non-tariff trade barriers.

USTR US trade representative is an official in the executive office of the president, with cabinet-level and ambassadorial rank, charged with advising the president and with leading and coordinating US government policy on international trade negotiations and the development of trade policy. USTR also designates the White House office which the representative heads.

Valuation The appraisal of the worth of imported goods by customs officials for the purpose of determining the amount of duty payable in the importing country. The GATT customs valuation code obligates governments that sign it to use the transaction value of imported goods – or the price actually paid or payable for them – as the principal basis for valuing the goods for customs purposes.

Variable levy A tariff subject to alterations as world market prices change. The alterations are designed to assure that the import price after payment of duty will equal a predetermined 'gate' price. The variable levy of the European Community, the best known example, equals the difference between the target price for domestic agricultural producers and lowest offers for imported commodities on a CIF basis. The amount of the levy is adjusted for changes in the world-market situation, daily in the case of grains, fortnightly for dairy products, and quarterly for pork. *See also* Deficiency payments

WIPO World Intellectual Property Organization.

World Bank *See* IBRD

SUGGESTIONS FOR FURTHER READING

Perhaps no subject has been as extensively studied and debated in Canada's history as Canada-US trade and economic relations. Various aspects of the issue have generated a large and interesting literature. The following suggestions for further reading, therefore, can do no more than point the way.

Prior to the negotiations, the most up-to-date and thorough examination of the issue of Canada-US freer trade could be found in the *Final Report* of the Royal Commission on the Economic Union and Development Prospects for Canada (the Macdonald Commission) and in its supporting research. In the report, the section on Canada-US freer trade is found on pp. 215-385 of vol. 1. Of the supporting research (all published by the University of Toronto Press in 1985), vol. 11, *Canada-United States Free Trade*, edited by J. Whalley; vol. 13, *Trade, Industrial Policy and International Competition*, by R. Harris; vol. 29, *The Politics of Canada's Economic Relationship with the United States*, edited by D. Stairs and G.R. Winham, which contains a good historical overview of the issue by J.L. Granatstein, 'The Issue That Will Not Go Away'; and vol. 53, *Canadian Economic Development and the International Trading System*, by M.M. Hart, are all of direct interest. Other volumes touch on related issues such as industrial policy and federal-provincial relations. The total output of seventy-one volumes remains a monumental statement of academic research and opinion on public policy in the mid-1980s. All are available in French. A popular summary of the Commission's report can be found in Rod McQueen, *Leap of Faith* (Toronto: Coward Company 1985).

A very readable and persuasive introduction to the issue of freer trade was prepared just prior to the negotiations by Richard G. Lipsey and Murray G. Smith, *Taking the Initiative: Canada's Trade Options in a Turbulent World* (Toronto: C.D. Howe Institute 1985). A somewhat shorter introduction to the freer trade issue can be found in Anthony Westell, 'Economic Integration with the United States,' *International Perspectives* (November/December 1984). Westell's essay is in large measure a response to Mitchell Sharp's 1972 third option paper ('Canadian-U.S. Relations: Options for the Future') which appeared as a special edition of *International Perspectives* when it was still the External Affairs' house organ. Sharp and Westell continued the debate in the pages of that journal in 1985. *Toronto Star* columnist Richard Gwyn provided a very personal account in *The 49th Paradox* (Toronto: McClelland and Stewart 1985). A popular but detailed criticism based on new left economics is found in James Laxer, *Free Trade and the Future of Canada* (Edmonton: Hurtig Publishers 1986).

The Senate Standing Committee on Foreign Affairs under the chairmanship of Senator George van Roggen examined Canada-US relations at great length between 1975 and 1982. Particularly pertinent is vol. III of its report, *Canada's Trade Relations with the United States* (Ottawa: Supply and Services 1982).

A handy overview of various perspectives on this issue prior to the negotiations, written before the public debate reached a fever pitch, can be found in a special supplement (VIII of October 1982) of *Canadian Public Policy*, edited by J.M. Curtis and A.R. Moroz, 'Canada-United States Trade and Policy Issues.' Particularly useful is an article in this supplement by R.S. Saunders, 'Continentalism and Economic Nationalism in the Manufacturing Sector: Seeking Middle Ground.' The supplement also includes an update by Ron and Paul Wonnacott of their pioneering 1967 economic analysis, *Free Trade Between the United States and Canada: The Potential Economic Effects* (Cambridge, MA: Harvard University Press 1967).

The best introduction to the GATT and Canada's place in the international economic system can be found in Frank Stone, *Canada, the GATT and the International Trade System* (Montreal: Institute for Research on Public Policy 1984). A more recent study focusing on some of the problems experienced by the GATT and the consequent challenge to US leadership can be found in Patrick Low, *Trading Free: The GATT and US Trade Policy* (New York: Twentieth Century Fund 1993).

Literature on the Uruguay Round remains uneven. The best overview of the negotiating issues can be found in a multi-author study sponsored by the World Bank and edited by J. Michael Finger and Andrzej Olechowski, *The Uruguay Round: A Handbook on the Multilateral Trade Negotiations* (Washington, DC: World Bank 1988). The first part of the negotiations was chronicled in Alan Oxley, *The Challenge of Free Trade* (London: Harvester Wheatsheaf 1990). Oxley was Australia's ambassador to the GATT from 1985 to 1989 and chair of the Contracting Parties in 1988. More detailed references can be found in 'The Uruguay Round,' in Fen Osler Hampson with Michael Hart, *Multilateral Negotiations: Lessons from Arms Control, Trade and the Environment* (Baltimore: John Hopkins University Press, 1995).

A good general introduction to Canadian trade policy is contained in the Department of External Affairs, *A Review of Canadian Trade Policy* (Ottawa: Supply and Services 1983). A more recent popular introduction can be found in Michael Hart, *Trade – Why Bother?* (Ottawa: Centre for Trade Policy and Law 1992).

For trade policymaking in Washington in the early 1980s, see Stephen L. Lande and Graig VanGrasstek, *The Trade and Tariff Act of 1984: Trade Policy in the Reagan Administration* (Lexington, MA: D.C. Heath 1986); Robert E. Baldwin, *The Political Economy of U.S. Import Policy* (Cambridge, MA: MIT Press 1985); and I.M. Destler, *American Trade Politics: System Under Stress* (Washington, DC: Institute for International Economics 1986).

Two studies by Rodney Grey set out the problems of the US system of contingency protection for exporters to the United States market: *Trade Policy in the 1980s: An Agenda for Canada-U.S. Trade Relations* (Montreal: C.D. Howe Institute 1981); and *United States Trade Policy Legislation: A Canadian View* (Montreal: Institute for Research on Public Policy 1982). Murray Smith (with Michael Aho and Gary Horlick) provided an update in a short study prepared for the Canadian-American Committee, *Bridging the Gap: Trade Laws in the Canadian-U.S. Negotiations* (Toronto: C.D. Howe Institute 1987). A popular but devastating study of the problems posed by the US trade remedy system can be found in James Bovard, *The Fair Trade Fraud* (New York: St. Martin's Press 1991). The subsidy dimension, from an American point of view, can be found in Gary Clyde Hufbauer and Joanna Shelton Erb, *Subsidies in International Trade* (Washington, DC: Institute for International Economics 1984). A US perspective on the Canadian desire to negotiate a new trade remedy regime is provided by Paul Wonnacott, *The United States and Canada: The Quest for Free Trade, an Examination of Selected Issues* (Washington, DC: Institute for International Economics 1987).

A good overview of the Canada-US relationship can be found in a collection of essays prepared for discussion at a symposium at Arden House in Harriman, New York, in November 1984 and edited by Charles F. Doran and John H. Sigler, *Canada and the United States: Enduring Friendship, Persistent Stress* (Englewood Cliffs, NJ: Prentice-Hall 1985). Doran's *Forgotten Partnership* (Baltimore: Johns Hopkins University Press 1984); and *Economic Interdependence, Autonomy, and Canadian/American Relations* (Montreal: Institute for Research on Public Policy 1983) are both good value. A less sympathetic overview is provided by Stephen Clarkson, *Canada and the Reagan Challenge* (Toronto: Canadian Institute for Public Policy, revised edition 1985). Also relevant are George A. Carver, ed., *The View from the South: A U.S. Perspective on Key Bilateral Issues Affecting U.S.-Canadian Relations* (Washington, DC: Center for Strategic and International Studies 1985); Willis and Louise Armstrong, *US Policy Towards Canada: The Neighbour We Cannot Take for Granted* (Washington, DC: The Atlantic Council 1981); and *US Policy Towards Canada: Guidelines for the Next Decade* (Washington, DC: The Atlantic Council 1987).

The Canadian-American Committee, jointly sponsored by the C.D. Howe Institute in Canada and the National Planning Association in the United States, has published many books and pamphlets advocating economic cooperation. Publications related to the FTA debate include David Leyton-Brown, *Weathering the Storm: Canadian-U.S. Relations, 1980-83* (Toronto and Washington 1985); Peter Morici and Laura L. Megna, *Canada-United States Trade and Economic Interdependence* (1980); Peter Morici, Arthur J.R. Smith, and Sperry Lea, *Canadian Industrial Policy* (1982); Peter Morici, *The Global Competitive Struggle: Challenges to the United States and Canada* (1984); Richard G. Lipsey and Murray G. Smith, *Global Imbalances and U.S. Policy Responses* (1987); and Peter Morici, *Meeting the Competitive Challenge: Canada and the United States in the Global Economy* (1987).

A series prepared under the auspices of the Norman Paterson School of International Affairs, *Canada Among Nations*, aims at providing an annual review of Canada in the world. Ten volumes, each edited by two members of the faculty, have now appeared (Toronto: James Lorimer 1985-1990; and Ottawa: Carleton University Press 1991-94). Each contains a series of essays by individual authors on the significant developments for Canada in such areas as trade, international development, industrial policy, and Canada-US relations. The series has become a handy overview of developments in Canada's international relations.

The best account of post-war Canada-US relations can be found in Robert Bothwell, *Canada and the United States: The Politics of Partnership* (Toronto: University of Toronto Press 1992). The relevant chapters in J.L. Granatstein and Norman Hillmer, *For Better or for Worse: Canada and the United States to the 1990s* (Toronto: Copp Clark Pitman 1991) also provide a balanced account. A more personal view can be found in John W. Holmes, *Life with Uncle: The Canadian-American Relationship* (Toronto: University of Toronto Press 1981).

Of the many general books written on Canada since 1945, one of the best is Robert Bothwell, Ian Drummond, and John English, *Canada Since 1945: Power, Politics, and Provincialism* (Toronto: University of Toronto Press 1981). In addition to being readable, it successfully weaves trade and economic events into the general political history and provides a balanced perspective on Canada's place in the world.

The Canada-U.S. autopact is considered in C.D. Arthur, *The Automotive Agreement in a Canada-United States Comprehensive Trade Arrangement* (Background paper prepared for the Department of External Affairs in 1985); Paul Wonnacott, *U.S. and Canadian Auto Policies in a Changing World Environment* (Toronto: C.D. Howe Institute 1987); and Carl Beigie, *The Canada-U.S. Automotive Agreement: An Evaluation* (Montreal: Canadian-American Committee of the Private Planning Association 1970).

The adjustment challenge is discussed by Ronald J. Wonnacott with Roderick Hill, *Canadian and U.S. Adjustment Policies* (Toronto: Canadian-American Committee 1987); Victoria Curzon Price, *Free Trade Areas, the European Experience: What Lessons for Canadian-U.S. Trade Liberalization?* (Toronto: C.D. Howe Institute 1987); G.E. Salembier, Andrew R. Moroz, and Frank Stone, *The Canadian Import File: Trade, Protection and Adjustment* (Montreal: Institute for Research on Public Policy 1987); and Michael J. Trebilcock, Marsha Chandler, and Robert Howse, *Trade and Transitions: A Comparative Analysis of Adjustment Policies* (London: Routledge 1990).

A basic set of documents was published by the federal government in December 1985 as *Canadian Trade Negotiations: Introduction, Selected Documents, Further Reading* (Ottawa: Supply and Services 1986). A more complete but somewhat jaundiced collection of documents is contained in Duncan Cameron, ed., *The Free Trade Papers* (Toronto: James Lorimer 1986). The text of the agreement as well as booklets containing general and sectoral and other assessments and analysis (such as on agriculture, fish, manufacturing, women, and consumer issues) were published by the government in 1988 and 1989. The C.D. Howe Institute issued a similar series of occasional papers on individual issues in 1988 and 1989 in its *Trade Monitor* and *Commentary* series, including assessments of the auto, agriculture, and women's issues.

Starting in the mid-1980s, there were a host of conferences and seminars devoted to various aspects of the free-trade issue. Collections of essays and papers arising out of these conferences and other collective efforts prepared before the negotiations, if nothing else, put the lie to the charge that the issue was not sufficiently debated. Many are still available and worth examining, including:

- Edward R. Fried and Philip H. Trezise, eds., *U.S. Canadian Economic Relations: Next Steps?* (Washington, DC: Brookings Institution 1984).
- David Conklin and Thomas J. Courchene, eds., *Canadian Trade at a Crossroads: Options for New International Agreements* (Toronto: Ontario Economic Council 1985).
- Deborah Fretz, Robert Stern, and John Whalley, eds., *Canada/United States Trade and Investment Issues* (Toronto: Ontario Economic Council 1986).
- D.H. Flaherty and W.R. McKercher, eds., *Southern Exposure: Canadian Perspectives on the United States* (Toronto: McGraw-Hill Ryerson 1986).
- Edward R. Fried, Frank Stone, and Philip H. Trezise, eds., *Building a Canadian-American Free Trade Area* (Washington, DC: Brookings Institution 1987).
- Robert M. Stern, Philip H. Trezise, and John Whalley, eds., *Perspectives on a U.S. Canadian Free Trade Agreement* (Washington, DC: Brookings Institution 1987).
- Maureen Irish and Emily F. Carasco, eds., *The Legal Framework for Canada-United States Free Trade* (Toronto: Carswell 1987).
- Allan Maslove and S. Winer, eds., *Knocking at the Back Door: Canadian Perspectives on the Political Economy of Freer Trade with the United States* (Halifax: Institute for Research on Public Policy 1987).
- A.R. Riggs and Tom Velk, eds., *Canadian-American Free Trade: Historical, Political and Economic Dimensions* (Halifax: Institute for Research on Public Policy 1987).
- Laurier LaPierre, ed., *If You Love this Country* (Toronto: McClelland and Stewart 1987) – a popular and not very profound collection of anti-free trade essays similar in content and sophistication to Keith Davey, ed., *Canada Not For Sale: The Case Against Free Trade* (Toronto: General Paperbacks 1987).

After the agreement was concluded, new conferences and seminars and multi-author efforts sought to provide new analysis and insight. Most involve short studies and comments by individual authors and lack thematic consistency, but do provide good insight into the debate. Post-agreement books include:

- Murray G. Smith and Frank Stone, eds., *Assessing the Canada-U.S. Free Trade Agreement* (Halifax: Institute for Research on Public Policy 1987) – the first post-agreement conference, prepared before the legal text was available.
- Jeffrey J. Schott and Murray G. Smith, eds., *The Canada-United States Free Trade Agreement: The Global Impact* (Washington, DC and Ottawa: Institute for International Economics and Institute for Research on Public Policy 1988) – contains some very good essays and includes the first serious assessment from a US perspective.
- William Diebold, Jr., ed., *Bilateralism, Multilateralism and Canada in U.S. Trade Policy* (New York: Council on Foreign Relations 1988) – an excellent study that places the agreement into its broader global and historical perspective.
- John Crispo, ed., *Free trade: the real story* (Toronto: Gage 1988) – a popular pro-free trade collection of essays examining the agreement, written as an antidote to the hysteria of the critics.
- Duncan Cameron, ed., *The Free Trade Deal* (Toronto: James Lorimer 1988) – the first serious anti-free trade analysis, based largely on new left economics and political science; some of the articles, however, do not rise much above polemics and analyze the agreement feared rather than the agreement negotiated.
- Marc Gold and David Leyton-Brown, eds., *Trade-offs on Free Trade: The Canada-U.S. Free Trade Agreement* (Toronto: Carswell 1988) – contains many essays both pro and con but is of uneven quality.
- Donald M. McRae and Debra P. Steger, *Understanding the Free Trade Agreement* (Halifax:

Institute for Research on Public Policy 1988) – reports on a January 1988 conference at the University of Ottawa and contains some thoughtful material by Canadian and international legal experts.

- Richard G. Dearden, Michael M. Hart, and Debra P. Steger, eds., *Living with Free Trade* (Ottawa: Centre for Trade Policy and Law 1989) – reports on a May 1989 conference that sought to provide an integrated view of the issues in the Uruguay Round and the post-FTA negotiating agendas.
- Peter Morici, ed., *Making Free Trade Work: The Canada-U.S. Agreement* (New York: Council on Foreign Relations 1990) – one of the few multi-author volumes that has a balance of Canadian and US perspectives.
- Earle Gray, ed., *Free Trade Free Canada* (Woodville, ON: Canadian Speeches 1988) – a handy collection of pro-free trade documents, speeches, and testimony before parliamentary committees.

More satisfactory and complete analyses can be found in integrated studies, whether for or against the agreement. These include:

- Richard G. Lipsey and Robert C. York, *Evaluating the Free Trade Deal: A Guided Tour through the Canada-U.S. Agreement* (Toronto: C.D. Howe Institute 1988) – the first comprehensive assessment written for a general audience by one of Canada's best economists; it continues to be a good overview.
- Peter Morici, *A New Special Relationship: Free Trade and U.S. Canada Economic Relations in the 1990s* (Ottawa and Halifax: Center for Trade Policy and Law and Institute for Research on Public Policy 1991) – a balanced and thoughtful assessment of the longer term implications of the new bilateral relationship ushered in by the agreement.
- Randall White, *Fur Trade and Free Trade: Putting the Canada-U.S. Trade Agreement in Historical Perspective* (Toronto: Dundurn Press 1988) – less a history of the issue and more a sophisticated and well-researched exploration of the historical roots of the themes and issues in the negotiations and public debate.
- Gilbert R. Winham, *Trading with Canada* (New York: Twentieth Century Fund 1988) – written by a Dalhousie University political science professor for a US audience, it is the first serious and dispassionate analysis of the issues in the negotiations. Its major flaw is that it is too short, leaving many issues only barely explored.
- Bruce Doern and Brian Tomlin, *Faith and Fear: The Free Trade Story* (Toronto: Stoddart 1991) – to date, the only serious study of the negotiations, based on hundreds of interviews and a careful sifting of the available record. While there is room for quibbling, the account is fair and balanced.
- John D. Richard and Richard G. Dearden, *The Canada-U.S. Free Trade Agreement: Final Text and Analysis* (Toronto: CCH Canadian 1988) – the first legal commentary available; its haste shows.
- Debra Steger, *A Concise Guide to the Canada-U.S. Trade Agreement* (Toronto: Carswell 1988) – a solid commentary on the agreement typical of the many prepared by legal firms in Canada and the United States for their clients.
- Jon R. Johnson and Joel S. Schachter, *The Free Trade Agreement: A Comprehensive Guide* (Toronto: Canada Law Book 1988) – the best, most detailed, and careful of the legal commentaries, includes the full text of the agreement. The legal commentary is sound; the policy background to the issues is barely touched.
- Judith H. Bello and Alan F. Holmer, eds., *Guide to the U.S.-Canada Free-Trade Agreement* (Englewood Cliffs, NJ: Prentice-Hall Law & Business 1990) – a looseleaf guide by two former senior counsels in USTR, providing the best legal overview from a US perspective.
- Marjorie Montgomery Bowker, *On Guard For Thee: An Independent Review of the Free Trade Agreement* (Hull, PQ: Voyageur Press 1988) – an obtuse diatribe by a well-meaning but hopelessly confused family court judge from Edmonton whose 'simple' guide to the agree-

lllènt was lionized by the media and became an overnight sensation. Mrs. Bowker's understanding of the agreement was in no way informed by any serious background reading and is akin to an explanation of the Income Tax Act by the average taxpayer venting his or her spleen in April.

- John W. Warnock, *Free Trade and the New Right Agenda* (Vancouver: New Star Books 1988) – a typical but reasonably serious example of the many anti-free trade books written by left-wing political scientists in Canada.
- Maude Barlow, *Parcel of Rogues: How Free Trade is Failing Canada* (Toronto: Key Porter Books 1990) – a political tract by a leading spokesperson for the anti-free trade forces, long on rhetoric and short on facts and analysis.
- Mel Hurtig, *The Betrayal of Canada* (Toronto: Stoddart 1991) – a fatuous account of the impact of free trade on Canada by the patron saint of the Pro-Canada Network.
- Linda McQuaig, *The Quick and the Dead: Brian Mulroney, Big Business and the Seduction of Canada* (Toronto: Viking 1991) – a best selling conspiracy novel by a slick journalist who knows what sells.
- Lawrence Martin, *Pledge of Allegiance: The Americanization of Canada in the Mulroney Years* (Toronto: McClelland and Stewart 1993) – a major disappointment by a journalist who should have known better and whose earlier work suggests that others rightly expected something more serious.
- Jeffrey Simpson, *Faultlines: Struggling for a Canadian Vision* (Toronto: HarperCollins 1993) – while not a free-trade book, it contains an excellent essay on Derek Burney and his vision for Canada as exemplified by the free-trade agreement.

It is not possible to comment in detail on the wide range of books and articles that have been written about Canada-US free trade. Three books, however, need some further comment, if only to set the record straight and warn readers. For students of journalism and political writing in Canada, there is room for some fun in comparing the account in these pages based on intense personal involvement and those found in the work of journalists like Linda McQuaig and Lawrence Martin. Both interviewed us at length, and what we told them was corroborated in discussions with many of the principals in the negotiations. They decided that what they had learned from these interviews did not fit their preconceived notions and would not hold popular appeal – in itself an interesting comment on their assessment of the intelligence of most of their readers. They thus decided to write works of fiction instead.

Martin's account (*Pledge of Allegiance*) is in the nature of a pop psychology thriller based on the rather dubious thesis that Canadians who live close to the US border and regularly travel back and forth imbibing US culture and values, are more likely to have developed a continentalist rather than a Canadian outlook. These so-called border boys see nothing wrong with pledging allegiance to the United States and hitching Canada's star to an American destiny. Given the realities of Canadian geography and demography, Martin must have found it hard to find anyone other than border boys and girls. Needless to say, his account leaves something to be desired for the serious student.

McQuaig's approach (*The Quick and the Dead*) stands in the long tradition of conspiracy books. Her Canadian nationalism, however, is so muddled that she cannot believe that any Canadian would have had either the intelligence or the drive to hatch let alone carry through this conspiracy. All the Canadians in her book are dupes. The authors of the conspiracy are to be found in the United States, starting with the chair of American Express, James Robertson, and including Ronald Reagan and his cabinet, all of whom skillfully manipulated such sell-out artists as Brian Mulroney, Simon Reisman, and Derek Burney. Her heroes are all Canadians, but they prove to be mere putty in the hands of these superior forces. Her tale proves to be no more uplifting nor informative than Martin's. For those interested, Michael Hart reviewed the book, as well as those by Barlow and Hurtig, in 'Nationalist Gobbledegook,' *bout de papier* 9, no. 2 (Spring 1992):13-16.

Both Martin and McQuaig's books are typical of the views of Canadian left-wing political journalists who are convinced that Canadians will only make it if the government does everything for them. Without the help of an all-knowing and all-doing federal government, Canada is doomed. Anything that in any way undermines the march towards this utopia needs to be resisted and rooted out. The FTA proved such a danger and therefore needed to be discredited in the most lurid terms. Facts and sober analysis of the rather complex world in which we live are but small nuisances to be dismissed to serve this greater good.

Not all journalists, of course, partake of this nonsense nor are all political books as shallow as these. Jeffrey Simpson's account of the negotiations in his chapter on Derek Burney in *Faultlines*, for example, has the merit of balance and reflects the result of careful interviews and a good ear. Unfortunately, Simpson has spent too much time in the company of other journalists and in the drawing rooms of Canada's glitterati. As a result, he holds the dubious view that both groups of people are as important and influential in the Canadian scheme of things as they themselves think. He introduces us, for example, to a precious breed of intellectuals, largely confined to the Annex in Toronto, whom he calls *gauchistes de fauteuil*. He asserts that these people were major players in the free-trade debate and in the development of Canadian public policy. Perhaps they are influential in and around the University of Toronto and in a few political science departments around the country, but certainly they were not major players in the free-trade story. Any account which gives them pride of place needs to be taken with a grain of salt.

By 1991, the appetite for conferences and studies on Canada-US free trade had run its course, particularly since attention increasingly focused on Mexico and the prospect for trilateral negotiations and, soon thereafter, on broader hemispheric negotiations. On the former see Michael Hart, *A North American Free Trade Agreement: The Strategic Implications for Canada* (Ottawa and Montreal: Centre for Trade Policy and Law and Institute for Research on Public Policy 1990); and Government of Canada, *NAFTA – What's it all about?* (Ottawa: External Affairs and International Trade 1993); on the latter, see Michael Hart, 'Canada Discovers its Vocation as a Nation of the Americas,' in Fen Osler Hampson and Christopher J. Maule, eds., *After The Cold War: Canada Among Nations 1990-91* (Ottawa: Carleton University Press 1991); and Michael Hart, 'A Western Hemisphere Free Trade Agreement: Policy or Pipedream?' in Rod Dobell and Michael Neufeld, eds., *Beyond NAFTA: The Western Hemisphere Interface* (Lantzville, BC: Oolichan Books 1993). A US perspective on the NAFTA, before and after, can be found in Gary Clyde Hufbauer and Jeffery J. Schott, *North American Free Trade: Issues and Recommendations* (Washington, DC: Institute for International Economics 1992) and *NAFTA: An Assessment* (Washington, DC: Institute for International Economics 1992). On the issues raised by broader hemispheric trade negotiations, see Sylvia Saborio, ed., *The Premise and the Promise: Free Trade in the Americas* (Washington, DC: Overseas Development Council 1992).

Sources for more specific issues are cited in the notes to the individual chapters.

CREDITS

Photographs

INDEX

Marketing boards. *See* Supply management

Martin, Bob 95, 127

Martin, Patrick 62

Martin, Richard 83

Masse, Marcel 104

Matsunaga, Spark 150, 204, 347

Mazankowski, Don 332, 337

Media coverage of free trade (Canadian) 20-1, 72, 101, 105-9, 110-11, 113, 131, 138-9, 140-2, 148, 157, 160-1, 163, 168-9, 172-3, 175, 184, 186-8, 196-7, 201, 203, 206, 211, 214, 224-6, 229-31, 238, 247, 249-50, 259, 261, 264-6, 269, 271, 273, 283, 288, 292-4, 297-8, 301, 323, 327, 330, 336-40, 345, 348-9, 354, 359-60, 362, 364, 375. *See also* individual journalists

Media coverage of free trade (US) 220, 319, 338, 346

Medicare 8, 113

Meech Lake 102, 157, 176, 179, 182, 184, 195

Meech Lake Accord 247

Mercantilism 23, 25-7, 36, 39, 42, 54, 67, 370-1

Merkin, Bill 63, 94-5, 98, 205, 220, 241, 264, 271, 278-9, 329, 354, 356

Mesley, Wendy 109

Mexico 102, 190, 255, 272, 367, 389

MFA. *See* Multifibre Agreement

MFN. *See* Most-Favoured-Nation Treatment

Michel, Bob 118

Miller, Frank 85

Millican, Harold 138

Mitchell, George 145

Mont Tremblant 157, 169-70, 172

Montreal 75, 83, 169, 245

Most-Favoured-Nation Treatment (MFN) 25-6, 61, 217, 377, 378

Moynihan, Daniel Patrick 48, 144, 347

Mulholland, William 29

Mulroney, Brian 35, 62-3, 67, 70, 73, 84, 88, 99, 102, 111, 117, 122, 129, 141-2, 149-50, 161, 212, 219, 230, 235, 243, 247, 266-6, 287, 289, 293, 316, 319, 320, 333, 337, 340, 346, 361; appoints Pat Carney trade minister, 175; appoints Simon Reisman chief negotiator 120-4; attitude towards free trade 72, 87, 98, 99, 320-2; decides to seek FTA with the United States 104-5; involvement in conclusion of negotiations 324-37; and meetings with the premiers 84, 128, 138-40, 228, 266, 287-8, 347, 364; meets with Vice President Bush to discuss trade irritants 163, 218; at Quebec Summit 69; 147; reaction to US restrictions on shakes and shin-

gles 161; reaction to US action on softwood lumber 197; and parliamentary debate 228-30; and Senate fast-track approval 147; shares his vision of free trade with Canadians in television address 141; and Shamrock II 143; and Shamrock III 233-5; signs free-trade agreement 366; takes charge of the negotiations 282, 317; and Venice summit 250-1; visits Washington in September 1985 63

Mulroney, Nicholas 102

Multifibre Agreement (MFA) 26, 156

Multilateral Trade Negotiations (MTN) 3, 46, 49, 59, 75, 83, 85, 92, 95, 125, 189-90

Murphy, Peter (CTV reporter) 109

Murphy, Peter (US chief negotiator) 117, 137, 143, 155-7, 160-1, 166-9, 172-3, 176, 183, 188, 190, 193, 199-201, 203-7, 210-11, 213-17, 220-1, 224, 233-4, 236-41, 243, 247, 249-51, 255-63, 265, 270-3, 278-81, 282, 285-6, 289-93, 314, 319, 321, 328, 329, 337, 338, 356-60; appointment of 117, 143, 156; and the autopact 167, 214; career background of 155-7; and dinner in New York with Reisman 220-1; and the final plenary 291-3; lack of political clout of 190, 193, 204; and relations with Congress 270-1; and relations with Reisman 314; and social programs 167;

Murray, Lowell 337

NAFTA. *See* North American Free Trade Agreement

Nason, Harry 138

National Association of Manufacturers (NAM – US) 162

National Energy Program (NEP) 16, 18

National Federation of Independent Business (NFIB) 256

National Policy 5, 55, 77, 340, 385-6

National Retail Federation (US) 256

National Revenue, Department of 197

National Security Council 289

National treatment 25-6, 97, 134, 141, 180, 183-4, 191, 195, 221, 223, 236, 277, 306-8, 374, 382

Native groups 113

New Brunswick 138-9, 168, 181, 347

New Democratic Party 23, 67, 84, 100, 168, 201, 214, 226, 230, 246, 266-7, 283, 347, 356, 377

Newall, Ted 77

Newfoundland 6, 138, 141, 288

Newman, Kevin 109

Nichols, Marjorie 108, 122, 266, 267, 316
Niles, Tom 157, 358
Nixon, Bob 365
Nixon, Richard 14, 40, 48, 50
Non-tariff barriers or measures 61, 77, 80-1, 85, 104, 185, 195, 218, 231, 232, 372-4, 379, 381
North American Free Trade Agreement (NAFTA) 367, 377, 389
North, Oliver 267
Nova Scotia 18, 138
Nymark, Alan 126, 227-8

O'Donnel, Joe 107
O'Neill, Juliet 108
O'Neill, Tip 219
OECD. *See* Organization for Economic Cooperation and Development
Ontario 29, 55, 71, 73, 75, 77, 85, 89, 99, 111, 128, 131-2, 135, 138-9, 181-2, 214-15, 227, 245, 264-6, 274-5, 277, 281, 283-4, 287-8, 362, 365, 377
Organization for Economic Cooperation and Development (OECD) 8, 16, 39, 40, 239, 268, 377
Organized labour 35, 67, 71, 73-6, 79, 82, 93, 109, 113, 130-1, 246, 255, 305, 312, 365. *See also* Canadian Auto Workers; Canadian Federation of Labour; Canadian Labour Congress; United Autoworkers
Osler, Hoskins and Harcourt 359
Ostry, Sylvia 63, 125
Ottawa 4, 18, 21, 53, 56, 58, 63, 67, 70-1, 78, 82-3, 85-6, 91, 93, 95, 98, 101, 107-9, 119-22, 126, 129, 133, 135-6, 138-9, 144, 147-8, 155, 157, 163, 166, 168-9, 176, 195, 199, 204-5, 218, 224, 226-7, 231, 238, 243, 245-6, 250, 256, 259, 261, 264-5, 269-70, 289, 291-3, 310, 312, 318, 322, 324, 326-7, 329, 333, 336, 338, 343, 347-8, 350-4, 356-9, 361-2, 366, 389
Ottawa Summit (Shamrock III) 191-2, 233-5, 238

Packwood, Robert 144-6, 148, 150, 347
Parliament 20, 63, 67, 87, 104, 110, 130, 227-9, 246, 324, 361. *See also* House of Commons; House of Commons Standing Committee on External Affairs and International Trade; Senate Standing Committee on Foreign Affairs
Parliamentary Committee, Special, on free trade and the US Strategic Defense Initiative (Hockin Committee) 82-3, 100, 372. *See also* House of Commons Standing

Committee on External Affairs and International Trade; Senate Standing Committee on Foreign Affairs
Parti Québecois 99
Pawley, Howard 84, 99, 228, 265, 267, 347
Pearson, Lester 23, 34, 91
Peckford, Brian 99, 288, 348
Peterson, David 99, 132, 138-40, 214, 228, 265-6, 274, 283-4, 287-8, 348, 362
Pharmaceuticals 147, 160, 165, 179, 306, 323, 335-6, 341, 353-4, 382. *See also* Drug patents; Intellectual property
Phillips, Roger 346
Polling 62, 71-3, 88-9, 111, 130-2, 174-5, 197, 212, 230, 244, 246, 283, 364
Pork 146, 254
Pornography 113
Powell, Jody 256
Predatory pricing 171
President (US). *See* Reagan, Ronald
Press coverage of free trade. *See* Media coverage of free trade
Price discrimination 27, 292, 345
Prime minister (Canada). *See* Mulroney, Brian
Prime Minister's Office (PMO) 21, 103, 141, 148, 212, 229, 235, 348
Prince Edward Island 141, 246
Priorities and Planning Committee of Cabinet (Canada) 98-9
Privy Council Office (PCO) 126, 293
Pro-Canada Network 246-7
Procurement. *See* Government procurement
Procurement Agreement (GATT) 180, 194, 304
Procurement Code. *See* Procurement Agreement
Protectionism 9, 161, 174, 197, 292, 313, 326, 345, 369
Protectionism, in United States 6, 9, 36-40, 42-7, 49-53, 56-7, 62, 65, 67, 73, 75-6, 78, 80, 83, 88, 92, 95, 110, 116-18, 123, 162, 175-6, 186, 188-91, 196-7, 203-4, 228, 230, 233-4, 242, 255, 267, 309, 347, 376, 382, 385
Pryor, David 146
Punta Del Este Conference 65, 190, 196, 268

Quantitative restriction (QR) 39, 158
Quebec 69-71, 75, 87, 89, 99, 108, 128, 131, 138-9, 161, 167-8, 182, 227, 229, 246, 293, 325, 347, 361
Quebec Chamber of Commerce 76

8, 39-40, 85, 93, 129, 138, 140, 216, 227, 299, 381
Toronto 3-4, 30, 35, 75-6, 83, 100, 103, 107, 109-
    10, 135, 141, 219, 245, 283, 326, 345, 349
Trade Act of 1974 (US) 40, 129, 166
Trade and Tariff Act of 1984 (US) 42
Trade liberalization 6, 15, 23, 28, 30, 40, 52, 57,
    65, 78, 81, 83, 195, 387
Trade Negotiations Office (TNO) 124-5, 133,
    135-7, 140-1, 157, 160, 176, 192, 195, 204, 213,
    219, 228-9, 234, 241, 273, 321, 328, 330, 338,
    340, 348-53, 356, 358-9
Trade-Related Investment Measures (TRIMs)
    184, 237
Trade remedies and trade remedy law 27-8,
    50, 52, 95-7, 112, 145, 170-2, 178, 186, 193, 234-
    5, 260, 272, 280, 285, 291, 298, 300, 302-3,
    306, 321, 325-6, 331-2, 334, 341, 346, 354, 359,
    371, 375-6, 379, 380-1, 383. *See also* Anti-
    dumping; Contingency protection;
    Countervail; Dumping; Emergency safe-
    guards; Subsidies
Trade subcommittee, US House 94, 96, 120,
    143, 271, 321
Trade subcommittee, US Senate 146
Trade unions. *See* Canadian Auto Workers;
    Canadian Federation of Labour; Canadian
    Labour Congress; Organized labour;
    United Autoworkers
Transfer of technology. *See* Intellectual prop-
    erty
Transparency 182. *See also* Dispute settlement
Transport, Department of (Canada) 93, 278
Transport Canada Training Institute,
    Cornwall (TCTI) 275, 277
Transportation, Department of (US) 268, 352
Transportation services 59, 176-7, 223, 255,
    267, 278, 305, 352, 355, 359-60, 378, 382
Treasury Department (US) 189, 195, 215, 236,
    268, 279, 323, 326, 328-30
Trent, John 246
Trezise, Phil 120, 123
Trudeau, Pierre Elliott 13, 16-17, 71, 88
Trueman, Peter 109
Turner, John 121-3, 141, 168, 230, 266

Unemployment 7, 42, 44, 76, 384
Unfair trade 44-5, 48, 135, 193, 244, 289, 379-80
United Auto Workers (UAW) 44. *See also*
    Canadian Auto Workers
United Nations Conference on Trade and
    Development (UNCTAD) 27
United States Trade Representative (USTR)

43, 45-8, 63, 69-71, 95-6, 117-18, 125, 143-4,
    148, 155-6, 188-90, 206, 219, 225, 242, 256,
    268, 285, 292, 294, 312, 323, 325, 327-31, 335-6,
    338, 346, 356, 358, 363, 373
Uruguay Round of GATT negotiations 39, 49,
    65, 190, 219, 242-3, 262, 319, 368
US Chamber of Commerce 70
US Court of International Trade (US CIT)
    162
US International Trade Commission
    (USITC) 43, 60, 83, 97, 115, 119, 135, 164, 194,
    215, 217, 302, 388
US-Israel free-trade agreement 46, 96, 244,
    255
USTR. *See* United States Trade Representative

Vancouver 75, 83, 84, 96, 98-9, 139, 228, 265,
    322
Vastel, Michel 108
Vaughn, Bev 285
Venice Summit 239, 250-1, 257, 259, 284
Von Finckenstein. *See* Finckenstein, Konrad
    von

Waddell, Christopher 108, 134, 238, 274, 340
Wallin, Pamela 321, 340
Warren, J.W. (Jake) 138, 227
Washington 8, 35, 38, 44-5, 53, 58, 63, 69, 76,
    84, 93-5, 98, 103-4, 107-8, 115, 117, 119-20,
    129-30, 143-5, 147-8, 155-7, 161-4, 169-70, 172,
    184, 188, 190, 196-7, 201, 203, 205, 207, 212-13,
    220, 224, 227, 236, 238, 241, 246, 251, 258,
    260, 262, 264, 267, 270, 275, 279, 282, 285-6,
    289-91, 293, 309-13, 315, 318, 320-5, 328, 330,
    333, 336-8, 343-4, 346, 351-2, 354, 355,-7, 359-
    60, 362-3, 366, 389
Washington Summit (Shamrock II) 143
Water, as natural resource 35, 121, 355
Watkins, Mel 67
Ways and Means Committee, US House 37,
    94, 96, 115, 143, 234, 309-10, 321, 333, 363, 366
Weaver, James 146
Webster, Jack 108
Weiss, George 120, 271, 310
Whalley, John 29-30, 34
White, Bob 246
Whitely, Don 108
Wilgress, Dana 56
Wills, Terrance 364
Wilson, Bill 175
Wilson, Michael 62-4, 69, 102, 162, 229, 289,
    290, 319, 322-3, 326-9, 335-8, 340, 346

Winder Building 164, 166, 205
Wine 194, 233, 255, 323, 379. *See also* Alcoholic
    beverages
Winham, Gil 30, 34
Winsor, Hugh 108, 168, 324
Wise, John 229
Women's issues 112, 246, 365. *See also* Feminist
    groups
Wonnacott, Paul 13
Wonnacott, Ron 13
World Bank (IBRD) 322

Yerxa, Rufus 94, 309
Yeutter, Clayton 48, 71, 97, 100, 117, 143-5, 148,
    155-7, 188, 190, 197, 200, 219-20, 225, 270,
    290, 294, 310, 321, 323, 325-9, 334, 338, 340,
    346, 362, 363, 373
Young, Christopher 122
Young, John 13, 14

ABOUT THE AUTHORS

The three authors are all officers in Canada's Department of Foreign Affairs and International Trade who served in the United States branch of the Department in the period leading up to the negotiations, and then moved to the Trade Negotiations Office in 1986 when negotiations began in earnest.

Michael Hart was responsible for much of the policy work leading up to the negotiations, pursued contingency protection during the negotiations, and in the closing stages did much of the legal drafting and preparation of explanatory material. He is currently senior advisor, trade policy studies. In twenty years with the federal government, he has been involved in various other trade negotiations and in advising the government on day-to-day trade policy issues. During assignments in Ottawa and at the Canadian Permanent Mission to the GATT in Geneva, he has pursued agricultural trade issues, the negotiation of textile and clothing restraint agreements, commodity agreements, bilateral air agreements, and the legislation and implementation of Canada's trade remedy laws. More recently, he has advised the NAFTA negotiating team and directed the Department's Economic Planning Unit.

Concurrently, he has also forged a career as an independent analyst of trade policy issues. He is widely published and much in demand as a speaker and seminar leader on trade policy issues. He embarked on this second career in 1982 when he undertook a study of Canada's trade policies while coordinating an interdepartmental team reviewing the challenges Canada would face on the trade policy front in the 1980s. The result was two books: *A Review of Canadian Trade Policy* and *Trade Policy for the 1980s: A Discussion Paper*. The following year, while on loan to the Institute for Research on Public Policy, he prepared one of the background research volumes for the Royal Commission on the Economic Union and Development Prospects for Canada (the Macdonald Commission), *Canadian Economic Development and the International Trading System: Constraints and Opportunities*. He then worked with the staff of the Commission in preparing its report, particularly the sections that deal with bilateral and multilateral trade negotiations.

In 1989, while on loan to Carleton University, he founded the Centre for Trade Policy and Law as a centre for the research and teaching of trade policy issues, in association with the Faculty of Law at the University of Ottawa and the Norman Paterson School of International Affairs at Carleton University. Since returning to government service in 1990, he has maintained his interest in teaching as an adjunct professor of international affairs at the Norman Paterson School.

In addition to his many papers and articles on various trade policy issues and his academic and government responsibilities, Mr. Hart has recently written *A North American Free Trade Agreement: The Strategic Implications for Canada* (1990); *Trade – Why Bother?* (1992), and *What's Next: Canada, the Global Economy and the New Trade Policy* (1994). He is currently at work on two major studies: one focuses on the implications of globalization for Canadian trade policy while the other, a study of the historical development of Canadian trade policy, brings together his academic training as an historian at Calvin College, the University of Virginia, and the University of Toronto and his practical experience in government.

Bill Dymond was responsible for guiding the preparatory task force and was lead negotiator on government procurement during the negotiations. Educated at the University of Toronto, he joined the Department of External Affairs in 1967 and, after an assignment with the Prices and Incomes Board, joined the Canadian Permanent Mission in Geneva responsible for GATT and UNCTAD trade policy issues. He returned to Ottawa in 1974 as chief of the Commodity Policy Division in the Department of Industry, Trade, and Commerce and served concurrently as chief of the GATT Division during the closing stages of the Tokyo Round of multilateral trade negotiations. In 1979 he was appointed deputy head of Canada's mission to the European Communities in Brussels. He returned in 1983 to the Department of External Affairs as director of the Western European Economic Relations Division. In 1984 he took on responsibility for the Canada-US sectoral trade initiative, and in 1985 co-authored the discussion paper *How to Secure and Enhance Canadian Access to Export Markets*, which in turn led to preparations for a more far-reaching initiative. He left the Trade Negotiations Office at the conclusion of formal negotiations to take up an assignment as minister-counsellor commercial in the Canadian Embassy in Washington, responsible for managing Canada-US trade relations. He is currently Canada's ambassador to Brazil.

Educated at the University of Manitoba and Carleton University, Colin Robertson joined the Department of External Affairs in 1977. After various assignments in New York, the Minister's Office, the Press Office, the Federal-Provincial Relations Division, with Petro-Canada International, and in the US Relations Branch, he joined the Trade Negotiations Office to work on US subsidies, communications, and speech-writing. From the end of 1987-92 he was counsellor and consul at the Canadian Commission in Hong Kong. After his return, he coordinated the parliamentary approval of the NAFTA and directed foreign policy communications at headquarters. Robertson has long been an active participant in the affairs of the Professional Association of Foreign Service Officers (PAFSO). For four years he was editor of *bout de papier*, transforming it from a newsletter into a lively journal of news and opinion with a circulation far beyond that of PAFSO's members and served as president until recently. He is currently on loan to the Department of Citizenship and Immigration as director general for communications.